Quantum Inspired Computational Intelligence

Quantum Inspired Computational Intelligence

Research and Applications

Edited by

Siddhartha Bhattacharyya

Ujjwal Maulik

Paramartha Dutta

AMSTERDAM • BOSTON • HEIDELBERG • LONDON
NEW YORK • OXFORD • PARIS • SAN DIEGO
SAN FRANCISCO • SINGAPORE • SYDNEY • TOKYO
Morgan Kaufmann is an imprint of Elsevier

Morgan Kaufmann is an imprint of Elsevier
50 Hampshire Street, 5th Floor, Cambridge, MA 02139, United States

Library of Congress Cataloging-in-Publication Data
A catalog record for this book is available from the Library of Congress

British Library Cataloguing-in-Publication Data
A catalogue record for this book is available from the British Library

ISBN: 978-0-12-804409-4

For information on all Morgan Kaufmann publications
visit our website at https://www.elsevier.com/

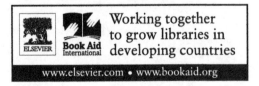

Publisher: Todd Green
Acquisition Editor: Brian Romer
Editorial Project Manager: Amy Invernizzi
Production Project Manager: Punithavathy Govindaradjane
Cover Designer: Victoria Pearson

Typeset by SPi Global, India

Siddhartha Bhattacharyya dedicates this book to his late father Ajit Kumar Bhattacharyya and his late mother Hashi Bhattacharyya, and his beloved wife Rashni.

Ujjwal Maulik dedicates this book to his son Utsav and all his students who have made this journey enjoyable.

Paramartha Dutta dedicates this book to his late father Arun Kanti Dutta and his mother Bandana Dutta.

Contents

List of Contributors

D. Anguita
University of Genoa, Genoa, Italy

A.S. Ashour
Tanta University, Tanta, Egypt

V.E. Balas
Aurel Vlaicu University of Arad, Arad, Romania

E.C. Behrman
Wichita State University, Wichita, KS, United States

S. Bhattacharyya
RCC Institute of Information Technology, Kolkata, WB, India

A. Chakrabarti
A.K. Choudhury School of Information Technology, University of Calcutta, Kolkata, WB, India

A. Choudhury
University Institute of Technology, Burdwan, WB, India

R. Das
Jadavpur University, Kolkata, WB, India

S. Das
Jadavpur University, Kolkata, WB, India

N. Dey
Techno India College of Technology, Kolkata, WB, India

S. Dey
Camellia Institute of Technology, Kolkata, WB, India

A.K. Dwivedi
Bhilai Institute of technology, Durg, CT, India

M.K. Ghose
Sikkim Manipal Institute of Technology, Rangpo, SK, India

Gursaran
Dayalbagh Educational Institute, Agra, UP, India

D.P. Hudedagaddi
SCOPE, VIT University, Vellore, TN, India

G. Klepac
Raiffeisenbank Austria d.d., Zagreb, Croatia

D. Konar
Sikkim Manipal Institute of Technology, Rangpo, SK, India

B.J. MacLennan
University of Tennessee, Knoxville, TN, United States

K. Mahata
Government College of Engineering and Leather Technology, Kolkata, WB, India

A. Mani
Amity School of Engineering and Technology, Amity University Uttar Pradesh, Noida, UP, India

N. Mani
Dayalbagh Educational Institute, Agra, UP, India

U. Maulik
Jadavpur University, Kolkata, WB, India

M. McCann
Wichita State University, Wichita, KS, United States

D.V. Medhane
School of Computing Science and Engineering, VIT University, Vellore, TN, India

N.H. Nguyen
Wichita State University, Wichita, KS, United States

L. Oneto
University of Genoa, Genoa, Italy

B.K. Panigrahi
Indian Institute of Technology Delhi, New Delhi, DL, India

R.N. Patel
SSTC, Bhilai, CT, India

S. Ridella
University of Genoa, Genoa, Italy

S.G. Roy
Techno India College of Technology, New Town, Kolkata, WB, India

S. Samanta
University Institute of Technology, Burdwan, WB, India

A.K. Sangaiah
School of Computing Science and Engineering, VIT University, Vellore, TN, India

A. Sarkar
Jadavpur University, Kolkata, WB, India

J.E. Steck
Wichita State University, Wichita, KS, United States

B.K. Tripathy
SCOPE, VIT University, Vellore, TN, India

About the Editors

Dr. Siddhartha Bhattacharyya (SMIEEE, SMACM, SMIETI, MIRSS, MIAENG, MACSE, MIAASSE, MCSTA, LMCSI, LMOSI, LMCEGR) obtained his bachelor's degree in physics, his bachelor's degree in optics and optoelectronics, and his master's degree in optics and optoelectronics from the University of Calcutta, India, in 1995, 1998, and 2000, respectively. He completed his PhD degree in computer science and engineering at Jadavpur University, India, in 2008. He is the recipient of the University Gold Medal from the University of Calcutta for his master's degree.

He is currently Professor and Head of Information Technology of RCC Institute of Information Technology, Kolkata, India. In addition, he has served as the Dean of Research and Development of the institute since November 2013. Before this, he was an associate professor of information technology at RCC Institute of Information Technology, Kolkata, India, from 2011 to 2014. Before that, he served as an assistant professor in computer science and information technology at the University Institute of Technology, the University of Burdwan, India, from 2005 to 2011. He was a lecturer in information technology at Kalyani Government Engineering College, India, from 2001 to 2005.

He was the convener of the AICTE-IEEE National Conference on Computing and Communication Systems (CoCoSys-09) in 2009. He was a member of the Young Researchers' Committee of the WSC 2008 Online World Conference on Soft Computing in Industrial Applications. He has been a member of the organizing and technical program committees of several national and international conferences. He was General Chair of the IEEE International Conference on Computational Intelligence and Communication Networks in 2014 and General Chair of the 2015 IEEE International Conference on Research in Computational Intelligence and Communication Networks in 2015. He is General Chair of the 2016 International Conference on Wireless Communications, Network Security, and Signal Processing in Chiang Mai, Thailand, in 2016, and General Chair of the 2016 Second IEEE International Conference on Research in Computational Intelligence and Communication Networks in 2016.

He is the coauthor of three books and the coeditor of five books and has more than 150 research publications in international journals and conference proceedings to his credit. He holds a patent on intelligent colorimeter technology. He is an editor of the *Journal of Pattern Recognition Research*. He is a member of the editorial board of *International Journal of Engineering, Science and Technology* and *ACCENTS Transactions on Information Security*. He has been an associate editor of the *International Journal of BioInfo Soft Computing* since 2013. He is a member of the editorial board of *Applied Soft Computing*. He is the lead guest editor of the special issue of *Applied Soft Computing* on hybrid intelligent techniques for image analysis and understanding (2015–16) and the special issue of the *International Journal of Computers and Applications* on computational intelligence and communications (2016).

His research interests include soft computing, pattern recognition, multimedia data processing, hybrid intelligence, and quantum computing.

Dr. Ujjwal Maulik has been a professor in the Department of Computer Science and Engineering, Jadavpur University, Kolkata, India, since 2004. He was awarded his bachelor's degrees in physics and computer science in 1986 and 1989, respectively, and was awarded his master's and PhD degrees in computer science in 1992 and 1997, respectively.

He chaired the Department of Computer Science and Technology, Kalyani Government Engineering College, Kalyani, India from 1996 to 1999. He worked at Los Alamos National Laboratory, Los Alamos, New Mexico, United States in 1997, the University of New South Wales, Sydney, Australia in 1999, the University of Texas at Arlington, United States, in 2001, the University of Maryland, Baltimore County, United States, in 2004, Fraunhofer Institute AiS, St Augustin, Germany, in 2005, Tsinghua University, China, in 2007, the University of Rome, Italy, in 2008, the University of Heidelberg, Germany, in 2009, the German Cancer Research Center (DKFZ) in 2010, 2011, and 2012, Grenoble Institute of Technology, France, in 2010, 2013, and 2014, the Interdisciplinary Centre for Mathematical and Computational Modelling, University of Warsaw, Poland, in 2013, the International Center of Theoretical Physics, Trieste, Italy, in 2014, the University of Padua, Italy, in 2014, Corvinus University Budapest, Hungary, in 2015, and the University of Ljubljana, Slovenia, in 2015. He has also visited many institutes and universities around the world for invited lectures and collaborative research. He has been invited to supervise doctoral students in well-known universities in France.

He was the recipient of Government of India BOYSCAST fellowship in 2001 and the Alexander von Humboldt Fellowship for Experienced Researchers in 2010, 2011, and 2012, and was a Senior Associate of the International Centre for Theoretical Physics, Italy, in 2012. He coordinators five Erasmus Mundus Mobility with Asia (EMMA) programs (European-Asian mobility program). He has been the program chair, the tutorial chair, and a member of the program committees of many international conferences and workshops.

He is a founder member of the IEEE Computational Intelligence Society Kolkata Section Chapter and worked as Secretary and Treasurer in 2011, as Vice Chair in 2012, and as Chair in 2013, 2014, and 2016. He is a fellow of the Indian National Academy of Engineering, the West Bengal Association of Science and Technology, the Institution of Engineering and Telecommunication Engineers, and the Institution of Engineers and a Senior Member of the IEEE.

He is the coauthor of seven books and more than 275 research publications. He is an associate editor of *IEEE Transactions on Fuzzy Systems* and *Information Sciences* and also on the editorial board of many journals, including *Protein & Peptide Letters*. Moreover, he has served as a guest coeditor of special issues of journals, including *IEEE Transactions on Evolutionary Computation*.

His research interests include computational intelligence, bioinformatics, combinatorial optimization, pattern recognition, data mining, and social networks.

Dr. Paramartha Dutta was awarded his bachelor's and master's degrees in statistics by the Indian Statistical Institute, Kolkata, in 1988 and 1990, respectively. He was awarded his master of technology degree in computer science by the same institute in 1993 and his PhD degree in engineering by the Bengal Engineering and Science University, Shibpur, in 2005. He has served in the capacity of research personnel in various projects funded by the Government of India, including at the Defence Research and Development Organization, the Council of Scientific and Industrial Research, and the Indian Statistical Institute, Kolkata. He is now a professor in the Department of Computer and System Sciences of Visva-Bharati University, Santiniketan, India. Before this, he served at Kalyani Government Engineering College and the College of Engineering in West Bengal as a full-time faculty member.

He has coauthored eight books and has also five edited books to his credit. He has published about 180 articles in various journals and conference proceedings, both international and national. He has guided three scholars who have already had been awarded their PhD degree. Presently he is supervising four PhD students. He is a Life Fellow of the Optical Society of India, the Computer Society of India, the Indian Science Congress Association, the Indian Society for Technical Education, and the Indian Unit of Pattern Recognition and Artificial Intelligence—the Indian affiliate of the International Association for Pattern Recognition—and a Senior Member of the Association for Computing Machinery, the IEEE Computer Society, and the International Association of Computer Science and Information Technology.

Dr. Paramartha Dutta was awarded his bachelor's and master's degrees in statistics by the Indian Statistical Institute, Kolkata, in 1988 and 1990, respectively. He was awarded his master of technology degree in computer science by the same institute in 1993 and his PhD degree in engineering by the Bengal Engineering and Science University, Shibpur, in 2005. He has served in the capacity of research personnel in various projects funded by the Government of India, including at the Defence Research and Development Organization, the Council of Scientific and Industrial Research, and the Indian Statistical Institute, Kolkata. He is now a professor in the Department of Computer and System Sciences of Visva-Bharati University, Santiniketan, India. Earlier, he has served at Kalyani Government Engineering College and the College of Engineering in West Bengal as a full-time faculty member.

He has coauthored eight books and has also five edited books to his credit. He has published about 180 articles in various journals and conference proceedings, both international and national. He has guided three scholars who have already been awarded their PhD degree. Presently, he is supervising four PhD students. He is a Fellow of the Optical Society of India, the Computer Society of India, the Indian Science Congress Association, the Indian Society for Technical Education, and the Indian Unit of Pattern Recognition and Artificial Intelligence—the Indian affiliate of the International Association for Pattern Recognition—and a Senior Member of the Association for Computing Machinery, the IEEE Computer Society, and the International Association of Computer Science and Information Technology.

Foreword

Inspiration is at the heart of every algorithm design. Recently we have experienced an increase in algorithm designs inspired no longer only by biology but by all disciplines of human culture, modeling, nature, and systems. One of these enterprises is quantum computing. The fundamental ideas of quantum physics to model microscopic phenomena have some implications for computing paradigms, as was found about 2 decades ago. As long as there is no observation, a system remains in a mixed state that is a superposition of all states in which it can be observed by some chance expressed in weighting factors for each particular state. A quantum computer is thought to be able to process the superposed states all at once, in parallel so to say. This way, encryption algorithms can be broken, and huge databases can be sampled in a fraction of the time conventional computing needs. However, the technical realization of a real-world quantum computer may take time. Nevertheless, there is steady progress.

Besides parallelism, there are other features of interest that have captured the attention of computer scientists. One is that a single register of a few qubits—as the information processing unit in quantum computing is called—can appear as any possible solution on observation or measurement. Of course, each different solution will appear with some specific probability. But what about having a qubit register that is likelier than others to produce better solutions on measurement? This could be the basis for optimization. All we need, it seems, is a smart way to modify the probabilities of each qubit by reasonable operations. Some of them were found quickly, now called "quantum gates": a collection of operators with some randomized component that allow the transformation of a qubit register into a new one according to some fitness or quality function. This sounds similar to the basic ideas behind evolutionary computation. There a population of individuals designed such that each encodes a solution of an optimization problem is repeatedly renewed. The new individuals are the results of selection of modified variants of the former generation. The modifications are done by application of various genetic operators, with crossover and mutation being the most famous and typical ones.

In the same sense, quantum computing can be embedded into evolutionary algorithms following this obvious similarity. If we do this, maybe will we lose only one thing about a real-world quantum computer: true parallelism. So, a quantum-inspired computation algorithm will not break RSA but it can boost conventional metaheuristic algorithms.

This said, quantum-inspired computing is not a single new algorithm. It is a technique to enhance existing metaheuristics in various ways, as well as other concepts of computer science. We will see this later. With regard to metaheuristics, quantum-inspired computing will replace the conventional bit strings used to encode solutions with a qubit register. The genetic operators will be replaced with quantum gate operators (most popular is a simple rotation). Measurements thus receiving bit strings finally that encode problem solutions will guide the selection. All these steps have enough flexibility to come up with many other variations. And they can be embedded in many other algorithms in a similar way, or in other ways, such as for particle swarm optimization. In the same sense, a bit string generated from sampling a qubit register can control all other aspects of an algorithm as well: topology, archiving, selections, repairing infeasible solutions, etc.

Quantum-inspired computing runs in three tiers. Tier 1 is the quantum physical models themselves. The history of quantum physics produced a number of alternative formulations of quantum physics that provide ways for variant computational paradigms. Tier 2 is the way a computation is modeled to make it open for quantum representations and operations. Tier 3 is the quantum-inspired algorithm itself that fully or partially—starting from a conventional effective algorithm—replaces and adjusts the processing steps according to the paradigms of quantum computing.

This book is about tiers 2 and 3, and a bit about tier 1 as the reference to the original quantum computer is needed to better understand where we are and where we will go. The book is divided into two main parts, the first part about research, the second about applications.

In the research part, containing four chapters, the focus is on the ways and means to interpret quantum physics in such a way that it can become the basis for new algorithms. In Chapter 1, entitled "Quantum neural computation of entanglement is robust to noise and decoherence," a link is made to the neural computation paradigm. In particular, this means learning and training from the perspective of quantum computing. Chapter 2, entitled "Quantum computing and supervised machine learning: training, model selection, and error estimation," focuses on the question of learning (here supervised learning) but from the viewpoint of explicit model construction.

Chapter 3, entitled "Field computation: A framework for quantum-inspired computing," presents field computation as a generalization of both quantum computing and neurocomputing, while following a pathway as described above, but now with field transformations replacing the quantum gates. In contrast to this, the topology is at the center of Chapter 4, entitled "Design of cellular quantum-inspired evolutionary algorithms with random topologies," by hinting at another aspect of quantum-inspired computing, the structure of the population and how it influences other steps of quantum-inspired computing.

The second part of this book includes nine chapters, more than in the theoretical part, and it shows that quantum-inspired computing is indeed able to produce algorithms to solve real-world problems. And it does not need to hide behind standard benchmark performance comparisons.

Chapter 5 is entitled "An efficient pure color image denoising using quantum parallel bidirectional self-organizing neural network architecture" and here we see for the first time an aspect that will appear more often in the following: that quantum-inspired computing provides guidance on modifying not only single algorithms but also hybrid algorithms and their embedding in an application domain. Here a variant of a self-organizing map is designed such that it can help solve an image-processing task of noise reduction or removal. But the task is extended at the same time to color images. The proposed algorithm takes advantage of the plurality representation in qubits that allows color spaces to be handled more easily. A related theme of thresholding is handled in Chapter 6, entitled "Quantum-inspired multiobjective simulated annealing for bilevel image thresholding," and this time the classical simulated annealing is shaped into a quantum-inspired version. A broader overview of such themes is given in Chapter 7, entitled "Quantum-inspired computational intelligence techniques in image segmentation." As mentioned earlier, a tier 2 line of development can tell us about other computational principles used for quantum-inspired computing. Chapter 8, entitled "Fuzzy evaluated quantum cellular automata approach for watershed image analysis," discusses the cellular automaton paradigm. This can serve as the basis to control immersion simulations that are used for image segmentation.

In Chapter 9, entitled "Quantum-inspired evolutionary algorithm for scaling factor optimization during manifold medical information embedding," the "standard" quantum-inspired evolutionary algorithm is used to optimize settings for digital watermarking (ie, the art of hiding information in media that can serve as being tamperproof with regard to manipulation), here for the case of medical data.

Chapter 10, entitled "Digital filter design using a quantum-inspired multiobjective cat swarm optimization algorithm," appears to stand on many legs. The central application theme is filter design but we also find the handling of this problem as a multiobjective optimization problem, and use of the novel cat swarm optimization as a base algorithm for "quantum inspiration." The result clearly outperforms the conventional cat swarm optimization. Chapter 11, entitled 'A novel graph clustering algorithm based on discrete-time quantum random walk," belongs to tier 2 in our simple terminology introduced above. This time it is random walk that gets a quantum-inspired twin assigned. This actually helps us handle a challenging recent problem in networking research, often called "community detection" or here simply "graph clustering." It illustrates further success of this ubiquitous principle of quantum-inspired computation.

Chapter 12, entitled "The Schrödinger equation as inspiration for a client portfolio simulation hybrid system based on dynamic Bayesian networks and the REFII model," corresponds to tier 1, and a different approach to do "quantum inspiration" is shown, together with a relevant practical application. Finally, Chapter 13, entitled "A quantum-inspired hybrid intelligent position monitoring system in wireless networks," approaches the position confidentiality problem, whenever a user of a wireless service is going to take advantage of location-based services but possibly at the price of giving up a bit of privacy. Also here, a hybrid intelligence algorithm enhanced with quantum-inspired computation helps with this intricate problem.

The designer of the quantum computer might smile a bit at the impatience shown by designers of quantum-inspired computations and their prospective failure of achieving the main promise of quantum computing, the intrinsic parallelism. This book will show that there is no reason to have such an impression: in addition to parallelism, quantum computing shows so many other features that it has provided much inspiration to work such as that presented in this book and work by many others.

I want to invite readers to enjoy this book and take most of its benefits. One could be to join the team of quantum-inspired algorithm designers and expand the repertoire, and also to bring about new insights into this new and challenging enterprise.

Mario Koeppen
Fukuoka

Preface

Imparting intelligence has become the focus of various computational paradigms. Thanks to evolving soft computing and artificial intelligence methods, scientists have been able to explain and understand real-life processes and practices which formerly remained unexplored by dint of their underlying imprecision, uncertainties, and redundancies, as well as the unavailability of appropriate methods for describing the inexactness, incompleteness, and vagueness of information representation. Computational intelligence tries to explore and unearth intelligence embedded in the system under consideration. From a historical perspective, researchers were involved in establishing artificial intelligence as a computational method acting as the artificial analogue of natural intelligence. Encouraged by the constructive outcome of such efforts, the question of imparting these ingredients of artificial intelligence within a computational device or a machine engulfed the focal point of relevant research efforts. This paved the way for the exploration of the domain of machine intelligence. Subsequent to this, developing the capability of the machine to carry out computation on its own in an intelligent manner became the challenge. Human civilization witnessed the growth of computational intelligence or intelligent computing. This is grossly the phenomenon of present-day research efforts. Serious research effort is being devoted in this direction. From this research status, a question that arises is: What form of research is going to unfold in the days to come? What will be the fate of the intelligent computing research paradigm? It is with this backdrop that our present endeavors are being conducted.

Although computational intelligence stemmed from needs in image processing and pattern recognition, lately scientists and researchers working on engineering, science, business, and financial applications have turned to computational intelligence for better investigation of throughput and end results. In fact, it is very difficult, if not impossible, to identify a current computationally intensive application that is devoid of the influence of "intelligent" approaches. No longer limited to computing-related disciplines, computational intelligence models may be applied to any endeavor which handles complex and meaningful information.

Quantum computing as a discipline to evolve computationally intensive systems came into existence in the late 1990s. Quantum-inspired computational intelligence refers to an emergent field of research that concentrates on applying the principles of quantum computing characterized by certain principles of quantum mechanics, such as standing waves, interference, quantum bits (*qubits*), coherence, decoherence, superposition of states, entanglement, and interference, to develop more efficient and more robust intelligent systems. Conventional computational intelligence or soft computing approaches, such as artificial neural networks, fuzzy systems, evolutionary computing, swarm intelligence, and hybrid soft computing methods, are thereby conjoined with quantum computing principles to achieve the objective. This volume offers a wide spectrum of research work done with soft computing combined with quantum computing systems.

In Chapter 1 the authors discuss the concept of noise-immune as well as decoherent quantum neural entanglement indicators where witnesses work on a more general class of states on one side and are devoid of a lengthy measurement procedure on the other. More interestingly, here the additional training overhead decreases with the growing size of the system.

The authors of Chapter 2 explore the strength of quantum computation as a alternative paradigm to mitigate the limitation of conventional computation techniques due to the growing size of datasets and the dimensionality issue of the input/output space thereof. They establish that quantum computation has been successful in addressing the computational aspects of building, tuning, and estimating the performance of a model of supervised learning of an unknown relation from input/output datasets.

Chapter 3, on the basis of the mathematical foundations of Hilbert space, provides field computation, basic field transformations, examples of field computation and their relation to neural networks, dimension reduction for the sake of physical realizability, cortical information processing in terms of fields, connections to the uncertainty principle, and minimal operations for universal field computation and general-purpose field computation.

Quantum-inspired evolutionary algorithms, characterized by qubit representation, variation operators such as rotation gates, measurement operators, and population structures, are designed by the integration of principles from quantum mechanics into the framework of evolutionary algorithms. Chapter 4 presents the design of cellular quantum-inspired evolutionary algorithms with static, dynamic, and adaptive random topologies that have been tested on a suite of standard benchmark problems and have been found to compare favorably with the current state-of-the-art algorithms.

A self-supervised learning network in a quantum environment, named a "quantum parallel bidirectional self-organizing neural network" (QPBDSONN) architecture appropriate for pure color image denoising that mimics the classical parallel bidirectional self-organizing neural network by the embedding of quantum computation is the main contribution of Chapter 5. It invokes the fundamental concepts and principles of quantum mechanics. The QPBDSONN comprises three quantum bidirectional self-organizing neural network architectures in the input layer to process three distinct color components (red, green, and blue) separately used in the color noisy images. The superiority of the proposed QPBDSONN is established by its application on synthetic and real-life wrench pure color images with different degrees of uniform noise and Gaussian noise by comparison with its classical parallel bidirectional self-organizing neural network counterpart, a supervised autoassociative Hopfield network, and a nonlinear technique named "median filter with adaptive discrete wavelet transformations." The results reveal that the QPBDSONN dominates its classical counterpart and the threefold parallel Hopfield network as far as timing efficiency is concerned and it also restores the shapes of extracted images with great accuracy compared with the median filter with adaptive discrete wavelet transformations. Finally, the statistical significance of the proposed QPBDSONN is provided by means of a two-sample Kolmogorov-Smirnov test.

A new quantum-based multiobjective simulated annealing for bilevel thresholding technique is developed in Chapter 6. The proposed approach, designed by the mingling of the basic quantum properties and a popular metaheuristic algorithm, called "simulated annealing," collectively on the core of multiobjective optimization, is applied on grayscale images and two steps are followed in succession to find the optimal threshold value of the input image. Firstly, two different objective functions (generally of conflicting type) are used to determine the set of nondominated solutions; thereafter, an objective function, called "Huang's method" is applied on these nondominated solutions to find the optimal threshold value for bilevel image thresholding. The superiority of proposed method over its counterpart is established in terms of the peak signal to noise ratio.

Quantum-inspired computational-based intelligent methods find several applications. One such major application-image segmentation is explained in Chapter 7. The authors of this chapter establish how such a technique is able to outperform classical methods of segmentation.

The authors of Chapter 8 propose a new unsupervised approach to pixel classification that is a hybrid of fuzzy *C*-means and partitioned quantum cellular automata methods and is able to detect clusters using a two-dimensional partitioned cellular automata model based on fuzzy segmentations. The clustered regions are compared with well-known fuzzy *C*-means and *K*-means methods and also with the ground truth knowledge. The results show the superiority of the new method.

Chapter 9 proposes a novel authentication system for robust biomedical content, which embeds multiple hospitals' logos or multiple electronic patient records within the medical image. The authors explore watermarking based on a hybrid combination of discrete cosine transformation, discrete wavelet transformation, and singular value decomposition teamed with optimization algorithms. With extensive experimentation, they establish the effectiveness of their findings.

In Chapter 10 the authors propose a quantum-inspired evolutionary cat swarm optimization technique for the design of filters. Hilbert transformers are designed with use of a multiobjective optimization approach. The applicability of the proposed approach is evaluated by comparison of the results obtained with the proposed algorithm with those obtained with other state-of-the-art evolutionary multiobjective algorithms. The reduction in power consumption is validated for real-time applications by implementation of the designed filters with use of a field-programmable gate array.

Chapter 11 explains how quantum random walk helps in graph-based clustering, and a new quantum clustering algorithm is proposed. The proposed quantum clustering algorithm is based on the discrete-time quantum random walk, which finds the clusters from a given adjacency matrix of a graph. The authors provide a quantum circuit model and Quantum Computing Language-based simulation of the algorithm and illustrate its faster rate of convergence. Simulation results for experimental graphs indicate that the proposed algorithm shows an exponential speedup over existing classical algorithms.

A novel method inspired by the Schrödinger equation for client portfolio simulation based on dynamic Bayesian networks and the REFII model is the novel finding in Chapter 12. A client portfolio is treated as a complex system with numerous potential states (variables), and those states can vary depending on the period over which the client portfolio is observed. Each state at a specific point in time can be expressed with a probability, and those probabilities depend on the states of other connected elements (variables or particles as interpreted in the Schrödinger equation method). The chapter also provides a real-life case study.

Finally, the authors of Chapter 13 propose a novel quantum-inspired hybrid intelligent position monitoring system in wireless networks with the aim of conserving confidentiality of an individual in real-time position-based services. They devise a quantum-inspired position monitoring system algorithm incorporating fuzzy logic and quantum computational theory so as to achieve computational intelligence in the problem of a mobile object's position confidentiality. The simulation results and case studies prove that the proposed quantum-inspired system can conserve confidentiality of the roaming user with reduced communication cost.

In the present scope the editors have tried to present a compilation of research on quantum-inspired intelligence—both theoretical and applied. This is particularly in keeping with view that in the days intelligent techniques based on the classical platform of computation will be duly replaced by the quantum computational paradigm. The editors hope that this endeavor will enthuse the relevant research community in that direction.

Siddhartha Bhattacharyya
Ujjwal Maulik
Paramartha Dutta
Kolkata, India

Acknowledgments

The success and the final outcome of this book in the present complete form required a lot of guidance and assistance from many people. We are extremely fortunate to have received this at all times during the preparation of this book. We wish to acknowledge those people behind the scenes who were a constant source of inspiration during the preparation of this book.

Firstly, we express our heartfelt thanks to the authors who have contributed to this edited volume, without whom this book would not have been possible. Thanks are also due to the reviewers who have helped to evaluate the authored contributions in spite of their busy schedules.

We express our respect and deep sense of gratitude to the Editorial Advisory Board members for their continuous supervision and inspiration. Words of encouragement and competent advice from their end were always invaluable during the preparation of this book.

We are highly elated to express our gratitude to Elsevier, which agreed to publish this book. It has been a joyful and learning experience in working with Elsevier. Special thanks are due to Amy Invernizzi, Editorial Project Manager, Elsevier, and Brian Romer, Senior Acquisitions Editor, Elsevier, without whom this project would not have become a reality. Their roles as stupendous mentors in detecting and rectifying faults in our efforts should not remain unmentioned.

We express our indebtedness to Mario Koeppen of Kyushu Institute of Technology, Japan, for writing the foreword for the book, adding to its scholarly content.

As the lead editor of this book, Siddhartha Bhattacharyya expresses his indebtedness to Sparsamani Chatterjee (Chairman), Arup Kumar Bhaumik (Principal), and Pradip Kumar Das (Dean, Academics) of the RCC Institute of Information Technology, Kolkata, India. They have been a constant source of inspiration to him.

Siddhartha Bhattacharyya also thanks the following colleagues at his institute: Biswanath Chakraborty, Pramatha Nath Basu, Anirban Mukherjee, Indrajit Pan, Hrishikesh Bhaumik, Dipankar Majumdar, Pankaj Pal, Abhijit Das, Hiranmoy Roy, Jhuma Ray, Soumyadip Dhar, Moumita Deb, Abantika Choudhury, Amit Khan, Sudarsan Biswas, Moumita Chatterjee, Ripan Mandal, Sudipta Bose (Nandi), and Arijit Majumdar.

Finally, we thank those whose names have not been mentioned here but who have helped us.

Siddhartha Bhattacharyya
Ujjwal Maulik
Paramartha Dutta

PART

I

Research

CHAPTER

Quantum neural computation of entanglement is robust to noise and decoherence

1

E.C. Behrman, N.H. Nguyen, J.E. Steck, M. McCann
Wichita State University, Wichita, KS, United States

1 INTRODUCTION AND LITERATURE BACKGROUND

The use and manipulation of entanglement is central to the exploitation of quantum computation (see, e.g., [1–8]). The quantum system obviously "knows" what its own entanglement is, although extraction of that information is not obvious; thus we use dynamic learning methods [9,10] to map this information onto a single experimental measurement which is our entanglement indicator [11]. Our method does not require prior state reconstruction or lengthy optimization [4,5] nor must the system be "close" to a given entangled state [7]. An entanglement witness emerges from the learning process. We use knowledge of the smaller two-qubit system as a means of "bootstrapping" to larger systems [12]. As the size of the system grows, the amount of additional training necessary diminishes [13,14], unlike in other methods, for example, which require knowledge or reconstruction of the density matrix [1–3]; thus our method potentially may be of general applicability even to large-scale quantum computers, once they have been built.

In any experimental implementation, we need also to consider that no setup is perfect: there will always be some uncertainty due to extraneous effects. The problem of fault tolerance in quantum computing has received considerable attention. One approach is to design fault-tolerant algorithms [15]. Another is to implement feedback control [16,17]. Still another is to use repeated weak measurement [18]. Dong et al. [19] use an approach in some ways similar to ours that they call "sampling-based learning control." Several authors have established robustness of quantum computing to noise [20]. In quantum systems there is also the problem of decoherence. Under certain conditions [17,21] or for certain classes of problems [20,22] quantum computers can be robust to decoherence.

Over the past couple of decades interest has grown in the use of a machine learning or neural network approach to quantum computing [23]. Several different approaches have been used [19,20,24–27]. For example, Bisio et al. [26] trained a

Quantum Inspired Computational Intelligence. http://dx.doi.org/10.1016/B978-0-12-804409-4.00001-2

network to reproduce an unknown (unitary) transformation. We imagine, instead, that we have a particular quantity (here the entanglement) that we wish to measure, and we train the network to give an indicator of that quantity.

Machine learning [19,24,25] shows particular promise for dealing with general problems. Classically learning systems such as neural networks have proven fault tolerant and robust to noise; they are also famously used for noise reduction in signals [28]. A machine learning approach would seem to be an excellent one for issues such as noise, decoherence, or missing or damaged data. Here we show that this is in fact the case, using as a test bed our entanglement indicator on the simple two-qubit system.

2 DYNAMIC LEARNING OF AN ENTANGLEMENT INDICATOR

In previous work we showed we could successfully train a quantum system to estimate its own degree of entanglement, by mapping a measurable output at the final time, to give an indicator of the entanglement of the prepared, initial state. Briefly, the method was as follows; for full details the reader is referred to [11,13,14,29,30]

We begin with the Schrödinger equation for the time evolution of the density matrix ρ [31]:

$$\frac{d\rho}{dt} = \frac{1}{i\hbar}[H, \rho], \tag{1}$$

where H is the Hamiltonian. We consider an N-qubit system whose Hamiltonian is

$$H = \sum_{\alpha=1}^{N} K_{\alpha}\sigma_{x\alpha} + \varepsilon_{\alpha}\sigma_{z\alpha} + \sum_{\alpha \neq \beta=1}^{N} \zeta_{\alpha\beta}\sigma_{z\alpha}\sigma_{z\beta}, \tag{2}$$

where $\{\sigma\}$ are the Pauli operators corresponding to each of the qubits, $\{K\}$ are the tunneling amplitudes, $\{\varepsilon\}$ are the biases, and $\{\zeta\}$ are the qubit-qubit couplings. We choose the usual "charge basis," in which each qubit's state is given as 0 or 1; for a system of N qubits there are 2^N states, each labeled by a bit string, each of whose numbers corresponds to the state of each qubit, in order. The amplitude for each qubit to tunnel to its opposing state (i.e., switch between the 0 and 1 states) is its K value; each qubit has an external bias represented by its ε value; and each qubit is coupled to each of the other qubits, with a strength represented by the appropriate ζ value. Note that, for example, the operator $\sigma_{x1} = \sigma_x \otimes I \ldots \otimes I$, where there are $(N-1)$ outer products, acts nontrivially only on qubit 1.

The parameter functions $\{K(t), \varepsilon(t), \zeta(t)\}$ direct the time evolution of the system in the sense that if at least one of them is changed, the way a given initial state will evolve in time will also change because of Eqs. (1) and (2). This is the basis for the use of our quantum system as a neural network. The role of the input vector is played by the initial density matrix $\rho(0)$, the role of the output is played by (some function of) the density matrix at the final time, $\rho(t_f)$, and the role of the "weights" of the network is played by the parameter functions of the Hamiltonian, $\{K, \varepsilon, \zeta\}$, all of which can be adjusted experimentally [8]. By adjusting these parameters using a machine learning algorithm, we can train the system to evolve in time from an input state to a set of particular final states at the final time t_f. Because the time evolution is quantum mechanical (and, we assume, coherent), a quantum mechanical function, like an entanglement witness of the initial state, can be mapped to an observable of the system's final state, a measurement made at the final time t_f. Complete details, including a derivation of the quantum dynamic learning paradigm using quantum backpropagation [9] in time [10], are given in [11]. We call this quantum system a "quantum neural network" (QNN).

We found [11,30] a set of parameter functions that successfully map the input (initial) state of a two-qubit system to a good approximation of the entanglement of formation of that initial state, using as the output the qubit-qubit correlation function at the final time, $\langle \sigma_{z1}(t_f)\sigma_{z2}(t_f)\rangle^2$. This set of parameter functions was relatively easily generalized to three- four-, and five-qubit systems [14]. Here we will consider the effect of noise on only the simplest case, of two qubits ($N = 2$), and for ease of notation we will call the two qubits A and B. With continuum [29,30] rather than piecewise constant parameter functions [11,14] training is more rapid and complete; see Fig. 1. The parameter functions are trained with a set of just four initial quantum states ("inputs"), as shown in Table 1: a fully entangled state ("Bell"), a "flat" state (equal amounts of all basis states), a product state "C" whose initial ($t = 0$) correlation function $\langle \sigma_{zA}\sigma_{zB}\rangle^2$ is nonzero, and a partially entangled state "P." Because of the symmetry in the Hamiltonian and in the training set, $K_A = K_B = K$, and

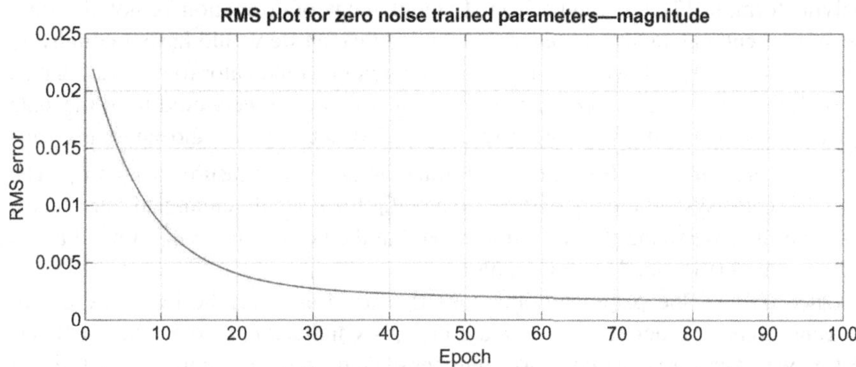

FIG. 1

Total root mean square (RMS) error for the training set as a function of epoch (pass through the training set), for the two-qubit system, with zero noise. Asymptotic error is 1.6×10^{-3}. For comparison, with piecewise constant functions a similar level of error required 2000 epochs.

Table 1 Training Data for a Quantum Neural Network Entanglement Witness

Input State $\|\Psi(0)\rangle$	Target	Trained	E_F
Bell = $\frac{1}{\sqrt{2}}(\|00\rangle + \|11\rangle) = \|\Phi_+\rangle$	1.0	0.998	1.0
Flat = $\frac{1}{2}(\|00\rangle + \|01\rangle + \|10\rangle + \|11\rangle)$	0.0	1.2×10^{-5}	0.0
C = $\frac{1}{\sqrt{1.25}}(0.5\|10\rangle + \|11\rangle)$	0.0	1.8×10^{-4}	0.0
P = $\frac{1}{\sqrt{3}}(\|00\rangle + \|01\rangle + \|10\rangle)$	0.44	0.44	0.55
RMS error		1.6×10^{-3}	
Epochs		100	

RMS, root mean square.

$\epsilon_A = \epsilon_B = \epsilon$. Each is a relatively simple function, well parametrized by only one frequency (ϵ, ζ) or two frequencies (K), as shown in Table 2 and plotted in Figs. 2–4. The (*input*, *output*) pairs are

$$\begin{aligned} input &= \rho(0) = |\Psi(0)\rangle\langle\Psi(0)|, \\ output &= \langle\sigma_{zA}(t_f)\sigma_{zB}(t_f)\rangle^2 \rightarrow target \end{aligned} \tag{3}$$

with prepared input states at zero time, and corresponding targets, given in Table 1, which also shows the QNN-indicated entanglement values after training has finished and, for comparison, the entanglement of formation, calculated with use of the analytic formula [2] for comparison. Entanglement of formation is not the only measure of entanglement, of course, but any one we chose would have qualitatively similar behavior, which we would like our entanglement indicator to imitate. That is, we seek here not exact *agreement* with E_F (in which case we would train the state $\frac{1}{\sqrt{3}}(|00\rangle + |01\rangle + |10\rangle)$ to a target value of 0.55) but a robust and internally self-consistent measure, which we hope will track an analytic measure such as E_F. The QNN indicator systematically underestimates E_F for partially entangled pure states; this is because we found through simulation that the net was naturally trained to the target value of 0.44; see [11] for details.

Once trained, the parameter functions that are found can be tested by use of the Hamiltonian so defined to calculate the QNN indicator for other initial states. Testing was therefore done on a large number of states not represented in the training set, including fully entangled states, partially entangled states, product (unentangled) states, and even *mixed* states. (Note that only *pure* states were present in the training sets.) The interested reader is referred to our previous work for the (extensive) testing results [11,14,30]. Note also that the testing was done with the fitted functions only.

Table 2 Curve Fit Coefficients for Parameter Functions K, ϵ, and ζ, for a Quantum Neural Network Entanglement Witness

Coefficient	K	ϵ	ζ
a_0	0.00248	9.89×10^{-5}	9.89×10^{-5}
a_1	3.68×10^{-6}	-4.96×10^{-6}	-1.46×10^{-5}
b_1	1.95×10^{-6}	4.55×10^{-6}	-2.34×10^{-5}
a_2	3.70×10^{-6}	–	–
b_2	8.68×10^{-7}	–	–
ω	0.0250	0.0250	0.0575
RMS error	9.77×10^{-7}	1.84×10^{-6}	7.29×10^{-6}

$f(t) = a_0 + a_1 \cos(\omega t) + b_1 \sin(\omega t) + a_2 \cos(2\omega t) + b_2 \sin(2\omega t)$.
RMS, root mean square.

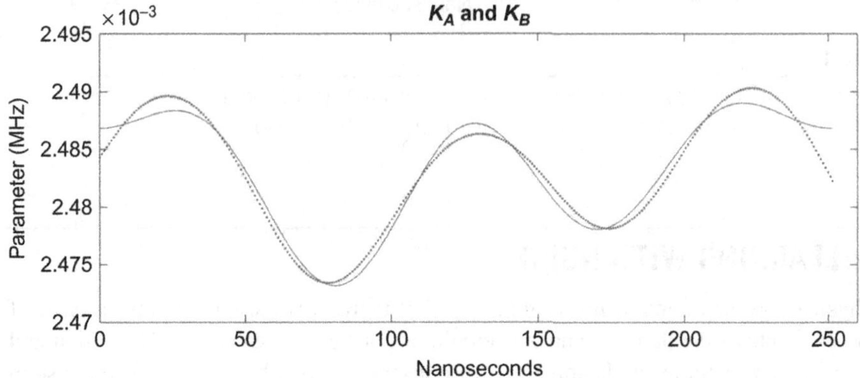

FIG. 2

Parameter function $K_A = K_B$ as a function of time (*data points*), as trained at zero noise for the entanglement indicator, and plotted with the Fourier fit (*solid line*).

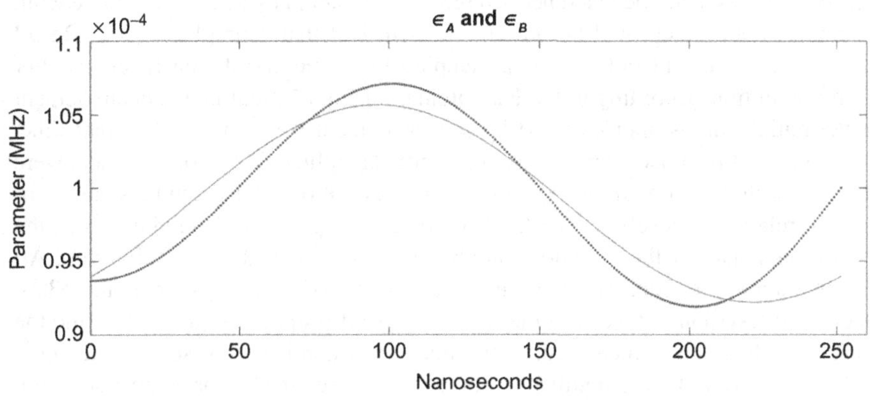

FIG. 3

Parameter function $\epsilon_A = \epsilon_B$ as a function of time (*data points*), as trained at zero noise for the entanglement indicator, and plotted with the Fourier fit (*solid line*).

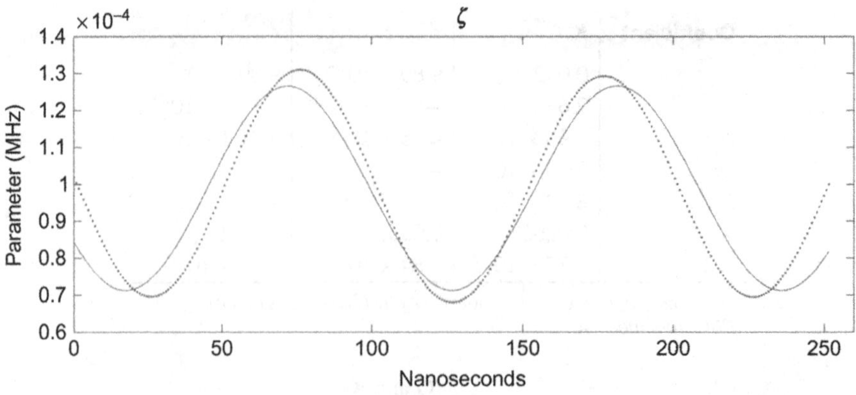

FIG. 4

Parameter function ζ as a function of time (*data points*), as trained at zero noise for the entanglement indicator, and plotted with the Fourier fit (*solid line*).

3 LEARNING WITH NOISE

Physical systems contain noise, meaning that there is some uncertainty in each of the elements of the density matrix (though, of course, it must remain Hermitian and positive semidefinite, with unit trace to conserve probability.) What if the system which is trained is somewhat noisy?

Let us first define our terms. Because we are working with simulations, we can isolate the different effects of "noise" and "decoherence": here we will use "noise" to refer to random (uncorrelated) magnitudes, of a given size, added to the density matrix elements, and "decoherence" to refer to random phases so added. In general, of course, both effects will be present; we will call that "complex" noise. Recall that our entanglement indicator is a mapping to a time correlation function, after evolution in time according to the Hamiltonian of Eq. (2); that is, the entanglement of the initial state is approximated by a measurement performed at the final time. To simulate white noise (zero mean and specified amplitude), random numbers were added at each timestep $\Delta t = 0.8$ ns of that time evolution. These numbers have zero time correlation themselves. The level of noise we report is the amplitude (i.e., the root-mean-square of these random numbers) that is imposed at each timestep. All the simulations were done for the same total time of 317 timesteps, or about 253 ns. Because the system evolves in time, the noise itself propagates, so by the time the correlation function is measured, at the final time, numbers that seem quite small can build up to destroy a significant amount of entanglement. For comparison with our testing results, we will always therefore include the entanglement of formation for the noisy density matrix, calculated with the Bennett-Wootters formula [1,2] and marked "BW" on our testing graphs (Figs. 12–17, 25–30, and 38–43).

We consider first the case of magnitude noise only. Fig. 5 shows a typical rms error training curve for a fairly large level of noise. As expected, asymptotic error for the training set increases with increasing noise. The parameter functions also become "noisy"; see Figs. 6–8.

Much of this variation is not meaningful though. In fact, the numbers in Table 2 are slightly different from the ones we found in [30]. Is that difference significant? To investigate this we tested the system with all but a selected one of the parameter functions' Fourier coefficients set to the trained values but with random numbers (of the right order of magnitude) assigned to the Fourier coefficients of the parameter function chosen. The system was remarkably insensitive to this procedure when the random function was the tunneling function K: as long as K was of the right order of magnitude, the indicator still tested extremely well—in fact for most of the testing the indicator results were identical. This was not true if ϵ or ζ was randomized, however: errors were substantial, particularly when the Fourier frequency ω was randomized. Still, exact agreement with the trained functions is not, apparently, necessary.

We can, as before, fit each function to a Fourier series, and tested the system using the fitted functions. Figs. 9, 10, and 11 show the Fourier coefficients for $K_A = K_B$, $\epsilon_A = \epsilon_B$, and ζ respectively as functions of increasing noise level. The Fourier components of the tunneling parameter function K are clearly the least sensitive to

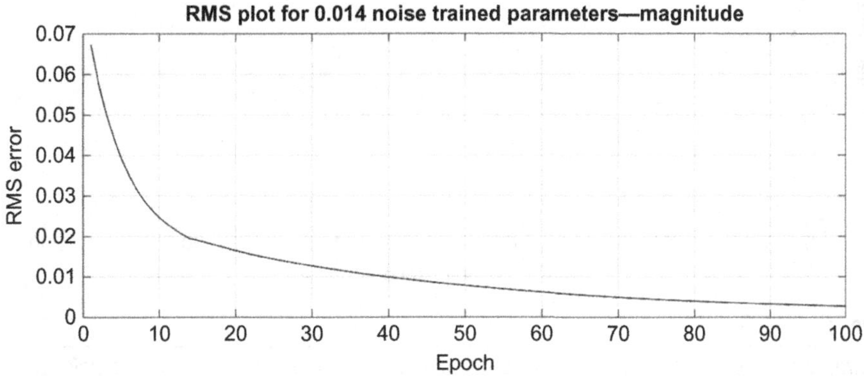

FIG. 5

Total root mean square (RMS) error for the training set as a function of epoch (pass through the training set), for the two-qubit system, with a (magnitude) noise level of 0.014 at each (of 317 in total) timestep. Asymptotic error is 3.1×10^{-3}, about double what it was with no noise.

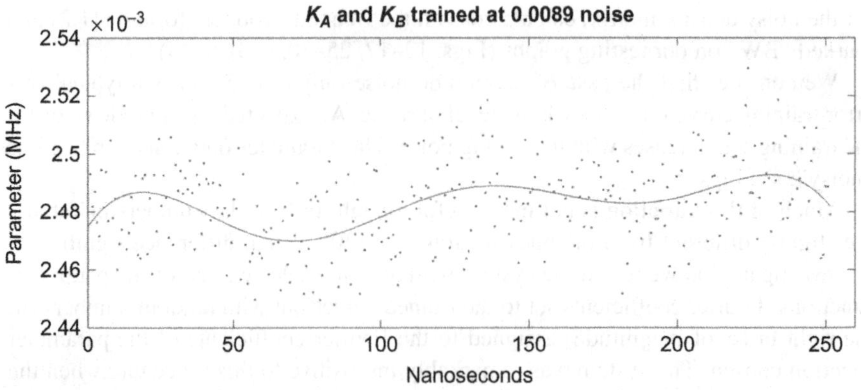

FIG. 6

Parameter function $K_A = K_B$ as a function of time, as trained at 0.0089 amplitude noise at each of the 317 timesteps, for the entanglement indicator (*data points*) and plotted with the Fourier fit (*solid line*). Note the change in scale from Fig. 2 because of the (much larger) spread of the noisy data: the Fourier fit is actually almost the same on this graph.

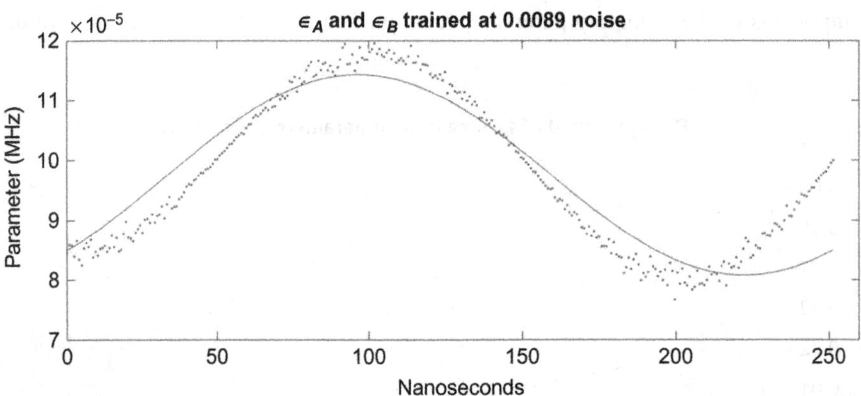

FIG. 7

Parameter function $\epsilon_A = \epsilon_B$ as a function of time, as trained at 0.0089 amplitude noise at each of the 317 timesteps, for the entanglement indicator (*data points*) and plotted with the Fourier fit (*solid line*).

the noise level, while for ϵ they are a bit more so and for ζ they are the most sensitive. This is in accordance with the observed insensitivity of the entanglement indicator to K: that is, it is true both that the indicator is relatively insensitive to the K function and that the K function's Fourier fit is insensitive to environmental noise.

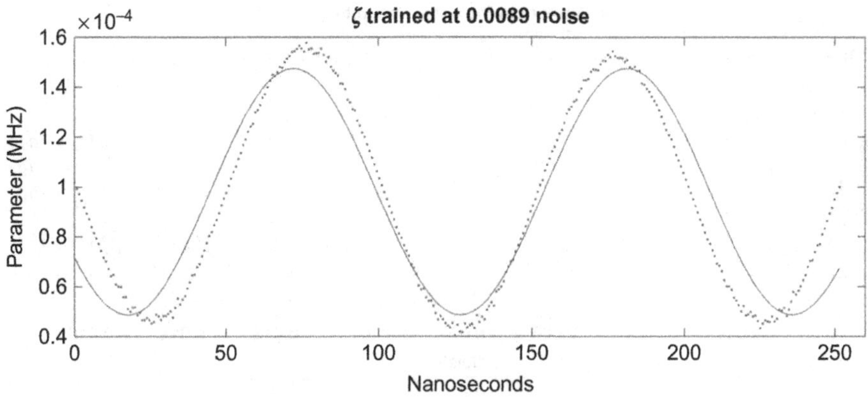

FIG. 8

Parameter function ζ as a function of time, as trained at 0.0089 noise at each of the 317 timesteps, for the entanglement indicator (*data points*) and plotted with the Fourier fit (*solid line*).

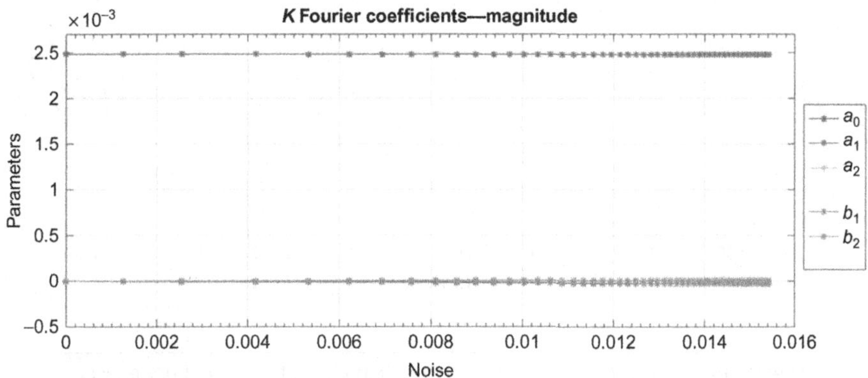

FIG. 9

Fourier coefficients for the tunneling parameter functions K as a function of noise level.

All of the parameters look fairly stable at these levels of noise from this point of view. But a more important question is: How much does noise interfere with the net's ability to detect entanglement?

Consider a pure state, specifically, the state $P(\gamma) = \frac{|00\rangle + |11\rangle + \gamma|01\rangle}{\sqrt{2+|\gamma|^2}}$. For $\gamma = 0$ this is, of course, the (fully entangled) Bell state; as γ increases, the entanglement decreases. $P(\gamma)$ is one of the states we used to test our system in our 2008 article [11], and, as we found then, the entanglement as computed by the QNN, without noise,

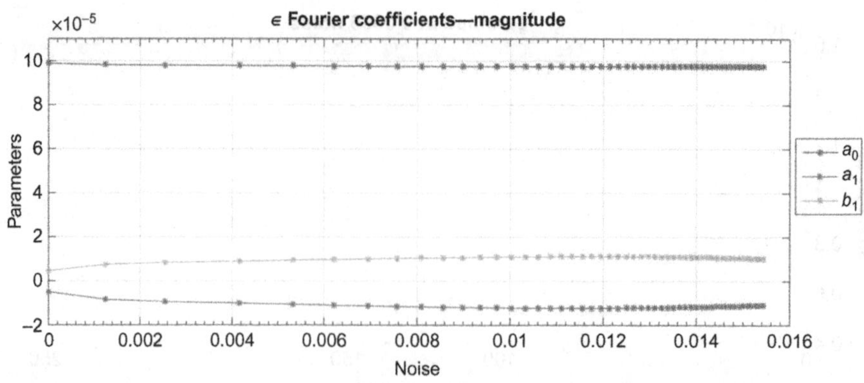

FIG. 10

Fourier coefficients for the bias parameter functions ϵ as a function of noise level.

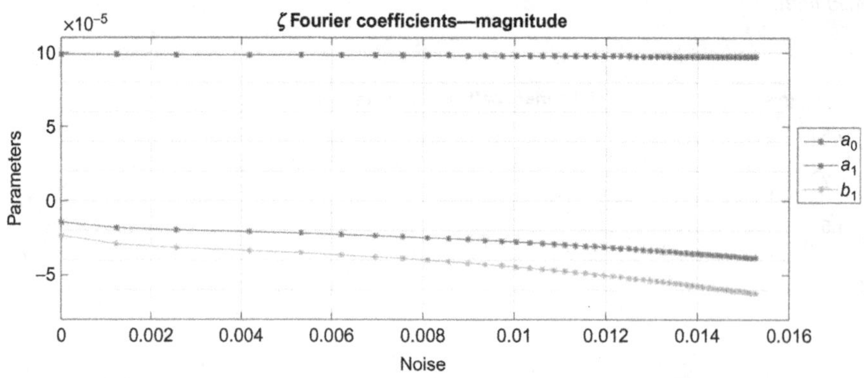

FIG. 11

Fourier coefficients for the coupling parameter function ζ as a function of noise level.

tracks the entanglement of formation very well. How much noise or uncertainty can the network tolerate? We answer this question in two ways. First, we suppose the QNN was trained on the perfect (zero noise) system of the four-pair training set, and we add increasing amounts of noise to test the system for various nonzero values of γ, and compare the results with the entanglement of formation both at zero noise and at 0.0069 noise (see Fig. 12). Then we suppose the QNN was trained on a noisy system and, again, test with increasing levels of noise. Figs. 13 and 14 show, respectively, an intermediate level and a high level of noise present during training the system. Recall that the noise should be understood as occurring over the total time evolution interval: that is, an independent (uncorrelated) noise at the given rms level was added at *each*

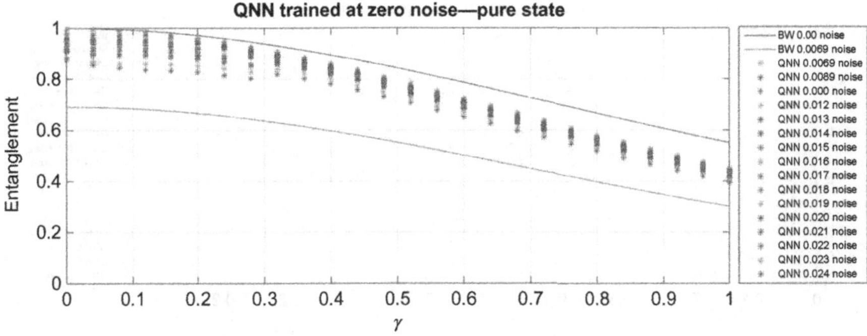

FIG. 12

Entanglement of the state P as a function of γ as calculated by the quantum neural network (QNN) and compared with the entanglement of formation (marked "BW") at zero noise (blue; dark gray top curve in print version) and at 0.0069 noise (orange; light gray bottom curve in print version). In each case the QNN was trained at zero noise but was tested at the given level.

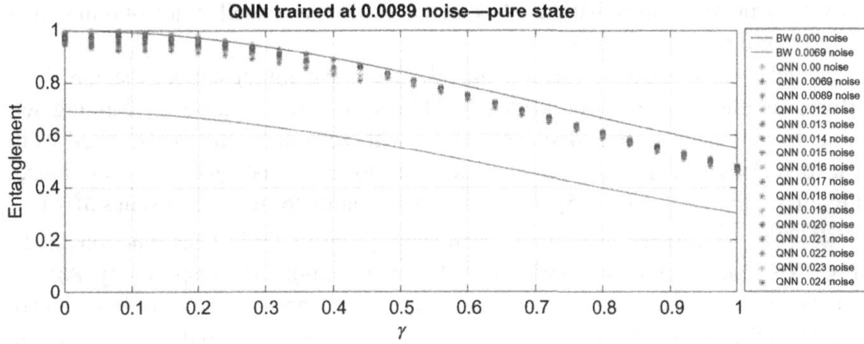

FIG. 13

Entanglement of the state P as a function of γ, as calculated by the quantum neural network (QNN), and compared with the entanglement of formation (marked "BW") at zero noise (blue; dark gray top curve in print version) and at 0.0069 noise (orange; light gray bottom curve in print version). In each case the QNN was trained at a noise level of 0.0089 and then tested at the given level.

timestep. The two curves showing the entanglement of formation can therefore be thought of as a kind of "error bar": the correct entanglement of the system should lie somewhere between the zero noise result and the result at maximum noise insofar as the QNN tracks well with the entanglement of formation. Presumably the presence of noise destroys entanglement, but since the measurement itself is noisy, it is not certain how much is destroyed and how much is simply a bad measurement. Still, it

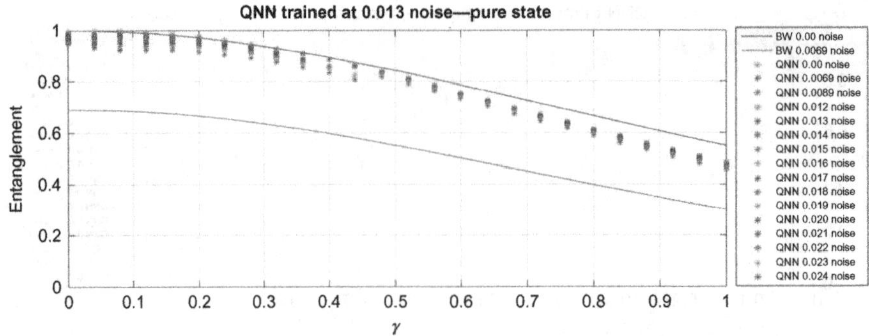

FIG. 14

Entanglement of the state P as a function of γ, as calculated by the quantum neural network (QNN), and compared with the entanglement of formation (marked "BW") at zero noise (blue; dark gray top curve in print version) and at 0.0069 noise (orange; light gray bottom curve in print version). In each case the QNN was trained at 0.013 noise and then tested at the given level.

is obvious from the results that the QNN technique does an excellent job of remaining robust to pure noise.

Second, we consider testing on mixed states. We might expect the QNN to perform significantly less well with these kinds of states because the training set (Table 1) contained no mixed states. In fact with zero noise the QNN tested well on several classes of mixed states [11]; we need to see if that success is maintained with noisy conditions. Figs. 15, 16, and 17 show results for the mixed states $M(\delta) = \frac{\delta|11\rangle\langle 11|+|\Phi^+\rangle\langle\Phi^+|}{\delta+1}$, where $|\Phi^+\rangle$ is the Bell state, given in Table 1, as functions of δ, for a QNN trained at zero, 0.0089, and 0.013 noise amplitude, respectively. Again, the entanglement of formation results can serve as an approximate error bound, and we see that the QNN's entanglement indicator is robust to noise. Indeed, comparison of these figures with the ones for pure states shows that the performance on mixed states is even better. Because of this we might expect the QNN indicator to show greater robustness to decoherence than to magnitude noise; we will see in the next section that this is the case.

4 DECOHERENCE

We now turn to the case of "pure" decoherence; that is, we introduce random phases to the elements of the density matrix, without changing their magnitudes. Fig. 18 shows a typical rms error training curve for a fairly large level of phase noise. Again asymptotic error for the training set increases with increasing phase noise (decoherence). The parameter functions also become "noisy" (see Figs. 19–21).

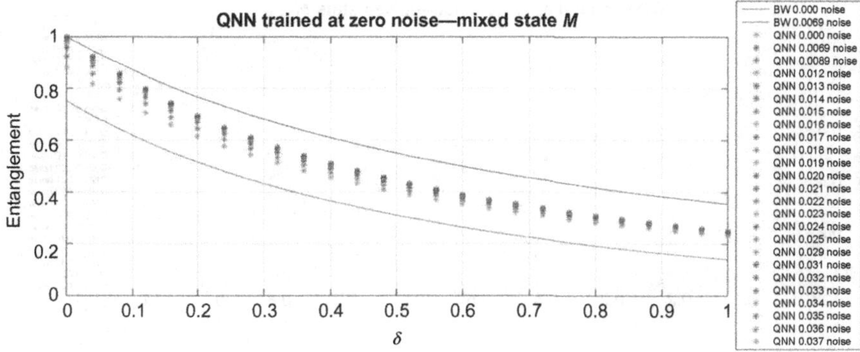

FIG. 15

Entanglement of the state M as a function of δ, as calculated by the quantum neural network (QNN), and compared with the entanglement of formation (marked "BW") at zero noise (blue; dark gray top curve in print version) and at 0.0069 noise (orange; light gray bottom curve in print version). In each case the QNN was trained at zero noise but tested at the given level.

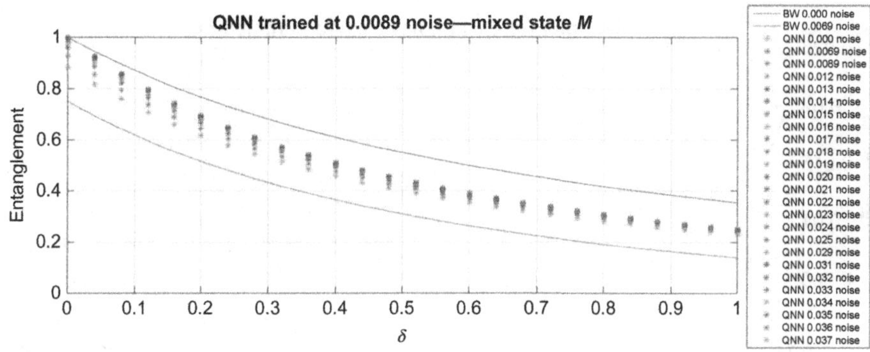

FIG. 16

Entanglement of the state M as a function of δ, as calculated by the quantum neural network (QNN), and compared with the entanglement of formation (marked "BW") at zero noise (blue; dark gray top curve in print version) and at 0.0069 noise (orange; light gray bottom curve in print version). In each case the QNN was trained at a noise level of 0.0089 and then tested at the given level.

Figs. 22, 23, and 24 show the Fourier coefficients for $K_A = K_B, \epsilon_A = \epsilon_B$, and ζ respectively as functions of increasing decoherence level. It is clear that in the case of decoherence the parameter functions are even stabler than in the previous case of noise.

Testing results for the pure state P subject to decoherence are shown in Figs. 25, 26, and 27, as trained, respectively, at zero, 0.0089, and 0.013 decoherence (phase

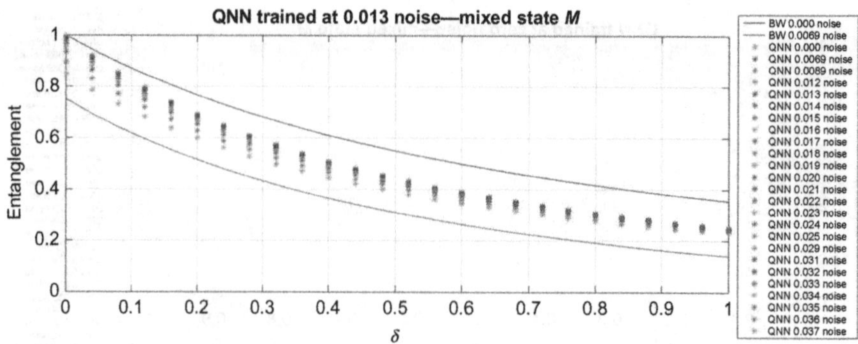

FIG. 17

Entanglement of the state M as a function of δ, as calculated by the quantum neural network (QNN), and compared with the entanglement of formation (marked "BW") at zero noise (blue; dark gray top curve in print version) and at 0.0069 noise (orange; light gray bottom curve in print version). In each case the QNN was trained at 0.013 noise and then tested at the given level.

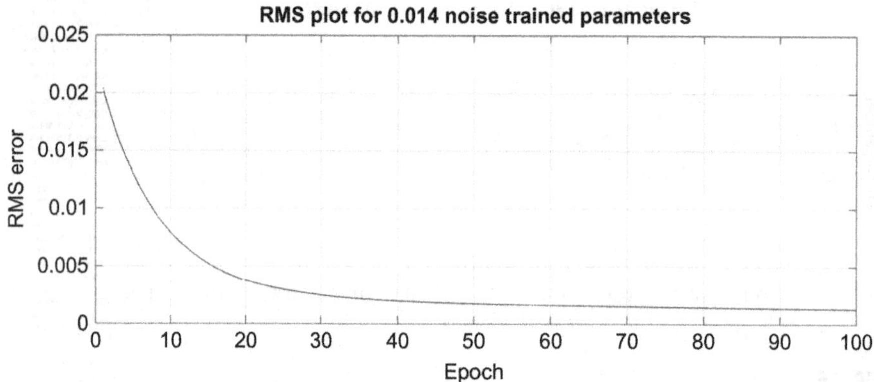

FIG. 18

Total root mean square (RMS) error for the training set as a function of epoch (pass through the training set), for the 2-qubit system, with a phase noise level of 0.014 at each (of 317 in total) timestep. Asymptotic error is 1.3×10^{-3}, approximately the same as with no noise.

noise) and tested with various levels of phase noise and compared with the entanglement of formation at zero and 0.0069 phase noise. The results are extremely good, better even than the ones in Figs. 12–14; clearly, the QNN is even better at dealing with decoherence than with "pure" noise. Possibly the various (random) phases tend to cancel each other; but since for *definite* phase shifts the QNN underestimates the entanglement, sometimes drastically [11,30], this was an unexpectedly good result.

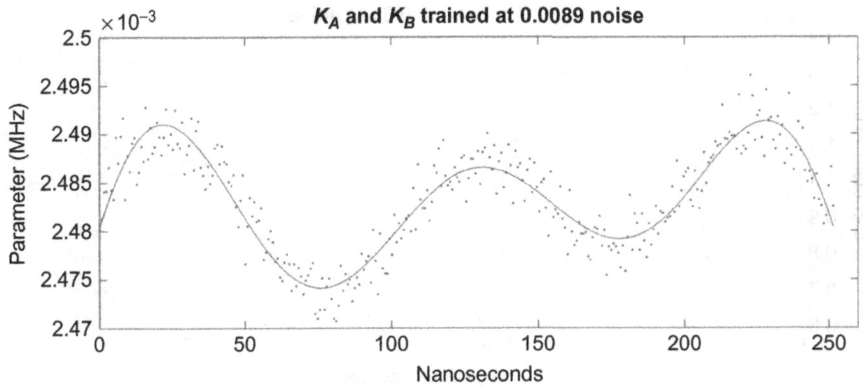

FIG. 19

Parameter function $K_A = K_B$ as a function of time, as trained at 0.0089 phase noise at each of the 317 timesteps, for the entanglement indicator *(data points)* and plotted with the Fourier fit (*solid line*).

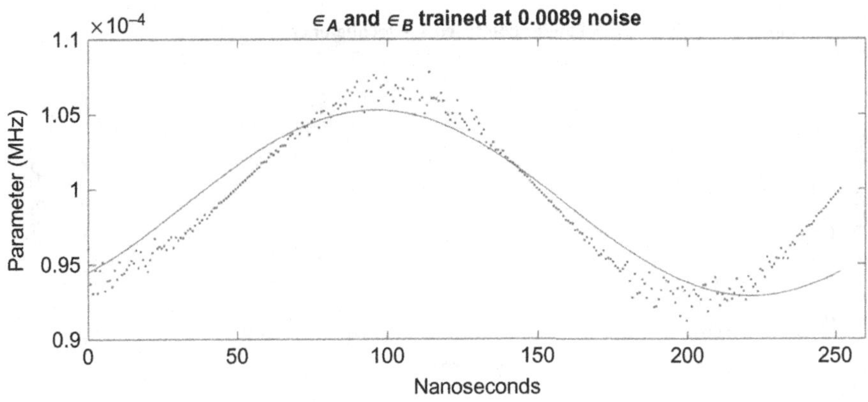

FIG. 20

Parameter function $\epsilon_A = \epsilon_B$ as a function of time, as trained at 0.0089 phase noise at each of the 317 timesteps, for the entanglement indicator (*data points*) and plotted with the Fourier fit (*solid line*).

Figs. 28, 29, and 30 show the performance of the QNN on the mixed state M, as trained, respectively, at zero, 0.0089, and 0.013 decoherence (phase noise) and tested with various levels of phase noise and compared with the entanglement of formation at zero and 0.0069 phase noise. Again we see that the QNN entanglement indicator is robust to decoherence.

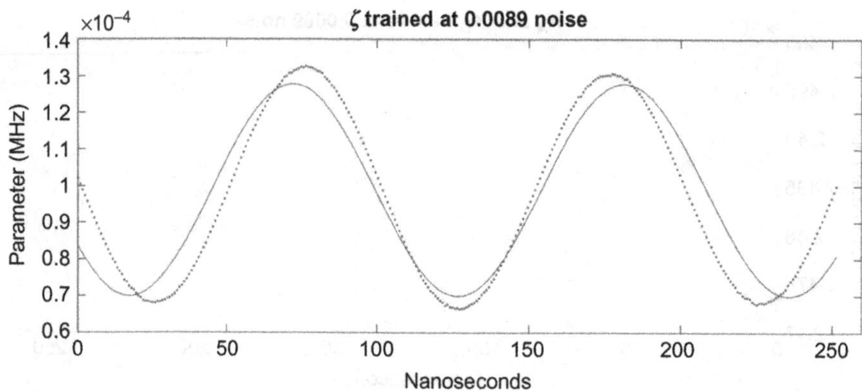

FIG. 21

Parameter function ζ as a function of time, as trained at 0.0089 phase noise at each of the 317 timesteps, for the entanglement indicator (*data points*) and plotted with the Fourier fit (*solid line*).

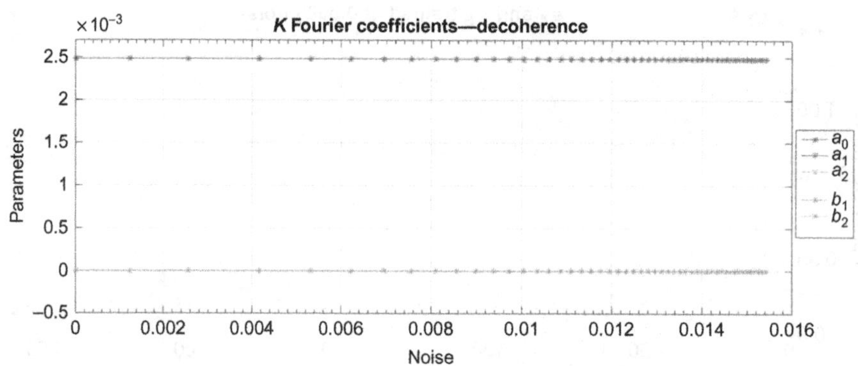

FIG. 22

Fourier coefficients for the tunneling parameter functions K as functions of the decoherence level.

5 NOISE PLUS DECOHERENCE

Finally we consider the case of noise plus decoherence; that is, what we are calling random complex noise. For this case we add both magnitude and phase noise. Fig. 31 shows a typical rms error training curve for the same level of complex noise as in Figs. 5 and 18. Again asymptotic error for the training set increases with increasing complex noise. The parameter functions again become "noisy" (see Figs. 32–34).

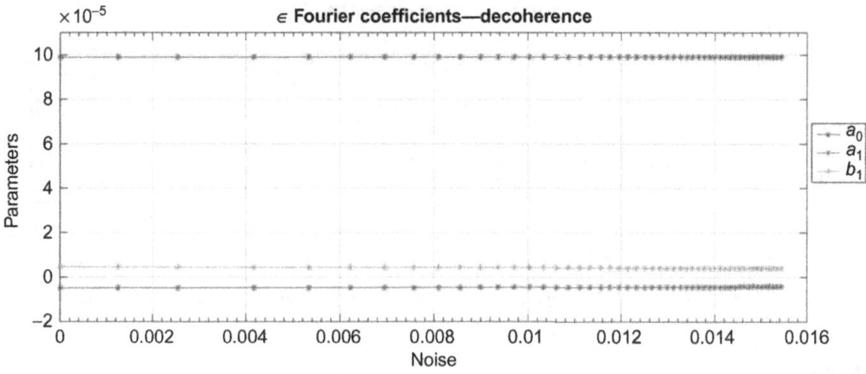

FIG. 23

Fourier coefficients for the bias parameter functions ϵ as functions of the decoherence level.

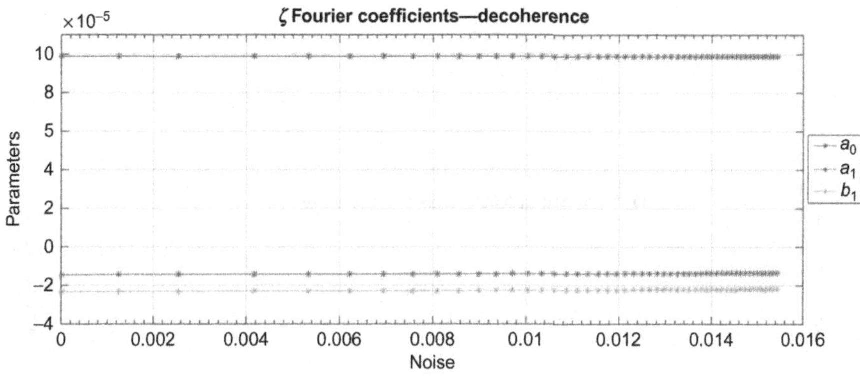

FIG. 24

Fourier coefficients for the coupling parameter function ζ as functions of the decoherence level.

Again we test to see how much the Fourier fit changes, this time with complex noise. Figs. 35, 36, and 37 show the Fourier coefficients as a function of the complex noise level for K, ϵ, and ζ, respectively. We can see that the indicator is, again, relatively stable.

Again we use the Fourier-fitted functions to test the performance of the QNN on both pure and mixed states. Figs. 38, 39, and 40 show the performance of the QNN on the entanglement of the state P, as trained, respectively, at zero, 0.0089, and 0.013 amplitude complex noise and tested with various levels of complex noise and compared with the entanglement of formation at zero and 0.0069 complex noise.

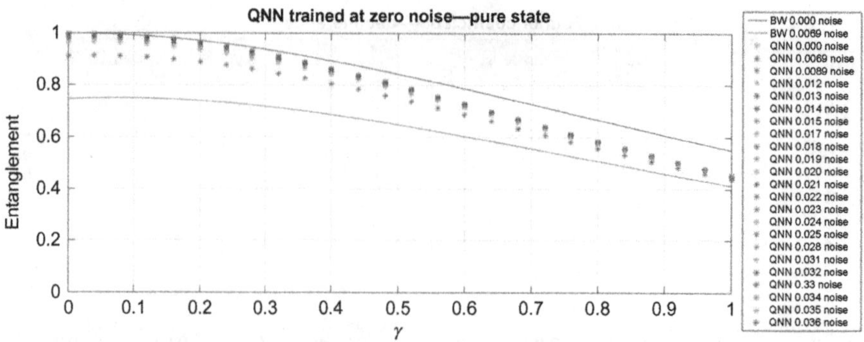

FIG. 25

Entanglement of the state P as a function of γ, as calculated by the quantum neural network (QNN), and compared with the entanglement of formation (marked "BW") at zero phase noise (blue; dark gray top curve in print version) and at 0.0069 phase noise (orange; light gray bottom curve in print version). In each case the QNN was trained at zero phase noise but was tested at the given level.

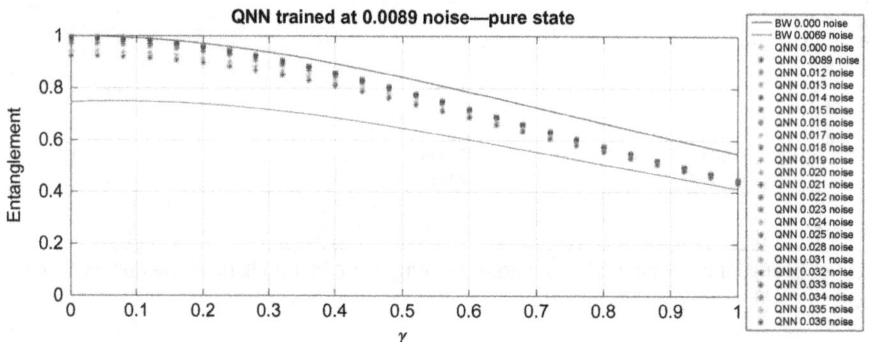

FIG. 26

Entanglement of the state P as a function of γ, as calculated by the quantum neural network (QNN), and compared with the entanglement of formation (marked "BW") at zero phase noise (blue; dark gray top curve in print version) and at 0.0069 phase noise (orange; light gray bottom curve in print version). In each case the QNN was trained at a phase noise level of 0.0089 and then tested at the given level.

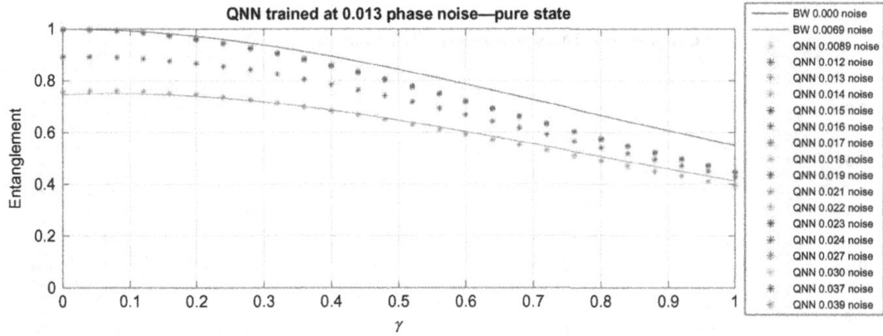

FIG. 27

Entanglement of the state P as a function of γ, as calculated by the quantum neural network (QNN), and compared with the entanglement of formation (marked "BW") at zero phase noise (blue; dark gray top curve in print version) and at 0.0069 phase noise (orange; light gray bottom curve in print version). In each case the QNN was trained at 0.013 phase noise and then tested at the given level.

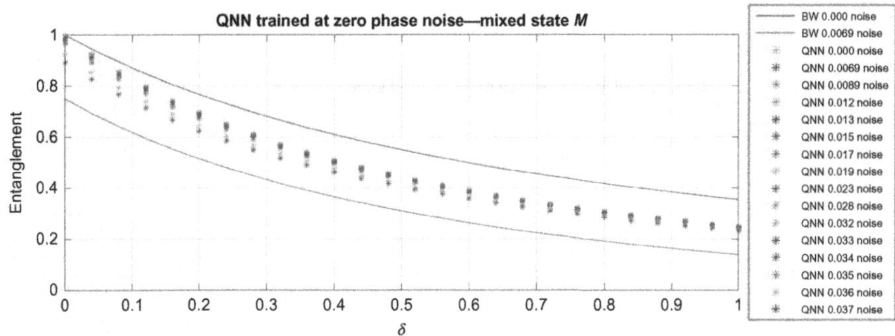

FIG. 28

Entanglement of the state M as a function of δ, as calculated by the quantum neural network (QNN), and compared with the entanglement of formation (marked "BW") at zero phase noise (blue; dark gray top curve in print version) and at 0.0069 phase noise (orange; light gray bottom curve in print version). In each case the QNN was trained at zero noise but was tested at the given level.

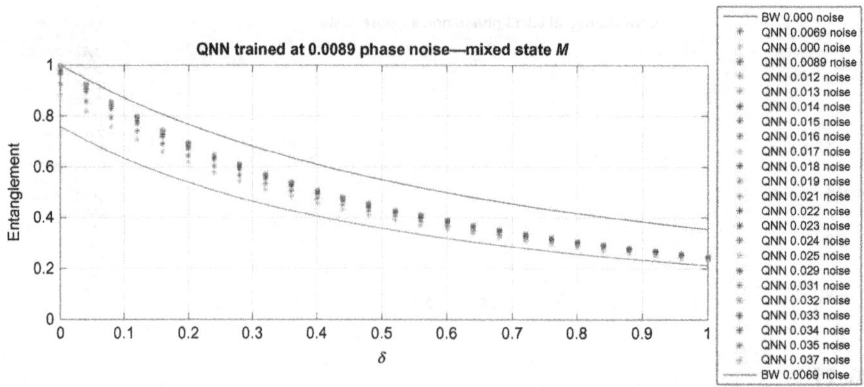

FIG. 29

Entanglement of the state M as a function of δ, as calculated by the quantum neural network (QNN), and compared with the entanglement of formation (marked "BW") at zero phase noise (blue; dark gray top curve in print version) and at 0.0069 phase noise (orange; light gray bottom curve in print version). In each case the QNN was trained at a phase noise level of 0.0089 and then tested at the given level.

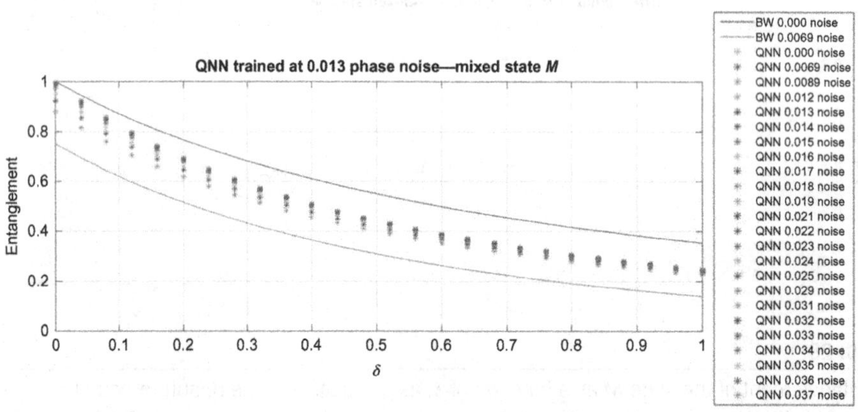

FIG. 30

Entanglement of the state M as a function of δ, as calculated by the quantum neural network (QNN), and compared with the entanglement of formation (marked "BW") at zero phase noise (blue; dark gray top curve in print version) and at 0.0069 phase noise (orange; light gray bottom curve in print version). In each case the QNN was trained at 0.013 phase noise and then tested at the given level.

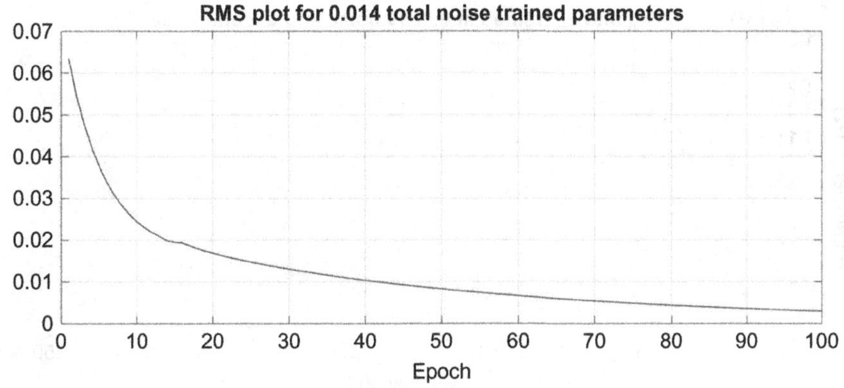

FIG. 31

Total root mean square (RMS) error for the training set as a function of epoch (pass through the training set), for the two-qubit system, with a complex noise level of 0.014 at each (of 317 in total) timestep. Asymptotic error is 3.0×10^{-3}, approximately the same as with only magnitude noise.

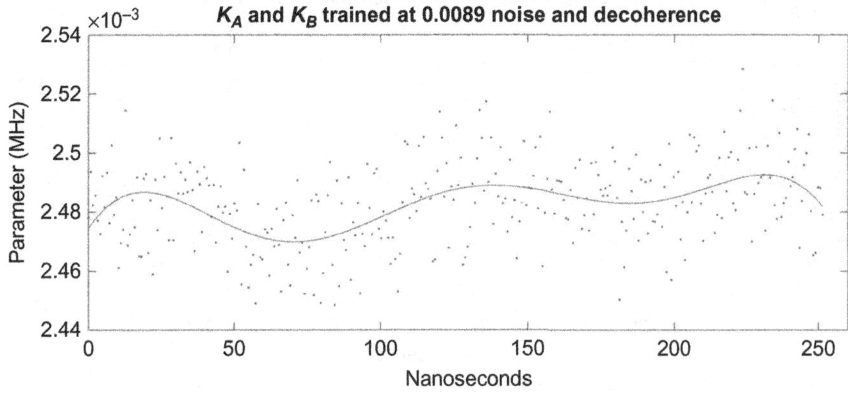

FIG. 32

Parameter function $K_A = K_B$ as a function of time, as trained at 0.0089 complex noise at each of the 317 timesteps, for the entanglement indicator (*data points*) and plotted with the Fourier fit (*solid line*). Note the change in scale from Fig. 2 because of the (much larger) spread of the noisy data: the Fourier fit is actually almost the same on this graph.

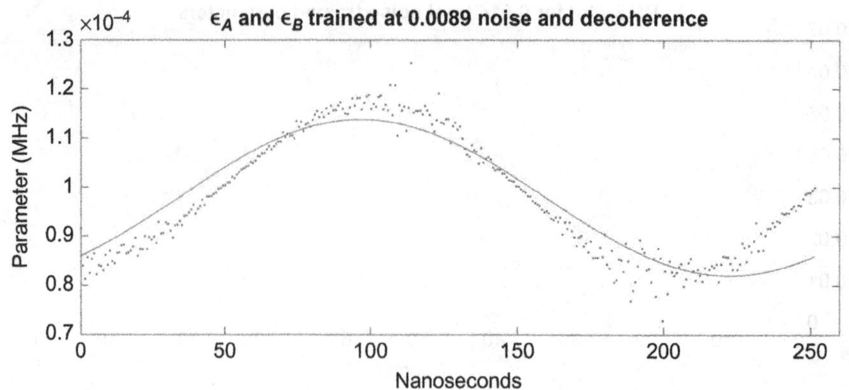

FIG. 33

Parameter function $\epsilon_A = \epsilon_B$ as a function of time, as trained at 0.0089 complex noise at each of the 317 timesteps, for the entanglement indicator (*data points*) and plotted with the Fourier fit (*solid line*).

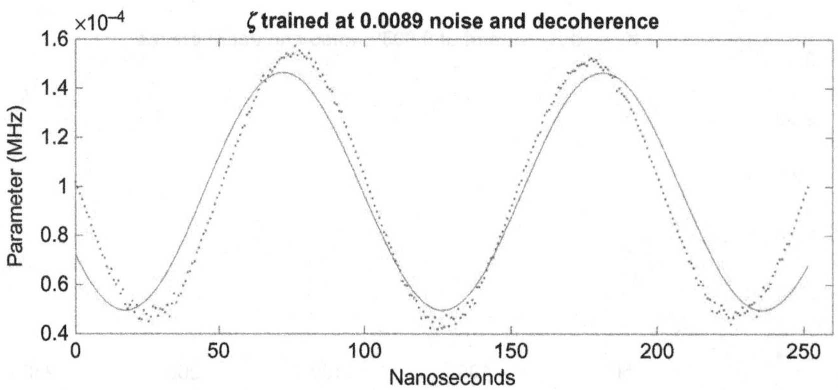

FIG. 34

Parameter function ζ as a function of time, as trained at 0.0089 complex noise at each of the 317 timesteps, for the entanglement indicator (*data points*) and plotted with the Fourier fit (*solid line*).

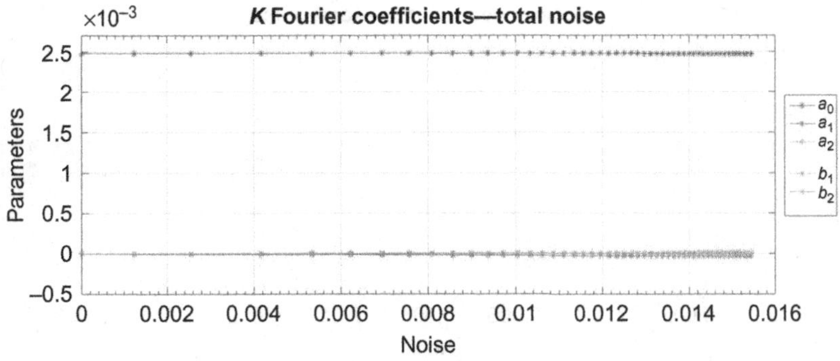

FIG. 35

Fourier coefficients for the tunneling parameter functions K as functions of the complex noise level.

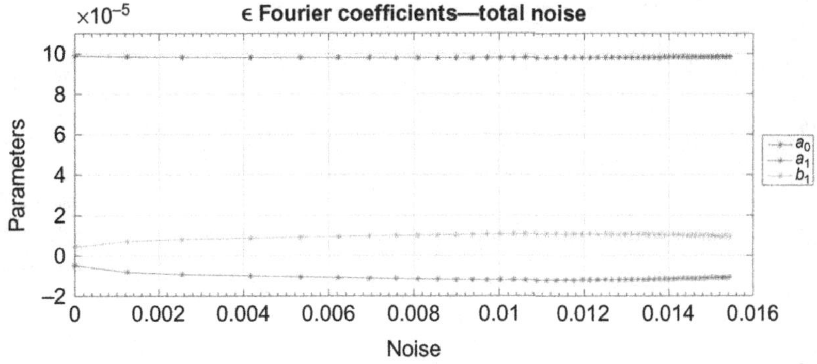

FIG. 36

Fourier coefficients for the bias parameter functions ϵ as functions of the complex noise level.

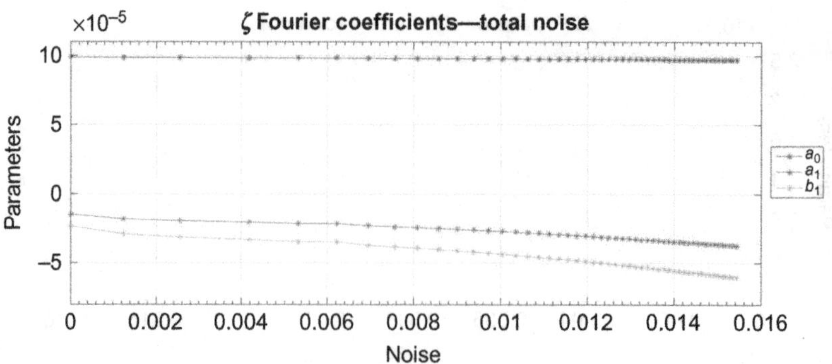

FIG. 37

Fourier coefficients for the coupling parameter function ζ as functions of the complex noise level.

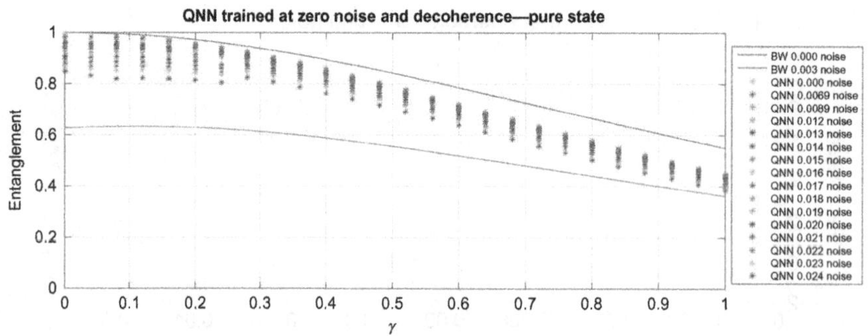

FIG. 38

Entanglement of the state P as a function of γ, as calculated by the quantum neural network (QNN), and compared with the entanglement of formation (marked "BW") at zero noise (blue; dark gray top curve in print version) and at 0.69% noise plus decoherence (orange; light gray bottom curve in print version). In each case the QNN was trained at zero noise but was tested at the given level.

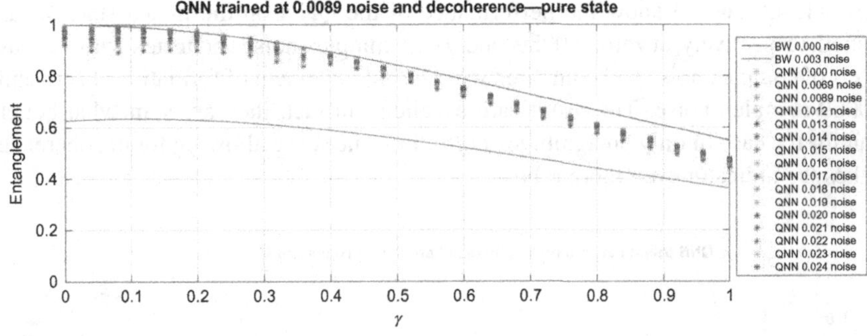

FIG. 39

Entanglement of the state *P* as a function of γ, as calculated by the quantum neural network (QNN), and compared with the entanglement of formation (marked "BW") at zero noise (blue; dark gray top curve in print version) and at 0.0069 noise plus decoherence (orange; light gray bottom curve in print version). In each case the QNN was trained at a complex noise level of 0.0089 and then tested at the given level.

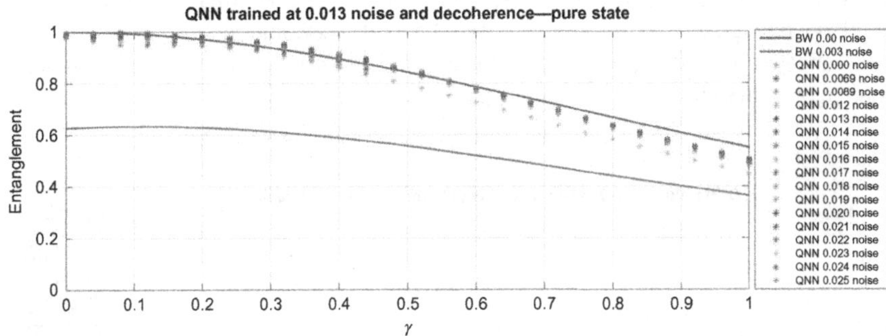

FIG. 40

Entanglement of the state *P* as a function of γ, as calculated by the quantum neural network (QNN), and compared with the entanglement of formation (marked "BW") at zero complex noise (blue; dark gray top curve in print version) and at 0.0069 noise plus decoherence (orange; light gray bottom curve in print version). In each case the QNN was trained at a complex noise level of 0.013 and then tested at the given level.

Figs. 41, 42, and 43 show the performance of the QNN on the mixed state *M*, as trained, respectively, at zero, 0.0089, and 0.013 complex noise and tested with various levels of complex noise and compared with the entanglement of formation at zero and 0.0069 complex noise. The results are excellent; in fact, they are somewhat better than for the case of only "magnitude" noise. In some sense allowing for decoherence makes the indicator even more robust.

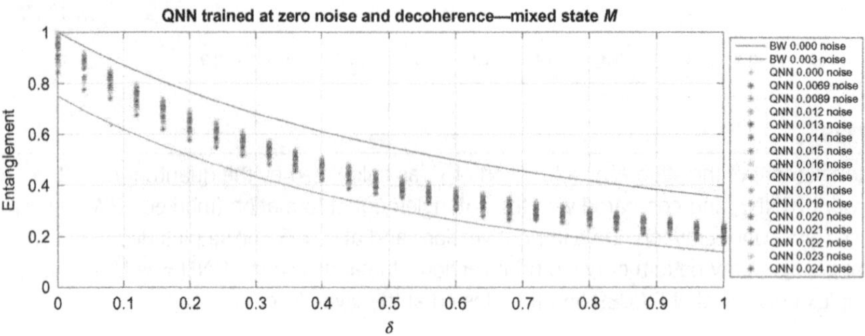

FIG. 41

Entanglement of the state *M* as a function of δ, as calculated by the quantum neural network (QNN), and compared with the entanglement of formation (marked "BW") at zero noise (blue; dark gray top curve in print version) and at 0.0069 noise plus decoherence(orange; light gray bottom curve in print version). In each case the QNN was trained at zero noise but was tested at the given level.

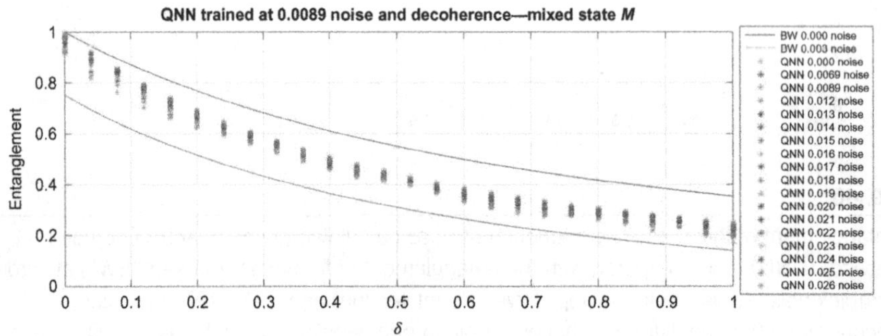

FIG. 42

Entanglement of the state *M* as a function of δ, as calculated by the quantum neural network (QNN), and compared with the entanglement of formation (marked "BW") at zero noise (blue; dark gray top curve in print version) and at 0.0069 noise plus decoherence (orange; light gray bottom curve in print version). In each case the QNN was trained at a complex noise level of 0.0089 and then tested at the given level.

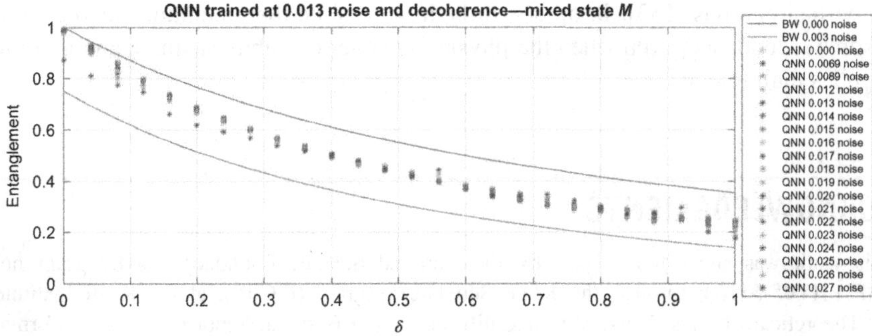

FIG. 43

Entanglement of the state M as a function of δ, as calculated by the quantum neural network (QNN), and compared with the entanglement of formation (marked "BW") at zero noise (blue; dark gray top curve in print version) and at 0.0069 noise plus decoherence (orange; light gray bottom curve in print version). In each case the QNN was trained at 0.013 complex noise and then tested at the given level.

6 CONCLUSIONS

In previous work we proposed an entanglement indicator for a general qubit system. This indicator is a quantum system that processes the state whose entanglement is to be estimated. The parameters of the quantum system are adjusted via a supervised learning process using a sparse training set of states whose entanglement is well defined. The learning is continued until sufficient training is achieved. The trained parameter functions are well represented by single frequency functions (first-order Fourier curve fit).

We have shown here that those functions are robust to fairly high levels of noise and decoherence. The QNN tests well on "unknown" states, both pure and mixed. The performance on decoherence in particular was excellent. We are reasonably confident that our results show that QNNs are well suited for dealing with these types of problems in quantum computing.

We are currently working to extend our results on noise and decoherence to multiple-qubit systems, using the well-known neural network technique of bootstrapping [12]. We also wish to understand exactly why the QNN is so robust to noise and decoherence. Classical neural networks are robust to noise and single neuron/synapse failure because of the multiple redundance of parallel computing. Here we have only a very small number of qubits/neurons, but we have designed our quantum network as operating over propagation in time, which can be written as a superposition of a very large number of definite time paths, by use of the Feynman path integral representation of quantum mechanics [32]. In this picture the instantaneous states of the quantum system at intermediate times, which are integrated over, play the role of "virtual neurons" [33]. In other words, it is possible that quantum superposition ensures redundance, even when the physical number of qubits is small, and thereby supplies fault tolerance.

ACKNOWLEDGMENTS

This work was supported in part by the National Science Foundation under grant no. NSF PHY05-51164, through the KITP Scholars program (E.C.B.), at the Kavli Institute for Theoretical Physics, University of California, Santa Barbara, Santa Barbara, California, United States.

REFERENCES

[1] C.H. Bennett, D.P. DiVincenzo, J.A. Smolin, W.K. Wootters, Mixed-state entanglement and quantum error correction, Phys. Rev. A 54 (1996) 3824–3851.

[2] W.K. Wootters, Entanglement of formation of an arbitrary state of two qubits, Phys. Rev. Lett. 80 (1998) 2245–2248.

[3] D.M. Greenberger, M.A. Horne, A. Zeilinger, in: M.A. Horne (Ed.), Bell's Theorem and the Conception of the Universe, Kluwer Academic, Dordrecht, 1989, p. 107.

[4] V. Vedral, M.B. Plenio, M.A. Rippin, P.L. Knight, Quantifying entanglement, Phys. Rev. Lett. 78 (1997) 2275–2279; V. Vedral, M.B. Plenio, Entanglement measures and purification procedures, Phys. Rev. A 57 (1998) 1619–1633; L. Henderson, V. Vedral, Classical, quantum and total correlations, J. Phys. A 34 (2001) 6899–6905.

[5] S. Tamaryan, A. Sudbery, L. Tamaryan, Duality and the geometric measure of entanglement of general multiqubit W states, Phys. Rev. A 81 (2010) 052319.

[6] H.S. Park, S.-S.B. Lee, H. Kim, S.-K. Choi, H.-S. Sim, Construction of optimal witness for unknown two-qubit entanglement, Phys. Rev. Lett. 105 (2010) 230404.

[7] R. Filip, Overlap and entanglement-witness measurements, Phys. Rev. A 65 (2002) 062320; F.G.S.L. Brando, Quantifying entanglement with witness operators, 2005, quant-ph/0503152.

[8] T. Yamamoto, Y.A. Pashkin, O. Astafiev, Y. Nakamura, J.S. Tsai, Demonstration of conditional gate operation using superconducting charge qubits, Nature 425 (2003) 941–944.

[9] Y. LeCun, A theoretical framework for back-propagation, in: D. Touretzky, G. Hinton, T. Sejnowski (Eds.), Proceedings of 1998 Connectionist Models Summer School, Morgan Kaufmann, San Mateo, 1988, pp. 21–28.

[10] P. Werbos, in: Handbook of Intelligent Control, Van Nostrand Reinhold, New York, 1992, pp. 79–80.

[11] E.C. Behrman, J.E. Steck, P. Kumar, K.A. Walsh, Quantum algorithm design using dynamic learning, Quantum Inf. Comput. 8 (2008) 12–29.

[12] B. Efron, R.J. Tibshirani, An Introduction to the Bootstrap, Chapman and Hall/CRC, Boca Raton, FL, 1994.

[13] E.C. Behrman, J.E. Steck, Dynamic learning of pairwise and three-way entanglement, in: Proceedings of the Third World Congress on Nature and Biologically Inspired

Computing (NaBIC, 2011), Salamanca, Spain, October 19–21, 2011, Institute of Electrical and Electronics Engineers, 2011.

[14] E.C. Behrman, J.E. Steck, Multiqubit entanglement of a general input state, Quantum Inf. Comput. 13 (2013) 36–53.

[15] H. Buhrman, I. Newman, H. Rohrig, R. deWolf, Robust polynomials and quantum algorithms, in: Proceedings of the 22nd Annual Symposium on Theoretical Aspects of Computer Science, Lecture Notes in Computer Science, vol. 3404, Springer, Berlin, 2005, pp. 593–604.

[16] S.-Y. Huang, H.-S. Goan, X.-Q. Li, G.J. Milburn, Generation and stabilization of a three-qubit entangled W state in circuit QED via quantum feedback control, 2013, arXiv:1311.6321v1.

[17] S.C. Hou, X.L. Huang, X.X. Yi, Suppressing decoherence and improving entanglement by quantum-jump-based feedback control in two-level systems, Phys. Rev. A 82 (2010) 012336.

[18] L. Xiang-Ping, F. Mao-Fa, F. Jian-Shu, Z. Qian-Quan, Preserving entanglement and the fidelity of three-qubit quantum states undergoing decoherence using weak measurement, Chin. Phys. B 23 (2014) 020304.

[19] D. Dong, M.A. Mabrok, I.R. Petersen, B. Qi, C. Chen, H. Rabitz, Sampling-based learning control for quantum systems with uncertainties, 2015, arXiv:1507.07190v1.

[20] A.W. Cross, G. Smith, J.A. Smolin, Quantum learning robust against noise, Phys. Rev. A 92 (2015) 012327.

[21] M.-L. Hu, H. Fan, Robustness of quantum correlations against decoherence, Ann. Phys. 327 (2012) 851–860.

[22] S. Roy, I.R. Petersen, E.H. Huntington, Robust adaptive quantum phase estimation, 2015, arXiv:1412.4963v3.

[23] E.C. Behrman, J. Niemel, J.E. Steck, S.R. Skinner, A quantum dot neural network, in: Proceedings of the Fourth Workshop on Physics and Computation (PhysComp96), vol. 22, 1996.

[24] E.C. Behrman, L.R. Nash, J.E. Steck, S.R. Skinner, A quantum Hopfield network, in: Proceedings of the Fifth Joint Conference on Information Sciences, vol. 1, 2000, p. 760; V.G. Chandrashekar, E.C. Behrman, J.E. Steck, Physical realizations of a temporal quantum neural computer, in: Proceedings of the 2001 International Joint Conference on Neural Networks (IJCNN01), Washington, DC, July 15–19, 2001, published on CD, ISBN 0-7803-7046-5.

[25] W. Zhu, H. Rabitz, Closed loop learning control to suppress the effects of quantum decoherence, J. Chem. Phys. 118 (2003) 6751.

[26] A. Bisio, G. Chiribelle, G.M. D'Ariano, S. Facchini, P. Perinotti, Optimal quantum learning of a unitary transformation, 2010, arXiv:0903.0543v2.

[27] S. Lloyd, M. Mohseni, P. Rebentrost, Quantum algorithms for supervised and unsupervised machine learning, 2013, arXiv:1307.0411.

[28] P.D. Wasserman, Advanced Methods in Neural Computing, Van Nostrand Reinhold, New York, 1993.

[29] E.C. Behrman, J.E. Steck, A quantum neural network computes its own relative phase, in: Proceedings of the IEEE Symposium on Computational Intelligence 2013, Singapore, April 15–19, 2013, Institute of Electrical and Electronics Engineers, 2013.

[30] E.C. Behrman, R.E.F. Bonde, J.E. Steck, J.F. Behrman, On the correction of anomalous phase oscillation in entanglement witnesses using quantum neural networks, IEEE Trans. Neural Netw. Learn. Syst. 25 (9) (2014) 1696–1703.

[31] A. Peres, Quantum Theory: Concepts and Methods, Kluwer, Dordrecht, The Netherlands, 1995.

[32] R.P. Feynman, An operator calculus having applications in quantum electrodynamics, Phys. Rev. 84 (1951) 108–128; R.P. Feynman, A.R. Hibbs, Quantum Mechanics and Path Integrals, McGraw-Hill, New York, 1965.

[33] E.C. Behrman, L.R. Nash, J.E. Steck, V.G. Chandrashekar, S.R. Skinner, Simulations of quantum neural networks, Inform. Sci. 128 (2000) 257–269.

CHAPTER

Quantum computing and supervised machine learning: Training, model selection, and error estimation

2

L. Oneto, S. Ridella, D. Anguita
University of Genoa, Genoa, Italy

1 INTRODUCTION

In the supervised learning (SL) framework, one builds a model by exploiting the available observations through a learning algorithm (LA) that is able to capture the information hidden in the data [1]. In other words, supervised machine learning (ML) algorithms infer an input-output relation from a set of data that consists of examples of this relation [2–5]. This phase is usually called the "training phase." Because of the rapid growth of the number of samples, of the dimensionality of the input and output space, and of the variety and structure of the data that are transferred, stored, and processed, the conventional ML methods started to show their limits [6–10]. Specifically, the problem of tuning the performance of the algorithms—namely, model selection (MS)—and rigorously estimating their performance—namely, error estimation (EE)—started to become a crucial issue from both the theoretical and the practical point of view [11–18]. Quantum computing (QC) [19] can be extremely useful in ML because it can significantly speed up computationally expensive procedures [20] and, at the same time, it can inspire new learning approaches [21,22] and pave the way to new methods for understanding the quality of the learned model.

The purpose of this chapter is to show the benefits of the use of QC for addressing the computational issues related to the training, MS, and EE phases in ML. Moreover, we show how QC can inspire new theoretical approaches which are not feasible with the standard computation paradigm.

In general, a learning process is at least subject to three different sources of error [23,24]: the approximation error, which depends mostly on a suboptimal tuning of the LA or on the suboptimal choice of the algorithm itself; the estimation error, which is linked to the availability of only a finite number of observations;

Quantum Inspired Computational Intelligence. http://dx.doi.org/10.1016/B978-0-12-804409-4.00002-4

and the implementation error, which is related to the restrictions of building and implementing the model on real-world devices.

The training phase can be seen as a minimization process [1,14]: given a class of functions (e.g., linear separators in a Hilbert space), a network architecture (e.g., a multilayer perceptron with several layers, each composed of several neurons), a model structure (e.g., a binary tree classifier of fixed depth), or a learning rule (e.g., k-local rule), we have to find the best configuration of the model parameters with reference to a loss function [25]. Every LA is the result of a trade-off between computational requirements and accuracy: some LAs are very accurate but do not scale well with the number of samples, while others are not able to capture the information hidden in the data if the number of samples is too small but are computationally inexpensive [26].

MS [11] addresses the problem of tuning an LA to the available data, so as to reduce the different sources of error (approximation, estimation, and implementation). This problem affects most of LAs because, in general, their effectiveness is controlled by one or more hyperparameters (e.g., the size of the Hilbert space, the number of layers and neurons for each layer in a multilayer perceptron, the depth of a binary tree, the k in the k-local rule), which must be tuned during the learning process to achieve optimal performance. The well-known no-free-lunch theorems [27,28] ensure that is not possible to aprioristically set these hyperparameters; consequently they must be tuned on the basis of the available samples. This process gives rise to both computational and theoretical issues: it is quite difficult to find an effective and computationally inexpensive MS strategy [12,29,30], but even without any computational constraint, MS remains a largely unsolved research problem [14,15,30].

EE addresses the problem of estimating the accuracy of a learned model, and is tightly linked to the training and MS phases [13]. In fact, the main objective of building an optimal model is to choose the parameters and hyperparameters that minimize its generalization error and, at the same time, to compute an estimate of this value for predicting its performance on future data. Statistical learning theory addresses exactly these issues by exploiting the most recent statistical results on concentration properties of empirical processes [31]. Differently from the other two phases, EE is still an unsolved theoretical problem which obviously has important practical implications [30,32–34].

QC [19,20,35–37] represents a promising paradigm for solving complex problems, such as large-number factorization [38], exhaustive search [39–41], optimization [42,43], and mean and median computation [20,44,45]. Its importance has increased very rapidly in recent decades since basic results from quantum theory ensure that any computation feasible on digital Turing machines can also be performed on quantum computers [46], and technology refinements have shown that quantum computers could soon become a reality [47–49]. The recent literature shows that QC can be very useful for building data-driven models [21,22,50–53]. The reason why QC is so appealing in many practical applications is the so-called quantum speedup [54–56]: basically, using quantum algorithms, one can reduce the computation time from $O(T)$ to $O\left(\sqrt{T}\right)$. While this effect is not theoretically fully understood, its impact on real-world problems is obvious.

In this chapter we will show how QC can help during the three phases of learning. For the training phase, it allows us to deal with complex optimization problems efficiently and effectively. Obviously, NP problems, which cannot be tackled with QC approaches [19], remain hard to solve, but QC provides an important speedup which allows us to deal with nonconvex problems and design new families of LAs. Dealing with nonconvex problems also allows us to rigorously apply many MS and EE techniques which require bounded error measures. Consequently, in this chapter we will show how QC can help in dealing with the MS and EE problems effectively. We will review all of the most recent MS and EE methods and how these methods can take advantage of the quantum speedup. In brief, among the several methods proposed in the literature for MS and EE, we will identify two main categories: out-of-sample and in-sample methods [13,14]. The first one works well in many situations and allows us to apply simple statistical techniques to estimate the quantities of interest by splitting the data into different sets, each one for different purposes: training, MS, and EE. Some examples of out-of-sample methods are the well-known hold-out, cross validation [15,57–59], leave-one-out, and bootstrap methods [12,16,60]. In-sample methods use the whole set of available data for training, MS, and EE, thanks to the application of rigorous statistical procedures. We will describe how in-sample methods can be further divided into two subgroups: the hypothesis space-based methods and the algorithm-based methods [30]. The first subgroup requires we know the class of functions from which the algorithm will choose the model. Some examples of these methods are the Vapnik-Chervonenkis (VC) theory [1], the (local) Rademacher complexity (RC) theory [11,32,34,61,62], and the PAC-Bayes theory [33,63–65]. The second subgroup of methods do not require we know in advance the class of functions; they just need to apply the algorithm on a series of modified training sets. Some examples are the compression bound [64,66] and algorithmic stability [30,67,68] methods.

This chapter is organized as follows. Section 2 recalls the classical SL framework and the problems of training a model, selecting the hyperparameters which produce the most accurate model, and finally accurately estimating the performance of the trained model. Section 3 introduces the QC framework, and shows the difference between the classical computing (CC) paradigm and the QC one by showing the computational advantages of one over the other. Section 4 shows that QC can be useful during the training phase, while Section 5 reviews the techniques for MS and EE and shows how these techniques can exploit the advantages of the QC paradigm. Finally, in Section 6 the conclusions and the future perspectives regarding the issues addressed in the chapter are presented.

2 THE SUPERVISED LEARNING PROBLEM: TRAINING, MODEL SELECTION, AND ERROR ESTIMATION

As first step let us recall the conventional SL framework, in particular the binary classification problem, and some common definitions [1,65,67]. Let us consider a set of labeled samples $\mathcal{D}_n = \{(X_1,Y_1),\ldots,(X_n,Y_n)\} = \{Z_1,\ldots,Z_n\}$ drawn to be independent and identically distributed (i.i.d.) according to an unknown probability distribution μ over the Cartesian product between the input space $\mathcal{X}$ and the output space $\mathcal{Y} = \{-1,+1\}$, defined as $\mathcal{Z} = \mathcal{X} \times \mathcal{Y}$. Let us consider a function in a possibly unknown set of functions $f \in \mathcal{F}$, where $f : \mathcal{X} \rightarrow \overline{\mathcal{Y}} = [-1,+1]$. The error of f in approximating μ is measured with reference to some $[0,1]$-bounded loss function $\ell : \mathcal{F} \times \mathcal{Z} \rightarrow [0,1]$. Then the risk of f can be defined as

$$L^{\ell}(f) = \mathbb{E}_Z\{\ell(f,Z)\}. \tag{1}$$

Since μ is unknown, $L^{\ell}(f)$ cannot be computed but we can compute its empirical estimators. Before defining them, we introduce two modified training sets:

$$\mathcal{D}_n^{\setminus i} = \{Z_1,\ldots,Z_{i-1},Z_{i+1},\ldots,Z_n\}, \tag{2}$$

$$\mathcal{D}_n^{i} = \{Z_1,\ldots,Z_{i-1},Z_i',Z_{i+1},\ldots,Z_n\}, \tag{3}$$

where the ith element is removed or replaced respectively by another sample Z_i', sampled i.i.d. from μ.

If $\hat{f} = \mathscr{A}_{(\mathcal{D}_n,\mathcal{H})}$, $\hat{f}^{\setminus i} = \mathscr{A}_{(\mathcal{D}_n^{\setminus i},\mathcal{H})}$, and $\hat{f}^{i} = \mathscr{A}_{(\mathcal{D}_n^{i},\mathcal{H})}$ are functions chosen from $\mathcal{F}$ according to some criteria, or algorithm $\mathscr{A}_{\mathcal{H}}$, and based respectively on $\mathcal{D}_n$, $\mathcal{D}_n^{\setminus i}$, and $\mathcal{D}_n^{i}$, we can define the empirical risk and the leave-one-out risk of a function $f \in \mathcal{F}$ [67] as, respectively,

$$\hat{L}^{\ell}(f) = \hat{L}^{\ell}_{\text{emp}}(f) = \frac{1}{n}\sum_{i=1}^{n}\ell(f,Z_i), \tag{4}$$

$$\hat{L}^{\ell}_{\text{loo}}(f) = \frac{1}{n}\sum_{i=1}^{n}\ell(\hat{f}^{\setminus i},Z_i). \tag{5}$$

$\hat{L}^{\ell}(f)$ and $\hat{L}^{\ell}_{\text{loo}}(f)$ are the commonest empirical estimators of $L^{\ell}(f)$. $\mathcal{H}$ is a set of hyperparameters which defines, implicitly or explicitly, $\mathcal{F}$ and must be tuned. Since in this work, for simplicity, we will deal with binary classification problems, we will employ the hard loss function:

$$\ell_{\text{H}}(f,Z) = [Yf(X) \leq 0], \tag{6}$$

where the Iverson bracket notation has been used. Instead of choosing $f \in \mathcal{F}$ according to an algorithm $\mathscr{A}$, we can use the approach proposed in the PAC-Bayes framework where the probability of selecting $f \in \mathcal{F}$ is defined. The result of defining a distribution over $\mathcal{F}$ instead of just picking a single $f \in \mathcal{F}$ is a randomized classifier called the "Gibbs classifier" [65]. To make this classifier deterministic we have to take its expected value over the defined distribution. The resulting weighted majority vote classifier is called the "Bayes classifier" [65]. Usually the Bayes classifier is preferred over the Gibbs classifier for two reasons: first, many practitioners dislike a learned model which may give different outputs given the same input, and, second, in many situations the Bayes classifier provides better performance than the Gibbs classifier [65].

Rigorously speaking, the Gibbs classifier draws an $f \in \mathcal{F}$, according to a probability distribution Q over $\mathcal{F}$, each time a label for an input $X \in \mathcal{X}$ is required. For the Gibbs classifier (namely, G_Q), we can define its expected risk together with its empirical counterpart [33]:

$$L^{\ell}(G_Q) = \mathbb{E}_{f \sim Q}\{L^{\ell}(f)\}, \tag{7}$$

$$\hat{L}^{\ell}(G_Q) = \hat{L}^{\ell}_{\text{emp}}(G_Q) = \mathbb{E}_{f \sim Q}\{\hat{L}^{\ell}_{\text{emp}}(f)\}. \tag{8}$$

Note that Q must be chosen on the basis of $\mathcal{D}_n$. The Bayes classifier [65] can then be defined as

$$B_Q(X) = \text{sign}\left[\mathbb{E}_{f \sim Q}\{f(X)\}\right]. \tag{9}$$

From this definition it is possible to express the generalization error of the Bayes classifier [33,65] as

$$L^{\ell}(B_Q) = \mathbb{E}_Z\left\{\ell(B_Q, Z)\right\}. \tag{10}$$

According to statistical learning theory [1], a learning process consists in selecting a priori an appropriate class of functions $\mathcal{F}$ and then choosing the most suitable model from it, on the basis of the available data. The former phase is the MS phase, while the latter is the training phase. In some cases these two phases cannot be so clearly divided since $\mathcal{F}$ may be unknown (i.e., neural networks [2], k-nearest neighbors [69], random forests [70], etc.). For example, $\mathcal{F}$ is implicitly defined in neural networks by their architecture, and the LAs (e.g., backpropagation) deal with the problem of selecting the best weights of the architecture, which represents the choice of a model $f \in \mathcal{F}$. Another example is represented by the Gibbs classifier where the class of functions $\mathcal{F}$ is clearly defined but the selection of $f \in \mathcal{F}$ is not. In this case this selection is implicitly defined by the process of selecting a distribution over $\mathcal{F}$ which fits the data. For this reason, let us introduce a more general notation which can better model all these situations. Let $\mathfrak{R}$ be a rule and $\mathcal{S}^{\mathfrak{R}}$ a set of rules. Consequently, for a deterministic classifier $\mathcal{S}^{\mathfrak{R}} = \mathcal{F}$ and $\mathfrak{R} = f \in \mathcal{F}$, while for probabilistic rules $\mathcal{S}^{\mathfrak{R}}$ is a set of distributions over all the possible functions (in this way by setting to zero the probability of selecting a function outside $\mathcal{F}$, we implicitly select also the class of functions) and $\mathfrak{R}$ is a particular distribution.

Ideally, the objective of the learning process would consist in selecting the function

$$\mathfrak{R}_{\mu} = \arg \min_{\mathfrak{R} \in \mathcal{S}^{\mathfrak{R}}_{\mu}} L^{\ell}(\mathfrak{R}), \tag{11}$$

where $\mathfrak{R}_{\mu}$ is the Bayes estimator, which allows us to minimize the posterior expected loss, and $\mathcal{S}^{\mathfrak{R}}_{\mu}$ is an aprioristically defined set of rules, such that it includes $\mathfrak{R}_{\mu}$. As $\mathcal{S}^{\mathfrak{R}}_{\mu}$ is generally unknown, a set of rules $\mathcal{S}^{\mathfrak{R}}$ different from $\mathcal{S}^{\mathfrak{R}}_{\mu}$ is selected, which

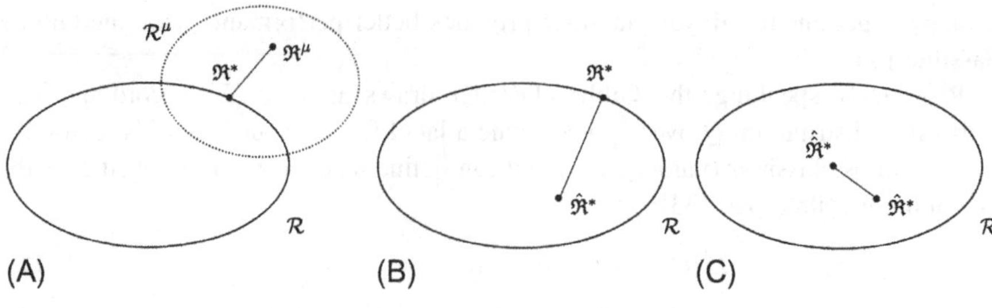

FIG. 1

(A) Approximation error, (B) estimation error, and (C) implementation error.

could not include $\mathfrak{R}_{\mu}$, in principle. Consequently the learning process targets the identification of the rule

$$\mathfrak{R}^* = \arg \min_{\mathfrak{R} \in \mathcal{S}^{\mathfrak{R}}} L^{\ell}(\mathfrak{R}); \tag{12}$$

namely, the best possible rule given the nonoptimal choice of the sets of rules. The distance between $\mathfrak{R}_{\mu}$ and $\mathfrak{R}^*$ is defined as the approximation error [23] (see Fig. 1A).

However, finding $\mathfrak{R}^*$ requires μ to be known in order to compute the generalization error. As μ is generally unknown, we have to resort to its empirical estimator $\hat{L}^{\ell}(\mathfrak{R})$ of $L^{\ell}(\mathfrak{R})$. Thus the learning process aims at searching for

$$\hat{\mathfrak{R}}^* = \arg \min_{\mathfrak{R} \in \mathcal{S}^{\mathfrak{R}}} \hat{L}^{\ell}(\mathfrak{R}). \tag{13}$$

The discrepancy between $\mathfrak{R}^*$ and $\hat{\mathfrak{R}}^*$ is defined as the estimation error [23] (see Fig. 1B).

It is also worth underlining that whenever we are dealing with real-world problems, $\hat{\mathfrak{R}}^*$ cannot be found exactly: for example, this could be because the resulting optimization problem is not convex and hence only a suboptimal solution can generally be found [71] (i.e., by our resorting to a convex relaxation of the problem or with other heuristic approaches [72–76]). In these cases only an approximation $\hat{\hat{\mathfrak{R}}}^*$ of $\hat{\mathfrak{R}}^*$ can be found: the discrepancy between $\hat{\mathfrak{R}}^*$ and $\hat{\hat{\mathfrak{R}}}^*$ is defined as the implementation error [76] (see Fig. 1C).

The training phase deals with the problem of reducing the approximation error by finding the best way of choosing the rule in the set of rules, while the MS phase deals with the problem of selecting the best sets of rules $\mathcal{S}^{\mathfrak{R}}$ in a set of r sets of rules $\mathcal{S}_r^{\mathcal{S}^{\mathfrak{R}}} = \{\mathcal{S}_1^{\mathfrak{R}}, \ldots, \mathcal{S}_r^{\mathfrak{R}}\}$ which minimize the approximation and estimation errors. Even though some heuristic methods for selecting the best set of rules exist [77–80], these methods are often characterized by poor performance with respect to the performance supported by statistical learning theory.

In particular, the problem of MS is strictly linked to the last problem of any SL procedure—namely, the EE problem, which aims to estimate (generally by deriving an upper bound which holds with high probability) the performance of the final rule in a reliable way. If a reliable method for estimating the generalization error (namely, $\breve{L}^{\ell}(\mathfrak{R})$) is available, the sets of rules which produce, through the training phase, the model characterized by the smaller estimated generalization error must be chosen. Then by solving the EE problem, one also solves the MS problem. Note that solving the EE problem is a much trickier task than just finding a good MS procedure, since the EE phase strives to achieve a tight estimate. For example, let us consider $\mathcal{S}_2^{\mathcal{S}^{\mathfrak{R}}} = \{\mathcal{S}_1^{\mathfrak{R}}, \mathcal{S}_2^{\mathfrak{R}}\}$. In these sets we select, respectively, $\mathfrak{R}_1 \in \mathcal{S}_1^{\mathfrak{R}}$ and $\mathfrak{R}_2 \in \mathcal{S}_2^{\mathfrak{R}}$ and we estimate their generalization error, $\breve{L}^{\ell}(\mathfrak{R}_1)$ and $\breve{L}^{\ell}(\mathfrak{R}_2)$ respectively. In Fig. 2 we report three different cases:

1. Fig. 2A shows the worst scenario, where, if $\mathfrak{R}^*$ is chosen on the basis of $\breve{L}^{\ell}(\mathfrak{R}_1)$ and $\breve{L}^{\ell}(\mathfrak{R}_2)$, the wrong set of rules and the wrong rule will be chosen and, moreover, the estimated generalization error will not be tight enough.
2. Fig. 2B shows the case when the estimator that we employ is not good enough for EE since it is not tight enough, but it is good for MS purposes. In fact if we select the set of rules on the basis of $\breve{L}^{\ell}(\mathfrak{R}_1)$ and $\breve{L}^{\ell}(\mathfrak{R}_2)$, the right class of rules will be chosen but the estimated generalization error will not be tight enough.
3. Fig. 2C shows the best case when the estimator is good for both MS and EE.

For this reason it is extremely important to obtain sharp estimates of the generalization error. In fact the sharper is the bound over $L^{\ell}(\mathfrak{R})$, the better will be the MS phase.

The are many theoretical approaches for addressing the EE problem. These approaches can be categorized:

- out-of-sample methods;
- in-sample methods, which can be further subdivided into:
  - methods that do not require knowledge of the set of rules;
  - methods that require knowledge of the set of rules, which can be further subdivided into:

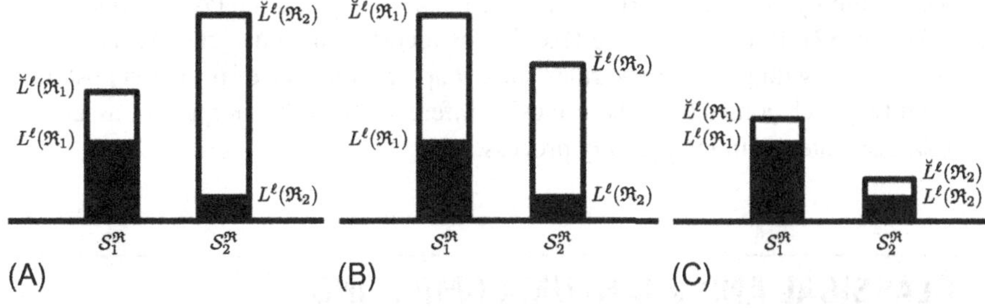

FIG. 2

Estimators of the generalization error: model selection (MS) and error estimation (EE): (A) bad for both MS and EE; (B) good for MS and bad for EE; (C) good for both MS and EE.

* methods for deterministic rules;
* methods for probabilistic rules.

Out-of-sample methods [14,81] are favored by practitioners because they work well in many situations and allow the application of simple statistical techniques for estimating the quantities of interest. Some examples of out-of-sample methods are the well-known hold-out, cross validation, leave-one-out, and bootstrap methods [15,16]. All these techniques rely on a similar idea: the original dataset is resampled, with or without replacement, to build two independent datasets called, respectively, the "training set" and the "validation set" (or "estimation set"). The first one is used for the training phase, while the second one is used to estimate training phase generalization error, so that the hyperparameters can be tuned to achieve generalization error minimum value and solve the MS problem. Note that both error estimates computed through the training and validation sets are, obviously, optimistically biased; therefore if the EE phase is desired, one has to build a third independent set, called the "test set," by nesting two of the resampling procedures mentioned above. Furthermore, the resampling procedure itself can introduce artifacts in the estimation process and therefore must be carefully designed.

In-sample methods [14,81], instead, allow the whole set of available data to be used for the training, MS, and EE phases thanks to the application of rigorous statistical procedures [1,11,32,63,66,67]. Despite their unquestionable advantage with respect to out-of-sample methods, their use is not widespread: one of the reasons is the common belief that although in-sample methods are very useful for gaining deep theoretical insights into the learning process or for developing new LAs, they are not suitable for practical purposes. However, recent advances in and deeper insights into these methods demonstrate that this is no longer true [82]. Among the in-sample methods we find methods that do not require knowledge of the set of rules $\mathcal{S}^{\mathfrak{R}}$, and hence these methods can be applied basically to any deterministic LA. The most important methods in this family are the algorithmic stability [30,67,68,83] and the compression bound [64,66,84] methods. Other methods require one to know a priori the set of rules, and hence they cannot be applied to algorithms such as neural networks or k-nearest neighbors. In this family the most important methods are the VC theory [1], the (local) RC theory [32,34,61,85], and the PAC-Bayes theory [33,63,65,86,87]. In particular, the PAC-Bayes theory is the only one that is able to deal effectively with probabilistic rules since it applies the idea of prior and posterior probability, which comes from the Bayesian inference, with the purpose of assessing the risk associated with the learning process.

3 CLASSICAL AND QUANTUM COMPUTING

QC is a beautiful combination of quantum physics, computer science, and information theory. In this section we will deal with the theory and the changes that occur when the classical model underpinning CC is replaced with QC. This means that we will not take into consideration the ongoing efforts to build quantum computers, since the latter is an active, yet young, area and it is not easy to predict which approaches will be the most successful ones [19,47–49]. In this section we review the quantum information processing notions that are relevant for understanding the algorithms that we will use in the SL framework. A detailed description of the topics can be found in [35,88].

In particular we will assume that the input of the quantum algorithms is given in the form of a black box B, or oracle, that can be accessed in quantum superposition. In practice, the quantum black box will be implemented as a quantum circuit that can have classical inputs and outputs. As we will see, the main feature of the QC paradigm is the possibility to decrease the number of calls, or evaluations, to the black box that are required with respect to the CC paradigm. Let

$$B : \{0, \dots, N-1\} \to \mathcal{B} \subseteq \mathbb{R} \tag{14}$$

be a function. Let $\bar{B}$ be its mean:

$$\bar{B} = \frac{1}{N} \sum_{i=0}^{N-1} B(i). \tag{15}$$

Let $B(i^*)$ be one of its minima,

$$i^* : \arg \min_{i \in \{1, \dots, N-1\}} B(i), \quad B(i^*) = B^*, \tag{16}$$

since, in general, there exists another $j \in \{1, \dots, N-1\} : B(j) = B(i^*)$ with $j \neq i$. In particular we suppose that the number of global minima is n_{B^*}.

3.1 CLASSICAL COMPUTING

With the CC paradigm it is possible to bound with high probability, under some hypothesis, the difference between $\bar{B}$ and one of its empirical estimators. In particular we define the empirical mean $\hat{\hat{B}}$ when the samples $\mathcal{B}_n = \{B_1, \dots, B_n\}$ are sampled with and without replacement, $\hat{\hat{B}}^{\text{rep}}$ and $\hat{\hat{B}}^{\text{no-rep}}$, respectively, from $\mathcal{B}_N = \{B(0), \dots, B(N-1)\}$:

$$\hat{\hat{B}} = \frac{1}{n} \sum_{i=1}^{n} B_i, \tag{17}$$

where we indicate with $\hat{\hat{B}}$ the case when the property holds for both $\hat{\hat{B}}^{\text{rep}}$ and $\hat{\hat{B}}^{\text{no-rep}}$.

In particular, if $\mathcal{B} = [lb, ub] \in \mathbb{R}$, it is possible to bound the difference between $\bar{B}$ and $\hat{\hat{B}}$ by use of the Hoeffding inequality [89].

Theorem 1 ([89]). *If $\mathcal{B} = [lb, ub]$, it is possible to state that*

$$\mathbb{P}\left\{\bar{B} - \hat{\hat{B}} \geq t\right\} \leq e^{-\frac{2nt^2}{(ub-lb)^2}}. \tag{18}$$

Alternatively, with probability $(1-\delta)$, *we can state that*

$$\bar{B} \leq \hat{\hat{B}} + (ub - lb)\sqrt{\frac{\ln\left(\frac{1}{\delta}\right)}{2n}}. \tag{19}$$

Moreover, it is possible to improve the previous result if we want to bound only the difference between $\bar{B}$ and $\hat{\hat{B}}^{\text{no-rep}}$ by using the Serfling inequality [90].

Theorem 2 ([90]). *If* $\mathcal{B} = [lb, ub]$, *it is possible to state that*

$$\mathbb{P}\left\{\bar{B} - \hat{\hat{B}}^{no\text{-}rep} \geq t\right\} \leq e^{-\frac{2nt^2}{\left(1-\frac{n-1}{N}\right)(ub-lb)^2}}. \tag{20}$$

Alternatively, with probability $(1-\delta)$, *we can state that*

$$\bar{B} \leq \hat{\hat{B}}^{no\text{-}rep} + (ub - lb)\sqrt{\frac{\left(1-\frac{n-1}{N}\right)\ln\left(\frac{1}{\delta}\right)}{2n}}. \tag{21}$$

When instead $\mathcal{B} = \{0, 1\}$, it is possible to improve the result of Theorems 1 and 2 by noting that $\hat{\hat{B}}^{\text{rep}}$ is distributed according to the binomial distribution and $\hat{\hat{B}}^{\text{no-rep}}$ is distributed according to the hypergeometric distribution. On the basis of these considerations we can recall the next two theorems. The first one bounds both $\bar{B} - \hat{\hat{B}}^{\text{rep}}$ and $\bar{B} - \hat{\hat{B}}^{\text{no-rep}}$.

Theorem 3 ([91]). *If* $\mathcal{B}_N = \{0, 1\}^N$, *it is possible to state that the following inequality holds with probability* $(1-\delta)$:

$$\bar{B} \leq \max_{p\in[0,1]}\left\{p : \sum_{i=0}^{n\hat{\hat{B}}}\binom{n}{i}p^i(1-p)^{n-i} \geq \delta\right\} \leq \hat{\hat{B}} + \sqrt{\frac{\ln\left(\frac{1}{\delta}\right)}{2n}}. \tag{22}$$

The second one bounds only $\bar{B} - \hat{\hat{B}}^{\text{no-rep}}$.

Theorem 4 ([92]). *If* $\mathcal{B}_N = \{0, 1\}^N$, *it is possible to state that the following inequality holds with probability* $(1-\delta)$:

$$\bar{B} \leq \max_{p\in[0,1]}\left\{p : \sum_{i=0}^{n\hat{\hat{B}}^{no\text{-}rep}}\frac{\binom{Np}{i}\binom{N-Np}{n-i}}{\binom{N}{n}} \geq \delta\right\} \leq \hat{\hat{B}}^{no\text{-}rep} + \sqrt{\frac{\left(1-\frac{n-1}{N}\right)\ln\left(\frac{1}{\delta}\right)}{2n}}. \tag{23}$$

Given the results of Theorems 1–4, it is possible to state that, on the basis of the CC paradigm, the mean value of the function B, if the function is bounded, can be estimated with high probability and the accuracy of the estimate converges to zero as $O\left(\sqrt{\frac{1}{n}}\right)$, where n are the number of observations of B.

There is a particular case where it is possible to show that the rate of convergence is faster with respect to the general case. In particular, if $\hat{\hat{B}}^{\text{rep}} = 0$ or $\hat{\hat{B}}^{\text{no-rep}} = 0$, thanks to Theorems 3 and 4 we have that with probability $(1 - \delta)$

$$\bar{B} \le \frac{\ln\left(\frac{1}{\delta}\right)}{n} \to O\left(\frac{1}{n}\right). \tag{24}$$

Anyway, $\hat{\hat{B}}^{\text{rep}} = 0$ and $\hat{\hat{B}}^{\text{no-rep}} = 0$ are the only cases when it is possible to achieve such a rate.

With the CC paradigm it is also possible to find, with high probability, the minima $B^* \in \mathcal{B}_N$. Since no assumption on B has been made, we have to resort to a Monte Carlo search. Consequently, it is possible to state the following theorem.

Theorem 5. *If n observations $\mathcal{B}_n$ out of the N possible ones $\mathcal{B}_N$ are made without replacement, the probability of finding a global minimum is*

$$\mathbb{P}\left\{B^* \in \mathcal{B}_n\right\} \ge 1 - \prod_{i=0}^{n-1}\left(1 - \frac{n_{B^*}}{N-i}\right) \ge 1 - \left(1 - \frac{n_{B^*}}{N}\right)^n. \tag{25}$$

Alternatively, we can state that $B^* \in \mathcal{B}_n$ with probability greater than $(1 - \delta)$ if

$$n \ge \frac{N \ln\left(\frac{1}{\delta}\right)}{n_{B^*}}. \tag{26}$$

Proof. To prove our statement let us note that the probability of extracting the minimum when only one element of $\mathcal{B}_N = \{B(0), \ldots, B(N-1)\}$ is observed is

$$\mathbb{P}\left\{B^* \in \mathcal{B}_1\right\} = \frac{n_{B^*}}{N}. \tag{27}$$

From this observation we can state that

$$\mathbb{P}\left\{B^* \notin \mathcal{B}_1\right\} = 1 - \frac{n_{B^*}}{N} \le 1 - \frac{1}{N}. \tag{28}$$

Moreover, the probability of not extracting the minimum by extracting two elements without replacement from $\mathcal{B}_N = \{B(0), \ldots, B(N-1)\}$ is

$$\mathbb{P}\left\{B^* \notin \mathcal{B}_2\right\} = \left(1 - \frac{n_{B^*}}{N}\right)\left(1 - \frac{n_{B^*}}{N-1}\right) \tag{29}$$

if during the first extraction the minimum was been extracted, otherwise it is zero. Consequently

$$\mathbb{P}\left\{B^* \notin \mathcal{B}_2\right\} \le \left(1 - \frac{n_{B^*}}{N}\right)\left(1 - \frac{n_{B^*}}{N-1}\right) \le \left(1 - \frac{n_{B^*}}{N}\right)^2. \tag{30}$$

By induction, the probability of not extracting the minimum when n observations without replacement of $\mathcal{B}_N = \{B(0), \ldots, B(N-1)\}$ are made is

$$\mathbb{P}\left\{B^* \notin \mathcal{B}_n\right\} \leq \prod_{i=0}^{n-1}\left(1 - \frac{n_{B^*}}{N-i}\right) \leq \left(1 - \frac{n_{B^*}}{N}\right)^n. \tag{31}$$

This concludes the proof of the first statement of the theorem. For the second statement let us note that

$$1 - \left(1 - \frac{n_{B^*}}{N}\right)^n \geq 1 - \delta \quad \rightarrow \quad \left(1 - \frac{n_{B^*}}{N}\right)^n \leq \delta, \tag{32}$$

but

$$\ln\left(1 - \frac{n_{B^*}}{N}\right)^n \leq -n\frac{n_{B^*}}{N}. \tag{33}$$

By combining Eqs. (32) and (33), we obtain our proof. □

Theorem 5 shows that, with the CC paradigm, to reach a desired probability of finding the minimum, the required number of Monte Carlo trials grows linearly with the number of elements in $\mathcal{B}_N$.

The next theorem is the equivalent of Theorem 5 but in this case the observations of $\mathcal{B}_n$ are made with replacement. Note that there is basically no difference between observing with or without replacement if N is large enough.

Theorem 6. *If n observations $\mathcal{B}_n$ out of the N possible ones $\mathcal{B}_N$ are made with replacement, the probability of find a global minimum is*

$$\mathbb{P}\left\{B^* \in \mathcal{B}_n\right\} \geq 1 - \left(1 - \frac{n_{B^*}}{N}\right)^n. \tag{34}$$

Alternatively, we can state that $B^* \in \mathcal{B}_n$ with probability greater than $(1-\delta)$ if

$$n \geq \frac{N \ln\left(\frac{1}{\delta}\right)}{n_{B^*}}. \tag{35}$$

Proof. As stated in the proof of Theorem 5, let us note that the probability of extracting the minimum when only one element of $\mathcal{B}_N = \{B(0), \ldots, B(N-1)\}$ is observed is

$$\mathbb{P}\left\{B^* \in \mathcal{B}_1\right\} = \frac{n_{B^*}}{N}. \tag{36}$$

From this observation we can state that

$$\mathbb{P}\left\{B^* \notin \mathcal{B}_1\right\} = 1 - \frac{n_{B^*}}{N} \leq 1 - \frac{1}{N}. \tag{37}$$

Since we are observing $\mathcal{B}_n$ elements from $\mathcal{B}_N = \{B(0), \ldots, B(N-1)\}$ with replacement, we have that

$$\mathbb{P}\left\{B^* \notin \mathcal{B}_n\right\} \leq \left(1 - \frac{n_{B^*}}{N}\right)^n. \tag{38}$$

By following the same argument as in the proof of Theorem 5, one can prove the statements of the theorem. □

3.2 QUANTUM COMPUTING

Without loss of generality, we assume throughout that N is a power of 2. The first theorem that we recall is, somehow, the counterpart of Theorems 1 and 2, but for the case of QC.

Theorem 7 ([44]). *If $\mathcal{B} = [0, 1]$, it is possible to state that there exists a quantum algorithm which returns an estimation $\bar{\bar{B}}$ of $\bar{B}$ such that*

$$\bar{B} \leq \bar{\bar{B}} + \frac{2\pi\sqrt{\bar{B}(1-\bar{B})}}{n} + \frac{\pi^2}{n^2}, \tag{39}$$

with probability at least $\frac{8}{\pi^2}$. The algorithm requires $O(n)$ evaluations of B.

The second theorem, instead, is the counterpart of Theorems 3 and 4 for the case of QC.

Theorem 8 ([44]). *If $\mathcal{B}$ can be expressed with κ bits, it is possible to state that there exists a quantum algorithm which returns an estimation $\bar{\bar{B}}$ of $\bar{B}$ such that*

$$\bar{B} \leq \bar{\bar{B}} + \frac{1}{N}\sum_{i=0}^{\kappa-1} \frac{\sqrt{\sum_{j=1}^{N} B_i(j)}}{2^i}, \tag{40}$$

where $B_i(j)$ is the ith bit, with $i \in \{0, \ldots, \kappa-1\}$, of the binary expansion of $B(j)$, with probability at least $\frac{2}{3}$. The algorithm requires $O\left(\sqrt{N}\kappa \ln \kappa\right)$ evaluations of B.

The problem with Theorems 7 and 8 is that it is not possible to set a different confidence level. To address this issue we need another preliminary result that allows us to derive two quantum algorithms for finding the mean value and where the desired level of confidence can be chosen a priori.

Theorem 9 ([93]). *Let us consider a classical or QC algorithm which aims to estimate some quantity θ and whose output $\hat{\theta}$ satisfies $|\theta - \hat{\theta}| \leq \epsilon$ but with probability $\gamma \leq \frac{1}{2}$. Then it is sufficient to repeat the algorithm $O\left(\ln\left(\frac{1}{\delta}\right)\right)$ times and take the median to obtain an estimate which is accurate within ϵ with probability $(1-\delta)$.*

By using Theorem 9, one can prove the counterparts of Theorems 1 and 2 in the framework of QC.

Theorem 10. *If $\mathcal{B} = [0, 1]$, it is possible to state that there exists a quantum algorithm which returns an estimation $\bar{\bar{B}}$ of $\bar{B}$ such that with probability $(1-\delta)$ we have*

$$\bar{B} \leq \frac{n^3}{n^3 + 4\pi^2 n}\bar{\bar{B}} + \frac{2\pi\sqrt{\bar{\bar{B}}n^4 - \bar{\bar{B}}^2 n^4 - 2\pi^2\bar{\bar{B}}n^2 + 2\pi^2 n^2 - \pi^4}}{n^3 + 4\pi^2 n} + \frac{3\pi^2 n}{n^3 + 4\pi^2 n} \tag{41}$$

$$\leq \bar{\bar{B}} + \frac{2\pi\sqrt{\bar{\bar{B}}}}{n} + \frac{6\pi^2}{n^2}. \tag{42}$$

The algorithm requires $O\left(n \ln\left(\frac{1}{\delta}\right)\right)$ *evaluations of B.*

Proof. To prove the statement of Eq. (41) we have to combine Theorems 7 and 9. In particular, we have to run the algorithm of Theorem 7 $O\left(\ln\left(\frac{1}{\delta}\right)\right)$ times and take as $\bar{\bar{B}}$ the median value of the output of the $O\left(\ln\left(\frac{1}{\delta}\right)\right)$ runs of the algorithm. Thus we apply Theorem 9 and eventually we have to solve Eq. (39) from Theorem 7 with respect to $\bar{B}$ to obtain Eq. (41). Instead, Eq. (42) comes from trivial upper bounds. □

Theorem 11. *If $\mathcal{B}$ can be expressed with κ bits, it is possible to state that there exists a quantum algorithm which returns an estimation $\bar{\bar{B}}$ of $\bar{B}$ such that with probability* $(1-\delta)$ *we have*

$$\bar{B} \leq \bar{\bar{B}} + \frac{1}{N} \sum_{i=0}^{\kappa-1} \frac{\sqrt{\sum_{j=1}^{N} B_i(j)}}{2^i}, \tag{43}$$

where $B_i(j)$ is the ith bit, with $i \in \{0, \ldots, \kappa-1\}$, of the binary expansion of $B(j)$. The algorithm requires $O\left(\sqrt{N}\kappa \ln \kappa \ln\left(\frac{1}{\delta}\right)\right)$ *evaluations of B.*

Proof. The proof is analogous to the one of Theorem 10 but here we have to combine Theorems 8 and 9 instead of Theorems 7 and 9. □

We can specialize Theorem 11 to the particular case of $\mathcal{B} = \{0,1\}$ to obtain insight into the result reported in that theorem.

Lemma 1. *If $\mathcal{B} = \{0,1\}$, it is possible to state that there exists a quantum algorithm which returns an estimation $\bar{\bar{B}}$ of $\bar{B}$ such that with probability* $(1-\delta)$ *we have*

$$\bar{B} \leq \bar{\bar{B}} + \frac{\sqrt{4\bar{\bar{B}}N+1}}{2N} + \frac{1}{2N} \leq \bar{\bar{B}} + \sqrt{\frac{\bar{\bar{B}}}{N}} + \frac{1}{N}. \tag{44}$$

The algorithm requires $O\left(\sqrt{N} \ln\left(\frac{1}{\delta}\right)\right)$ *evaluations of B.*

Proof. The proof consists in considering Theorem 11 and noting that, if $\mathcal{B} = \{0,1\}$, $\sum_{j=1}^{N} B_i(j) = \bar{B}$. Then by solving Eq. (43) with respect to $\bar{B}$, one proves the statement. □

Given the results of Theorems 10 and 11 and Lemma 1, it is possible to state that with the QC paradigm the mean value of the function B can be estimated with high probability and the accuracy of the estimate converges to zero as $O\left(\frac{1}{n}\right)$, where n is the number of observations of B. There is a particular case when the rate of convergence is faster with respect to the general case: when $\bar{\bar{B}} = 0$, the accuracy of the estimate converges to zero as $O\left(\frac{1}{n^2}\right)$. Anyway, $\bar{\bar{B}} = 0$ is the only case when it is possible to achieve such a rate.

As reported for the case of CC, we want to show how to find the minimum $B^* \in \{B(0), \ldots, B(N-1)\}$ with a QC approach. For this reason we have to use the following theorem (which can be found in [42]), which was inspired by the seminal work of Grover [20,39].

Theorem 12 ([42,44]). *There exists a quantum algorithm which is able to find the minimum $B^* \in \{B(0), \ldots, B(N-1)\}$. The algorithm finds a correct answer with probability at least $\frac{2}{3}$ after $O\left(\sqrt{N}\right)$ observations of the set $\{B(0), \ldots, B(N-1)\}$.*

Analogously to the QC algorithms for finding the mean value, Theorem 12 does not allow us to control the level of confidence. Therefore to increase the success probability we have to run the algorithms of Theorem 12 multiple times. With this approach the total number of repetitions, which is related to the computational cost for the quantum machine, is proportional to the number of runs multiplied by the computational cost of the algorithm reported in Theorem 12. From this observation we can state the following theorem.

Theorem 13. *There exists a quantum algorithm which is able to find the minimum $B^* \in \{B(0), \ldots, B(N-1)\}$. The algorithm finds a correct answer with probability at least $(1-\delta)$ after $O\left(\sqrt{N}\ln\left(\frac{1}{\delta}\right)\right)$ observations of the set $\{B(0), \ldots, B(N-1)\}$.*

Proof. By using Theorem 12, we know that if we run the algorithm k times and take the minimum with respect to the k minimums $\{\tilde{B}_1^*, \ldots, \tilde{B}_k^*\}$ found during the k runs, we can state that the probability of not finding the minimum in one run is

$$\mathbb{P}\left\{B^* \neq \tilde{B}_1^*\right\} \leq \left(1 - \frac{2}{3}\right). \tag{45}$$

Then the probability of not finding it in k runs is

$$\mathbb{P}\left\{B^* \neq \min\{\tilde{B}_1^*, \ldots, \tilde{B}_k^*\}\right\} \leq \left(1 - \frac{2}{3}\right)^k. \tag{46}$$

Consequently we can state that

$$\mathbb{P}\left\{B^* \in \{\tilde{B}_1^*, \ldots, \tilde{B}_k^*\}\right\} \geq 1 - \left(1 - \frac{2}{3}\right)^k. \tag{47}$$

From this result we can observe that

$$1 - \left(1 - \frac{2}{3}\right)^k \geq 1 - \delta \quad \rightarrow \quad \left(1 - \frac{2}{3}\right)^k \leq \delta, \tag{48}$$

but

$$\ln\left(1 - \frac{2}{3}\right)^k \leq -\frac{2k}{3}. \tag{49}$$

By combining Eqs. (48) and (49), we have that

$$k \geq \frac{3\ln\left(\frac{1}{\delta}\right)}{2}, \tag{50}$$

and this concludes the proof. □

Note that the main difference with respect to the CC algorithms reported in Theorems 5 and 6 is that to reach a desired probability of finding the minimum, the QC algorithm of Theorem 13 requires that the number of observations of $\mathcal{B}_N$ grows sublinearly with the number of elements in $\mathcal{B}_N$.

4 QUANTUM COMPUTING FOR TRAINING

As described in Section 2, the training phase can be seen as a minimization process. From this observation it is clear that QC can be extremely useful in this context. In particular, many problems result in a search between a finite number of possibilities $N = 2^p$; with CC approaches, tackling these problems in a reasonable time is not feasible for p greater than approximately 30–40 [75]. In these cases QC can be useful since, even if QC does not break the NP problems (see Section 3), it can speed up the computation by making these problems tractable for reasonable values of p [21,37]. On the other hand, there are cases where the training phase requires the computation of a model which is the result of a mean value between the output of a finite, but extremely large, number of models; in this case again QC can speed up the computation thanks to the results reported in Section 3. In this section we will present a series of training problems which result in minimization processes or in the computation of a mean value which can take advantage of the QC paradigm.

4.1 BOUNDED LOSS FUNCTIONS

In this subsection we will deal with one of the major problems, related to the training phase of a classifier. Since we consider binary classification problems, the hard loss function, which counts the number of misclassified examples, is used to measure the quality of the different classifiers. Consequently, the choice of a rule in a set of rules is based on the following principle:

$$\hat{\mathfrak{R}}^* = \arg \min_{\mathfrak{R} \in \mathcal{S}^{\mathfrak{R}}} \hat{L}^{\ell_{\mathrm{H}}}(\mathfrak{R}). \tag{51}$$

Unfortunately Problem of Eq. (51) is NP-hard and hence cannot be tackled with the CC paradigm. For this reason, convex relaxations of the hard loss function are used [25]. Unfortunately, they may cause unintended effects which can compromise the quality of the learned model. Moreover, the hard loss function does not allow accurate control of the set of rules [1]. Consequently, the ideal approach it to approximate the hard loss function with bounded but smooth losses which allow one to have better control of the set of rules.

To better understand these concepts, let us consider an example of a learning approach where it is possible to show all the above-mentioned problems, the state-of-the-art solutions for addressing them, and how QC can help us face this problem with a more direct approach. Let us consider the case when $\mathcal{S}^{\mathfrak{R}} = \mathcal{F}$ is composed of all the possible linear separators in the input space $\mathcal{X} = \mathbb{R}^d$. Consequently

$\mathfrak{R} = f : \mathbb{R}^d \to \{-1, 1\}$ and in particular $f(X) = \text{sign}\left(w^T X + b\right)$, where $w \in \mathbb{R}^d$ and $b \in \mathbb{R}$. In this case the problem in Eq. (51) becomes

$$\min_{w,b} \sum_{i=1}^{n} \left[Y_i(w^T X_i + b) \leq 0 \right]. \tag{52}$$

The problem of this formulation is that, in general, it admits infinite solutions, and consequently the problem is ill posed [1,94–97]. For this reason a regularization term must be inserted to give a criterion for selecting the best solution over the infinite possible ones or, from another point of view, one may want to have more accurate control over the class of functions $\mathcal{F}$. To make this process possible, we have to make the hard loss smoother. One possibility is to upper bound it with the so-called trimmed loss or ramp loss [98,99]:

$$\left[w^T X_i + b \neq Y_i \right] \leq \max\left\{0, \min\left\{1, \left[1 - Y_i(w^T X_i + b)\right]\right\}\right\}. \tag{53}$$

Consequently, on the basis of the Ivanov regularization principle [95], we can better control $\mathcal{F}$ by defining it as all the possible linear separator with $\|w\|_2^2 \leq w_{\max}^2$. In this case Eq. (52) becomes

$$\min_{w,b} \sum_{i=1}^{n} \max\left\{0, \min\left\{1, 1 - Y_i(w^T X_i + b)\right\}\right\} \tag{54}$$
$$\text{subject to} \quad \|w\|_2^2 \leq w_{\max}^2.$$

Eq. (54) is harder to solve with respect to its Tikhonov-based regularization version [94]. In particular, there exists a value of C which makes Eq. (54) equivalent to the Tikhonov version [97,100]:

$$\min_{w,b} \frac{1}{2}\|w\|_2^2 + C \sum_{i=1}^{n} \max\left\{0, \min\left\{1, 1 - Y_i(w^T X_i + b)\right\}\right\}, \tag{55}$$

where $\mathcal{F}$ is implicitly defined by the constant C. In particular, if $C = 0$ (which is equivalent to $w_{\max}^2 = 0$), we have that $\mathcal{F}$ contains just two functions $\mathcal{F} = \{1, -1\}$; if instead $C = \infty$ (which is equivalent to $w_{\max}^2 = \infty$), we have that $\mathcal{F}$ is composed of all the possible linear separators in the input space $\mathcal{X} = \mathbb{R}^d$.

Eq. (55) is one of the state-of-the-art approaches for classification [1,98,99,101, 102], and its extension to nonlinear classifiers is trivial by use of the kernel trick [1,103,104].

Unfortunately, Eq. (55) is not convex and this limits its application to real-world issues. To solve Eq. (55) one has to resort to some concave-convex optimization procedures [72], which obviously do not guarantee that the global minimum can be found in reasonable time. Thus a convex relaxation of the problem is required and results in probably the most well-known and widespread classification algorithm, the support vector machines for binary classification [105]:

$$\min_{w,b} \quad \frac{1}{2}\|w\|_2^2 + C\sum_{i=1}^{n} \max\left\{0, 1 - Y_i(w^T X_i + b)\right\}, \tag{56}$$

which is a convex constrained quadratic programming problem that is very easy to solve [106] even for huge values of n [107–109].

The convex relaxation adopted for switching from Eq. (55) to Eq. (56) generates many problems as underlined in Section 4.1.1.

On the basis of these considerations we propose a method for solving Eq. (55) which uses QC where CC cannot provide a feasible alternative. Hence let us reformulate Eq. (54) as follows:

$$\begin{aligned} P_1(w,b,\xi,\zeta) \doteq \min_{w,b,\xi,\zeta} \quad & \frac{1}{n}\sum_{i=1}^{n}(\xi_i + \zeta_i) \\ \text{subject to} \quad & \|w\|_2^2 \le w_{\max}^2, \\ & Y_i(w^T X_i + b) \ge 1 - \xi_i - [1 - Y_i(w^T X_i + b)]\zeta_i, \quad i \in \{1,\dots,n\}, \\ & \xi_i \ge 0, \quad i \in \{1,\dots,n\}, \\ & \zeta_i \in \{0,1\}, \quad i \in \{1,\dots,n\}. \end{aligned} \tag{57}$$

Note that the problem is still not convex and CC cannot help us. But let us note that if the vector ζ is set a priori to one of its possible 2^n values so that $\zeta = \hat{\zeta}$, Eq. (57) becomes

$$\begin{aligned} P_2(w,b,\xi,\hat{\zeta}) \doteq \min_{w,b,\xi} \quad & \frac{1}{n}\sum_{i=1}^{n}(\xi_i + \hat{\zeta}_i) \\ \text{subject to} \quad & \|w\|_2^2 \le w_{\max}^2, \\ & Y_i(w^T X_i + b) \ge 1 - \xi_i - [1 - Y_i(w^T X_i + b)]\hat{\zeta}_i, \quad i \in \{1,\dots,n\}, \\ & \xi_i \ge 0, \quad i \in \{1,\dots,n\}, \end{aligned} \tag{58}$$

which is convex. Consequently, solving Eq. (57) results in

$$P_1(w,b,\xi,\zeta) = \min_{\hat{\zeta} \in \{0,1\}^n} P_2(w,b,\xi,\hat{\zeta}). \tag{59}$$

Consequently P_2 can be considered as a black box such that $P_2 : \{\hat{\zeta}_1, \dots, \hat{\zeta}_{2^n}\} \to [0,1]$ where $\hat{\zeta}_i$ is a vector which represents the unsigned binary number i. But this is exactly a problem that can be faced with the tool presented in Section 3 and that can take advantage of the QC speedup. Consequently, QC can find, with high probability, the solution of Eq. (57).

4.1.1 Example: The problems behind the convex relaxation

This section presents an example showing that the convex relaxation adopted for switching from Eq. (55) to Eq. (56) generates many problems. First, let us reformulate Eq. (56) as follows:

$$\min_{w,b,\xi} \quad \frac{1}{2}\|w\|_2^2 + C\sum_{i=1}^{n} \xi_i \tag{60}$$
$$\text{subject to} \quad Y_i(w^T X_i + b) \geq 1 - \xi_i, \quad i \in \{1, \ldots, n\},$$
$$\xi_i \geq 0, \quad i \in \{1, \ldots, n\}.$$

Then we introduce a one-dimensional dataset for the purpose of illustrating the effects of the convex relaxation in taking into account possible misclassified samples. The dataset is built as follows: The points belonging to one class, say, the positive one, are concentrated at the origin; the negative-labeled ones are concentrated at $X = -1$. One outlier for the latter class is also present at $X = \lambda$ (Fig. 3). Let us suppose that the negative class is composed of n_1 samples plus the outlier and the positive class is composed of n_2 samples. Rewriting Eq. (60) for this specific setting, we have that

$$\min_{w,b,\xi} \quad \frac{1}{2}\|w\|_2^2 + C\,(n_1\xi_1 + n_2\xi_2 + \xi_3) \tag{61}$$
$$\text{subject to} \quad w - b = 1 + \mu_1 - \xi_1, \quad b = 1 + \mu_2 - \xi_2, \quad -\lambda w - b = 1 + \mu_3 - \xi_3,$$
$$\xi_1, \xi_2, \xi_3, \mu_1, \mu_2, \mu_3 \geq 0.$$

With simple computations [105] it is possible to see that the solution can be expressed as

$$w = n_1\alpha_1 - \lambda\alpha_3, \quad -\alpha_1 + \alpha_2 - \alpha_3 = 0, \quad \alpha_1, \alpha_2, \alpha_3 \geq 0, \quad \alpha_1, \alpha_2, \alpha_3 \leq C. \tag{62}$$

The goal is to find when the error measured with the convex relaxation and caused by the outlier is large enough to draw the separation threshold beyond the positive class, thus causing its misidentification. The required conditions are $w = 0$ and $b = -1$. From Eq. (61) it follows that

$$0 = \mu_1 - \xi_1, \quad -2 = \mu_2 - \xi_2, \quad 0 = \mu_3 - \xi_3, \quad \xi_1, \xi_2, \xi_3, \mu_1, \mu_2, \mu_3 \geq 0. \tag{63}$$

By combining Eqs. (62) and (63), we obtain

$$\mu_1 = \xi_1 = \mu_3 = \xi_3 = \mu_2 = 0,\ \xi_2 = 2,\ \alpha_2 = C = \frac{n_1\alpha_1 + \alpha_3}{n_2},\ \xi_1, \xi_2, \xi_3, \mu_1, \mu_2, \mu_3 \geq 0. \tag{64}$$

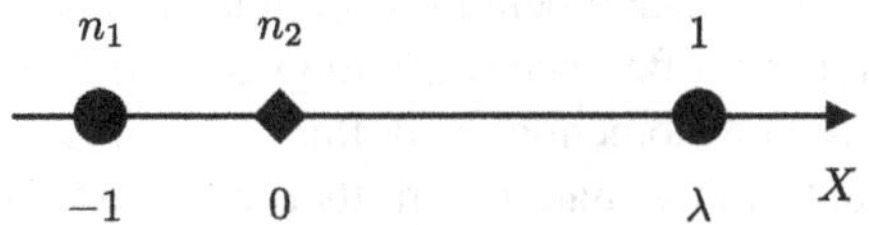

FIG. 3

Outliers might affect the classifier accuracy during support vector machines training.

Consequently we can state that

$$\alpha_3 = C\frac{n_2}{1+\lambda} \leq C, \quad \alpha_1 = \frac{\alpha_3 \lambda}{n_1} = \frac{\lambda}{1+\lambda}\frac{n_2}{n_1}C \leq C. \tag{65}$$

Thus if the conditions

$$n_2 \leq 1+\lambda, \quad \lambda n_2 \leq (1+\lambda) n_1 \tag{66}$$

hold, there is no way of finding the right classifier with Eq. (56). Obviously there is not this issue with Eq. (55).

4.2 ENERGY-EFFICIENT MODELS

QC may also be useful when one has to build models which have to be implemented in situations where limited computational complexity or energy efficiency is required. Most state-of-the-art ML algorithms do not consider the computational constraints of implementing the learned model on a real device [24,75,76]. The capability of a learning procedure to select simple models (i.e., functions which can be described with a limited amount of information) is of paramount importance as well (e.g., refer to results on minimum description length [110,111]). For example, some resource-limited devices are not equipped with floating point processing units to avoid battery draining, to speed up computation, or to reduce the size of the chip: consequently, it is important to learn models which can be described with a few bits in a fixed point format [75,112–122]. This implies revising and restructuring the training phase, which will use rules that can be described with a fixed number of bits κ: the smaller is κ, the simpler and the more energy efficient will be the resulting model [24,76].

On the basis of these considerations let us give an example and show how QC can help in addressing this issue. Let us consider again Eq. (52). In particular let us force the linear separator to be expressed just with a finite number of bits κ:

$$\begin{aligned} \min_{w,b} \quad & \frac{1}{n}\sum_{i=1}^{n}\left[Y_i(w^T X_i + b) \leq 0\right] \\ \text{subject to} \quad & w_j \in \{-2^{k-1}+1, \ldots, 0, \ldots, 2^{k-1}-1\}, \quad j \in \{1, \ldots, d\}, \\ & b \in \{-2^{k-1}+1, \ldots, 0, \ldots, 2^{k-1}-1\}. \end{aligned} \tag{67}$$

Previous studies [24,76,123–125] showed that limiting the number of bits leads to a beneficial regularization effect, allowing the learning of simpler models which outperform more complex ones, while being less computationally demanding. Broadly speaking, only a few bits are often necessary to guarantee that a learning procedure captures the underlying phenomenon, and this capability remains substantially unchanged if the amount of information is further increased. This concept is strictly linked to the Kolmogorov theory [110] and, in particular, the minimum description length principle [111], which states that the smaller the number of bits used to describe the model, the more significant is the result of the learning process. For this reason many approaches have tried to emulate the reduction of the number of bits used to learn the model: noise injection into the data or into the model is one of the most successful approaches [126–129].

Moreover, analogously to what we did in the previous section, let us make the loss smoother, by using the ramp loss, and formulate the associated Ivanov-based regularization problem:

$$\begin{aligned}
\min_{w,b} \quad & \frac{1}{n}\sum_{i=1}^{n} \max\left\{0, \min\left\{1, 1 - Y_i(w^T X_i + b)\right\}\right\} \\
\text{subject to} \quad & \|w\|_2^2 \leq w_{\max}^2, \\
& w_j \in \{-2^{k-1}+1, \dots, 0, \dots, 2^{k-1}-1\}, \quad j \in \{1, \dots, d\}, \\
& b \in \{-2^{k-1}+1, \dots, 0, \dots, 2^{k-1}-1\}.
\end{aligned} \tag{68}$$

This is obviously an NP-hard problem, which cannot be tackled with the CC paradigm and only suboptimal solutions can be found [75,76]. If we reformulate it as

$$\begin{aligned}
\min_{w,b,\xi,\zeta} \quad & \frac{1}{n}\sum_{i=1}^{n} (\xi_i + \zeta_i) \\
\text{subject to} \quad & \|w\|_2^2 \leq w_{\max}^2, \\
& Y_i(w^T X_i + b) \geq 1 - \xi_i - [1 - Y_i(w^T X_i + b)]\zeta_i, \quad i \in \{1, \dots, n\}, \\
& \xi_i \geq 0, \quad i \in \{1, \dots, n\}, \\
& \zeta_i \in \{0, 1\}, \quad i \in \{1, \dots, n\}, \\
& w_j \in \{-2^{k-1}+1, \dots, 0, \dots, 2^{k-1}-1\}, \quad j \in \{1, \dots, d\}, \\
& b \in \{-2^{k-1}+1, \dots, 0, \dots, 2^{k-1}-1\},
\end{aligned} \tag{69}$$

this problem can be seen as the search among all the possible finite set of values of w, b, and ζ, and thus among $2^{\kappa(d+1)+n}$ possibilities. By using again the tools presented in Section 3 (analogously to the problem expressed in Eq. 57), one can take advantage of the QC speedup and find, with high probability, the solution of this problem.

We can derive the nonlinear extension of Eq. (68) by mapping the input space $\mathbb{R}^d$ into another possibly unknown space $\mathbb{R}^D$ through a nonlinear function $\phi : \mathbb{R}^d \to \mathbb{R}^D$ and then searching for the best linear separator $f(X) = w^T\phi(X)$ in this new space. The bias term b has been disregarded thanks to the results of [130]. For this purpose, by drawing inspiration from the representer theorem [131–133] (which does not hold for Eq. 68), and choosing to express w as a linear combination of the points in the dataset projected onto $\mathbb{R}^D$, we have

$$w = \sum_{i=1}^{n} \alpha_i \phi(X_i). \tag{70}$$

With this substitution we are not able to control the weights $w_j \in \{-2^{k-1}+1,\dots,0,\dots,2^{k-1}-1\}$ for all $j \in \{1,\dots,D\}$. What we can control, instead, are the $\alpha_i \in \{-2^{k-1}+1,\dots,0,\dots,2^{k-1}-1\}$, with $i \in \{1,\dots,n\}$. Thanks to the kernel trick [1,4,104,134], the mapping function ϕ does not even need to be known. Indeed, it is possible to select a hardware-friendly kernel, such as the Laplacian kernel proposed in [75], to obtain

$$f(X) = w^T\phi(X) = \sum_{i=1}^{n} \alpha_i \phi(X_i)^T \phi(X) = \sum_{i=1}^{n} \alpha_i K(X_i, X) = \sum_{i=1}^{n} \alpha_i 2^{-\gamma \|X_i - X\|_1}. \tag{71}$$

The hardware-friendly kernel $K(X_i, X) = 2^{-\gamma\|X_i-X\|_1}$ requires only adders and shifters for it to be implemented if γ in an integer value; alternatively, if $\gamma \in \mathbb{R}$, we can use a lookup table [75,124].

Thanks to these result we are able to formulate the nonlinear extension of Eq. (68):

$$\begin{aligned} &\min_{\alpha} \frac{1}{n} \sum_{i=1}^{n} \max\left\{0, \min\left\{1, 1 - Y_i \sum_{j=1}^{n} \alpha_j K(X_j, X_i)\right\}\right\} \\ &\text{subject to} \quad \sum_{i=1}^{n}\sum_{j=1}^{n} \alpha_i \alpha_j K(X_i, X_j) \le w_{\max}^2, \\ &\qquad \alpha_i \in \{-2^{k-1}+1,\dots,0,\dots,2^{k-1}-1\}, \quad i \in \{1,\dots,n\}. \end{aligned} \tag{72}$$

Given the nature of the learning process and whenever a hardware-friendly kernel is chosen, the implementation of the model $f(X) = \sum_{i=1}^{n} \alpha_i K(X_i, X)$ is easy and efficient even on resource-limited systems [76]. Unfortunately, Eq. (72) is again an NP-hard problem [76]. If we reformulate it as

$$\begin{aligned} \min_{\alpha,\xi,\zeta} \quad & \frac{1}{n} \sum_{i=1}^{n} (\xi_i + \zeta_i) \\ \text{subject to} \quad & \sum_{i=1}^{n}\sum_{j=1}^{n} \alpha_i \alpha_j K(X_i, X_j) \le w_{\max}^2, \\ & Y_i \sum_{j=1}^{n} \alpha_j K(X_j, X_i) \ge 1 - \xi_i - \left[Y_i \sum_{j=1}^{n} \alpha_j K(X_j, X_i) \right] \zeta_i, \quad i \in \{1,\dots,n\}, \\ & \xi_i \ge 0, \quad i \in \{1,\dots,n\}, \\ & \zeta_i \in \{0,1\}, \quad i \in \{1,\dots,n\}, \\ & \alpha_i \in \{-2^{k-1}+1,\dots,0,\dots,2^{k-1}-1\}, \quad i \in \{1,\dots,n\}, \end{aligned} \tag{73}$$

Eq. (72) can be seen as the search among all the possible finite set of $2^{(\kappa+1)n}$ values of α and ζ. By using again the tools presented in Section 3 (analogously to what was presented for Eq. 57), we can take advantage of the QC speedup and find, with high probability, the solution of Eq. (73).

4.3 SPARSE SOLUTIONS

Another key feature in learning is the notion of sparsity. Sparsity allows one, for example, to perform an automatic detection of the most relevant features of the input space $\mathcal{X}$ in the set of the d possible ones for the particular learning task [135]. In other situations, sparsity is required for computational reasons, in the sense that sparse models can be deployed with reduced computational effort [76,124,136]. Finally, previous studies [24,76] showed that increasing the sparsity of the solution leads to a beneficial regularization effect, allowing simpler models to be learned which outperform more complex ones while being less computationally demanding.

Regarding the use of the sparsity for feature selection tasks, let us consider Eq. (52) and let us force the linear separator to take into account all the linear separators which lie in a subspace $\mathbb{R}^s$ of the original space $\mathbb{R}^d$. On the basis of this consideration, Eq. (52) can be reformulated as follows:

$$\begin{aligned} \min_{w,b} \quad & \frac{1}{n}\sum_{i=1}^{n}\left[Y_i(w^T X_i + b) \leq 0\right] \\ \text{subject to} \quad & \sum_{j=1}^{d}[w_j \neq 0] \leq s. \end{aligned} \tag{74}$$

By adopting the ramp loss and reformulating Eq. (74) according to the Ivanov-based philosophy, we have that

$$\begin{aligned} \min_{w,b} \quad & \sum_{i=1}^{n} \max\left\{0, \min\left\{1, 1 - Y_i(w^T X_i + b)\right\}\right\} \\ \text{subject to} \quad & \|w\|_2^2 \leq w_{\max}^2, \\ & \sum_{j=1}^{d}[w_j \neq 0] \leq s. \end{aligned} \tag{75}$$

Eq. (75) is NP-hard and there are mainly two state-of-the-art solutions for addressing this issue. The first one involves the least absolute shrinkage and selection operator (LASSO) regularization technique plus relaxation of the ramp loss to its convex counterpart [137]:

$$\begin{aligned} \min_{w,b} \quad & \frac{1}{n}\sum_{i=1}^{n} \max\left\{0, 1 - Y_i(w^T X_i + b)\right\} \\ \text{subject to} \quad & \|w\|_1 \leq w_{\max}. \end{aligned} \tag{76}$$

Eq. (76) is convex since $\|w\|_1$ is the Manhattan norm and, thanks to the geometry of the constraint $\|w\|_1 \leq w_{\max}$, many w_j, with $j \in \{1, \ldots, d\}$, tend to be zero. Unfortunately Eq. (76) has some drawbacks: first we cannot enforce a priori the constraint $\sum_{j=1}^{d}[w_j \neq 0] \leq s$ [124,137,138], and second the solution tends to be unstable [139,140]. For the first issue there is currently no definitive solution

[76,124]. For the second issue the elastic net regularization approach [141,142] is used. It consists in combining the stabilization effect of the $\|w\|_2^2$ with the sparsity effect of the $\|w\|_1$. The result is the reformulation of Eq. (76) into the following one:

$$\min_{w,b} \quad \frac{1}{n}\sum_{i=1}^{n} \max\left\{0, 1 - Y_i(w^T X_i + b)\right\} \tag{77}$$
$$\text{subject to} \quad (1-\lambda)\|w\|_1 + \lambda\|w\|_2^2 \le w_{\max},$$

where $\lambda \in [0,1]$ is a constant which balances the stabilization effect of the $\|w\|_2^2$ with the sparsity effect of the $\|w\|_1$ [143]. Eq. (77) is convex and can be solved for large values of n with the CC paradigm.

Eqs. (76) and (77), although effective in many practical situations, are just attempts to solve and approximations of Eq. (75), the original problem. Anyway, Eq. (75) can be reformulated as follows:

$$P_1(w,b,\xi,\zeta^n,\zeta^d) \doteq \min_{w,b,\xi,\zeta^n,\zeta^d} \quad \frac{1}{n}\sum_{i=1}^{n}(\xi_i + \zeta_i^n) \tag{78}$$

$$\begin{aligned}
&\text{subject to } \|w\|_2^2 \le w_{\max}^2,\\
&\quad Y_i([\mathrm{diag}(\zeta^d)w]^T X_i + b) \ge 1 - \xi_i - [1 - Y_i([\mathrm{diag}(\zeta^d)w]^T X_i + b)]\zeta_i^n, i \in \{1,\dots,n\},\\
&\quad \xi_i \ge 0, \quad i \in \{1,\dots,n\},\\
&\quad \zeta_i^n \in \{0,1\}, \quad i \in \{1,\dots,n\},\\
&\quad \zeta_j^d \in \{0,1\}, \quad j \in \{1,\dots,d\},
\end{aligned}$$

and if the vectors ζ^n and ζ^d are set a priori to one of their possible 2^{n+d} values ($\zeta^n = \hat{\zeta}^n$ and $\zeta^d = \hat{\zeta}^d$), Eq. (78) becomes

$$P_2(w,b,\xi,\hat{\zeta}^n,\hat{\zeta}^d) \doteq \min_{w,b,\xi} \quad \frac{1}{n}\sum_{i=1}^{n}(\xi_i + \hat{\zeta}_i^n) \tag{79}$$

$$\begin{aligned}
&\text{subject to} \|w\|_2^2 \le w_{\max}^2,\\
&\quad Y_i([\mathrm{diag}(\hat{\zeta}^d)w]^T X_i + b) \ge 1 - \xi_i - [1 - Y_i([\mathrm{diag}(\hat{\zeta}^d)w]^T X_i + b)]\hat{\zeta}_i^n, \ i \in \{1,\dots,n\},\\
&\quad \xi_i \ge 0, \quad i \in \{1,\dots,n\},\\
&\quad \hat{\zeta}_i^n \in \{0,1\}, \quad i \in \{1,\dots,n\},\\
&\quad \hat{\zeta}_j^d \in \{0,1\}, \quad j \in \{1,\dots,d\},
\end{aligned}$$

which is convex, and $\mathrm{diag}(\hat{\zeta}^d)$ is the diagonal matrix whose elements on the diagonal are the ones in the vector $\hat{\zeta}^d$. Consequently, by solving the problem expressed in Eq. (78), we have that

$$P_1(w,b,\xi,\zeta^n,\zeta^d) = \min_{\hat{\zeta}^n,\hat{\zeta}^d} P_2(w,b,\xi,\hat{\zeta}^n,\hat{\zeta}^d). \tag{80}$$

Thus the optimization problem P_2 can be considered as a black box such that $P_2 : \{[\hat{\xi}^n, \hat{\xi}^d]_1, \ldots, [\hat{\xi}^n, \hat{\xi}^d]_{2^{n+d}}\} \rightarrow [0, 1]$, where $[\hat{\xi}^n, \hat{\xi}^d]_1$ is a vector which represents the integer binary number i. This is exactly a problem that can be faced with the tools presented in Section 3 and that can take advantage of the QC speedup. Consequently, one can find the solution to Eq. (78) with high probability by using QC.

For the problem of learning a model that needs to be sparse to have better computational properties, let us consider the nonlinear formulation of Eq. (75). Analogously to what was done in the previous section for Eq. (72), we can reformulate Eq. (75) as follows:

$$\begin{aligned} \min_{\alpha} \quad & \sum_{i=1}^{n} \max\left\{0, \min\left\{1, 1 - Y_i \sum_{j=1}^{n} \alpha_j K(X_j, X_i)\right\}\right\} \\ \text{subject to} \quad & \sum_{i=1}^{n} \sum_{j=1}^{n} \alpha_i \alpha_j K(X_j, X_i) \leq w_{\max}^2, \\ & \sum_{j=1}^{n} [\alpha_i \neq 0] \leq s, \end{aligned} \tag{81}$$

where, to compute $f(X) = \sum_{i=1}^{n} \alpha_i K(X_i, X)$, we have to sum just over the subset of s samples instead of the whole n, and this can drastically reduce the computational burden.

Eq. (81) is NP-hard, and one of the state-of-the-art solutions for addressing it is to switch from the combinatorial constraint $\sum_{j=1}^{n} [\alpha_i \neq 0] \leq s$ to a LASSO regularization and to relax the ramp loss to its convex counterpart [137]. To further simplify the problem and increase the sparsity of the solution, the constraint $\sum_{i=1}^{n} \sum_{j=1}^{n} \alpha_i \alpha_j K(X_j, X_i) \leq w_{\max}^2$ is disregarded:

$$\begin{aligned} \min_{\alpha} \quad & \sum_{i=1}^{n} \max\left\{0, 1 - Y_i \sum_{j=1}^{n} \alpha_j K(X_j, X_i)\right\} \\ \text{subject to} \quad & \|\alpha\|_1 \leq \alpha_{\max}. \end{aligned} \tag{82}$$

Eq. (82) uses the LASSO regularization to obtain a sparse solution, even though obviously we cannot enforce it to be zero as much as would like to. On the other hand, Eq. (82) is convex and can be solved even for large values of n with the CC paradigm. Moreover, Eq. (82), although effective in many situations, is just an attempt to solve Eq. (81). If, instead, we reformulate Eq. (81) as

$$
\begin{aligned}
&\min_{\alpha,\zeta^\xi,\zeta^\alpha} \frac{1}{n}\sum_{i=1}^{n}(\xi_i+\zeta_i^\xi) \qquad (83)\\
&\text{subject to}\quad Y_i\sum_{j=1}^{n}\zeta_i^\alpha\alpha_jK(X_j,X_i)\geq 1-\xi_i-\left[1-Y_i\sum_{j=1}^{n}\zeta_i^\alpha\alpha_jK(X_j,X_i)\right]\zeta_i,\quad i\in\{1,\ldots,n\},\\
&\qquad \xi_i\geq 0,\quad i\in\{1,\ldots,n\},\\
&\qquad \zeta_i^\xi\in\{0,1\},\quad i\in\{1,\ldots,n\},\\
&\qquad \zeta_i^\alpha\in\{0,1\},\quad i\in\{1,\ldots,n\},
\end{aligned}
$$

this problem becomes analogous to the one expressed in Eq. (78). Eq. (83) can be tackled with QC approaches since it can be modeled as a search between the minima of 2^{2n} convex problems, analogously to what we did for Eq. (75).

4.4 GIBBS AND BAYES CLASSIFIERS

Let us consider a probabilistic rule $\mathfrak{R} \in \mathcal{S}^{\mathfrak{R}}$, where $\mathcal{S}^{\mathfrak{R}}$ is a set of distributions over a class of functions $\mathcal{F}$. The model built through the support vector machines formulation of Eq. (56) is a deterministic classifier and, in its linear formulation, it can be expressed as:

$$
f(X) = \text{sign}\left([w^*]^T X + b^*\right), \qquad (84)
$$

where $f \in \mathcal{F}$ and $\mathcal{F}$ is composed of all the linear separators in the input space $\mathcal{X} = \mathbb{R}^d$ with $\|w\|_2^2 \leq w_{\max}^2$; w^*, b^* is the solution to Eq. (56). On the basis of PAC-Bayes theory [33,63,65,86,87] (see Section 5.4), some recent studies [64,144–146] suggest transforming the deterministic classifier of support vector machines into a randomized classifier. The proposal is to adopt as Q the density function $q(w) = c_q e^{-\gamma\|w^*-w\|^2}$, which is a multidimensional Gaussian distribution centered at w^*. γ regulates the variance of the Gaussian distribution, and $c_q = \int_w e^{-\gamma\|w^*-w\|^2} dw$ is a normalization factor. In this case the Gibbs classifier is easily implementable and the Bayes classifier can be computed in closed form [144,145].

Nevertheless if, instead of Eq. (56), we want to use Eq. (68), or in other words we want to use just the linear separators that can be represented with a finite number of bits, we can take advantage of QC from two perspectives. Let us denote with w^*, b^* the solution of Eq. (68) based on the QC approach of Eq. (69); in this way we can take advantage of the ability of QC to find minima of problems that cannot be tackled with CC approaches. Moreover, let us start from [64,144–146] and define the following distribution:

$$
q(w) = \begin{cases} c_q e^{-\gamma\|w^*-w\|^2} & \text{if}\quad w_j \in \mathcal{K}\quad \forall j \in \{1,\ldots,d\},\\ 0 & \text{otherwise,}\end{cases} \qquad (85)
$$

where $\mathcal{K} = \{-2^{k-1}+1,\ldots,0,\ldots,2^{k-1}-1\}$. The associated Gibbs and Bayes classifiers are, on the basis of the concepts described in Section 4.2, energy efficient since they can be implemented with a finite number of bits and a lookup table. But to implement the Gibbs classifier we need to know $q(w)$, while to implement the Bayes classifier we need to compute the following quantity:

$$\int_{w} \operatorname{sign}\left(wX + b^{*}\right) q(w) dw. \tag{86}$$

To compute $q(w)$ we need to estimate the quantity

$$\sum_{w_1\in\mathcal{K}} \sum_{w_2\in\mathcal{K}} \cdots \sum_{w_d\in\mathcal{K}} e^{-\gamma\|w^{*}-w\|^2}. \tag{87}$$

If d and κ are small, $q(w)$ can be computed in closed form, otherwise it must be estimated. Then it is easy to see that we can take advantage of the QC speedup (see Section 3) to estimate $q(w)$ since we are searching for a mean value of a function which assumes values in a finite set of possibilities (in particular $2^{\kappa d}$). The same reasoning can be made for the Bayes classifier of Eq. (86).

Contrary to the problem of finding the minima, which is the commonest problem during the training phase, it is not so common to find problems, during the training phase, that can take advantage of QC speedup in finding the mean value of a function. As we will see in the next section, there are many problems in MS and EE that require the computation of a mean value over a finite set of possible values of a particular function.

5 QUANTUM COMPUTING FOR MODEL SELECTION AND ERROR ESTIMATION

In Section 4 we showed that the training phase of an LA, which is the process of selecting the best rule in a set of rules, can fully exploit the QC properties to speed up the computation. In this section we will consider the MS and EE processes, which deal respectively with the problem of choosing the best set of rules among different sets of rules $\mathcal{S}_{\text{MS}}^{\mathfrak{R}} \in \mathcal{S}_r^{\mathcal{S}^{\mathfrak{R}}}$ and with the problem of estimating the generalization error of the rule chosen in the best set of rules $\mathfrak{R}_{\text{MS}} \in \mathcal{S}_{\text{MS}}^{\mathfrak{R}}$ during the training phase. In particular, as described in Section 2, we will review all of the most important approaches to the solution of this problem, but with particular focus on the computational issues that can take advantage of the QC paradigm. For this reason, in some cases, we will report simplified results with respect to the state of the art so as to keep the discussion more focused on the computational aspects than on the statistical properties which characterize these estimators.

5.1 OUT-OF-SAMPLE METHODS: HOLD-OUT, CROSS VALIDATION, AND BOOTSTRAP

Out-of-sample methods, as described in Section 2, rely on a similar idea: the original dataset $\mathcal{D}_n$ is resampled once or many (n_r) times, with or without replacement, to build three independent datasets called "learning, validation, and test sets" respectively, $\mathcal{L}_l^i$, $\mathcal{V}_v^i$, and $\mathcal{T}_t^i$, with $i \in \{1, \ldots, n_r\}$. Note that $\mathcal{L}_l^i \cap \mathcal{V}_v^i = \oslash$, $\mathcal{L}_l^i \cap \mathcal{T}_t^i = \oslash$, and $\mathcal{V}_v^i \cap \mathcal{T}_t^i = \oslash \forall i \in \{1, \ldots, n_r\}$. To select the best set of rules $\mathcal{S}_{\text{MS}}^{\mathfrak{R}}$ in a set of possible ones $\mathcal{S}_r^{\mathcal{S}^{\mathfrak{R}}}$ or, in other words, to perform the MS phase, we have to apply the following procedure:

$$\mathcal{S}_{\text{MS}}^{\mathfrak{R}} : \quad \min_{\mathcal{S}^{\mathfrak{R}} \in \mathcal{S}_r^{\mathcal{S}^{\mathfrak{R}}}} \frac{1}{n_r} \sum_{i=1}^{n_r} \frac{1}{v} \sum_{Z \in \mathcal{V}_v^i} \ell(\mathfrak{R}^i, Z), \tag{88}$$

where $\mathfrak{R}^i$ is the result of the training phase with $\mathcal{S}^{\mathfrak{R}}$ and $\mathcal{L}_l^i$. Note that $\mathcal{S}^{\mathfrak{R}}$ might also not be explicitly known since we just need to apply the training phase to a series of different training sets. Moreover the procedure and the following results hold for any [0, 1]-bounded loss function. Since the samples in $\mathcal{L}_l^i$ are i.i.d. from the ones in $\mathcal{V}_v^i$, the idea is that $\mathcal{S}_{\text{MS}}^{\mathfrak{R}}$ should be the set of rules from which the LA selects rules during the training phase which allow one to achieve a small error on a dataset that is independent of the training set [14].

The EE phase is performed as follows:

$$L(\mathfrak{R}_{\text{MS}}) \leq \frac{1}{n_r} \sum_{i=1}^{n_r} \frac{1}{t} \sum_{Z \in \mathcal{T}_t^i} \ell(\mathfrak{R}^i, Z) + \sqrt{\frac{\ln\left(\frac{1}{\delta}\right)}{2t}}, \tag{89}$$

where the bound holds with probability $(1 - \delta)$. This result can be derived since the data in $\mathcal{L}_l^i$ and $\mathcal{V}_v^i$ are i.i.d. from the ones in $\mathcal{T}_t^i$; thus Theorem 1 can be used [14]. Note that after the best set of hyperparameters has been found, in practice, one can select as $\mathfrak{R}_{\text{MS}}$ the one obtained when the training phase is performed over the whole set of data $\mathcal{D}_n$ [14,57,58].

If $n_r = 1$, if l, v, and t are aprioristically set such that $n = l + v + t$, and if the resampling procedure is performed without replacement, we obtain the hold-out method [14]. For implementation of the complete k-fold cross validation, we have to set $n_r = \binom{n}{k}\binom{n-\frac{n}{k}}{k}$, $l = (k-2)\frac{n}{k}$, $v = \frac{n}{k}$, and $t = \frac{n}{k}$, and the resampling must be done without replacement [14,15,57]. Finally, for implementation of the bootstrap method, $l = n$ and $\mathcal{L}_l^i$ must be sampled with replacement from $\mathcal{D}_n$, while $\mathcal{V}_v^i$ and $\mathcal{T}_t^i$ are sampled without replacement from the sample of $\mathcal{D}_n$ that has not been sampled in $\mathcal{L}_l^i$ [14,16]. Note that for the bootstrap procedure $n_r = \binom{2n-1}{n}$. It is worthwhile noting that the only hypothesis needed to rigorously apply the out-of-sample technique is the i.i.d. hypothesis on the data contained in $\mathcal{D}_n$ and that all these techniques work both for deterministic and for probabilistic rules.

The out-of-sample methods can take full advantage of the QC speedup. To compute the quantities involved in the MS and EE phases, which are basically mean values of a complex procedure (see Eqs. 88 and 89), we have to perform many training phases to obtain the errors of $\mathfrak{R}^i$ over the validation and test sets, $\mathcal{V}_v^i$ and $\mathcal{T}_t^i$ respectively, and then take the average of these results (note that each training phase can itself take advantage of the QC, as reported in Section 4). These averages take into account $n_r \approx n!$ values and must be recomputed for each $\mathcal{S}^{\mathfrak{R}} \in \mathcal{S}_r^{\mathcal{S}^{\mathfrak{R}}}$. This procedure is computationally expensive, and hence one usually adopts an estimate of the quantities of Eqs. (88) and (89) by setting n_r to a reasonable value (e.g., in k-fold cross validation $n_r = k$ [57,58] or in the bootstrap method n_r is set to some hundreds [14]). QC approaches (see Section 3) can obtain a more accurate estimate with the same n_r or the same accuracy with a smaller n_r since we are searching for a mean value of functions which assume values in a finite set of possibilities $n_r \approx N!$ (in fact, $n_r = \binom{n}{k}\binom{n-\frac{n}{k}}{k}$ for the complete k-fold cross validation procedure, and $n_r = \binom{2n-1}{n}$ for the bootstrap MS procedure). This issue is even more crucial if we consider the k in the complete k-fold cross validation and the number of samples to resample during the bootstrap procedure as hyperparameters to be tuned [29,147–150].

5.2 VAPNIK-CHERVONENKIS THEORY

The VC theory was one of the first attempts to develop an in-sample method for MS and EE [1]. As described in Section 2, in-Sample methods use the whole set of data for training, MS, and EE. In particular, the VC theory requires we know in advance the set of rules $\mathcal{S}^{\mathfrak{R}} \in \mathcal{S}_r^{\mathcal{S}^{\mathfrak{R}}}$, and deals with a deterministic function $\mathfrak{R} = f$ which belongs to a class of functions $\mathcal{S}^{\mathfrak{R}} = \mathcal{F}$ chosen in a set of classes of functions $\mathcal{S}_r^{\mathcal{S}^{\mathcal{R}}} = \mathcal{S}_r^{\mathcal{F}} = \{\mathcal{F}_1, \ldots, \mathcal{F}_r\}$. The following analysis holds just for the binary classification problems where the hard loss function ℓ_{H} is used. The extension to real-valued loss functions can be found in [1], but it is rarely used because it has been superseded by the RC theory, which will be presented in Section 5.3. In this section we will present the VC theory approach to the selection of the best class of functions in a set of classes of functions $\mathcal{F}_{\mathrm{MS}} \in \mathcal{S}_r^{\mathcal{F}}$ and to the estimation of the generalization error of a function chosen in the best class of functions $f_{\mathrm{MS}} \in \mathcal{F}_{\mathrm{MS}}$.

In the VC theory the following quantity associated with a class of functions $\mathcal{F}$ is defined:

$$\mathcal{F}|_{\mathcal{D}_n} = \{\{\mathrm{sign}[f(X_1)], \ldots, \mathrm{sign}[f(X_n)]\} \,|\, f \in \mathcal{F}\}, \tag{90}$$

which is the set of distinct functions in $\mathcal{F}$ which shatter the dataset $\mathcal{D}_n$. Then the VC entropy $H_n(\mathcal{F})$ and the annealed VC entropy $A_n(\mathcal{F})$, together with their empirical counterparts $\hat{H}_n(\mathcal{F})$ and $\hat{A}_n(\mathcal{F})$ [1], can be recalled:

$$\hat{H}_n(\mathcal{F}) = \ln\left(\left|\mathcal{F}|_{\mathcal{D}_n}\right|\right), \quad H_n(\mathcal{F}) = \mathbb{E}_{X_1,\ldots,X_n} \hat{H}_n(\mathcal{F}), \tag{91}$$

$$\hat{A}_n(\mathcal{F}) = \hat{H}_n(\mathcal{F}), \quad A_n(\mathcal{F}) = \ln\left(\mathbb{E}_{X_1,\ldots,X_n} \left|\mathcal{F}|_{\mathcal{D}_n}\right|\right). \tag{92}$$

On the basis of the above definitions, it is possible to introduce the growth function and the VC dimension, $G_n(\mathcal{F})$ and $d_{VC}(\mathcal{F})$ respectively, as [1]

$$G_n(\mathcal{F}) = \max_{X_1,\ldots,X_n} \ln\left(\left|\mathcal{F}|_{\mathcal{D}_n}\right|\right), \quad d_{VC}(\mathcal{F}) = \max_n \{n : G_n(\mathcal{F}) = 2^n\}. \tag{93}$$

Note that [1]

$$H_n(\mathcal{F}) \le A_n(\mathcal{F}) \le G_n(\mathcal{F}) \le d_{VC}(\mathcal{F}) \ln n. \tag{94}$$

From these definitions it is possible to prove the following theorem.

Theorem 14 ([151]). *Given a class of functions $\mathcal{F}$, it is possible to state that the following inequalities hold with probability* $(1-\delta)$*:*

$$L^{\ell_H}(f) \le \hat{L}^{\ell_H}(f) + \sqrt{\frac{A_{2n}(\mathcal{F})}{n}} + \sqrt{\frac{\ln\left(\frac{4}{\delta}\right)}{n}} \tag{95}$$

$$\le \hat{L}^{\ell_H}(f) + \sqrt{\frac{d_{VC}(\mathcal{F}) \ln n}{n}} + \sqrt{\frac{\ln\left(\frac{4}{\delta}\right)}{n}}, \quad \forall f \in \mathcal{F}. \tag{96}$$

Moreover, if $\mathcal{F}$ is chosen in a set of r classes of functions $\mathcal{S}_r^{\mathcal{F}}$, we have that the following inequality holds with probability $(1-2\delta)$*:*

$$L^{\ell_H}(f) \le \hat{L}^{\ell_H}(f) + \sqrt{\frac{d_{VC}(\mathcal{F}) \ln n}{n}} + \sqrt{\frac{\ln\left(\frac{4}{\delta}\right)}{n}} + \sqrt{\frac{\ln r}{n}}, \quad \forall f \in \mathcal{F} \in \mathcal{S}_r^{\mathcal{F}}. \tag{97}$$

The VC theory is basically a more refined form of the union bound [1,152] which is able to deal with classes of functions which contain an infinite number of functions. In particular, the entropies and the growth function measure the number of distinct functions with respect to the distribution of the data, while d_{VC} is a measure of dimensionality for a general nonlinear class of functions [1,153]. Unfortunately the bounds of Theorem 14 are data independent or take into account quantities that cannot be estimated from the data.

The following theorem has been proved recently [31,154].

Theorem 15 ([31,154]). *The following statement holds with probability* $(1-\delta)$*:*

$$A_{2n}(\mathcal{F}) \le 4\hat{A}_n(\mathcal{F}) + 8\ln\left(\frac{1}{\delta}\right) = 4\hat{H}_n(\mathcal{F}) + 8\ln\left(\frac{1}{\delta}\right). \tag{98}$$

Consequently, by combining Theorems 14 and 15, we obtain the empirical counterpart of the inequality in Eq. (95).

Theorem 16. *Given a class of functions $\mathcal{F}$, it is possible to state that the following inequality holds with probability* $(1-3\delta)$*:*

$$L^{\ell_H}(f) \le \hat{L}^{\ell_H}(f) + \sqrt{\frac{4\hat{A}_n(\mathcal{F})}{n}} + \sqrt{\frac{9\ln\left(\frac{4}{\delta}\right)}{n}}, \quad \forall f \in \mathcal{F}. \tag{99}$$

Moreover, if $\mathcal{F}$ is chosen such that $\mathcal{F} \in \mathcal{S}_r^{\mathcal{F}}$, we can state that the following inequality holds with probability $(1-2\delta)$*:*

$$L^{\ell_H}(f) \leq \hat{L}^{\ell_H}(f) + \sqrt{\frac{4\hat{A}_n(\mathcal{F})}{n}} + \sqrt{\frac{9\ln\left(\frac{4}{\delta}\right)}{n}} + \sqrt{\frac{9\ln r}{n}}, \quad \forall f \in \mathcal{F} \in \mathcal{S}_r^{\mathcal{F}}. \tag{100}$$

Note that, thanks to the results of Theorems 14 and 16, we have an upper bound of the generalization error of any function $f \in \mathcal{F}$ for any class of function $\mathcal{F}$ chosen such that $\mathcal{F} \in \mathcal{S}_r^{\mathcal{F}}$. Consequently, we can present the two MS and EE procedures based on the VC theory. In particular, the original approach based on Theorem 14 suggests we choose

$$f_{\text{MS}}, \mathcal{F}_{\text{MS}} : \arg \min_{f \in \mathcal{F} \in \mathcal{S}_r^{\mathcal{F}}} \hat{L}^{\ell_H}(f) + \sqrt{\frac{d_{\text{VC}}(\mathcal{F}) \ln n}{n}} + \sqrt{\frac{\ln\left(\frac{4}{\delta}\right)}{n}} + \sqrt{\frac{\ln r}{n}}, \tag{101}$$

while the second approach, based on Theorem 16, suggests we choose

$$f_{\text{MS}}, \mathcal{F}_{\text{MS}} : \arg \min_{f \in \mathcal{F} \in \mathcal{S}_r^{\mathcal{F}}} \hat{L}^{\ell_H}(f) + \sqrt{\frac{4\hat{A}_n(\mathcal{F})}{n}} + \sqrt{\frac{9\ln\left(\frac{4}{\delta}\right)}{n}} + \sqrt{\frac{9\ln r}{n}}. \tag{102}$$

Note that Eqs. (101) and (102) both also suggest we choose in $\mathcal{F}_{\text{MS}}$ the function f_{MS} with the smallest empirical error. This approach is known in the literature as "data-dependent structural risk minimization" [1,152].

Unfortunately, d_{VC} is data independent since it does not take into account the distribution of the data [1]. For this reason the MS procedure of Eq. (102) should be preferred [31,153,154] but to apply it we need to compute $\hat{A}_n(\mathcal{F})$. In particular we will show that this task can take advantage of the QC speedup. For this purpose, let us consider $\mathcal{F}$ as the set of linear classifiers in the space defined by the function $\phi : \mathbb{R}^d \to \mathbb{R}^D$, where $X \in \mathcal{X} \subseteq \mathbb{R}^d$ and $f(X) = w^T\phi(X) + b$, with $w \in \mathbb{R}^D$ and $b \in \mathbb{R}$. As described above, d_{VC} is not distribution dependent; indeed it is trivial to show that[1]

$$d_{\text{VC}} \leq D + 1. \tag{103}$$

To be able to take into account the distribution of the data, we have to use the VC entropy. Note that to perform the MS procedure of Eq. (102) with the VC entropy, we need to compute $\hat{A}_n(\mathcal{F}_{\mathcal{H}})$, which is the number of configurations of the labels that can be shattered by $\mathcal{F}_{\mathcal{H}}$. Consequently, let $\sigma_j \in \{-1, 1\}^n$ be one of the possible $j \in \{1, \ldots, 2^n\}$ configurations of the labels; we have to find how many of them can

[1]The result can be found in [1] but note that $d_{\text{VC}} < D + 1$ only if the data-generating distribution assumes values in a subspace of $\mathbb{R}^D$.

be shattered by a linear separator in the space defined by ϕ; thus we have to check for how many of problems

$$\min_{w,b} \quad 0, \quad \text{subject to} \quad \sigma_{i,j}(w^T\phi(X_i)+b) \geq 1, \quad \forall i \in \{1,\ldots,n\}, \tag{104}$$

at least one solution exists. Note that the above problem is a linear programming problem [71]. Searching for a feasible solution of a linear programming problem is again a linear programming problem [71], which can be solved in polynomial time [71]. Unfortunately we have to solve 2^n problems, and this represents an NP problem. The issue can be circumvented by our noting that we can estimate $\frac{\hat{A}_n(\mathcal{F}_\mathcal{H})}{n}$ in Eq. (102) through the approaches in Section 3 by checking just a subset of the 2^n possible configurations of the labels [153]. In this way we can take advantage of the QC speedup in computing the mean value of the function which assumes values in a finite number of possibilities (in this case 2^n possibilities). Note that there is no reason to use QC also for solving the problem expressed by Eq. (104) since it is convex and therefore can be solved by CC linear programming solvers [71].

5.3 (LOCAL) RADEMACHER COMPLEXITY THEORY

RC theory is based the powerful data-dependent notion of complexity [61,85,155]. RC has been shown to be able to provide deep insight into the learning process [85, 153] and to be useful in many real-world applications [14,24,76]. RC theory works in the same hypotheses of the VC theory but the results hold for any [0, 1]-bounded loss function [85]. Moreover, we will also show an evolution of the RC theory,—namely the Local RC (LRC) theory [32,34,156]—motivated by a drawback of the RC theory: the latter in fact takes into account all the functions in $\mathcal{F}$, and also the ones that will never been chosen from $\mathcal{F}$ because of their high error. LRC, instead, is able to take into account just the functions with small error [32].

Let us recall the notion of RC [14,85,155]:

$$\hat{R}_n(\mathcal{F}) = \mathbb{E}_\sigma \sup_{f\in\mathcal{F}} \frac{2}{n}\sum_{i=1}^{n} \sigma_i \ell(f, Z_i), \tag{105}$$

$$\sigma_i \in \{\pm 1\}, \quad \mathbb{P}\{\sigma_i = +1\} = \mathbb{P}\{\sigma_i = -1\} = \frac{1}{2}, \quad \forall i \in \{1,\ldots,n\}.$$

RC measures the ability of the class of functions to fit random labels [11]. More refined interpretations and the advantages and disadvantages with respect to the VC theory can be found in [153]. From this definition of RC it is possible to state the following theorem.

Theorem 17 ([85]). *If a function f is chosen in a class of functions $\mathcal{F}$, and the class of functions is selected in a set of classes of functions $\mathcal{S}_r^\mathcal{F}$, the following inequality holds with probability* $(1-\delta)$:

$$L^\ell(f) \le \hat{L}^\ell(f) + \hat{R}_n(\mathcal{F}) + 3\sqrt{\frac{\ln(\frac{2}{\delta})}{2n}} + 3\sqrt{\frac{\ln r}{2n}}, \quad \forall f \in \mathcal{F} \in \mathcal{S}_r^{\mathcal{F}}. \tag{106}$$

Since the bound reported in Theorem 17 holds for all $f \in \mathcal{F} \in \mathcal{S}_r^{\mathcal{F}}$, the RC theory suggests the following MS and EE procedure:

$$f_{\text{MS}}, \mathcal{F}_{\text{MS}}: \quad \arg \min_{f \in \mathcal{F} \in \mathcal{S}_r^{\mathcal{F}}} \hat{L}^\ell(f) + \hat{R}_n(\mathcal{F}) + 3\sqrt{\frac{\ln(\frac{2}{\delta})}{2n}} + 3\sqrt{\frac{\ln r}{2n}}. \tag{107}$$

As one can see from Theorem 17, the RC-based bound of Eq. (106) takes into account all the $f \in \mathcal{F}$. LRC, instead, is able to discard those functions from $\mathcal{F}$ which will never be chosen by the LA because of their high error [32,34,156]. The following result is the LRC-based counterpart of Theorem 17.

Theorem 18 ([32,34]). *Under the same hypothesis of Theorem 17, the following inequality holds with probability* $(1 - \delta)$*:*

$$L^\ell(f) \le \min_{K \in (1,\infty)} \frac{K}{K-1}\hat{L}^\ell(f) + Kp + \sqrt{\frac{\ln\left(\frac{3r}{\delta}\right)}{2n}}, \quad \forall f \in \mathcal{F} \in \mathcal{S}_r^{\mathcal{F}}. \tag{108}$$

$$\textit{subject to} \quad \sup_{\alpha \in [0,1]} \alpha \left[LR + \sqrt{\frac{2\ln(\frac{3r}{\delta})}{n}} \right] \le \frac{p}{K}, \quad p \ge 0,$$

$$LR \le \hat{R}\left(\left\{ f : f \in \mathcal{F}, \hat{L}^\ell(f) \le \frac{p}{\alpha} + LR + \sqrt{\frac{\ln(\frac{3r}{\delta})}{2n}} \right\} \right) + \sqrt{\frac{2\ln(\frac{3r}{\delta})}{n}},$$

where K, α, and p must be found with a numerical procedure such that all the previous conditions are satisfied.

Using the LRC-based result is much harder than using the RC-based one [32, 34,61]; nevertheless Theorem 18, analogously to Theorem 17, inspires the following MS and EE procedure:

$$f_{\text{MS}}, \mathcal{F}_{\text{MS}}: \quad \arg \min_{f \in \mathcal{F} \in \mathcal{S}_r^{\mathcal{F}}} \min_{K \in (1,\infty)} \frac{K}{K-1}\hat{L}(f) + Kp + \sqrt{\frac{\ln\left(\frac{3r}{\delta}\right)}{2n}} \tag{109}$$

$$\text{subject to} \quad \sup_{\alpha \in [0,1]} \alpha \left[LR + \sqrt{\frac{2\ln(\frac{3r}{\delta})}{n}} \right] \le \frac{p}{K}, \quad p \ge 0,$$

$$LR \le \hat{R}\left(\left\{ f : f \in \mathcal{F}, \hat{L}(f) \le \frac{p}{\alpha} + LR + \sqrt{\frac{\ln(\frac{3r}{\delta})}{2n}} \right\} \right) + \sqrt{\frac{2\ln(\frac{3r}{\delta})}{n}}.$$

In the following presentation we will show that RC and LRC can take full advantage of the QC approaches described in Section 3. In particular, to apply the MS procedures of Eqs. (107) and (109), we have to compute $\hat{R}_n(\mathcal{F})$ and $\hat{R}_n\left(\left\{f : f \in \mathcal{F}, \hat{L}(f) \leq \beta\right\}\right)$ (note that LRC is equal to RC if $\beta = 1$) and these quantities can be estimated faster thanks to the powerful QC approaches described in Section 3. Let us consider the same framework depicted in Section 5.2, where $\mathcal{F}$ is the set of linear classifiers in the space defined by the function $\phi : \mathbb{R}^d \to \mathbb{R}^D$, where $X \in \mathcal{X} \subseteq \mathbb{R}^d$, $f(X) = w^T\phi(X) + b$, with $w \in \mathbb{R}^D$ and $b \in \mathbb{R}$, and the hard loss function is used, $\ell(f, Z) = \frac{1-Y\text{sign}[f(X)]}{2}$. Then we can rewrite the LRC as follows:

$$\begin{aligned}
&\hat{R}_n\left(\left\{f : f \in \mathcal{F}, \hat{L}(f) \leq \beta\right\}\right) \qquad (110)\\
&= \mathbb{E}_\sigma \sup_{f \in \left\{f : f \in \mathcal{F}, \hat{L}(f) \leq \beta\right\}} \frac{2}{n} \sum_{i=1}^{n} \sigma_i \ell(f, Z_i) \\
&= -\mathbb{E}_\sigma \inf_{f \in \left\{f : f \in \mathcal{F}, \hat{L}(f) \leq \beta\right\}} \frac{2}{n} \sum_{i=1}^{n} \sigma_i \ell(f, Z_i) \\
&= -\mathbb{E}_\sigma \inf_{f \in \left\{f : f \in \mathcal{F}, \frac{1}{n}\sum_{i=1}^{n} \frac{1-Y_i\text{sign}[f(X_i)]}{2} \leq \beta\right\}} \frac{2}{n} \sum_{i=1}^{n} \frac{1-\sigma_i \text{sign}[f(X_i)]}{2} \\
&= -\mathbb{E}_\sigma \min_{\substack{w \in \mathbb{R}^D, b \in \mathbb{R}, \\ w,b \in \left\{w,b : \frac{1}{n}\sum_{i=1}^{n} \frac{1-Y_i\text{sign}[w^T\phi(X_i)+b]}{2} \leq \beta\right\}}} \frac{2}{n} \sum_{i=1}^{n} \frac{1-\sigma_i \text{sign}[w^T\phi(X_i)+b]}{2}.
\end{aligned}$$

Consequently, to compute the RC and LRC, we have to solve the following problem or check if the solution exists for all the 2^n configurations of the $\sigma_j \in \{-1, 1\}^n$ with $j \in \{1, \ldots, 2^n\}$:

$$\begin{aligned}
&P_1(w, b, \zeta^Y, \zeta^\sigma) \doteq \min_{w,b} \sum_{i=1}^{n} \zeta^\sigma \qquad (111)\\
&\text{subject to} \quad \frac{1}{n}\sum_{i=1}^{n} \zeta_i^Y \leq \beta, \\
&\qquad Y_i(w^T\phi(X_i)+b) \geq 1 - \left[1 - Y_i(w^T\phi(X_i)+b)\right]\zeta_i^Y, \quad i \in \{1, \ldots, n\}, \\
&\qquad \sigma_i(w^T\phi(X_i)+b) \geq 1 - \left[1 - \sigma_i(w^T\phi(X_i)+b)\right]\zeta_i^\sigma, \quad i \in \{1, \ldots, n\}, \\
&\qquad \zeta_i^Y \in \{0, 1\}, \quad i \in \{1, \ldots, n\}, \\
&\qquad \zeta_i^\sigma \in \{0, 1\}, \quad i \in \{1, \ldots, n\},
\end{aligned}$$

which is an NP-hard problem. If the vectors ζ^Y and ζ^σ are set a priori to one of their possible 2^{2n} values ($\zeta^Y = \hat{\zeta}^Y$ and $\zeta^\sigma = \hat{\zeta}^\sigma$), Eq. (111) becomes

$$P_2(w, b, \hat{\zeta}^Y, \hat{\zeta}^\sigma) \doteq \min_{w,b} \sum_{i=1}^{n} \hat{\zeta}^\sigma \qquad (112)$$

$$\text{subject to} \quad \frac{1}{n}\sum_{i=1}^{n}\zeta_i^Y \leq \beta,$$
$$Y_i(w^T\phi(X_i)+b) \geq 1 - \left[1 - Y_i(w^T\phi(X_i)+b)\right]\hat{\xi}_i^Y, \quad i \in \{1,\ldots,n\},$$
$$\sigma_i(w^T\phi(X_i)+b) \geq 1 - \left[1 - \sigma_i(w^T\phi(X_i)+b)\right]\hat{\xi}_i^\sigma, \quad i \in \{1,\ldots,n\},$$

which is convex. Consequently, to solve Eq. (111) we can use Eq. (112) as follows:

$$P_1(w,b,\zeta^Y,\zeta^\sigma) = \min_{\hat{\xi}^Y,\hat{\xi}^\sigma} P_2(w,b,\hat{\xi}^Y,\hat{\xi}^\sigma). \tag{113}$$

Thus to solve this problem with a QC approach, P_2 can be considered as a black box such that $P_2 : \{[\hat{\xi}^Y,\hat{\xi}^\sigma]_1,\ldots,[\hat{\xi}^Y,\hat{\xi}^\sigma]_{2^{2n}}\} \to [0,1]$, where $[\hat{\xi}^Y,\hat{\xi}^\sigma]_i$ is a vector which represents the integer binary number i. This is exactly a problem that can be tackled with the tools presented in Section 3 and that can take advantage of the QC speedup. Consequently, the solution to Eq. (111) can be found with high probability by use of the QC paradigm to improve the rate of convergence of the estimate with respect to the case when CC is used. Moreover, we can again use the QC algorithm to estimate the mean value over the possible 2^n configurations of the possible $\sigma_i \in \{0,1\}^n$ with $j \in \{1,\ldots,2^n\}$ (see the expectation with respect to σ in the definition of RC and LRC).

5.4 PAC-BAYES THEORY

The PAC-Bayes theory is the last major theory in the context of hypothesis space-based in-sample methods. PAC-Bayes theory, differently from the VC and RC theories, bounds the error of the Gibbs classifier and the Bayes classifier [33,63,65,157–159]. This framework allows one to deal with probabilistic classifiers and ensemble methods [65], such as bagging [70,160], and boosting [161,162]. PAC-Bayes analysis holds for both the hard loss function and the linear loss function:

$$\ell_S(f,Z) = \min\left\{1, \max\left\{0, \frac{1-Yf(X)}{2}\right\}\right\}. \tag{114}$$

Note that, if $f_B \in \mathcal{F}_B$ is a binary classifier $f_B : \mathcal{X} \to \{-1,1\}$, we have that $\ell_S(f_B,Z) = \ell_H(f_B,Z)$. In this section we indicate with ℓ the case when both ℓ_H and ℓ_S can be used.

In particular, given two probability distributions Q and P over $\mathcal{F}$, let us define the expected disagreement [65] of $f \in \mathcal{F}$ with respect to Q, together with its empirical counterpart:

$$d_Q = \frac{1}{2} - \frac{1}{2}\mathbb{E}_X\left\{[\mathbb{E}_{f\sim Q}\{f(X)\}]^2\right\}, \quad \hat{d}_Q = \frac{1}{2} - \frac{1}{2m}\sum_{i=1}^{m}[\mathbb{E}_{f\sim Q}\{f(X_i)\}]^2. \tag{115}$$

The expected joint error [65] of $f \in \mathcal{F}$ with respect to Q and its empirical counterpart are

$$e^{\ell}_{Q} = \mathbb{E}_{Z, f_1 \sim Q, f_2 \sim Q} \{\ell(f_1, Z)\ell(f_2, Z)\}, \tag{116}$$

$$\hat{e}^{\ell}_{Q} = \mathbb{E}_{f_1 \sim Q, f_2 \sim Q} \left\{ {}^{1}\!/\!_{n} \sum_{i=1}^{n} [\ell(f_1, Z_i)\ell(f_2, Z_i)] \right\}. \tag{117}$$

Note that in [65] it is proved that

$$d_Q \leq 2\left(\sqrt{e_Q} - e_Q\right). \tag{118}$$

We denote with $\mathtt{KL}[Q||P]$ the Kullback-Leibler divergence [163] between P and Q, while $\mathtt{kl}[q||p]$ and $\mathtt{kl}\left[\begin{smallmatrix} q_1 \\ q_2 \end{smallmatrix} || \begin{smallmatrix} p_1 \\ p_2 \end{smallmatrix}\right]$ are, respectively, the Kullback-Leibler divergence for the binomial and trinomial distributions [86]:

$$\mathtt{kl}[q||p] = q \ln\left[\frac{q}{p}\right] + [1-q] \ln\left[\frac{1-q}{1-p}\right], \tag{119}$$

$$\mathtt{kl}\left[q_1, q_2 || p_1, p_2\right] = q_1 \ln\left[\frac{q_1}{p_1}\right] + q_2 \ln\left[\frac{q_2}{p_2}\right] + [1 - q_1 - q_2] \ln\left[\frac{1 - q_1 - q_2}{1 - p_1 - p_2}\right].$$

Thanks to Pinsker's inequality [163], we can state that $|q - p| \leq \sqrt{{}^{1}\!/\!_{2}\mathtt{kl}(q||p)}$. Finally, let us recall the definition of the last fundamental quantity in the PAC-Bayes framework [86,164]:

$$\xi_n = \sum_{k=0}^{n} \binom{n}{k} \left(\frac{k}{n}\right)^k \left(1 - \frac{k}{n}\right)^{n-k} \leq 2\sqrt{n}, \tag{120}$$

which will appear in many of the results presented. A lot of work has been done to bound the risk of the Bayes classifier and the Gibbs classifier; in particular, it is possible to identify five state-of-the-art milestone results. The first one bounds the risk of the Gibbs classifier in terms of its empirical estimate.

Theorem 19 ([63,86]). *For any probability distribution P over $\mathcal{F}$, chosen before seeing $\mathcal{D}_n$, for all Q we have that the following inequality holds with probability* $(1 - \delta)$*:*

$$L^{\ell}(G_Q) \in \left[\inf \mathcal{I}^{\ell}_{0}(\delta, P, Q, n), \sup \mathcal{I}^{\ell}_{0}(\delta, P, Q, n)\right], \tag{121}$$

where

$$\mathcal{I}^{\ell}_{0}(\delta, P, Q, n) = \left\{ r : r \in [0,1], \mathtt{kl}\left[\hat{L}^{\ell}(G_Q)||r\right] \leq \frac{\mathtt{KL}[Q||P] + \ln\left(\frac{\xi_n}{\delta}\right)}{n} \right\}.$$

The second result bounds the risk of the Bayes classifier and is commonly known as the "$\mathcal{C}$-bound." Unfortunately, this bound involves only quantities that cannot be computed from the data.

Theorem 20 ([65,159]). *Given the risk of the Gibbs classifier, the expected disagreement, and the expected joint error of Q over $\mathcal{F}$, we have that*

$$L^{\ell}(B_Q) \leq 1 - \frac{[1-2L^{\ell}(G_Q)]^2}{1-2d_Q} = 1 - \frac{[1-(2e^{\ell}_Q + d_Q)]^2}{1-2d_Q}. \tag{122}$$

This bound holds for both $\ell = \ell_S$ and $\ell = \ell_H$. Moreover, $L^{\ell}(B_Q) \leq 2L^{\ell_S}(G_Q)$.

By using Theorems 19 and 20, one can obtain the third milestone result, which is an empirical bound over the risk of the Bayes classifier.

Theorem 21. *For any probability distribution P over $\mathcal{F}$, chosen before seeing $\mathcal{D}_n$, with probability $(1-\delta)$ and for all Q, we have that*

$$L^{\ell}(B_Q) \leq 2\min\left[{}^1\!/\!_2, \sup \mathcal{I}^{\ell}_0(\delta, P, Q, n)\right]. \tag{123}$$

This bound holds for both $\ell = \ell_S$ and $\ell = \ell_H$.

The next lemma bounds the expected disagreement in terms of its empirical counterparts, and its proof is very similar to the proof of Theorem 19.

Lemma 2 ([65,165]). *For any probability distribution P over $\mathcal{F}$, chosen before seeing $\mathcal{D}_n$ and $\mathcal{D}_u$, with probability $(1-\delta)$ and for all Q, we have that*

$$d_Q \in [\inf \mathcal{I}_1(\delta, P, Q, m), \sup \mathcal{I}_1(\delta, P, Q, m)], \tag{124}$$

where

$$\mathcal{I}_1(\delta, P, Q, m) = \left\{ r : r \in \left[0, \frac{1}{2}\right], \mathtt{kl}\left[\hat{d}_Q \| r\right] \leq \frac{2\mathrm{KL}[Q\|P] + \ln\left(\frac{\xi_m}{\delta}\right)}{m} \right\}. \tag{125}$$

On the basis of Theorems 19 and 20 and Lemma 2, it is possible to prove the fourth milestone result, which bounds the risk of the Bayes classifier.

Theorem 22 ([65]). *For any probability distribution P over $\mathcal{F}$, chosen before seeing $\mathcal{D}_n$ and $\mathcal{D}_u$, with probability $(1-2\delta)$ and for all Q, we have that*

$$L^{\ell}(B_Q) \leq 1 - \frac{\left(1 - 2\min\left[{}^1\!/\!_2, \sup \mathcal{I}^{\ell}_0(\delta, P, Q, n)\right]\right)^2}{1 - 2\inf \mathcal{I}_1(\delta, P, Q, m)}. \tag{126}$$

This bound holds for both $\ell = \ell_S$ and $\ell = \ell_H$.

Finally, the fifth milestone result, which is also the most recent one in PAC analysis, is as follows.

Theorem 23 ([65]). *For any probability distribution P over $\mathcal{F}$, chosen before seeing $\mathcal{D}_n$ and $\mathcal{D}_u$, with probability $(1-\delta)$ and for all Q, we have that*

$$L^{\ell}(B_Q) \leq \sup_{(e,d) \in \mathcal{I}^{\ell}_2(\delta, P, Q, n)} 1 - \frac{(1-\min[1,(2e+d)])^2}{1-2d}, \tag{127}$$

where

$$\mathcal{I}_2^{\ell}(\delta, P, Q, n) = \left\{ (e,d) : \begin{array}{c} e, d \in [0,1], d \leq 2\left(\sqrt{e} - e\right), \\ \mathtt{kl}\left[\hat{d}_Q, \hat{e}_Q^{\ell_S} || d, e\right] \leq \frac{2\mathrm{KL}[Q||P] + \ln\left(\frac{\xi_n + n}{\delta}\right)}{n} \end{array} \right\}. \tag{128}$$

This bound holds for both $\ell = \ell_S$ and $\ell = \ell_H$.

Note that all the bounds involve the Kullback-Leibler divergence between P and Q and the main problem of the PAC-Bayes theory is represented by their choice. On one hand, Q should fit our observations, but on the other hand, Q should be close to P to the minimize the Kullback-Leibler divergence. The milestone result of [87], later extended in [33], proposes the use of a Boltzmann prior distribution P which depends on the data-generating distribution μ. In particular, let us suppose that the density function associated with P is

$$p(f) = c_p e^{-\gamma L^{\ell}(f)}, \tag{129}$$

where $\gamma \in [0, \infty)$ and c_p is a normalization term. Basically, this distribution gives more importance to functions that have small risk.

Now let us choose as posterior Q a distribution with the following density function:

$$q(f) = c_q e^{-\gamma \hat{L}^{\ell}(f)}, \tag{130}$$

where c_q is a normalization term. In this case, we give more importance to functions with small empirical risk, and the following theorem can be proved.

Theorem 24 ([33]). *Given P defined in Eq. (129) and Q defined in Eq. (130), with probability* $(1-\delta)$, *we have that*

$$\mathrm{KL}[Q||P] \leq \mathrm{KL}_1(\gamma, \delta, n) = \frac{\gamma^2}{n} + \gamma \sqrt{\frac{2\ln\left(\frac{\xi_n}{\delta}\right)}{n}}. \tag{131}$$

Consequently, with probability $(1-2\delta)$, *we have that*

$$\mathtt{kl}\left[\hat{L}^{\ell}(G_Q) || L^{\ell}(G_Q)\right] \leq \frac{\mathrm{KL}_1(\gamma, \delta, n) + \ln\left(\frac{\xi_n}{\delta}\right)}{n}. \tag{132}$$

The loss ℓ that we use for P and Q can be different from the one that we use for $\hat{L}^{\ell}(G_Q)$ and $L^{\ell}(G_Q)$.

Note that in PAC-Bayes theory we have to compute many times a Q-weighted average of different quantities: for example, when we have to compute the Bayes classifier, or when we have to compute the empirical error of the Gibbs classifier, or when we have to compute the empirical expected disagreement and the expected joint error, or when we want to adopt the approach of Catoni [87], we have to estimate Q on the basis of Eq. (130). Moreover, usually when one uses the PAC-Bayes theory, the class of functions $\mathcal{F}$ takes into account not an infinite number of functions but a large, but finite, number of functions. The PAC-Bayes theory is usually suited for the analysis of a weighted combination of simpler classifiers [65]: bagging [70,160], boosting [161,162], and Bayesian approaches [166] or even kernel methods [1] and neural networks [2]. Consequently we can adopt the same strategy depicted in Section 4.4 to take advantage of the QC speedup for the computation of this Q-weighted average.

5.4.1 Algorithmic stability

Algorithmic stability is an in-sample method which circumvents the problem of knowing the class of functions, which is needed to apply the VC, RC, and PAC-Bayes theories, by defining the properties that an algorithm should fulfill to achieve good generalization performance [30,67,68,76,83,167]. Hence in this section we do not search for the right class of functions $\mathcal{F}$ in a set of possible ones $\mathcal{S}_r^{\mathcal{F}}$, but we search for the right combination of hyperparameters $\mathcal{H}$ in a set of r possible configurations of these hyperparameters $\mathcal{S}_r^{\mathcal{H}}$ of an LA $\mathscr{A}$. $\mathcal{H}$ implicitly defines the unknown $\mathcal{F}$, and in this section we will deal just with deterministic LAs [30,67]. Finally, all the following results hold for any bounded loss function $\ell : \mathcal{F} \times \mathcal{Z} \to [0, 1]$.

The algorithmic stability theory states mainly two results, which are reported in Theorems 25 and 27.

Theorem 25 ([67]). *Given an algorithm $\mathscr{A}$ where its hyperparameters $\mathcal{H}$ are chosen such that $\mathcal{H} \in \mathcal{S}_r^{\mathcal{H}}$, the following bounds hold with probability* $(1 - \delta)$*:*

$$L^{\ell}(\mathscr{A}_{(\mathcal{D}_n,\mathcal{H})}) \leq \hat{L}^{\ell}_{emp}(\mathscr{A}_{(\mathcal{D}_n,\mathcal{H})}) + \sqrt{\frac{r}{2n\delta} + \frac{3r\beta_{emp}}{\delta}}, \quad \forall \mathcal{H} \in \mathcal{S}_r^{\mathcal{H}}, \tag{133}$$

$$L^{\ell}(\mathscr{A}_{(\mathcal{D}_n,\mathcal{H})}) \leq \hat{L}^{\ell}_{loo}(\mathscr{A}_{\mathcal{H}}) + \sqrt{\frac{r}{2n\delta} + \frac{3r\beta_{loo}}{\delta}}, \quad \forall \mathcal{H} \in \mathcal{S}_r^{\mathcal{H}}, \tag{134}$$

where

$$\beta_{emp}(\mathscr{A}_{\mathcal{H}}, n) = \mathbb{E}_{\mathcal{D}_n, Z_i'} \left| \ell(\mathscr{A}_{(\mathcal{D}_n,\mathcal{H})}, Z_i) - \ell(\mathscr{A}_{(\mathcal{D}_n^i,\mathcal{H})}, Z_i) \right|, \tag{135}$$

$$\beta_{loo}(\mathscr{A}_{\mathcal{H}}, n) = \mathbb{E}_{\mathcal{D}_n, Z} |\ell(\mathscr{A}_{(\mathcal{D}_n,\mathcal{H})}, Z) - \ell(\mathscr{A}_{(\mathcal{D}_n^{\setminus i},\mathcal{H})}, Z)|. \tag{136}$$

Basically, the algorithmic stability theory states that if an algorithm selects similar functions even if the training set is slightly changed, then the algorithm will have good generalization performance [68].

It has been proven recently [30] that $\beta_{loo}(\mathscr{A}_{\mathcal{H}}, n)$, which is usually called "hypothesis stability," can be estimated directly from the data if $\beta_{loo}(\mathscr{A}_{\mathcal{H}}, n)$ decreases with n. We wish to highlight that this property is a desirable requirement for any LA, since we need this to be able to prove the learnability in the algorithmic stability framework,

$$\lim_{n\to\infty} \beta_{emp}(\mathscr{A}_{\mathcal{H}}, n) = 0 \quad \text{or} \quad \lim_{n\to\infty} \beta_{loo}(\mathscr{A}_{\mathcal{H}}, n) = 0, \tag{137}$$

or that, in other words, the impact on the learning procedure of removing or replacing one sample from $\mathcal{D}_n$ should decrease, on average, as n grows. Numerous researchers have already studied this property. In particular, it is related to the consistency concept [168]. However, connections can also be identified with the trend of the learning curves of an algorithm [169]. Such a quantity is also strictly linked to the concept of a smart rule [168]. It is worth underlining that in many of the above-cited studies the required property is proved to be satisfied by many well-known algorithms, such as least squares, regularized least squares, and kernelled regularized least squares [169–172].

Thanks to the property of Eq. (137) it is possible to prove the following theorem.

Theorem 26 ([30]). *The following inequality holds with probability* $(1-\delta)$*:*

$$\beta_{loo}(\mathscr{A}_{\mathcal{H}}, n) \leq \frac{8}{n\sqrt{n}} \sum_{i,j,k=1}^{\sqrt{n}/2} |\ell(\mathscr{A}_{(\check{\mathcal{D}}^k_{\sqrt{n}/2},\mathcal{H})}, \check{Z}^k_j) - \ell(\mathscr{A}_{(\check{\mathcal{D}}^{k\backslash i}_{\sqrt{n}/2},\mathcal{H})}, \check{Z}^k_j)| + \sqrt{\frac{\ln\left(\frac{1}{\delta}\right)}{\sqrt{n}}}, \tag{138}$$

where

$$\check{\mathcal{D}}^k_{\sqrt{n}/2} : \{Z_{(k-1)\sqrt{n}+1}, \ldots, Z_{(k-1)\sqrt{n}+\sqrt{n}/2}\}, \quad k \in \{1, \ldots, \sqrt{n}/2\}, \tag{139}$$

$$;\check{Z}^k_j : Z_{(k-1)\sqrt{n}+\sqrt{n}/2+j}, \quad k \in \{1, \ldots, \sqrt{n}/2\}. \tag{140}$$

By plugging the result of Theorem 26 into Theorem 25, we obtain the fully empirical algorithmic stability bound of [30], where every quantity involved in the bound can be estimated from the available data.

The bounds of Eqs. (133) and (134) are polynomial bounds in n (so not very tight when n is small), while β_{emp} and β_{loo} are two versions of 'hypothesis stability which are able to take into account both the properties of the algorithm and the property of the distribution that has generated the data $\mathcal{D}_n$ [30,67]. It is possible to improve the bounds of Eqs. (133) and (134) by use of a stronger notion of algorithmic stability, known as the "uniform stability."

Theorem 27 ([67]). *Given an algorithm* $\mathscr{A}$ *where its hyperparameters* $\mathcal{H}$ *are chosen such that* $\mathcal{H} \in \mathcal{S}^{\mathcal{H}}_r$*, the following bounds hold with probability* $(1-\delta)$*:*

$$L^{\ell}(\mathscr{A}_{(\mathcal{D}_n,\mathcal{H})}) \leq \hat{L}^{\ell}_{emp}(\mathscr{A}_{(\mathcal{D}_n,\mathcal{H})}) + \beta^i + (4n\beta^i + 1)\sqrt{\frac{\ln(\frac{r}{\delta})}{2n}}, \quad \forall \mathcal{H} \in \mathcal{S}^{\mathcal{H}}_r, \tag{141}$$

$$L^{\ell}(\mathscr{A}_{(\mathcal{D}_n,\mathcal{H})}) \leq \hat{L}^{\ell}_{loo}(\mathscr{A}_{\mathcal{H}}) + \beta^{\backslash i} + (4n\beta^{\backslash i} + 1)\sqrt{\frac{\ln(\frac{r}{\delta})}{2n}}, \quad \forall \mathcal{H} \in \mathcal{S}^{\mathcal{H}}_r, \tag{142}$$

where

$$\beta^i = \left|\ell(\mathscr{A}_{(\mathcal{D}_n,\mathcal{H})}, \cdot) - \ell(\mathscr{A}_{(\mathcal{D}^i_n,\mathcal{H})}, \cdot)\right|_{\infty}, \beta^{\backslash i} = |\ell(\mathscr{A}_{(\mathcal{D}_n,\mathcal{H})}, \cdot) - \ell(\mathscr{A}_{(\mathcal{D}^{\backslash i}_n,\mathcal{H})}, \cdot)|_{\infty}. \tag{143}$$

Unfortunately, the uniform stability (β^i or $\beta^{\backslash i}$) is not able to take into account the properties of the distribution that has generated the data $\mathcal{D}_n$ and sometimes is not even able to capture the properties of the algorithm because it deals with a worst-case learning scenario [30].

All four algorithmic stability-based bounds of Theorems 25 and 27 inspire an MS and EE procedure. In particular, all the bounds are in the form $L^{\ell}(\mathscr{A}_{(\mathcal{D}_n,\mathcal{H})}) \leq \breve{L}^{\ell}(\mathscr{A}_{\mathcal{H}}, \mathcal{D}_n, n, \delta, r)$. To perform the MS and EE procedure, we have

$$\mathscr{A}_{(\mathcal{D}_n,\mathcal{H}^*)}, \mathcal{H}^* : \quad \arg \min_{\mathcal{H} \in \mathcal{S}_r^{\mathcal{H}}} \breve{L}^{\ell}(\mathscr{A}_{\mathcal{H}}, \mathcal{D}_n, n, \delta, r). \tag{144}$$

The procedure of Eq. (144) can be used with any LA for which it is possible to compute one notion of algorithmic stability. In the literature this approach is called "algorithmic risk minimization" [30,76].

Note that usually the uniform stability is not used in real-world applications because it is not data dependent and the bound is too loose in practice. Instead, the fully empirical algorithmic stability-based bound of [30], which is the result of the combination of Theorem 26 and Theorem 25, is very effective in practice for solving real-world problems [29,30,76]. Nevertheless, to use this MS and EE procedure we need to compute the leave-one-out error and the empirical hypothesis stability (see Theorem 26). For the leave-one-out error we can use the QC speedup (as described in Section 5.1) since the leave-one-out error is a particular case of the complete k-fold cross validation with k equal to the number of samples, $k = n$. For the empirical hypothesis stability, it is again an average over a finite number of possibilities. Then when n is large, computing that quantity can be quite a computationally expensive task [29,30] that can take advantage of the QC speedup.

5.4.2 Compression bound

The compression bound is the result of the approximation of the Kolmogorov theory [110] and, in particular, the minimum description length principle [111]. The compression bound theory [66,84] states that, for a fixed quality of the learned model, the fewer data from $\mathcal{D}_n$ we need for learning the rule, the better will be its generalization performance [64,173]. In particular, given a set of rules $\mathcal{S}^{\mathfrak{R}}$, it is possible to state the following theorem.

Theorem 28 ([64,66]). *Let us consider a set of rules $\mathcal{S}^{\mathfrak{R}}$. If the criteria for selecting the rule $\mathfrak{R} \in \mathcal{S}^{\mathfrak{R}}$ based on $\mathcal{D}_n$ returns the same rule $\mathfrak{R}$ based on a subset $\mathcal{D}'_{n'}$ of the whole data $\mathcal{D}_n$, or in other words, $\mathcal{D}'_{n'} \subseteq \mathcal{D}_n$, the following bound holds with probability $(1-\delta)$:*

$$L(\mathfrak{R}) \leq \frac{1}{n''} \sum_{Z \in \mathcal{D}''_{n''}} \ell(\mathfrak{R}, Z) + \sqrt{\frac{\ln\left(\frac{1}{\delta}\right)}{2n''}} + \sqrt{\frac{\ln\left(n\binom{n}{n'}\right)}{2n''}}, \quad \forall \mathfrak{R} \in \mathcal{S}^{\mathfrak{R}}, \tag{145}$$

where $\mathcal{D}''_{n''} = \mathcal{D}_n \setminus \mathcal{D}'_{n'}$, $n'' = n - n'$ and any $[0,1]$-bounded loss function can be used.

Moreover, if we choose the set of rules $\mathcal{S}^{\mathfrak{R}} \in \mathcal{S}_r^{\mathcal{S}^{\mathfrak{R}}}$, it is possible to derive the following result.

Theorem 29 ([64,66]). *Under the same assumptions as for Theorem 28, if we choose the set of rules $\mathcal{S}^{\mathfrak{R}} \in \mathcal{S}_r^{\mathcal{S}^{\mathfrak{R}}}$ on the basis of $\mathcal{D}_n$, the following bound holds with probability* $(1-\delta)$*:*

$$L(\mathfrak{R}) \le \frac{1}{n''} \sum_{Z \in \mathcal{D}''_{n''}} \ell(\mathfrak{R}, Z) + \sqrt{\frac{\ln\left(\frac{1}{\delta}\right)}{2n''}} + \sqrt{\frac{\ln\left(n\binom{n}{n'}\right)}{2n''}} + \sqrt{\frac{\ln r}{2n''}}, \quad \forall \mathfrak{R} \in \mathcal{S}^{\mathfrak{R}} \in \mathcal{S}_r^{\mathcal{S}^{\mathfrak{R}}}. \tag{146}$$

The problem with Theorem 28 (and consequently also with Theorem 29) is that it applies the union bound with respect to all the possible rules that can be created with n'' of n samples. For this reason in [84,173] it is proposed to take into account just the rules with small empirical error (this is analogous to the improvement of LRC over RC).

Theorem 30 ([84,173]). *Under the same assumption as in Theorem 29, we can state that the following inequality holds with probability* $(1-\delta)$*:*

$$L(\mathfrak{R}) \le \frac{1}{n''} \sum_{Z \in \mathcal{D}''_{n''}} \ell(\mathfrak{R}, Z) + \sqrt{\frac{\ln\left(\frac{4}{\delta}\right)}{2n''}} + \sqrt{\frac{\ln(ns)}{2n''}} + \sqrt{\frac{\ln r}{2n''}}, \quad \forall \mathfrak{R} \in \mathcal{S}^{\mathfrak{R}} \in \mathcal{S}_r^{\mathcal{S}^{\mathfrak{R}}}, \tag{147}$$

where s is the cardinality of the subset of all the $\binom{n}{n'}$ rules chosen from $\mathcal{S}^{\mathfrak{R}}$ based on all the possible $\mathcal{D}'_{n'}$ datasets of cardinality n' sampled from $\mathcal{D}'_{n'}$ such that

$$\left| \frac{1}{n''} \sum_{Z \in \mathcal{D}''_{n''}} \ell(\mathfrak{R}, Z) - \frac{1}{n} \sum_{Z \in \mathcal{D}_n} \ell(\mathfrak{R}', Z) \right| \le \frac{1}{n} + \sqrt{\frac{\ln\left(\frac{16n^2}{\delta}\right)}{2n-1}}. \tag{148}$$

The compression bounds of Theorems 29 and 30 can be used to select the best set of rules $\mathcal{S}^{\mathfrak{R}} \in \mathcal{S}_r^{\mathcal{S}^{\mathfrak{R}}}$. In particular, all the bounds are in the form $L(\mathfrak{R}) \le \breve{L}(\mathfrak{R}, \mathcal{S}^{\mathfrak{R}}, \mathcal{D}_n, n, n', \delta, r)$, even when the set of rules is not known explicitly, since we just have to apply the LAs many times to a series of subsets of the training set. To perform the MS and EE procedure we have

$$\mathfrak{R}_{\text{MS}}, \mathcal{S}^{\mathfrak{R}}_{\text{MS}} : \quad \arg \min_{\mathcal{S}^{\mathfrak{R}} \in \mathcal{S}_r^{\mathcal{S}^{\mathfrak{R}}}} \breve{L}(\mathfrak{R}, \mathcal{S}^{\mathfrak{R}}, \mathcal{D}_n, n, n', \delta, r). \tag{149}$$

The procedure of Eq. (149) can be used with any LA.

In the compression bound-based MS and EE approach, as for the out-of-sample MS and EE methods, we need to train the algorithm on a large series of training sets, in particular $\binom{n}{n'}$, and check what percentage of functions trained with $\mathcal{D}'_{n'}$ has small empirical error on $\mathcal{D}''_{n''}$ to obtain an estimate of s in Theorem 30. This procedure can take advantage of the QC speedup since we have a logical function which assumes 0's or 1's based on Eq. (148) on a finite number of possibilities $\binom{n}{n'}$. This is exactly a problem that is suited for being tackled with a QC approach, as can be seen in Section 3. Therefore also the compression bound in-sample-based method can take advantage of the QC speedup as for the other MS and EE methods presented in this chapter.

6 CONCLUSIONS

QC is acquiring growing importance mostly because of the recent technological breakthrough in the implementation of quantum computers. On the other hand, ML techniques, which are needed to build the predictive models for a large number of applications ranging from medical to industrial ones, are asked to solve more and more complex problems given the rapid growth of the number of samples, of the dimensionality of the input and output space, and of the variety and structure of the data that are transferred, stored, and processed on a daily basis. In this chapter we have shown how QC techniques can open up new scenarios for the solution of SL problems. QC can open the way to new, more powerful, more refined, and more advanced ways of extracting knowledge from the data. In particular, we have shown that QC can be extremely useful in all three main aspects of an automatic learning process: from the training phase, which mostly results in an optimization problem, to the MS and EE phases, which aim to select the model with the best generalization performance by upper bounding its risk. This is a starting point, and more work is necessary in this direction for us to be ready to fully exploit the future generation of quantum computers as soon as they become available.

REFERENCES

[1] V.N. Vapnik, Statistical Learning Theory, Wiley-Interscience, New York, 1998.
[2] C.M. Bishop, Pattern Recognition and Machine Learning, Springer, Berlin, 2006.
[3] C. Alippi, M. Polycarpou, Handbook on Computational Intelligence, Part D: Neural Networks, Springer, Berlin, 2015.
[4] J. Shawe-Taylor, N. Cristianini, Kernel Methods for Pattern Analysis, Cambridge University Press, Cambridge, 2004.
[5] T.G. Dietterich, Ensemble methods in machine learning, in: Multiple Classifier Systems, Springer, Berlin, 2000.
[6] V. Cherkassky, F.M. Mulier, Learning From Data: Concepts, Theory, and Methods, John Wiley & Sons, New York, 2007.
[7] Y. Zhai, Y.S. Ong, I.W. Tsang, The Emerging "Big Dimensionality", IEEE Comput. Intell. Mag. 9 (3) (2014) 14–26.
[8] E. Cambria, H. Wang, B. White, Guest Editorial: big social data analysis, Knowl.-Based Syst. 69 (2014) 1–2.
[9] X. Wu, X. Zhu, G.Q. Wu, W. Ding, Data mining with big data, IEEE Trans. Knowl. Data Eng. 26 (1) (2014) 97–107.
[10] G.B. Huang, E. Cambria, K.A. Toh, B. Widrow, Z. Xu, New trends of learning in computational intelligence [Guest Editorial], IEEE Comput. Intell. Mag. 10 (2) (2015) 16–17.

[11] P.L. Bartlett, S. Boucheron, G. Lugosi, Model selection and error estimation, Mach. Learn. 48 (1–3) (2002) 85–113.
[12] A. Kleiner, A. Talwalkar, P. Sarkar, M.I. Jordan, A scalable bootstrap for massive data, J. R. Stat. Soc. Ser. B Stat. Methodol. 76 (4) (2014) 795–816.
[13] I. Guyon, A. Saffari, G. Dror, G. Cawley, Model selection: beyond the Bayesian/frequentist divide, J. Mach. Learn. Res. 11 (2010) 61–87.
[14] D. Anguita, A. Ghio, L. Oneto, S. Ridella, In-sample and out-of-sample model selection and error estimation for support vector machines, IEEE Trans. Neural Netw. Learn. Syst. 23 (9) (2012) 1390–1406.
[15] R. Kohavi, A study of cross-validation and bootstrap for accuracy estimation and model selection, in: International Joint Conference on Artificial Intelligence, 1995.
[16] B. Efron, R.J. Tibshirani, An Introduction to the Bootstrap, CRC Press, Boca Raton, FL, 1994.
[17] C. Alippi, A probably approximately correct framework to estimate performance degradation in embedded systems, IEEE Trans. Comput. Aided Des. Integr. Circuits Syst. 21 (7) (2002) 749–762.
[18] L. Oneto, I. Orlandi, D. Anguita, Performance assessment and uncertainty quantification of predictive models for smart manufacturing systems, in: IEEE International Conference on Big Data (IEEE BIG DATA), 2015.
[19] E.G. Rieffel, W.H. Polak, Quantum Computing: A Gentle Introduction, MIT Press, Cambridge, MA, 2011.
[20] L.K. Grover, A framework for fast quantum mechanical algorithms, in: Proceedings of the Thirtieth Annual ACM Symposium on Theory of Computing, 1998.
[21] M. Schuld, I. Sinayskiy, F. Petruccione, Quantum computing for pattern classification, in: PRICAI: Trends in Artificial Intelligence, Springer, Berlin, 2014.
[22] D. Anguita, S. Ridella, F. Rivieccio, R. Zunino, Quantum optimization for training support vector machines, Neural Netw. 16 (5) (2003) 763–770.
[23] E.D. Vito, L. Rosasco, A. Caponnetto, U.D. Giovannini, F. Odone, Learning from examples as an inverse problem, J. Mach. Learn. Res. 6 (2005) 883–904.
[24] L. Oneto, A. Ghio, D. Anguita, S. Ridella, Learning resource-aware models for mobile devices: from regularization to energy efficiency, Neurocomputing 169 (2015) 225–235.
[25] L. Rosasco, E. De Vito, A. Caponnetto, M. Piana, A. Verri, Are loss functions all the same? Neural Comput. 16 (5) (2004) 1063–1076.
[26] O. Bousquet, L. Bottou, The tradeoffs of large scale learning, in: Advances in Neural Information Processing Systems, 2008.
[27] D.H. Wolpert, The lack of a priori distinctions between learning algorithms, Neural Comput. 8 (7) (1996) 1341–1390.
[28] D.H. Wolpert, W.G. Macready, No free lunch theorems for optimization, IEEE Trans. Evol. Comput. 1 (1) (1997) 67–82.
[29] L. Oneto, B. Pilarz, A. Ghio, D. Anguita, Model selection for big data: algorithmic stability and bag of little bootstraps on GPUs, in: European Symposium on Artificial Neural Networks, Computational Intelligence and Machine Learning, 2015.
[30] L. Oneto, A. Ghio, D. Anguita, S. Ridella, Fully empirical and data-dependent stability-based bounds, IEEE Trans. Cybern. 45 (9) (2015) 1913–1926.
[31] S. Boucheron, G. Lugosi, P. Massart, Concentration Inequalities: A Nonasymptotic Theory of Independence, Oxford University Press, Oxford, 2013.

[32] P.L. Bartlett, O. Bousquet, S. Mendelson, Local Rademacher complexities, Ann. Stat. (2005) 1497–1537.
[33] G. Lever, F. Laviolette, J. Shawe-Taylor, Tighter PAC-Bayes bounds through distribution-dependent priors, Theor. Comput. Sci. 473 (2013) 4–28.
[34] L. Oneto, A. Ghio, D. Anguita, S. Ridella, Local Rademacher complexity: sharper risk bounds with and without unlabeled samples, Neural Netw. 65 (2015) 115–125.
[35] M.A. Nielsen, I.L. Chuang, Quantum Computation and Quantum Information, Cambridge University Press, Cambridge, 2010.
[36] A.O. Pittenger, An Introduction to Quantum Computing Algorithms, vol. 19, Springer Science & Business Media, Berlin, 2012.
[37] S. Aaronson, Quantum Computing Since Democritus, Cambridge University Press, Cambridge, 2013.
[38] M.B. Plenio, P.L. Knight, Realistic lower bounds for the factorization time of large numbers on a quantum computer, Phys. Rev. A 53 (5) (1996) 2986.
[39] L.K. Grover, A fast quantum mechanical algorithm for database search, in: Proceedings of the Twenty-Eighth Annual ACM Symposium on Theory of Computing, 1996.
[40] L.K. Grover, Quantum mechanics helps in searching for a needle in a haystack, Phys. Rev. Lett. 79 (2) (1997) 325.
[41] L.K. Grover, From Schrodinger's equation to the quantum search algorithm, Am. J. Phys. 69 (7) (2001) 769–777.
[42] C. Durr, P. Hoyer, A quantum algorithm for finding the minimum, 1996, arXiv preprint quant-ph/9607014.
[43] T. Hogg, D. Portnov, Quantum optimization, Inform. Sci. 128 (3) (2000) 181–197.
[44] G. Brassard, F. Dupuis, S. Gambs, A. Tapp, An optimal quantum algorithm to approximate the mean and its application for approximating the median of a set of points over an arbitrary distance, 2011, arXiv preprint arXiv:1106.4267.
[45] R.R. Tucci, Quantum circuit for calculating mean values via Grover-like algorithm, 2014, arXiv preprint arXiv:1404.0668.
[46] D. Deutsch, Quantum theory, the Church-Turing principle and the universal quantum computer, Proc. R. Soc. Lond. A: Math. Phys. Eng. Sci. 400 (1818) (1985) 97–117.
[47] T.D. Ladd, F. Jelezko, R. Laflamme, Y. Nakamura, C. Monroe, L.L. O'Brien, Quantum computers, Nature 464 (7285) (2010) 45–53.
[48] A.D. Córcoles, E. Magesan, S.J. Srinivasan, A.W. Cross, M. Steffen, J.M. Gambetta, J.M. Chow, Demonstration of a quantum error detection code using a square lattice of four superconducting qubits, Nat. Commun. 6 (2015).
[49] R. Barends, J. Kelly, A. Megrant, D. Sank, E. Jeffrey, Y. Chen, Y. Yin, B. Chiaro, J. Mutus, C. Neill, Coherent Josephson qubit suitable for scalable quantum integrated circuits, Phys. Rev. Lett. 111 (8) (2013).
[50] D. Anguita, S. Ridella, F. Rivieccio, R. Zunino, Training support vector machines: a quantum-computing perspective, in: International Joint Conference on Neural Networks, 2003.
[51] P. Gastaldo, S. Ridella, R. Zunino, Prospects of quantum-classical optimization for digital design, Appl. Math. Comput. 179 (2) (2006) 581–595.
[52] P. Rebentrost, M. Mohseni, S. Lloyd, Quantum support vector machine for big data classification, Phys. Rev. Lett. 113 (13) (2014) 130503.
[53] S. Lloyd, M. Mohseni, P. Rebentrost, Quantum algorithms for supervised and unsupervised machine learning, 2013, arXiv preprint arXiv:1307.0411.

[54] G. Castagnoli, D.R. Finkelstein, Theory of the quantum speed-up, Proc. R. Soc. Lond. A: Math. Phys. Eng. Sci. 457 (2012) (2001) 1799–1806.
[55] G. Castagnoli, The 50% advanced information rule of the quantum algorithms, Int. J. Theor. Phys. 48 (8) (2009) 2412–2426.
[56] G. Castagnoli, Highlighting the mechanism of the quantum speedup by time-symmetric and relational quantum mechanics, 2013, arXiv preprint arXiv:1308.5077.
[57] S. Arlot, A. Celisse, A survey of cross-validation procedures for model selection, Stat. Surv. 4 (2010) 40–79.
[58] D. Anguita, A. Ghio, S. Ridella, D. Sterpi, K-fold cross validation for error rate estimate in support vector machines, in: International Conference on Data Mining, 2009.
[59] D. Anguita, A. Ghio, L. Oneto, S. Ridella, In-sample model selection for support vector machines, in: IEEE International Joint Conference on Neural Networks (IJCNN), 2011.
[60] B. Efron, Bootstrap methods: another look at the jackknife, Ann. Stat. 7 (1) (1979) 1–26.
[61] L. Oneto, A. Ghio, D. Anguita, S. Ridella, Global Rademacher complexity bounds: from slow to fast convergence rates, Neural Process. Lett. 43 (2) (2016) 567–602.
[62] D. Anguita, A. Ghio, L. Oneto, S. Ridella, Unlabeled patterns to tighten Rademacher complexity error bounds for kernel classifiers, Pattern Recognit. Lett. 37 (2014) 210–219.
[63] D.A. McAllester, Some PAC-Bayesian theorems, in: Computational Learning Theory, 1998.
[64] J. Langford, Tutorial on practical prediction theory for classification, J. Mach. Learn. Res. 6 (2005) 273–306.
[65] P. Germain, A. Lacasse, F. Laviolette, M. Marchand, J.-F. Roy, Risk bounds for the majority vote: from a PAC-Bayesian analysis to a learning algorithm, J. Mach. Learn. Res. 16 (4) (2015) 787–860.
[66] S. Floyd, M. Warmuth, Sample compression, learnability, and the Vapnik-Chervonenkis dimension, Mach. Learn. 21 (3) (1995) 269–304.
[67] O. Bousquet, A. Elisseeff, Stability and generalization, J. Mach. Learn. Res. 2 (2002) 499–526.
[68] T. Poggio, R. Rifkin, S. Mukherjee, P. Niyogi, General conditions for predictivity in learning theory, Nature 428 (6981) (2004) 419–422.
[69] P. Klesk, M. Korzen, Sets of approximating functions with finite Vapnik-Chervonenkis dimension for nearest-neighbors algorithms, Pattern Recognit. Lett. 32 (14) (2011) 1882–1893.
[70] L. Breiman, Random forests, Mach. Learn. 45 (1) (2001) 5–32.
[71] S. Boyd, L. Vandenberghe, Convex Optimization, Cambridge University Press, Cambridge, 2004.
[72] A.L. Yuille, A. Rangarajan, The concave-convex procedure, Neural Comput. 15 (4) (2003) 915–936.
[73] E.L. Lawler, D.E. Wood, Branch-and-bound methods: a survey, Oper. Res. 14 (4) (1966) 699–719.
[74] M. Muselli, On convergence properties of pocket algorithm, IEEE Trans. Neural Netw. 8 (3) (1997) 623–629.
[75] D. Anguita, A. Ghio, S. Pischiutta, S. Ridella, A support vector machine with integer parameters, Neurocomputing 72 (1) (2008) 480–489.
[76] L. Oneto, S. Ridella, D. Anguita, Learning hardware-friendly classifiers through algorithmic stability, ACM Trans. Embed. Comput. 15 (2) (2016) 23:1–23:29.

[77] B.L. Milenova, J.S. Yarmus, M.M. Campos, SVM in oracle database 10g: removing the barriers to widespread adoption of support vector machines, in: International Conference on Very Large Data Bases, 2005.

[78] T. Joachims, Text Categorization With Support Vector Machines: Learning With Many Relevant Features, Springer, Berlin, 1998.

[79] J.X. Liu, H.P. Cai, Y.J. Tan, Heuristic Algorithm for Tuning Hyperparameters in Support Vector Regression, J. Syst. Simul. 7 (2007) 1–32.

[80] S. Walczak, N. Cerpa, Heuristic principles for the design of artificial neural networks, Inf. Softw. Technol. 41 (2) (1999) 107–117.

[81] A. Inoue, L. Kilian, In-sample or out-of-sample tests of predictability: which one should we use? Econ. Rev. 23 (4) (2005) 371–402.

[82] S. Shalev-Shwartz, S. Ben-David, Understanding Machine Learning: From Theory to Algorithms, Cambridge University Press, Cambridge, 2014.

[83] A. Elisseeff, T. Evgeniou, M. Pontil, L.P. Kaelbing, Stability of randomized learning algorithms, J. Mach. Learn. Res. 6 (1) (2005).

[84] J. Langford, D. McAllester, Computable shell decomposition bounds, J. Mach. Learn. Res. 5 (2004) 529–547.

[85] P.L. Bartlett, S. Mendelson, Rademacher and Gaussian complexities: risk bounds and structural results, J. Mach. Learn. Res. 3 (2003) 463–482.

[86] P. Germain, A. Lacasse, F. Laviolette, M. Marchand, PAC-Bayesian learning of linear classifiers, in: International Conference on Machine Learning, 2009.

[87] O. Catoni, PAC-Bayesian Supervised Classification. Lecture Notes–Monograph Series, vol. 56, Institute of Mathematical Statistics, Beachwood, Ohio, USA, 2007.

[88] D. Aharonov, Quantum computation, Annu. Rev. Comput. Phys. 6 (1998) 259–346.

[89] W. Hoeffding, Probability inequalities for sums of bounded random variables, J. Am. Stat. Assoc. 58 (301) (1963) 13–30.

[90] R.J. Serfling, Probability inequalities for the sum in sampling without replacement, Ann. Stat. 2 (1) (1974) 39–48.

[91] C.J. Clopper, E.S. Pearson, The use of confidence or fiducial limits illustrated in the case of the binomial, Biometrika 26 (4) (1934) 404–413.

[92] G. Casella, R.L. Berger, Statistical Inference, vol. 2, Duxbury, Pacific Grove, CA, 2002.

[93] M.R. Jerrum, L.G. Valiant, V.V. Vazirani, Random generation of combinatorial structures from a uniform distribution, Theor. Comput. Sci. 43 (1986) 169–188.

[94] A.N. Tikhonov, V.I.A. Arsenin, F. John, Solutions of Ill-Posed Problems, Winston, Washington, DC, 1977.

[95] V.V. Ivanov, The theory of approximate methods and their application to the numerical solution of singular integral equations, Springer, Berlin, 1976.

[96] V.A. Morozov, Z. Nashed, A. Aries, Methods for Solving Incorrectly Posed Problems, Springer, New York, 1984.

[97] L. Oneto, S. Ridella, D. Anguita, Tikhonov, Ivanov and Morozov regularization for support vector machine learning, Mach. Learn. 103 (1) (2016) 103–136.

[98] R. Collobert, F. Sinz, J. Weston, L. Bottou, Trading convexity for scalability, in: International Conference on Machine Learning, 2006.

[99] D. Anguita, A. Ghio, L. Oneto, S. Ridella, Selecting the hypothesis space for improving the generalization ability of support vector machines, in: IEEE International Joint Conference on Neural Networks (IJCNN), 2011.

[100] K. Pelckmans, J. Suykens, B. De Moor, Morozov, Ivanov and Tikhonov regularization based LS-SVMs, in: Neural Information Processing Systems, 2004.

[101] L. Wang, H. Jia, J. Li, Training robust support vector machine with smooth ramp loss in the primal space, Neurocomputing 71 (13) (2008) 3020–3025.
[102] J.P. Brooks, Support vector machines with the ramp loss and the hard margin loss, Oper. Res. 59 (2) (2011) 467–479.
[103] B. Scholkopf, A.J. Smola, Learning With Kernels: Support Vector Machines, Regularization, Optimization, and Beyond, MIT Press, Cambridge, MA, 2001.
[104] B. Scholkopf, The kernel trick for distances, in: Advances in Neural Information Processing Systems, 2001.
[105] C. Cortes, V. Vapnik, Support-vector networks, Mach. Learn. 20 (3) (1995) 273–297.
[106] J. Shawe-Taylor, S. Sun, A review of optimization methodologies in support vector machines, Neurocomputing 74 (17) (2011) 3609–3618.
[107] M. Zaharia, M. Chowdhury, T. Das, A. Dave, J. Ma, M. McCauley, M.J. Franklin, S. Shenker, I. Stoica, Resilient distributed datasets: a fault-tolerant abstraction for in-memory cluster computing, in: USENIX Conference on Networked Systems Design and Implementation, 2012.
[108] S. Shalev-Shwartz, Y. Singer, N. Srebro, A. Cotter, Pegasos: primal estimated subgradient solver for SVM, Math. Program. 127 (1) (2011) 3–30.
[109] J.L. Reyes-Ortiz, L. Oneto, D. Anguita, Big data analytics in the cloud: spark on Hadoop vs MPI/OpenMP on Beowulf, in: INNS International Conference on Big Data (INNS BIG DATA), 2015.
[110] M. Li, P.M.B. Vitanyi, An Introduction to Kolmogorov Complexity and Its Applications, Springer, Berlin, 2009.
[111] P.D. Grunwald, I.J. Myung, M.A. Pitt, Advances in Minimum Description Length: Theory and Applications, MIT Press, Cambridge, MA, 2005.
[112] B. Parhami, Computer Arithmetic: Algorithms and Hardware Designs, Oxford University Press, Inc., Oxford, 2009.
[113] D. Anguita, A. Boni, S. Ridella, A digital architecture for support vector machines: theory, algorithm, and FPGA implementation, IEEE Trans. Neural Netw. 14 (5) (2003) 993–1009.
[114] A. Ghio, S. Pischiutta, A support vector machine based pedestrian recognition system on resource-limited hardware architectures, in: Research in Microelectronics and Electronics Conference PRIME, 2007.
[115] K. Irick, M. DeBole, V. Narayanan, A. Gayasen, A hardware efficient support vector machine architecture for FPGA, in: International Symposium on Field-Programmable Custom Computing Machines, 2008.
[116] B. Lesser, M. Mücke, W.N. Gansterer, Effects of reduced precision on floating-point SVM classification accuracy, Procedia Comput. Sci. 4 (2011) 508–517.
[117] M.G. Epitropakis, V.P. Plagianakos, M.N. Vrahatis, Hardware-friendly higher-order neural network training using distributed evolutionary algorithms, Appl. Soft Comput. 10 (2) (2010) 398–408.
[118] C. Orsenigo, C. Vercellis, Discrete support vector decision trees via tabu search, Comput. Stat. Data Anal. 47 (2) (2004) 311–322.
[119] O. Pina-Ramfrez, R. Valdes-Cristerna, O. Yanez-Suarez, An FPGA implementation of linear kernel support vector machines, in: IEEE International Conference on Reconfigurable Computing and FPGA's, 2006.
[120] J. Manikandan, B. Venkataramani, V. Avanthi, FPGA implementation of support vector machine based isolated digit recognition system, in: IEEE International Conference on VLSI Design, 2009.

[121] T. Luo, L.O. Hall, D.B. Goldgof, A. Remsen, Bit reduction support vector machine, in: IEEE International Conference on Data Mining, 2005.

[122] E.S. Larsen, D. McAllister, Fast matrix multiplies using graphics hardware, in: ACM/IEEE conference on Supercomputing, 2001.

[123] M. Höhfeld, S.E. Fahlman, Probabilistic rounding in neural network learning with limited precision, Neurocomputing 4 (6) (1992) 291–299.

[124] D. Anguita, A. Ghio, L. Oneto, S. Ridella, A support vector machine classifier from a bit-constrained, sparse and localized hypothesis space, in: International Joint Conference on Neural Networks, 2013.

[125] D. Anguita, B.A. Gomes, Mixing floating-and fixed-point formats for neural network learning on neuroprocessors, Microproc. Microprog. 41 (10) (1996) 757–769.

[126] J. Sum, C.S. Leung, K. Ho, Convergence analyses on on-line weight noise injection-based training algorithms for MLPs, IEEE Trans. Neural Netw. Learn. Syst. 23 (11) (2012) 1827–1840.

[127] I. Takanami, M. Sato, Y.P. Yang, A fault-value injection approach for multiple-weight-fault tolerance of MNNs, in: IEEE International Joint Conference on Neural Networks, 2000.

[128] Y. Grandvalet, S. Canu, S. Boucheron, Noise injection: theoretical prospects, Neural Comput. 9 (5) (1997) 1093–1108.

[129] K. Matsuoka, Noise injection into inputs in back-propagation learning, IEEE Trans. Syst. Man Cybern. 22 (3) (1992) 436–440.

[130] T. Poggio, S. Mukherjee, R. Rifkin, A. Rakhlin, A. Verri, b, in: Uncertainty in Geometric Computations, 2002.

[131] B. Scholkopf, R. Herbrich, A.J. Smola, A generalized representer theorem, in: Computational Learning Theory, 2001.

[132] F. Dinuzzo, B. Schölkopf, The representer theorem for Hilbert spaces: a necessary and sufficient condition, in: Advances in Neural Information Processing Systems, 2012.

[133] F. Dinuzzo, M. Neve, G. De Nicolao, U.P. Gianazza, On the representer theorem and equivalent degrees of freedom of SVR, J. Mach. Learn. Res. 8 (10) (2007).

[134] J. Mercer, Functions of positive and negative type, and their connection with the theory of integral equations, Philos. Trans. R. Soc. Lond. Ser. A Contain. Pap. Math. Phys. Character (1909) 415–446.

[135] I. Guyon, A. Elisseeff, An introduction to variable and feature selection, J. Mach. Learn. Res. 3 (2003) 1157–1182.

[136] J. Zhu, S. Rosset, T. Hastie, R. Tibshirani, 1-Norm support vector machines, Adv. Neural Inf. Process. Syst. 16 (1) (2004) 49–56.

[137] R. Tibshiranit, Regression shrinkage and selection via the LASSO, J. R. Stat. Soc. Ser. B: Methodol. 58 (1) (1996) 267–288.

[138] N. Meinshausen, P. Bühlmann, High-dimensional graphs and variable selection with the LASSO, Ann. Stat. 34 (3) (2006) 1436–1462.

[139] N. Meinshausen, P. Bühlmann, Stability selection, J. R. Stat. Soc. Ser. B: Stat. Methodol. 72 (4) (2010) 417–473.

[140] H. Zou, T. Hastie, R. Tibshirani, On the degrees of freedom of the LASSO, Ann. Stat. 35 (5) (2007) 2173–2192.

[141] H. Zou, T. Hastie, Regularization and variable selection via the elastic net, J. R. Stat. Soc. Ser. B: Stat. Methodol. 67 (2) (2005) 301–320.

[142] C. De Mol, E. De Vito, L. Rosasco, Elastic-net regularization in learning theory, J. Complex. 25 (2) (2009) 201–230.

[143] D. Anguita, A. Ghio, L. Oneto, J.L. Reyes-Ortiz, S. Ridella, A novel procedure for training L1-L2 support vector machine classifiers, in: International Conference on Artificial Neural Networks (ICANN), 2013.

[144] J. Shawe-Taylor, J. Langford, PAC-Bayes & margins, in: Advances in Neural Information Processing Systems, 2003.

[145] E. Parrado-Hernández, A. Ambroladze, J. Shawe-Taylor, S. Sun, PAC-Bayes bounds with data dependent priors, J. Mach. Learn. Res. 13 (1) (2012) 3507–3531.

[146] R.H.T. Graepel, A PAC-Bayesian margin bound for linear classifiers: why SVMs work, in: Advances in Neural Information Processing Systems, 2001.

[147] D. Anguita, L. Ghelardoni, A. Ghio, L. Oneto, S. Ridella, The 'K' in K-fold cross validation, in: European Symposium on Artificial Neural Networks, Computational Intelligence and Machine Learning (ESANN), 2012.

[148] A. Kleiner, A. Talwalkar, P. Sarkar, M.I. Jordan, A scalable bootstrap for massive data, J. R. Stat. Soc. Ser. B: Stat. Methodol. 76 (4) (2014) 795–816.

[149] A. Kleiner, A. Talwalkar, P. Sarkar, M.I. Jordan, The big data bootstrap, in: International Conference on Machine Learning, 2012.

[150] A. Kleiner, A. Talwalkar, P. Sarkar, M.I. Jordan, Bootstrapping big data, in: Advances in Neural Information Processing Systems, Workshop: Big Learning: Algorithms, Systems, and Tools for Learning at Scale, 2011.

[151] V.N. Vapnik, S. Kotz, Estimation of Dependences Based on Empirical Data, vol. 41, Springer-Verlag, New York, 1982.

[152] J. Shawe-Taylor, P.L. Bartlett, R.C. Williamson, M. Anthony, Structural risk minimization over data-dependent hierarchies, IEEE Trans. Inf. Theory 44 (5) (1998) 1926–1940.

[153] D. Anguita, A. Ghio, L. Oneto, S. Ridella, A deep connection between the Vapnik-Chervonenkis entropy and the Rademacher complexity, IEEE Trans. Neural Netw. Learn. Syst. 25 (12) (2014) 2202–2211.

[154] S. Boucheron, G. Lugosi, P. Massart, A sharp concentration inequality with applications, Random Struct. Algorithms 16 (3) (2000) 277–292.

[155] V. Koltchinskii, Rademacher penalties and structural risk minimization, IEEE Trans. Inf. Theory 47 (5) (2001) 1902–1914.

[156] V. Koltchinskii, Local Rademacher complexities and oracle inequalities in risk minimization, Ann. Stat. 34 (6) (2006) 2593–2656.

[157] D.A. McAllester, PAC-Bayesian stochastic model selection, Mach. Learn. 51 (1) (2003) 5–21.

[158] F. Laviolette, M. Marchand, PAC-Bayes risk bounds for stochastic averages and majority votes of sample-compressed classifiers, J. Mach. Learn. Res. 8 (7) (2007) 1461–1487.

[159] A. Lacasse, F. Laviolette, M. Marchand, P. Germain, N. Usunier, PAC-Bayes bounds for the risk of the majority vote and the variance of the Gibbs classifier, in: Advances in Neural Information Processing Systems, 2006.

[160] L. Breiman, Bagging predictors, Mach. Learn. 24 (2) (1996) 123–140.

[161] R.E. Schapire, Y. Freund, P. Bartlett, W.S. Lee, Boosting the margin: a new explanation for the effectiveness of voting methods, Ann. Stat. 26 (5) (1998) 1651–1686.

[162] R.E. Schapire, Y. Singer, Improved boosting algorithms using confidence-rated predictions, Mach. Learn. 37 (3) (1999) 297–336.

[163] A.B. Tsybakov, Introduction to Nonparametric Estimation, Springer Science & Business Media, Berlin, 2008.

[164] A. Maurer, A note on the PAC Bayesian theorem, 2004, arXiv preprint cs/0411099.

[165] M. Younsi, Proof of a combinatorial conjecture coming from the PAC-Bayesian machine learning theory, 2012, arXiv preprint arXiv:1209.0824.

[166] A. Gelman, J.B. Carlin, H.S. Stern, D.B. Rubin, Bayesian Data Analysis, vol. 2, Taylor & Francis, United Kingdom, 2014.

[167] A. Rakhlin, S. Mukherjee, T. Poggio, Stability results in learning theory, Anal. Appl. 3 (04) (2005) 397–417.

[168] L. Devroye, L. Györfi, G. Lugosi, A Probabilistic Theory of Pattern Recognition, Springer, Berlin, 1996.

[169] R. Dietrich, M. Opper, H. Sompolinsky, Statistical mechanics of support vector networks, Phys. Rev. Lett. 82 (14) (1999) 2975.

[170] M. Opper, W. Kinzel, J. Kleinz, R. Nehl, On the ability of the optimal perceptron to generalise, J. Phys. A: Math. Gen. 23 (11) (1990) L581.

[171] M. Opper, Statistical mechanics of learning: generalization, in: The Handbook of Brain Theory and Neural Networks, 1995, pp. 922–925.

[172] S. Mukherjee, P. Tamayo, S. Rogers, R. Rifkin, A. Engle, C. Campbell, T.R. Golub, J.P. Mesirov, Estimating dataset size requirements for classifying DNA microarray data, J. Comput. Biol. 10 (2) (2003) 119–142.

[173] J. Langford, D.A. McAllester, Computable shell decomposition bounds, in: Computational Learning Theory, 2000.

CHAPTER

Field computation: A framework for quantum-inspired computing

3

B.J. MacLennan
University of Tennessee, Knoxville, TN, United States

1 INTRODUCTION

This chapter develops the theory of *field computation*, a model of computation that uses the mathematics of quantum mechanics to describe information representation and processing in massively parallel neural networks in both cortical tissue and neuromorphic computers. Field computation can be implemented in a variety of technologies, including massively parallel analog and digital electronics, full wavefront optical computing, and continuous-value quantum computing [1]. This chapter presents the basic concepts, definitions, and theorems of field computation, and discusses its applications in neuroscience, artificial intelligence, and quantum computing. (Prior and related work is cited throughout this chapter where it is relevant to the discussion.)

Informally, a *field* can be defined as a spatially continuous distribution of continuous quantity. Examples include real-valued and complex-valued scalar and vector fields, but we also consider fields with values in other continuous algebraic fields. In terms of physical realization, field computation includes both *physical fields*, which are mathematically continuous (e.g., electromagnetic and gravitational fields, quantum mechanical wave functions), and *phenomenological fields*, which are discrete, but sufficiently dense to be treated mathematically as though continuous (e.g., fluids, macroscopic objects, cortical tissue, massive arrays of discrete electrical components). Recent neuron counts reveal primate cortical densities ranging from 56,000 to 127,000 neurons per square millimeter [2]. Therefore, even a 0.1-mm^2 patch of human cerebral cortex might contain enough neurons to be treated as a field. A mathematical theory of cortical processing was the original motivation for the work described here [3], but the theory is more widely applicable, and in particular provides a mathematical foundation for quantum-inspired artificial intelligence and quantum computing. The quantum wave function is a field, in the sense defined

Quantum Inspired Computational Intelligence. http://dx.doi.org/10.1016/B978-0-12-804409-4.00003-6

above, and a suitable medium for field computation, but fields can be implemented classically as well and used as a medium for quantum-inspired computation.

Field computation may be defined as computation in which the state is represented by one or more physical or phenomenological fields [4]. It has a long history, for although most analog computers were used to integrate systems of ordinary differential equations, already in the nineteenth and early twentieth centuries systems of partial differential equations were being solved with use of the *field analogy method* [4,5]. In these computers fields were represented in continuous media such as electrolytic tanks or rubber sheets, or in dense arrays of discrete components such as capacitors.

2 FIELDS

Fields are described mathematically as continuous functions over (typically one-dimensional, two-dimensional, or three-dimensional) extended domains. If ϕ is a field over a domain Ω, then its value at a point $u \in \Omega$ can be written $\phi(u)$, but we usually use the subscript notation ϕ_u, which helps us to think of fields as continuously indexed vectors. Occasionally it will be convenient to use Dirac's notation $\langle u \mid \phi \rangle$ for the value of ϕ at u. The value of a time-varying field ϕ at point u and time t is written $\phi_u(t)$, and the value of the field as a whole at a particular time t is written $\phi(t)$. Fields take their values in some algebraic field, usually the real or complex numbers, but also finite-dimensional vectors of real or complex numbers. (In general, we use uppercase and lowercase Greek letters for fields, lowercase roman letters for scalars and vectors, and uppercase roman letters for functions, including field transformations.)

Physically realizable fields have additional properties. For example, they have a bounded range of variation: $|\phi_u| \leq b$ for some bound $b \in \mathbb{R}$ and all $u \in \Omega$. Typically their domains are finite in size, but sometimes we use fields that are extended in the time dimension. Physically realizable fields are usually *band limited* because the physical media cannot sustain unlimited rates of spatial variation, and phenomenological (nonphysical) fields have some finite discrete grain size. We write $\Phi_K(\Omega)$ for a space of physically realizable K-valued fields over the domain Ω; when the fields' codomain is clear from the context, as is usually the case, we write $\Phi(\Omega)$.

Generally we treat fields as elements of a separable Hilbert space, in particular as square-integrable functions over Ω, and we treat a field space $\Phi_K(\Omega)$ as an appropriate subspace of the Hilbert space $\mathcal{H}(\Omega, K)$ (leaving the Lebesgue measure unspecified). Therefore the mathematics of field computation is the same as the mathematics of quantum mechanics, and thus field computation is an example of quantum-inspired computation. However, although field computation includes the usual apparatus of quantum computation (e.g., qubits and quantum gates), it goes beyond them by focusing on the greater information representation capacity of the spatially extended wave function, which is analogous to cortical information representations. Field computation also applies to large spatial arrays of discrete quantum systems such as quantum dots. Therefore field computation expands the familiar range of quantum computation and brings it closer to neural information processing.

Since a Hilbert space is an inner product space, we define the inner product of fields in the usual way. If ϕ and ψ are two real-valued or complex-valued fields with a common domain, $\phi, \psi \in \Phi(\Omega)$, then their inner product is

$$\langle \phi \mid \psi \rangle = \int_{\Omega} \phi_u^* \psi_u du,$$

where ϕ_u^* is the complex conjugate of ϕ_u. This inner product is extended to vector-valued fields, $\boldsymbol{\phi}, \boldsymbol{\psi} \in \Phi_{\mathbb{C}^n}(\Omega)$, as follows:

$$\langle \boldsymbol{\phi} \mid \boldsymbol{\psi} \rangle = \int_{\Omega} \boldsymbol{\phi}_u^{\dagger} \boldsymbol{\psi}_u du,$$

where $\boldsymbol{\phi}_u^{\dagger}$ is the conjugate transpose (adjoint) of the column vector $\boldsymbol{\phi}_u$. Given the inner product, we define the norm $\|\phi\|$ in the usual way:

$$\|\phi\| = \sqrt{\langle \phi \mid \phi \rangle}.$$

The elements of a Hilbert space must have a finite norm (i.e., to be square integrable): $\|\phi\| < \infty$ for all $\phi \in \Phi(\Omega)$. A quantum wave function is, of course, normalized: $\|\phi\| = 1$.

Occasionally we use the constant-valued fields $\mathbf{0}$ and $\mathbf{1}$, which are defined as $\mathbf{0}_u = 0$ and $\mathbf{1}_u = 1$ for all $u \in \Omega$. We write $\mathbf{0}_{\Omega}$, $\mathbf{1}_{\Omega}$, etc., when it is necessary to be explicit about the field's domain. Conversely, since some field operations return or operate on a single real or complex number, it is useful to treat these numbers as degenerate fields (i.e., as functions whose domains are singleton sets). For example, we define $\Phi^0 = \Phi_{\mathbb{C}}(\{0\})$ to be the field space of complex numbers. Because $\mathbb{C}$ and Φ^0 are isomorphic ($\mathbb{C} \cong \Phi^0$), we treat them as equivalent when confusion is unlikely.

3 FIELD COMPUTATION

Field computation is the application of *field transformations* to one or more fields in discrete or continuous steps. Since fields are functions in a Hilbert space, field transformations are operators on Hilbert spaces, which is also the mathematics of quantum mechanics. In short, since *quantum-inspired computation* is computation over Hilbert spaces, field computation includes quantum-inspired computation [6]. Quantum transformations are, of course, unitary, but field computation is not limited to quantum implementations, and so it permits the use of nonunitary and even nonlinear operations. Moreover, any quantum process can be simulated with classical field computation (by classical computation in the Hilbert space), and therefore any local quantum computation can be implemented on a classical field computer but it can be computationally very expensive to do so. Nevertheless, field computation provides an overarching framework for designing and programming hybrid classical-quantum computer systems.

In this section we define the principal operations of field computation. In a field computer these operations operate in parallel on entire fields, and thus they are constant-time operations. (Space complexity is addressed in terms of the required spatial bandwidth of the fields involved in the computation, or in terms of the size of the basis.)

The simplest field operations are *local transformations*, which apply the same function at each point of a field. That is, if the input field is $\phi \in \Phi_J(\Omega)$ and the function is $f : J \to K$, then the output field $\psi \in \Phi_K(\Omega)$ is defined as $\psi_u = f(\phi_u)$. We use the notation $\overline{f} : \Phi_J(\Omega) \to \Phi_K(\Omega)$ for the local transformation, and therefore write $\psi = \overline{f}(\phi)$, but write $\psi = f(\phi)$ when confusion is unlikely.

Matrix-vector products are fundamental to the description of neural computation, and their extensions to the continuous domain are similarly fundamental for they are simple linear operators. Let $\phi \in \Phi(\Omega)$ and $L \in \Phi(\Omega' \times \Omega)$ be square-integrable fields (which are continuous analogs of a vector and a matrix). We define the *field product* $L\phi = \psi \in \Phi(\Omega')$ by

$$\psi_u = \int_\Omega L_{uv}\phi_v dv.$$

Although we call it a "product," it is not in general associative. Rather, it is an *integral operator of Hilbert-Schmidt type* with a *kernel L*. Because physically realizable fields are band limited, physically realizable linear operators have a Hilbert-Schmidt kernel [7]. Unitary field products can be approximated by a small set of fixed quantum operations [8, Section 4.5].

Let $L : \Phi(\Omega) \to \mathbb{C}$ be a continuous functional (scalar-valued linear operator). Then the Riesz representation theorem [e.g., 9, Section 12.4] says that L has a *representer*, which is a field $\rho \in \Phi(\Omega)$ such that $L\phi = \langle \rho \mid \phi \rangle$. If we use Dirac's bracket notation for fields, $|\rho\rangle = \rho$, then $L = \langle \rho|$, which is the dual of the field $|\rho\rangle$. This theorem applies to all field functionals because linear operators are continuous if and only if they are bounded, and realizable field transformations are bounded (i.e., there is a b such that $\|L\phi\| \leq b\|\phi\|$ for all $\phi \in \Phi(\Omega)$).

We extend the field product to multilinear operators in the obvious way. Let $\phi^k \in \Phi(\Omega_k)$ for $k = 1, \ldots, n$ and let $M \in \Phi(\Omega' \times \Omega_n \times \cdots \times \Omega_2 \times \Omega_1)$. Then we define $M\phi^1\phi^2 \cdots \phi^n = \psi \in \Phi(\Omega')$:

$$\psi_u = \int_{\Omega_n} \cdots \int_{\Omega_2} \int_{\Omega_1} M_{uv_n \cdots v_2 v_1} \phi^1_{v_1} \phi^2_{v_2} \cdots \phi^n_{v_n} dv_1 dv_2 \cdots dv_n.$$

In the absence of parentheses, these products associate to the left.

As in quantum mechanics, an *outer product* is also useful in field computation but we define it a little differently so that it is more generally useful. Let $\phi \in \Phi(\Omega)$ and $\psi \in \Phi(\Omega')$; then the outer product $\phi \wedge \psi \in \Phi(\Omega \times \Omega')$ is defined as $(\phi \wedge \psi)_{(u,v)}$

$= \phi_u \psi_v$ for all $u \in \Omega, v \in \Omega'$. Since the space $\Phi(\Omega \times \Omega')$ is isomorphic to the space $\Phi(\Omega) \otimes \Phi(\Omega')$ of tensor products $\phi \otimes \psi$, we can treat the outer and tensor products as effectively identical, and in this chapter use the tensor product, which is more familiar from quantum mechanics. Note also that the field outer product $\phi \wedge \psi$ is the kernel of the dyad or Dirac outer product $|\phi\rangle\langle\psi^*|$. (The tensor product operator will never be elided, as is common in quantum mechanics, because that could be confused with a field product.)

The following relationships hold among the inner, outer (tensor), and field products for all $\phi, \chi \in \Phi(\Omega)$ and $\psi \in \Phi(\Omega')$:

$$\phi(\chi \otimes \psi) = \langle \phi^* \mid \chi \rangle \psi = \psi \langle \chi^* \mid \phi \rangle = (\psi \otimes \chi)\phi.$$

(Note that $\langle \phi^* \mid \chi \rangle = \langle \chi^* \mid \phi \rangle$ is a scalar.)

Two closely related, useful field operators, which often have direct physical implementations, are cross-correlation and convolution. The *cross-correlation* of two fields over the same domain is defined as

$$(\psi \star \phi)_u = \int_\Omega \psi^*_{v-u} \phi_v dv. \tag{1}$$

Therefore, $(\psi \star \phi)_u$ is an inner product-based comparison of ϕ with ψ displaced by u; that is, $(\psi \star \phi)_u = \langle \psi_{-u} \mid \phi \rangle$, where ψ_{-u} is ψ displaced by u. Thus cross-correlation compares the two fields (in an inner-product sense) in all possible relative positions and returns a field of those comparisons. The *convolution* of the two fields is similar:

$$(\psi * \phi)_u = \int_\Omega \psi_{u-v} \phi_v dv. \tag{2}$$

It has simpler algebraic properties than the cross-correlation. Moreover, convolutional neural networks have proved very valuable in practical applications. With field computation hardware (e.g., optical implementations), convolution and cross-correlation are typically constant-time operations.

4 DERIVATIVES OF FIELD TRANSFORMATIONS

It is useful to take the derivatives of field transformations, which are equivalent to the derivatives of operators over function spaces [10, Section 251G]. There are two alternative notions of differentiation of operators on Banach spaces, and therefore also on Hilbert spaces: the Fréchet and Gâteaux derivatives. They are the same for field transformations because of the requirements of physical realizability [7]. We begin with the Fréchet differential, which is an operator in $\mathcal{L}(\Phi(\Omega), \Phi(\Omega'))$, the space of bounded linear operators from $\Phi(\Omega)$ to $\Phi(\Omega')$.

Let $F : \Phi(\Omega) \to \Phi(\Omega')$ be any field transformation and let U be an open subset of $\Phi(\Omega)$. Then $D \in \mathcal{L}(\Phi(\Omega), \Phi(\Omega'))$ is the *Fréchet differential* of F at $\phi \in U$ if for all $\alpha \in \Phi(\Omega)$ such that $\phi + \alpha \in U$ there is an $E : \Phi(\Omega) \to \Phi(\Omega')$ such that

$$F(\phi + \alpha) = F(\phi) + D(\alpha) + E(\alpha)$$

and

$$\lim_{\|\alpha\| \to 0} \frac{\|E(\alpha)\|}{\|\alpha\|} = 0.$$

Further, the *Fréchet derivative* $F' : \Phi(\Omega) \to \mathcal{L}(\Phi(\Omega), \Phi(\Omega'))$ is defined by $F'(\phi) = D$, which provides a locally linear approximation to F at ϕ.

For the same F and U, we define $dF : \Phi(\Omega) \times \Phi(\Omega) \to \Phi(\Omega')$ to be the *Gâteaux derivative* of F if for all $\alpha \in U$ the following limit exists:

$$dF(\phi, \alpha) = \lim_{s \to 0} \frac{F(\phi + s\alpha) - F(\phi)}{s} = \left. \frac{dF(\phi + s\alpha)}{ds} \right|_{s=0}.$$

In general, if the Fréchet derivative exists, then it is identical to the Gâteaux derivative; that is, $dF(\phi, \alpha) = F'(\phi)(\alpha)$ for all $\alpha \in \Phi(\Omega)$.

Since a Fréchet differential is a linear operator, it has a kernel field $K \in \Phi(\Omega' \times \Omega)$ satisfying $K\alpha = F'(\phi)(\alpha)$ for all α in $\Phi(\Omega)$. Therefore we define the *operator gradient* to be this kernel, $\nabla F(\phi) = K$. The analog in field computation of a directional derivative is then defined:

$$\nabla_\alpha F(\phi) = [\nabla F(\phi)]\alpha = F'(\phi)(\alpha).$$

Recalling that $\Phi^0 = \Phi(\{0\}) \cong \mathbb{C}$, we can see that the gradient of a functional $F : \Phi(\Omega) \to \Phi^0$ is the two-dimensional field $\nabla F(\phi) \in \Phi(\{0\} \times \Omega)$. With slight abuse of notation we can define $\nabla F(\phi) = \rho \in \Phi(\Omega)$, where ρ is the representer of $F'(\phi)$. Then $F'(\phi)(\alpha) = \langle \rho \mid \alpha \rangle = \langle \nabla F(\phi) \mid \alpha \rangle$.

Successively higher-order operator derivatives are operators of successively higher types. For example, if $F : \Phi(\Omega) \to \Phi(\Omega')$, then $dF : \Phi(\Omega)^2 \to \Phi(\Omega')$, where $\Phi(\Omega)^2 = \Phi(\Omega) \times \Phi(\Omega)$. In general, $d^n F : \Phi(\Omega)^{n+1} \to \Phi(\Omega')$. Similarly, as $F' : \Phi(\Omega) \to \mathcal{L}(\Phi(\Omega), \Phi(\Omega'))$, so $F'' : \Phi(\Omega) \to \mathcal{L}(\Phi(\Omega), \mathcal{L}(\Phi(\Omega), \Phi(\Omega')))$. In general,

$$F^{(n)} : \Phi(\Omega) \to \overbrace{\mathcal{L}(\Phi(\Omega), \mathcal{L}(\Phi(\Omega), \ldots, \mathcal{L}(\Phi(\Omega)}^{n}, \Phi(\Omega')) \cdots)).$$

Higher-order differentials are computed by products of "directional gradients":

$$\begin{aligned} dF^n(\phi, \alpha_1, \ldots, \alpha_n) &= \nabla^n F(\phi) \alpha_1 \cdots \alpha_n \\ &= \nabla^n F(\phi)(\alpha_n \otimes \cdots \otimes \alpha_1) \\ &= \nabla_{\alpha_n} \cdots \nabla_{\alpha_1} F(\phi). \end{aligned}$$

The chain rules for Fréchet and Gâteaux derivatives complete this introduction to the derivatives of field transformations. Let $F : \Phi(\Omega') \to \Phi(\Omega'')$ and $G : \Phi(\Omega) \to \Phi(\Omega')$; then

$$(F \circ G)'(\phi)(\alpha) = F'[G(\phi)][G'(\phi)(\alpha)], \tag{3}$$

$$d(F \circ G)(\phi, \alpha) = dF[G(\phi), dG(\phi, \alpha)]. \tag{4}$$

In field computation we are often interested in the approximation of nonlinear field transformations, and for this purpose we can use a well-known analog of Taylor's theorem for Hilbert spaces (in fact for any Banach space), which allows us to express a nonlinear operator as a sum of multilinear operators.

Theorem 1 (Taylor). *Let U be any open subset of $\Phi(\Omega)$. Suppose that $F : \Phi(\Omega) \to \Phi(\Omega')$ is a field transformation and that its first n derivatives exist in U. Let $\phi \in U$ be the field around which we will expand F. If $\alpha \in \Phi(\Omega)$ is such that $\phi + s\alpha \in U$ for all $s \in [0, 1]$, then*

$$F(\phi + \alpha) = \sum_{k=0}^{n-1} \frac{d^k F(\phi, \overbrace{\alpha, \dots, \alpha}^{k})}{k!} + R_n(\phi, \alpha),$$

where the remainder term is

$$R_n(\phi, \alpha) = \int_0^1 \frac{(1-s)^{n-1} d^n F(\phi + s\alpha, \overbrace{\alpha, \dots, \alpha}^{n})}{(n-1)!} ds.$$

For notational convenience we have defined $d^0 F(\phi) = F(\phi)$.

The Taylor expansion can be expressed in terms of directional gradients as

$$F(\phi + \alpha) = F(\phi) + \sum_{k=1}^{n-1} \frac{\nabla_\alpha^k F(\phi)}{k!} + R_n(\phi, \alpha),$$

where we define $\nabla_\alpha^k F(\phi) = \nabla^k F(\phi) \alpha^{\otimes k}$, and where $\alpha^{\otimes k}$ is the k-fold tensor product:

$$\alpha^{\otimes k} = \overbrace{\alpha \otimes \alpha \otimes \cdots \otimes \alpha}^{k}.$$

This approximation is obviously analogous to a polynomial expansion, and we can strengthen the analogy by expressing the derivatives by products with coefficient fields. Therefore if we define the fields $\Gamma_k = \nabla^k F(\phi)$, the approximation takes the form

$$F(\phi + \alpha) \approx F(\phi) + \sum_{k=1}^{n-1} \frac{\Gamma_k \alpha^{\otimes k}}{k!}.$$

To avoid redundant computation of tensor powers of α, we can compute the approximation recursively by an analog of "Horner's rule": $F(\phi + \alpha) \approx G_0(\alpha)$, where

$$G_k(\alpha) = \Gamma_k + \frac{G_{k+1}(\alpha)}{k+1}\alpha$$

for $k = 0, \ldots, n-1$, $\Gamma_0 = F(\phi)$, and $G_n(\alpha) = 0$. This formulation facilitates computation by a series of neural network-like layers.

5 EXAMPLES OF FIELD COMPUTATION

In this section we present several examples of field computation with applications in artificial intelligence, neural modeling, and quantum computation. We begin with noniterative computations, and in particular with the simplest case, a feed-forward pipeline of field transformations. In this case we apply a sequence of transformations $F_1, \ldots, F_n$ to an input field ϕ to yield an output field ψ: $\psi = F_n(\cdots F_1(\phi)\cdots)$. We can think of the output field ψ as a function of a particular input field ϕ, or if the input field is a signal changing in discrete or continuous time, $\phi(t)$, then the field transformation operates as a memoryless filter to produce the output signal $\psi(t)$: $\psi(t) = F_n(\cdots F_1(\phi(t))\cdots)$.

5.1 NEURAL NETWORK-STYLE COMPUTATION

Multilayer feed-forward neural networks are good examples of this style of neural computation. In typical artificial neural networks, the activity y_i of neuron i in one layer is a simple function of the activities, $x_1, \ldots, x_n$, of the neurons in another layer. In general,

$$y_i = s\left(\sum_{j=1}^{N} W_{ij}x_j + b_i\right), \tag{5}$$

where W_{ij} is the weight (connection strength) to neuron i from neuron j, b_i is a *bias* (negative threshold), and $s : \mathbb{R} \to \mathbb{R}$ is a *sigmoid function* (i.e., a nondecreasing, bounded continuous function).

Neural network-style computation can be applied to continuous fields, such as images, or to dense arrays of neurons treated as phenomenological fields. In these cases we may speak of *neural fabrics* or *cortical arrays*. Suppose ϕ is the field representing the activity over an input neural region Ω and ψ is a field representing the activity over an output region Ω'. Then the activity ψ_u of neuron u ($u \in \Omega'$) is defined by the activities ϕ_v of the neurons v ($v \in \Omega$) by the integral equation

$$\psi_u = \int_\Omega L_{uv}\phi_v dv + \beta_u,$$

where $L \in \Phi(\Omega' \times \Omega)$ is an *interconnection kernel* or *projection field* (representing the synaptic weights) and $\beta \in \Phi(\Omega')$ is a *bias field* (representing neural thresholds). With the addition of a sigmoid activation function we have $\psi = \overline{s}(L\phi + \beta)$.

Clearly, an N-layer-deep neural network is implemented in the same way. Let $\phi_0 \in \Phi(\Omega_0)$ be the input field and $\phi_N \in \Phi(\Omega_N)$ be the output field. For $k = 1, \ldots, N$, let $L_k \in \Phi(\Omega_k \times \Omega_{k-1})$ be the interconnection kernel (projection field) from layer $k - 1$ to layer k, and let $\beta_k \in \Phi(\Omega_k)$ be the bias field for layer k. Then $\phi_k = \bar{s}(L_k \phi_{k-1} + \beta_k)$.

5.2 DISCRETE BASIS FUNCTION NETWORKS

Many cortical neurons are broadly tuned, which means that they respond maximally to a certain input pattern or sensory stimulus, but their response falls off gradually for other inputs (its *receptive field profile*). This results in a representation of an input signal in terms of the joint activity of a population of broadly tuned neurons. If the number of neurons in the representation is small, we may talk of a discrete set of (possibly nonorthogonal) basis fields. One important class of these is *radial basis function networks* [11,12].

Suppose we have a set of radial basis functions, $r_1, r_2, \ldots, r_N$, where $r_j : \Phi(\Omega) \to [0, 1]$. This means that each function responds maximally to a particular input field η_j, its optimal input. Its value $r_j(\phi)$ represents how close ϕ is to its optimal input η_j. In many cases the radial basis functions have an identical receptive field profile $r : [0, \infty) \to [0, 1]$, which maps distance into neural activity, $r_j(\phi) = r(\|\phi - \eta_j\|)$. We assume that r is monotonically decreasing with $r(0) = 1$ and $r(x) \to 0$ as $x \to \infty$.

The inner product functions as a measure of similarity, as we can see by expanding the squared difference:

$$\|\phi - \eta_j\|^2 = \|\phi\|^2 - \langle \phi \mid \eta_j \rangle - \langle \eta_j \mid \phi \rangle + \|\eta_j\|^2.$$

In many cases the input and focal fields are real valued and normalized ($\|\phi\| = 1 = \|\eta_j\|$; see Section 7.1), in which case there is a simple inverse relation between squared distance and inner product: $\|\phi - \eta_j\|^2 = 2 - 2\langle \phi \mid \eta_j \rangle$. (Quantum states are, of course, normalized by definition.)

Since for real-valued normalized fields $\langle \phi \mid \eta_j \rangle \in [-1, 1]$, we can define radial basis functions with an identical response curve in terms of a fixed monotonically increasing function $s : [-1, 1] \to [0, 1]$ applied to the inner product, $r_j(\phi) = s(\langle \phi \mid \eta_j \rangle)$, which equals 1 when $\phi = \eta_j$ and equals 0 when the fields are maximally different ($\phi = -\eta_j$). This is a special case of neural network-style computation, in which s is the sigmoidal activation function (see Eq. 5). For complex-valued normalized fields, we use $r_j(\phi) = s(\langle \phi \mid \eta_j \rangle - \langle \phi \mid \eta_j^* \rangle)$, which makes use of conjugate weight fields η_j and η_j^*. Radial basis functions model *coarse coding* in the nervous system in which populations of broadly tuned neurons collectively represent an input pattern [e.g., 13,14, pp. 91–96]. We can define this population code explicitly as a finite-dimensional vector function $\mathbf{p}(\phi)$ given by $p_j(\phi) = r_j(\phi)$.

Hilbert function spaces are isomorphic to ℓ_2, the space of square-summable sequences; in particular, there is a one-to-one correspondence between fields and the (square-summable) infinite sequences of their generalized Fourier coefficients. Therefore, let $|1\rangle, |2\rangle, \ldots$ be an orthonormal basis of $\Phi(\Omega)$ and define $\mathbf{p} : \Phi(\Omega) \to \ell_2$ by the projections $p_j(\phi) = \langle j \mid \phi \rangle$. In practice, we can use a finite-dimensional projection, since there is a dimension m that will achieve any desired degree of accuracy. We will use $\mathbf{p}^m : \Phi(\Omega) \to \mathbb{C}^m$ for an m-dimensional representation:

$$\mathbf{p}^m(\phi) = (p_1(\phi), p_2(\phi), \ldots, p_m(\phi))^{\mathrm{T}}.$$

Equivalently this is the (unnormalized) result of a quantum mechanical projection into the subspace spanned by $|1\rangle, |2\rangle, \ldots, |m\rangle$, which is obtained with probability $\|\mathbf{p}^m(\phi)\|^2$ by our measuring in this subspace.

5.3 CONTINUA OF BASIS FUNCTIONS

One goal of field computation is to describe cortical maps with large numbers of neurons. In these cases we may think of a spatially organized *continuum* of basis functions rather than a discrete array of them. Suppose that the input space is $\Phi(\Omega)$ and the output space is $\Phi(\Omega')$. At each point $u \in \Omega'$ we want to apply to the input a different functional $R(u, \text{—})$, with a different focal field. Therefore let $\phi \in \Phi(\Omega)$ and $\psi \in \Phi(\Omega')$, and suppose $R : \Omega' \times \Phi(\Omega) \to \Phi(\Omega')$. The output field is then given by $\psi_u = R(u, \phi)$. More specifically, suppose that ψ_u is computed by neural network-style computation with a continuum of weight fields η^u; that is, $\psi_u = s(\langle \eta^u \mid \phi \rangle)$. The inner product is computed as $\langle \eta^u \mid \phi \rangle = \int_\Omega (\eta_v^u)^* \phi_v dv$. Therefore define the field $\mathrm{H} \in \Phi(\Omega' \times \Omega)$ by $\mathrm{H}_{uv} = (\eta_v^u)^*$. The output field is computed by the following field computation: $\psi = \bar{s}(\mathrm{H}\phi)$.

An important special case occurs when each field in the continuum has the same shape but centered at a different point $u \in \Omega$; that is, the fields η^u are defined as $\eta_v^u = \varrho(v - u)$ and therefore the kernel is $\mathrm{H}_{uv} = \varrho^*(v - u)$. It is apparent that $\mathrm{H}\phi = \varrho \star \phi$, the cross-correlation of the receptive field with the input field (see Eq. 1). If the receptive field ϱ is even, $\varrho(-x) = \varrho(x)$, then $\psi = \bar{s}(\varrho^* * \phi)$, which is a simple convolutional neural network (see Eq. 2). In these cases, if the kernel H is unitary, then $\mathrm{H}\phi$ can be computed by quantum operations.

5.4 APPROXIMATIONS OF SPATIAL INTEGRATION AND DIFFERENTIATION

In this section we describe field computation approximations of spatial integrals and derivatives by convolutions. For a simple example, suppose that $\phi \in \Phi([-1, 1])$ is a one-dimensional field. The integral $\psi = \int \phi$, which is defined as $\psi_x = \int_0^x \phi_y dy$, can be computed by a convolution $\psi = \upsilon * \phi$ with the *Heaviside* or *unit step field* on $\mathbb{R}$:

$$\upsilon_x = \begin{cases} 1 & \text{if } x \geq 0, \\ 0 & \text{if } x < 0. \end{cases}$$

Next consider the spatial derivative $\phi'_u = d\phi_u/du$ for $\phi \in \Phi([-1,1])$. To derive its kernel we need the *Dirac delta function* or *unit impulse function*, which is the probability density of an ideal (dimensionless) particle located at the origin. It is defined by the properties

$$\delta(0) = +\infty,$$
$$\delta(x) = 0, x \neq 0,$$
$$\int_{-\infty}^{+\infty} \delta(x)dx = 1.$$

It is the derivative of the unit step function, $\delta(x) = \upsilon'(x)$, and satisfies the "sifting equation":

$$\phi(x) = \int_{-\infty}^{+\infty} \delta(x-y)\phi(y)dy.$$

Therefore it is an identity for the convolution operation: $\phi = \delta * \phi$.

Next we express the derivative as a convolution:

$$\begin{aligned} \phi'(x) &= \frac{d}{dx}\int_{-\infty}^{+\infty} \delta(x-y)\phi(y)dy \\ &= \int_{-\infty}^{+\infty} \delta'(x-y)\phi(y)dy, \end{aligned}$$

where δ' is the *unit doublet*, the derivative of the Dirac delta function. This function is zero everywhere except infinitesimally below the origin, where it equals $+\infty$, and infinitesimally above it, where it equals $-\infty$. Therefore the derivative is computed by the convolution $\phi' = \delta' * \phi$.

Generalized functions, such as the unit impulse and unit doublet, are not physically realizable fields but they can be approximated as closely as required, for example, by impulses or doublets of narrow but nonzero width. Alternatively, we can approximate the delta function with a sufficiently sharp Gaussian field $\gamma_x = \sqrt{r/\pi}\exp(-rx^2)$. Using it instead of δ produces Gaussian-smoothed operations. Thus Gaussian-smoothed sifting, $\phi \approx \gamma * \phi$, implements Gaussian smoothing. The Gaussian-smoothed spatial derivative is computed by the convolution with the *derivative of the Gaussian* field: $\phi' \approx \gamma' * \phi$, where $\gamma'_x = d\gamma_x/dx$.

Spatial and temporal differentiation must be used with caution, since they amplify high-frequency noise; in particular we have to be careful in applying spatial differentiation to phenomenological fields with an underlying discrete physical structure, which constitutes high-frequency noise. Therefore, in practice, differentiation is often done with a low-pass filter, such as Gaussian smoothing, to eliminate this noise.

These same kernel techniques can be extended to partial spatial derivatives. For example, suppose that $\psi \in \Phi(\mathbb{R}^2)$ is a two-dimensional field. Convolution with $\delta' \otimes \delta$ will take the derivative along the first dimension, and convolution with $\delta \otimes \delta'$ will take it along the second dimension. To see this,

$$\begin{aligned}
[(\delta' \otimes \delta) * \Psi](x,y) &= \int_{-\infty}^{\infty}\int_{-\infty}^{\infty} (\delta' \otimes \delta)(x-u, y-v)\Psi(u,v)dvdu \\
&= \int_{-\infty}^{\infty} \delta'(x-u) \int_{-\infty}^{\infty} \delta(y-v)\Psi(u,v)dvdu \\
&= \int_{-\infty}^{\infty} \delta'(x-u)\Psi(u,y)du \\
&= \partial\Psi(x,y)/\partial x.
\end{aligned}$$

Obviously, the kernels $\gamma' \otimes \gamma$ and $\gamma \otimes \gamma'$ can be used to approximate these partial derivatives, and the technique extends to higher dimensions.

These methods of approximating spatial derivatives can be used to compute the gradient or divergence of a field. Since the gradient is a vector field, we define $\mathbf{i} \in \Phi_{\mathbb{R}^2}(\mathbb{R}^2)$ to be a constant vector field of unit vectors in the x direction, $\mathbf{i}_{(x,y)} = (1,0)$, and similarly, $\mathbf{j}_{(x,y)} = (0,1)$. Then the gradient field is defined as

$$\nabla\psi = [(\delta' \otimes \delta) * \psi]\mathbf{i} + [(\delta \otimes \delta') * \psi]\mathbf{j}.$$

A Gaussian-smoothed approximation is

$$\nabla\psi \approx [(\gamma' \otimes \gamma) * \psi]\mathbf{i} + [(\gamma \otimes \gamma') * \psi]\mathbf{j}. \tag{6}$$

Computing the divergence of a vector field depends on how the vector field is represented. For example, a vector field $\Psi \in \Phi_{\mathbb{R}^2}(\mathbb{R}^2)$ can be represented by a pair of scalar fields $\chi, \psi \in \Phi_{\mathbb{R}}(\mathbb{R}^2)$ that are its Cartesian components, $\Psi = \chi\mathbf{i} + \psi\mathbf{j}$. The divergence is the sum of the partial derivatives of the individual components:

$$\nabla \cdot \Psi = (\delta' \otimes \delta) * \chi + (\delta \otimes \delta') * \psi \approx (\gamma' \otimes \gamma) * \chi + (\gamma \otimes \gamma') * \psi.$$

If the vector field is represented directly (i.e., as a physical vector field), then it can be separated into its scalar Cartesian components and the divergence computed as above.

The Laplacian operator can be computed directly from the second derivatives. Consider the second derivative of a one-dimensional field: $\phi'' = \delta' * (\delta' * \phi) = (\delta' * \delta') * \phi = \delta'' * \phi$, where δ'' is the second derivative of the unit impulse (a "unit triplet"). Therefore the Laplacian operator of a two-dimensional field is

$$\nabla^2\psi = (\delta'' \otimes \delta + \delta \otimes \delta'') * \psi \approx (\gamma'' \otimes \gamma + \gamma \otimes \gamma'') * \psi, \tag{7}$$

where γ'' is the second derivative of the Gaussian field. The latter, a so-called Mexican hat function (inverted in this case), has the center-surround receptive-field profile exhibited by many neurons.

5.5 ITERATIVE FIELD COMPUTATION

Like conventional computations, many field computations are iterative. In the simplest case field operations can be performed sequentially, as on a conventional computer, but operating on all field elements in parallel. Field programs look like ordinary digital computer programs except that the variables hold fields and the operators are field operations. For example, an iterative diffusion algorithm might contain an assignment statement such as this, which updates a field variable ϕ and uses a field operator ∇^2 (with $d > 0$):

$$\phi := \phi + d\nabla^2\phi.$$

5.6 FIELD DIFFERENTIAL EQUATIONS

More commonly, as in conventional analog computers, field computers operate in continuous time by integrating partial differential equations. For example, a simple first-order field-valued differential equation is written as $\dot{\phi} = F(\phi)$, which is field-computation notation for $\partial\phi_u(t)/\partial t = F_u[\phi(t)]$. The computation is performed by continuous-time field integrators, which solve the initial-value problem $\phi(T) = \phi(0) + \int_0^T F[\phi(t)]dt$.

Gradient ascent provides a useful example of field computation; it can be implemented by sequential or continuous iteration. Suppose we are beginning with an initial field ϕ^0 (say, a corrupted image) and we are given a functional $F : \Phi(\Omega) \to \mathbb{R}$, a "figure of merit," which expresses the "goodness" of an image. Then the image can be improved by gradient ascent either sequentially $[\phi := \phi + r\nabla F(\phi)]$ or continuously $[\dot{\phi} = r\nabla F(\phi)]$ by use of the field gradient ∇ (see Section 4).

Diffusion has many applications in artificial intelligence—for example, optimization and constraint-satisfaction in motion estimation and image processing [15,16], and breadth-first path planning [17]—but is expensive to simulate on a sequential computer. A diffusion equation, such as $\dot{\phi} = d\nabla^2\phi$, can be implemented directly on a continuous-time field computer, in which the Laplacian operator is computed in constant time; sequential-time iteration ($\phi := \phi + d\nabla^2\phi$) is no different. As we have seen (Section 5.4, Eq. 7), the Laplacian operator can be approximated by convolution with a simple kernel if it is not a primitive operation.

5.7 REACTION-DIFFUSION COMPUTATION

Another important use of diffusion is in reaction-diffusion computing [18,19]. In these systems fields are realized in (generally two-dimensional) distributions of chemical concentration, but they can also be implemented in other physical systems. Chemical reaction-diffusion systems have been applied to image processing [18, pp. 26–31] and to collision-free and shortest-path planning [19, Chapter 2]. In general, we have n chemical concentration fields $\phi^1, \ldots, \phi^n \in \Phi(\Omega)$, each represented by a different chemical species. The system is defined by a system of partial differential equations such as the following:

$$\begin{aligned}\dot{\phi}^1 &= \overline{F_1}(\phi^1,\ldots,\phi^n) + d_1\nabla^2\phi^1,\\ \dot{\phi}^2 &= \overline{F_2}(\phi^1,\ldots,\phi^n) + d_2\nabla^2\phi^2,\\ &\vdots\\ \dot{\phi}^n &= \overline{F_n}(\phi^1,\ldots,\phi^n) + d_n\nabla^2\phi^n,\end{aligned}$$

where the d_k are positive diffusion rates, and the local reactions $\overline{F_k}$ occur at each point $u \in \Omega$ of the fields: $F_k(\phi_u^1,\ldots,\phi_u^n)$. This system can be expressed compactly in terms of vector fields: $\dot{\boldsymbol{\phi}} = \overline{\mathbf{F}}(\boldsymbol{\phi}) + \mathrm{D}\nabla^2\boldsymbol{\phi}$, where $\mathrm{D} = \mathrm{diag}(d_1,\ldots,d_n)$ is a diagonal matrix of the diffusion constants. Field computation can be used to simulate reaction-diffusion systems modeling the behavior of massive swarms of agents [4].

6 CHANGE OF FIELD DOMAIN

Mathematically, fields can be defined over any compact spaces, but physically realizable fields will be extended over at most three spatial dimensions and perhaps one time dimension. Quantum systems are an exception, for separate quantum systems with states in $\Phi(\Omega_1),\ldots,\Phi(\Omega_n)$ can be assembled into a composite system with the state space $\Phi(\Omega_1)\otimes\cdots\otimes\Phi(\Omega_n)$, which is isomorphic to $\Phi(\Omega_1\times\cdots\times\Omega_n)$. There is no theoretical limit to the dimension of such systems.

For classical systems, however, we may need to reduce the spatial dimension, and the techniques used may be applicable to quantum systems as well. To understand the problem, suppose we are using field computation to process images represented as two-dimensional fields in $\Phi(\Omega)$, where Ω is a bounded subset of two-dimensional Euclidean space. In general, a linear operation for processing these images will have a kernel in $\Phi(\Omega \times \Omega)$, a space of four-dimensional fields, which are in general physically unrealizable.

One solution to this problem is, for example, to represent the two-dimensional images by one-dimensional fields on which we can operate with a two-dimensional kernel. To accomplish this rerepresentation, we use generalized Fourier decompositions of the fields. For example, suppose $|1\rangle, |2\rangle, \ldots$ is an orthonormal basis for $\Phi(\Omega)$, a space of two-dimensional fields, and suppose $|1'\rangle, |2'\rangle, \ldots$ is an orthonormal basis for $\Phi(\Omega')$, a space of one-dimensional fields. A one-dimensional representation $\psi \in \Phi(\Omega')$ of an arbitrary $\phi \in \Phi(\Omega)$ can be computed:

$$|\psi\rangle = \sum_k |k'\rangle\langle k \mid \phi\rangle = \left(\sum_k |k'\rangle\langle k|\right)|\phi\rangle.$$

This invertible transformation is implemented by the three-dimensional kernel $K = \sum_k |k'\rangle\langle k|$.

Since the original and reduced fields have the same generalized Fourier coefficients, the fields have (by the Parseval equality) the same norms, and so the transformation is isometric and preserves inner products. Obviously, $KK^\dagger = I$ and $K^\dagger K = I$ (but with different identity operators). Therefore K is unitary and can be implemented by quantum gates.

Of course, reducing the dimension of the operand fields will not do much good unless we can also reduce the dimension of the kernel that is to operate on them. To see how to do this, suppose $L : \Phi(\Omega) \to \Phi(\Omega')$ is a Hilbert-Schmidt linear operator. Use the kernel $\mathrm{H} = \sum_k |k'\rangle\langle k| \in \Phi([0,1] \times \Omega)$ to reduce the two-dimensional input to a one-dimensional field in $\Phi([0,1])$ with orthonormal basis $|1'\rangle, |2'\rangle, \ldots$. Similarly, use the kernel $\Theta = \sum_j |j''\rangle\langle j'| \in \Phi(\Omega' \times [0,1])$, where $|1''\rangle, |2''\rangle, \ldots$ is an orthonormal basis for $\Phi(\Omega')$, to transform the one-dimensional output representation into the two-dimensional output space. The actual computation has a two-dimensional kernel, for it transforms a one-dimensional input representation to a one-dimensional output representation. The two-dimensional kernel $K \in \Phi([0,1]^2)$ to perform the computation on the one-dimensional fields is just the sum of the matrix elements times the corresponding dyads:

$$K = \sum_{j,k} \langle j'' \mid L \mid k \rangle |j'\rangle\langle k'|.$$

In summary, the two-dimensional to two-dimensional operator can be executed by means of one-dimensional fields by a composition of three field computations using at most three-dimensional kernels: $L = \Theta K \mathrm{H}$. Of course, nothing comes for free. The spatial bandwidth of the one-dimensional fields will be approximately the square of the bandwidth of the two-dimensional fields. That is, the dimension (in terms of basis elements) of the one-dimensional field is the product of the dimensions (in basis elements) of the two-dimensional field's two spatial dimensions. The same approach applies to fields of any dimension, provided the generalized Fourier coefficients of the input can be extracted and provided the output can be constructed from its coefficients.

In some cases it may be necessary to factor a field computation through a finite-dimensional space. This may occur in the brain when a relatively small number of neurons have no significant spatial relationship (i.e., the spatial relationships among them do not convey information). Suppose, for example, that $L : \Phi(\Omega) \to \Phi(\Omega')$, that $|k\rangle, k = 1, \ldots, m$, constitute an orthonormal basis for $\Phi(\Omega)$, and that $|j'\rangle, j = 1, \ldots, n$, constitute an orthonormal basis for $\Phi(\Omega')$. (Physically realizable fields are finite-dimensional.) Consider $|\psi\rangle = L|\phi\rangle$. Let $\mathbf{c}$ be the vector of generalized Fourier coefficients of the input, $c_k = \langle k \mid \phi\rangle$, and let $\mathbf{d}$ be the coefficients of the output, $d_j = \langle j' \mid \psi\rangle$. The Hilbert-Schmidt theorem shows that $\mathbf{d} = \mathbf{M}\mathbf{c}$, where $M_{jk} = \langle j' \mid L \mid k\rangle$. To put this in neural network terms, we have an input layer of m neurons with receptive fields $|k\rangle, k = 1, \ldots, m$. They are connected through weights M_{jk} to an second layer of n neurons with projection fields $|j'\rangle, j = 1, \ldots, n$, which are summed to produce the output, $\psi = \sum_{j=1}^{n} d_j |j'\rangle$. The numbers m and n could be quite large, but we do not treat these neural layers as fields because they do not have significant spatial structure.

A partial reduction of dimension is sometimes useful. In these cases some of the spatial dimensions are reduced through a discrete set of basis functions, as described above, but the others remain unreduced. Let $L : \Phi(\Omega) \to \Phi(\Omega')$ be a linear operator with kernel $K \in \Phi(\Omega' \times \Omega)$. We suppose that $\Omega = \Omega_1 \times \Omega_2$ has physically unrealizable dimension. Letting $\psi = K\phi$ and treating $\phi_v = \phi_{xy}$ as a function of y, $\phi_x(y)$, we expand the product:

$$\psi_u = \int_{\Omega} K_{uv}\phi_v dv = \int_{\Omega_1}\int_{\Omega_2} K_{uxy}\phi_x(y)dydx, \tag{8}$$

Next we expand ϕ_x in a generalized Fourier series in terms of $|1\rangle, |2\rangle, \ldots$, an orthonormal basis of $\Phi(\Omega_2)$: $\phi_x = \sum_k |k\rangle\langle k \mid \phi_x\rangle$. With some abuse of notation, the Fourier coefficients are given by

$$\langle k \mid \phi_x\rangle = \int_{\Omega_2} \phi_{xy}\langle k|_y dy = (\phi\langle k|)_x,$$

where the field product $\phi\langle k| \in \Phi(\Omega_1)$. We substitute the formula for the Fourier coefficients into the series, and the result into Eq. (8) to get

$$\psi_u = \sum_k \int_{\Omega_1}\int_{\Omega_2} K_{uxy}|k\rangle_y(\phi\langle k|)_x dydx = \sum_k [K|k\rangle(\phi\langle k|)]_u.$$

That is, $\psi = \sum_k K|k\rangle(\phi\langle k|)$. (The parentheses are required because the field product is not associative.) Therefore, let $J_k = K|k\rangle$ to obtain a field computation $L(\phi) = \sum_k J_k(\phi\langle k|)$, which makes use of kernels $J_k \in \Phi(\Omega' \times \Omega_1)$ of lower dimension than $K \in \Phi(\Omega' \times \Omega)$.

In this reduction we discretized $\Phi(\Omega_2)$, but $\Phi(\Omega_1)$ can be discretized in the same way, and moreover several dimensions can be discretized. Usually, we discretize those dimensions that have the fewest nonnegligible Fourier coefficients (smallest bandwidth).

The preceding example reduced the kernel dimension by discretizing one dimension of the input space, but sometimes it is preferable to discretize an output dimension. For example, suppose $L : \Phi(\Omega) \to \Phi(\Omega')$ with kernel $K \in \Phi(\Omega' \times \Omega)$, where $\Omega' = \Omega_1 \times \Omega_2$. Let $|1\rangle, |2\rangle, \ldots$ be an orthonormal basis for $\Phi(\Omega_1)$. Consider an output value $\psi_u = \psi_{xy}$ as a function of x, expand the products, and rearrange the sum as before:

$$\begin{aligned}
\psi_{xy} &= \sum_k |k\rangle_x \int_{\Omega_1} \langle k|_{x'} \psi_{x'y} dx' \\
&= \sum_k |k\rangle_x \int_{\Omega} \int_{\Omega_1} \langle k|_{x'} K_{x'yv} dx' |\phi\rangle_v dv \\
&= \sum_k |k\rangle_x (\langle k \mid K \mid \phi\rangle)_y \\
&= \sum_k (|k\rangle \otimes \langle k \mid K \mid \phi\rangle)_{xy}.
\end{aligned}$$

Therefore $\psi = \sum_k |k\rangle \otimes \langle k \mid K \mid \phi\rangle$. Define the kernel $J_k = \langle k|K \in \Phi(\Omega_2 \times \Omega)$, and we can compute the operator with lower-dimensional fields: $L(\phi) = \sum_k |k\rangle \otimes J_k|\phi\rangle$.

In the above examples we were concerned with reducing the dimension of fields so that they are physically realizable, and we saw that one way to do this is to represent a continuous field by a discrete set of generalized Fourier coefficients. However, it is sometimes useful to go in the opposite direction, and use a constant-time field product to implement a finite-dimensional matrix-vector product.

Let M be an $m \times n$ matrix, let $\mathbf{c} \in \mathbb{R}^n$ be the input vector, and suppose that our intention is to compute $\mathbf{d} = \mathrm{M}\mathbf{c}$ by a field product $|\psi\rangle = K|\phi\rangle$. That is, we will represent the input vector by a field $|\phi\rangle \in \Phi(\Omega)$ in a field space $\Phi(\Omega)$ containing n physically realizable orthonormal fields $|1\rangle, \ldots, |n\rangle$. The input field is defined as $|\phi\rangle = \sum_{k=1}^{n} c_k|k\rangle$, and the output field $\psi \in \Phi(\Omega')$ is defined as $|\psi\rangle = \sum_{j=1}^{m} d_j|j'\rangle$ for physically realizable orthonormal fields $|1'\rangle, \ldots, |m'\rangle$ of $\Phi(\Omega')$. The matrix-vector multiplication is implemented by a kernel $K \in \Phi(\Omega' \times \Omega)$ that is given by $K = \sum_{j=1}^{m} \sum_{k=1}^{n} M_{jk}|j'\rangle\langle k|$. To see this, observe

$$\begin{aligned}
K|\phi\rangle &= \left(\sum_{j,k} M_{jk}|j'\rangle\langle k| \right) |\phi\rangle \\
&= \sum_{j,k} M_{jk}|j'\rangle\langle k \mid \phi\rangle \\
&= \sum_j |j'\rangle \sum_k M_{jk} c_k \\
&= \sum_j |j'\rangle d_j \\
&= |\psi\rangle.
\end{aligned}$$

7 CORTICAL FIELD COMPUTATION

Field computation has proved useful in describing neural systems underlying motor control and in formulating *dynamic field models* of many cognitive processes [20,21]. Moreover, field computation on cortical maps shows how neural systems can implement nonlinear operations on multiple inputs in superposition, analogous to quantum computation [22]. The complex coefficients can encode additional pragmatic information, such as probability, confidence, or importance.

7.1 INFORMATION FIELDS

It is often useful to distinguish the meaning of a message, which is defined by syntax and semantics, from its pragmatics, which is conveyed by other aspects of this signal. For example, the loudness of an utterance does not affect its meaning, but it could affect the likelihood of its reception or its effect on a hearer's behavior. Similarly, repeating a signal does not affect its information content but it might affect the reliability of its transmission. Often we can say that it is the "shape" of a signal that conveys information, and it is its "size" and other bulk properties (e.g., color, pitch, brightness) that convey pragmatics. For example, Hopfield [23] remarked that in some neural systems the phase of impulses conveyed the information but the frequency of the impulses conveyed pragmatic characteristics, such as urgency, importance, or certainty. Therefore we may define an *information field* to be a normalized field, or alternatively a field whose magnitude does not matter (i.e., a *ray* in a projective Hilbert space), just like a quantum state vector. We can think of an ordinary field ϕ as comprising two components, $\phi = p\psi$, a pragmatic magnitude, $p = \|\phi\|$, and an information-bearing form, $\psi = \phi/p$. Similarly, in quantum mechanical systems Bohm and Hiley [24, pp. 35–36] distinguish a *form*, which *guides* the action, and a *magnitude*, which determines the *amount* of action.

7.2 NONLINEAR COMPUTATION BY TOPOGRAPHIC MAPS

Much of the information in the brain is organized in *topographic maps* in which sensory properties or other information is systematically mapped to spatial location. For example, there are *tonotopic maps* that systematically map pitch and *retinotopic maps* that reflect the organization of the retina. Information processing in topographic maps is naturally described by field computation, and topographic mapping facilitates the computation of nonlinear transformations of the information.

In these maps, activity in a region represents the information by its location within the region. That is, a particular value $x \in \Omega$ is represented by a corresponding field in $\Phi(\Omega)$ that is distinctly peaked at x. Mathematically, this field can be approximated by a Dirac delta function $\delta(u - x)$ located at x; as in quantum mechanics, we will write it as $|x\rangle$. It corresponds to the wave function of an idealized particle with its probability density concentrated at x.

Now consider an arbitrary function $f : \Omega \to \Omega'$. Its value for a particular $x, f(x)$, is represented by a delta function with its peak at the location corresponding to this value; that is, $|f(x)\rangle$. In neural terms, each neuron representing an $x \in \Omega$ is connected to the neuron $y \in \Omega'$ representing $y = f(x)$. Investigation of this in field computation terms will reveal some of the advantages of computing with topographic maps [22].

Given an arbitrary $f : \Omega \to \Omega'$ we will use a corresponding kernel $K \in \Phi(\Omega' \times \Omega)$ so that for all $x \in \Omega$, $|f(x)\rangle = K|x\rangle$. Since the delta functions are orthonormal, this is simply

$$K = \int_{\Omega} |f(x)\rangle\langle x| dx, \tag{9}$$

which is, in essence, the *graph* of the function f; the computation is a sort of table lookup.

The delta functions can be approximated by the point-to-point neural connections described above, but they are not physically realizable in general. Therefore it will be worthwhile to reexpress this computation in terms of realizable kernels. To accomplish this, expand the delta functions in terms of an orthonormal basis; for example, $|x\rangle = \sum_k |k\rangle\langle k \mid x\rangle$ and therefore $\langle x| = \sum_k \langle x \mid k\rangle\langle k|$. Similarly, $|f(x)\rangle = \sum_j |j'\rangle\langle j' \mid f(x)\rangle$. Substitute the latter two Fourier series into Eq. (9) to get

$$\begin{aligned} K &= \int_\Omega \left(\sum_j |j'\rangle\langle j' \mid f(x)\rangle \right) \otimes \left(\sum_k \langle x \mid k\rangle\langle k| \right) dx \\ &= \sum_{j,k} |j'\rangle \otimes |k\rangle \int_\Omega \langle j' \mid f(x)\rangle\langle x \mid k\rangle dx \\ &= \sum_{j,k} |j'\rangle \otimes |k\rangle\langle j' \circ f \mid k\rangle, \end{aligned}$$

where $|j' \circ f\rangle$ is the composition of $|j'\rangle$ and f: $|j' \circ f\rangle_x = |j'\rangle_{f(x)}$.

Computing with topographic maps has several interesting properties, one of which is that it uses a linear operator to compute a possibly nonlinear function. Several useful properties follow from linearity. For example, the map is able to operate on a superposition of two or more simultaneous inputs to produce a superposition of their outputs: $K(|x\rangle + |x'\rangle) = |f(x)\rangle + |f(x')\rangle$. Since inputs and outputs are represented by the locations of the peaks rather than their heights, the magnitude of the impulse (or its quantum probability amplitude) can be used to represent a pragmatic property of the input value, such as its certainty or importance (see Section 7.1). Topographic computation passes these pragmatic characteristics from the inputs to the outputs: $K(p|x\rangle) = p|f(x)\rangle$. If we have two (or more) inputs $x, x' \in \Omega$ with corresponding pragmatic weights $p, p' \in \mathbb{R}$, perhaps reflecting confidence or importance, then the outputs carry the same weights: $K(p|x\rangle + p'|x'\rangle) = p|f(x)\rangle + p'|f(x')\rangle$. If multiple simultaneous inputs, each with its own weight, happen to lead to the same output, then their weights will combine; for example, if $f(x) = f(x')$, then $K(p|x\rangle + p'|x'\rangle) = (p + p')|f(x)\rangle$. In this way individually uncertain or unimportant inputs may jointly lead to an output of much greater certainty or importance.

These observations extend naturally to the continuum case. Suppose the real field $\varpi \in \Phi(\Omega)$ represents the probability or other pragmatic characteristics of the information, so that ϖ_x is the pragmatic weight of $x \in \Omega$. If we think of the input field as a weighted superposition of delta functions, $|\varpi\rangle = \int_\Omega \varpi_x |x\rangle dx$, then we can see that the output will reflect these weights: $K|\varpi\rangle = \int_\Omega \varpi_x |f(x)\rangle dx \in \Phi(\Omega')$. The pragmatic weight of each output point will be the sum of the weights of all inputs leading to that output:

$$\langle y \mid K \mid \varpi\rangle = (K\varpi)_y = \int_{\{x|y=f(x)\}} \varpi_x dx = \int_{f^{-1}(y)} \varpi_x dx.$$

If f is not bijective, then K will not be unitary and therefore not quantum computable. In this case we can use instead $K = \int_\Omega (|f(x)\rangle \otimes |x\rangle)(\langle 0| \otimes \langle x|)dx$, where $|0\rangle \in \Phi(\Omega')$.

7.3 FIELD REPRESENTATIONS OF DISCRETE SYMBOLS

Quantum-inspired Hilbert-space models are illuminating aspects of human categorical cognition and may lead to improved use of concepts in artificial intelligence systems. For example, Pothos and Busemeyer [25] have presented compelling evidence that quantum probability provides a better model than classical probability for many cognitive processes. We have argued that this is because these cognitive processes are implemented in cortex by field computation, since it is described by the same mathematics as quantum probability [26]. Aerts et al. [27] have used the mathematics of quantum mechanics to explain how humans combine concepts and use them in context.

Most concepts have indefinite boundaries and are context sensitive; they are modeled well by connectionist theories, but the *words* that denote these concepts are discrete, analogous to particles. For the most part, words have a discrete topology; that is, as lexical entities (not strings of letters or phonemes) they are either the same or completely different: $d(x,x) = 0$ and $d(x,y) = 1$ for $x \neq y$. Therefore words (and other particular things that must be kept distinct) are naturally represented by orthonormal fields, which have exactly this property. Such orthogonal representations emerge through self-organizing processes from the essentially continuous underlying adaptive and learning mechanisms in the brain.

7.4 GABOR REPRESENTATION AND THE UNCERTAINTY PRINCIPLE

The well-known Heisenberg uncertainty principle applies to nonquantum systems, as shown by Gabor [28], who applied the Heisenberg-Weyl derivation to arbitrary square-integrable signals of finite duration and bandwidth; it is thus applicable to field computation. It quantifies the degrees of freedom of physically realizable fields.

Suppose that ψ is a field over n-dimensional space, $\psi \in \Phi(\Omega)$. The spread, or uncertainty, of the field along each spatial dimension x_k can be measured by the root mean square deviation of x_k (assumed to have zero mean):

$$\Delta x_k = \|x_k \psi(\mathbf{x})\| = \sqrt{\int_\Omega \psi^*_\mathbf{x} x_k^2 \psi_\mathbf{x} d\mathbf{x}},$$

where $\mathbf{x} = (x_1, \ldots, x_n)^\mathrm{T} \in \Omega \subset \mathbb{R}^n$. Let $\Psi(\mathbf{u})$ be the Fourier transform of $\psi(\mathbf{x})$, and define in a similar way the uncertainty, or spread, in the frequency domain:

$$\Delta u_k = \|(u_k - \bar{u})\Psi(\mathbf{u})\| = \sqrt{\int_\Omega \Psi^*_\mathbf{u} u_k^2 \Psi_\mathbf{u} d\mathbf{u}}.$$

Gabor proved that $\Delta x_k \Delta u_k \geq 1/4\pi$, which may be called the *Gabor uncertainty principle* (for an informal introduction, see [29]).

The minimum joint spread in the space and spatial frequency domains, $\Delta x_k \Delta u_k = 1/4\pi$, is achieved by the *Gabor elementary fields*, which are Gaussian-modulated complex exponentials (i.e., *wave packets*):

$$g_{\mathbf{pu}}(\mathbf{x}) = \exp\left[-\pi \|\mathrm{A}(\mathbf{x}-\mathbf{p})\|^2\right] \exp[2\pi i \mathbf{u} \cdot (\mathbf{x}-\mathbf{p})].$$

This is a family of fields parameterized by $\mathbf{p}$, which is the center of the Gaussian envelope, and $\mathbf{u}$, which is a *wave vector* defining the frequency and phase of the complex exponential. All members of the family share a common Gaussian envelope whose shape is defined by a diagonal *aspect matrix* $\mathrm{A} = \mathrm{diag}(\alpha_1, \ldots, \alpha_n)$. It defines the common spread of the wave packets in the space and frequency domains: $\Delta x_k = \alpha_k/(2\sqrt{\pi})$ and $\Delta u_k = \alpha_k^{-1}/(2\sqrt{\pi})$.

We can characterize a field (function) by its amplitude at various points in *Gabor space*; that is, at different combinations of spatial location and frequency $(\mathbf{x}, \mathbf{u})$. But the Gabor uncertainty principle shows that these amplitudes cannot be localized more closely than cells of size $\prod_{k=1}^{n} \alpha_k/(2\sqrt{\pi})\alpha_k^{-1}/(2\sqrt{\pi}) = (4\pi)^{-n}$. Gabor referred to these elementary units of (complex-valued) information as *logons*, and the number of them in a field of finite extent and bandwidth as its *logon content*. It measures the maximum information (degrees of freedom) that can be represented by such a function (and Gabor's original purpose was to analyze the information-carrying capacity of the transatlantic cable). If X_k is a field's extent along the kth axis and U_k is its bandwidth on that axis, then the field's Gabor-space volume is $V_G = \prod_{k=1}^{n} X_k U_k$ and its logon content is $L = (4\pi)^n V_G$.

Gabor showed that any square-integrable function with a finite Gabor-space volume could be expanded into a superposition of Gabor elementary functions [30, pp. 656–657]: $\psi = \sum_{k=1}^{L} c_k g_k$, where for convenience I have indexed the Gabor functions sequentially. That is, any physically realizable field can be analyzed as a superposition of wave packets, and the L complex coefficients c_k constitute the information content of the field. Since the Gabor elementary functions are not orthogonal, these coefficients cannot be computed directly by an inner product, $\langle g_k \mid \psi \rangle$. With appropriate choice of parameters, however, the Gabor elementary functions constitute a *tight frame*, which allows the coefficients to be approximated by the inner product [31, p. 1275]. Alternatively, they can be computed directly by least-squares approximation (see Section 8) or by gradient descent on the error of approximation, $\mathcal{E} = \|\hat{\psi}(\mathbf{c}) - \psi\|^2$, where $\hat{\psi}(\mathbf{c}) = \sum_{k=1}^{L} c_k g_k$. Since $\partial \mathcal{E}/\partial c_k = 2\langle g_k \mid \hat{\psi}(\mathbf{c}) - \psi \rangle$, gradient descent is $\dot{c}_k \propto \langle g_k \mid \psi - \hat{\psi}(\mathbf{c}) \rangle$.

8 UNIVERSAL FIELD COMPUTATION

An important question, with both theoretical and practical implications, is whether there can be a *universal field computer*; that is, a field computer that can be programmed to do any field computation in a large, significant class of computations. This question can be answered from the perspective of the ordinary theory of computation but it does not address the key questions in an informative way. Since, in mathematical terms, fields are continuous functions, it is more natural to address universal field computation from the perspective of approximation theory in Hilbert spaces.

For example, as explained in Section 4 (Theorem 1), there is an analog of Taylor's theorem for Hilbert spaces, and this theorem allows us to expand field transformations in sums of multilinear operators, which are analogous to the polynomials of the familiar Taylor theorem [3,4,22,32]. This shows how to compute a wide class of field transformations with a small set of operations: field product, field addition, and field scaling. The required gradient kernels may be of high spatial dimension, but we have discussed ways of reducing dimension (see Section 6).

Another approach to the question comes from various universal approximation theorems for real-valued and complex-valued functions [e.g., 33, pp. 166–168, 219–220, 236–239, 323–326]. They can be extended to physically realizable fields, which have a finite number of non-zero Fourier coefficients. These theorems show how to approximate field transformations with a limited repertoire of basic field operations.

For example, suppose that we want to interpolate a real-valued field transformation $F : \Phi(\Omega) \to \Phi(\Omega')$ given by the input-output samples (ϕ^k, ψ^k), where $F(\phi^k) = \psi^k$, $k = 1, \dots, P$ with an interpolating function of the form

$$\hat{\psi} = \sum_{j=1}^{H} r_j(\phi)\alpha_j \tag{10}$$

for some H. The operators $r_j : \Phi(\Omega) \to \mathbb{R}$ are fixed nonlinear functionals (e.g., radial basis functions) that weight the output projection fields $\alpha_j \in \Phi(\Omega')$. These fields can be computed by use of the least-squares algorithm to minimize the approximation error, $\mathcal{E} = \sum_{k=1}^{P} \|\hat{\psi}^k - \psi^k\|^2$, where $\hat{\psi}^k = \sum_{j=1}^{H} r_j(\phi^k)\alpha_j$, as explained next.

By Parseval's identity, $\|\hat{\psi}^k - \psi^k\|^2$ is equal to the sum of the squares of the generalized Fourier coefficients of $\hat{\psi}^k - \psi^k$. Therefore let $|1\rangle, |2\rangle, \dots$ be a basis for $\Phi(\Omega')$, and compute them:

$$\begin{aligned} \langle i \mid \hat{\psi}^k - \psi^k\rangle &= \left\langle i \,\middle|\, \sum_{j=1}^{H} r_j(\phi^k)\alpha_j - \psi^k \right\rangle \\ &= \left[\sum_{j=1}^{H} r_j(\phi^k)\langle i \mid \alpha_j\rangle\right] - \langle i \mid \psi^k\rangle. \end{aligned}$$

Since physically realizable fields have finite bandwidth, and for any fields we can pick a number N of Fourier coefficients to approximate them as closely as we like, we can reduce this to a finite-dimensional least-squares problem. Define a $P \times H$ matrix R of the basis functional values for each input sample: $R_{kj} = r_j(\phi^k)$. Let A be an $H \times N$ matrix (to be determined) of the Fourier coefficients of the projection fields, $A_{ji} = \langle i \mid \alpha_j \rangle$, and let Y be a $P \times N$ matrix of the Fourier coefficients of the output samples, $Y_{ki} = \langle i \mid \psi^k \rangle$. In these terms,

$$\langle i \mid \hat{\psi}^k - \psi^k \rangle = \sum_{j=1}^{H} R_{kj} A_{ji} - Y_{ki}.$$

Therefore let the error matrix $\mathrm{E} = \mathrm{RA} - \mathrm{Y}$ so that $\|\hat{\psi}^k - \psi^k\|^2 = \sum_{i=1}^{N} E_{ki}^2$, and the total error is the squared Frobenius norm: $\hat{\mathcal{E}} = \sum_{k,i} E_{ki}^2 = \|\mathrm{E}\|_F^2$.

This is an ordinary least-squares problem, and the error is minimized by $\mathrm{A} = \mathrm{R}^+\mathrm{Y}$, where R^+ is the *Moore-Penrose pseudoinverse*, $\mathrm{R}^+ = (\mathrm{R}^\mathrm{T}\mathrm{R})^{-1}\mathrm{R}^\mathrm{T}$ [e.g., 34, pp. 371–373]. The solution matrix A contains the Fourier coefficients of the output projection fields that minimize the error: $\alpha_j = \sum_{i=1}^{N} A_{ji} |i\rangle$.

Thus we can determine the projection fields that minimize the error, but for universal approximation we need to be able to make the error as small as we like. This depends on the number and shape of the basis functionals r_j. One suitable class of functions is the radial basis functions, $r_j(\phi) = r(\|\phi - \eta_j\|)$, where each focal field η_j causes the maximal response of the corresponding basis function r_j. In fact we can choose $H = P$ and $\eta_j = \phi^j$, and the matrix R will be invertible for many radial functions r [33, pp. 238–239]. Therefore these radial basis functionals (for which convolution might be used), together with field scaling and summation (in order to evaluate Eq. 10) are sufficient to approximate any realizable field transformation.

These radial basis function approximations are like continuum neural networks, and other neural network-like field computations are also universal, such as basis functionals of the form $r_j(\phi) = s(\langle \omega_j \mid \phi \rangle + b_j)$. The weight fields ω_j and the bias values b_j are determined by an approximation algorithm [33, pp. 166–168]. In this case the operations required for universality are field scaling and summation for Eq. (10), and inner product, scalar addition, and the sigmoid s for computation of the basis functionals.

9 GENERAL-PURPOSE FIELD COMPUTERS

It remains to say a little about general-purpose field computers. These can take many forms. The most familiar arrangement is to supplement an ordinary digital computer with hardware for performing a repertoire of field operations. Fields are stored in appropriate registers (one-dimensional, two-dimensional, or three-dimensional) like numbers in ordinary computers. Computation proceeds in sequential steps with loops, conditionals, and the other familiar apparatus of computer programming.

The most natural implementation of field computation (historically common, but less familiar nowadays) is the continuous-time analog computer. Programs are, in effect, partial differential equations, and the field computer integrates them with respect to time. In addition to initial-value and boundary-value problems, such computers can process continuous input signals and generate continuous output signals for control applications. This is closest to the function of the nervous system, which depends heavily on field computation.

In Section 8 we saw that a few operations are sufficient for universal computation: field summation ($\phi + \psi$), field scaling ($z\phi$), inner product ($\langle \phi \mid \psi \rangle$), field product ($K\phi$), and simple radial basis functionals. More specifically, perceptron net-style approximation requires the inner product and any nonconstant, bounded, monotone-increasing scalar function (i.e., a sigmoid function), and radial basis approximation requires the norm (which can be computed with the inner product) and any nonconstant, bounded, monotone-decreasing scalar function. Reduction of dimension may require the tensor/outer product ($\phi \otimes \psi$). Other useful operations which are easy to implement in some technologies include convolution ($\phi * \psi$), cross-correlation ($\phi \star \psi$), various local operators (e.g., $\overline{\log}$, $\overline{\exp}$), and vector field operations (∇, $\nabla \cdot$, ∇^2). Other vector field operations can be implemented in terms of their Cartesian or polar components. Scalar analog computation is implemented by field computation on zero-dimensional fields in Φ^0.

10 CONCLUSIONS AND FUTURE WORK

Hilbert spaces provide the mathematical foundations of quantum mechanics, and quantum-inspired computation can be identified with computation in Hilbert spaces. In particular, the concept of a *field*, a continuous spatial distribution of quantity, can be used as a model both of information representations in neural cortex and of quantum wave functions. Field computation thus provides a unifying framework for quantum-inspired cognition, both natural and artificial. A relatively small number of field operations, which have natural physical implementations, are sufficient for universal field computation and correspond to simple neural networks.

Research in field computation is progressing in many directions simultaneously. For example, continuing progress in neuroscience is illuminating cortical information representation and processing. These processes, many of which depend on cortical maps with high neuron densities, can be expressed naturally as field transformations and therefore implemented on current and future field computers. As we strive to reach and to surpass human-scale artificial intelligence, the most direct route will be to implement these processes by means of field-computing hardware. Quantum computation is also a kind of field computation, and therefore field computation provides a unifying framework for neural computation and quantum computation. In particular, field computation provides a path by which techniques from neural computation (over normalized vectors) can be brought into quantum computation, implementing computation over dense neural arrays by physical operations on quantum wave functions. Finally, field computation is a theory of massively parallel (or, more correctly, continuously parallel) analog computation, which can be implemented in a variety of current and future technologies. Implementation on conventional digital computers and graphical processing units has been and will continue to be a convenient medium for field computation. Other computational media, however, promise more direct implementations. These include nonlinear optical computation, continuous variable quantum computation, chemical computation, and massively parallel analog computation. Quantum-inspired field computation is thus a theoretical foundation for both natural and artificial intelligence.

REFERENCES

[1] S. Lloyd, S.L. Braunstein, Quantum computation over continuous variables, Phys. Rev. Lett. 82 (1999) 1784–1787, http://dx.doi.org/10.1103/PhysRevLett.82.1784.

[2] C.E. Collins, D.C. Airey, N.A. Young, D.B. Leitch, J.H. Kaas, Neuron densities vary across and within cortical areas in primates, Proc. Natl. Acad. Sci. 107 (36) (2010) 15927–15932, http://dx.doi.org/10.1073/pnas.1010356107.

[3] B.J. MacLennan, Technology-independent design of neurocomputers: the universal field computer, in: M. Caudill, C. Butler (Eds.), Proceedings of the IEEE First International Conference on Neural Networks, vol. 3, IEEE Press, New York, 1987, pp. 39–49.

[4] B.J. MacLennan, Field computation in natural and artificial intelligence, in: R. Meyers, et al. (Eds.), Encyclopedia of Complexity and System Science, Chapter 6, entry 199, Springer, Berlin, 2009, pp. 3334–3360, http://dx.doi.org/10.1007/978-0-387-30440-3_199.

[5] B.J. MacLennan, The promise of analog computation, Int. J. Gen. Syst. 43 (7) (2014) 682–696, http://dx.doi.org/10.1080/03081079.2014.920997.

[6] B.J. MacLennan, The nature of computing—computing in nature, Tech. Rep. UT-CS-05-565, Department of Computer Science, University of Tennessee, Knoxville, 2005, also available from web.eecs.utk.edu/~mclennan (November 25, 2005).

[7] B.J. MacLennan, Field computation: a theoretical framework for massively parallel analog computation, parts I–IV, Tech. Rep. CS-90-100, Department of Computer Science, University of Tennessee, Knoxville, 1990, also available from web.eecs.utk.edu/~mclennan.

[8] M.A. Nielsen, I.L. Chuang, Quantum Computation and Quantum Information, tenth ed., Cambridge University Press, Cambridge, 2010.

[9] G. Brachman, L. Narici, Functional Analysis, Academic Press, New York, 1966.

[10] Mathematical Society of Japan, in: S. Iyanaga, Y. Kawada (Eds.), Encyclopedic Dictionary of Mathematics, MIT Press, Cambridge, 1980.

[11] W. Light, Ridge functions, sigmoidal functions and neural networks, in: E. Cheney, C. Chui, L. Schumaker (Eds.), Approximation Theory VII, Academic Press, Boston, 1992, pp. 163–206.

[12] M. Powell, Radial basis functions for multivariable interpolation: a review, in: IMA Conference on Algorithms for the Approximation of Functions and Data, RMCS, Shrivenham, UK, 1985, pp. 143–167.

[13] T. Sanger, Probability density estimation for the interpretation of neural population codes, J. Neurophysiol. 76 (1996) 2790–2793.

[14] D.E. Rumelhart, J.L. McClelland, The PDP Research Group, Parallel Distributed Processing: Explorations in the Microstructure of Cognition, MIT Press, Cambridge, MA, 1986.

[15] M. Miller, B. Roysam, K. Smith, J. O'Sullivan, Representing and computing regular languages on massively parallel networks, IEEE Trans. Neural Netw. 2 (1991) 56–72.

[16] P. Ting, R. Iltis, Diffusion network architectures for implementation of Gibbs samplers with applications to assignment problems, IEEE Trans. Neural Netw. 5 (1994) 622–638.

[17] O. Steinbeck, A. Tóth, K. Showalter, Navigating complex labyrinths: optimal paths from chemical waves, Science 267 (1995) 868–871.

[18] A. Adamatzky, Computing in Nonlinear Media and Automata Collectives, Institute of Physics Publishing, Bristol, 2001.

[19] A. Adamatzky, B. De Lacy Costello, T. Asai, Reaction-Diffusion Computers, Elsevier, Amsterdam, 2005.

[20] B.J. MacLennan, Field computation in motor control, in: P.G. Morasso, V. Sanguineti (Eds.), Self-Organization, Computational Maps and Motor Control, Elsevier, Amsterdam, 1997, pp. 37–73, also available from web.eecs.utk.edu/~mclennan.

[21] J.P. Spencer, G. Schöner (Eds.), Dynamic Thinking: A Primer on Dynamic Field Theory, Oxford University Press, New York, NY, 2015.

[22] B.J. MacLennan, Field computation in natural and artificial intelligence, Inf. Sci. 119 (1999) 73–89, also available from web.eecs.utk.edu/~mclennan.

[23] J. Hopfield, Pattern recognition computation using action potential timing for stimulus response, Nature 376 (1995) 33–36.

[24] D. Bohm, B. Hiley, The Undivided Universe: An Ontological Interpretation of Quantum Theory, Routledge, London/New York, 1993.

[25] E.M. Pothos, J.R. Busemeyer, Can quantum probability provide a new direction for cognitive modeling? Behav. Brain Sci. 36 (2013) 255–327, http://dx.doi.org/10.1017/S0140525X12001525.

[26] B.J. MacLennan, Cognition in Hilbert space, Behav. Brain Sci. 36 (3) (2013) 296–297, http://dx.doi.org/10.1017/S0140525X1200283X.

[27] D. Aerts, L. Gabora, S. Sozzo, Concepts and their dynamics: a quantum-theoretic modeling of human thought, Top. Cogn. Sci. 5 (2013) 737–772.

[28] D. Gabor, Theory of communication, J. Instit. Electr. Eng. 93 (Part III) (1946) 429–457.

[29] B.J. MacLennan, Gabor representations of spatiotemporal visual images, Tech. Rep. CS-91-144, Department of Computer Science, University of Tennessee, Knoxville, 1991, also available from web.eecs.utk.edu/~mclennan.

[30] C. Heil, D. Walnut, Continuous and discrete wavelet transforms, SIAM Rev. 31 (4) (1989) 628–666.

[31] I. Daubechies, A. Grossman, Y. Meyer, Painless non-orthogonal expansions, J. Math. Phys. 27 (1986) 1271–1283.

[32] B.J. MacLennan, Field computation in the brain, in: K. Pribram (Ed.), Rethinking Neural Networks: Quantum Fields and Biological Data, Lawrence Erlbaum, Hillsdale, NJ, 1993, pp. 199–232, also available from web.eecs.utk.edu/~mclennan.

[33] S. Haykin, Neural Networks and Learning Machines, third ed., Pearson Education, New York, 2008.

[34] S. Leon, Linear Algebra With Applications, second ed., Macmillan, New York, 1986.

CHAPTER

Design of cellular quantum-inspired evolutionary algorithms with random topologies 4

N. Mani[a], Gursaran[a], A. Mani[b]

Dayalbagh Educational Institute, Agra, UP, India[a]

Amity School of Engineering and Technology, Amity University Uttar Pradesh, Noida, UP, India[b]

1 INTRODUCTION

Quantum-inspired evolutionary algorithms (QEAs) are population-based metaheuristics which have been designed by the integration of principles from quantum mechanics into the framework of evolutionary algorithms. They have been successfully used to solve difficult search and optimization problems such as automatic color detection [1], image segmentation [2], bandwidth [3], circuit testing [4], software testing [5], economic dispatch [6,7], engineering design optimization [8], design of digital filters [9], and process optimization [10].

The primary components of QEAs are quantum bit representation, Q-bit, variation operators such as rotation gates, and measurement operators and can search with a few individuals and even with one individual [11]. The performance of canonical QEAs has been improved through modifications in operators (e.g., real observation QEAs [7], quantum crossover [12], quantum mutation [13] and neighborhood operators [14,15]) and population structure (e.g., versatile QEAs, vQEA [16,17]).

It was shown [16–18] that population structure influences the performance of QEAs. Further, it was shown [17] that a QEA with a cellular population model, also known as a "fine-grained population model," performs better than a QEA with panmictic and coarse-grained population models on a set of benchmark problem suites. The cellular model admits many different kinds of topologies, which can be divided into two broad categories (i.e., random and spatial). In random topologies the position of the individuals in relation to the other individuals in the population is assigned randomly, whereas in the case of spatial topologies the position of the individuals in relation to the other individuals in the population is assigned on the

Quantum Inspired Computational Intelligence. http://dx.doi.org/10.1016/B978-0-12-804409-4.00004-8

basis of some spatial information, which could be derived from the fitness landscape, phenotype or genotype space, or a combination of them [19]. Some attempts were recently made to measure the effect of static random topologies on the performance of fine-grained QEAs [20]. This chapter describes the design of cellular QEAs with random topologies.

The popular random topologies are the Gbest, ring, and von Neumann topologies, and they have been widely investigated in particle swarm optimization (PSO) [21]. Von Neumann topology has also been investigated with square, rectangular, and narrow cellular structure in genetic algorithms (GAs) [22]. That work implements the above-mentioned topologies by randomly distributing the individuals in the population without considering spatial information and empirically compares their relative performance. Three versions of random population topologies were implemented (i.e., static, dynamic, and adaptive). The static random population topology computes its neighborhood list only once during the initialization stage and maintains the structure throughout the execution of the algorithm. The dynamic random population topology changes its structure during the execution of the algorithm on the basis of the preprogrammed number of generations. The adaptive random population topology changes its structure during the execution of the program on the basis of the feedback from the search process in terms of changes in average fitness and entropy of the fitness of the solution vectors from one generation to the next. Some attempts were made recently to measure the effect of static random topologies on the performance of fine-grained QEAs [20] but they did not consider the impact of dynamic and adaptive random topologies, whereas this chapter investigates both dynamic and adaptive random topologies for the design of cellular QEAs.

The chapter is organized as follows. Section 2 describes population topologies and grid shapes. Static cellular QEAs (SCLQEAs), dynamic cellular QEAs (DCLQEAs), and adaptive cellular QEAs (ACLQEAs) are described in Section 3. Benchmark problems are described in Section 4. Section 5 discusses testing and results. Section 6 concludes the chapter.

2 LITERATURE SURVEY

Most of the attempts to integrate quantum mechanical concepts into an evolutionary algorithms framework have focused on designing algorithms that run on conventional computers instead of quantum computers and have been appropriately classified as quantum inspired. Narayan and Moore [23] used parallel verses interpretation of quantum mechanics to design their quantum-inspired GA. A number of other hybridizations have also been proposed, of which the most popular is the proposal by Han and Kim [24], termed a "canonical QEA." It uses a Q-bit as the smallest unit of information and a Q-bit individual as a string of Q-bits for genotype representation. Experimental results show that the canonical QEA performs better than the conventional GA. Platlet et al. [16] identified a weakness of QEAs and proposed a new algorithm, called a "versatile quantum-inspired evolutionary algorithm" (vQEA) that always adapts the search toward the last promising solution found, thus leading to a smoother and more efficient exploration. This claim is supported by experimental evaluations. The vQEA [16] could improve on the performance of QEAs [24] without introducing the improvements suggested in [25] by using a different kind of population model [17].

Some attempts have also been made to use structured populations to improve the performance of evolutionary algorithms [22]. The structure of a population is classified as panmictic, coarse grained, or fine grained. The canonical QEA proposed by Han and Kim [24] has an island or coarse-grained population model. The performance of this algorithm was improved by a change of the global update strategy [16] and was named a "versatile quantum-inspired evolutionary algorithm" (vQEA). The modification to convert a QEA into a vQEA can be also viewed as equivalent to changing the population structure from a coarse-grained model in a QEA to panmictic in a vQEA. The improvement attained by the vQEA over the QEA indicates the impact of population structure on the performance of the QEA. Further, it was shown [17] that a QEA with a fine-grained or cellular population model performs better than other models. The cellular population model admits different types of topologies, such as von-Neumann topology, which were implemented in a QEA and tested on P-PEAKS problem instances with encouraging results [20].

Extensive studies have been conducted on the influence of topologies for interaction between particles in PSO [21]. These studies have shown that global interactions lead to fast but suboptimal results. On the other hand, topologies with local interaction only lead to slower convergence, but the results are likelier to be in the optimal region. In PSO the search starts with a randomly generated population of solutions called the "swarm of particles" in d-dimensional solution space. Each particle i is represented by its position denoted by $X_i = (x_{i1}, x_{i2}, \ldots, x_{id})$ in a d-dimensional space. A velocity vector $V_i = (v_{i1}, v_{i2}, \ldots, v_{id})$ is associated with every particle i.

The position of the particle is updated by use of its current velocity and previous position. The velocity equation is

$$V_i(t+1) = V_i(t) + c_1\varphi_1(p_{\text{ibest}} - X_i(t)) + c_2\varphi_2(p_{\text{Gbest}} - X_i(t)), \tag{1}$$

where $V_i(t+1)$ is the velocity of particle i at the $(t+1)$th iteration, $X_i(t)$ is the position of particle i at the tth iteration; $p_{\text{ibest}} = (p_{i1}, p_{i2}, \ldots, p_{id})$ is the best position of particle i achieved so far, $p_{\text{Gbest}} = (p_{g1}, p_{g2}, \ldots, p_{gd})$ is the best position of the swarm achieved so far by any particle of the swarm, c_1 and c_2 are positive learning constants which determine the rate at which the particle moves toward the its best position and the global best position respectively, and φ_1 and φ_2 are random numbers in the range (0,1). The position equation of the particle is

$$X_i(t+1) = X_i(t) + V_i(t+1). \tag{2}$$

The position is updated until a stopping criterion is met or the maximum number of iterations has been reached. Many improvements have been suggested over the canonical PSO that attempt to overcome problems such as explosion [21].

Considerable research on PSO is centered around the Gbest PSO model, where a particle is attracted toward the best position found in the entire swarm. The Gbest PSO, however, is susceptible to premature and/or false convergence over multimodal fitness landscapes [21,26]. To overcome the problems faced with the Gbest version of PSO, a neighborhood is identified for each particle. The PSO is then modified so that the social influence is dictated by the best position found in the neighborhood of each individual. The relationship of influence is thus defined by a social network, which is called a "population topology" [21,26–28]. A number of topologies have been proposed in the literature. The most commonly used topologies are the Gbest, Lbest, ring, and von Neumann topologies. Fig. 1 shows these topologies. In the Lbest topology, each particle is stochastically attracted to the best solution that any particle in its neighborhood has found.

As Shi [29] notes, the global version of PSO (i.e., Gbest) converges fast, but with potential to converge to a local minimum, while Lbest versions of PSO may have a better chance of finding the solutions slowly. Kennedy [30] also claims that PSO with small neighborhoods might perform better on complex problems, whereas PSO with large neighborhoods performs better for simple problems. Others [27] have recommended that a PSO with von Neumann topology be used as it may perform better than other PSOs with regularly shaped neighborhoods. Several experiments have now shown that topologies may play an important role in the performance of a PSO and its variants [21,26–30].

More recent proposals are the nonclique static topology [31], the singly linked topology [32] in which members share information at different rates, and the stochastic star topology [33] in which the communication structure is probabilistically defined. Further, in an attempt at hybridization, Hamdan [34] has proposed combining, star, ring, and von Neumann topologies in the same algorithm. The algorithm combines the idea of the Gbest model with the idea of the Lbest model. Typical topologies use static arrangements of particles. Topologies may also allow restructuring with some limitations. Jones and Soule [35] have shown that dynamically redefining a topology by stochastically reorganizing the swarm at periodic intervals improves performance for certain types of problems.

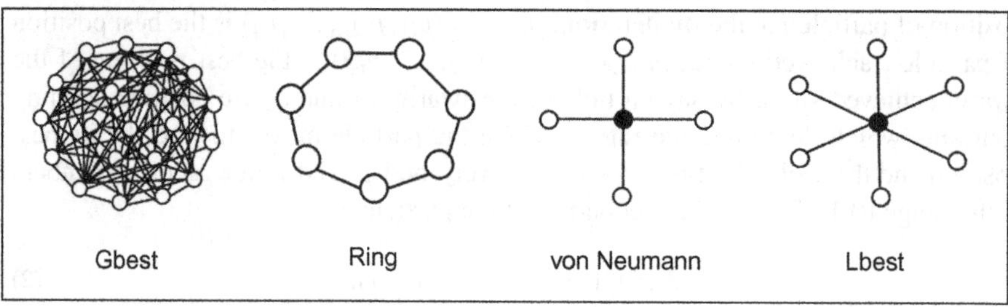

FIG. 1

Topologies.

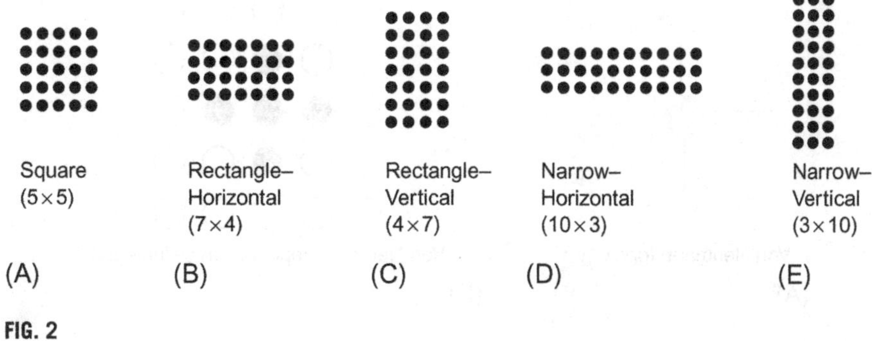

FIG. 2

Cellular grid structures.

The variation operator (rotation gate [24]) in a QEA requires an attractor to determine the direction of rotation of the chosen Q-bit to update it. Thus the selection of attractors plays an important role in the evolution process in a QEA and is dependent on local and global migrations in a canonical QEA [16]. The idea of population topologies has been borrowed from PSO and has been implemented in the selection of attractors in a canonical QEA [17]. The local migration [24] is related to topologies in this work by restriction of the selection of Lbest to the neighborhood defined by the topology [21,22].

Von Neumann topology has been primarily investigated and implemented with three types of cellular/fine-grained structure (i.e., square, rectangular, and narrow) as shown in Fig. 2. Every individual is located in a unique position on a two-dimensional toroidal grid. The size of the grid is G_xXG_y, where G_x is the number of rows and G_y is the number of columns. The neighborhood on the grid is defined by von Neumann topology, which has five individuals (i.e., the current individual and its immediate north, east, west, and south neighbors). Thus it is also called "NEWS neighborhood topology" or "linear5 (L5) neighborhood topology." The individual is linked to four others in its neighborhood in a cubic lattice-type arrangement as shown in Fig. 3. This work investigates the effect of static, dynamic, and adaptive topologies in random form on the performance of quantum-inspired algorithms.

3 CELLULAR QUANTUM-INSPIRED EVOLUTIONARY ALGORITHMS

QEAs are characterized by Q-bit representation and variation operators such as rotation gates. A QEA maintains a population of individuals in Q-bits. A Q-bit coded individual can probabilistically represent a linear superposition of states in

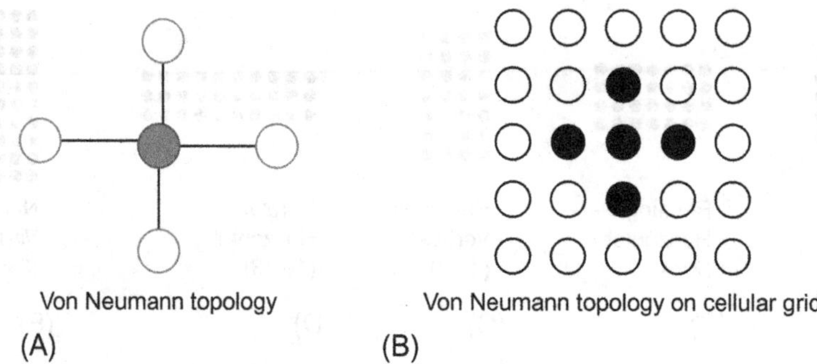

FIG. 3

Von Neumann topology.

the search space. Thus it has better characteristics of population diversity than other representations [24]. A Q-bit is represented as follows:

$$q_i = \begin{bmatrix} \alpha_i \\ \beta_i \end{bmatrix}, \tag{3}$$

where $|\alpha_i|^2$ is the probability of Q-bit q_i being in state 0, $|0\rangle$ and $|\beta_i|^2$ is the probability of Q-bit q_i being in state 1, $|1\rangle$, and

$$|\alpha_i|^2 + |\beta_i|^2 = 1. \tag{4}$$

Further, α_i and β_i are real numbers for QEA implementations discussed in this chapter.

In a binary-coded QEA, each individual vector is represented by a set of Q-bits in a chromosome string as [24]

$$Q(t) = \begin{bmatrix} \alpha_1 & \alpha_2 & \ldots & \alpha_n \\ \beta_1 & \beta_2 & \ldots & \beta_n \end{bmatrix}, \tag{5}$$

such that $|\alpha_i|^2 + |\beta_i|^2 = 1$, where $i = 1$ to n.

Measurement is a process of generating binary strings from the Q-bit string, Q. To observe the Q-bit string (Q), a string consisting of random numbers between 0 and 1 (R) is generated. The ith element of the binary string, b_i, is set to 0 if the ith random number, r_i, is less than $|\alpha_i|^2$ and is set to 1 otherwise.

A quantum gate is used to update the elements of the Q-bit so that they move toward the attractor [16]. Thus there is a higher probability of generating solution strings which are similar to the attractor in subsequent iterations. One such quantum gate is the rotation gate, which is unitary in nature and updates the Q-bit as follows:

$$\begin{bmatrix} {\alpha_i}^{t+1} \\ {\beta_i}^{t+1} \end{bmatrix} = \begin{bmatrix} \cos(\Delta\theta_i) & -\sin(\Delta\theta_i) \\ \sin(\Delta\theta_i) & \cos(\Delta\theta_i) \end{bmatrix} \begin{bmatrix} {\alpha_i}^{t} \\ {\beta_i}^{t} \end{bmatrix}, \quad (6)$$

where ${\alpha_i}^{t+1}$ and ${\beta_i}^{t+1}$ denote probabilities of the ith Q-bit in the $(t+1)$th iteration, and $\Delta\theta_i$ is the angle of rotation. The magnitude of $\Delta\theta_i$ is a tunable parameter and is problem specific, and the sign $(+/-)$ is dependent on the attractor (i.e., it rotates the Q-bit in the direction of the attractor so as to improve the probability of the Q-bit collapsing in the same state as the attractor on measurement). It takes into account the relative current fitness level of the individual and the attractor and also their binary bit values for determination of the magnitude and direction of rotation. The lookup table for selection of $\Delta\theta_i$ is given in [24] as Table 1. Thus the quantum gate supports elitism, whereas the measurement operator helps to preserve diversity by probabilistic collapse to state 0 or state 1.

Initialization of Q-bits has been performed randomly (i.e., Q-bits have been assigned values between -1 and $+1$ by our generating them randomly, while taking into account the normalization criteria described in Eq. (4). The termination condition is based on the number of generations.

The algorithm for the static random topology is similar to that given in [17,20] for the fine-grained population model, except that the size of the toroidal grid has been changed to accommodate square, rectangular, and narrow grids. The algorithm with static random topology is as follows:

1. $t = 0$; population size $= N$, topology $=$ type, neighborhood size $=$ NS, grid size $= G_x \times G_y$;
2. initialize $Q_1(t), \ldots, Q_N(t)$ and compute *Neighborhood_list*();
3. make $P_1(t), \ldots, P_N(t)$ by observing the states of $Q_1(t), \ldots, Q_N(t)$ respectively;
4. if repair is required, then repair $P_i(t)$, $i = 1, \ldots, N$;
5. evaluate $P_1(t), \ldots, P_N(t)$ and store the result in $OP_1(t), \ldots, OP_N(t)$;
6. store the global, neighborhood, and individual best solutions in $GB(t)$, $NB_i(t-1)$, and $IB_i(t)$ respectively, $i = 1, \ldots, N$;
while (termination condition is not met) {
7. $t = t + 1$;
for each individual $i = 1, \ldots, N$ {
8. determine attractor $A_i(t) = NB_i(t-1)$;
9. apply quantum gate(s) on $Q_i(t-1)$ to update it to $Q_i(t)$;
10. make $P_i(t)$ by observing the states of $Q_i(t)$;
11. if repair is required, then repair $P_i(t)$;
12. evaluate $P_i(t)$ and store the result in $OP_i(t)$;
13. store the best solutions among $IBi(t-1)$ and $OP_i(t)$ in $IB_i(t)$;
14. store the neighborhood best solution among $NB_i(t-1)$ and $Best\_Neighbor_i(t)$ in $NB_i(t-1)$;

15. store the Gbest solution $GB(t-1)$ among $IB_i(t)$ in$GB(t)$; }}

In step 1, initialize the population size N, the type of topology (i.e., Von Neumann, GBest, or ring), the size of the neighborhood, and the grid size in the case of von Neumann topology. In step 2 the Q-bit register $Q(t)$ containing Q-bit strings $Q_1(t), \ldots, Q_N(t)$ is initialized randomly and the neighborhood list is computed on the basis of the topology, neighborhood size, and grid size. In step 3 the binary solutions represented by $P_1(t), \ldots, P_N(t)$ are constructed by measurement of the states of $Q_1(t), \ldots, Q_N(t)$ respectively. In step 4, if repair is required in binary solutions $P_i(t)$, then repair is performed. Repair is required in the case of knapsack problems, in which a random repair strategy is used (i.e., when the weight of selected items exceeds the capacity of the knapsack, then items are chosen randomly from the selected items and are removed until the weight of items in the knapsack is not less than the capacity of the knapsack. In step 5 the binary solution is evaluated to give a measure of its fitness $OP_i(t)$, where $OP_i(t)$ represents the objective function value. In step 6 the initial global, neighborhood, and individual best solutions are selected among the binary solutions $OP_i(t)$, and are stored in $GB(t)$, $NB_i(t-1)$, and $IB_i(t)$ respectively; the neighborhood best solution is determined from the individuals in the neighborhood list of every individual. In step 8 the attractor $A_i(t)$ for the ith individual as the $NB_i(t-1)$. In step 9, update $Q_i(t-1)$ to $Q_i(t)$ using quantum gates, which are quantum rotation gates. In step 10 the binary solutions in $P_i(t)$ are formed by measurement of the states of $Q_i(t)$ as in step 3. In step 11, if repair is required, then it is performed as in step 4, and in step 12, each binary solution is evaluated for the fitness as in step 5. In steps 13, 14, and 15 the global, neighborhood, and individual best solutions are selected and stored in $GB(t)$, $NB_i(t-1)$ and $IB_i(t)$ respectively on the basis of a comparison between previous and current best solutions.

The algorithm for the dynamic random topology is the same as that for the static random topology except that when a prespecified number of generations, termed the "transitional generation number" (TGN), have been executed, then the structure of the grid is changed (i.e., the neighborhood list is changed according to a preprogrammed structure, e.g., narrow to square/rectangular and square/rectangular to narrow). This leads to migration of individuals as the neighbors migrate and form new neighborhoods. Only one fixed transition point was reported in [22] (i.e., at half the total number of generations required to solve a problem). However, to understand the impact of dynamic changes in the shape of the grid on the performance of any algorithm, a number of transition points should be tested, which was not done in [22] but has been done in this work. Further, we have also empirically investigated the impact of interleaving two different grid shapes until a fixed number of generations before switching to exploitation using different grid shapes. The extensive testing of various dynamic random topologies has led to the selection of the best performing combination of grid shapes, which have been used as the basis for investigating adaptive random topologies.

To elaborate further, the QEA with dynamic random topology differs from the algorithm for static random topology in step 1, where we consider two grid sizes, say, A and B. In step 1 of dynamic random topology, we initialize the two grid sizes and also specify the value of the TGN at which transition will occur from grid size A to grid size B and an additional step in the while loop is introduced as step 13 given below:

13. **If** *t* is less than the TGN **then**
grid size = A;
Compute *Neighborhood_list*();
else
grid size = B;
Compute *Neighborhood_list*();
End

In step 13, in the while loop, if the current generation *t* is less than the TGN, then grid size A would be used, otherwise grid size B would be used and neighborhood list would be computed accordingly.

The algorithm for the adaptive random topology is same as that for the static random topology except that when the rate of convergence determined by the change in parameters such as the average fitness and entropy of the fitness of the individuals in the population from one generation to the next crosses prespecified threshold values, then the structure of the grid is changed (i.e., the neighborhood list is changed according to a predecided structure, e.g., narrow to square/rectangular and square/rectangular to narrow). It has been reported [22] that a narrow structure leads to better exploration and a square structure leads to more exploitation; thus whenever slow convergence is observed along with an increase in the entropy of the fitness of solution vectors, then the shape is changed to squarer so that exploitation can be improved. Similarly, whenever fast convergence is observed with a decrease in the entropy of the fitness of solution vectors, then the shape is changed to narrower so that exploration can be improved.

To elaborate further, the QEA with adaptive random topology differs from the algorithm for static random topology in step 1, where we consider two grid sizes, say, A and B. In step 1 of the adaptive random topology, we initialize the two grid sizes and also specify the value of the transition threshold ϵ, at which transition will either occur from narrow grid size A to square grid size B or vice versa and an additional step in the while loop is introduced as step 13 given below:

13. **If** Slow_Convergence **then**
grid size = B; //square
else if Fast_Convergence **then**
grid size = A; //narrow
else
continue without changing grid size;
End

In step 13, in the while loop, if the convergence rate is slower than the prespecified threshold value, then square grid size B would be used; however, if the convergence rate is faster than the prespecified threshold value, then narrow grid size A would be used, otherwise the grid size being used is not changed.

Three feedback parameters have been used for implementation of adaptive topology in this study (i.e., average fitness of the population, entropy of the fitness of the best solution vector of individuals in the population, and a combination of both). The rate of convergence determines slow and fast convergence and has been computed with use of threshold ϵ [22].

The change in the feedback parameter of the population is computed between the current generation and the previous generation. That is, let ${y_{av}}^t$ be the feedback parameter of the population at the current tth generation and ${y_{av}}^{t-1}$ be the feedback parameter of the population at the previous $(t-1)$th generation. Then $\Delta {y_{av}}^t = {y_{av}}^t - {y_{av}}^{t-1}$, and $\Delta {y_{av}}^{t-1} = {y_{av}}^{t-1} - {y_{av}}^{t-2}$. The condition for slow convergence is satisfied if $\Delta {y_{av}}^t < (1+\epsilon) \times \Delta {y_{av}}^{t-1}$ and the condition for fast convergence is satisfied if $\Delta {y_{av}}^t > (2-\epsilon) \times \Delta {y_{av}}^{t-1}$ [22].

4 BENCHMARK PROBLEMS

P-PEAKS and knapsack problem instances have been used as test cases for determining the performance of the SCLQEA, the DCLQEA, and the ACLQEA.

4.1 P-PEAKS PROBLEMS

The idea of P-PEAKS [36] is to generate P random N-bit strings that represent the location of P peaks in the search space. The fitness value of a string, x, is the hamming distance (*Ham_Dist*) between this string and the closest peak, divided by N as shown in Eq. (7):

$$f_{\text{P-PEAKS}}(\bar{x}) = \frac{1}{N} \max_{1 \le i \le n} \{N - Ham\_Dist(\bar{x}, Peak_i)\}. \tag{7}$$

Using a higher (or lower) number of peaks, we obtain more (or less) epistatic problems. The maximum fitness value for the problem instances is 1.0 [22]. It is a multimodal problem generator, which is an easily parameterizable task with a tunable degree of difficulty. The advantage of using a problem generator is that it removes the opportunity to hand-tune algorithms to a particular problem, thus allowing a large fairness while one is comparing the performance of different algorithms or different instances of the same algorithm. It helps in evaluating the algorithms on a high number of random problem instances so that the predictive power of the results for the problem class as a whole is very high. Two P-PEAKS problems have been used in this work with a size of 1000 and 20 peaks in the first instance and 1000 peaks in the second instance.

4.2 0-1 KNAPSACK PROBLEMS

These are profit maximization problems in which there are n items of different profit and weight available for selection. The selection is made to maximize the profit while keeping the weight of the selected items below the capacity of the knapsack [37]. The problem is formulated as follows.

Given a set of n items and a knapsack of capacity C, select a subset of the items to maximize the profit $f(x)$:

$$f(x) = \sum Pt_i \times x_i \tag{8}$$

subject to the condition

$$\sum Wt_i \times x_i \leq C, \tag{9}$$

where $x_i = (x_1, \ldots, x_n)$, x_i is 0 or 1, Pt_i is the profit of item i, and Wt_i is the weight of item i. If the ith item is selected for the knapsack, $x_i = 1$, otherwise $x_i = 0$.

We have used 34 different types of problem instances reported in [38] with uncorrelated, weakly correlated, strongly correlated, multiple strongly correlated, profit ceiling, and circle data sets with different dimensions. The problems are described as follows:

1. Uncorrelated instances: The weights Wt_i and the profits Pt_i are random integers uniformly distributed in [10, 100]. The problem instances used in this work are given in Table 1 (KP1 to KP7).
2. Weakly correlated instances: The weights Wt_i are random integers uniformly distributed in [10, 100] and the profits Pt_i are random integers uniformly distributed in $[Wt_i - 10, Wt_i + 10]$. The problem instances used in this work are given in Table 2 (KP8 to KP14).
3. Strongly correlated instances: The weights Wt_i are random integers uniformly distributed in [10, 100] and the profits Pt_i are set to $Wt_i + 10$. The problem instances used in this work are given in Table 3 (KP15 to KP19).
4. Multiple strongly correlated instances: The weights Wt_i are randomly distributed in [10, 100]. If the weight Wt_i is divisible by 6, then we set $Pt_i = Wt_i + 30$, otherwise we set $Pt_i = Wt_i + 20$. The problem instances used in this work are given in Table 4 (KP20 to KP24).
5. Profit ceiling instances: The weights Wt_i are randomly distributed in [10, 100] and the profits Pt_i are set to $Pt_i = 3Wt_i/3$. The problem instances used in this work are given in Table 5 (KP25 to KP29).
6. Circle instances: The weights Wt_i are randomly distributed in [10, 100] and the profits Pt_i are set to $Pt_i = d \times \sqrt{(4R^2 - (Wt_i - 2R)^2)}$. We choose $d = 2/3$, $R = 10$. The problem instances used in this work are given in Table 6 (KP30 to KP34).

   For each data set, the value of the capacity $C = 0.75 \times \sum Wt_i$.

Table 1 Uncorrelated Knapsack Problem Instances

Problem	Dimension	Target Weight	Total Weight	Total Value
KP1	150	6471	8628	8111
KP2	200	8328	11,104	10,865
KP3	300	12,383	16,511	16,630
KP4	500	20,363	27,150	28,705
KP5	800	33,367	44,489	44,005
KP6	1000	41,948	55,930	54,764
KP7	1200	49,485	65,980	66,816

Table 2 Weakly correlated knapsack problem instances

Problem	Dimension	Target Weight	Total Weight	Total Value
KP8	150	6403	8538	8504
KP9	200	8358	11,144	11,051
KP10	300	12,554	16,739	16,778
KP11	500	20,758	27,677	27,821
KP12	800	33,367	44,489	44,491
KP13	1000	41,849	55,799	55,683
KP14	1200	49,808	66,411	56,811

Table 3 Strongly Correlated Knapsack Problem Instances

Problem	Dimension	Target Weight	Total Weight	Total Value
KP15	300	12,247	16,329	19,329
KP16	500	21,305	28,407	33,406
KP17	800	33,367	44,489	52,489
KP18	1000	40,883	54,511	64,511
KP19	1200	50,430	67,240	79,240

Table 4 Multiple Strongly Correlated Knapsack Problem Instances

Problem	Dimension	Target Weight	Total Weight	Total Value
KP20	300	12,908	17,211	23,651
KP21	500	20,259	27,012	37,903
KP22	800	32,767	43,689	61,140
KP23	1000	42,442	56,589	77,940
KP24	1200	50,222	66,963	92,653

Table 5 Profit Ceiling Knapsack Problem Instances

Problem	Dimension	Target Weight	Total Weight	Total Value
KP25	300	12,666	16,888	17,181
KP26	500	19,811	26,415	26,913
KP27	800	32,011	42,681	43,497
KP28	1000	42,253	56,337	57,381
KP29	1200	50,208	66,944	68,157

Table 6 Circle Knapsack Problem Instances

Problem	Dimension	Target Weight	Total Weight	Total Value
KP30	300	12,554	16,739	26,448
KP31	500	20,812	27,749	43,880
KP32	800	32,581	43,441	69,527
KP33	1000	42,107	56,143	88,220
KP34	1200	49,220	65,627	104,287

5 TESTING, RESULTS, AND ANALYSIS

The testing was performed to evaluate the performance of cellular QEAs with random Von Neumann population topology. The set of parameters used for testing cellular QEAs has been widely used in work reported in the literature [11] and is given in Table 7. Further, the SCLQEA with Von Neumann topology was converted to dynamic and adaptive versions as suggested in [22] and tested to study the effect of such a change on the performance of QEAs. Moreover, a comparative study was performed between the ACLQEA and a GA, differential evolution (DE), classic cuckoo search (CS), and a hybrid CS algorithm with an improved shuffled frog leaping algorithm (CSISFLA) [38] on a set of 34 knapsack problems (KP1 to KP34).

5.1 STATIC RANDOM TOPOLOGIES

The value of the parameters used for all the instances of the SCLQEA in all the problems are given in Table 7. A population size of 48 (due to the grid size) and 1 as the number of observation per Q-bit in each generation were used in all the algorithms. The local migration period is one generation for all the algorithms. Different toroidal grid sizes with von Neumann topology having a neighborhood size of five individuals were used to study its effect on the performance of QEAs. The different toroidal grid sizes were selected so that the population size remained at 48. The stopping criterion is the maximum number of permissible iterations, which depends on the problem.

Table 7 Value of Parameters

Parameter	Value
θ_1 to θ_8	$0, 0, 0.01\pi, 0, -0.01\pi, 0, 0, 0$ respectively
Population size	48
Number of observations	1
Local migration period (iterations)	1
Neighborhood topology	Von Neumann
Neighborhood size	5
Stopping criterion (iterations)	Problem specific

Table 8 Comparative Study of the Static Cellular Quantum-Inspired Evolutionary Algorithm on P-PEAKS Problem Instances With Size 1000 and 20 or 1000 Peaks

Peaks	Population Size	Grid Shape	Best	Worst	Average	Median	Standard Deviation	Average NFEs
20	48	8 × 6	1.00	1.00	1.00	1.00	0.00	79,440
	48	12 × 4	1.00	1.00	1.00	1.00	0.00	83,709
	48	4 × 12	1.00	1.00	1.00	1.00	0.00	83,923
	48	6 × 8	1.00	1.00	1.00	1.00	0.00	84,586
	48	3 × 16	1.00	1.00	1.00	1.00	0.00	89,699
	48	16 × 3	1.00	1.00	1.00	1.00	0.00	94,216
1000	48	8 × 6	1.00	1.00	1.00	1.00	0.00	88,506
	48	6 × 8	1.00	1.00	1.00	1.00	0.00	92,218
	48	4 × 12	1.00	1.00	1.00	1.00	0.00	94,621
	48	12 × 4	1.00	1.00	1.00	1.00	0.00	97,272
	48	16 × 3	1.00	1.00	1.00	1.00	0.00	108,709
	48	3 × 16	1.00	1.00	1.00	1.00	0.00	113,245

NFEs, number of function evaluations.

5.1.1 P-PEAKS problems

The results of our testing the SCLQEA on P-PEAKS problem instances are presented in Table 8. Thirty independent runs of each instance of the algorithm were executed, and the best, worst, average, median, and standard deviation of the fitness along with the average number of function evaluations were recorded. The maximum number of generations was 3000.

5.1.2 0-1 knapsack problems

The results of our testing the SCLQEA on uncorrelated (KP1), strongly correlated (KP16), and profit ceiling (KP28) instances of 0-1 knapsack problems are presented in Table 9. Thirty independent runs of every instance of the algorithm were executed

Table 9 Comparative Study of the Static Cellular Quantum-Inspired Evolutionary Algorithm in KP1, KP16, and KP28

Problem	Grid Shape	Best	Worst	Average	Median	Standard Deviation	Average NFEs
KP1	8 × 6	7498	7493	7496.6	7497	1.33	33,838.4
	6 × 8	7498	7494	7496.8	7497	1.06	36,188.8
	4 × 12	7498	7490	7496.5	7497	1.66	36,246.4
	16 × 3	7498	7493	7496.8	7497	1.05	38,864
	12 × 4	7498	7487	7496.7	7497	1.93	40,144
	3 × 16	7498	7494	7497.1	7497	0.69	40,297.6
KP16	12 × 4	25,525	25,495	25,515	25,515	6.43	54,038.4
	8 × 6	25,525	25,505	25,519.3	25,515	5.68	54,201.6
	4 × 12	25,525	25,505	25,517.7	25,515	6.40	55,430.4
	6 × 8	25,525	25,505	25,518	25,515	5.96	55,475.2
	16 × 3	25,525	25,505	25,514.3	25,515	6.40	58,948.8
	3 × 16	25,525	25,505	25,517	25,515	5.51	63,233.6
KP28	8 × 6	43,284	43,272	43,277.6	43,278	3.50	90,804.8
	6 × 8	43,284	43,272	43,278	43,278	2.61	92,790.4
	4 × 12	43,281	43,269	43,274.1	43,275	3.45	92,134.4
	12 × 4	43,278	43,266	43,273.3	43,273.5	3.02	92,782.4
	3 × 16	43,275	43,263	43,269.4	43,269	3.02	90,996.8
	16 × 3	43,272	43,263	43,267.6	43,269	3.02	91,798.4

NFEs, number of function evaluations.

and the best, worst, average, median, and standard deviation of the fitness along with average number of function evaluations were recorded. The maximum number of generations was 2000.

In Table 9 the performance of six instances of the SCLQEA are sorted according to their fitness and average number of function evaluations. The performance of the SCLQEA with various topologies varies with the problem instances. In general, the SCLQEA with 8 × 6 grid shape performed better than all other five instances of the SCLQEA as it was able to reach optima quickly in KP1 and KP28. It was slightly slower than the SCLQEA with 12 × 4 grid shape in KP16 but has better average and worse fitness than the SCLQEA with 12 × 4 grid shape. It appears that, in general, rectangular grid shapes closer to a square perform better than narrow grid shapes, indicating that the exploitation provided by the grid shape is helping the SCLQEA locate the optimum quickly in knapsack problem instances.

5.2 DYNAMIC RANDOM TOPOLOGY

The 8 × 6 grid shape performed the best in static random topology for a P-PEAKS problem of size 1000 and 20 peaks, so it was chosen for implementation of dynamic random topology along with 16 × 3 and 12 × 4 grid shapes. Initially, we performed the testing by taking two of them as pairs (i.e., the QEA would run with the first grid shape and then switch to the other grid shape at a fixed generation number, the TGN. The different pairs used in testing were 8 × 6 and 16 × 3; 16 × 3 and 8 × 6 ; and 12 × 4 and 8 × 6. They were tested to identify the best performing pair and investigate their exploration and exploitation behavior. Further, we also studies the effect of a change in the TGN by varying it from 100 to 250, 500, 750, 1000, and 1200.

The P-PEAKS problem instance with size 1000 and 20 peaks and knapsack problem KP20 were used for a detailed study of the effect of variations in the TGN in dynamic random topology. Table 10 presents the results of the study with 8 × 6 and 16 × 3 grid shapes; that is, the DCLQEA starts with von Neumann topology and 8 × 6 gird shape and then transitions to 16 × 3 grid shape at a prespecified TGN. All the DCLQEA instances were able to reach the optimum in all 30 runs. The fastest DCLQEA instance has a TGN of 1000; however, it is still slower than the with 8 × 6 grid shape with no transition or the TGN as the maximum number of generations (i.e., 3000). However, all the other instances are faster than the with 16 × 3 grid shape (i.e., when the TGN is zero, i.e., the transition occurs before even a single generation has been executed). Thus this suggests that dynamic topology is able to improve on the performance of the 16 × 3 grid shape. Further, it was suggested [22] that square/rectangular grid shapes with von Neumann topology can better exploit and narrow grid shapes with von Neumann topology can better explore the search space. The results indicate that the behavior of grid shapes with the DCLQEA is also same as it was with the cellular GA in [22]. The poor performance with a TGN of 100, 250, or 500 as compared with the other values can be explained as the DCLQEA is first doing exploitation and then switching to exploration, whereas it should be the other way around (i.e., the QEA should first explore and then do exploitation). The performance of the DCLQEA with a TGN of zero is also testimony that a narrow grid

Table 10 Performance of the Dynamic Cellular Quantum-Inspired Evolutionary Algorithm With Dynamic Random Topology (8 × 6 to 16 × 3) on the P-PEAKS Problem Instance With Size 1000 and 20 Peaks

Grid Shape	TGN	Best	Worst	Median		Standard Deviation	Average NFEs
8 × 6	100	1.00	1.00	1.00	1.00	0.00	82,571
	250	1.00	1.00	1.00	1.00	0.00	84,390
to	500	1.00	1.00	1.00	1.00	0.00	82,754
	750	1.00	1.00	1.00	1.00	0.00	81,032
16 × 3	1000	1.00	1.00	1.00	1.00	0.00	79,696
	1200	1.00	1.00	1.00	1.00	0.00	81,573
8 × 6	No transition	1.00	1.00	1.00	1.00	0.00	79,440
16 × 3	0	1.00	1.00	1.00	1.00	0.00	94,216

NFEs, number of function evaluations; TGN, transitional generation number.

shape is focused mainly on exploration so it is consuming a greater average number of function evaluations to reach the optimum.

To verify the explanation for the behavior of the DCLQEA with different TGNs as shown by the results in Table 10, we decided to investigate the behavior of the DCLQEA with 16 × 3 and 8 × 6 grid shapes with von Neumann topology using the same variations in the TGN. The results of the investigation are presented. in Table 11.

In Table 11 it can be seen that all the DCLQEA instances were able to reach the optimum in all 30 runs. The fastest DCLQEA instance has a TGN of 100; however, it is still slower than the DCLQEA with 8 × 6 grid shape with a TGN of zero (i.e., the transition occurs before even a single generation has been executed). However, all the other instances except for that with a TGN of 1000 are faster than the instance with 16 × 3 grid shape (i.e., when there is no transition or with the TGN as the maximum number of generations, i.e., 3000). Thus this suggests that dynamic topology is able to improve on the performance of the DCLQEA with 16 × 3 grid shape. It was also observed that as the TGN was increased, the performance deteriorated (i.e., if the explanation to describe the behavior shown in Table 10 is correct, then more exploration is slowing down the convergence of the DCLQEA). This points to further reduction of the exploration, which one can do can either by lowering the TGN to 50 or by changing the grid shape to narrower such as 12 × 4. Table 12 presents the results for the performance of the DCLQEA with a TGN of 50. It can be seen that the performance of the DCLQEA has deteriorated as compared with its performance with a TGN of 100. Therefore we investigated replacement of 16 × 3 grid shape with 12 × 4 grid shape.

Table 13 presents the results of the study with 12 × 4 and 8 × 6 grid shapes. All the DCLQEA instances were able to reach the optimum in all 30 runs. The fastest DCLQEA instance has a TGN of 100, and is faster than the DCLQEA with 8 × 6 grid

Table 11 Performance of the Dynamic Cellular Quantum-Inspired Evolutionary Algorithm With Dynamic Random Topology (16 × 3 to 8 × 6) on the P-PEAKS Problem Instance With Size 1000 and 20 Peaks

Grid Shape	TGN	Best	Worst	Average	Median	Standard Deviation	Average NFEs
8 × 6	100	1.00	1.00	1.00	1.00	0.00	83,408
	250	1.00	1.00	1.00	1.00	0.00	85,876
to	500	1.00	1.00	1.00	1.00	0.00	89,737
	750	1.00	1.00	1.00	1.00	0.00	91,083
16 × 3	1000	1.00	1.00	1.00	1.00	0.00	95,275
	1200	1.00	1.00	1.00	1.00	0.00	93,257
8 × 6	0	1.00	1.00	1.00	1.00	0.00	79,440
16 × 3	No transition	1.00	1.00	1.00	1.00	0.00	94,216

NFEs, number of function evaluations; TGN, transitional generation number.

Table 12 Performance of the Dynamic Cellular Quantum-Inspired Evolutionary Algorithm With Dynamic Random Topology (16 × 3 to 8 × 6) With a Transitional Generation Number (TGN) of 100 or 50 on the P-PEAKS Problem Instance With Size 1000 and 20 Peaks

Grid Shape	TGN	Best	Worst	Average	Median	Standard Deviation	Average NFEs
16 × 3 to 8 × 6	100	1.00	1.00	1.00	1.00	0.00	83,408
	50	1.00	1.00	1.00	1.00	0.00	84,857

NFEs, number of function evaluations.

Table 13 Performance of the Dynamic Cellular Quantum-Inspired Evolutionary Algorithm With Dynamic Random Topology (12 × 4 to 8 × 6) on the P-PEAKS Problem Instance With Size 1000 and 20 Peaks

Grid Shape	TGN	Best	Worst	Average	Median	Standard Deviation	Average NFEs
12 × 4 to 8 × 6	100	1.00	1.00	1.00	1.00	0.00	79,257
	250	1.00	1.00	1.00	1.00	0.00	80,990
	500	1.00	1.00	1.00	1.00	0.00	82,515
	750	1.00	1.00	1.00	1.00	0.00	83,044
	1000	1.00	1.00	1.00	1.00	0.00	84,992
	1200	1.00	1.00	1.00	1.00	0.00	83,406
8 × 6	0	1.00	1.00	1.00	1.00	0.00	79,440
12 × 4	No transition	1.00	1.00	1.00	1.00	0.00	83,709

NFEs, number of function evaluations; TGN, transitional generation number.

shape and a TGN of zero as well as that with 12 × 4 grid shape (i.e., when the TGN is the maximum number of generations, i.e., 3000). Thus this suggests that dynamic topology is able to improve on the performance of the 8 × 6 and 12 × 4 grid shapes. Further, it justifies the explanation and validates the suggestion made in [22] that square/rectangular grid shapes with von Neumann topology can better exploit and narrow grid shapes with von Neumann topology can better explore the search space. The results indicate that the behavior of grid shapes with the DCLQEA is also same as that with the cellular GA in [22].

It was suggested [22] that self-adaptive random topologies are better than dynamic random topologies as they require less parameter tuning. To design an effective cellular QEA with adaptive random topologies, we further investigated the behavior of the QEA. We used 12 × 4 and 8 × 6 grid shapes from the previous study of dynamic topology with a single point transition. The impact on the performance of the DCLQEA was studied when the grid shapes were interleaved until a fixed number of generations before it finally switched to only a square/rectangular grid shape for exploitation.

The results of the investigations of interleaving grid shapes are presented in Table 14. The DCLQEA was run for 100 generations with 12 × 4 grid shape and then switched to 8 × 6 grid shape and was run for another 100 generations and then again switched back and forth until a fixed number of generations, which was varied from until generation number 1100, 1300, 1500, and till the generation at which optimum value is reached. The performance of the DCLQEA improved considerably after interleaving was applied, which indicates that the nature of the QEA is such that alternate emphasis on exploration and exploitation improved the speed of convergence through still more improvement in the balance between exploration and exploitation. This further encourages the use of the adaptive technique suggested in [22] which might improve the performance of the cellular QEA even further.

Table 15 presents the results of the study on KP20, which has 8×6 and 16×3 grid shapes; that is, the DCLQEA starts with von Neumann topology and 8 × 6 gird shape and then transitions to 16 × 3 grid shape at a prespecified TGN. All the DCQEA instances reached the same best and median solutions in their 30 runs. The fastest DCLQEA instance has a TGN of 500. Thus this suggests that dynamic topology is able to improve on the performance of 8 × 6 and 16 × 3 grid shapes.

Table 16 presents the results of the study on KP20, which has 16 × 3 and 8 × 6 grid shapes; that is, the DCLQEA starts with von Neumann topology and 16 × 3 gird shape and then transitions to 8 × 6 grid shape at a prespecified TGN. All the DCLQEA instances reached the same best and median solutions in their 30 runs. The fastest DCLQEA instance has a TGN of 500. Thus this suggests that dynamic topology is able to improve on the performance of 8 × 6 and 16 × 3 grid shapes. Further, the DCLQEA with 16 × 3 to 8 × 6 grid shape required a greater number of function evaluations than the DCLQEA with 8 × 6 to 16 × 3 grid shape to reach the same best and median solutions, which suggests that the DCLQEA with 16 × 3 to

Table 14 Performance of the Dynamic Cellular Quantum-Inspired Evolutionary Algorithm With Interleaved Dynamic Random Topology (12 × 4 to 8 × 6) on the P-PEAKS Problem Instance With Size 1000 and 20 Peaks

Grid Shape	Interleaving Until	Best	Worst	Average	Median	Standard Deviation	Average NFEs
12 × 4 to 8 × 6	1100	1.00	1.00	1.00	1.00	0.00	75,675
	1300	1.00	1.00	1.00	1.00	0.00	74,789
	1500	1.00	1.00	1.00	1.00	0.00	73,946
	The end	1.00	1.00	1.00	1.00	0.00	73,931
	100	1.00	1.00	1.00	1.00	0.00	79,257
8 × 6	0	1.00	1.00	1.00	1.00	0.00	79,440
12 × 4	No transition	1.00	1.00	1.00	1.00	0.00	83,709

NFEs, number of function evaluations.

Table 15 Performance of the Dynamic Cellular Quantum-Inspired Evolutionary Algorithm With Dynamic Random Topology (8 × 6 to 16 × 3) on the KP20 Problem Instance

Grid Shape	TGN	Best	Worst	Average	Median	Standard Deviation	Average NFEs
8 × 6 to 16 × 3	100	18,388	18,348	18,371	18,368	10	36,412
	250	18,388	18,348	18,373	18,368	10	37,699
	500	18,388	18,348	18,369	18,368	9	31,961
	750	18,388	18,368	18,371	18,368	8	33,064
	1000	18,388	18,368	18,373	18,368	9	35,038
	1200	18,388	18,368	18,373	18,368	9	35,217
8 × 6	No transition	18,388	18,368	18,373	18,368	9	35,217
16 × 3	0	18,388	18,348	18,367	18,368	7	34,531

NFEs, number of function evaluations; TGN, transitional generation number.

Table 16 Performance of the Dynamic Cellular Quantum-Inspired Evolutionary Algorithm With Dynamic Random Topology (16 × 3 to 8 × 6) on the KP20 Problem Instance

Grid Shape	TGN	Best	Worst	Average	Median	Standard Deviation	Average NFEs
8 × 6 to 16 × 3	100	18,388	18,348	18,371	18,368	10	36,412
	250	18,388	18,368	18,373	18,368	9	34,939
	500	18,388	18,368	18,369	18,368	5	32,083
	750	18,388	18,348	18,369	18,368	7	35,744
	1000	18,388	18,348	18,371	18,368	9	39,184
	1200	18,388	18,348	18,369	18,368	9	39,633
8 × 6	0	18,388	18,368	18,373	18,368	9	35,217
16 × 3	No transition	18,388	18,348	18,367	18,368	7	34,531

NFEs, number of function evaluations; TGN, transitional generation number.

8 × 6 grid shape is doing more exploration than the DCLQEA with 8 × 6 to 16 × 3 grid shape.

Table 17 presents the results of the study on KP20, which has 12 × 4 and 8 × 6 grid shapes; that is, the DCLQEA starts with von Neumann topology and 12 × 4 gird shape and then transitions to 8 × 6 grid shape at a prespecified TGN. All the DCLQEA instances reached the same best and median solutions in their 30 runs. The fastest DCLQEA instance has a TGN of 250. Thus this suggests that dynamic topology is able to improve on the performance of 8 × 6 and 12 × 4 grid shapes. Further, the DCLQEA with 12 × 4 to 8 × 6 grid shape required a lower number of function evaluations than the DCLQEA with 8 × 6 to 16 × 3 and 16 × 3 to 8 × 6 grid

Table 17 Performance of the Dynamic Cellular Quantum-Inspired Evolutionary Algorithm With Dynamic Random Topology (12 × 4 to 8 × 6) on the KP20 Problem Instance

Grid Shape	TGN	Best	Worst	Average	Median	Standard Deviation	Average NFEs
12 × 4 to 8 × 6	100	18,388	18,348	18,369	18,368	7	32,310
	250	18,388	18,368	18,370	18,368	6	31,224
	500	18,388	18,348	18,369	18,368	9	31,980
	750	18,388	18,368	18,375	18,368	10	36,475
	1000	18,388	18,368	18,371	18,368	8	34,617
	1200	18,388	18,368	18,373	18,368	9	37,030
8 × 6	0	18,388	18,368	18,373	18,368	9	35,217
12 × 4	No transition	18,388	18,368	18,373	18,368	9	37,584

NFEs, number of function evaluations; TGN, transitional generation number.

Table 18 Performance of the Dynamic Cellular Quantum-Inspired Evolutionary Algorithm With Interleaved Dynamic Random Topology (12 × 4 to 8 × 6) on the KP20 Problem Instance

Grid Shape	Interleaving Until	Best	Worst	Average	Median	Standard Deviation	Average NFEs
12 × 4 to 8 × 6	750	18,388	18,368	18,374	18,368	9	32,200
	1100	18,388	18,368	18,376	18,368	10.0	34,371
	1300	18,388	18,368	18,376.7	18,368	10.1	35,177
	1500	18,388	18,368	18,378.7	18,388	10.1	38,878
	The end	18,388	18,368	18,379.3	18,388	10.1	40,726
8 × 6	0	18,388	18,348	18,370	18,368	9.6	33,676
12 × 4	No transition	18,388	18,368	18,372.7	18,368	8.6	37,584

NFEs, number of function evaluations.

shapes to reach the same best and median solutions. Further, it has better average and worst solutions as is evident from Tables 15–17, which suggests that the DCLQEA with 12 × 4 to 8 × 6 grid shape has more balanced exploration and exploitation than the DCLQEA with 8 × 6 to 16 × 3 and 16 × 3 to 8 × 6 grid shapes.

The result of the investigations of interleaving grid shapes on KP20 is presented in Table 18. The DCLQEA was run for 100 generations with 12 × 4 grid shape and then switched to 8 × 6 grid shape and was run for another 100 generations and then again switched back and forth until fixed number of generations, which was varied from 500 to the maximum number of generations, to study its impact. The performance with regard to the average fitness value in 30 runs of the DCLQEA improved considerably after interleaving was applied, which indicates that the nature of the QEA is such that alternate emphasis on exploration and exploitation improves the average fitness value, although the average number of function evaluations has increased, through still more improvement in the balance between exploration and exploitation.

5.3 ADAPTIVE RANDOM TOPOLOGY

We implemented the adaptive random topology by changing the grid shape after receiving feedback from the search process as the case [22]; that is, if the convergence rate is too slow, then the grid shape is changed to the shape that supports more exploitation, whereas if the convergence rate is too fast, this means that the grid shape should be switched to the shape that supports exploration as too fast convergence may cause the population to lose diversity quickly. The feedback is either the change in the average fitness value of the population from one generation to the next or the change in the entropy of the fitness of binary solution vectors from one generation to the next, or both.

Table 19 presents the results of the investigation with average fitness as the feedback parameter in the ACLQEA. The feedback threshold, ϵ, was varied from 0.005 to 0.15 and 12×4 and 8×6 grid shapes were used. The performance of the ACLQEA with adaptive random topology with average fitness as the feedback parameter is much better than the performance of the DCLQEA with interleaved dynamic random topology. The ACLQEA performed best when ϵ was less than or equal to 0.02. As ϵ increases from 0.02, the ACLQEA takes more time to reach the

Table 19 Performance of the Adaptive Cellular Quantum-Inspired Evolutionary Algorithm With 12×4 to 8×6 Grid Shape and Average Fitness as Feedback on the P-PEAKS Problem Instance With Size 1000 and 20 Peaks

Grid Shape	ϵ	Best	Worst	Average	Median	Standard Deviation	Average NFEs
12×4 to 8×6	0.005	1.00	1.00	1.00	1.00	0.00	67,806
	0.008	1.00	1.00	1.00	1.00	0.00	67,806
	0.010	1.00	1.00	1.00	1.00	0.00	67,806
	0.015	1.00	1.00	1.00	1.00	0.00	67,806
	0.020	1.00	1.00	1.00	1.00	0.00	67,806
	0.023	1.00	1.00	1.00	1.00	0.00	68,419
	0.025	1.00	1.00	1.00	1.00	0.00	68,688
	0.050	1.00	1.00	1.00	1.00	0.00	69,962
	0.100	1.00	1.00	1.00	1.00	0.00	70,864
	0.150	1.00	1.00	1.00	1.00	0.00	71,058

NFEs, number of function evaluations.

optimum, and this indicates that quick appropriate changes in grid shape help the ACLQEA find the peak quickly.

Table 20 presents the results of the investigation with fitness entropy in the ACLQEA. The feedback threshold, ϵ, was varied from 0.015 to 0.2 and 12×4 and 8×6 grid shapes were used. The overall performance of the ACLQEA with fitness entropy as the feedback parameter is better than the performance of the ACLQEA with average fitness as the feedback parameter. The ACLQEA using fitness entropy performed best when ϵ was 0.02. As ϵ increases or decreases from 0.02, the ACLQEA takes more time to reach the optimum; this indicates that quick appropriate changes in grid shape help the ACLQEA find the peak quickly.

Table 21 presents the results of the investigation with both average fitness and fitness entropy as the feedback parameters in the ACLQEA. The feedback

Table 20 Performance of the Adaptive Cellular Quantum-Inspired Evolutionary Algorithm With 12 × 4 to 8 × 6 Grid Shape and Fitness Entropy as Feedback on the P-PEAKS Problem Instance With Size 1000 and 20 Peaks

Grid Shape	ϵ	Best	Worst	Average	Median	Standard Deviation	Average NFEs
12 × 4 to 8 × 6	0.015	1.00	1.00	1.00	1.00	0.000	66,046
	0.020	1.00	1.00	1.00	1.00	0.000	65,621
	0.023	1.00	1.00	1.00	1.00	0.000	66,070
	0.025	1.00	1.00	1.00	1.00	0.000	66,070
	0.050	1.00	1.00	1.00	1.00	0.000	67,552
	0.100	1.00	1.00	1.00	1.00	0.000	66,731
	0.150	1.00	1.00	1.00	1.00	0.000	66,298
	0.200	1.00	1.00	1.00	1.00	0.000	67,309

NFEs, number of function evaluations.

Table 21 Performance of the Adaptive Cellular Quantum-Inspired Evolutionary Algorithm With 12 × 4 to 8 × 6 Grid Shape and Combined Average Fitness and Fitness Entropy as Feedback on the P-PEAKS Problem Instance With Size 1000 and 20 Peaks

Grid Shape	ϵ	Best	Worst	Average	Median	Standard Deviation	Average NFEs
12 × 4 to 8 × 6	0.025	1.00	1.00	1.00	1.00	0.00	72,842
	0.050	1.00	1.00	1.00	1.00	0.00	72,443
	0.100	1.00	1.00	1.00	1.00	0.00	70,442
	0.150	1.00	1.00	1.00	1.00	0.00	69,496
	0.200	1.00	1.00	1.00	1.00	0.00	71,126

NFEs, number of function evaluations.

Table 22 Performance of the Adaptive Cellular Quantum-Inspired Evolutionary Algorithm With 12 × 4 to 8 × 6 Grid Shape and Combined Average Fitness and Fitness Entropy as Feedback on the P-PEAKS Problem Instance With Size 1000 and 20 Peaks

Grid Shape	Feedback	ϵ	Best	Worst	Average	Median	Standard Deviation	Average NFEs
12 × 4	Fitness	0.015	18,388	18,368	18,376	18,368	9.9	31,536
		0.020	18,388	18,368	18,376	18,368	10.0	30,926
		0.025	18,388	18,368	18,376	18,368	10.1	31,816
to	Entropy	0.015	18,388	18,368	18,381	18,388	9.6	33,042
		0.020	18,388	18,368	18,383	18,388	9.0	32,242
		0.025	18,388	18,368	18,381	18,388	9.6	33,123
8 × 6	Fitness and entropy	0.100	18,388	18,368	18,371	18,368	6.9	34,024
		0.150	18,388	18,368	18,371	18,368	6.9	34,024
		0.200	18,388	18,368	18,371	18,368	6.9	34,024

NFEs, number of function evaluations.

threshold, ϵ, was varied from 0.025 to 0.200 and 12 × 4 and 8 × 6 grid shapes were used. The ACLQEA performed best when ϵ was 0.150. As ϵ increases or decreases from 0.15, the ACLQEA takes more time to reach the optimum; this indicates that appropriate changes in the grid shape help the ACLQEA find the peak in quickly. The performance of the ACLQEA with combined average fitness and fitness entropy as feedback was not as good as that with either of them individually but the performance was still better than that of interleaved dynamic random topologies.

The DCLQEA with interleaved dynamic topologies performed better than the SCLQEA with static random topologies (i.e., six static random topology configurations were investigated to arrive at the best one). The ACLQEA with adaptive random topologies performed better than the DCLQEA with dynamic random topologies. The ACLQEA with fitness entropy as the feedback parameter and feedback threshold $\epsilon = 0.02$ performed better than all the topologies investigated in this work for the P-PEAKS problem of size 1000 and with 20 peaks.

Similarly, Table 22 shows that the ACLQEA with fitness entropy as the feedback parameter and feedback threshold $\epsilon = 0.02$ performed better than all the topologies investigated in this work for knapsack problem instance KP20.

The cellular QEA with random topologies was used to solving the P-PEAKS problem with problem size 1000 and 1000 peaks, with the best configurations and parameters derived from experiments reported in Tables 8–21. Table 23 presents the result of the study and shows that adaptive random topology with fitness entropy as the feedback parameter and $\epsilon = 0.02$ performs the best. The dynamic random topology with continuous interleaving performs better than the dynamic random topology with a TGN of 100 as well as the best performing static random topology.

Table 23 Performance of Cellular Quantum-Inspired Evolutionary Algorithm With All the Random Topologies (12 × 4 to 8 × 6) on the P-PEAKS Problem Instance With Size 1000 and 1000 Peaks

Nature of Random Topology	Grid Shape	Best	Worst	Average	Median	Standard Deviation	Average NFEs
Static	8 × 6	1.00	1.00	1.00	1.00	0.00	88,506
Dynamic (transition—100)	12 × 4 to 8 × 6	1.00	1.00	1.00	1.00	0.00	87,891
Dynamic (interleaving—continuous)	12 × 4 to 8 × 6	1.00	1.00	1.00	1.00	0.00	85,403
Adaptive (fitness, $\epsilon = 0.02$)	12 × 4 to 8 × 6	1.00	1.00	1.00	1.00	0.00	78,016
Adaptive (entropy, $\epsilon = 0.02$)	12 × 4 to 8 × 6	1.00	1.00	1.00	1.00	0.00	74,139

NFEs, number of function evaluations.

5.4 COMPARATIVE STUDY

The performance of the ACLQEA with fitness entropy as the feedback parameter and $\epsilon = 0.02$ was compared with that of state-of-the-art techniques, which include the GA [39], DE [40,41], CS [42], and CSISFLA [38], with the parameters given in Table 24 on 34 knapsack benchmark problems (KP1 to KP34) detailed in Tables 2–6. The remaining parameters of the ACLQEA, with grid shape of 12 × 4 and 8 × 6, are same as those given in Table 7. Thirty independent runs of the ACLQEA were executed for 2000 generations, and the best, worst, average, median, and standard deviation of the fitness were recorded.

Tables 25 and 26 present the statistical results of the five algorithms on seven uncorrelated instances of the knapsack problem (KP1 to KP7). The ACLQEA outperforms GA, DE, CS and CSISFLA on KP1 to KP6 on all the statistical parameters. In KP7, CSISFLA has better Best and Worst solutions and CS has a better best solution than ACLQEA, however, ACLQEA has better median and average solution than all other algorithms.

Table 27 and 28 presents the statistical results for the five algorithms on seven weakly correlated instances of the knapsack problem (KP8 to KP14). ACLQEA outperforms the GA for all the statistical parameters in all seven weakly correlated problem instances. However, the ACLQEA performance is inferior to DE and CSISFLA on small-dimension problems such as KP8 and KP9. DE produced better results in KP10. CS produced better best results in KP12, KP13, and KP14, but

Table 24 Parameter Settings of the Genetic Algorithm (GA) [39], Differential Evolution (DE) [40,41], Cuckoo Search (CS) [42], and Cuckoo Search Algorithm With an Improved Shuffled Frog Leaping Algorithm (CSISFLA) [38]

Algorithm	Parameter	Value
GA [39]	Population size	100
	Crossover probability	0.6
	Mutation probability	0.001
DE [40,41]	Population size	100
	Crossover probability	0.9
	Amplification factor	0.3
CS [42]	Population size	40
	Egg laying probability	0.25
CSISFLA [38]	Memeplexes	4
	Frogs	10
	Mutation probability	0.15

Table 25 Comparative Study Between the Genetic Algorithm (GA), Differential Evolution (DE), Cuckoo Search (CS), Cuckoo Search Algorithm With an Improved Shuffled Frog Leaping Algorithm (CSISFLA), and Adaptive Cellular Quantum-Inspired Evolutionary Algorithm (ACLQEA) Using Statistical Results on Uncorrelated Knapsack Problem Instances

Problem	Algorithm	Best	Worst	Average	Median	Standard Deviation
KP1	GA	7316	6978	7200	7208	75.78
	DE	7475	7433	7471	7473	7.68
	CS	7472	7358	7403	7405	27.82
	CSISFLA	7475	7467	7473	7474	1.56
	ACLQEA	7498	7495	7497	7497	0.81
KP2	GA	9673	9227	9503	9507	97.39
	DE	9865	9751	9854	9865	22.52
	CS	9848	9678	9737	9734	33.22
	CSISFLA	9865	9837	9856	9858	7.23
	ACLQEA	10,052	10,034	10,039	10,039	3.02
KP3	GA	15,022	14,275	14,756	14,795	158.91
	DE	15,334	15,088	15,287	15,301	54.45
	CS	15,224	15,024	15,092	15,081	51.37
	CSISFLA	15,327	15,248	15,297	15,302	18.48
	ACLQEA	15,378	15,363	15,375	15,375	3.01

Table 25 Comparative Study Between the Genetic Algorithm (GA), Differential Evolution (DE), Cuckoo Search (CS), Cuckoo Search Algorithm With an Improved Shuffled Frog Leaping Algorithm (CSISFLA), and Adaptive Cellular Quantum-Inspired Evolutionary Algorithm (ACLQEA) Using Statistical Results on Uncorrelated Knapsack Problem Instances—cont'd

Problem	Algorithm	Best	Worst	Average	Median	Standard Deviation
KP4	GA	25,882	25,212	25,498	25,493	150.68
	DE	26,333	25,751	26,099	26,096	135.88
	CS	26,208	25,786	25,936	25,911	103.40
	CSISFLA	26,360	26,193	26,284	26,277	38.54
	ACLQEA	26,446	26,420	26,436	26,437	6.92
KP5	GA	39,528	38,462	38,976	39,014	243.62
	DE	39,652	39,215	39,410	39,399	113.28
	CS	40,223	39,416	39,565	39,514	179.98
	CSISFLA	40,290	39,885	40,072	40,081	91.97
	ACLQEA	40,509	40,476	40,492	40,492	8.56

Table 26 Comparative Study Between the Genetic Algorithm (GA), Differential Evolution (DE), Cuckoo Search (CS), Cuckoo Search Algorithm With an Improved Shuffled Frog Leaping Algorithm (CSISFLA), and Adaptive Cellular Quantum-Inspired Evolutionary Algorithm (ACLQEA) Using Statistical Results on Uncorrelated Knapsack Problem Instances

Problem	Algorithm	Best	Worst	Average	Median	Standard Deviation
KP6	GA	49,072	47,835	48,483	48,570	316.62
	DE	49,246	48,835	48,989	48,979	101.11
	CS	49,767	49,024	49,164	49,142	143.08
	CSISFLA	49,893	49,567	49,744	49,737	97.52
	ACLQEA	50,351	50,276	50,333	50,338	16.91
KP7	GA	59,793	58,351	59,135	59,225	370.86
	DE	59,932	59,488	59,707	59,727	110.39
	CS	60,629	59,708	59,939	59,884	166.43
	CSISFLA	60,779	60,264	60,443	60,420	130.56
	ACLQEA	60,611	59,720	60,479	60,524	200.52

Table 27 Comparative Study Between the Genetic Algorithm (GA), Differential Evolution (DE), Cuckoo Search (CS), Cuckoo Search Algorithm With an Improved Shuffled Frog Leaping Algorithm (CSISFLA), and Adaptive Cellular Quantum-Inspired Evolutionary Algorithm (ACLQEA) Using Statistical Results on Weakly Correlated Knapsack Problem Instances

Problem	Algorithm	Best	Worst	Average	Median	Standard Deviation
KP8	GA	6627	6531	6593	6593	20.63
	DE	6676	6657	6674	6676	4.80
	CS	6660	6637	6648	6646	6.79
	CSISFLA	6673	6663	6668	6668	2.23
	ACLQEA	6661	6657	6659	6659	1.14
KP9	GA	8658	8501	8588	8590	33.38
	DE	8743	8743	8743	8743	0.00
	CS	8717	8644	8676	8671	18.23
	CSISFLA	8728	8701	8714	8714	6.87
	ACLQEA	8706	8689	8693	8692	4.06
KP10	GA	13,062	12,939	12,997	12,991	30.64
	DE	13,202	13,158	13,186	13,186	9.76
	CS	13,157	13,069	13,094	13,087	21.91
	CSISFLA	13,168	13,120	13,145	13,145	11.90
	ACLQEA	13,182	13,175	13,178	13,178	1.30
KP11	GA	21,671	21,470	21,571	21,576	48.85
	DE	21,951	21,745	21,858	21,859	37.61
	CS	21,935	21,670	21,746	21,722	76.53
	CSISFLA	21,827	21,756	21,788	21,787	16.66
	ACLQEA	21,860	21,851	21,856	21,856	2.39
KP12	GA	34,587	34,314	34,488	34,499	63.23
	DE	34,814	34,578	34,721	34,718	64.50
	CS	34,987	34,621	34,697	34,654	100.38
	CSISFLA	34,818	34,721	34,760	34,758	22.87
	ACLQEA	34,949	34,923	34,934	34,934	6.52

the ACLQEA performed better for all other statistical parameters (worst, median, average, standard deviation—i.e., apart from best) than all the other algorithms.

Table 29 presents the statistical results for the five algorithms on five strongly correlated instances of the knapsack problem (KP15 to KP19). The ACLQEA outperforms the GA, DE, CS, and CSISFLA in all the strongly correlated problem instances for all the statistical parameters, except in KP15, where CSISFLA and CS performed better than the ACLQEA.

Table 28 Comparative Study Between the Genetic Algorithm (GA), Differential Evolution (DE), Cuckoo Search (CS), Cuckoo Search Algorithm With an Improved Shuffled Frog Leaping Algorithm (CSISFLA), and Adaptive Cellular Quantum-Inspired Evolutionary Algorithm (ACLQEA) Using Statistical Results on Weakly Correlated Knapsack Problem Instances

Problem	Algorithm	Best	Worst	Average	Median	Standard Deviation
KP13	GA	43,241	42,938	43,082	43,073	75.51
	DE	43,327	43,162	43,217	43,211	43.64
	CS	43,737	43,216	43,340	43,264	166.53
	CSISFLA	43,409	43,312	43,367	43,368	27.23
	ACLQEA	43,723	43,689	43,702	43,700	8.81
KP14	GA	51,472	50,414	51,058	51,135	265.56
	DE	51,947	51,444	51,600	51,569	108.83
	CS	53,333	51,601	51,831	51,788	299.35
	CSISFLA	52,403	52,077	52,267	52,264	86.19
	ACLQEA	52,535	52,157	52,475	52,502	100.75

Table 29 Comparative Study Between Genetic Algorithm (GA), Differential Evolution (DE), Cuckoo Search (CS), Cuckoo Search Algorithm With an Improved Shuffled Frog Leaping Algorithm (CSISFLA), and Adaptive Cellular Quantum-Inspired Evolutionary Algorithm (ACLQEA) Using Statistical Results on Strongly Correlated Knapsack Problem Instances

Problem	Algorithm	Best	Worst	Average	Median	Standard Deviation
KP15	GA	14,785	14,692	14,754	14,762	25.93
	DE	14,797	14,781	14,789	14,787	4.90
	CS	14,804	14,791	14,797	14,797	2.43
	CSISFLA	14,807	14,795	14,798	14,797	3.46
	ACLQEA	14,787	14,787	14,787	14,787	0.00
KP16	GA	25,486	25,402	25,458	25,465	21.61
	DE	25,502	25,481	25,492	25,493	4.21
	CS	25,514	25,502	25,506	25,505	3.49
	CSISFLA	25,515	25,505	25,510	25,512	3.94
	ACLQEA	25,535	25,525	25,529	25,525	4.90

Continued

Table 29 Comparative Study Between Genetic Algorithm (GA), Differential Evolution (DE), Cuckoo Search (CS), Cuckoo Search Algorithm With an Improved Shuffled Frog Leaping Algorithm (CSISFLA), and Adaptive Cellular Quantum-Inspired Evolutionary Algorithm (ACLQEA) Using Statistical Results on Strongly Correlated Knapsack Problem Instances—cont'd

Problem	Algorithm	Best	Worst	Average	Median	Standard Deviation
KP17	GA	40,087	39,975	40,039	40,041	28.33
	DE	40,111	40,068	40,089	40,088	8.66
	CS	40,107	40,096	40,103	40,105	3.88
	CSISFLA	40,117	40,098	40,111	40,113	5.12
	ACLQEA	40,170	40,146	40,151	40,147	6.71
KP18	GA	49,332	49,225	49,300	49,309	27.26
	DE	49,363	49,333	49,346	49,345	7.50
	CS	49,380	49,350	49,364	49,363	7.04
	CSISFLA	49,393	49,362	49,373	49,373	7.90
	ACLQEA	49,407	49,383	49,396	49,393	5.60
KP19	GA	60,520	60,418	60,482	60,489	26.62
	DE	60,540	60,501	60,519	60,519	8.55
	CS	60,558	60,530	60,542	60,540	6.77
	CSISFLA	60,562	60,539	60,549	60,550	5.70
	ACLQEA	60,600	60,580	60,593	60,590	5.04

Table 30 presents the statistical results for the five algorithms on five multiple strongly correlated instances of the knapsack problem (KP20 to KP24). The ACLQEA outperforms the GA, DE, CS, and CSISFLA for all the statistical parameters, except in KP20, where CSISFLAS matched the performance of the ACLQEA for the best and worst solutions; however, the ACLQEA has better median and average solutions than all the other algorithms.

Table 31 presents the statistical results for the five algorithms on five profit ceiling instances of the knapsack problem (KP25 to KP29). The ACLQEA outperforms the GA, DE, CS, and CSISFLA for all the statistical parameters, except in KP25, where CSISFLA matched the performance of the ACLQEA.

Table 32 presents the statistical results for the five algorithms on five circle instances of the knapsack problem (KP30 to KP34). The ACLQEA outperforms the GA, DE, CS, and CSISFLA for all the statistical parameters, except in KP34, where CS produced a better best solution than the other algorithms.

The ACLQEA produced better results than the GA in all 34 knapsack problem instances. It produced better results than DE in 30 of the 34 knapsack problem instances, better results than CS in 25 of the 34 knapsack problem instances, and better results than CSISFLA in 30 of the 34 knapsack problem instances.

Table 30 Comparative Study Between the Genetic Algorithm (GA), Differential Evolution (DE), Cuckoo Search (CS), Cuckoo Search Algorithm With an Improved Shuffled Frog Leaping Algorithm (CSISFLA), and Adaptive Cellular Quantum-Inspired Evolutionary Algorithm (ACLQEA) Using Statistical Results on Multiple Strongly Correlated Knapsack Problem Instances

Problem	Algorithm	Best	Worst	Average	Median	Standard Deviation
KP20	GA	18,346	18,172	18,284	18,288	38.39
	DE	18,387	18,335	18,354	18,348	15.25
	CS	18,386	18,355	18,368	18,368	4.73
	CSISFLA	18,388	18,368	18,381	18,386	8.03
	ACLQEA	18,388	18,368	18,383	18,388	9.00
KP21	GA	29,525	29,387	29,461	29,462	31.97
	DE	29,548	29,488	29,519	29,520	14.10
	CS	29,589	29,527	29,555	29,549	13.94
	CSISFLA	29,609	29,562	29,581	29,585	12.38
	ACLQEA	29,669	29,649	29,651	29,649	5.31
KP22	GA	47,645	47,494	47,568	47,575	39.72
	DE	47,704	47,620	47,659	47,657	20.68
	CS	47,727	47,673	47,696	47,695	15.09
	CSISFLA	47,757	47,697	47,732	47,736	13.02
	ACLQEA	47,834	47,797	47,802	47,797	10.15
KP23	GA	60,529	60,312	60,455	60,463	47.39
	DE	60,572	60,508	60,534	60,530	13.98
	CS	60,607	60,540	60,576	60,574	16.96
	CSISFLA	60,650	60,579	60,615	60,612	15.75
	ACLQEA	60,732	60,692	60,714	60,712	8.25
KP24	GA	72,063	71,725	71,914	71,917	64.42
	DE	72,072	71,973	72,018	72,018	19.38
	CS	72,094	72,031	72,058	72,057	15.93
	CSISFLA	72,151	72,070	72,112	72,111	21.20
	ACLQEA	72,272	72,242	72,253	72,252	5.81

Therefore the ACLQEA is a competitive algorithm as compared with other state-of-art techniques for solving knapsack problems.

6 CONCLUSIONS AND FUTURE WORK

QEAs are population-based metaheuristics, developed by integration of principles from quantum mechanics into the framework of evolutionary algorithms, and have

Table 31 Comparative Study Between the Genetic Algorithm (GA), Differential Evolution (DE), Cuckoo Search (CS), Cuckoo Search Algorithm With an Improved Shuffled Frog Leaping Algorithm (CSISFLA), and Adaptive Cellular Quantum-Inspired Evolutionary Algorithm (ACLQEA) Using Statistical Results on Profit Ceiling Knapsack Problem Instances

Problem	Algorithm	Best	Worst	Average	Median	Standard Deviation
KP25	GA	12,957	12,948	12,955	12,957	2.53
	DE	12,957	12,951	12,953	12,954	1.83
	CS	12,957	12,954	12,957	12,957	0.76
	CSISFLA	12,957	12,957	12,957	12,957	0.00
	ACLQEA	12,957	12,957	12,957	12,957	0.00
KP26	GA	20,295	20,268	20,285	20,286	7.37
	DE	20,301	20,292	20,294	20,294	2.17
	CS	20,304	20,295	20,299	20,298	1.86
	CSISFLA	20,307	20,298	20,304	20,304	2.28
	ACLQEA	20,307	20,307	20,307	20,307	0.00
KP27	GA	32,796	32,769	32,785	32,787	6.99
	DE	32,802	32,793	32,797	32,796	2.63
	CS	32,811	32,799	32,803	32,802	3.12
	CSISFLA	32,820	32,808	32,812	32,811	3.34
	ACLQEA	32,841	32,823	32,826	32,826	3.10
KP28	GA	43,248	43,215	43,234	43,236	8.76
	DE	43,257	43,245	43,249	43,248	3.57
	CS	43,269	43,251	43,257	43,254	4.41
	CSISFLA	43,272	43,260	43,266	43,266	2.88
	ACLQEA	43,296	43,290	43,292	43,293	1.79
KP29	GA	51,378	51,348	51,364	51,366	7.25
	DE	51,384	51,372	51,378	51,378	3.04
	CS	51,399	51,378	51,385	51,384	4.32
	CSISFLA	51,399	51,390	51,396	51,396	3.10
	ACLQEA	51,417	51,411	51,413	51,414	1.83

been successful in solving difficult search and optimization problems. They are uniquely characterized by their solution representation, variation operators, and population structure. QEAs have been implemented in panmictic, coarse-grained, and cellular population structures, of which cellular population structures have been the most successful. A cellular population structure admits many topologies. The effect of static, dynamic, and adaptive random topologies on the performance of cellular QEAs was investigated in detail in this chapter. P-PEAKS and 0-1 knapsack problem instances were used to test the cellular QEA with random topologies. The

Table 32 Comparative Study Between the Genetic Algorithm (GA), Differential Evolution (DE), Cuckoo Search (CS), Cuckoo Search Algorithm With an Improved Shuffled Frog Leaping Algorithm (CSISFLA), and Adaptive Cellular Quantum-Inspired Evolutionary Algorithm (ACLQEA) Using Statistical Results on Circle Knapsack Problem Instances

Problem	Algorithm	Best	Worst	Average	Median	Standard Deviation
KP30	GA	21,194	20,899	21,086	21,096	71.44
	DE	21,333	21,192	21,264	21,277	32.46
	CS	21,333	21,194	21,261	21,261	18.57
	CSISFLA	21,333	21,263	21,300	21,295	34.04
	ACLQEA	21,460	21,459	21,460	21,460	0.50
KP31	GA	35,262	34,982	35,112	35,124	82.25
	DE	35,343	35,184	35,247	35,267	38.08
	CS	35,345	35,271	35,297	35,277	31.29
	CSISFLA	35,414	35,342	35,354	35,345	23.23
	ACLQEA	35,425	35,420	35,423	35,423	1.77
KP32	GA	55,976	55,451	55,746	55,771	116.83
	DE	56,063	55,914	55,964	55,954	44.95
	CS	56,280	55,988	56,057	56,061	55.01
	CSISFLA	56,273	56,130	56,185	56,201	38.65
	ACLQEA	56,423	56,415	56,417	56,417	1.55
KP33	GA	70,739	70,247	70,487	70,456	113.53
	DE	70,806	70,641	70,696	70,684	38.21
	CS	70,915	70,729	70,789	70,797	42.50
	CSISFLA	71,008	70,867	70,924	70,939	41.17
	ACLQEA	71,371	71,366	71,368	71,368	1.21
KP34	GA	83,969	83,339	83,723	83,757	142.75
	DE	84,040	83,820	83,912	83,899	56.64
	CS	84,645	83,954	84,055	84,033	121.94
	CSISFLA	84,244	84,099	84,175	84,181	38.36
	ACLQEA	84,492	84,423	84,437	84,434	16.43

ACLQEA with entropy as a feedback parameter performed better than the other cellular QEA implementations. A comparative study was also performed between the ACLQEA with entropy as the feedback parameter and state-of-the-art algorithms such as a GA, DE, CS, and CSISFLA. The cellular QEA, in general, and its adaptive version with entropy as the feedback parameter are a set of competitive metaheuristics as compared with the other state-of-the-art techniques for solving 0-1 knapsack problems. The work reported here can be extended by consideration of spatial topologies instead of random topologies. Further, more complex real-world problems can be solved with the ACLQEA proposed in this chapter.

ACKNOWLEDGMENTS

We are thankful to anonymous reviewers for giving insightful comments, which helped improve the manuscript. Nija Mani is thankful to her department and University Grants Commission, Government of India (UGC) for supporting her PhD degree through a Meritorious Student's Fellowship.

REFERENCES

[1] D.H. Kim, Y.H. Yoo, S.J. Ryu, W.Y. Go, J.H. Kim, Automatic color detection for MiroSOT using quantum-inspired evolutionary algorithm, in: Intelligent Robotics Systems: Inspiring the NEXT, Communications in Computer and Information Science, vol. 376, 2013, pp. 11–20, http://dx.doi.org/10.1007/978-3-642-40409-2_2.

[2] Y. Li, S. Feng, X. Zhang, L. Jiao, SAR image segmentation based on quantum-inspired multiobjective evolutionary clustering algorithm, Inf. Process. Lett. 114 (6) (2014) 283–293, http://dx.doi.org/10.1016/j.ipl.2013.12.010.

[3] H. Xing, Y. Ji, L. Bai, X. Liu, Z. Qu, X. Wang, An adaptive-evolution-based quantum-inspired evolutionary algorithm for QOS multicasting in IP/DWDM networks, Comput. Commun. 32 (6) (2009) 1086–1094, http://dx.doi.org/10.1016/j.comcom.2008.12.036.

[4] H. Lei, K. Qin, Quantum-inspired evolutionary algorithm for analog test point selection, Analog Integr. Circuits Signal Process. Comput. Commun. 75 (3) (2013) 491–498.

[5] A.C. Kumari, K. Srinivas, M.P. Gupta, Software requirements selection using quantum-inspired elitist multi-objective evolutionary algorithm, in: International Conference on Advances in Engineering, Science and Management (ICAESM), vol. 1, 2012, pp. 782–787.

[6] G.S.S. Babu, D.B. Das, C. Patvardhan, Real-parameter quantum evolutionary algorithm for economic load dispatch, IET Gener. Transm. Dis. 2 (1) (2008) 22–31, http://dx.doi.org/10.1049/iet-gtd:20060495.

[7] Q. Niu, Z. Zhou, T. Zeng, A hybrid quantum-inspired particle swarm evolution algorithm and SQP method for large-scale economic dispatch problems, IET Gener. Transm. Dis. 6840 (2012) 207–214, http://dx.doi.org/10.1007/978-3-642-24553-4_29.

[8] A. Mani, C. Patvardhan, A hybrid quantum evolutionary algorithm for solving engineering optimization problems, Int. J. Hybrid Intell. Syst. 7 (3) (2010) 225–235.

[9] W. Fang, J. Sun, W. Xu, Design IIR digital filters using quantum-behaved particle swarm optimization, in: Advances in Natural Computation, Lecture Notes in Computer Science, vol. 4222, 2006, pp. 637–640, http://dx.doi.org/10.1007/11881223_78.

[10] A. Mani, C. Patvardhan, An improved model of ceramic grinding process and its optimization by adaptive quantum inspired evolutionary algorithm, Int. J. Simul. Syst. Sci. Technol. 11 (6) (2012) 76–85.

[11] G. Zhang, Quantum-inspired evolutionary algorithms: a survey and empirical study, J. Heuristics 17 (2011) 303–351, http://dx.doi.org/10.1007/s10732-010-9136-0.

[12] S. Zhao, G. Xu, T. Tao, L. Liang, Real-coded chaotic quantum-inspired genetic algorithm for training of fuzzy neural networks, Comput. Math. Appl. 57 (2009) 2009–2015, http://dx.doi.org/10.1109/CEC.2004.1330874.

[13] Q. Yang, S.C. Ding, Methodology and case study of hybrid quantum-inspired evolutionary algorithm for numerical optimization, Proc. ICNC 1 (2007) 634–638, http://dx.doi.org/10.1109/ICNC.2007.471.

[14] C. Patvardhan, A. Narain, A. Srivastava, Enhanced quantum evolutionary algorithm for difficult knapsack problems, in: Proceedings of International Conference on Pattern Recognition and Machine Intelligence, Lecture Notes in Computer Science, Springer-Verlag, Kolkata, 2007, pp. 252–260, http://dx.doi.org/10.1007/978-3-540-77046-6_31.

[15] L. Kliemann, O. Kliemann, C. Patvardhan, V. Sauerland, A. Srivastav, A new QEA computing near-optimal low-discrepancy colorings in the hypergraph of arithmetic progressions, in: Experimental Algorithms, 12th International Symposium, SEA, Lecture Notes in Computer Science, vol. 7933, 2013, pp. 67–78, http://dx.doi.org/10.1007/978-3-642-38527-8_8.

[16] M.D. Platelt, S. Schliebs, N. Kasabov, A versatile quantum-inspired evolutionary algorithm, in: 2007 IEEE Congress on Evolutionary Computation, 2007, pp. 423–430, http://dx.doi.org/10.1109/CEC.2007.4424502.

[17] N. Mani, Gursaran, A.K. Sinha, A. Mani, Effect of population structures on quantum-inspired evolutionary algorithm, Appl. Comput. Intell. Soft Comput. 2014 (976202) (2014) 22, http://dx.doi.org/10.1155/2014/976202.

[18] N. Mani, Gursaran, A.K. Sinha, A. Mani, An evaluation of cellular population model for improving QEA, in: Proceedings of GECCO, vol. 1, 2012, pp. 1437–1438, http://dx.doi.org/10.1145/2330784.2330976.

[19] J. Lane, A. Engelbrecht, J. Gain, Particle swarm optimization with spatially meaningful neighbours, in: Swarm Intelligence Symposium, SIS 2008. IEEE, vol. 1, 2008, pp. 21–23, http://dx.doi.org/10.1109/SIS.2008.4668281.

[20] N. Mani, Gursaran, A. Mani, Performance of static random topologies in fine-grained QEA on P-PEAKS problem instances, in: Proceedings of the 2015 IEEE International Conference on Research in Computational Intelligence and Communication Network, vol. 1, 2015, pp. 163–168.

[21] R. Mendes, Population topologies and their influence in particle swarm performance, Ph.D. Dissertation, University of Minho, 2004.

[22] E. Alba, B. Dorronsoro, The exploration/exploitation tradeoff in dynamic cellular genetic algorithms, IEEE Trans. Evol. Comput. 8 (2) (2005) 126–142, http://dx.doi.org/10.1109/TEVC.2005.843751.

[23] A. Narayanan, M. Moore, Quantum-inspired genetic algorithms, in: Proceedings of IEEE International Conference on Evolutionary Computation, vol. 1, 1966, pp. 61–66, http://dx.doi.org/10.1109/ICEC.1996.542334.

[24] K.H. Han, J.H. Kim, Quantum-inspired evolutionary algorithm for a class of combinatorial optimization, IEEE Trans. Evol. Comput. 6 (2002) 580–593, http://dx.doi.org/10.1109/TEVC.2002.804320.

[25] K.H. Han, J.H. Kim, Quantum-inspired evolutionary algorithms with a new termination criterion, Hε gate and two phase scheme, IEEE Trans. Evol. Comput. 8 (2) (2004) 156–168, http://dx.doi.org/10.1109/TEVC.2004.823467.

[26] J. Kennedy, R. Mendes, Neighborhood topologies in fully informed and best of neighborhood particle swarms, in: Proceedings of the 2003 IEEE International Workshop Soft Computing in Industrial Applications, vol. 1, 2003, pp. 45–50.

[27] J. Kennedy, R. Mendes, Population structure and particle swarm performance, in: Proceeding of the 2002 Congress on Evolutionary Computation, vol. 2, 2002, pp. 1671–1676, http://dx.doi.org/10.1109/CEC.2002.1004493.

[28] S. Ghosh, D. Kundu, K. Suresh, S. Das, A. Abraham, K. Panigrahi, V. Snasel, On some properties of the lbest topology in particle swarm optimization, in: Ninth International Conference on Hybrid Intelligent Systems, vol. 3, 2009, pp. 370–375, http://dx.doi.org/10.1109/HIS.2009.288.

[29] Y. Shi, Particle swarm optimization, in: CiteSeerX—Scientific Literature Digital Library and Search Engine, 2008.

[30] J. Kennedy, Small world and mega minds: effects of neighborhood topology on particle swarm performance, in: Proceeding of the 1999 Conference on Evolutionary Computation, vol. 3, 1999, pp. 1931–1938, http://dx.doi.org/10.1109/CEC.1999.785509.

[31] Z. Chen, Z. He, C. Zhang, The non-clique particle swarm optimizer, in: Proceedings of the First ACM/SIGEVO Summit on Genetic and Evolutionary Computation, 2009, pp. 61–66, http://dx.doi.org/10.1145/1543834.1543844.

[32] A.E.M. Zavala, A.H. Aguirre, E.R.V. Diharce, The singly-linked ring topology for the particle swarm optimization algorithm, in: Proceedings of the 11th Annual Conference on Genetic and Evolutionary Computation (Montreal, Quebec, Canada, July 08–12, 2009). GECCO '09, 2009, pp. 65–72, http://dx.doi.org/10.1145/1569901.1569911.

[33] V. Miranda, H. Keko, A.J. Duque., Stochastic star communication topology in evolutionary particle swarms (EPSO), Int. J. Comput. Intell. Res. 4 (2008) 105–116, http://dx.doi.org/10.5019/j.ijcir.2008.130.

[34] S.A. Hamdan, Hybrid particle swarm optimiser using multi-neighborhood topologies, J. Comput. Sci. 4 (2008) 36–44.

[35] F. Jones, T. Soule, Dynamic particle swarm optimization via ring topologies, in: Proceedings of the 11th Annual Conference on Genetic and Evolutionary Computation (Montreal, Quebec, Canada, July 08–12, 2009). GECCO '09, 2009, pp. 1745–1746, http://dx.doi.org/10.1145/1569901.1570138.

[36] K.D. Jong, M. Potter, W. Spears, Using problem generators to explore the effects of epistasis, in: Proceedings of the 7th International Conference on Genetic Algorithms, vol. 1, 1997, pp. 338–345.

[37] D. Pisinger, Where are the hard knapsack problems, Comput, Oper. Res. 32 (2004) 2271–2284, http://dx.doi.org/10.1016/j.cor.2004.03.002.

[38] Y. Feng, G. Wang, Q. Feng, X. Zhao, an effective hybrid cuckoo search algorithm with improved shuffled frog leaping algorithm for 0-1 knapsack problems, Comput. Intell. Neurosci. 2014 (2014) 1–17, http://dx.doi.org/10.1155/2014/857254.

[39] Z. Michalewicz, Genetic Algorithms + Data Structures = Evolution Programs, Springer, Berlin, Germany, 1996.

[40] S. Das, P.N. Suganthan, Differential evolution: a survey of the state-of-the-art, IEEE Trans. Evol. Comput. 15 (2011) 4–31, http://dx.doi.org/10.1109/TEVC.2010.2059031.

[41] R. Mallipeddi, P.N. Suganthan, Q.K. Pan, M.F. Tasgetiren, Differential evolution algorithm with ensemble of parameters and mutation strategies, Appl. Soft Comput. J. 11 (2) (2011) 1679–1696, http://dx.doi.org/10.1016/j.asoc.2010.04.024.

[42] A. Gherboudj, A. Layeb, S. Chikhi, Solving 0-1 knapsack problems by a discrete binary version of cuckoo search algorithm, Int. J. Bio-Inspired Comput. 4 (2012) 229–236, http://dx.doi.org/10.1504/IJBIC.2012.048063.

PART

Applications

II

CHAPTER

An efficient pure color image denoising using quantum parallel bidirectional self-organizing neural network architecture

5

D. Konar[a], S. Bhattacharyya[b], B.K. Panigrahi[c], M.K. Ghose[a]

Sikkim Manipal Institute of Technology, Rangpo, SK, India[a] RCC Institute of Information Technology, Kolkata, WB, India[b] Indian Institute of Technology Delhi, New Delhi, DL, India[c]

1 INTRODUCTION

In the rising phase of the multimedia data revolution, color image denoising is an essential preprocessing procedure for multichannel information processing applications. Recent years have witnessed the emerging popularity of digital media for color visual information transmission from the sender to the receiver end as digital images, but very often during transmission the image pixels get corrupted with noise. The noisy colored image obtained after transmission requires filtering or removal of noise before its use in applications. Moreover, in the field of pattern recognition and computer vision, it is necessary to analyze color images and extract interesting objects. Color image denoising involves the process of extraction of a pure color object from a noisy environment. In this image denoising procedure, a digital image is segmented into distinct regions in the image feature space comprising the image pixels with identical features such as color, intensity, and texture. In the computer vision community, pure color image denoising is always a daunting task owing to the wide variation in visual information. Along with the increasing demand for the development of modern digital imaging devices, there are increasing requirements for efficient image denoising algorithms with greater image quality and their real-time applications. Typical real-time applications include defense, content-based image retrieval, surveillance, and biomedical applications, to name a few. To segment the nonredundant useful foreground region from the larger background area of color images, plentiful linear and nonlinear classical smoothing filters [1] in both the

Quantum Inspired Computational Intelligence. http://dx.doi.org/10.1016/B978-0-12-804409-4.00005-X

spatial and the temporal domain have been developed over the decades. Distance regularized level set evolution and graph cuts-based approaches [2,3] relying on optimization of an energy function are a notable contribution in this direction to intrinsically maintain the level set function and reduce computational cost. Color image denoising approaches in the frequency domain and primitive smoothing filters have also contributed significantly in this field of research. Recently, wavelet [4,5], curvelet [6], and ridgelet [7] transformation-based techniques have become popular for color image denoising. Of late, boundary fragment-connecting methods [8] operating on fragments contained in the subset for extraction of perceptually salient closed boundaries in images to produce a closed boundary for the relevant object have been reported. Because of additive noise with uniform power and a Gaussian probability distribution, the pixels of color images get corrupted [9]. To denoise the images affected by uniform and Gaussian noise, linear smoothing filters such as the nonlocal mean filter, shape-adaptive transform [10], bilateral filtering [11,12], nonlocal mean-based methods [13,14], and nonlocal collaborative filtering [15,16] can be used. The inherent drawback with these linear filtering approaches is blurring effects and therefore poor quality of images extracted from noisy versions. Wavelet thresholding has proved to be efficient in reducing blurring effects by means of a discrete wavelet transform, a discrete Fourier transform, or a discrete cosine transform [17], to name a few methods. To facilitate the object extraction procedure, these transformation techniques decompose an image application in the spatial domain into multiple scales of different time-frequency components. A recently developed adaptive wavelet thresholding accomplished with a median filter [18] has been extensively applied on two-dimensional digital images for image denoising. Owing to the inherent nonlinearity offered by the median filter, it is efficient in preserving the edges of the object from a noisy perspective. Although these approaches stand in good stead in some cases, they seldom pay any heed to the human visual perception system, resulting in their being undesirable in cluttered or noisy environments.

This chapter is organized as follows: Section 2 provides a detailed literature survey focusing on color image denoising and extraction of a pure colored object. The principal objective of the research reported in this chapter is given in Section 3. Section 4 elucidates the fundamental overview of fuzzy sets and their necessary operations. A brief explanation of basic concepts of quantum computing necessary for this chapter is provided in Section 5. Section 6 sheds light on the parallel architecture and its principle of its operation in a parallel bidirectional self-organizing neural network (PBDSONN) [19,20]. Section 7 briefly introduces the operation of the supervised autoassociative threefold parallel Hopfield network [21]. Section 8 focuses on the proposed quantum PBDSONN (QPBDSONN) architecture. A vivid explanation of the network dynamics of the functioning and the operation related to adjustments of weighted interconnections of the network of the QPBDSONN architecture is included in this section. The comparative results of the suggested QPBDSONN architecture, the PBDSONN architecture [19,20], the Hopfield network architecture [21], and the median filter with adaptive wavelet thresholding [18] on an artificial synthetic pure color image and on a real-life wrench pure color image affected by various levels of uniform and Gaussian noise are reported in Section 9. Finally, the one-sided Kolmogorov-Smirnov (KS) test is performed to show the statistical superiority of the proposed method. Section 10 concludes with the scope of future research.

2 REVIEW OF THE LITERATURE

In the last few decades, color image denoising has become a promising field of research which exploits the extraction of a color and grayscale object from its noisy environment. Saliency-based object extraction relying on a saliency procedure has attracted the attention of many computer vision researchers in cluttered and noisy environments. The success behind the emerging popularity of this technique lies in the fact that it accords very well with human visual perception. The most admired contribution in the pattern recognition community in this regard is that of Itti et al. [22]. By combining the primary features of a multiscale image, in their article, they used a dynamic neural network to diminish the saliency map and a single topographical saliency map.

Nowadays, a wavelet transform [23] has been widely incorporated in the diversified field of image denoising applications [4–6,17,18]. A wavelet transform decomposes a color or grayscale noisy image into various gray or color levels to suppress noise using some thresholding [24] and statistical modeling [25,26]. In spite of the high efficiency of wavelet thresholding in color image denoising, it relies on the fixed wavelet basics using dilation and translation operations on the image application. In consequence of this fixed wavelet basics, a wavelet transform may suffer from various visual artifacts generated in the denoised output image. To obviate wavelet thresholding, Muresan and Parks [27] suggested a spatially adaptive principal component analysis image denoising algorithm guided by the locally fitted basis to transform the image. The sparse and redundant representation and K-SVD-based denoising algorithm proposed by Elad et al. [28,29] trained a highly overcomplete dictionary. Foi et al. [10] presented an improved image denoising algorithm based on a shape-adaptive discrete cosine transform of the neighborhood to represent the image in a sparse fashion which leads to efficient denoising.

A wavelet and minimum cut-based approach was adopted by Lian and Zagorodnov [30] to exploit both the interscale and intrascale correlations of wavelet coefficients. The efficiency of the proposed method was up to 5-dB gain in the peak signal-to-noise ratio for color images and leads to fewer visual color artifacts. In contrast to this suggested approach, another image denoising technique, named "nonlocal means" [31], finds the mean of identical image pixels according to the intensity distance. Bilateral filtering [11,12] also uses the same kind of techniques as nonlocal means by exploiting both the spatial and the intensity similarity for pixel averaging (i.e., each pixel is computed as the weighted mean of all the pixels in the image and the weights are guided by the similarity between the pixels). However, these approaches achieve remarkable results in terms of denoised output but the algorithms are complex in terms of implementation.

Ma and Zhang [32] proposed a fuzzy image contrast growing approach inspired by a saliency map to obtain denoised objects. Recently, a novel salient detection method combined with adaptive thresholding assisted by a frequency-tuned saliency map was suggested to preserve the well-defined edges of salient objects efficiently [33]. To construct a saliency map, Hou and Zhang [34] adopted a visual saliency detection method which examines the log-spectrum of an image. However, saliency-inspired approaches suffer from inherent drawbacks of integrity, in spite of their popularity among researches. The problem of integrity results in compromise of the redundant region of the background image in an object extraction procedure. A complementary saliency map offers the solution to this problem of integrity by resorting to the integration of envelope-like maps and sketch-like maps [35].

Artificial neural networks (ANNs) have been widely used to solve a large number of unorganized machine learning problems, such as pattern recognition, pattern association, color image processing, and computer vision. Because of inherent features of parallelism and graceful adaption, a basic ANN became popular in the field of pattern recognition research. The significant contribution of ANNs combined with fuzzy logic in object extraction deserves special mention [36,37]. Different supervised and unsupervised neural network architectures, differing in topology and the principles of operation, have been invented to produce real-time outputs.

Because of their ability to automatically retrieve dominant color components of color images, self-organizing maps [38,39] can be extensively used in color image segmentation. Owing to enormity and wide variations in the color space and spatial features, plenty of self-organizing map (SOM) have been used to cluster color image. Finally, to obtain the desired denoised output image, the clustered images are fused.

Bhattacharyya et al. [40] adopted a parallel multilayer self-organizing neural network architecture appropriate for both pure and true color object denoising and segmentation. The uniform thresholding used in the parallel multilayer self-organizing neural network architecture assumes the homogeneity of the pure color image therein. Because of wide variations in and the enormity of the intensity distribution prevalent in the color gamut of true color real-life images, the need for multilevel thresholding parameters in the image segmentation is obvious. An exhaustive list of solutions for true color object segmentation/extraction and pattern recognition problems was reported in [41]. It provides an extensive survey of the use and applications of supervised and self-supervised self-organizing neighborhood-based neural network architectures for the purpose of intelligent decision making. Examples include the parallel multilayer self-organizing neural network architecture [40] and the PBDSONN architecture [19].

A time-efficient PBDSONN appropriate for pure color image denoising in a real-time environment was suggested by Bhattacharyya et al. [19]. The PBDSONN architecture comprises three PBDSONNs in the input layer to process three distinct color components (red, green, blue) separately used in the color noisy images. The principle of the operation of this PBDSONN architecture is posed as a cluster of three PBDSONNs after isolation of these three distinct basic color components from the pure noisy color images in the initial phase. Afterward, the basic color components obtained from the input noisy color images are fed simultaneously thorough three parallel different basic color component PBDSONNs for subsequent processing. Finally, a fusion operation merges the processed color image components in the sink layer and produces the true color output image. The basic color components obtained from the input noisy color images are fed simultaneously thorough three parallel different basic color component bidirectional self-organizing neural networks (BDSONNs) for subsequent processing. Because of the self-supervised behavior of the PBDSONN, no of supervision or training is needed. The key operation of the PBDSONN comprises mainly the propagation of fuzzified information of the network intermediate outputs to the intermediate layer for self-organization. The constituent neurons of every layer of the network follow a cellular network architecture. Each constituent BDSONN of the PBDSONN architecture is arranged as follows: an input layer receiving fuzzified information, a hidden layer, and an output layer for the generation of processed final outputs. The number of neurons in the different network layers is representative of the number of pixels in the image region. On the reading of the fuzzy membership information from the three different color gamuts in the input layer, information is propagated to the subsequent network layers for further processing. The neurons of the three layers for each PBDSONN are replicated by fuzzy membership values. The neurons in each network layer are fully linked with unit weight and thereby form a cellular architecture. The weighted interlinked connections are interconnected to successive layers of neurons through second-order neighborhood-based mapping. The relative fuzziness measure at the central seed neuron yields the interlinked strength between two successive layers of neurons. The network is said to outperform the parallel multilayer self-organizing neural network architecture [41] in terms of the quality of the objects extracted from a noisy perspective.

Owing to its inherent micro quantum property, quantum computing has the ability to perform computational tasks exponentially faster than classical computing [42]. The quantum ANN lies at the intersection of an ANN and quantum computing, emerging as a powerful computing paradigm in problems such as pattern classification. Matsui et al. [43] developed a quantum neural model which exhibits the capability of impeccable quantum learning efficiency. This learning paradigm allows the evolution of a quantum multilayer feed forward neural network [44] in problems such as nonlinear control by exhibiting the effects of quantum mechanics [45]. An automated object extraction system relying on a quantum ANN architecture was developed by Aytekin et al. [46]. The novel quantum neural network architecture of Ezhov [47] was evolved to solve problems such as classification by replicating quantum associative memory architecture through quantum entanglement. A wide variety of research is done in the domain of the ANN resorting to quantum associative memory [48–52]. The superiority of quantum ANNs over classical ANNs was demonstrated by Menneer [53] and Perus [54] in the field of machine learning. A quantum replica of a parallel self-organizing map was developed by Weigang [55].

In the domain of computer vision and pattern recognition research, Hu [56] deciphered that the error incurred in the process of quantum measurement in a quantum ANN is reduced to half that compared with classical counterparts. A time-efficient binary image extraction using a quantum multilayer self-organizing neural network architecture was suggested by Bhattacharyya et al. [41,57], and it outperformed the classical multilayer self-organizing neural network [58]. They reported the efficacy of the suggested architecture on binary images affected by different types of noise. The proposed quantum multilayer self-organizing neural network architecture adjusts its weighted interconnections represented as quantum rotation gates by means of a proposed quantum back-propagation algorithm. The quantum multilayer self-organizing neural network was found to be more time-efficient than the classical multilayer self-organizing neural network architecture [58] in object extraction, and the shape of the extracted objects is retained with high precision. However, the inherent drawback of the proposed architecture lies in the use of a time complex back-propagation algorithm. To obviate the need for the back-propagation algorithm, Konar et al. [59] suggested an efficient quantum BDSONN (QBDSONN) architecture for binary image denoising guided by counterpropagation of the network states. The QBDSONN is superior to the classical BDSONN [60] and the quantum multilayer self-organizing neural network [41,57].

3 PROPOSED WORK

This chapter focuses on a fast and efficient parallel neural network applicable for pure color object extraction from a noisy environment, referred to as a "quantum parallel bidirectional self-organizing neural network (QPBDSONN) architecture." Like a PBDSONN [19], the suggested QPBDSONN architecture comprises three parallel constituent QBDSONNs [59] with quantum added characteristic. The input layer of each constituent QBDSONN is processes three distinct color components (red, green, blue) separately used in the color noisy images. The principle of the operation of this QPBDSONN architecture is posed as a cluster of three parallel QBDSONNs after isolation of these three distinct basic color components from the pure noisy color images in the initial phase. Afterward, the basic color components obtained from the input noisy color images are fed simultaneously thorough three parallel different basic color component QBDSONNs for subsequent processing. Each constituent QBDSONN comprises three network layers—the input layer, the hidden layer, and the output layer—each of which has fully linked neurons. The weighted interlinked connections and corresponding activations are updated by a rotation gate. The quantum measurements were performed to reduce the quantum states into either of the basis states of 0 or 255 guided by the probability. Finally, a fusion operation merges the processed color image components in the sink layer and produces the true color output image. Interested readers may consult [59] to learn more about the QBDSONN architecture and its operation.

Given the enormity of the noise levels in artificial synthetic and real-life wrench pure color images corrupted by an additive uniform and Gaussian distribution, we performed experiments. Thus it generalizes the robustness of the suggested QPBDSONN architecture to a wide variety of noise. A compact analysis with the outcome of the classical PBDSONN [19], the supervised threefold parallel Hopfield network [21], and the median filter with adaptive wavelet thresholding [18] was conducted. The comparative results show that the QPBDSONN architecture outperforms both the self-supervised classical PBDSONN [19] and the supervised threefold parallel Hopfield network [21] with regard to processing time. The QPBDSONN also outperforms the nonlinear median filter with adaptive wavelet thresholding [18] as far as the quality of the denoised pure color image is concerned.

4 FUNDAMENTALS OF FUZZY SETS

The basic concepts of fuzzy sets related to the current work are discussed in this section.

4.1 FUZZY SET CONCEPTS

The generalization of a crisp set is the concept of fuzzy set theory [61,62]. It is formulated as a collection of well-defined ordered pairs $(y_i, \mu_{Fz}(y_i))\forall y_i \in U$ and $0.0 \leq \mu_{Fz}(y_i) \leq 1.0$, where $\mu_{Fz}(y_i)$ corresponds to the membership value for y_i of the fuzzy set Fz. A high membership value, $\mu_F(y_i)$, refers to the greater belongingness of containment of its element y_i in the fuzzy set Fz. A membership value of 1 corresponds to strong belongingness and weak belongingness is represented by a membership value of 0. Formally, fuzzy set Fz can be defined as follows [61];

$$Fz = \left\{ \sum_{y_i \in U} \frac{\mu_{Fz}(y_i)}{y_i} : \forall y_i \in U \text{and } 0.0 \leq \mu_{Fz}(y_i) \leq 1.0 \right\}. \tag{1}$$

4.2 FUZZY SET OPERATIONS

The fundamental operations include union, intersection, and complement operating on either one or two fuzzy sets by extending the operations of a crisp set. Consider y, an element belonging the universe of discourse U, defines two fuzzy sets R and S as

$$\text{Union}: \mu_{R\cup S}(y) = \max\{\mu_R(y), \mu_S(y)\}, \quad \forall y \in U \tag{2}$$

$$\text{Intersection}: \mu_{R\cap S}(y) = \min\{\mu_R(y), \mu_S(y)\}, \quad \forall y \in U \tag{3}$$

$$\text{Complement}: \mu_{\overline{R}}(y) = 1 - \mu_R(y), \quad \forall y \in U \tag{4}$$

4.3 FUZZY CARDINALITY

Consider a fuzzy set $Fz = \{\sum_{y_i \in U} \frac{\mu_{Fz}(y_i)}{y_i} : \forall y_i \in U \text{and } 0.0 \leq \mu_{Fz}(y_i) \leq 1.0, \}$. Fuzzy cardinality can be defined as the summation of the membership values of the finite number of elements [62] as

$$\xi_{Fz} = \sum_{i=1}^{n} \mu_F(y_i). \tag{5}$$

Fuzzy cardinality is the measurable quantity for the degree of belongingness.

5 QUANTUM COMPUTING FUNDAMENTALS

Quantum computing originated from studies in the field of quantum mechanics and the functioning of quantum mechanical devices. This becomes evident through operations such as coherence, decoherence, and superposition on the constituent basis states which are characterized by quantum mechanical properties [63]. The fact that in quantum mechanical systems the linear combination of each possible solution outputs another solution is asserted through the property of superposition. "Coherence" refers to the correlation of basis states.

5.1 CONCEPT OF QUBITS

Unlike traditional computing, which is based on the binary number system, the smallest unit of information in quantum computing is a *qubit*, or quantum bit [42], formed by the linear superposition of *eigenstates* $|0\rangle$ and $|1\rangle$. It can be defined as

$$|Q\rangle = m|0\rangle + n|1\rangle. \tag{6}$$

Squares of the complex numbers m and n correspond to the probability of the occurrence of eigenstates $|0\rangle$ and $|1\rangle$ such that

$$|m|^2 + |n|^2 = 1. \tag{7}$$

The basic operations on qubits in discrete space are referred to as "linear unitary Hilbert operators," and various logic quantum gates [64] realized by the unitary operations reportedly qualify as quantum computation.

5.2 FUNDAMENTALS OF A ROTATION GATE

Formally, a single qubit rotation gate can be defined as follows:

$$Rot(\alpha) = \begin{bmatrix} \cos\alpha & -\sin\alpha \\ \sin\alpha & \cos\alpha \end{bmatrix} \tag{8}$$

A single qubit rotation gate operates on a single qubit as

$$Rot(\alpha) = \begin{bmatrix} \cos\alpha & -\sin\alpha \\ \sin\alpha & \cos\alpha \end{bmatrix} \times \begin{bmatrix} \cos Q_0 \\ \sin Q_0 \end{bmatrix} = \begin{bmatrix} \cos(\alpha + Q_0) \\ \sin(\alpha + Q_0) \end{bmatrix}. \tag{9}$$

5.3 QUANTUM MEASUREMENT

Unlike classical mechanics, where the position $\vec{x}(t)$ and momentum $\vec{p}(t)$ describe the state of the constituent particle in a simple system, the quantum state aptly describes a quantum mechanical system. It forms an abstract infinite-dimensional vector space through the entailment of the probabilities of all possible positions and momenta of a particle. Such an infinite-dimensional space is known as a "Hilbert space" and is characterized by a state vector always representing the pure state.

During laboratory preparation of a quantum system, the position or energy of the constituent states is measured and thereafter the quantum state of a system is destroyed by its conversion into one of the basic states 0 or 1 depending on the measurement. Repeated measurements without further evolution of the quantum state lead to identical results. However, repeated preparations followed by measurements show different results.

The measurement can be predicted sufficiently from the statistical expectation of the prepared system [65] by use of quantum state operators. This probability distribution may be continuous (e.g., position and momentum) or discrete (e.g., spin), and it also depends on the measured quantity owing to the inherent indeterministic and random nature of the quantum measurement procedure.

To be precise, "collapse," or "wave function collapse" [65], is the process leading to the quantum state taking the value for one of the eigenstates and the operator corresponding to the measured observable. As a result, the eigenstate finally appears to have a probability equal to the square of its overlap with the original state, though at random.

6 PARALLEL BIDIRECTIONAL SELF-ORGANIZING NEURAL NETWORK ARCHITECTURE

The PBDSONN architecture [19] is a parallel form of the BDSONN architecture [60]. The PBDSONN architecture comprises three BDSONNs in the input layer to process three distinct color components (red, green, blue) separately used in the color noisy images. The key operation of this PBDSONN architecture is posed as a cluster of three parallel BDSONNs after isolation of these three distinct basic color components from the pure noisy color images in the initial phase. The basic color components obtained from the input noisy color images are fed simultaneously thorough three parallel different basic color component BDSONNs for subsequent processing. Because of the self-supervised behavior of the PBDSONN, no supervision or training is needed. The key operation of the PBDSONN consists mainly in the propagation of fuzzified information from the network intermediate outputs to the intermediate layer for self-organization. A diagram of the PBDSONN architecture is shown in Fig. 1.

The source layer in the PBDSONN architecture feeds the basic color gamut to the trinity of parallel BDSONNs. The sink layer in the PBDSONN architecture combines all three basic processed color component images to obtain a pure color image. Each constituent BDSONN of the PBDSONN architecture is arranged as

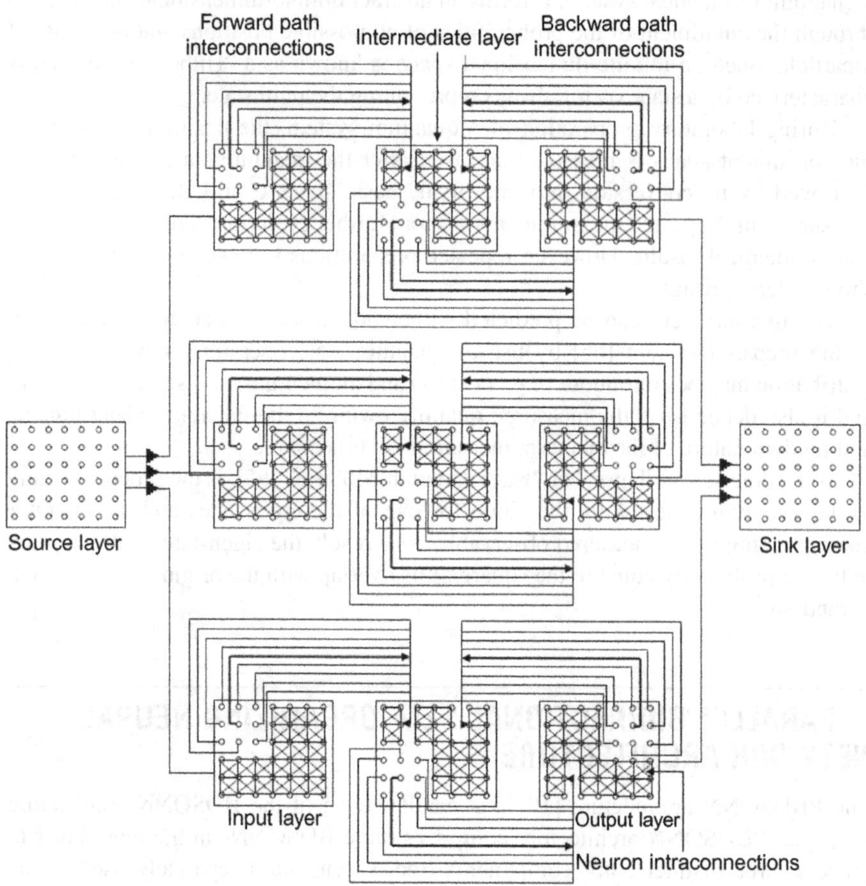

FIG. 1

A parallel bidirectional self-organizing neural network architecture.

S. Bhattacharyya, U. Maullik, P. Dutta, A parallel bi-directional self-organizing neural network (PBDSONN) architecture for color image extraction and segmentation, Neurocomputing 86, 17 and Figure No: 16, 2012.

follows: an input layer receiving fuzzified information, a hidden layer, and an output layer for the generation of processed final outputs. The number of neurons in the different network layers is representative of the number of pixels in the image region. On the reading of the fuzzy membership information from the three different color gamuts in input layer, information is propagated to the subsequent network layers for further processing. The neurons of the three layers for each parallel BDSONN are replicated by fuzzy membership values. The neurons in each network layer are fully linked with unit weight and thereby form a cellular architecture. The weighted interlinked connections are interconnected to successive layers of neurons through second-order neighborhood-based mapping. The relative fuzziness measure at the central seed neuron yields the interlinked strength between two successive layers of neurons. Let us consider the membership value of the ith central seed neuron of a specific network layer is μ_i and the membership value of each second-order (eight-connected) neighbor j (say) is μ_{ij} with respect to the ith seed neuron in the same layer. Therefore the weighted interlinking between subsequent layers corresponding to the ith central seed neuron is determined by the fuzzy complement operator as

$$w_{iji'} = \overline{(\mu_i - \mu_{ij})}. \tag{10}$$

The PBDSONN uses bilevel sigmoid activation functions in the different layers for extraction of pure color objects from a noisy perspective [19]. The input layer neurons of each parallel BDSONN in the PBDSONN architecture propagate the fuzzy membership values to the hidden layer in the forward direction for further processing. In the intermediate and output layers of each BDSONN, the summation of inputs accumulated at a particular seed neuron m is

$$I_m = \sum_i w_{ijm}\mu_{ij}. \tag{11}$$

The fuzzy membership value of the jth neighbor of the ith central seed neuron of the preceding network layer is represented by μ_{ij} and the interlinked strength between them is given by w_{ij}.

The binary sigmoid function $fsig(I)$ is used in this architecture to allow propagation between successive network layers as

$$fsig(I) = \frac{1}{1 + \mathrm{e}^{-\eta(I-\sigma)}}. \tag{12}$$

The gradient of the sigmoid function $fsig$ is considered represented by η and the activation to allow transfer of information is given by χ, known as "fuzzy context-sensitive thresholding." The accumulation of fuzzy information for all eight neighborhood neurons of the ith central seed neuron of the network layer provides the activation value.

The input-output association at the mth neuron of the hidden layer and the output layer is given by

$$Y = fsig(I_m). \tag{13}$$

Intersected readers should refer to [19,20,66] to learn more about the classical BDSONN and PBDSONN architectures and their primary operation.

7 HOPFIELD NETWORK

Proposed by John Hopfield in 1982, the Hopfield network [21] is a recurrent content-addressable memory that has binary threshold nodes which are supposed to yield a local minimum. It is a fully autoassociative architecture with symmetric weights without any self-loop. However, a problem with this network is that it tends to converge to the global minima instead. In a Hopfield network the weight between unit i and unit j is equal to that between unit j and unit i (i.e., $w_{ij} = w_{ji}$ and $w_{ii} = 0$ for all i, j). Since the weighted interconnections between two processing nodes are bidirectional, there is a feedback flow which forms a recurrent network. Fig. 2 shows the structure of a three-node Hopfield network. At any given time, a processing node may be an "active" or "inactive" state relying on the activation values. The state of the network is initialized by a random input pattern for the processing nodes (x_1, x_2, x_3), keeping some nodes "active" or "firing" and others "inactive," where a node is said to have fired if the output is "1," which occurs when the evaluated value of the activation function exceeds the threshold. The network performs by transforming itself at every instance through a transition to the next state, which is easily done by considering all neighboring nodes which output "1" or "active" processing nodes. Therefore a processing node x_i in the next network phase fires or outputs "1" if the

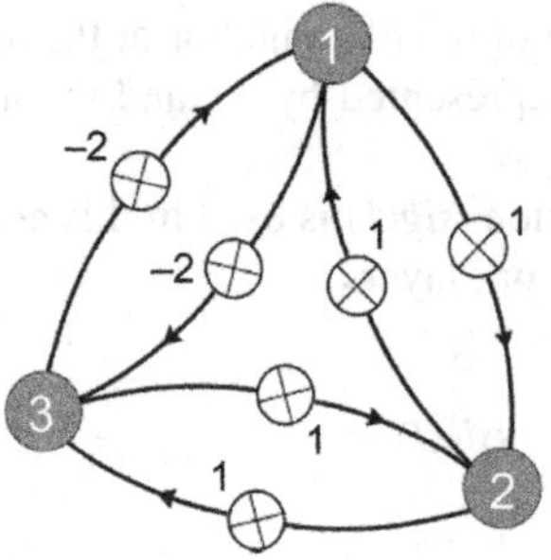

FIG. 2

Structure of a three-node fully connected Hopfield network.

S. Bhattacharyya, P. Pal, S. Bhowmick, Binary image denoising using a quantum multilayer self-organizing neural network, Appl. Soft Comput. 24, 720 and Figure No: 1, 2014.

total weight connected to x_i is greater than the activation value. This phenomenon is repeated until the network changes its state and stabilizes or does not transform any further.

The Hopfield network is characterized well by an energy function. In a situation where two processing nodes i and j in the network are connected by a positive weight, where node j outputs a "0" and node i outputs a "1," if node j is given a chance to update or fire, the contribution to its activation from node i is positive. Thus one can surmise that the weight is a constraint between nodes i and j that forces them to change the outputs to "1." Similarly, a negative weight would enforce opposite outputs. Thus the network behaves as a constraint satisfaction network. For the principle of the operation of the network dynamics of the Hopfield network, interested researchers may refer to [21,57] for details.

8 QUANTUM PARALLEL BIDIRECTIONAL SELF-ORGANIZING NEURAL NETWORK ARCHITECTURE

Since the QPBDSONN architecture is the quantum replica of the PBDSONN architecture [19], the QPBDSONN architecture similarly comprises three parallel QBDSONNs [59] for processing of three distinct basic color components (red, green, and blue). When the source layer of the QPBDSONN architecture receives pure color information from an input image scene, it segregates the three basic color components of the input pure color image for subsequent parallel processing. The information-processing neurons of the trinity of layers for each QBDSONN are represented by qubits. In contrast, information-processing neurons of the source and sink layers of the QPBDSONN architecture are represented as classical information without any quantum interference. Fig. 3 shows a diagram of the QPBDSONN architecture. The input, hidden, and output layers of each constituent QBDSONN in a quantum sense are illustrated by use of the matrix representation

$$\begin{pmatrix} |I_{11}\rangle & |I_{12}\rangle & |I_{13}\rangle & \dots & |I_{1n}\rangle \\ \dots & \dots & \dots & \dots & \dots \\ \dots & \dots & \dots & \dots & \dots \\ \dots & \dots & \dots & \dots & \dots \\ |I_{m1}\rangle & |I_{m2}\rangle & |I_{m3}\rangle & \dots & |I_{mn}\rangle \end{pmatrix}$$

for the input layer,

$$\begin{pmatrix} |H_{11}\rangle & |H_{12}\rangle & |H_{13}\rangle & \dots & |H_{1n}\rangle \\ \dots & \dots & \dots & \dots & \dots \\ \dots & \dots & \dots & \dots & \dots \\ \dots & \dots & \dots & \dots & \dots \\ |H_{m1}\rangle & |H_{m2}\rangle & |H_{m3}\rangle & \dots & |H_{mn}\rangle \end{pmatrix}$$

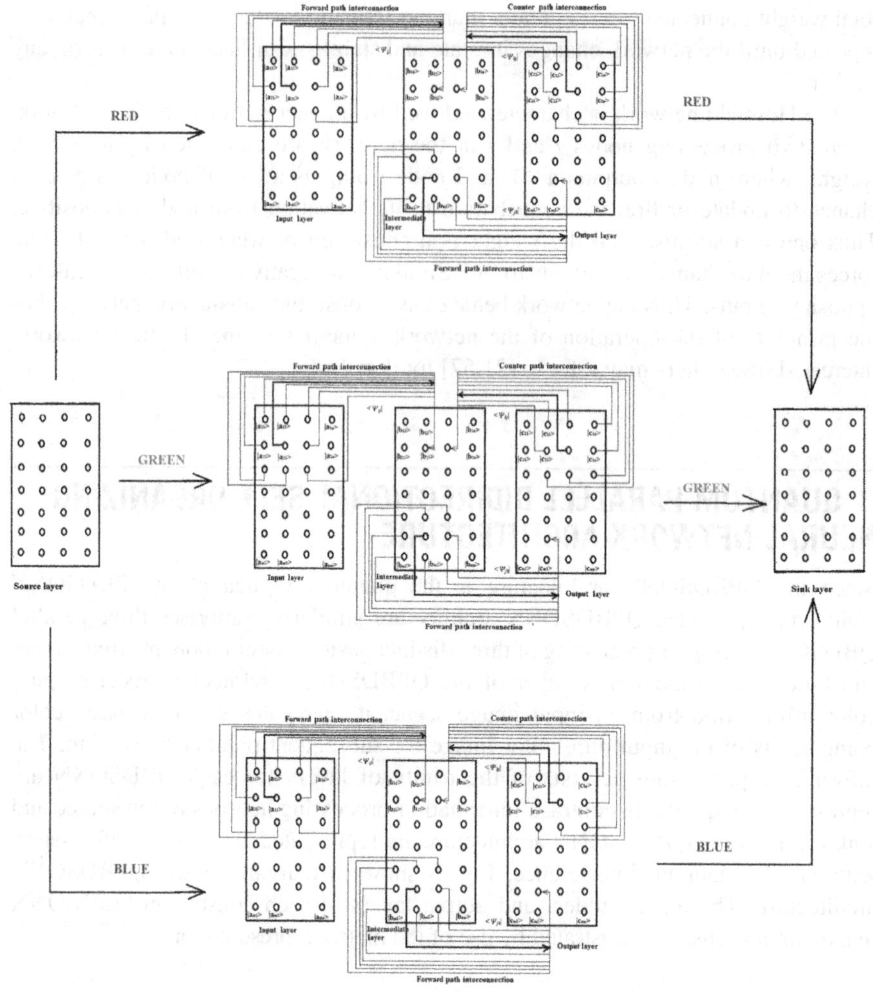

FIG. 3

Quantum parallel bidirectional self-organizing neural network architecture.

for the hidden layer, and

$$\begin{pmatrix} |O_{11}\rangle & |O_{12}\rangle & |O_{13}\rangle & \cdots & |O_{1n}\rangle \\ \cdots & \cdots & \cdots & \cdots & \cdots \\ \cdots & \cdots & \cdots & \cdots & \cdots \\ \cdots & \cdots & \cdots & \cdots & \cdots \\ |O_{m1}\rangle & |O_{m2}\rangle & |O_{m3}\rangle & \cdots & |O_{mn}\rangle \end{pmatrix}$$

for the output layer.

On receiving the basic color component from the source layer of the QPBDSONN, trinity of basic color component information is converted into quantum states. The switching layer or input layer of each constituent QBDSONN propagates the inputs to subsequent quantum layers for next-level further processing. The basic color components in terms of qubits are received in the switching input layer. Fully intralinked neurons are associated with weighted intralink $\frac{\pi}{2}$ (quantum 1 logic). Thus the central seed pixel (neuron) for each layer of the QBDSONN accumulates eight-connected neighborhood pixels with quantum fuzziness measure. The quantum fuzzy context-sensitive thresholding scheme is incorporated to enable the binary sigmoid transfer function and therefore allows the forward propagation and counterpropagation of information on the basis of activation values. Motivated by the use of forward propagation and counterpropagation of quantum states, the dynamics of the network self-organizes interconnected weights between subsequent layers of neurons. The input or switching layer of each QBDSONN in the QPBDSONN architecture abstains from any kind of further information processing after reading information from the image scene.

A two-way strategy is adopted for weighted interlayer connections in the suggested QPBDSONN architecture. A rotation gate is introduced for these weighted interconnections between subsequent quantum layers of the network. The rotation angle is driven by relative fuzzy measures in the quantum sense at the constituent neurons. A bilevel sigmoid function governing the computational efficacy of the trinity of neural layers present in the architecture is a notable feature in the proposed QPBDSONN. The output of the self-organized network architecture is obtained by use of the counterpropagation of quantum information. The QPBDSONN network stabilizes after processing the three distinct basic color components of the input pure color noisy image by employing three parallel QBDSONN. Finally, the sink layer of the proposed network architecture concatenates all these three color components and results extracted image.

8.1 DYNAMICS OF NETWORKS

When the pixel color values in fuzzy membership form are received from the image scene, the source layer of the QPBDSONN primarily segregates the pure color input image with dimension 256×256 into a three basic color component image and transforms the fuzzified pixel intensity $[0, 255]$ into the quantum level $[0, \frac{\pi}{2} \times 255]$.

R_i, G_i, and B_i are information in the fuzzy sense received by the input layers of all constituent QBDSONNs [59] dedicated to processing the three basic color component information red, green, and blue respectively, and RQ_i, GQ_i, and BQ_i are the corresponding quantum fuzzified inputs. Then

$$RQ_i = \frac{\pi}{2} R_i, \tag{14}$$

$$GQ_i = \frac{\pi}{2} G_i, \tag{15}$$

$$BQ_i = \frac{\pi}{2} B_i \tag{16}$$

qubits are used in the QPBDSONN architecture to describe the weighted interconnection and its activation. The angle of rotation for the interconnection weight and the activation value or threshold are α and β respectively, where the activation $|\theta\rangle$ can be expressed as

$$|\omega\rangle = \begin{bmatrix} \cos\beta \\ \sin\beta \end{bmatrix}. \tag{17}$$

For each constituent QBDSONN in the QPBDSONN architecture, the relation between the input and output of a neuron for each layer can be described as

$$|y_R\rangle = fsig\left(\sum_i^n RQ_i\langle\theta_i|\omega_k\rangle\right) = fsig\left(\sum_i^n RQ_i\cos(\alpha_i - \beta)\right), \tag{18}$$

$$|y_G\rangle = fsig\left(\sum_i^n GQ_i\langle\theta_i|\omega_k\rangle\right) = fsig\left(\sum_i^n GQ_i\cos(\alpha_i - \beta)\right), \tag{19}$$

$$|y_B\rangle = fsig\left(\sum_i^n BQ_i\langle\theta_i|\omega_k\rangle\right) = fsig\left(\sum_i^n BQ_i\cos(\alpha_i - \beta)\right). \tag{20}$$

The bilevel sigmoid function *fsig* used in the above equations is defined as

$$fsig(x) = \frac{1}{1 + e^{-\xi(x-\beta)}}. \tag{21}$$

Two key parameters used in the *fsig* function are $|\beta\rangle$ and ξ. These parameters control the gradient of *fsig*. $|y_R\rangle$, $|y_G\rangle$, and $|y_B\rangle$ are the true output generated in the output layer of each QBDSONN [59] in the QPBDSONN architecture.

Let us consider u_{R_j}, u_{G_j}, and u_{B_j} to be the intermediate layer's output of each QBDSONN used in the QPBDSONN of the jth candidate neuron and where $|R_k\rangle$, $|G_k\rangle$, and $|B_k\rangle$ are the kth candidate neuron's output in the output layer of each parallel QBDSONN, red, green, and blue respectively. The weighted interconnection between the input layer and the hidden layer is $|\theta_{ij}\rangle$ and that between the hidden, or intermediate, layer and the output layer of each parallel QBDSONN is $|\theta_{jk}\rangle$. The activation values in the intermediate and output layers are $|\omega_j\rangle$ and $|\omega_k\rangle$ respectively.

For each constituent QBDSONN of the QPBDSONN, for $i = 1$ to m input neurons and for $j = 1$ to n hidden neurons [67]

$$|R_k\rangle = fsig\left(\sum_j^n u_{R_j}\langle\theta_{jk}|\omega_k\rangle\right) = fsig\left(\sum_j^n fsig\left(\sum_i^m RQ_i\langle\theta_{ij}|\omega_j\rangle\right)\langle\theta_{jk}|\omega_k\rangle\right), \tag{22}$$

$$|G_k\rangle = fsig\left(\sum_j^n u_{G_j}\langle\theta_{jk}|\omega_k\rangle\right) = fsig\left(\sum_j^n fsig\left(\sum_i^m GQ_i\langle\theta_{ij}|\omega_j\rangle\right)\langle\theta_{jk}|\omega_k\rangle\right), \tag{23}$$

$$|B_k\rangle = fsig\left(\sum_j^n u_{B_j}\langle\theta_{jk}|\omega_k\rangle\right) = fsig\left(\sum_j^n fsig\left(\sum_i^m BQ_i\langle\theta_{ij}|\omega_j\rangle\right)\langle\theta_{jk}|\omega_k\rangle\right); \tag{24}$$

that is,

$$|R_k\rangle = fsig\left(\sum_j^n fsig\left(\sum_i^m RQ_i \cos(\alpha_{ij} - \beta_j)\right)\cos(\alpha_{jk} - \beta_k)\right) \tag{25}$$

$$|G_k\rangle = fsig\left(\sum_j^n fsig\left(\sum_i^m GQ_i \cos(\alpha_{ij} - \beta_j)\right)\cos(\alpha_{jk} - \beta_k)\right) \tag{26}$$

$$|B_k\rangle = fsig\left(\sum_j^n fsig\left(\sum_i^m BQ_i \cos(\alpha_{ij} - \beta_j)\right)\cos(\alpha_{jk} - \beta_k)\right) \tag{27}$$

Finally, in the output layer of each constituent QBDSONN, the outputs are generated in terms of quantum states. To reduce the quantum states, a quantum measurement is done and converted into pure color outputs $[0, 255]$ in the output layer and stored for further processing until the network converges. The outcomes being measured in terms of the three basic color component image having identical dimension 256×256 are fused in the sink layer to obtain true outputs.

8.2 NETWORK WEIGHT ADJUSTMENT

For each constituent QBDSONN [59] in the QPBDSONN architecture, a single qubit rotation gate is used to tune the strengths of the weighted interconnections and the quantum thresholding as

$$|\theta(i+1)\rangle = \begin{pmatrix} \cos\Delta\alpha & -\sin\Delta\alpha \\ \sin\Delta\alpha & \cos\Delta\alpha \end{pmatrix}|\theta(i)\rangle, \tag{28}$$

$$|\omega(i+1)\rangle = \begin{pmatrix} \cos\Delta\beta & -\sin\Delta\beta \\ \sin\Delta\beta & \cos\Delta\beta \end{pmatrix}|\omega(i)\rangle, \tag{29}$$

where

$$\alpha(i+1) = \alpha(i) + \Delta\alpha_i \tag{30}$$

and

$$\beta(i+1) = \beta(i) + \Delta\beta_i. \tag{31}$$

The selection of suitable rotation angles, $\Delta\alpha_t$ and $\Delta\beta_i$, drives the sequences of the iteration as given in Eqs. (30) and (31) superlinearly converge. However, the superlinearity of convergence of the network interoperability is established by stabilization of the network.

The error incurred by each constituent QBDSONN in the QPBDSONN architecture is illustrated as

$$Err = \frac{1}{2}\sum(ICW[i+1] - ICW[i])^2. \tag{32}$$

The weighted interconnection strength at a particular iteration, or epoch (i), is $ICW(i)$, which is obtained after operation through quantum measurement of $|\theta(i+1)\rangle$. Err is a continuous coherent function of α and β.

It can be assumed that $\alpha(i) \to \overline{\alpha}$, $\beta(i) \to \overline{\beta}$.

$$\sigma(i) = \alpha(i) - \overline{\alpha}, \tag{33}$$

$$\nu(i) = \beta(i) - \overline{\beta}, \tag{34}$$

$$\vartheta(i) = \alpha(i+1) - \alpha(i) = \sigma(i+1) - \sigma(i), \tag{35}$$

and

$$\kappa(t) = \beta(i+1) - \beta(i) = \nu(i+1) - \nu(i). \tag{36}$$

However, superlinear convergence of the sequences $\{\alpha(i)\}$ and $\{\beta(i)\}$ can be shown subject to the following:

$$\lim_{i\to\infty} \frac{||\alpha(i+1) - \overline{\alpha}||}{||\alpha(i) - \overline{\alpha}||} \le 1, \tag{37}$$

$$\lim_{i\to\infty} \frac{||\beta(i+1) - \overline{\omega}||}{||\beta(i) - \overline{\beta}||} \le 1. \tag{38}$$

The formulations in Eqs. (37) and (38) can be shown as

$$||\sigma(i+1)|| = O||\vartheta(i)||, \tag{39}$$

$$||\nu(i+1)|| = O||\kappa(i)||. \tag{40}$$

Moreover, the angles of rotation $\Delta\alpha$ and $\Delta\beta$ are determined as follows:

$$\Delta\alpha = -\lambda\left(\frac{\partial Err(\alpha(i), \beta(i))}{\partial\alpha(i)}(Err(\alpha(i), \beta(i)))\right)^{\frac{1}{\gamma}}, \tag{41}$$

$$\Delta\beta = -\lambda\left(\frac{\partial Err(\alpha(i),\beta(i))}{\partial\alpha(i)}(Err(\alpha(i),\beta(i)))\right)^{\frac{1}{\gamma}}. \tag{42}$$

The rate of learning in self-organization and self-supervision is λ and $\gamma > 2$. The learning rate λ is determined by the relative measure of quantum fuzzy information which is computed after quantum measurement at an individual neuron.

According to Thaler's formula,

$$Err(\alpha(i{+}1),\ \beta\,(i+1))\ Err(\alpha(i)\beta\,(i)) \tag{43}$$

$$=\left[\ \Delta\alpha(i)\quad \Delta\beta(i)\ \right]\begin{bmatrix}\frac{\partial Err(\alpha(i),\beta(i))}{\partial\alpha(i)}\\ \frac{\partial Err(\alpha(i),\beta(i))}{\partial\beta(i)}\end{bmatrix}+O\left[\ ||\Delta\alpha(i)\quad \Delta\beta(i)||\ \right]$$

$$\approx\lambda\left(\left(\frac{\partial Err(\alpha\,(i)\,,\beta(i))}{\partial\alpha(i)}\right)^2+\left(\frac{\partial Err\,(\alpha\,(i)\,,\beta\,(i))}{\partial\beta\,(i)}\right)\right)^2(Err(\alpha(i)\ ,\beta\,(i)))^{\frac{1}{\gamma}}. \tag{44}$$

Therefore $Err(\alpha(i+1),\beta(i+1)) - Err(\alpha(i),\beta(i)) \leq 0$ reflects monotonically decreasing behavior of the corresponding iterative sequences $\{\alpha(i)\}$ and $\{\beta(i)\}$. The coherent nature of the continuous function $Err(\alpha(i),\beta(i))$ is as follows:

$$\lim_{i\to\infty} Err(\alpha(i),\beta(i)) = (\overline{\alpha},\overline{\beta}). \tag{45}$$

Eq. (45) elucidates the rapid convergent behavior of the iterative sequences $\{\alpha(i)\}$ and $\{\beta(i)\}$ owing to

$$\lim_{i\to\infty}\frac{||Err(\alpha(i+1),\beta(i+1)) - (\overline{\alpha},\overline{\beta})||}{||Err(\alpha(i),\beta(i)) - (\overline{\alpha},\overline{\beta})||} \leq 1. \tag{46}$$

The superlinearity of convergence can be illustrated with use of the underlying section [68]. Let us assume $\zeta = \frac{\partial Err(\alpha(i),\beta(i))}{\partial\alpha(i)}$; then

$$\frac{||\sigma(i+1)||}{||\vartheta(i)||} = \frac{||\alpha(i+1)-\overline{\alpha}||}{||-\lambda\left(\frac{\partial Err(\alpha(i),\beta(i))}{\partial\alpha(i)}Err(\alpha(i),\beta(i))\right)^{\frac{1}{\gamma}}||} \geq \frac{||\alpha(i+1)-\overline{\alpha}||}{\lambda\zeta(Err(\alpha(i),\beta(i)))^{\frac{1}{\gamma}}}. \tag{47}$$

Since $Err(\alpha(i),\beta(i))$ is the quadratic equation of $\alpha(i)$ and $\beta(i)$, where $\gamma > 2$,

$$||\alpha(i+1)-\overline{\alpha}|| = O((Err(\alpha(i),\beta(i)))^{\frac{1}{\gamma}}). \tag{48}$$

Therefore $||(\sigma(i+1))|| = O||(\vartheta(i))||$ proves the superlinear convergence of the iterative sequence $\{\alpha(i)\}$. Similarly, the iterative sequence $\{\beta(i)\}$ can also be proved to be superlinearly convergent.

8.3 NETWORK PARALLEL SELF-SUPERVISION ALGORITHM

The input-output association and the principle of the functioning in a quantum environment are described by the self-organizing and self-supervising algorithm of the QPBDSONN. The operations of the self-organizing procedure execute in five stages: (1) initialization of the network; (2) image segregation; (3) quantum input; (4) forward propagation; and (5) counterpropagation.

The operations of the self-supervision algorithm for the suggested QPBDSONN are summarized as follows [19,59]:

SELF-SUPERVISION ALGORITHM

1. Begin

Initialization of network stage

2. For each constituent QBDSONN, initialize all the weighted intralayer connection matrices between constituent neurons for all three layers to $\frac{\pi}{2}$, $IW[x][i]; x = R, G, B; i = 1, 2, 3$.

Image segregation stage

3. Perform separation on input pure color image fuzzy intensity values of size $a \times b$ into the trinity of distinct basic color component images as

$$Im[a][b] \Rightarrow I[x][i][a][b], x = R, G, B;$$

Quantum input stage

4. For each constituent QBDSONN of the QPBDSONN architecture, pure basic color fuzzy intensity values $[0, 255]$ are received by the input layer of each QBDSONN $I[x][i][a][b], x = R, G, B; i = 1$; from the segmented basic color component images of the input image scene of identical sizes $a \times b$.

5. Transform fuzzy input values $[0, 255]$ from the basic image plane $I[x][i][a][b]$ into quantum states $[0, \frac{\pi}{2} \times 255]$. Quantum fuzzy information $QI[x][i][a][b]$ in terms of qubits is transformed as

$$QI[x][i][a][b] = \frac{\pi}{2} \times I[x][i][a][b], x = R, G, B; i = 1.$$

Input layers of each constituent QBDSONN of the QPBDSONN architecture receive quantum fuzzified image information $QI[x][1][a][b]$ as inputs.

Forward propagation stage

6. In this phase the angle of rotation for weighted interconnections and the activations in each layer of the constituent QBDSONN of the QPBDSONN network are initialized as

$$\alpha = 2\pi \times \left(\frac{\pi}{2} - (QI[x][i][s][t] - QI[x][i][p][q])\right),$$

$$\beta = 2\pi \times Th[x][i+1][p][q],$$

$$|\theta\rangle = \begin{bmatrix} \cos\alpha \\ \sin\alpha \end{bmatrix},$$

$$|\omega\rangle = \begin{bmatrix} \cos\beta \\ \sin\beta \end{bmatrix}.$$

At a particular epoch (e), the ith network layer's second neighborhood-based $[s, t]$th quantum neuron or qubit of each constituent QBDSONN is $QI[x][i][s][t]$ and the value of the $[p, q]$th

central seed neuron is $QI[x][i][p][q]$. The thresholding value of the ith layer is computed by accumulating quantum fuzzified information at the $(i+1)$th network layer's $[p,q]$th central seed neuron and stored at $Th[x][i+1][p][q]$.
7. The update procedure for weighted interconnections for each constituent QBDSONN of the QPBDSONN architecture uses a rotation gate:

$$W[x][e+1][i][i+1][s][t] = \begin{bmatrix} \cos\alpha & -\sin\alpha \\ \sin\alpha & \cos\alpha \end{bmatrix} \times W[x][e][i][i+1][s][t].$$

In a specific epoch (e), for each QBDSONN in the QPBDSONN architecture, $W[x][e][i][i+1][s][t]$ defines the interconnection weight.
8. The outputs for each constituent QBDSONN of the QPBDSONN architecture are produced by updating of the interconnection weights and activation values using a rotation gate as

$$QI[x][i+1][p][q] = \sum [fsig(QI[x][i][s][t] * W[x][e][i][i+1][s][t])],$$

where $*$ is the inner product operator.
9. Repeat steps 5, 6, and 7 with intermediate layer quantum states of each QBDSONN.
Counterpropagation stage
10. For each QBDSONN, the rotation angle for interconnection strengths and the thresholds in the output layers are initialized as

$$\alpha = 2\pi \times \left(\frac{\pi}{2} - (QP[x][i][s][t] - QP[x][i][p][q])\right),$$

$$\beta = 2\pi \times Th[x][i-1][p][q],$$

$$|\theta\rangle = \begin{bmatrix} \cos\alpha \\ \sin\alpha \end{bmatrix},$$

$$|\omega\rangle = \begin{bmatrix} \cos\beta \\ \sin\beta \end{bmatrix},$$

where the ith layer's thresholding value $Th[x][i+1][p][q]$ is accumulated at the $[p,q]$th central seed neuron of the $(i-1)$th network layer for the xth QBDSONN.
11. For processing of the three basic color components of each constituent QBDSONN, compute the interconnection weight using a rotation gate as follows:

$$W[x][e+1][i][i+1][s][t] = \begin{bmatrix} \cos\alpha & -\sin\alpha \\ \sin\alpha & \cos\alpha \end{bmatrix} \times W[x][e][i][i+1][s][t],$$

where the interconnection weight at the specific epoch (e) of the xth QBDSONN is $W[x][e][i][i+1][s][t]$.
12.

$$QI[x][i-1][p][q] = \sum [fsig(QI[x][i][s][t] * W[x][e][i][i-1][s][t])].$$

13. Repeat until $((W[x][e+1][i][i+1][s][t] - W[x][e][i][i+1][s][t]) < \epsilon_0)$, where ϵ_0 is the tolerance error.
14. End

The interconnection weights and the processed outputs as pure color intensity information are obtained on application of the quantum measurement in the output layers of each of all three constituent QBDSONNs. Finally, the trinity of the primary pure color components red, green, and blue are combined in the sink layer of the suggested QPBDSONN architecture with use of an additive fusion technique to obtain the true pure color extracted output image.

9 EXPERIMENTAL RESULTS

Experiments were performed rigorously on a sufficient number of Gaussian noise-affected artificial synthetic and real-life wrench pure color images with various intensities with mean of 0 and standard deviation $\sigma = 8, 10, 12, 14$, and 16 [58]. The test was also conducted on test images identical to the aforementioned ones affected by noise of degree 64%, 100%, 144%, 196%, and 256% [19,36,40]. Fig. 4 shows the target test images. Figs. 5–8 reflect the input pure color version of images affected by uniform and Gaussian noise. The denoised pure color versions of the output images extracted from the Gaussian noisy versions by means of the classical PBDSONN architecture [19], the proposed QPBDSONN architecture, the supervised threefold parallel Hopfield network [21], and the median filter with adaptive discrete wavelet transformations (DWTs) [18] are provided in Figs. 11, 15, 19, 23 and 12, 16, 20, 24. Figs. 9, 13, 17, 21 and 10, 14, 18, 22 shows denoised pure color version of the output images extracted from the uniform noisy versions by means of the classical PBDSONN [19] architecture, the proposed QPBDSONN architecture, the supervised threefold parallel Hopfield network [21] and the median filter with adaptive DWTs [18].

From Figs. 9–24 it can be summarized that the proposed QPBDSONN architecture incurs minimum distortion in the shape of the extracted objects from the noisy perspective compared with the classical PBDSONN architecture and the median

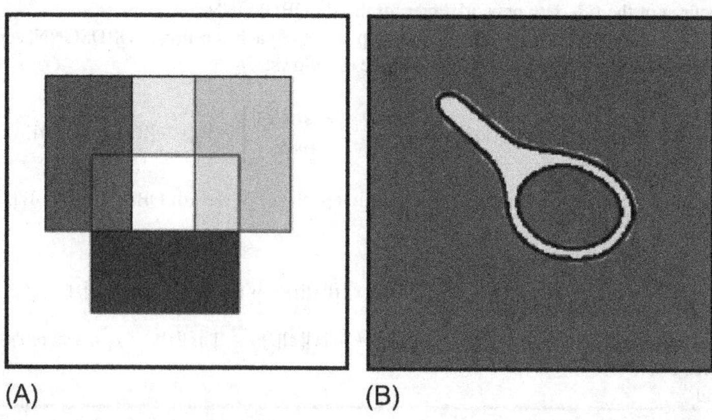

FIG. 4

Target test images: (A) artificial synthetic pure color image; (B) real-life wrench pure color image.

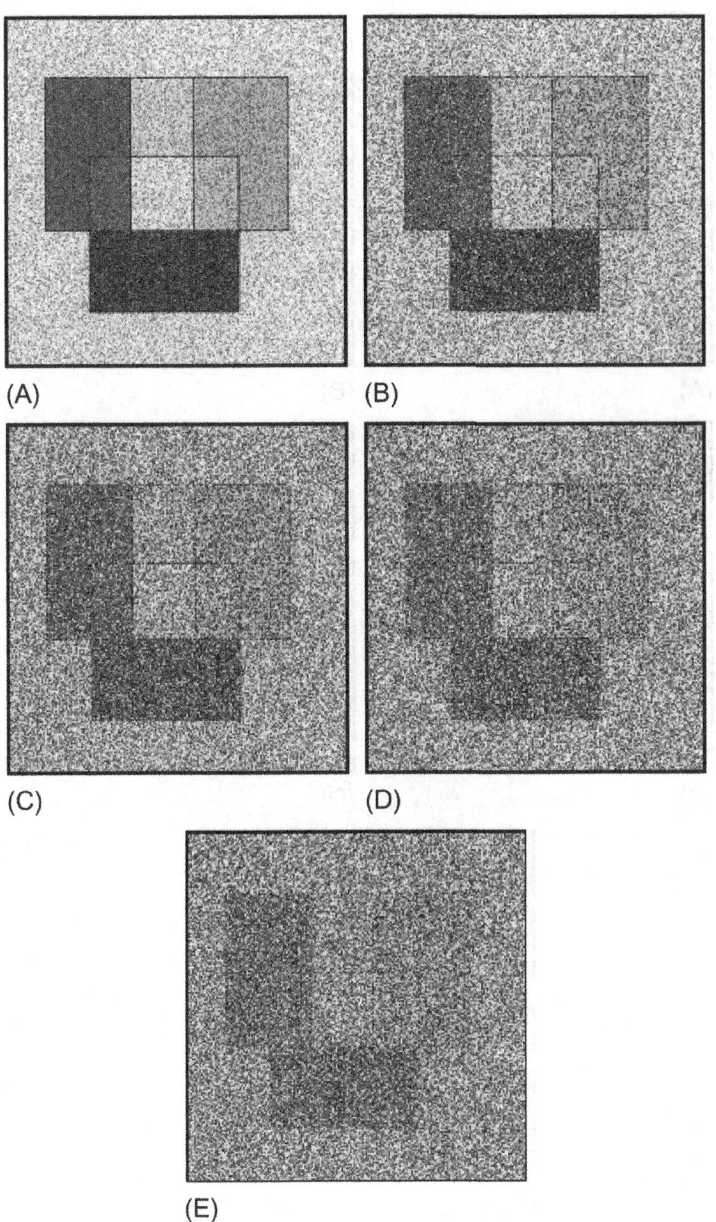

FIG. 5

Test synthetic artificial pure color images with uniform noise with degrees 64% (A), 100% (B), 144% (C), 196% (D), and 256% (E).

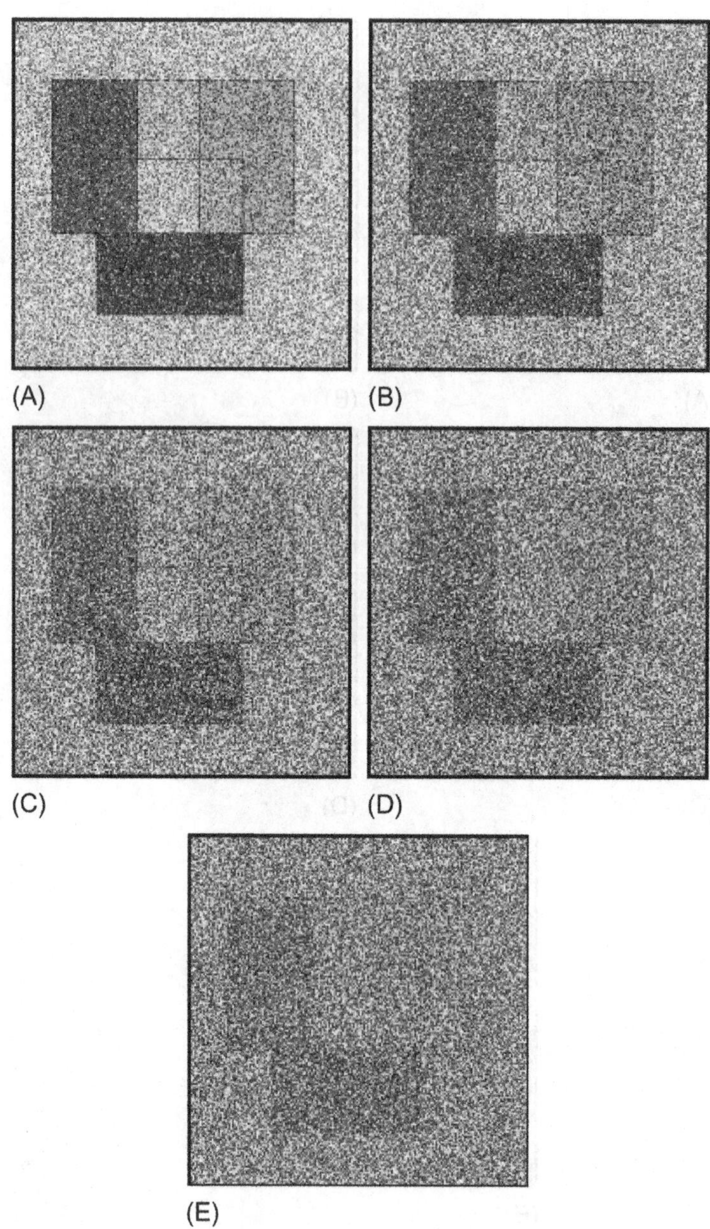

FIG. 6

Test synthetic artificial pure color images with Gaussian noise at $\sigma = 8$ (A), $\sigma = 10$ (B), $\sigma = 12$ (C), $\sigma = 14$ (D), and $\sigma = 16$ (E).

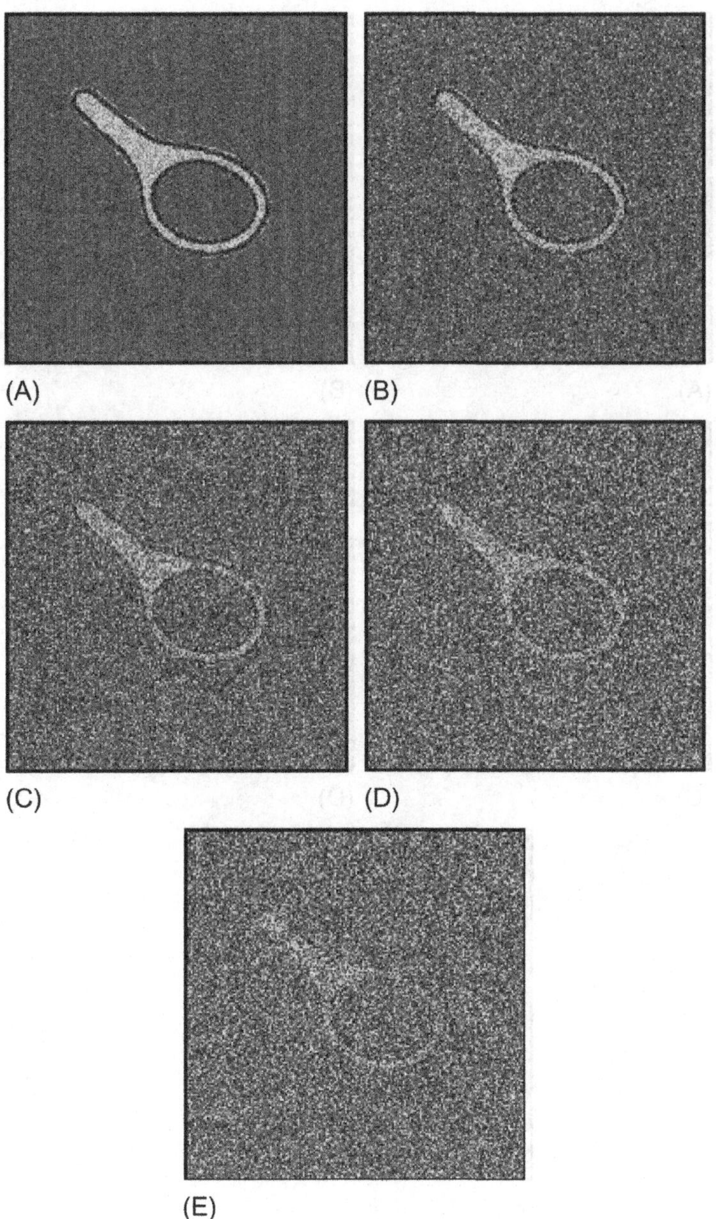

FIG. 7

Test real-life wrench pure color images with uniform noise with degree 64% (A), 100% (B), 144% (C), 196% (D), and 256% (E).

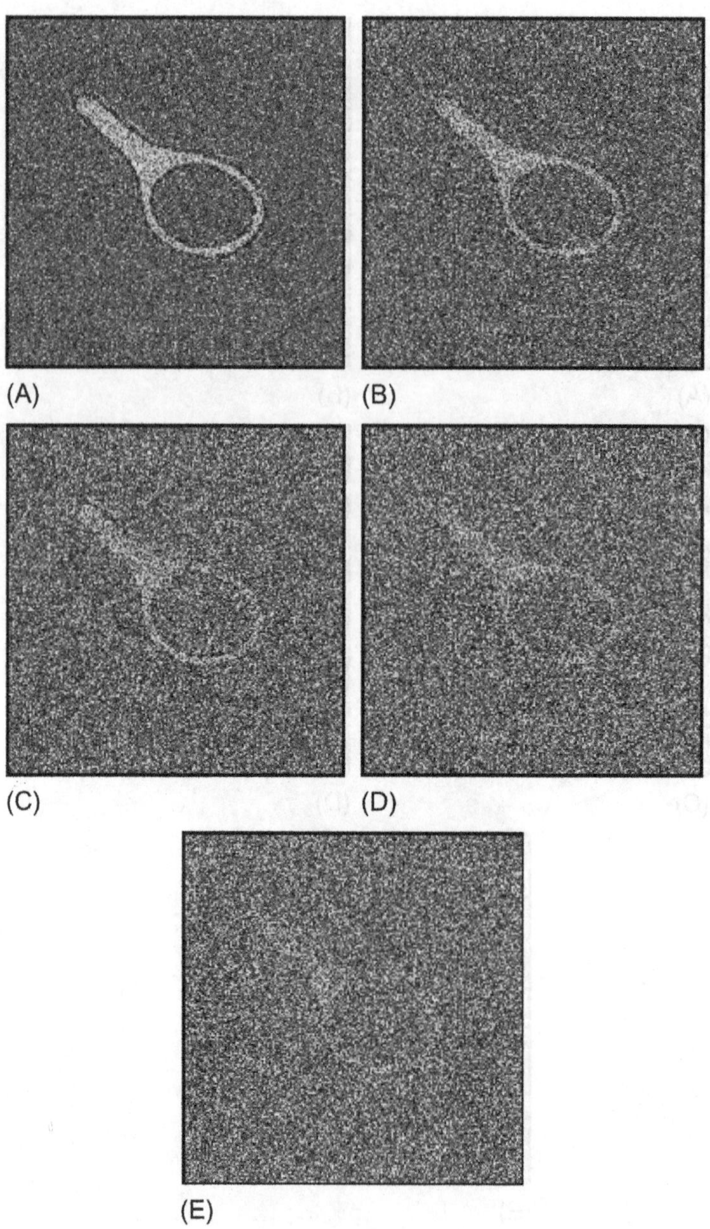

FIG. 8

Test real-life wrench pure color images with Gaussian noise at $\sigma = 8$ (A), $\sigma = 10$ (B), $\sigma = 12$ (C), $\sigma = 14$ (D), and $\sigma = 16$ (E).

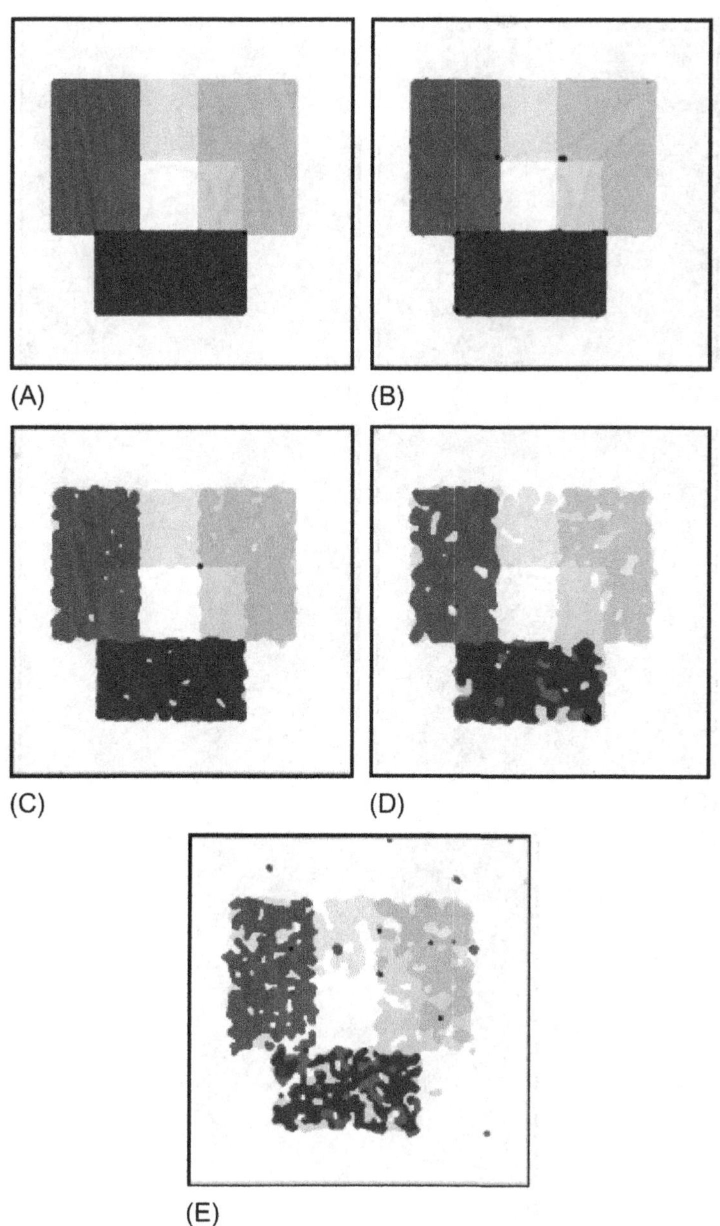

FIG. 9

Parallel bidirectional self-organizing neural network-extracted output pure color images from the test artificial synthetic pure color images with uniform noise.

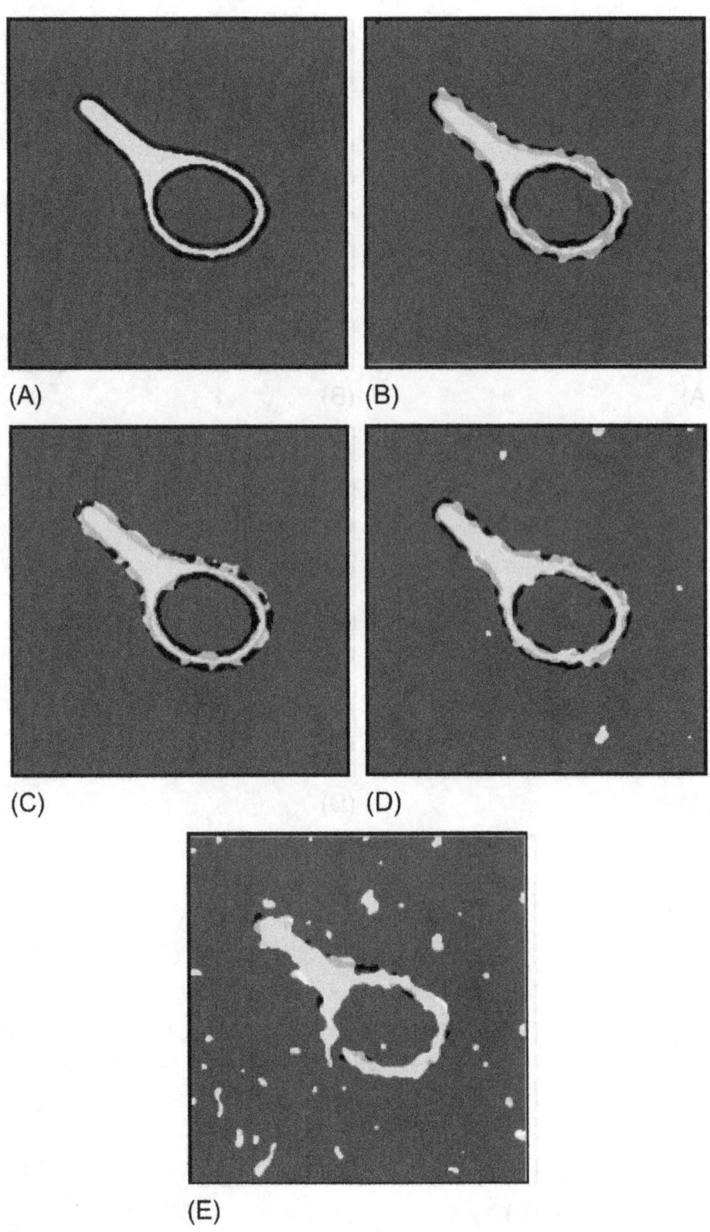

FIG. 10

Parallel bidirectional self-organizing neural network-extracted output pure color images from the test real-life wrench pure color images with uniform noise.

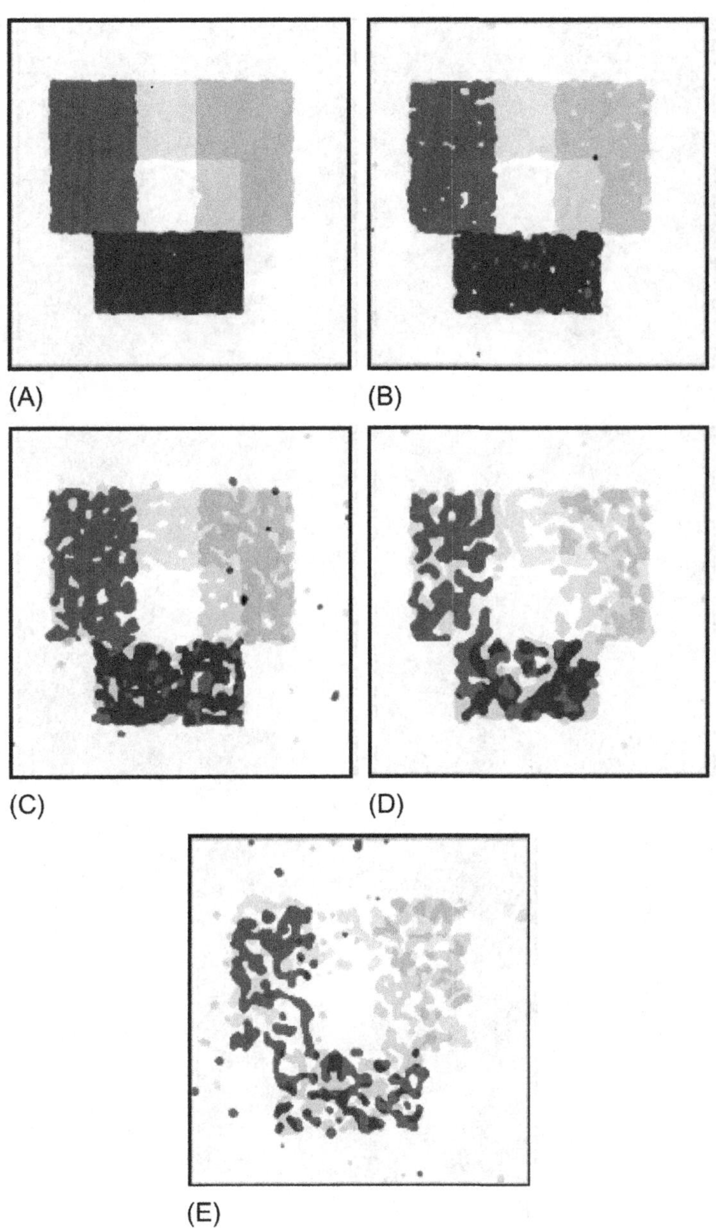

FIG. 11

Parallel bidirectional self-organizing neural network-extracted output pure color images from the test artificial synthetic pure color images with Gaussian noise.

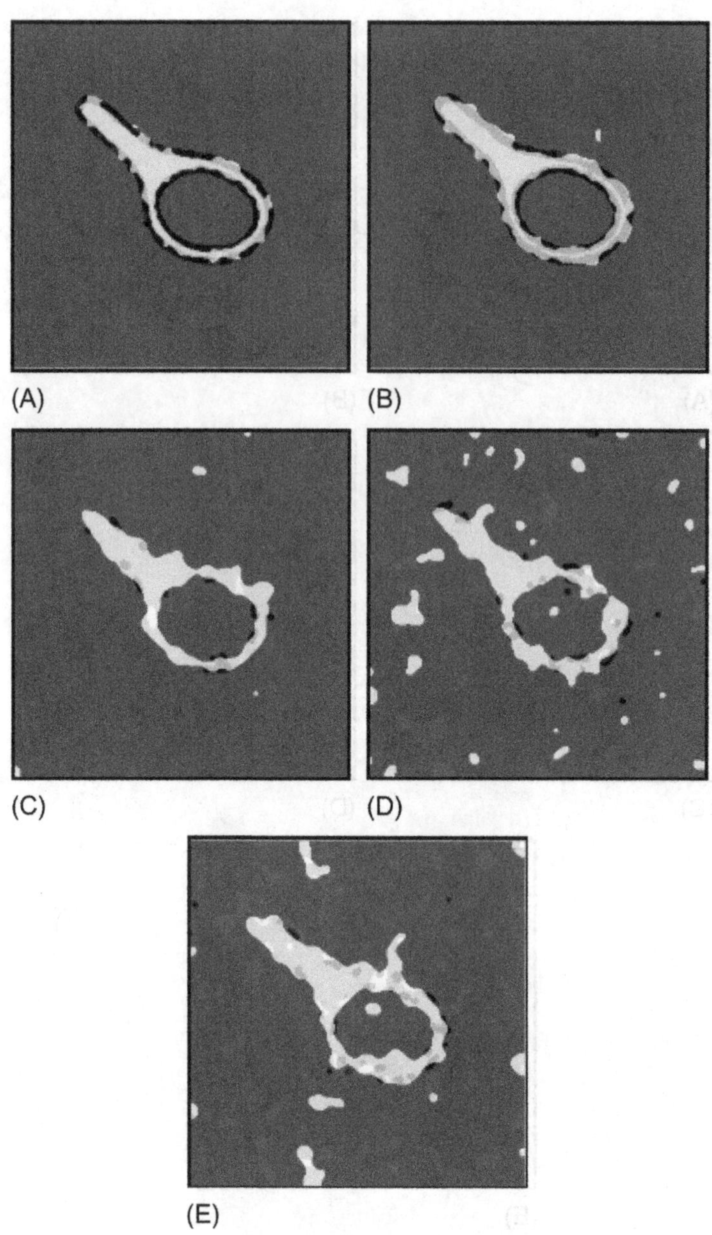

FIG. 12

Parallel bidirectional self-organizing neural network-extracted output pure color images from the test real-life wrench images with Gaussian noise.

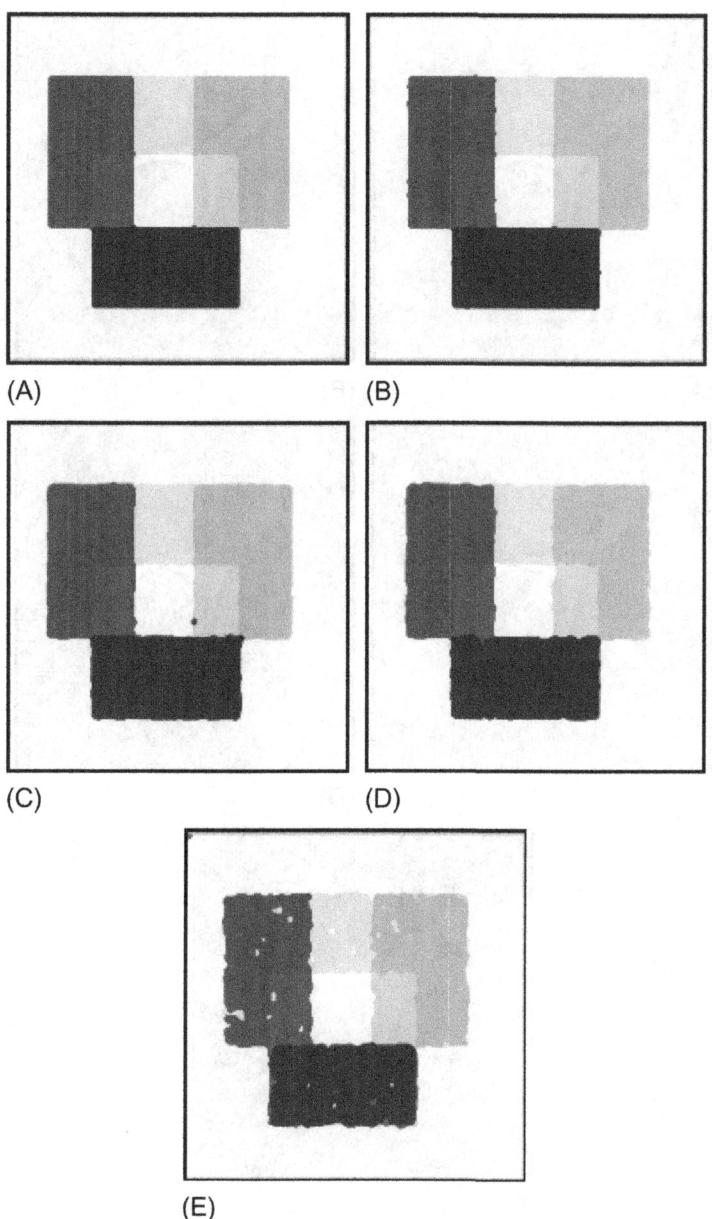

FIG. 13

Quantum parallel bidirectional self-organizing neural network-extracted output pure color images from the test artificial synthetic pure color images with uniform noise.

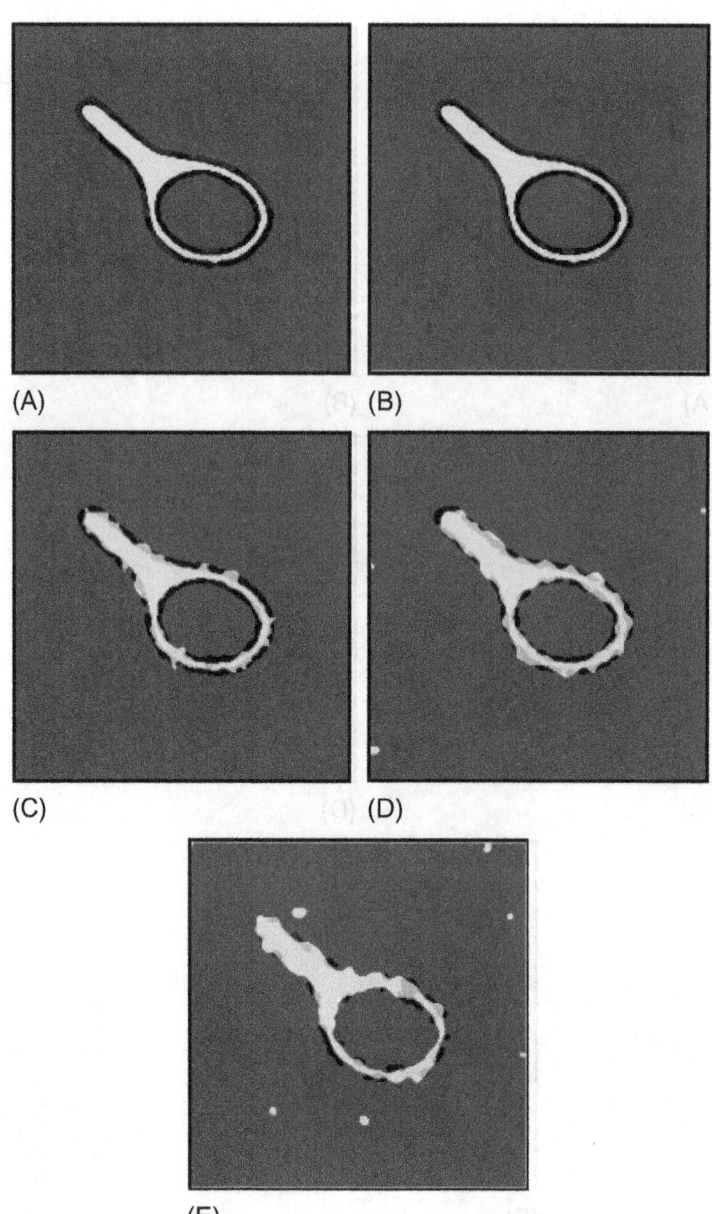

FIG. 14

Quantum parallel bidirectional self-organizing neural network-extracted output pure color images from the test real-life wrench pure color images with uniform noise.

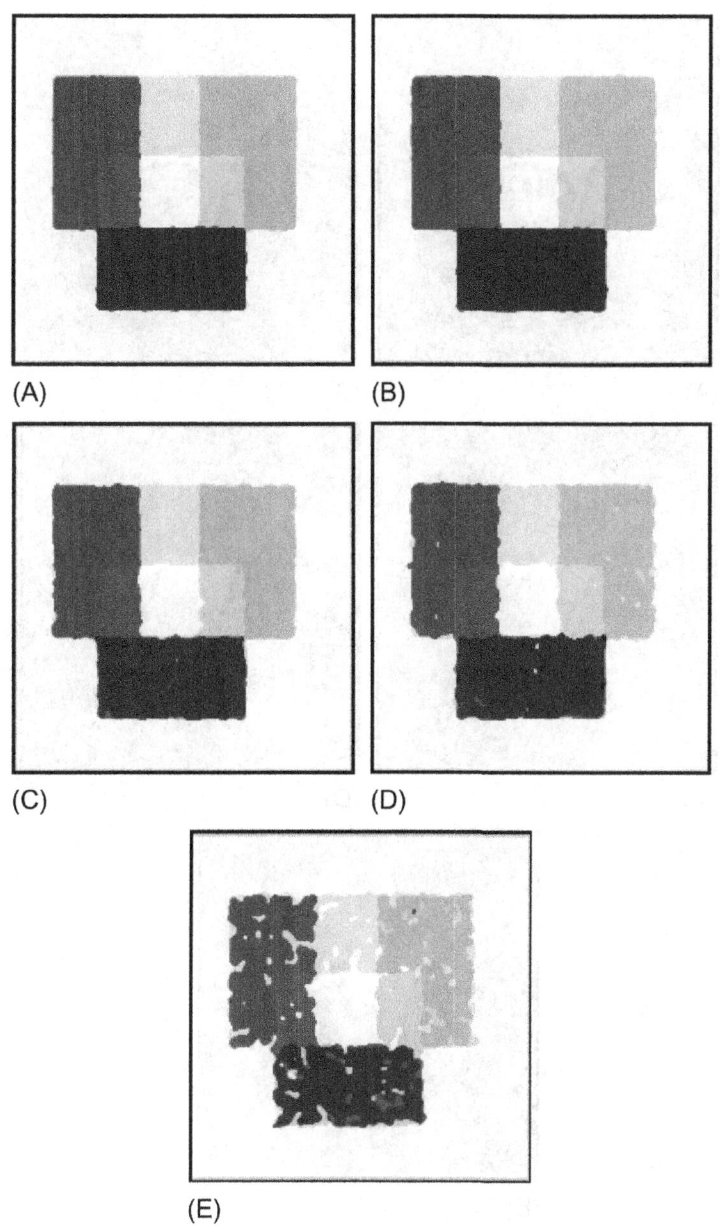

FIG. 15

Quantum parallel bidirectional self-organizing neural network-extracted output pure color images from the test artificial synthetic pure color images with Gaussian noise.

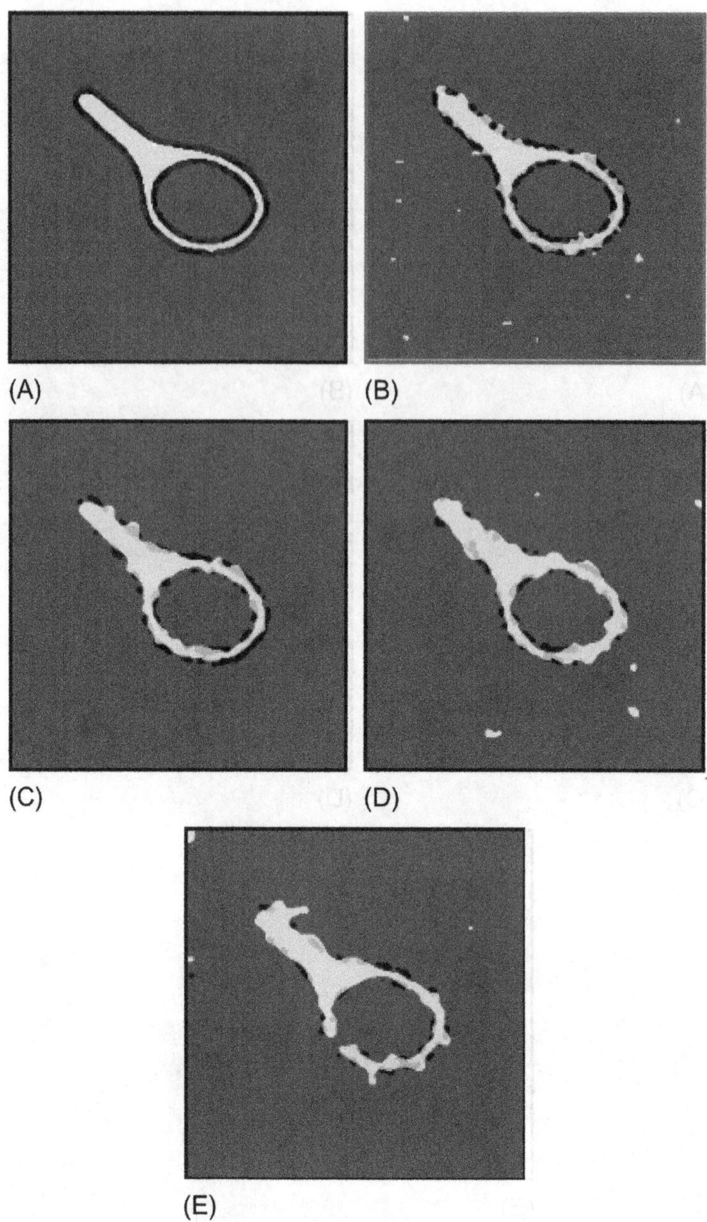

FIG. 16

Quantum parallel bidirectional self-organizing neural network-extracted output pure color images from the test real-life wrench images with Gaussian noise.

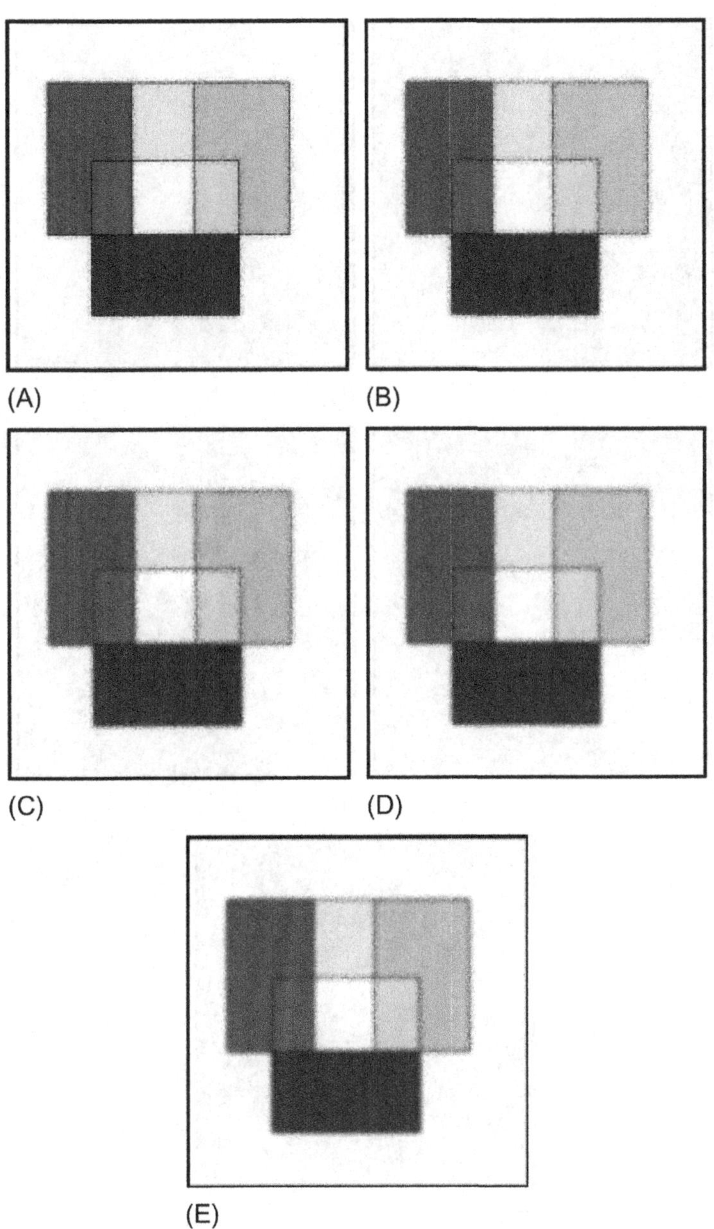

FIG. 17

Hopfield net-extracted output pure color images from the test artificial synthetic pure color images with uniform noise.

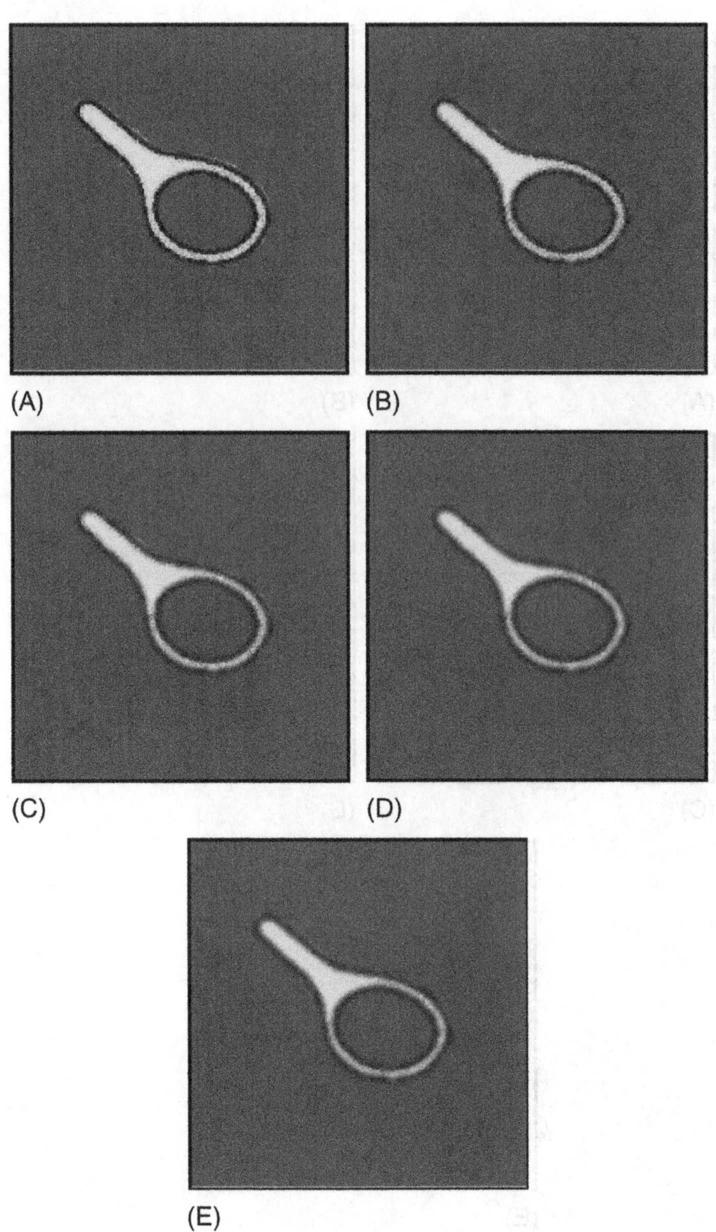

FIG. 18

Hopfield net-extracted output pure color images from the test real-life wrench pure color images with uniform noise.

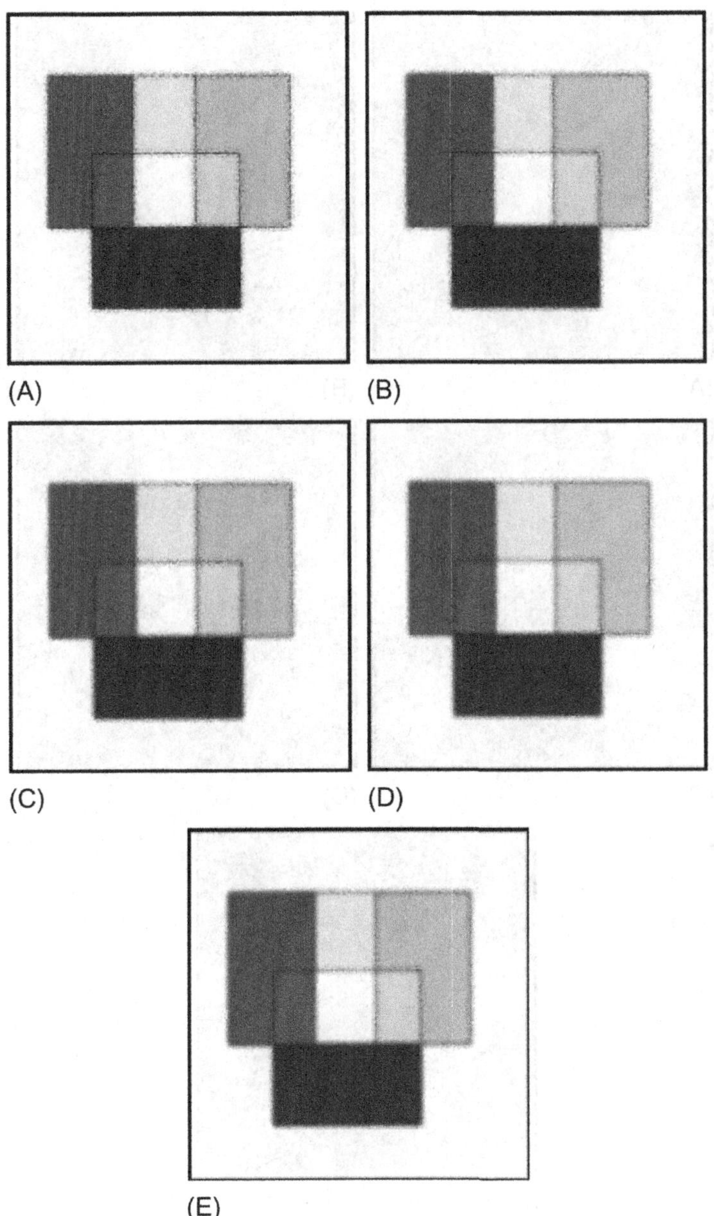

FIG. 19

Hopfield net-extracted output pure color images from the test artificial synthetic pure color images with Gaussian noise.

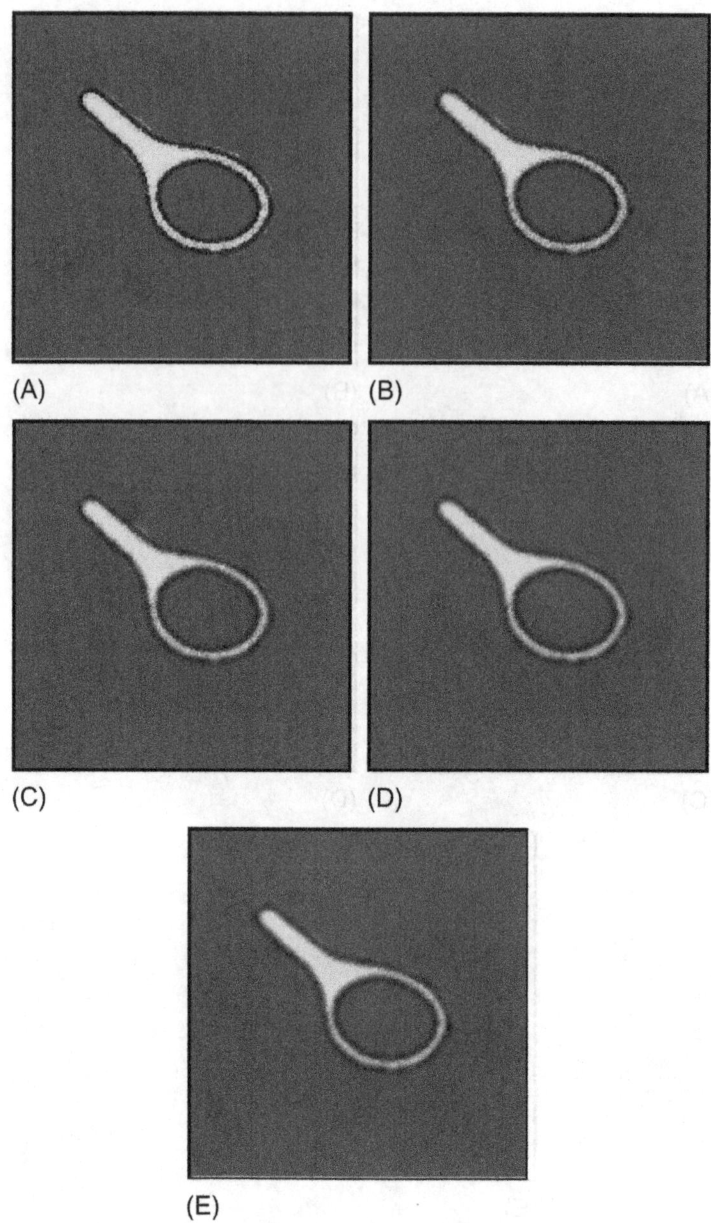

FIG. 20

Hopfield net-extracted output pure color images from the test real-life wrench images with Gaussian noise.

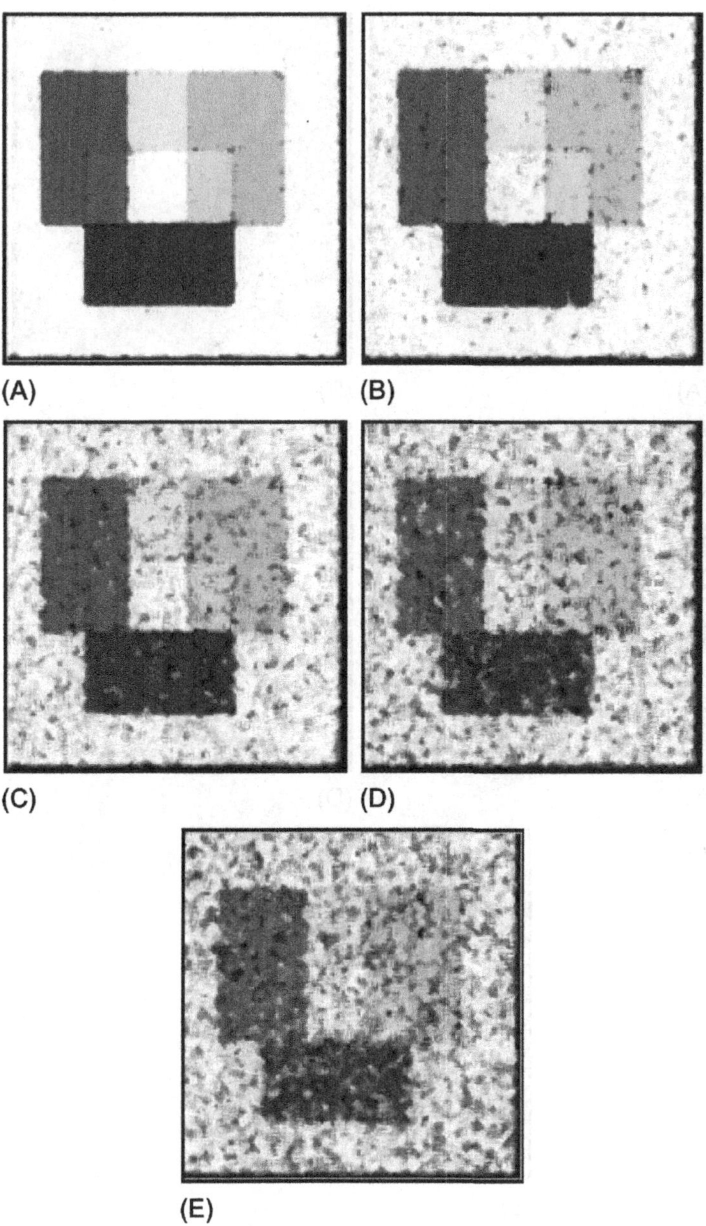

FIG. 21

Median filter with adaptive discrete wavelet transformation-extracted output pure color images from the test artificial synthetic pure color images with uniform noise.

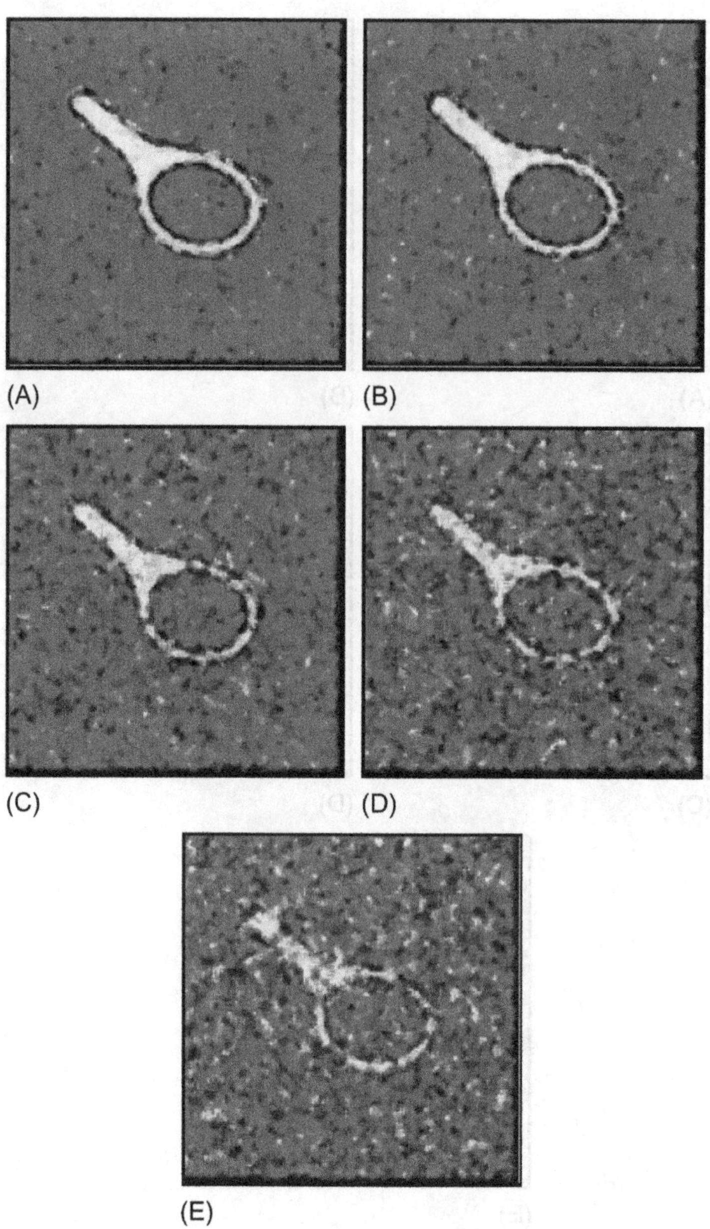

FIG. 22

Median filter with adaptive discrete wavelet transformation-extracted output pure color images from the test real-life wrench pure color images with uniform noise.

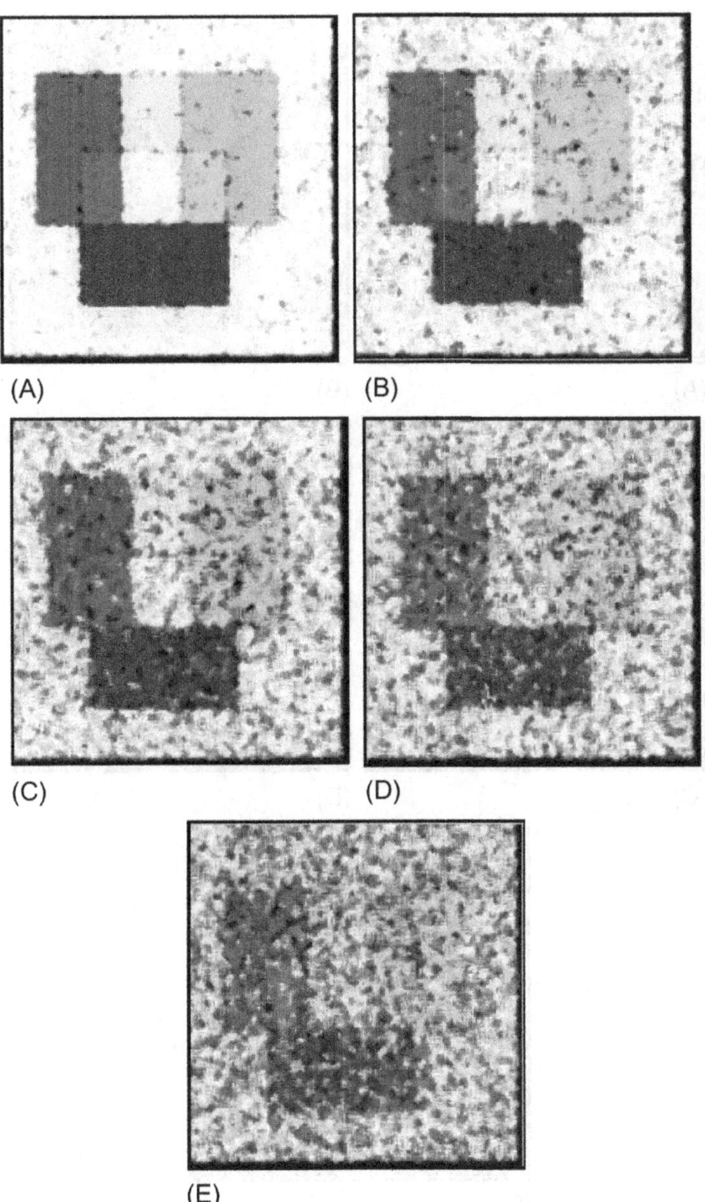

FIG. 23

Median filter with adaptive discrete wavelet transformation-extracted output pure color images from the test artificial synthetic pure color images with Gaussian noise.

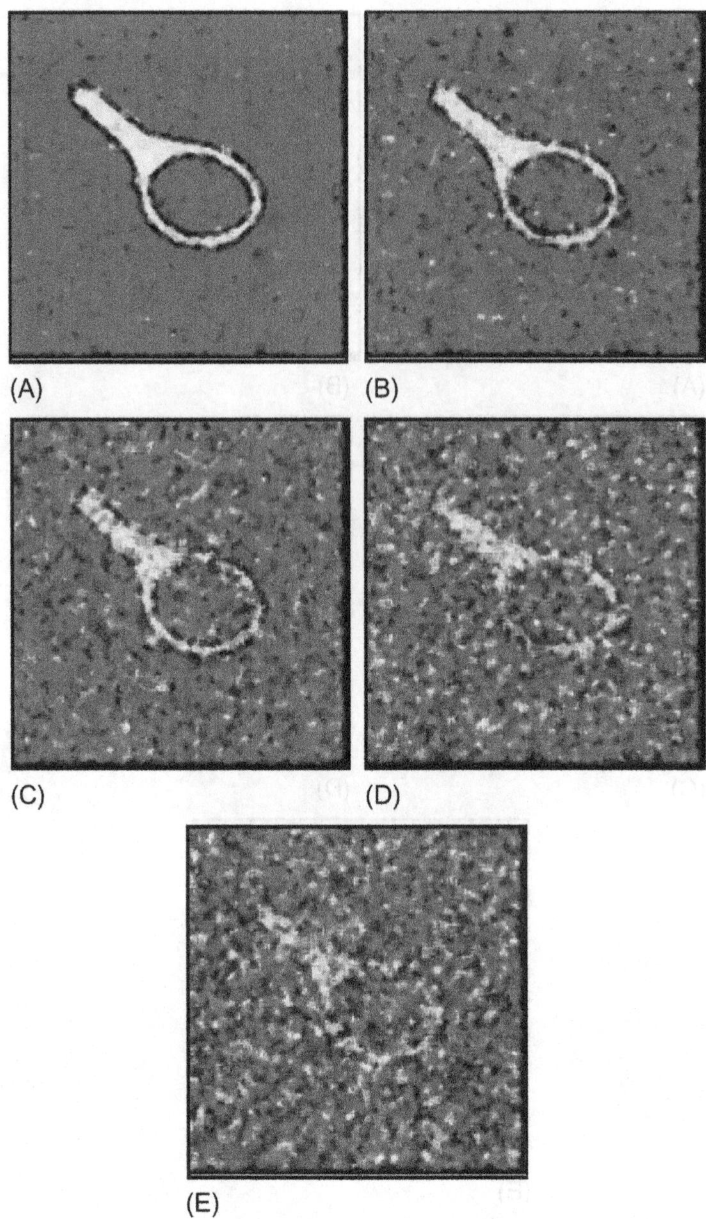

FIG. 24

Median filter with adaptive discrete wavelet transformation-extracted output pure color images from the test real-life wrench images with Gaussian noise.

filter. Since the Hopfield network architecture operates in a supervised fashion, it is an observable fact that the threefold parallel Hopfield network retains the object with great precision and also the noise characteristics should be known in advance.

The percentage of correct classification of pixels (*pcc*) [58] is applied to measure the distortion incurred in the object extraction process. Moreover, because processing is done in real time, the extraction time is an significant aspect considered for all three network architectures and the median filter. Using the suggested QPBDSONN architecture, the classical PBDSONN architecture, the threefold parallel Hopfield network, and the median filter, we measured *pcc* and the extraction times (t) during experiments for Gaussian noise-affected and uniform noise-affected artificial synthetic pure color images and real-life wrench pure color images; see Tables 1 and 2 respectively.

Considering the usefulness in real-time applications, it can be concluded from Tables 1 and 2 that the proposed QPBDSONN architecture is superior to its classical counterpart as well as the threefold parallel Hopfield network [21] with respect to processing that it and outperforms median filtering techniques in terms of the quality of extracted pure color images.

Table 1 Comparative Results for the Quantum Parallel Bidirectional Self-Organizing Neural Network, the Parallel Bidirectional Self-Organizing Neural Network, the Hopfield Network, and the Median Filter With Adaptive Discrete Wavelet Transformations on the Gaussian Noise-Affected Test Images

	QPBDSONN		PBDSONN		Hopfield Network		Median Filter	
σ	*t* (s)	*pcc*	*t* (s)	*pcc*	*t* (s)	*pcc*	*t* (s)	*pcc*
Synthetic pure color image								
8	39.392	97.2743	49.445	89.8415	259.592	87.8770	2.056	93.8029
10	37.765	95.0622	85.784	82.9816	280.930	87.3810	2.310	82.0939
12	43.830	88.1259	94.962	69.2010	324.445	85.7091	2.087	67.1440
14	50.761	83.5452	152.512	62.7172	307.599	85.6583	2.044	61.7952
16	59.074	69.9641	161.774	56.7617	507.955	85.6481	3.068	55.8972
Real-life pure color image								
8	31.711	93.3398	41.223	88.6004	308.972	88.5356	2.023	86.5215
10	46.365	86.7268	68.461	84.4909	234.824	88.3748	1.996	75.2301
12	59.976	77.0859	87.006	67.4328	350.697	88.3377	1.992	61.0614
14	70.595	74.8825	178.439	58.8354	313.524	88.2940	1.979	53.4000
16	79.394	68.1352	211.205	49.2178	419.632	88.2751	1.971	40.4764

PBDSONN, parallel bidirectional self-organizing neural network; QPBDSONN, quantum parallel bidirectional self-organizing neural network.

Table 2 Comparative Results for the Quantum Parallel Bidirectional Self-Organizing Neural Network, the Parallel Bidirectional Self-Organizing Neural Network, the Hopfield Network, and the Median Filter With Adaptive Discrete Wavelet Transformations on the Uniform Noise-Affected Test Pure Color Images

QPBDSONN			PBDSONN		Hopfield Network		Median Filter	
σ	*t* (s)	*pcc*	*t* (s)	*pcc*	*t* (s)	*pcc*	*t* (s)	*pcc*
Synthetic pure color image								
8	36.747	99.8943	45.696	98.4639	246.671	91.8849	1.882	94.2424
10	37.326	95.2140	69.833	94.2485	246.259	87.4242	2.167	83.2856
12	45.456	86.1874	85.507	79.5222	289.064	85.9990	2.985	70.9032
14	52.687	81.926	141.423	63.0662	393.163	85.7824	3.044	66.7594
16	57.070	73.3856	120.147	59.6064	357.456	85.6771	3.143	53.3949
Real-life pure color image								
8	35.436	94.6602	47.711	90.1882	308.177	89.2054	1.995	85.7774
10	43.930	91.8357	80.671	79.8631	338.155	88.4995	2.008	85.4956
12	51.624	82.7558	101.697	75.4374	410.745	88.3575	1.970	74.3970
14	47.377	78.5921	179.448	73.2350	411.369	88.3179	1.992	60.4500
16	61.601	72.3958	195.347	60.7693	387.114	88.2848	2.036	46.7864

PBDSONN, parallel bidirectional self-organizing neural network; QPBDSONN, quantum parallel bidirectional self-organizing neural network.

9.1 KOLMOGOROV-SMIRNOV TEST

The one-sided (KS) test is suitable to determine the statistical significance of a sample data set whose distribution is not known in advance and nonparametric in nature. To perform comparative analyses between two distinct samples described by empirical cumulative distribution functions, the KS test is preferred as a statistical significance test. Basically, the shapes and location of the statistical difference between two empirical cumulative distribution functions of samples X and Y are the key factors in the KS test. The one-sided KS test is aims at evaluating the statistically significant dissimilarity between two samples X and Y [69]. However, the KS test comprises two significant hypotheses: the null hypothesis H_0 and the alternative hypothesis H_t. If two samples X and Y are statistically equivalent ($X = Y$), then it is known as the "null hypothesis." In contrast, against the null hypothesis, if the samples X and Y are distinguishable, this reveals the statistical dissimilarity of the samples X and Y, known as the "alternative hypothesis" H_t.

Consider two randomly generated samples $x_1, x_2, x_3, x_4, \ldots, x_p$ and $y_1, y_2, y_3, y_4, \ldots, y_q$ drawn from the unknown one-dimensional probability distributions $M(x)$ and $N(x)$. The null hypothesis H_0, therefore, can be defined as H_0: $M(x) = N(x)$, against the alternative hypothesis H_t: $M(x) \neq N(x)$. By the one-sided KS test, stochastic dissimilarity between two samples X and Y (whether $X > Y$ or $X < Y$)

can be evaluated. Therefore, the statistically significant distances D_{qp}^{+}, D_{qp}^{-}, and D_{qp} are determined by the one-sided KS test. The computation of the necessary empirical cumulative distribution functions of samples X and Y is as follows:

$$S_1(x) - S_2(x) = \frac{\text{number of observed } x\text{'s} \leq x}{p} - \frac{\text{number of observed } y\text{'s} \leq x}{q}, \tag{49}$$

where $S_1(x)$ and $S_2(x)$ denote the empirical cumulative distribution functions of samples X and Y.

$$S_2(x) - S_1(x) = \frac{\text{number of observed } y\text{'s} \leq x}{p} - \frac{\text{number of observed } x\text{'s} \leq x}{q}. \tag{50}$$

The test statistics D_{qp}, D_{qp}^{+}, and D_{qp}^{-} can be obtained as

$$D_{qp} = \sup_x |S_1(x) - S_2(x)|, \tag{51}$$

$$D_{qp}^{+} = \sup_x (S_1(x) - S_2(x)), \tag{52}$$

$$D_{qp}^{-} = \sup_x (S_2(x) - S_1(x)). \tag{53}$$

Given the *critical value* [70] K_α, if $D_{qp} < K_\alpha$, the null hypothesis H_0 fails to reject. Assuming the significance level $\alpha = 0.05$ for a sample size of 5, the critical value K_α is 0.860, which reveals 95% confidence in favor of the experimental results in the KS test. Details of the KS test can be found in [70]. To investigate the statistical significance among the suggested QPBDSONN architecture and the existing classical PBDSONN architecture, the Hopfield network and adaptive wavelet thresholding, the KS test was performed. The comparative statistical significance is shown in Table 3, and the superiority of the QPBDSONN architecture is well established from the KS test results in terms of statistical significance over the classical counterparts.

If the sample size is not large enough, then any statistical test will fail to yield the optimal result. The statistical performance may be explored with the data in Table 3, which reveals that the QPBDSONN architecture offers the same quality of the extracted image as the PBDSONN in terms of *pcc*. The numerical outcome produced is in sheer contrast to the experimental results given in Tables 1 and 2. However, except for this stray case, it may be concluded from the KS test results that the suggested QPBDSONN architecture is superior in terms of processing time over the classical counterparts and therefore is statistically significant.

Apart from the results of the statistical significance test, graphical comparisons are also presented between the proposed QPBDSONN and the classical PBDSONN, the Hopfield network, and the median filter with adaptive DWTs considering the cumulative distribution and normal distribution of the sample outcome (see Figs. 25–30).

Table 3 Two-Sample One-Sided Kolmogorov-Smirnov Test Results With Respect to the Quantum Parallel Bidirectional Self-Organizing Neural Network for the Quantum Parallel Bidirectional Self-Organizing Neural Network, the Hopfield Network, and the Median Filter With Adaptive Discrete Wavelet Transformations

		PBDSONN	Hopfield Network	Median Filter
Synthetic image				
Uniform noise	*pcc*	=	=	=
	Time	>	>	<
Gaussian noise	*pcc*	=	=	=
	Time	>	>	<
Real-life image				
Uniform noise	*pcc*	=	=	=
	Time	>	>	<
Gaussian noise	*pcc*	=	<	=
	Time	=	>	<

PBDSONN, parallel bidirectional self-organizing neural network.

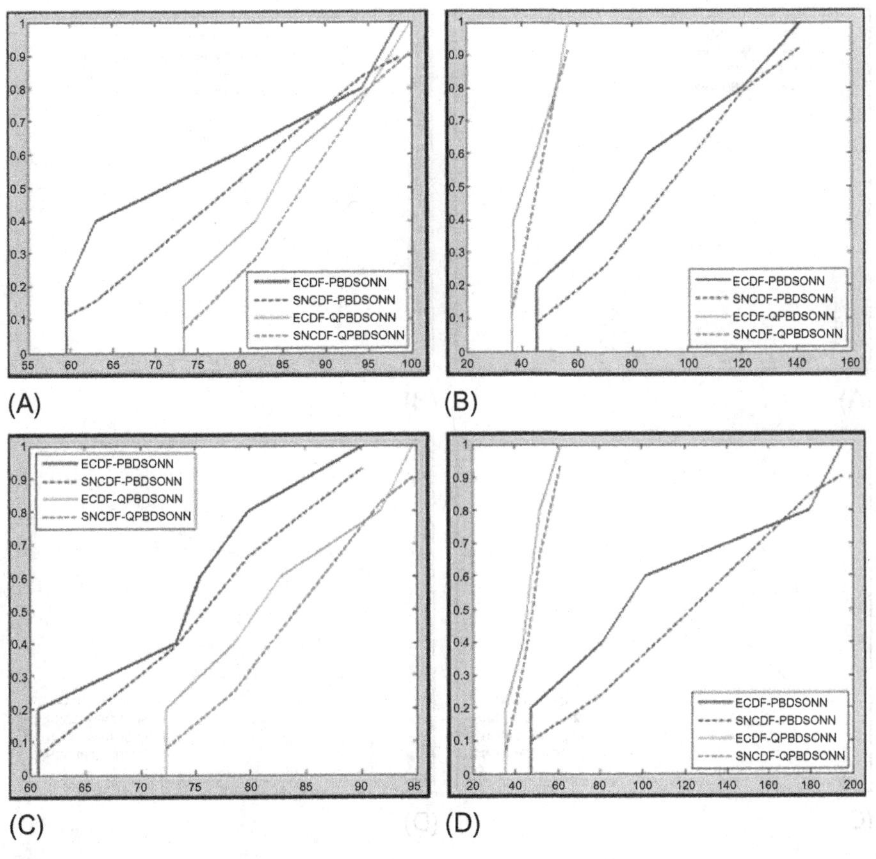

FIG. 25

Graphical comparison for *pcc* and time considering the empirical cumulative distribution function (ECDF) and standard normal cumulative distribution function (SNCDF) between the quantum parallel bidirectional self-organizing neural network (QPBDSONN) and the parallel bidirectional self-organizing neural network (PBDSONN) on pure color images affected by uniform noise. The data and the cumulative probability are plotted on the *x*-axis and the *y*-axis respectively. (A) The plot shows the difference between the *empirical cdf* of the PBDSONN and QPBDSONN on *pcc* of a synthetic object with uniform noise and the *cdf* of the *standard normal distribution.* (B) The plot shows the difference between the *empirical cdf* of the PBDSONN and QPBDSONN on *time (s)* of a synthetic object with uniform noise and the *cdf* of the *standard normal distribution.* (C) The plot shows the difference between the *empirical cdf* of the PBDSONN and QPBDSONN on *pcc* of a wrench with uniform noise and the *cdf* of the *standard normal distribution.* (D) The plot shows the difference between the *empirical cdf* of the PBDSONN and QPBDSONN on *time (s)* of a wrench with uniform noise and the *cdf* of the *standard normal distribution. cdf,* cumulative distribution function.

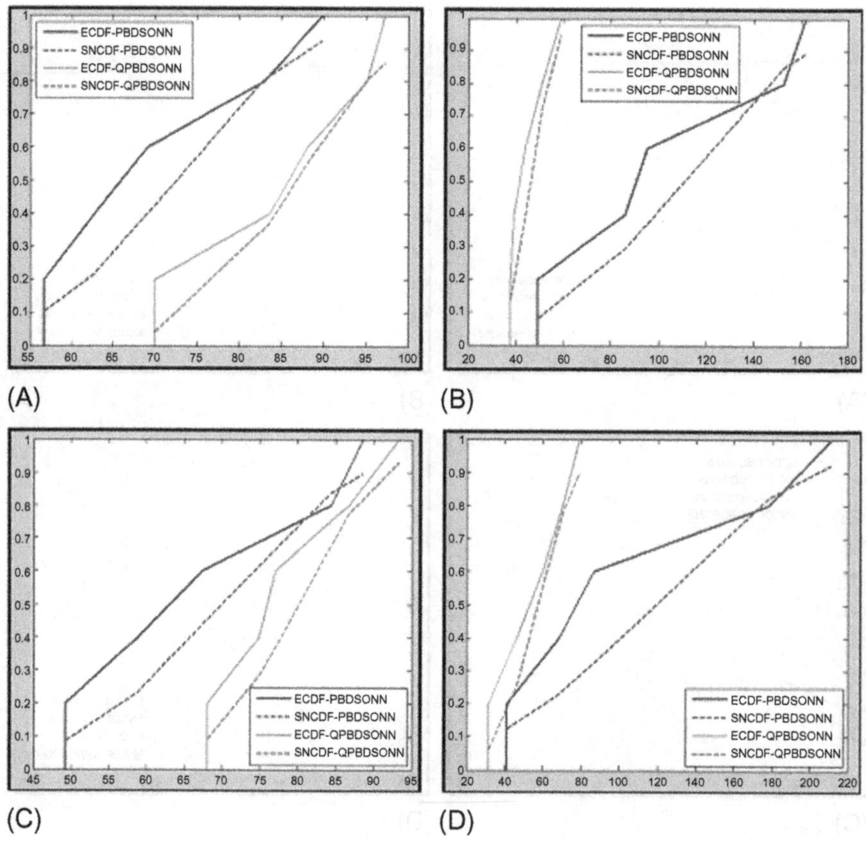

FIG. 26

Graphical comparison for *pcc* and time considering the empirical cumulative distribution function (ECDF) and the standard normal cumulative distribution function (SNCDF) between the quantum parallel bidirectional self-organizing neural network (QPBDSONN) and the parallel bidirectional self-organizing neural network (PBDSONN) on pure color images affected by Gaussian noise. The data and the cumulative probability are plotted on the *x*-axis and the *y*-axis respectively. (A) The plot shows the difference between the *empirical cdf* of the PBDSONN and QPBDSONN on *pcc* of a synthetic object with Gaussian noise and the *cdf* of the *standard normal distribution.* (B) The plot shows the difference between the *empirical cdf* of the PBDSONN and QPBDSONN on *time (s)* of a synthetic object with Gaussian noise and the *cdf* of the *standard normal distribution.* (C) The plot shows the difference between the *empirical cdf* of the PBDSONN and QPBDSONN on *pcc* of a wrench with Gaussian noise and the *cdf* of the *standard normal distribution.* (D) The plot shows the difference between the *empirical cdf* of the PBDSONN and QPBDSONN on *time (s)* of a wrench with Gaussian noise and the *cdf* of the *standard normal distribution. cdf,* cumulative distribution function.

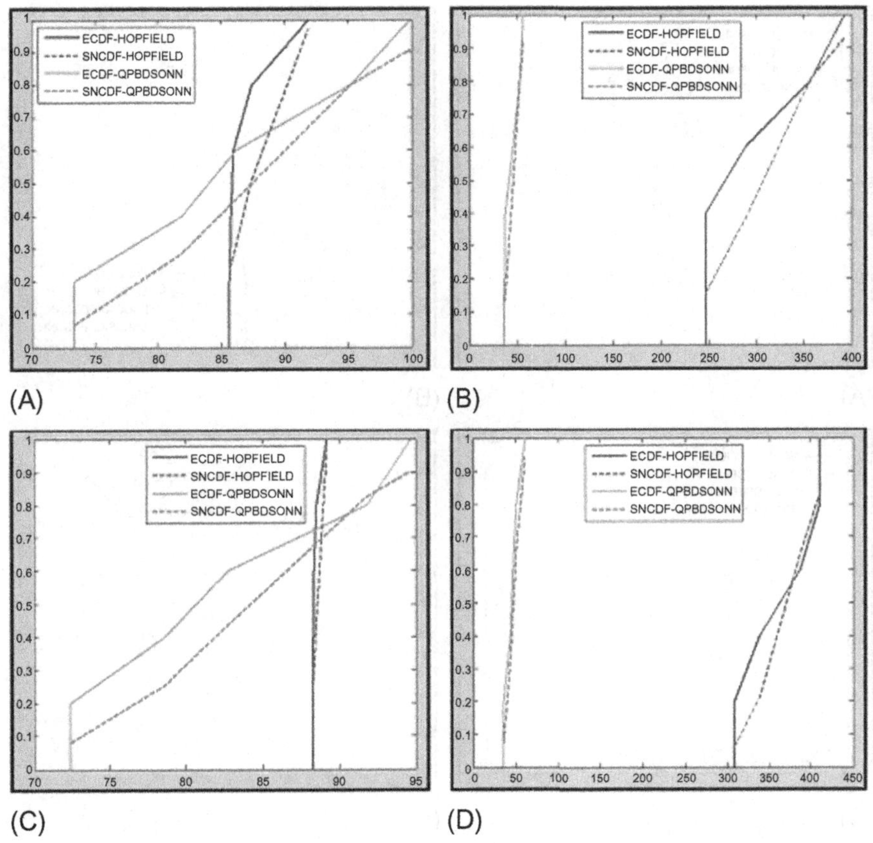

FIG. 27

Graphical comparison for *pcc* and time considering the empirical cumulative distribution function (ECDF) and the standard normal cumulative distribution function (SNCDF) between the quantum parallel bidirectional self-organizing neural network (QPBDSONN) and the Hopfield network on pure color images affected by uniform noise. The data and the cumulative probability are plotted on the *x*-axis and the *y*-axis respectively. (A) The plot shows the difference between the *empirical cdf* of the Hopfield and QPBDSONN on *pcc* of a synthetic object with uniform noise and the *cdf* of the *standard normal distribution.* (B) The plot shows the difference between the *empirical cdf* of the Hopfield and QPBDSONN on *time (s)* of a synthetic object with uniform noise and the *cdf* of the *standard normal distribution.* (C) The plot shows the difference between the *empirical cdf* of the Hopfield and QPBDSONN on *pcc* of a wrench with uniform noise and the *cdf* of the *standard normal distribution.* (D) The plot shows the difference between the *empirical cdf* of the Hopfield and QPBDSONN on *time (s)* of a wrench with uniform noise and the *cdf* of the *standard normal distribution. cdf,* cumulative distribution function.

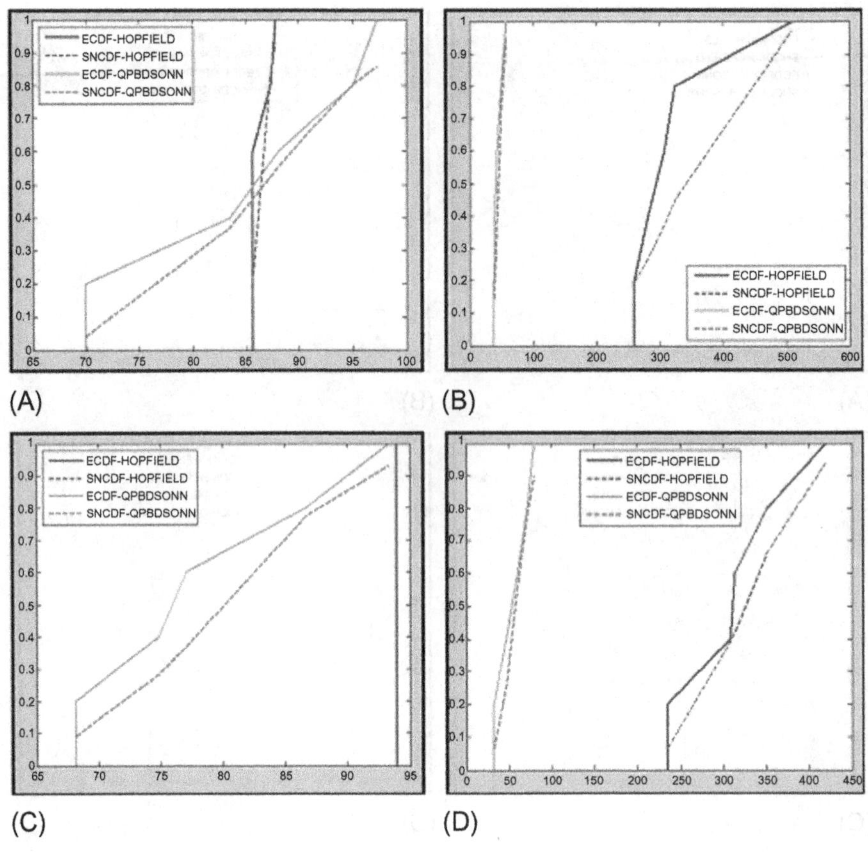

FIG. 28

Graphical comparison for *pcc* and time considering the empirical cumulative distribution function (ECDF) and the standard normal cumulative distribution function (SNCDF) between the quantum parallel bidirectional self-organizing neural network (QPBDSONN) and the Hopfield network on pure color images affected by Gaussian noise. The data and the cumulative probability are plotted on the *x*-axis and the *y*-axis respectively. (A) The plot shows the difference between the *empirical cdf* of the Hopfield and QPBDSONN on *pcc* of a synthetic object with Gaussian noise and the *cdf* of the *standard normal distribution*. (B) The plot shows the difference between the *empirical cdf* of the Hopfield and QPBDSONN on *time (s)* of a synthetic object with Gaussian noise and the *cdf* of the *standard normal distribution*. (C) The plot shows the difference between the *empirical cdf* of the Hopfield and QPBDSONN on *pcc* of a wrench with Gaussian noise and the *cdf* of the *standard normal distribution*. (D) The plot shows the difference between the *empirical cdf* of the Hopfield and QPBDSONN on *time (s)* of a wrench with Gaussian noise and the *cdf* of the *standard normal distribution*. *cdf*, cumulative distribution function.

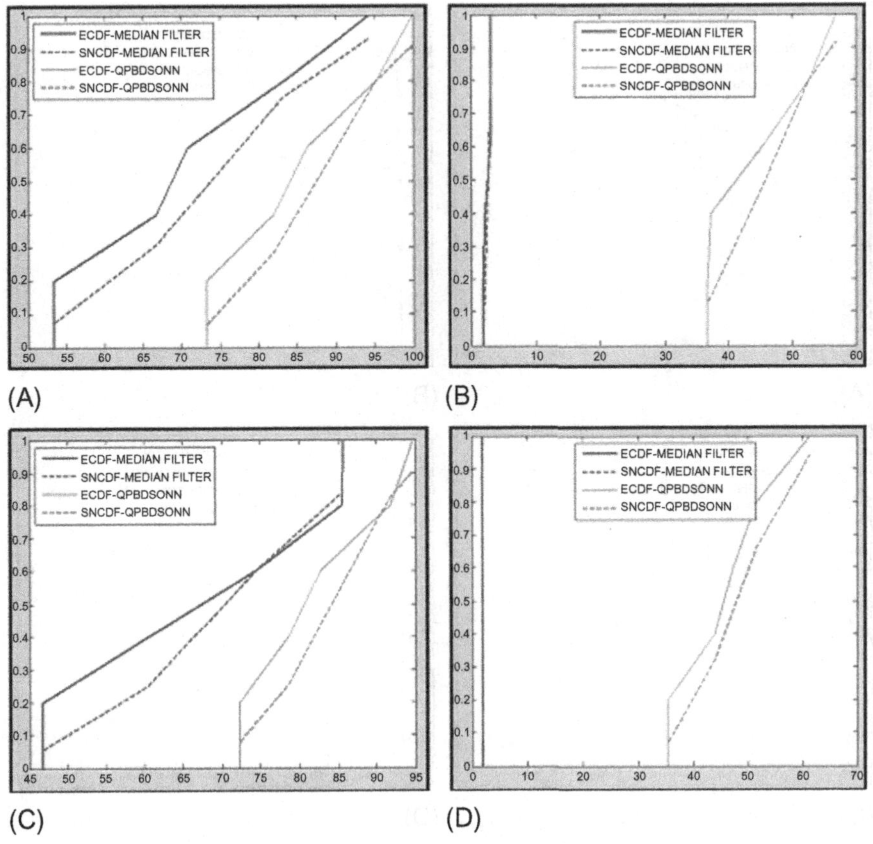

FIG. 29

Graphical comparison for *pcc* and time considering the empirical cumulative distribution function (ECDF) and the standard normal cumulative distribution function (SNCDF) between the quantum parallel bidirectional self-organizing neural network (QPBDSONN) and the adaptive discrete wavelet transformation (DWT) on pure color images affected by uniform noise. The data and the cumulative probability are plotted on the *x*-axis and the *y*-axis respectively. (A) The plot shows the difference between the *empirical cdf* of the Median filter with DWT and QPBDSONN on *pcc* of a synthetic object with uniform noise and the *cdf* of the *standard normal distribution.* (B) The plot shows the difference between the *empirical cdf* of the Median filter with DWT and QPBDSONN on *time (s)* of a synthetic object with uniform noise and the *cdf* of the *standard normal distribution.* (C) The plot shows the difference between the *empirical cdf* of the Median filter with DWT and QPBDSONN on *pcc* of a wrench with uniform noise and the *cdf* of the *standard normal distribution.* (D) The plot shows the difference between the *empirical cdf* of the Median filter with DWT and QPBDSONN on *time (s)* of a wrench with uniform noise and the *cdf* of the *standard normal distribution. cdf*, cumulative distribution function.

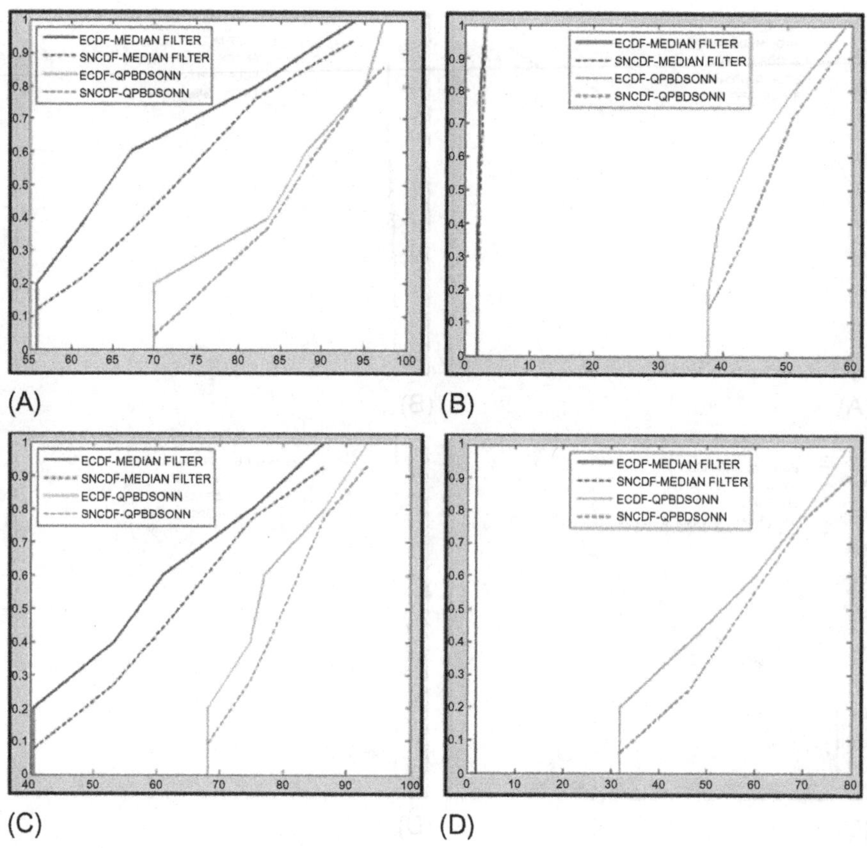

FIG. 30

Graphical comparison for *pcc* and time considering the empirical cumulative distribution function (ECDF) and the standard normal cumulative distribution function (SNCDF) between the quantum parallel bidirectional self-organizing neural network (QPBDSONN) and the adaptive discrete wavelet transformation (DWT) on pure color images affected by Gaussian noise. The data and the cumulative probability are plotted on the *x*-axis and the *y*-axis respectively. (A) The plot shows the difference between the *empirical cdf* of the Median filter with DWT and QPBDSONN on *pcc* of a synthetic object with Gaussian noise and the *cdf* of the *standard normal distribution.* (B) The plot shows the difference between the *empirical cdf* of the Median filter with DWT and QPBDSONN on *time (s)* of a synthetic object with Gaussian noise and the *cdf* of the *standard normal distribution.* (C) The plot shows the difference between the *empirical cdf* of the Median filter with DWT and QPBDSONN on *pcc* of a wrench with Gaussian noise and the *cdf* of the *standard normal distribution.* (D) The plot shows the difference between the *empirical cdf* of the Median filter with DWT and QPBDSONN on *time (s)* of a wrench with Gaussian noise and the *cdf* of the *standard normal distribution. cdf,* Cumulative distribution function.

10 CONCLUSION

An efficient quantum parallel self-organization algorithm referred to as a "quantum parallel bidirectional self-organizing neural network (QPBDSONN) architecture" for object extraction in real time from a noisy environment was illustrated in this chapter. The proposed architecture mimics the classical PBDSONN architecture in a quantum environment. The novelty of the suggested network architecture lies in the functioning and suitable tuning of interconnection weights, resulting in faster computation. In the current work the processing nodes of each constituent QBDSONN component used in the proposed architecture were represented by qubits and rotation gates, dedicated to weighted interconnections between different layers to reduce the processing time of the counterpropagation of quantum fuzzified information exhibited by the quantum thresholding. In the output layer of each constituent QBDSONN in the proposed architecture, quantum measurement was done to obtain three distinct basic pure color components—red, green, and blue—by conversion of the qubits or quantum states into one of the classical bits 0 or 255 depending on the probability. To produce true output as an extracted pure color image from a noisy background, an additive fusion technique was used. The efficacy of the suggested network architecture was established by comparative analysis of the results as far as the quality of the extracted output images was concerned and the extraction time over the classical PBDSONN, the supervised Hopfield network, and the median filter with adaptive DWTs.

The future direction of research into the suggested QPBDSONN architecture is aimed at gray level and true color image segmentation. Currently, the authors are engaged in this new horizon of research.

REFERENCES

[1] R.C. Gonzalez, R.E. Woods, Digital Image Processing, Prentice-Hall, Englewood Cliffs, NJ, 2002.

[2] C. Li, C. Xu, C. Gui, M.D. Fox, Level set evolution without reinitialization: a new variational formulation, IEEE Trans. Image Process. 19 (12) (2010) 3243–3254.

[3] N. Xu, R. Bansal, N. Ahuja, Object segmentation using graph cuts based active contours, IEEE Trans. Pattern Anal. Mach. Intell. 27 (2005) 546–561.

[4] S.G. Chang, B. Yu, M. Vetterli, Spatially adaptive wavelet thresholding with context modeling for image denoising, IEEE Trans. Image Process. 9 (2000) 1522–1531.

[5] J. Portilla, V. Strela, M.J. Wainwright, E.P. Simoncelli, Image denoising using scale mixtures of Gaussians in the wavelet domain, IEEE Trans. Image Process. 12 (2003) 1338–1351.

[6] J.L. Starck, E.J. Candes, D.L. Donoho, The curvelet transform for image denoising, IEEE Trans. Image Process. 11 (2002) 670–684.

[7] G.Y. Chen, B. Kegl, Image denoising with complex ridgelets, Pattern Recognit. 40 (2007) 578–585.

[8] S. Wang, T. Kubota, J.M. Siskind, J. Wangl, Salient closed boundary extraction with ratio contour, IEEE Pattern Anal. Mach. Intell. 27 (2003).

[9] B. Goossens, A.P. Zurica, W. Philips, Image denoising using mixtures of projected Gaussian scale mixtures, IEEE Trans. Image Process. 18 (2009).

[10] A. Foi, V. Katkovnik, K. Egiazarian, Point wise shape-adaptive DCT for high-quality denoising and deblocking of grayscale and color images, IEEE Trans. Image Process. 16 (2007).

[11] C. Tomasi, R. Manduchi, Bilateral filtering for gray and colour images, in: IEEE International Conference on Computer Vision, 1998, pp. 839–846.

[12] D. Barashi, A fundamental relationship between bilateral filtering, adaptive smoothing and the non-linear diffusion equation, IEEE Trans. Pattern Anal. Mach. Intell. 24 (2002) 844–847.

[13] A. Buades, B. Coll, J.M. Morel, A review of image denoising algorithms with a new one, Multiscale Model. Simul. 4 (2005) 490–530.

[14] C. Kervrann, J. Boulangerl, Optimal spatial adaptation for patch based image denoising, IEEE Trans. Image Process. 15 (2006) 2866–2878.

[15] S. Lee, Digital image enhancement and noise filtering by use of local statistics, IEEE Trans. Pattern Anal. Mach. Intell. 2 (1980) 165–168.

[16] K. Dabov, A. Foi, V. Katkovnik, K. Egiazarian, Image denoising by sparse 3D transform-domain collaborative filtering, IEEE Trans. Image Process. 16 (2007) 2080–2095.

[17] A. Fathi, A.R. Naghsh-Nilchi, Efficient image denoising method based on a new adaptive wavelet packet thresholding function, IEEE Trans. Pattern Anal. Mach. Intell. 21 (9) (2012).

[18] V. Dhanushree, M.G. Srinivasa, Image de-noising using median filter and DWT adaptive wavelet threshold, IOSR J. VLSI Signal Process. 5 (3) (2015).

[19] S. Bhattacharyya, U. Maulik, P. Dutta, A parallel bi-directional self-organizing neural network (PBDSONN) architecture for color image extraction and segmentation, Neurocomptuting 86 (2012) 1–23.

[20] S. Bhattacharyya, U. Maulik, Soft Computing for Image and Multi-media Data Processing, Springer, Berlin, 2013.

[21] P.D. Scott, S.S. Young, N.M. Nasrabadi, Object recognition using multilayer Hopfield neural network, IEEE Trans. Image Process. 6 (3) (1997) 357–372.

[22] L. Itti, C. Koch, E. Niebur, A model of saliency-based visual attention for rapid scene analysis, IEEE Pattern Anal. Mach. Intell. 20 (11) (1998) 1254–1259.

[23] S. Mallat, A Wavelet Tour of Signal Processing, Academic Press, New York, 1998.

[24] R.R. Coifman, D.L. Donoho, De-noising by soft thresholding, IEEE Trans. Inf. Theory 41 (1995) 613–627.

[25] M.K. Mihcak, I. Kozintsev, K. Ramchandran, P. Moulin, Low-complexity image denoising based on statistical modeling of wavelet coefficients, IEEE Trans. Inf. Theory 6 (12) (1999) 300–303.

[26] S.G. Chang, B. Yu, M. Vetterli, Spatially adaptive wavelet thresholding with context modeling for image denoising, IEEE Trans. Image Process. 9 (9) (2000) 1522–1531.

[27] D.D. Muresan, T.W. Parks, Adaptive principal components and image denoising, in: Proceedings of the 2003 International Conference on Image Processing, vol. 1 (9), 2003, pp. 1101–1104.

[28] M. Elad, M. Aharon, Image denoising via sparse and redundant representations over learned dictionaries, IEEE Trans. Image Process. 15 (12) (2006) 3736–3745.

[29] M. Aharon, M. Elad, A.M. Bruckstein, The K-SVD: an algorithm for designing of over complete dictionaries for sparse representation, IEEE Trans. Signal Process. 54 (11) (2006) 4311–4322.

[30] N.X. Lian, V. Zagorodnov, Color image denoising using wavelets and minimum cut analysis, IEEE Signal Process. Lett. 12 (11) (2005) 741–745.

[31] L.P. Yaroslavsky, Digital Signal Processing—An Introduction, Springer, address, 1985.

[32] Y. Ma, H. Zhang, Contrast-based image attention analysis by using fuzzy growing, in: ACM Trans. on Multimedia, 2003.

[33] R. Achanta, S. Hemami, F. Estrada, S. Susstrunk, Frequency-tuned salient region detection, in: IEEE CVPR, 2009.

[34] X. Hou, L. Zhang, Saliency detection: a spectral residual approach, in: IEEE Conference on Computer Vision and Pattern, 2007.

[35] H. Yu, J. Li, Y. Tian, T. Huang, Automatic Interesting Object Extraction From Images Using Complementary Saliency Maps, in: Proc. MM10, Firenze, Italy, 2010.

[36] S. Bhattacharyya, P. Dutta, U. Maulik, A self-supervised bidirectional neural network (BDSONN) architecture for object extraction guided by beta activation function and adaptive fuzzy context sensitive thresholding, Int. J. Intell. Technol. 4 (2006) 345–365.

[37] B. Kosko, Neural Networks and Fuzzy Systems: A Dynamical Systems Approach to Machine Intelligence, Prentice-Hall, Englewood Cliffs, NJ, 1998.

[38] S.H. Ong, N.C. Yeo, K.H. Lee, Y.V. Venkatesh, D.M. Cao, Segmentation of color images using a two-stage self-organizing network, Image Vis. Comput. 20 (11) (2002) 279–289.

[39] J. Vesanto, E. Alhoniemi, Clustering of the self-organizing map, IEEE Trans. Pattern Anal. Mach. Intell. 11 (3) (2000) 279–289.

[40] S. Bhattacharyya, K. Dasgupta, Color object extraction from noisy background using parallel multi-layer self-organizing neural networks, in: Proceedings of CSI-YITPA(E), 2003, pp. 32–36.

[41] S. Bhattacharyya, P. Dutta, U. Maulik, P.K. Nandi, Multi-level activation functions for true color image segmentation using a self-supervised parallel self-organizing neural network (PSONN) architecture: a comparative study, Int. J. Comput. Sci. 2 (1) (2007) 9–21.

[42] D. Mcmohan, Quantum Computing Explained, John Wiley and Sons, New York, 2008.

[43] N. Matsui, M. Takai, H. Nishimura, A network model based on qubit-like neuron corresponding to quantum circuit, in: The Institute of Electronics Information and Communications in Japan (Part III: Fundamental Electronic Science), vol. 83 (10), 2000, pp. 67–73.

[44] N. Kouda, M. Takai, H. Nishimura, A multilayered feedforward network based on qubit neuron model, Syst. Comput. Jpn. 35 (13) (2004) 43–51.

[45] N. Kouda, M. Takai, H. Nishimura, F. Peper, An examination of qubit neural network in controlling an inverted pendulum, Neural Process. Lett. 22 (3) (2005) 277–290.

[46] C. Aytekin, S. Kiranyaz, M. Gabbouj, Quantum mechanics in computer vision: automatic object extraction, in: Proc. ICIP 2013, 2013, pp. 2489–2493.

[47] A.A. Ezhov, Pattern recognition with quantum neural networks, in: Advances in Pattern Recognition ICAPR 2001, Springer, Berlin/Heidelberg, 2001, pp. 60–71.

[48] R. Chrisley, Quantum learning new directions in cognitive science, in: Proceedings of the International Symposium, Saariselka, Lapland, Finland, Helsinki, Finnish Association of Artificial Intelligence, 1995, pp. 77–89.
[49] S. Kak, Quantum neural computing, in: Advances in Imaging and Electron Physics, vol. 94, 1995, pp. 259–313.
[50] T. Menneer, A. Narayanan, Quantum-Inspired Neural Networks, Department of Computer Science, University of Exeter, Exeter, United Kingdom, 1995.
[51] E.C. Behrman, J. Niemel, J.E. Steck, S.R. Skinner, Quantum neural computing, IEEE Trans. Neural Netw. 94 (1996) 259–313.
[52] D. Ventura, T. Martinez, Quantum associative memory, in: IEEE Transactions on Neural Networks, 1998.
[53] T. Menneer, Quantum artificial neural networks, Ph.D. Thesis, University of Exeter, UK, 1998, pp. 259–313.
[54] M. Perus, Neural networks as a basis for quantum associate networks, Neural Netw. World 10 (6) (2000) 1001–1013.
[55] L. Weigang, A study of parallel self-organizing map, 1998, e-print: http://xxx.lanl.gov/abs/quant-ph/9808025.
[56] Z.Z. Hu, Quantum computation via neural networks applied to image processing and pattern recognition, Ph.D. Thesis, University of Western Sydney, Australia, 2001.
[57] S. Bhattacharyya, P. Pal, S. Bhowmik, A quantum multilayer self-organizing neural network for object extraction from a noisy background, in: Proceedings of the Fourth International Conference on Communication Systems and Network Technologies, 2014, pp. 512–518.
[58] A. Ghosh, N.R. Pal, S.K. Pal, Self-organization for object extraction using a multilayer neural network and fuzziness measures, IEEE Trans. Fuzzy Syst. 1 (1) (1993) 54–68.
[59] D. Konar, S. Bhattacharyya, N. Das, B.K. Panigrahi, A quantum bi-directional self-organizing neural network (QBDSONN) for binary image denoising, in: Proc. ICACCI, 2015, pp. 54–68.
[60] S. Bhattacharyya, P. Pal, S. Bhowmick, Binary image denoising using a quantum multilayer self-organizing neural network, Appl. Soft Comput. 24 (6) (2014) 717–729.
[61] L. Zadeh, Fuzzy sets, Inf. Control 8 (1965) 338–353.
[62] T. Ross, T. Ross, Fuzzy Logic With Engineering Applications, McGraw Hill College Div, New York, 1965.
[63] D. Ventura, T. Martinez, An artificial neuron with quantum mechanical properties, in: Proceedings of International Conference on Artificial Neural Networks and Genetic Algorithms, 1997, pp. 482–485.
[64] M.A. Nielson, I.L. Chung, Quantum Computation and Quantum Information, vol. 3, Cambridge University Press, Cambridge, 2000.
[65] J.J. Sakurai, Modern Quantum Mechanics, Addison Wesley, Reading, MA, 1994.
[66] S. Bhattachrayya, P. Dutta, U. Maulik, Binary object extraction using bi-directional self-organizing neural network (BDSONN) architecture with fuzzy context sensitive thresholding, Pattern Anal. Appl. 10 (2007) 345–360.
[67] D. Mu, Z. Guan, H. Zhang, Learning algorithm and application of quantum neural networks with quantum weights, in: IJCTE, vol. 5, 2013.

[68] X.H. L.J. Zhen, D. Huang, Super-linearly convergent BP learning algorithm for feed forward neural networks, J. Softw. 11 (2000) 1094–1096.
[69] P. Dutta, D.D. Majumder, Performance Analysis of Evolutionary Algorithm, Lambert Academic Publishers, Saarbrücken, Germany, 2012, ISBN 978-3-659-18349-2.
[70] M.H. Gail, S.B. Green, Critical values for the one-sided two-sample Kolmogorov-Smirnov statistic, J. Am. Stat. Assoc. 71 (355) (1976) 757–760.

CHAPTER

6 Quantum-inspired multi-objective simulated annealing for bilevel image thresholding*

S. Dey[a], S. Bhattacharyya[b], U. Maulik[c]

Camellia Institute of Technology, Kolkata, WB, India[a] RCC Institute of Information Technology, Kolkata, WB, India[b] Jadavpur University, Kolkata, WB, India[c]

1 INTRODUCTION

Segmentation

The fundamental step of digital image processing is possibly segmentation of an image into numerous regions. The basic rule of image segmentation is that the regions to be segmented must be separate and homogeneous in nature. The segmentation is performed on the basis of one or more features of the input image [1,2]. For example, the color of an image or its texture or any other relevant feature may be used for this purpose. The image segmentation method is very effective for a wide range of applications. Several authors have successfully applied the image segmentation method in different areas, such as image retrieval [3], face detection [4], and object recognition [5]. Pal and Pal [5] presented a comprehensive and useful review of this method.

Thresholding

There are a number of different methods for image segmentation. Thresholding is the most used, simplest, most accurate, and most robust tool in this category [5–7]. The objective of thresholding is to group the pixel intensity values of an image in contrast to a set of threshold values. Many researchers have proposed different thresholding methods in image segmentation [7–14]. Among the different methods available for image thresholding, Otsu's method [15], Kapur's method [16], and Pun's method [17] are possibly the most used methods in this category.

*Fully documented templates are available in the elsarticle package on http://www.ctan.org/tex-archive/macros/latex/contrib/elsarticleCTAN.

Quantum Inspired Computational Intelligence. http://dx.doi.org/10.1016/B978-0-12-804409-4.00006-1

A comprehensive literature survey has been presented by Sezgin and Sankur [8]. The thresholding method is fundamentally divided into two parts: bilevel thresholding and multilevel thresholding. The number of classes required to perform bilevel thresholding is 2, and for multilevel thresholding the number required depends on the level of computation [18,19].

Quantum computing

The term "quantum computing" (QC) alludes to the building of a new-generation computer, known as quantum mechanical computer, which was designed in the light of quantum mechanics focusing on the computational paradigm. QC uses quantum mechanical phenomena for computing operations on various data. This kind of system was introduced in the early 1980s [20,21] but actual formalization occurred in the late 1980s and 1990s [22–24]. The fascinating feature in the context of quantum computation is that the basic principles of quantum mechanics can be applied to represent data, which can be used later for the execution of different operations [25–28]. A few QC paradigms include a polynomial time factoring algorithm developed by Shor [23] and an algorithm for searching databases developed by Grover [24]. These quantum-based algorithms prove the superiority of QC over classical computing in terms of computational capability.

Metaheuristic algorithm

In the field of computer science, "metaheuristic" can be coined as a computational method, which is used to optimize different combinatorial problems. In its way, it iteratively explores a few chosen search spaces to uncover possible solutions. This type of method always puts its best effort into improving the quality of the candidate solution with reference to a specific fitness function, taken as a measure of reference. Generally, no or very few assumptions (intelligence) are required beforehand for the problem selected for optimization. Although a metaheuristic does not ensure an optimal solution, sometimes it reaches a near optimal solution [29–31]. A comparative review of different metaheuristic methods is available [32].

Optimization

"Optimization" can be defined as the study of specific problems where a single or several objectives are minimized or maximized to get the best possible outcome. This technique is divided into two parts on the basis of the number of objective functions used for optimization: single-objective optimization and multi-objective optimization. The former type of optimization technique optimizes one objective at the most, whereas, more than one objective function is optimized simultaneously in the latter type [33,34]. The foremost objective of optimization is to follow a methodical way to find the best possible value of one or more objective functions in a specific domain. In multi-objective optimization the solutions of the set of objective functions are called "Pareto-optimal solutions" [35,36].

2 LITERATURE SURVEY

Several authors have applied different simulated annealing (SA) approaches in single-objective and multi-objective optimization. In 1989 Glover and Greenberg [37] used the approaches applied in a genetic algorithm, tabu search, neural networks, targeted analysis, and SA and summarized them. Coello Coello [38,39] and van Veldhuizen and Lamont [40,41] presented literature surveys on different methods based on a number of metaheuristic and evolutionary algorithms. Collins et al. [42], Rutenbar [43], and Eglese [44] also performed surveys on single-objective SA in different time frames. The performance of SA has been studied in the multi-objective framework in recent years. In this chapter, a survey on both kinds of optimization strategies based on SA is presented.

Several researchers used SA to solve different operational research problems. Chen et al. [45] combined the Hopfield neural network and the theory of SA and reported a novel approach to build a new plan on prismatic parts. Sridhar and Rajendran [46] used SA in a cellular manufacturing system. They solved its scheduling problem by introducing three new perturbation patterns to create new sequences. Suresh and Sahu [47] applied SA in an assembly line balancing program. It was designed only to solve problems on a single objective. According to their observations the performance of SA was as good as that of similar approaches. Meller and Bozer [48] used SA to solve facility layout problems comprising either single or multiple floors. These are a kind of combinatorial problem. The difficulty one may face in solving such problems is that one generally encounters local minima at different times. In 1988 Mukhopadhyay et al. [49] presented an approach related to a flexible manufacturing system. They used SA to reduce the system imbalance as much as possible. Kim et al. [50] introduced a method to regulate vehicles' routes in a transportation system with a multistop facility in a multiperiod time frame. They considered a multiretailer distribution system (one warehouse) for this purpose. The system can also determine the delivery capacities for each retailer.

Researchers started applying SA as an optimization technique to solve a variety of combinatorial optimization problems. Afterward, SA was familiarized in a multi-objective structure because of the easiness of its use and its ability to create a Pareto solution set in one run by adjusting a diminutive computational cost. Serafini [51,52] first developed multi-objective type of SA. To develop this algorithm, he modified the acceptance condition of solutions in the basic algorithm. A number of alternative conditions have been investigated to enhance the acceptance probability of nondominated solutions. A combined form of several conditions was introduced to improve the search capacity on these nondominated solutions. In 1994 Ulungu and Teghem [53] used the idea of probability in multi-objective optimization. Serafini [54] also applied SA on the multi-objective structure. Later, Ulungu et al. [55] introduced a comprehensive multi-objective SA algorithm and tested this algorithm on a multi-objective version of a combinatorial problem, where a weighted combining function was used to evaluate the fitness value of solutions. An improved version of this method was developed and comprehensively tested by Ulungu et al. [56]. A variant of the SA approach was introduced by Suppapitnarm and Parks [57] to handle multi-objective problems, called the "SMOSA method." Tuyttens et al. [58] applied the theory of the multi-objective SA method to solve a bicriteria assignment problem. The annealing process regulates each temperature in an independent way on the basis of the performance of the outcome for each criterion. Czyiak et al. [59] proposed a different way to use SA in a multi-objective optimization framework, called the "Pareto SA method." Czyiak and Jaszkiewicz [60] collectively used a unicriterion genetic algorithm and SA to produce effectual solutions of a multicriteria-based shortest path problem. Suman [61,62] developed two dissimilar SA-based methods, called "weight-based multi-objective SA" and "Pareto domination-based multi-objective SA," to handle the multi-objective constrained problems. Suman [62] also examined five different SA methods for system reliability optimization problems. Suman [63] further presented an improved version of the multi-objective methods (SA based) where the user is not required to furnish the number of iterations beforehand. A detailed survey of different quantum-inspired metaheuristic algorithms has been presented by Dey et al. [64].

3 OVERVIEW OF SIMULATED ANNEALING

SA [65] is a compact, accurate, and powerful technique which provides admirable solutions to an extensive range of optimization problems. This method is very much popular because of its simplicity, efficiency, and robustness. SA is a probabilistic method which was introduced by Kirkpatrick et al. [65]. It is equally effective in both kinds of optimization frameworks (either single-objective or multi-objective). This optimization method is very useful to solve such problems which are complex in nature. At each iteration, the objective function of this method is used to find the fitness values of the existing solution and a recently selected solution. Thereafter, these two values are compared to get the best fitted solution between them. SA always accepts an improved solution at each iteration. The nonimproved solutions may also be accepted in the expectation of evasion of the local optimal value in the hunt for global optima. The acceptance of these inferior solutions at each iteration may depend on a temperature-dependent probability criterion.

"Annealing" may be coined as a process or heat treatment where a metal is first allowed to be heated to a stipulated temperature and afterward is allowed to be cooled gradually. SA is a similar technique for optimization. This method is commonly described with regard to thermodynamics. SA starts exploring its search space for an improved solution with a very high temperature parameter setting. After each iteration the temperature is gradually decreased and SA continues its search until the temperature reaches its predefined low value. As this method approaches very low temperature, it appears to be very greedy. As the temperature decreases, worsening steps occurs less as well.

Basically, the whole process of annealing involves the following steps [65]:

- The temperature is first increased to a extreme value at which the solid starts to melt.
- Afterward, the temperature is reduced carefully until the particles of the solid assemble themselves in its ground state.

In this method, the decision to accept the better/worsening move is taken by following the procedure described here. First, a temperature parameter (T) (real valued) is invoked and a very high value is assigned to it. Suppose N is the current configuration (assignment) and $h_1(N)$ is its evaluated (fitness) value. Hoping for better movement of its search space, SA impartially chooses a neighbor first. Let the new assignment be N'. Assuming a minimization problem, if $h_1(N') \leq h_1(N)$, SA accepts the new assignment and sets it as the current assignment. Otherwise this assignment can be accepted only with a probability $\exp(h_1(N) - h_1(N'))/T$.

4 MULTI-OBJECTIVE OPTIMIZATION

As its name suggest, the multi-objective optimization technique is a kind of optimization problem which optimizes at minimum two objective functions (generally of conflicting type) simultaneously. Multi-objective optimization is typically suitable in such problems where decisions regarding optimal solutions are taken by consideration of the trade-offs between the conflicting objectives [66]. Problems in multi-objective optimization are mostly found in fields such as economics, engineering, and logistics. Generally, there are very few single solutions that optimize each objective function simultaneously. Rather, there may be an infinite set of nondominated/Pareto-optimal solutions in multi-objective optimization. Formally, a multi-objective optimization problem is formulated as

$$\begin{aligned} \mathcal{M}_{\text{op}}(\mathbf{y}) &= g(\mathbf{z}) = [g_1(\mathbf{z}), g_2(\mathbf{z}), \ldots, g_q(\mathbf{z})]^{\text{T}} \\ \text{subject to } \varphi_m(\mathbf{z}) &\geq 0, \quad m = 1, 2, \ldots, r, \\ \upsilon_n(\mathbf{x}) &= 0, \quad n = 1, 2, \ldots, s. \end{aligned} \tag{1}$$

For multi-objective optimization, $\mathcal{M}_{\text{op}}$ is either a maximization or a minimization problem. Here, $\mathbf{z} = (z_1, z_2, \ldots, z_u) \in Z$ signifies a decision vector of u decision variables and $\mathbf{y} = (y_1, y_2, \ldots, y_v) \in Y$ is an objective vector. Z is the parameter space and Y is the objective space.

Dominance between individuals is possibly the most important concept in multi-objective optimization. Suppose a solution in a multi-objective optimization problem is assumed to be $\mathcal{D} = \{d_1, d_2, \ldots, d_r\}$. Let, $d_i, d_j \in \mathcal{D}$. Theoretically, the d_i dominate the d_j if (assuming we have a minimization multi-objective problem)

1. $g_\kappa(d_i) \leq g_\kappa(z_j)$ for all $\kappa \in 1, 2, \ldots, \mathcal{E}$,
2. $g_\kappa(d_i) < g_\kappa(d_j)$ if three exists at least one $\kappa \in 1, 2, \ldots, \mathcal{E}$,

where $\mathcal{E}$ is the number of objective functions. To find the set of nondominated solutions of a multi-objective optimization problem, it must satisfy both of the above criteria. Any multi-objective optimization technique accepts Pareto-optimal solutions for its optimization.

5 QUANTUM COMPUTING OVERVIEW

Unlike a classical computer, which solely uses classical mechanics, such as a dedicated circuit diagram for flowing electrical voltage, gates etc., a quantum computer requires quantum mechanical features to perform its operations on data. Since quantum computers are able to perform their memory-oriented tasks and process data at the atomic and subatomic level, they are more efficient and powerful than their classical counterparts [67,69]. They can have parallel processing capability, and these types of machines can process millions of different operations simultaneously. The term "quantum computer" can be defined as a computer system which is designed on basis of quantum theory. Some studies on quantum computers have already been presented [23,70]. The basic component of QC is known as a "qubit." It is a unit vector defined over two-dimensional Hilbert space [71,72]. The superposition can be defined as the linear combination of the basic states in QC. It can be represented by

$$|\psi\rangle = b_1|0\rangle + b_2|1\rangle, \tag{2}$$

where $|0\rangle$ is called the "ground state," $|1\rangle$ is known as the "excited state," and $(b_1, b_2) \in \mathbb{C}$. In general, for a z-state quantum system the feature of QC called "quantum orthogonality" must satisfy, as given by [73,74],

$$\sum_{k=1}^{z} b_k = 1. \tag{3}$$

The property of QC called "quantum entanglement" is defined as an inimitable correlation between quantum states. Theoretically, it can be defined as the tensor product between these states, as given by $|\vartheta_1\rangle \otimes |\vartheta_2\rangle$.

Let, during an intermediate period of execution, u be the number of qubits in a superposed form. The transformation of this form into a corresponding single state is called "quantum measurement." With reference to Eq. (2), the probability of transforming $|\psi\rangle$ into $|0\rangle$ and $|1\rangle$ is $|b_1|^2$ and $|b_2|^2$ respectively [75,76].

In QC a quantum register $(\mathcal{Q}_p) = n$ signifies that the register ID is formed with n qubits. The equivalent decimal number of these qubits is given by [77]

$$\underbrace{|1\rangle \otimes |0\rangle \otimes \cdots \otimes |0\rangle \otimes |1\rangle}_{m \text{ qubits}} \equiv |\underbrace{10 \cdot \cdot 01}_{m \text{ bits}}\rangle \equiv |\mathcal{Z}\rangle,$$

where $\mathcal{Z}$ is the decimal number. Note that $\otimes$ signifies the tensor product.

Like the conventional system, different quantum gates are used in QC. Quantum gates are hardware devices. Like the conventional system, n inputs produces n outputs in QC. A quantum gate follows the rules by

$$U^{+} = U^{-1}, UU^{+} = U^{+}U = I \quad \text{and} \quad U = e^{iHt}, \tag{4}$$

where U and H are the unitary operator and the Hermitian operator respectively. As an example, the quantum rotation gate is a popular gate in QC, and can be described by the following equation:

$$\begin{bmatrix} \alpha_j' \\ \beta_j' \end{bmatrix} = \begin{bmatrix} \cos(\theta_j) - \sin(\theta_j) \\ \sin(\theta_j) \cos(\theta_j) \end{bmatrix} \begin{bmatrix} \alpha_j \\ \beta_j \end{bmatrix}, \tag{5}$$

where the jth qubit is represented by (α_j, β_j). Here a rotation angle θ_j is invoked to update this qubit to (α_j', β_j') [71,72]. There are a number of quantum gates in quantum computing, such as the Fredkin gate, the NOT gate, the Toffoli gate, the Hadamard gate, the controlled NOT gate, and the controlled phase-shift gate.

6 THRESHOLDING TECHNIQUE

A number of image thresholding techniques have been introduced in the literature. Sezgin and Sankur [8] presented a comprehensive survey of different types of these techniques and evaluated their performance. In this chapter, Huang's method [78] has been used as the image thresholding technique to evaluate the proposed method. The details of Huang's method are described in brief in the following section.

6.1 HUANG'S METHOD FOR BILEVEL IMAGE THRESHOLDING

Huang and Wang [78] introduced a popular image thresholding technique called "Huang's method." This method can be applied proficiently in bilevel image thresholding to find the optimal threshold value, which can also be effectively used in multilevel thresholding as well with an additional computational complexity. Huang's method is a optimization method which finds the optimal threshold value by minimizing the measures of fuzziness. Then, a measure called the "membership function" is used to show the characteristic relationship between a pixel and its region. Huang's method is described below in details

Let $\mathcal{I}_{m\times n}$ denote an image set having L gray level values. Also, suppose that the intensity of the (a,b)th pixel is symbolized as i_{ab}. Let the membership value in $\mathcal{I}$ be denoted by $\mu_{\mathcal{I}(i_{ab})}$. This membership value can be noted as a characteristic function to express the fuzziness of the (a,b)th pixel in $\mathcal{I}_{m\times n}$. Now, the notation of a fuzzy set is used to describe $\mathcal{I}$:

$$\mathcal{I} = \{(i_{ab}, \mu_{\mathcal{I}(i_{ab})})\}, \tag{6}$$

where $\mu_{\mathcal{I}(i_{ab})} \in [0,1]$, $a = 0, 1, \ldots, (m-1)$ and $b = 0, 1, \ldots, (n-1)$.

Let the pixels in the image be grouped into exactly two classes (for bilevel image thresholding), $\mathcal{C} = \{C_0, C_1\}$, on the basis of their intensity values. Also, suppose that the mean gray levels of C_0 and C_1 are symbolized by μ_0 and μ_1 respectively.

Now μ_0 and μ_1 are defined as follows:

$$\mu_0 = \frac{\sum_{v=0}^{T_r} vh(v)}{\sum_{v=0}^{T_r} h(v)},$$

$$\mu_1 = \frac{\sum_{v=T_r+1}^{L} vh(v)}{\sum_{v=T_r+1}^{L} h(v)}, \tag{7}$$

where $h(v)$ represents the frequency of the vth pixel.

The aforesaid membership function for the (a, b)th pixel can expressed as follows:

$$\begin{aligned} \mathcal{I}(i_{ab}) &= \frac{1}{1 + |i_{ab} - \mu_0|/\varsigma}, i_{ab} \in [0, T_r], \\ &= \frac{1}{1 + |i_{ab} - \mu_1|/\varsigma}, i_{ab} \in [T_r + 1, L], \end{aligned} \tag{8}$$

where ς is a constant, $\mathcal{I}(i_{ab}) \in [1/2, 1]$.

Let $\overline{\mathcal{I}}$ be the complement of $\mathcal{I}$. The distance between $\mathcal{I}$ and its complement is defined by

$$\mathcal{D}_q(\mathcal{I}, \overline{\mathcal{I}}) = \left[\sum_a \sum_b |\mathcal{I}(i_{ab}) - \overline{\mathcal{I}}(i_{ab})|^q \right]^{\frac{1}{q}}, \quad q = 1, 2, \ldots, L-1, \tag{9}$$

where $\overline{\mathcal{I}}(i_{ab}) = 1 - \mathcal{I}(i_{ab})$. Therefore the measure of fuzziness of $\mathcal{I}$ is given by

$$\mathcal{W} = 1 - \frac{\mathcal{D}_q(\mathcal{I}, \overline{\mathcal{I}})}{(m \times n)^{\frac{1}{q}}}. \tag{10}$$

Minimization of $\mathcal{W}$ leads to the optimal threshold values for this method (as given in Eq. (10)).

7 PROPOSED METHOD

In this chapter a quantum-inspired SA-based multi-objective optimization (QISAMO) technique is introduced for bilevel image thresholding. This technique is basically designed in such a way that it can efficiently determine the optimal threshold value in the basis of the multi-objective arrangement. The outline of the QISAMO is described below.

The symbols used in the proposed QISAMO are:

- τ_s, the starting temperature;
- τ_c, the closing temperature;
- ι, the number of iterations;
- ϵ, the reduction fraction;
- φ_r, objective functions required to find the nondominated set of solutions, where r represents the number of such functions;
- ϕ, the objective function used on the set of Pareto-optimal solutions to find the optimal threshold value;
- $\mathcal{S}_r$, the nondominated set of solutions;
- θ, the optimal threshold value.

The first seven of these symbols are called "input symbols" and the last symbol is called an "output symbol."

The short description of QISAMO is given next.

In QISAMO, firstly, an initial population comprising one configuration ($\mathcal{P}$) is generated by randomly choosing pixel intensity values from the image. The length of the configuration is selected as $\mathcal{L} = \lceil \max(\sqrt{L}) \rceil$, L being the pixel intensity value. Then each pixel of this configuration is encoded with a real value between 0 and 1 at random with use of the basic theory of QC to create $\mathcal{P}'$. A basic quantum property, called "quantum orthogonality," is applied on $\mathcal{P}'$ to create $\mathcal{P}''$. Afterward, a quantum *rotation gate* is applied on $\mathcal{P}''$ to get quick convergence. Then, on the basis of a probability measure, all positions in the configuration are selected to find solutions. Let this create $\mathcal{P}^+$. Thereafter, a Pareto-optimal solution set ($\mathcal{S}_r$) is determined with use of a number of (say, r) fitness functions (φ_r). Initially, the proposed technique starts exploring its search space at a high temperature (τ_s). At each temperature this technique is executed for a successive number of iterations (ι). Thereafter the temperature is reduced with use of a reduction fraction (ϵ) as given in step 24. Better movement toward the optimal solution is always accepted. If ($\mathcal{F}(\mathcal{Q}^+) > \mathcal{F}(\mathcal{S}_r^+)$) (as shown in step 21), the configurations $\mathcal{Q}^+$ and $\mathcal{Q}$ are accepted, otherwise these newly created configurations can also be accepted for nonimproving movement with probability $\exp(-(\mathcal{F}(\mathcal{S}_r^+) - \mathcal{F}(\mathcal{Q}^+)))/\mathcal{T}$. The algorithm stops its execution when the temperature crosses a predefined low temperature value (τ_c). The details of QISAMO are illustrated below:

1. In the first step a population of a single configuration ($\mathcal{P}$) is initially created by random selection of a pixel intensity value from the input image. The length of this configuration is taken as $\mathcal{L} = \lceil \max(L) \rceil$, where L is the pixel intensity value of the image.
2. For pixel encoding, each pixel in $\mathcal{P}$ is encoded with a random real number between 0 and 1 by use of the theory of qubits in QC. Let this pixel-encoding scheme create a new arrangement, called $\mathcal{P}'$.
3. Afterward, the property of QC, called *quantum orthogonality*, is maintained for each location of the configuration in $\mathcal{P}$, which creates $\mathcal{P}''$.

4. Then, for faster convergence, each position of the configuration in $\mathcal{P}''$ is updated by application of a quantum rotation gate in the quantum computer.
5. Each position of the configuration in $\mathcal{P}''$ may contribute a possible solution. A particular location which contains a value greater than a randomly generated number between 0 and 1 is competent to be a possible solution. Let the set of all possible solutions in $\mathcal{P}''$ create $\mathcal{P}^+$.
6. Count the number of such positions and save it in ℓ.
7. Chose a number $\jmath$ between 1 and ℓ at random.
8. With use of $\mathcal{P}^+$, $\jmath$ threshold values in the form of pixel intensity are computed as solutions. Let this create $\mathcal{P}^*$.
9. For $g = 1$ to r, perform the following two steps.
10. (a) The threshold values in $\mathcal{P}^+$ are evaluated r times to find the fitness values with use of r fitness functions, φ_r; (b) the best solution for each fitness function is found and recorded in $\mathcal{S}_g$.
11. The Pareto-optimal solution set is determined with use of $\mathcal{S}_g$ and then these solutions are recorded in $\mathcal{S}_r$.
12. The fitness value of each configuration in $\mathcal{S}_r$ is computed with use of ϕ. Let it be denoted by $\mathcal{F}(\mathcal{S}_r)$.
13. Store the best configuration, $b_s \in \mathcal{P}''$, its threshold value in $T_s \in \mathcal{S}_r$ and the corresponding fitness value in F_s.
14. Repeat steps 2–5 to create $\mathcal{S}_r^+$.
15. Set $\mathcal{T} = \tau_s$.
16. Run the following steps (steps 17–24) until $\mathcal{T} \geq \tau_c$
17. For $h = 1$ to ι, perform the following steps (steps 18–23).
18. Perturb $\mathcal{S}_r$. Let this make $\mathcal{Q}$.
19. Repeat steps 2–5 to create $\mathcal{Q}^+$.
20. Repeat steps 6–12 and use Eq. (10) to calculate the fitness value $\mathcal{F}(\mathcal{Q}^+, T)$.
21. If $(\mathcal{F}(\mathcal{Q}^+) - \mathcal{F}(\mathcal{S}_r^+) > 0)$ holds
22. Set $\mathcal{S}_r^+$=$\mathcal{Q}^+$,$\mathcal{S}_r$=$\mathcal{Q}$ and $\mathcal{F}(\mathcal{S}_r^+)$=$\mathcal{F}(\mathcal{Q}^+)$.
23. Otherwise set $\mathcal{S}_r^+$=$\mathcal{Q}^+$,$\mathcal{S}_r$=$\mathcal{Q}$ and $\mathcal{F}(\mathcal{S}_r^+)$=$\mathcal{F}(\mathcal{Q}^+)$ with probability $\exp(-(\mathcal{F}(\mathcal{S}_r^+) - \mathcal{F}(\mathcal{Q}^+)))/\mathcal{T}$.
24. $\mathcal{T} = \mathcal{T} \times \epsilon$.
25. Report the optimal threshold value, $\theta = \mathcal{S}_r^+$.

7.1 COMPLEXITY ANALYSIS

Stepwise analysis of time complexity (worst case) of the proposed QISAMO is given below:

- Initially (step 1), the population ($\mathcal{P}$) of the QISAMO is formed with a single configuration of length $\mathcal{L} = \lceil \max(\sqrt{L}) \rceil$, where L represents the pixel intensity of a grayscale image. For performance of this step, the time complexity is $O(\mathcal{L})$.
- For the pixel-encoding part (as described in step 2), the time complexity is $O(\mathcal{L})$.

- The time complexity to conduct each of the next three steps (steps 3–5) is $O(\mathcal{L})$.
- Similarly, the time complexity to perform step 8 is $O(\mathcal{L})$.
- The nondominated set of solutions is determined through steps 10 and 11. The overall time complexity for performance of these steps is $O(\mathcal{L})$.
- Similarly, the time complexity to perform the next step (step 12) is $O(\mathcal{L})$.
- In step 14, steps 2–5 are repeated. To execute each of these steps, the time complexity is $O(\mathcal{L})$.
- Steps 18–20 are executed for ι iterations. For each iteration the time complexity to execute each step is $O(\mathcal{L})$.
- Let the outer loop (step 15) and the inner loop (step 16) of this algorithm be executed ξ and ι times respectively. The time complexity to execute these steps of the proposed technique is therefore $\xi \times \iota$. If the steps stated above are aggregated (summarized), the overall time complexity (worst case) of the QISAMO is $\mathcal{L} \times \xi \times \iota$.

8 EXPERIMENTS AND DISCUSSION

The proposed QISAMO technique was implemented (coded) in MATLAB on a system consisting of a Toshiba Intel Core i3, 2.53-GHz PC with 2GB RAM and Microsoft Windows 7. To have an apposite implementation of the QISAMO technique, predefined parameters (after proper tuning) are required, and these are presented in a parameter specification table (see Table 1). Twelve real images named "Airplane,", "Anhinga," "Baboon," "Barbara," "Boat," "Cameraman," "Couple," "Desert," "Grnpeace," "Monolake," "Oldmill," and "Stonehse," each of dimension 256 × 256, were used to conduct the required experiments. The original versions of these images are shown in Fig. 1. The results obtained were compared with those obtained with the classical counterpart of the proposed technique.

Table 1 Parameter Specification for Quantum-Inspired Simulated Annealing-Based Multi-objective Optimization and Simulated Annealing-Based Multi-objective Optimization

Parameter	QISAMO	SAMO
Starting temperature, τ_S	1000	1000
Closing temperature, τ_C	0.5	0.5
Number of iterations, ι	40	500
Reduction fraction, ϵ	0.95	0.95

QISAMO, quantum-inspired simulated annealing-based multi-objective optimization; SAMO, simulated annealing-based multi-objective optimization.

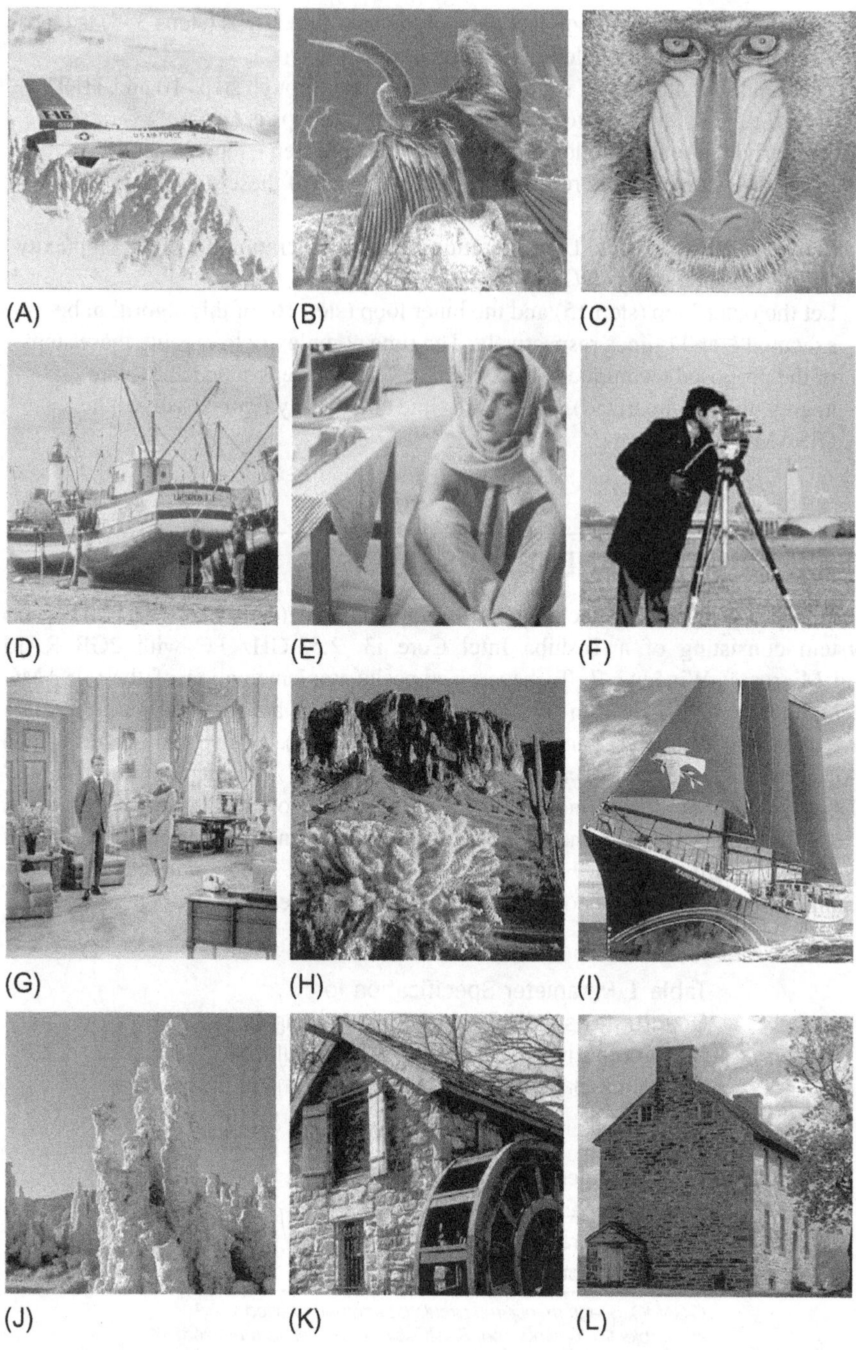

FIG. 1

Original test images: (A) Airplane, (B) Anhinga, (C) Baboon, (D) Barbara, (E) Boat, (F) Cameraman, (G) Couple, (H) Desert, (I) Grnpeace, (J) Monolake, (K) Oldmill, and (L) Stonehse.

8.1 THRESHOLDING RESULTS OF THE TECHNIQUES INVESTIGATED

In this section the best results of the proposed QISAMO and SAMO are reported for bilevel image thresholding. Each technique was executed separately for 40 different runs for all test images. The best fitness value ($\mathcal{V}_b$) and its corresponding optimal threshold (θ) for each technique are presented in Table 2. The proposed QISAMO is designed for bilevel thresholding using the wrapper of the multi-objective optimization technique. Two different objective function (of conflicting type) were applied to find the Pareto-optimal or nondominated set of solutions. Finally, Huang's method [78] was applied on the set of nondominated solutions to get the final results. The thresholded images are presented in Figs. 2–7.

Table 2 Best Results for Quantum-Inspired Simulated Annealing-Based Multi-objective Optimization and Simulated Annealing-Based Multi-objective Optimization for Bilevel Thresholding of Airplane, Anhinga, Baboon, Barbara, Boat, Cameraman, Couple, Desert, Grnpeace, Monolake, Oldmill, and Stonehse

	QISAMO		SAMO	
Image	θ	$\mathcal{V}_b$	θ	$\mathcal{V}_b$
Airplane	136	0.176456	133	0.176661
Anhinga	139	0.165477	129	0.166681
Baboon	130	0.194270	132	0.194300
Barbara	128	0.171788	125	0.171969
Boat	110	0.176947	112	0.176956
Cameraman	128	0.176734	135	0.177782
Couple	108	0.190757	109	0.190770
Desert	135	0.169047	138	0.169265
Grnpeace	143	0.166374	149	0.166985
Monolake	158	0.175334	154	0.176172
Oldmill	125	0.164389	124	0.164437
Stonehse	143	0.167608	146	0.167961

QISAMO, quantum-inspired simulated annealing-based multi-objective optimization; SAMO, simulated annealing-based multi-objective optimization.

8.2 EFFICIENCY OF TECHNIQUES INVESTIGATED

The average fitness ($\mathcal{V}_{av}$) and the standard deviation (σ) were computed for each method over all runs. The results of these measures are presented in Table 3. QISAMO has encouraging results with regard to both mean fitness (very close to the best fitness) and standard deviation of the best values over different runs. QISAMO always provides better results for these two measures than SAMO This proves the stability and sturdiness of the proposed method. The computational time of QISAMO seems to be much faster than that of SAMO for each image. The quality

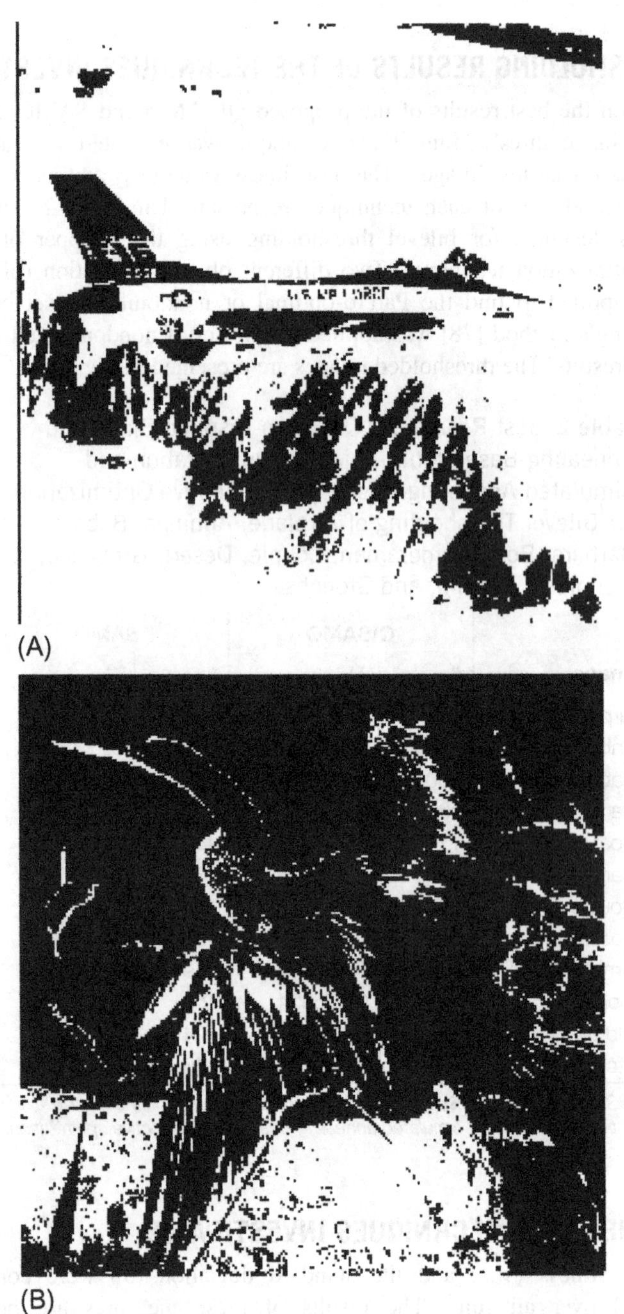

FIG. 2

Thresholded images for (A) Airplane and (B) Anhinga for Huang's method.

L. Huang, M. Wang, Image thresholding by minimizing the measures of fuzziness, Pattern Recognit. 28 (1) (1995) 41–51.

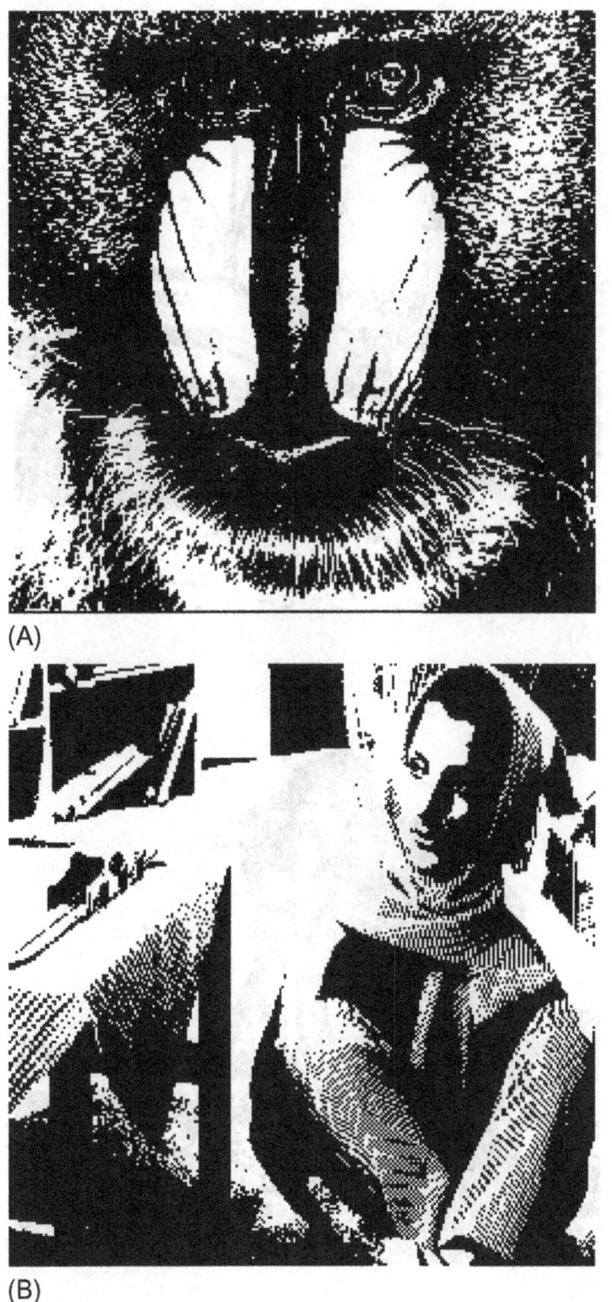

FIG. 3

Thresholded images for (A) Baboon and (B) Barbara for Huang's method.

L. Huang, M. Wang, Image thresholding by minimizing the measures of fuzziness, Pattern Recognit. 28 (1) (1995) 41–51.

(A)

(B)

FIG. 4

Thresholded images for (A) Boat and (B) Cameraman for Huang's method.

L. Huang, M. Wang, Image thresholding by minimizing the measures of fuzziness, Pattern Recognit. 28 (1) (1995) 41–51.

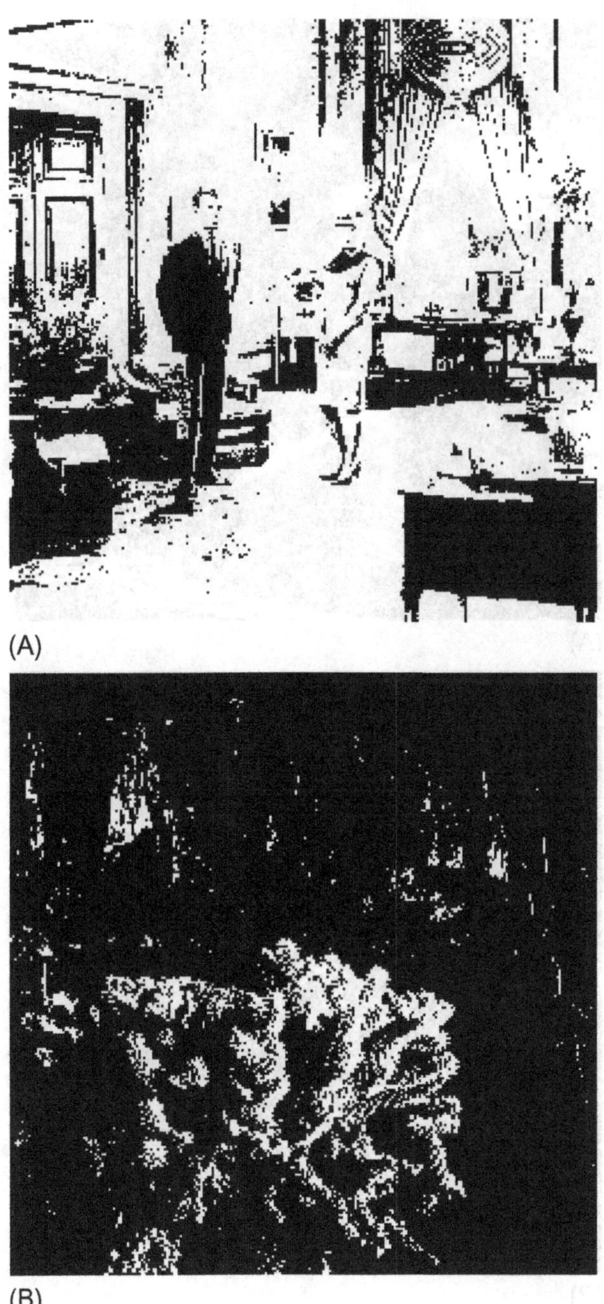

FIG. 5

Thresholded images for (A) Couple and (B) Desert for Huang's method.

L. Huang, M. Wang, Image thresholding by minimizing the measures of fuzziness, Pattern Recognit. 28 (1) (1995) 41–51.

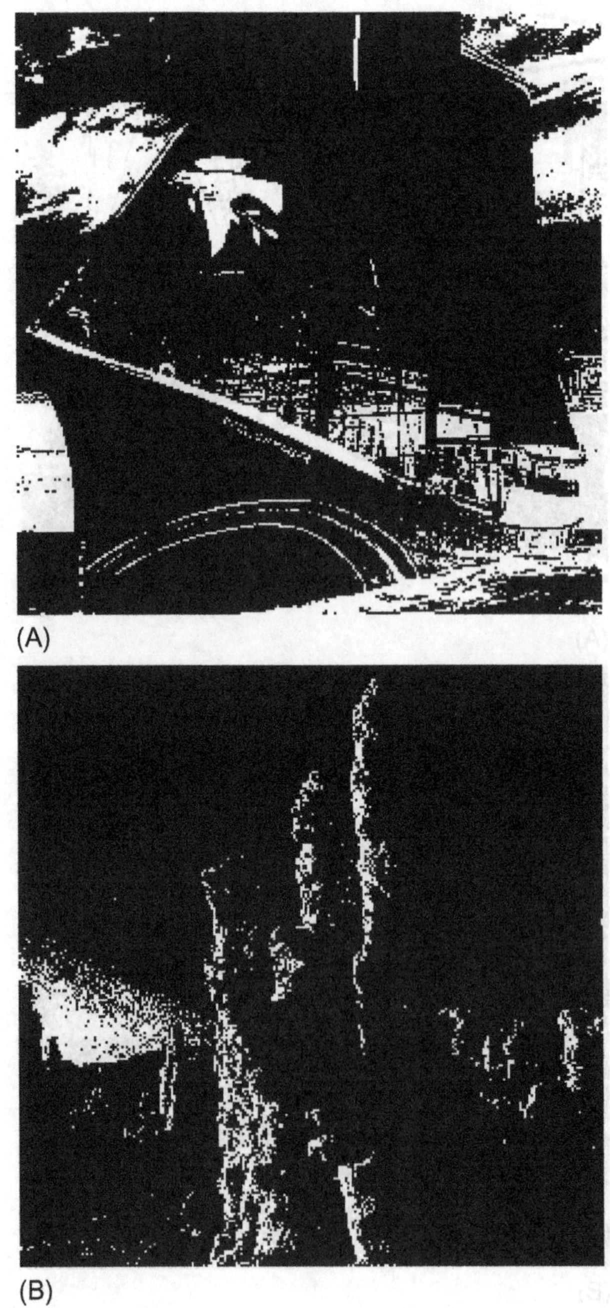

(A)

(B)

FIG. 6

Thresholded images for (A) Grnpeace and (B) Monolake for Huang's method.

L. Huang, M. Wang, Image thresholding by minimizing the measures of fuzziness, Pattern Recognit. 28 (1) (1995) 41–51.

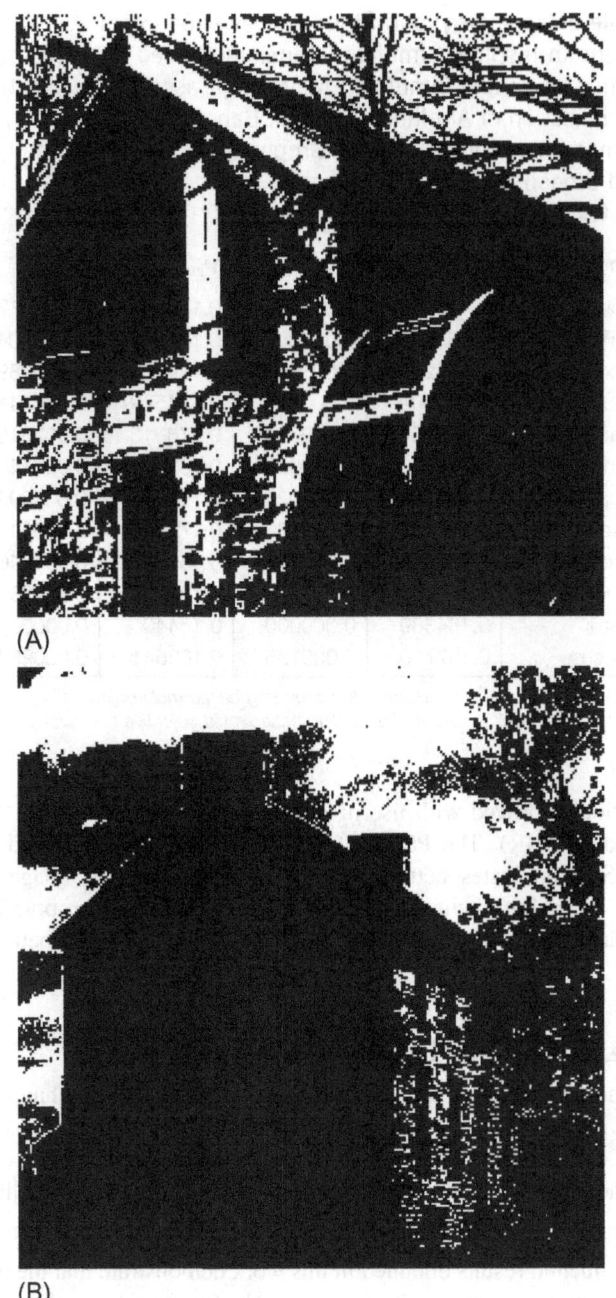

(A)

(B)

FIG. 7

Thresholded images for (A) Oldmill and (B) Stonehse for Huang's method.

L. Huang, M. Wang, Image thresholding by minimizing the measures of fuzziness, Pattern Recognit. 28 (1) (1995) 41–51.

Table 3 Mean ($\mathcal{V}_{av}$) and Standard Deviation (σ) of Quantum-Inspired Simulated Annealing-Based Multi-objective Optimization and Simulated Annealing-Based Multi-objective Optimization of Airplane, Anhinga, Baboon, Barbara, Boat, Cameraman, Couple, Desert, Grnpeace, Monolake, Oldmill, and Stonehse

	QISAMO		SAMO	
Image	$\mathcal{V}_{av}$	σ	$\mathcal{V}_{av}$	σ
Airplane	0.176493	0.000063	0.179513	0.005877
Anhinga	0.165505	0.000069	0.168902	0.007204
Baboon	0.194296	0.000063	0.194374	0.006089
Barbara	0.171809	0.000051	0.174579	0.006741
Boat	0.176959	0.000024	0.178913	0.002810
Cameraman	0.171809	0.000051	0.182707	0.008145
Couple	0.190768	0.000023	0.192895	0.004393
Desert	0.169143	0.000130	0.178247	0.018049
Grnpeace	0.166405	0.000060	0.167743	0.001246
Monolake	0.175467	0.000220	0.187234	0.009932
Oldmill	0.164389	0.000000	0.16440	0.000008
Stonehse	0.167710	0.000125	0.168541	0.000952

QISAMO, quantum-inspired simulated annealing-based multi-objective optimization; SAMO, simulated annealing-based multi-objective optimization.

of segmentation is proved with use of a special measure, called the "peak signal to noise ratio" (PSNR). The PSNRs for both methods are presented in Table 4. A greater PSNR indicates better quality of segmentation in image processing. Hence from the point of view of image segmentation, the proposed method is better compared than the other method (since QISAMO finds a better PSNR for all images).

8.3 CONCLUSION AND FUTURE PROSPECTS

We have proposed a novel quantum-inspired multi-objective SA technique for bilevel thresholding on real grayscale images. This method has been compared with its conventional counterpart in all respects. The effectiveness of the proposed scheme can be affirmed as novel and also computationally efficient owing to the following facts:

1. The experimental results obtained in this work demonstrate that the proposed approach achieves better results in terms of the fitness value and computational time than the conventional approach.
2. From the segmentation point of view, the PSNR of the proposed method provides better results for all test images than its classical counterpart.

Table 4 Peak Signal to Noise Ratio and Computational Time for the Best Results of Quantum-Inspired Simulated Annealing-Based Multi-objective Optimization and Quantum-Inspired Simulated Annealing-Based Multi-objective Optimization of Airplane, Anhinga, Baboon, Barbara, Boat, Cameraman, Couple, Desert, Grnpeace, Monolake, Oldmill, and Stonehse for Huang's Method

	QISAMO		SAMO	
Image	**PSNR**	***t***	**PSNR**	***t***
Airplane	20.4128	2.01	20.310	8.15
Anhinga	18.6295	2.29	18.2940	7.48
Baboon	16.4678	1.58	16.4674	7.12
Barbara	17.4023	1.49	17.4015	8.12
Boat	17.6201	2.37	17.5175	7.52
Cameraman	16.0488	2.12	15.6279	8.00
Couple	15.7973	2.02	15.7467	8.38
Desert	17.0052	2.21	16.9312	8.07
Grnpeace	16.5847	1.51	16.4109	7.25
Monolake	17.3693	1.52	17.2862	7.45
Oldmill	11.4236	2.00	11.4179	8.30
Stonehse	16.9577	1.49	16.8155	8.19

PSNR, peak signal to noise ratio; QISAMO, quantum-inspired simulated annealing-based multi-objective optimization; SAMO, simulated annealing-based multi-objective optimization.
L. Huang, M. Wang, Image thresholding by minimizing the measures of fuzziness, Pattern Recognit. 28 (1) (1995) 41–51.

3. The stability and accuracy of the proposed approach are evident from the encouraging results for the mean fitness value and the standard deviation respectively.

Summarizing all of these statements, we can assert that the proposed method is more effective than its classical counterpart. As we have tried to walk in a new direction, this chapter should generate adequate interest and induce other researchers toward the advancement of this novel work.

REFERENCES

[1] W. Kang, K. Wang, Q. Wang, D. An, Segmentation method based on transition region extraction for coronary angiograms, in: Proceedings of IEEE International Conference on Mechatronics and Automation, 2009, 905–909.

[2] J. Yang, L.H. Staib, V. Duncan, Neighborhood-constrained segmentation with level based 3-D deformable models, IEEE Trans. Med. Imaging 23 (8) (2004) 940–948.

[3] A.A. Younes, I. Truck, H. Akdaj, Color image profiling using fuzzy sets, Turk. J. Electr. Eng. 13 (3) (2005) 343–359.

[4] L. Lanzarini, J.L. Battaglia, J. Maulini, W. Hasperue, Face recognition using SIFT and binary PSO descriptors, in: 32nd International Conference on Information Technology Interfaces (ITI), 2010, 557–562.

[5] N.R. Pal, S.K. Pal, A review on image segmentation techniques, Pattern Recognit. 26 (9) (1993) 1277–1294.

[6] F. Chan, F. Lam, H. Zhuj, Adaptive thresholding by variational method, IEEE Trans. Image Process. 7 (3) (1998) 468–473.

[7] P. Sahoo, S. Soltani, A. Wongj, A survey of thresholding techniques, Comput. Vis. Graph. Image Process. 41 (1988) 233–260.

[8] M. Sezgin, B. Sankur, Survey over image thresholding techniques and quantitative performance evaluation, J. Electron. Imaging 13 (1) (2004) 146–165.

[9] H. Cheng, Y. Chen, X. Jiang, Thresholding using twodimensional histogram and fuzzy entropy principle, IEEE Trans. Image Process. 9 (2000) 732–735.

[10] J. Chang, H. Liao, M. Hor, J. Hsieh, M. Chem, New automatic multi-level threshold images, Image Vis. Comput. 15 (1997) 23–34.

[11] N. Papamarkos, C. Strouthopoulos, I. Audreadis, Multi-thresholding of color and grey level images through a neural network technique, Image Vis. Comput. 18 (2000) 213–222.

[12] P. Yin, Maximum entropy-based optimal threshold selection using deterministic reinforcement learning with controlled randomization, Signal Process. 82 (2002) 993–1006.

[13] P.S. Liao, T.S. Chen, P.C. Chung, A fast algorithm for multilevel thresholding, J. Inf. Sci. Eng. 17 (2001) 713–727.

[14] A. Nakiba, H. Oulhadja, P. Siarry, Image thresholding based on Pareto multiobjective optimization, Eng. Appl. Artif. Intell. 23 (3) (2010) 313–320.

[15] N. Otsu, A threshold selection method from grey-level histograms, IEEE Syst. Man Cybern. 9 (1) (1979) 62–66.

[16] J.N. Kapur, P.K. Sahoo, A.K.C. Wong, A new method for gray-level picture thresholding using the entropy of the histogram, Comput. Vis. Graph. Image Process. 29 (1985) 273–285.

[17] T. Pun, A new method for gray-level picture thresholding using the entropy of the histogram, Signal Process. 2 (1980) 223–237.

[18] D. Sen, S.K. Pal, Gradient histogram thresholding in a region of interest for edge detection, Image Vis. Comput. 28 (2010) 677–695.

[19] M.K. Kundu, S.K. Pal, Thresholding for edge detection using human psycho-visual phenomena, Pattern Recognit. Lett. 4 (6) (1986) 433–441.

[20] P. Benioff, The computer as a physical system: a microscopic quantum mechanical Hamiltonian model of computers as represented by Turing machines, J. Stat. Phys. 22 (1980) 563–591.

[21] R. Feynman, Simulating physics with computers, Int. J. Theor. Phys. 21 (6/7) (1982) 467–488.

[22] D. Deutsch, Quantum theory, the Church-Turing principle and the universal quantum computer, Proc. R. Soc. Lond. Ser. A: Math. Phys. Sci. 400 (1818) (1985) 97–117.

[23] P. Shor, Polynomial-time algorithms for prime factorization and discrete algorithms on a quantum computer, in: Proceedings of the 35th Annual Symposium on Foundations of Computer Science, IEEE Computer Society Press, New York, 1994, pp. 124–134.

[24] L.K. Grover, A fast quantum mechanical algorithm for database search, in: Proceedings of ACM Symposium on TOC, Philadelphia, 1996, pp. 212–219.

[25] M.A. Nielsen, I.L. Chuang, Quantum Computation and Quantum Information, Cambridge University Press, Cambridge, 2006.

[26] S. Dey, S. Bhattacharyya, U. Maullik, Chaotic map model based interference employed in quantum inspired genetic algorithm to determine the optimum gray level image thresholding, in: Global Trends in Intelligent Computing Research and Development, 2013, pp. 68-110.

[27] S. Bhattacharyya, P. Dutta, S. Chakraborty, R. Chakraborty, S. Dey, Determination of optimal threshold of a gray-level image using a quantum inspired genetic algorithm with interference based on a random map model, in: Proceedings of 2010 IEEE International Conference on Computational Intelligence and Computing Research (ICCIC 2010), Coimbatore, India, 2010, pp. 422–425.

[28] S. Dey, S. Bhattacharyya, U. Maullik, Optimum gray level image thresholding using a quantum inspired genetic algorithm, in: Advanced Research on Hybrid Intelligent Techniques and Applications, 2015, pp. 349–377.

[29] C. Blum, A. Roli, Metaheuristic in combinatorial optimization: overview and conceptual comparison, Technical Report, IRIDIA, 2001–2013.

[30] F. Glover, G.A. Kochenberger, Handbook on Metaheuristics, Kluwer Academic Publishers, Dordrecht, 2003.

[31] E.-G. Talbi, Metaheuristic: From Design to Implementation, John Wiley & Sons, New York, NY, 2009.

[32] K. Hammouche, M. Diaf, P. Siarry, A comparative study of various meta-heuristic techniques applied to the multilevel thresholding problem, Eng. Appl. Artif. Intell. 23 (2010) 678–688.

[33] J.L. Cohon, Multiobjective Programming and Planning, Academic Press, New York, 1978.

[34] D. Goldberg, Genetic Algorithms in Search, Optimization and Machine Learning, Addison Wesley, Reading, MA, 1989.

[35] D.A.V. Veldhuizen, G.B. Lamont, Multiobjective evolutionary algorithms: analyzing the state-of-the-art, J. Evol. Comput. 8 (2) (2000) 125–147.

[36] K. Deb, Multi-Objective Optimization Using Evolutionary Algorithms, Wiley, Chichester, UK, 2001.

[37] F. Glover, H.J. Greenberg, New approaches for heuristic search: a bilateral linkage with artificial intelligence, Eur. J. Oper. Res. 39 (1989) 119–130.

[38] C.A. Coello Coello, An empirical study of evolutionary technique for multiobjective optimization in engineering design, Ph.D. Thesis, Department of Computer Science, Tulane University, New Orleans, LA, 1996.

[39] C.A. Coello Coello, A comprehensive survey of evolutionary based multiobjective optimization techniques, Knowl. Inf. Syst. 1 (1999) 269–308.

[40] D.A.V. Veldhuizen, Multiobjective evolutionary algorithm research: a history and analysis, Technical Report TR-98-03, Department of Electrical and Computer Engineering, Graduate School of Engineering, Air Force Institute of Technology, Wright-Patterson Air Force Base, Ohio, 1998.

[41] D.A.V. Veldhuizen, Evolutionary computing conference to a Pareto front, in: J.R. Koza (Ed.), Late Breaking Papers at the Genetic Programming. Conference, Stanford University, California, July 1998, Stanford University Bookstore, Stanford, California, 1998, pp. 221–228.

[42] N.E. Collins, R.W. Eglese, B.L. Golden, Simulated annealing—an annotated bibliography, Am. J. Math. Manage. Sci. 8 (1988) 209–307.

[43] R.A. Rutenbar, Simulated annealing algorithms: an overview, IEEE Circ. Dev. Mag. 5 (1) (1989) 19–26.

[44] R.W. Eglese, Simulated annealing: a tool for operational research, Eur. J. Oper. Res. 46 (1990) 271–281.

[45] J. Chen, Y.F. Zhang, A.Y.C. Nee, Setup planning using Hopfield net and simulated annealing, Int. J. Prod. Res. 36 (1988) 981–1000.

[46] J. Sridhar, C. Rajendran, Scheduling in a cellular manufacturing system: a simulated annealing approach, Int. J. Prod. Res. 31 (1993) 2927–2945.

[47] G. Suresh, S. Sahu, Stochastic assembly line balancing using simulated annealing, Int. J. Prod. Res. 32 (1994) 1801–1810.

[48] R.D. Meller, Y.A. Bozer, A new simulated annealing algorithm facility layout problem, International Journal of Production Research 34 (1996) 1675–1692.

[49] S.K. Mukhopadhyay, M.K. Singh, R. Srivastava, FMS machine loading: a simulated annealing approach, Int. J. Prod. Res. 36 (1998) 1529–1547.

[50] J.U. Kim, Y.D. Kim, S.O. Shim, Heuristic algorithms for a multi-period multi-stop transportation planning problem, J. Oper. Res. Soc. 53 (1998) 1027–1037.

[51] P. Serafini, Mathematics of multi-objective optimization, in: CISM Courses and Lectures, vol. 289, Springer-Verlag, Berlin, 1985.

[52] P. Serafini, Simulated annealing for multiple objective optimization problems, in: Proceedings of the Tenth International Conference on Multiple Criteria Decision Making, Taipei, 1992, pp. 87–96.

[53] L.E. Ulungu, Multiobjective combinatorial optimization problems: a survey, J. Multi-Crit. Decis. Anal. 3 (1994) 83–104.

[54] P. Serafini, Simulated annealing for multiple objective optimization problems, in: G.H. Tzeng, H.F. Wang, V.P. Wen, P.L. Yu (Eds.), Multiple Criteria Decision Making. Expand and Enrich the Domains of Thinking and Application, Springer-Verlag, Berlin, 1994, pp. 283–292.

[55] L.E. Ulungu, J. Teghem, P. Fortemps, D. Tuyttens, MOSA method: a tool for solving multiobjective combinatorial optimization problems, J. Multi-Crit. Decis. Anal. 8 (1999) 221–236.

[56] L.E. Ulungu, J. Teghem, C. Ost, Interactive simulated annealing in a multiobjective framework: application to an industrial problem, J. Oper. Res. Soc. 49 (1998) 1044–1050.

[57] A. Suppapitnarm, T. Parks, Simulated annealing: an alternative approach to true multiobjective optimization, in: Genetic and Evolutionary Computation Conference. Conference Workshop Program, Orlando, Florida, 1999, pp. 406–407.

[58] D. Tuyttens, J. Teghem, P. Fortemps, K.V. Nieuwenhuyze, Performance of the MOSA method for the bicriteria assignment problem, J. Heuristics 6 (3) (2000) 295–310.

[59] P. Czyzak, M. Hapke, A. Jaszkiewicz, Application of the Pareto-simulated annealing to the multiple criteria shortest path problem, Technical Report, Politechnika Poznanska Instytut Informatyki, Poland, 1994.

[60] P. Czyzak, A. Jaszkiewicz, Pareto simulated annealing—a metaheuristic technique for multiple-objective combinatorial optimization, J. Multi-Crit. Decis. Anal. 7 (1998) 34–47.

[61] B. Suman, multi-objective simulated annealing—a metaheuristic technique for multiobjective optimization of a constrained problem, Found. Comput. Decis. Sci. 27 (2002) 171–191.

[62] B. Suman, Simulated annealing based multiobjective algorithm and their application for system reliability, Eng. Optim. 35 (2003) 391–416.

[63] B. Suman, Self-stopping PDMOSA and performance measure in simulated annealing based multiobjective optimization algorithms, Comput. Chem. Eng. 29 (2004) 1131–1147.

[64] S. Dey, S. Bhattacharyya, U. Maullik, Quantum behaved swarm intelligent techniques for image analysis: a detailed survey, in: Handbook of Research on Swarm Intelligence in Engineering, 2015, pp. 1–39.

[65] S. Kirkpatrik, C.D. Gelatt, M.P. Vecch, Optimization by simulated annealing, Science 220 (1983) 671–680.

[66] S. Dey, S. Bhattacharyya, U. Maulik, Quantum inspired automatic clustering for multi-level image thresholding, in: Proceedings of International Conference On Computational Intelligence and Communication Networks (ICCICN 2014), RCCIIT, Kolkata, India, 2014, 242–246.

[67] S. Dey, S. Bhattacharyya, U. Maulik, Quantum inspired genetic algorithm and particle swarm optimization using chaotic map model based interference for gray level image thresholding, Swarm Evol. Comput. 15 (2014) 38–57.

[68] S. Dey, I. Saha, S. Bhattacharyya, U. Maulik, Multi-level thresholding using quantum inspired meta-heuristics, Knowl. Based Syst. 67 (2014) 373–400.

[69] S. Dey, S. Bhattacharyya, U. Maulik, New quantum inspired tabu search for multi-level colour image thresholding, in: Proceedings of 8th International Conference On Computing for Sustainable Global Development (INDIACom-2014), BVICAM, New Delhi, 2014, 311–316.

[70] D. Deutsch, R. Jozsa, Rapid solution of problems by quantum computation, Proc. R. Soc. Lond. Ser. A: Math Phys. Sci. 439 (1907) (1992) 553–558.

[71] D. Mcmohan, Quantum Computing Explained, John Wiley & Sons, Inc., Hoboken, NJ, 2008.

[72] V. Vendral, M.B. Plenio, M.A. Rippin, Quantum Entanglement, Phys. Rev. Lett. 78 (12) (1997) 2275–2279.

[73] S. Dey, S. Bhattacharyya, U. Maulik, Quantum inspired automatic clustering for multi-level image thresholding, in: Proceedings of International Conference On Computational Intelligence and Communication Networks (ICCICN 2014), RCCIIT, Kolkata, India, 2014, pp. 247–251.

[74] S. Dey, S. Bhattacharyya, U. Maulik, New quantum inspired tabu search for multi-level colour image thresholding, in: Proceedings of 8th International Conference On Computing for Sustainable Global Development (INDIACom-2014), BVICAM, New Delhi, 2014, pp. 311–316.

[75] S. Bhattacharyya, S. Dey, An efficient quantum inspired genetic algorithm with chaotic map model based interference and fuzzy objective function for gray level image thresholding, in: Proceedings of 2011 International Conference on Computational Intelligence and Communication Systems (CICN 2011), Gwalior, India, 2011, pp. 121–125.
[76] K.H. Han, J.H. Kim, Quantum-inspired evolutionary algorithm for a class combinational optimization, IEEE Trans. Evol. Comput. 6 (6) (2002) 580–593.
[77] S. Dey, S. Bhattacharyya, U. Maulik, New quantum inspired meta-heuristic methods for multi-level thresholding, in: Proceedings of 2013 International Conference on Advances in Computing, Communications and Informatics (ICACCI), Mysore, 2013, pp. 1236–1240.
[78] L. Huang, M. Wang, Image thresholding by minimizing the measures of fuzziness, Pattern Recognit. 28 (1) (1995) 41–51.

CHAPTER

7

Quantum inspired computational intelligent techniques in image segmentation

D.P. Hudedagaddi, B.K. Tripathy
SCOPE, VIT University, Vellore, TN, India

1 INTRODUCTION

Quantum is a buzzword which is often found on the jargon list. Nowadays, quantum mechanics (QM) successfully paved its way into most of the trend setting technologies (e.g., semiconductors and lasers). Although astonishing, it is a fact that technology has had a paradigm shift from the theoretical stage. Quantum computational intelligence is an area that has roots in quantum physics and theoretical computer science. In the early 1980s, Richard Feynman questioned the possibility of designing a universal quantum computer because of the overhead involved. The overhead was exponential to the size of the system when QM simulations were performed on a conventional computer. The simulated time was also considered as an overhead.

Turing machines—and all types of computers in the present era—depend on traditional material science. However, current quantum material science asserts that the world acts in an unexpected way. A quantum framework can be considered as a superposition of a wide range of states. Also, spatially isolated quantum frameworks might be entrapped with one another and operations on it might have "nonneighborhood" impacts. QC is the field that studies the computational ability and different properties of computers with respect to QM standards. An important goal is to discover quantum computations that are fundamentally quicker than any computation technique which tackles the same issue.

Unlike customary computers which store data in binary form, a quantum computer uses qubits—which can be 1, 0, or both. Quantum tunneling, along with quantum superposition, makes computations more powerful and faster in quantum computers (i.e., it manipulates all the combinations of bits simultaneously). Qubits do not depend on the customary binary nature of computing. Conventional computers

Quantum Inspired Computational Intelligence. http://dx.doi.org/10.1016/B978-0-12-804409-4.00007-3

encode information in binary. The conventional computers perform calculations on a set of numbers. However, quantum computers encode information as a sequence of QM states (e.g., orientations of electrons or polarization of a photon), which may be a 1, 0, a combination of the two, or a number indicating a condition of the qubit that lies somewhere around 1 and 0, or a superposition of an extensive variety of numbers. Unlike a normal computer that uses the binary system, a quantum computer is capable of simultaneously reversing all the numbers in the classical computation. It also possesses the ability to produce interference between various numbers. By performing calculations on a wide range of numbers and even meddling the outcomes to get a solitary reply, a quantum computer can possibly be more effective than a similar size conventional computer. By using only a single handling unit, a quantum computer can actually perform hordes of operations in parallel.

1.1 COMPUTATIONAL INTELLIGENCE (CI)

CI, a branch of artificial intelligence (AI) which includes the study of versatile components to empower or encourage savvy practices in intricate and evolving situations. CI is an aggregation of major computational paradigms, which is different from intelligent systems (IS). CI covers all parts of AI and emphasizes on the improvement and development of real world applications. CI highly relies on numerical information supplied by manufacturers and does not depend on "knowledge." On the contrary, AI depends on human experts for deriving its knowledge. The intelligence or knowledge displayed by CI is self-developing and unconstrained, unlike in AI where it is synthetic and artificial [1].

CI is a relatively new branch of AI. The branches vary from reasoning, neurobiology, developmental science, sociology, finance, political science, control engineering, to anthropology and many more have been examining intelligence over a longer period. The study of CI could be depicted as synthetic psychology, experimental philosophy, or computational epistemology. It can be a new approach to ponder the old issue of the way of learning and insight. However, it has a more effective exploratory device than that was already accessible. Rather than having the capacity to observe just the outer behavior of intelligent frameworks, as in philosophy, psychology, economics, and sociology, CI possesses the capacity to try different things with executable models of intelligent behavior. These models are open to examination, updation, and experimentation in a complete and thorough way. This means we now have an approach to develop the models that logicians could only theorize about. A person can try different things with these models, rather than simply talking about its theoretical properties. The goal of aerodynamics was not just to synthesize flying birds; but was to understand the concept of flying. However, to comprehend the wonder of flying machines, CI's definitive objective is not the full-scale reproduction of human knowledge. The thought of psychological legitimacy isolates CI work into two classifications: the one which is concerned with mimicking human intelligence called cognitive modeling and the other which is not.

CI is directly connected with computer science. Most CI (or AI) research is carried out in software engineering or computer science labs. This has been a more appropriate location for the study of computation, which is fundamental to CI. It is vital to comprehend algorithms, data structures, and combinatorial complexities in order to build intelligent machines. It is surprising to know the extensive involvement of computer science in AI and CI, starting from the traditional computer systems to the recent evolving systems.

In days to come, CI can be seen under the umbrella of cognitive science. Cognitive science combines different disciplines that study discernment and thinking, from psychology to semantics to human sciences to neuroscience. CI separates itself from cognitive science because it gives tools to fabricate intelligence, as opposed to simply considering the external behavior or dissecting the inner workings of IS [2].

1.2 QUANTUM COMPUTING (QC)

QC is an emerging field of computer science. Recently, several researchers are involved in extensive research in this field. It takes its inceptions from the establishments of the quantum material science. It also brings in parallelism that clearly diminishes the effect of algorithmic multifaceted nature. Such a capacity of parallel processing can be used proficiently in finding solutions for optimization issues. As there is a lack of efficient quantum machines, alternatives have been recommended, such as simulating quantum calculations on conventional computers or linking them to existing strategies. A blend of evolutionary algorithms and QC principles has officially demonstrated its handiness in addressing numerous issues, such as the *N*-queens problem, the traveling salesman problem, and image registration and so on [3].

QC is the area that concentrates on creating computers taking into account the standards of quantum hypothesis. It includes the behavior of matter and energy on quantum (subatomic, nuclear) level. Developments in quantum computer will result in a paradigm shift from a computer to an advanced supercomputer. It would come with an execution performance which is extremely high. This quantum computer, implements the law of quantum physics, enhances the processing ability through its capacity to be in different levels. It can also perform assignments utilizing every single conceivable change all the while. IBM, MIT, and the Oxford University are some of the famous centers for research in QC.

Paul Benio's work at Argonne National Labs, in 1981 laid the foundation for finding the key components of QC. He came up with a conventional computer that worked with standards of QM. However, David Deutsch gave the foundations for research on quantum processing. It was at a conference that he began pondering the likelihood of outlining a computer that can be built solely in the light of quantum standards. He then put forward his findings a couple of months later. With this as the beginning, there has been an extensive amount of knowledge available in the field of quantum world.

1.2.1 Quantum theory

Quantum theory's evolution started in 1900. Max Planck presented the thought which included him stating energy existed in forms of individual units called "quanta" at the German Physical Society. Further improvements by various researchers over the last 30 years prompted the present day understanding of quantum theory.

1.2.2 Quantum theory's essential elements

1. Energy, similar to matter, comprises of discrete units rather than a wave.
2. Elementary particles behave like a particle or wave depending on the condition.
3. Movement of elementary particles is random and unpredictable.
4. Concurrent estimation of two integral values, for example, the position and energy of an elementary particle, is unpreventably defective. The higher the precision in one value leads to higher flaw in the other value.

Neils Bohr stated that objective reality is a myth. This means a principle called superposition claims that every single object is in its conceivable state simultaneously. To represent the hypothesis, Schrödinger's cat analogy can be used. To start with, a living cat is placed in a thick box made of lead. At initial stage, it is confirmed for the cat to be alive. Later, a vial of cyanide is dropped and the case is sealed. The status of the cat is now unknown. It can either be alive or might have died after breaking the cyanide. Because there is no idea about the cat being alive or dead, it is considered that the cat is in both states—according to superposition of states in quantum law. The superposition can be lost, and the cat's status (of living or dead) can only be known once the box is opened.

Another elucidation of quantum theory is the many-worlds theory. Moreover, there is a system for association between these universes that finds a way of allowing all states to be available, and for every single conceivable state to be influenced in some way. Hawking and Feynman have strongly believe in the many-worlds theory.

1.2.3 Differences between conventional and QC

Conventional computing relies on standards communicated by Boolean variable based mathematics. It works—more often than not—with a 7-mode logical gate. However, it is possible to work with three modes (AND, NOT, and COPY). Information is to be handled in a restrictive double state anytime—which is either 0 or 1. These quantities are bits. Large numbers of transistors and capacitors present in the computers must be in one state at a given time—it can either be a 0 or 1. The preceding exchange of states presently quantify in billionths of a second. Still, a limitation exists in the matter of how rapidly these gadgets switch state.

The quantum computer, by differentiation, works with a two-mode rationale door: XOR and a mode called QO1. In a quantum computer, various natural particles (e.g., electrons or photons) can be used with its charge as a representation of 0 and/or 1. Each of these particles is called as a quantum bit (also called a qubit). Their nature forms the premise of QC. The significant parts of quantum physics are standards of entanglement and superposition.

1.3 IMAGE SEGMENTATION

The objective of image segmentation is to group pixels into notable regions, that is, locales relating to individual surfaces, objects, or common parts of objects. In this way, having diverse segmentation results might permit considering distinctively the image in the accompanying stages. This will be more profitable if the present day parallel processing techniques are exploited [4].

The segmentation process partitions an image into distinct clusters, each containing pixels of similar qualities. The success rate of image analysis relies on dependability of the segments; however, an exact division of an image is generally a difficult issue.

Segmentation techniques may be either contextual or noncontextual. The noncontextual segmentation technique takes no account of spatial connections between components in an image and groups pixels together on the premise of some global quality (e.g., grey level or color). Contextual techniques exploit these connections (e.g., it groups together pixels with comparable grey levels and close spatial areas).

Segmentation has two objectives. The first objective is to disintegrate the image into parts for further investigation. The segmentation in facial images is reliable, if the individual's attire or background does not have the same color as the individual's face. In complex cases, for example, separating a complete street system from a greyscale aerial picture, the segmentation issue can be extremely troublesome and might require using a lot of space.

Second, the objective of segmentation is to perform a change of representation. The pixels of the image must be composed into high-level units that are either more significant or more productive for further investigation (or both). A basic issue is regardless of whether segmentation can be performed for a wide range of spaces utilizing general bottom up techniques that do not use any unique domain knowledge. It is highly improbable of having a solitary division framework function admirably for all issues. Research has demonstrated that a practitioner of machine vision applications must have the capacity to look over a toolset of strategies and may be tailor an answer utilizing knowledge of the application.

2 QUANTUM INSPIRED CI TECHNIQUES

Quantum inspired computing is an emerging field that was established in 1995. It focuses on examining QC which incorporates with specific standards of QM, and CI to benefit engineering issues with cyclic or recurrent behavior [5]. The hypothesis of QC is identified with a theory of reversible computing, uniting thoughts from established information theory, software engineering, and quantum material science. Since the 1990s, research is being done to apply standards of QC in enhancing the design of AI. The technologies inspired by quantum are as follows:

1. neural network
2. fuzzy system
3. evolutionary methods

2.1 INSPIRED BY NEURAL NETWORK

Quantum inspired neural network (QNN) alludes to NN models, depending on standards inspired from QM. The class of QNN that uses ideas from QC remains at a hypothetical level because it requires an utilitarian quantum system for execution. Researchers proposed a few models in which a neuron is demonstrated as quantum bit and quantum associative memory (QAM). Another class incorporates models of natural NN explaining the extraordinary execution of biological brain by using concepts from QM and QC.

A simple QNN was presented by Kak [6] and Kasabov [7]. It included a wave capacity whose properties were illustrated by neuron coherence and decoherence [8]. Later relationships, based on dynamics, were talked about [9] in demonstrating storage capacity [10,11].

Matsuda [12] presented the idea of quantized values (e.g., integers or whole numbers) in NNs—instead of binary values (i.e., 0 or 1)—to avoid neighborhood minima. It was noticed that the number of neurons and associations in the middle of neurons, and calculation time diminished significantly in comparison with customary strategies. Purushothaman et al. [13] interpreted quantum states superposition to propose QNN taking into account multilevel activation function that directs superposition of sigmoid functions in the hidden layer.

Meng et al. [14] presented artificial neural network (ANN) model in view of quantum computational multiagent system [15] with a reinforcement learning algorithm in which every neuron acts as a dynamic parallel processing specialist to build its rate, computational power, and learning capacity. A predictive model of QNN, to be specific generalized QNN for nondirect frameworks has been created taking into account proportional–integral–derivative (PID), NN, and QC [16]. A suitable training algorithm will enable the multilevel activation function systems to apply for versatile clustering of the specimens with fuzzy limit [17–21].

2.2 INSPIRED BY FUZZY SYSTEM

Among different prospects of research seen most recently, extensive focus is laid on creating basic new preprocessing platforms, with managing instability, were QM and fuzzy set hypothesis contrast from those used as a part of traditional probability theory. Vulnerabilities in QM and fuzzy sets were managed through frameworks [22]. Similarities between the two theories, including mathematical and dynamic investigation of the systems, were underlined and demonstrated favorable by numerous specialists. In another way, phenomenal elements like nonappearance of the continuous "square root of not" operation in fuzzy rationale was analyzed by Kreinovich et al. [23].

Accelerating fuzzy inference was accomplished because of the substitution of serial operations between frameworks of extensive dimensionality by one-stage quantum expansion or a quantum subtraction by Rigatos and Tzafestas [24]. The thought of using string of fuzzy bits to indicate superposition of crisp values was presented by Hannachi et al. (e.g., using the likeness in the middle of fuzzy and quantum rationale). Creators have additionally built up a 2-D fuzzy qubit model, which was further used for actualizing QAM learning and retrieval algorithms [25].

Wave function formalism was accommodated membership function of fuzzy c-means (FCM) with a translation of the presence of cryptical wave function in it. It brought together nature of FCM and a nonparametric unsupervised clustering method. Hongjian et al. [26] in quantum hypothesis demonstrated difficult issues in model determination of nonlinear complex data [27]. Inspired by quantum hypothesis of estimation, quantum semantics, an augmentation of fuzzy logic was induced development of a semantic refining algorithm suitable for mapping dataset with less statistical variability between samples, into a graph thereby analyzing its properties [28].

2.3 INSPIRED BY EVOLUTIONARY METHODS

Algorithms inspired by natural evolution have been utilized for building solutions to optimization-related problems and issues related to approximated solutions. To overcome the different inadequacies in the established transformative techniques, analysts have introduced the quantum thought into traditional algorithms to perform effective parallel computations. For algorithm proficiency, it would be best if it kept running on a quantum computer, as the development of the same is yet progressing and hence, simulations of the quantum-based algorithms on a conventional computer can be especially resource consuming. Subsequently, specialists began working toward developing quantum inspired evolutionary computing algorithms for traditional computers rather than developing quantum algorithms for quantum computers.

The quantum inspired evolutionary algorithms are placed at the crossing point of two subareas of software engineering, QC and evolutionary computing (see Fig. 1). Contrary to "genuine" quantum algorithms, the considered algorithms do not require a useful quantum computer for its proficient execution. Rather, the algorithms misuse extra level of irregularity inspired by ideas and standards drawn from QM frameworks, such as, qubits, impedance, or superposition of states.

Primary proposal of evolutionary algorithm taking into account the ideas and standards of QC was introduced in [9] and this range is still seriously considered. Other early cases of quantum inspired evolutionary algorithms which use binary quantum representation in view of qubits are because of Han and Kim [29–31]. In the previous decade, a few other variants [31–34] of quantum evolutionary algorithms have been added. In Fig. 2, the pseudo-code of general quantum inspired evolutionary algorithm is introduced. Here, $Q(t)$ signifies tth generation of quantum populace.

It can be clearly seen how classical evolutionary algorithm has direct correspondence to that of quantum inspired evolutionary algorithm. However, the main stages of this are modeled with respect to concepts and principles of QC.

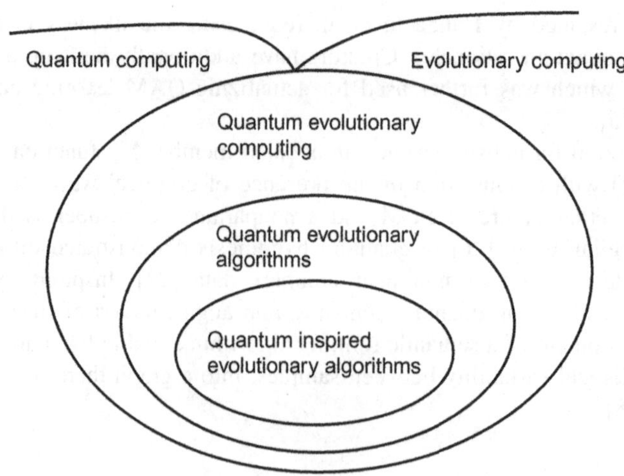

FIG. 1

Subfields of quantum and evolutionary computing.

Start
Initialize t to 0 and $Q(0)$
While termination criteria is unsatisfied do
Increment t by 1
Calculate $Q(t)$
Do genetic operation on $Q(t)$
Terminate while
End

FIG. 2

Quantum inspired evolutionary algorithm.

3 IMAGE SEGMENTATION USING QUANTUM INSPIRED EVOLUTIONARY METHODS

Image segmentation comprises basically of two stages. A split technique utilizing the established k-means; followed by a combining procedure which uses a quantum inspired evolutionary algorithm for finding of nondominated solutions set [35]. Evolutionary algorithm (EA) [34] is a subset of evolutionary algorithm, a nonexclusive generic population-based metaheuristic evolutionary algorithm including selection operation as per their level of fitness and other nature motivated operations. Genetic programming, evolutionary programming, evolution system are the other EA techniques [36].

EA often provides well approximating results for a wide range of issues. Because it assumes to be in an idealistic world, it does not make presumptions about the underlying fitness landscape [37]. The segmentation process in the component space of an image can be viewed as an optimization issue. Recent results have shown that the clustering techniques, utilizing single objective may not provide suitable result to one sort of corresponding dataset. Quantum inspired multiobjective evolutionary clustering algorithm (QMEC) [35], can be utilized to manage the issue of image segmentation, where two objectives are optimized at the same time. Based on the ideas and standards of QC [38], the multistate quantum bits are used to represent individuals and quantum rotation strategy system is used to redesign the probabilistic individual. These algorithms exploit the multiobjective optimization mechanism and the superposition of quantum states, and hence have a good population diversity. Because of a set of nondominated solutions in multiobjective clustering issues, a straightforward heuristic strategy can be adopted [39].

3.1 CASE STUDY 1: QUANTUM INSPIRED MULTIOBJECTIVE EVOLUTIONARY CLUSTERING ALGORITHM (QMEC)

Li et al. [36] developed the QMEC algorithm. The major steps of QMEC are described below.

3.1.1 The qubit individuals population initialization

A new qubit representation, probabilistic representation is used that represents a linear superposition of states and has a better characteristic of population diversity when compared to other representations. If there is a system of n-qubits, the system can represent 2^n state at the same time. One qubit is defined with a pair of numbers $[\alpha, \beta]$, satisfying $|\alpha|^2 + |\beta|^2 = 1$, where $|\alpha|^2$ gives probability that qubit will be found in "0" state, and $|\beta|^2$ gives probability that qubit will be found in "1" state. $Q(t) = \{q_1^t, q_2^t, \ldots, q_n^t\}$ is the qubit individual population, where

$$q_i^t = \begin{cases} \alpha_{i1}^t, \alpha_{i2}^t, \ldots, \alpha_{im}^t \\ \beta_{i1}^t, \beta_{i2}^t, \ldots, \beta_{im}^t \end{cases} \qquad (i = 1, 2, \ldots, n)$$

is a qubit individual, n gives size of population and m is length of individual. In initialization step, the qubit individuals are with the same probability of $1/\sqrt{2}$. The QMEC procedure is as follows.

1. Initialize individual qubit population $Q(t), t = 0$.
2. Classical population production $P(t)$ by noting $Q(t)$.
3. Calculate $P(t)$ fitness.
4. Capture nondominated solutions in $P(t)$ to $A(t)$.
5. Increment t by 1.
   (a) Observe $P(t)$ from state of $Q(t)$.
   (b) Evaluate fitness of $P(t)$.
   (c) Select n individuals from $P(t)UP(t-1)$ as new population $P(t)$.

(d) Store nondominated solutions in $P(t)$ to active population $A(t)$.
(e) Update $Q(t)$ using Q-gates.

6. If stop condition is satisfied then output Pareto solution from $P(t)$. Else go to step 5.
7. Decode solutions as labels and evaluate their quality.

3.1.2 Observing operator

In step 2, it is observed that $Q(t)$ produces classical binary population $P(t) = \{x_1^t, x_2^t, \ldots, x_n^t\}$, where x_i^t $(i = 1, 2, \ldots, n)$ of length m is a binary string that is observed from q_i^t. A random number $r \in [0, 1]$ is generated; if r is larger than $|\alpha_i^t|^2$, the corresponding bit in x_i^t takes "1", else takes "0." The bit "1" in *tαe* is the clustering center of the corresponding point.

3.1.3 Fitness function

The compactness and connectedness of clusters were chosen separately. Cluster compactness is calculated as distance between data points and their respective cluster center.

$$\text{Dev}\,(x) = \sum_{x_k \epsilon X} \sum_{i \epsilon x_k} \delta\,(i, \mu_k)$$

where μ_k indicates cluster centers x_k, x denotes the set of all clusters, and $\delta(s, \mu_k)$ is the Euclidean distance between kth center and ith data point in that cluster. The function should be minimized and reduced. The connectedness metric evaluates degree to which the neighboring data points are in the same cluster, which can be defined as follows

$$\text{Conn}\,(x) = \sum_{i=1}^{m} \left(\sum_{j=1}^{L} x_j^i \right)$$

where m is the clustered dataset size, and L is a parameter determining number of neighbors; $x_{i,j}$ represents the relationship of point i and its jth nearest neighbor; when they are not in the same cluster $x_i, j = 1/j$, else $x_{i,j} = 0$. The connectedness metric should be minimized.

3.1.4 Nondominate sort and elitism

In step 4, fast nondominated sort method was used to select n (population size) individuals from $P(t) \cup P(t-1)$ as new elitism population for Q gate updating to generate offspring. Front rank and corresponding crowding distance were calculated for each individual in $P(t) \cup P(t-1)$. Then first n individuals with smallest front rank and largest crowding distance were selected. The individuals with front rank being equal to 1 were served as the active population $A(t)$ to guide Q-gate updating.

3.1.5 Q-gate updating

Quantum rotation gate is similar to genetic operators but works on quantum bits and uses quantum properties. The property used in this technique is the superposition of quantum state which has better diversity compared with common genetic operators.

Individuals inactive population $A(t)$ were used to guide the qubit population for updation. Table 1 is the reference rotation angle. In Table 2, x_i is ith bit of current chromosome, best_i is ith bit of the guide individual which is chosen from active population $A(t)$ randomly. $\Delta\theta$ is the rotation step which controls convergence speed. $s(\alpha_i, \beta_i)$ is the direction of rotation angle and can guarantee convergence of algorithm. $\otimes$ represents whether the gene is 0 or 1. Comparing x_i with best_i, the rotation direction is obtained. The new qubit is $q_i^t = U(\Delta\theta) \times q_i^{t-1}$, where $U(\Delta\theta) = \begin{pmatrix} \cos(\Delta\theta) & -\sin(\Delta\theta) \\ \sin(\Delta\theta) & \cos(\Delta\theta) \end{pmatrix}$.

When the evolutionary process arrives to a particular extent, most of the individuals in the population are nondominate to each other. It is rotated to x_i or best_i with equal probability at this condition. This step is equivalent to the local disturbance.

3.1.6 Solution selection scheme

A set of nondominated solution was obtained. There was a need to select a preferred solution as the optimal solution. To overcome the time-consuming weakness of model based solutions election method, a simple heuristic method to select a preferred solution was obtained. Firstly, those solutions with given cluster number by the user were selected from the Pareto front as the candidate solutions, then sum

Table 1 Reference Rotation Angle

				$s(\alpha_i, \beta_i)$			
x_i	best_i	$f(x) > f(\text{best})$	$\Delta\theta_i$	$\alpha_i\beta_i > 0$	$\alpha_i\beta_i < 0$	$\alpha_i = 0$	$\beta_i = 0$
0	$\otimes$	T	0.01π	−1	+1	±1	0
1	$\otimes$	T	0.01π	+1	−1	0	±1
$\otimes$	0	F	0.01π	−1	+1	±1	0
$\otimes$	1	F	0.01π	+1	+1	0	±1

Table 2 The Clustering Correct Rate and Index I on Simulated SAR Image

	Algorithms			
Evaluate Index	QMEC	MOCK	GAC	KM
CCR %	95.10	93.66	93.27	93.39
$I(e^{-10})$	3.9638	3.8805	3.7398	3.7580

of two fitness function about those candidate solutions were computed. The minimum one was selected as the preferred output solution.

3.1.7 Evaluate indexes

The clustering correct rate (CCR) applied to evaluate the result provided by algorithms is defined as:

$$\mathrm{CCR}(T \cdot S) = \frac{1}{m}\sum_{i=1}^{T} \max \mathit{Confusion}(i,j) \quad (i = 1,\ldots,T; j = 1,\ldots,S)$$

where m represents total number of datapoints; T represents the true clusters; S represents the obtained clusters and $\mathit{Confusion}(i,j)$ represents the confusion matrix. Because one true class may be divided into more than one cluster by an algorithm, the larger class is taken as the statistic input. CCR is in the interval of [0, 1].

The other metric used in this study is the validity index I. It is defined as,

$$E_K = \sum_{k=1}^{K}\sum_{j=1}^{n} u_{kj} D(x_j, z_k)$$

and $D_K = \max_{i,j=1}^{K}\{D(z_i, z_j)\}$. Larger value of I implies better solution. It is reported that I index has been shown to provide a superior performance when compared to several other validity indexes.

$$I(K) = \left(\frac{1}{K} \times \frac{E_1}{E_K} \times D_K\right)^2$$

3.1.8 The complexity of computations

Here, the worst-case time complexity of QMEC is analyzed. If population size is n, size of dataset is m (generally $m > n$) and data dimensionality is d, then the time complexity of the algorithm is computed as follows.

The observing and repairing time complexity are $O(nm)$ and $O(n)$, respectively; the complexity of the individual evaluations, which consists of decoding step and computation of two clustering objectives, is $O(nmd)$; the time complexity for identifying nondominated individuals in the merging population is $O((n+n))^2$; the worst time complexity for nondominated neighbor-based selection is $O((n+n)log(n+n))$.

Complexity for Q-gate updating is $O(nm)$. So worst total time complexity is:

$$O(nm) + O(n) + O(nmd) + O(n+n)^2 + O(n+n)\log(n+n) + O(nm).$$

The worst time complexity of one generation for QMEC is: $O(nmd)$.

3.1.9 Experimental setup

SAR image and two remote sensing images with size 256 × 256 were used to validate the developed algorithm. The results were compared with MOCK, GAC, and KM. All the algorithms use the same preprocessing, 30 independent runs on each test image are performed. Experimental results are evaluated by two external indexes, the CCR and the index I. For both of them, the larger the index value is, the better the performance. Figs. 3–5 give the typical partition result selected by the largest index I over 30 independent runs.

For QMEC, the number of generations is 50, population size 30, observation time is 1 and maximum clusters is v_m where m is total number of watershed regions and minimum number of clusters is 2. For MOCK, the number of generations is 100, external and internal population size is 50, cross over probability is 0.7, and mutation probability is $1/N$. For GAC, the number of generation is 100, population size is 50, cross over probability is 0.7, and mutation probability is 0.1. For KM, the maximum iterative number is 500, and the stop threshold is 10-10.

3.1.10 Results on simulated SAR image

A simulated SAR image was processed. The generation of simulated SAR image was based on radar image formation. The ground truth image comes from a two-class Gibbs field, and corresponding three-look noisy image is generated by averaging three independent realizations of speckle respectively. Table 2 gives the average statistic values of clustering correct rate and validity index I.

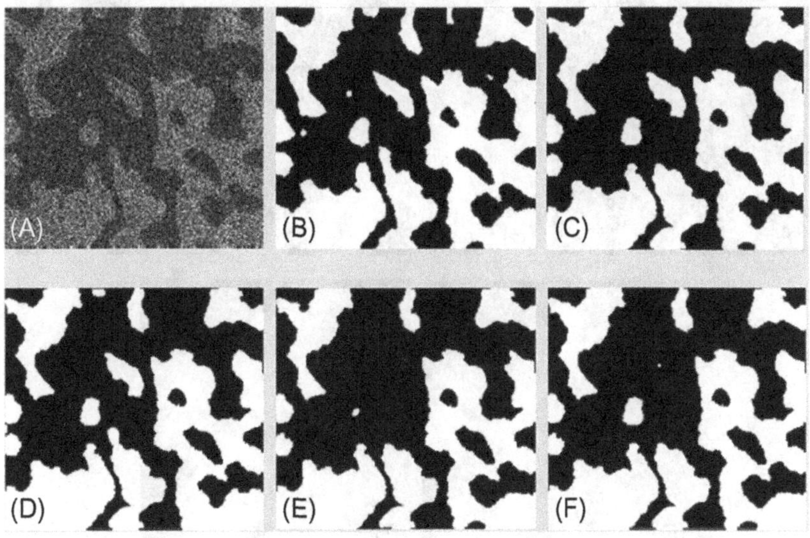

FIG. 3

(A) Simulated SAR image. (B) Ground truth. Result by (C) QMEC, (D) MOCK, (E) GAC, and (F) KM.

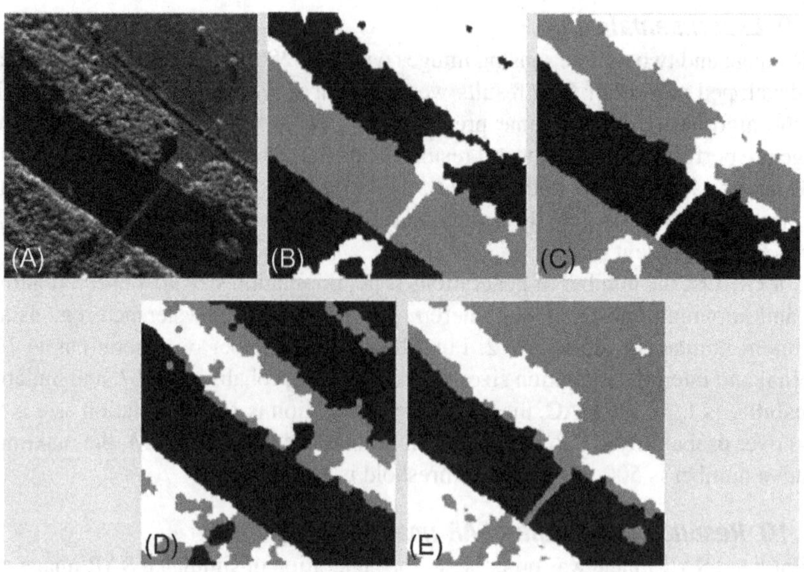

FIG. 4

Segmentation results of SAR image with three categories. (A) Is the original image and (B) to (E) are the segmentation results by QMEC, MOCK, GAC, and KM, respectively.

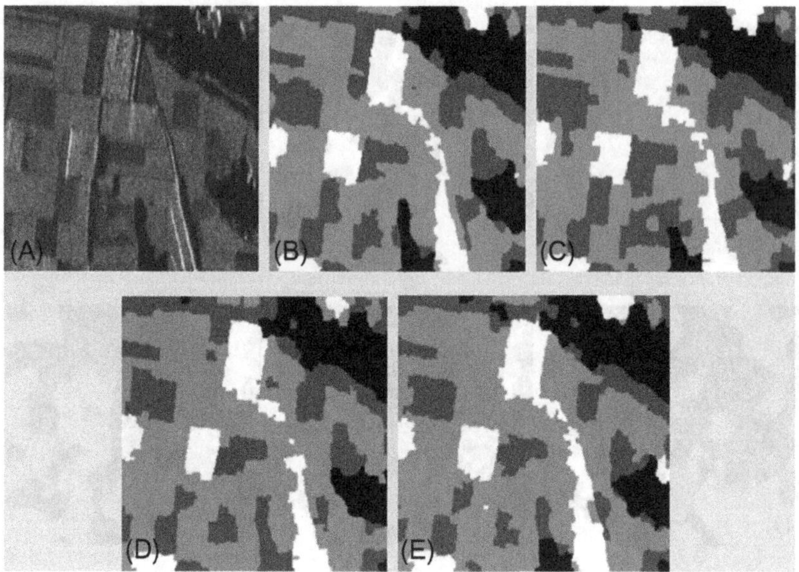

FIG. 5

Segmentation results of the SAR image with four categories. (A) Original image and (B) to (E) are segmentation results by QMEC, MOCK, GAC, and KM, respectively.

Visually, two center regions of the image are wrongly grouped by GAC in Fig. 3E, and one middle region of the image is misclassified by KM in Fig. 3F, respectively. The two multiobjective algorithms, QMEC and MOCK, perform better than the two single objective methods GAC and KM, as shown in Fig. 3C and D. So the multiobjective clustering is more efficient than the single objective clustering. When compared to MOCK, the QMEC exactly segments the black region in bottom right of the image, but does not correctly obtain the white region in top left, and the MOCK does it oppositely. From Table 2, it is obvious that MOCK and QMEC are superior to KM and GAC in both the clustering correct rate and index I. The clustering correct rate is improved about 1.5%, 1.7%, and 1.8% by using QMEC compared to MOCK, KM, and GAC, which illustrates that the QMEC is more precise. The index I increases along with the rise of the correct clustering rates. The index I was used to evaluate the performance of algorithms in SAR image segmentation without ground truth.

3.1.11 Results on remote sensing images

To demonstrate the performance of the QMEC, experiments were performed on two remote sensing images. The ground truth corresponding to the real SAR images are difficult to obtain. Hence, the evaluation of the segmentation result was based on index I and visual inspection. Table 3 is the average index I values of thirty runs on the two images by different algorithms.

Fig. 4A is a part of a Ku-band SAR original image with 1m spatial resolution in the area of Rio Grande River. Table 3 shows Index I of the two remote sensing images of different algorithms nearby Albuquerque, New Mexico. This image consists of three types of land cover, namely, river, vegetation, and crop. We can see that vegetation and crop are as a remixed together which is hard to distinguish. The GAC as shown in Fig. 4D does not find the pipeline and is land in the water region, and misclassified big part of the crop (gray) on the top right as the water (black). The result of KM is better than that of GAC, but the boundary between water and vegetation area are not correctly defined. The segmentation obtained by MOCK in Fig. 4C, improves the uniformity in the water region, and the segmentation on crop is improved greatly. However, some small part of vegetation is not detected. QMEC gets the best segmentation result, as shown in Fig. 4B, and it makes the river bank clear, and generates more homogeneous vegetation part than MOCK does. The boundaries between vegetation and crops are well defined, and the segmentation of QMEC on three types of land cover is closer to reality in comparison to the other

Table 3 Comparison of Four Algorithms

	Algorithms			
Index $I(e^{-10})$	**QMEC**	**MOCK**	**GAC**	**KM**
Fig. 4	5.0386	4.5855	1.8412	2.5655
Fig. 5	3.6501	3.5882	2.7122	2.1304

three algorithms. Table 3 presents the index I value of the four algorithms. It was observed that the QMEC obtains the largest value I, which is agreement with the visual partition results.

Fig. 5A is a SAR image of China's western area. The land cover includes three types of crops and several regions of water. The challenge here was to classify three different types of crops. The dark gray crops on the upper left are only correctly partitioned by QMEC, but it can be seen from Fig. 5B that it confuses the same on the middle bottom. MOCK as shown in Fig. 5C does not locate the dark on the bottom accurately. GAC and KM have serious misclassification on the middle bottom water region, and most of the dark gray crops are misclassified as light gray ones. As a whole, QMEC and MOCK have obtained the better partitions than GAC and KM. The result in Table 3 also shows that the two multiobjective clustering algorithms have higher index I, which indicates that their segmentation results are better.

3.2 CASE STUDY 2: A QUANTUM INSPIRED EVOLUTIONARY ALGORITHM FOR MULTIOBJECTIVE IMAGE SEGMENTATION

Talbi et al. [35] developed an evolutionary algorithm for multiobjective segmentation of images based on quantum theory and computations.

Split/merge technique forms the basis for completing the task of multiobjective image segmentation (Fig. 6). The split method comprises k-means algorithm as it is comparatively quicker when compared to algorithms which are fuzzy based. Pappas [4] observed that the value $k = 4$ gives right results for most images in k means.

Pixels which are a part of a cluster may not necessarily be next to each other. Here, k-means output was applied to verify for regions whose number was more than k. To reduce search space and also because of noise, the tiny regions were removed and were made a part of immediate neighbors with same chromatic properties. A region was taken out or dropped if it has less than 10 pixels [40]. This stage provided R regions and N edges. The image partition result that was obtained was fed for the multiobjective quantum inspired evolutionary algorithm as input. This algorithm intends to obtain a set of nondominated segmentations. Every segmentation result was produced by combining some neighboring regions. The algorithm makes use of three quantum chromosomes. Each chromosome is a sequence of N qubits.

A chromosome is depicted in Fig. 7.

Initially, random generation of chromosomes happen. One solution is contained in nondominated solution set. Then four operations are applied cyclically (Fig. 8).

The first operation includes quantum interference. This provides a shift of each qubit toward corresponding bit value. This has minimal Euclidean distance from chromosome's derived solution. The interference is got by applying a unitary quantum operator. This achieves a rotation (Fig. 9) whose angle is function of α_i, β_i. Value of the respective bit in selected nondominated solution is given in Table 4.

$\delta\theta$ is equal to $\pi/8$ after exploring different values.

Quantum mutation is the operation that is followed. This is performed on some qubits, depending on mutation rate, and a permutation between its α_t and β_i values.

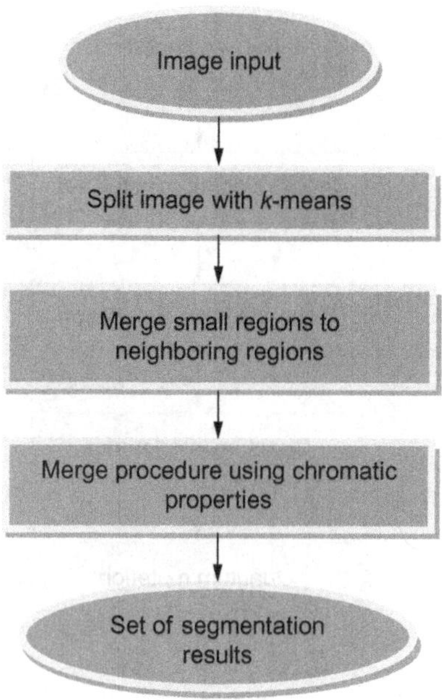

FIG. 6

Broad classification of an algorithm.

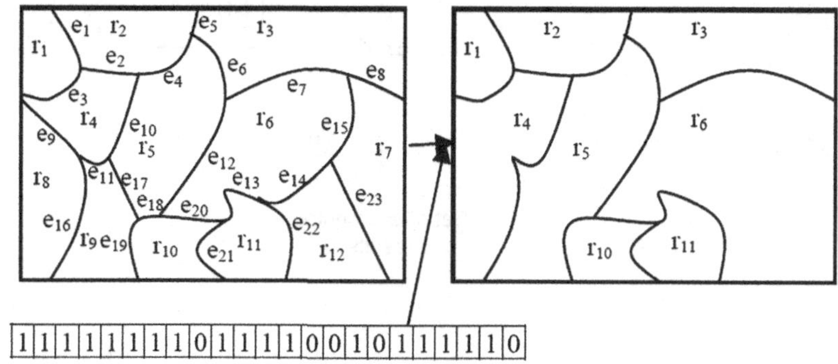

FIG. 7

Example of a binary solution representation.

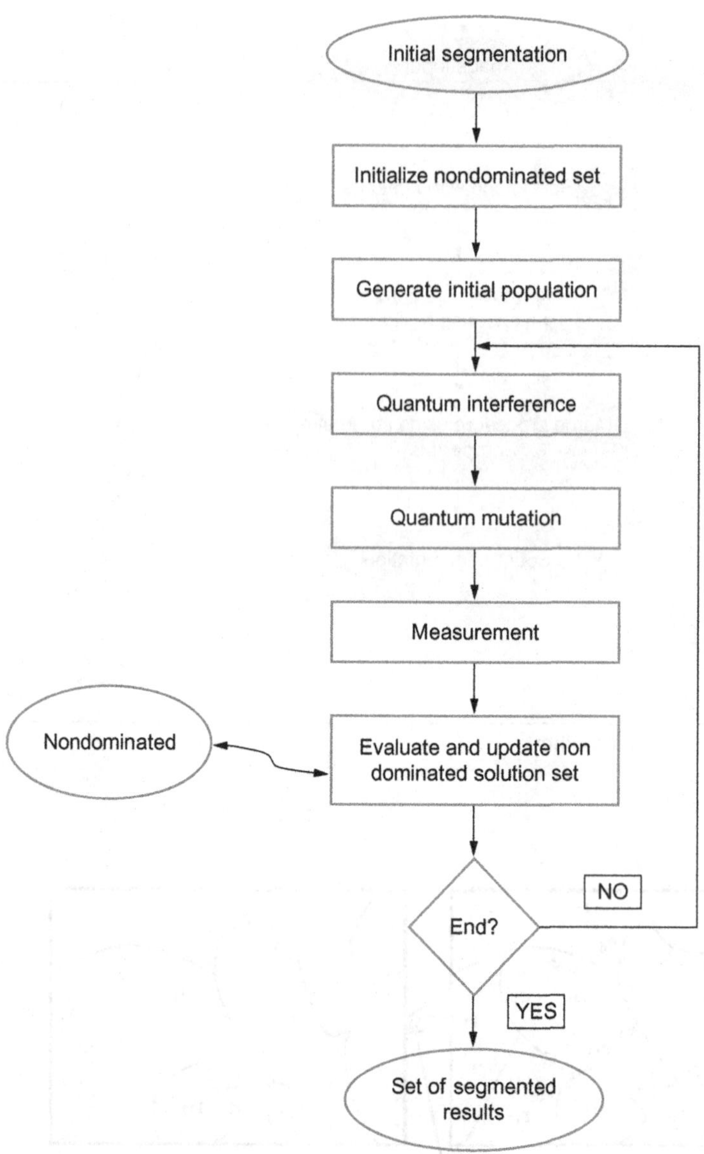

FIG. 8

The QEA for multiobjective image segmentation.

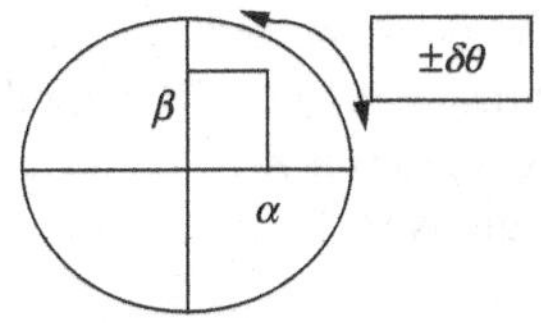

FIG. 9

Quantum interference.

Table 4 Rotation Angle Lookup Table

α	β	Bit Value Reference	Angle of Rotation
>0	>0	1	$+\delta\theta$
>0	>0	0	$-\delta\theta$
>0	<0	1	$-\delta\theta$
>0	<0	0	$+\delta\theta$
<0	>0	1	$-\delta\theta$
<0	>0	0	$+\delta\theta$
<0	<0	1	$+\delta\theta$
<0	<0	0	$-\delta\theta$

This provides the probabilities of having the values 0 and 1. The below matrices is an example to show the mutation. The interchange in values of matrices can be observed.

$$\begin{bmatrix} 0.7446 & -0.6833 & 0.1338 & \mathbf{0.3705} & -0.0272 & 0.6831 \\ -0.6675 & 0.7301 & 0.9901 & -0.9288 & -0.9996 & 0.7303 \end{bmatrix}$$

$$\begin{bmatrix} 0.7446 & -0.6833 & 0.1338 & \mathbf{-0.9288} & -0.0272 & 0.6831 \\ -0.6675 & 0.7301 & 0.9901 & 0.3705 & -0.9996 & 0.7303 \end{bmatrix}$$

In the next stage, a measurement on each chromosome to find superposition is applied. Since this algorithm operates on a conventional computer, it is possible to have all possible solutions in superposition for the forthcoming iterations. At the end of this operation, three binary solutions issued from the three quantum chromosomes are obtained. The fourth stage is updation of nondominated solutions set. Each existing solution dominated by a new solution is removed from the nondominated solutions set. If a new solution is not overpowered by any other solution, it gets added into the set of the nondominated solutions. The intraregion and interregion heterogeneity form the basis of evaluation.

Let R indicate number of regions, m_i indicate pixels mean value belonging to region i, var_i indicate variance inside region i. The number of maintained edges is ne and the number of the resulting regions is nr.

The homogeneity of intraregions is:

$$\text{Hom} = -\frac{1}{nr}\sum_{i=1}^{nr} var_i$$

The heterogeneity of inter-regions is:

$$\text{Het} = \frac{1}{ne}\sum_{i,j}^{nr} (m_i - m_j)^2$$

3.2.1 Results of the experiment

Developed algorithm was tested on several images. The results were obtained by applying the developed algorithm on a 256 × 256 pixels image (Fig. 10). The developers have also implemented a classical multiobjective genetic algorithm (MOGA) [25] with similar encoding method in parallel. For this, a population of 25 chromosomes and with a crossover operation was considered.

FIG. 10

Image "cameraman," size 256 × 256.

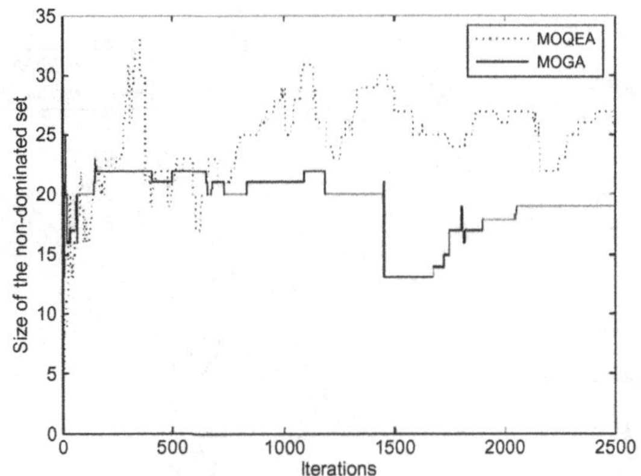

FIG. 11

Evolution of the size of nondominated solutions set.

Table 5 Summary About the Nondominated Set Dynamics

	Number of Iterations Inserting Nondominated Solutions	**Number of Iterations Removing Solutions From the Nondominated Set**	**Total Number of Insertions**	**Total Number of Deletions**
MOQEA	209	111	235	210
MOGA	67	41	140	120

Fig. 11 depicts the evolving size of nondominated solution set.

It was noticed that MOQEA provided more nondominated solutions though it had a smaller population size. Hence it is more dynamic than MOGA. Table 5 depicts dynamics of these two algorithms.

It was observed that MOQEA explored the search space more efficiently. In Fig. 12, the qualitative comparison of two algorithms is depicted.

It was noticed that most of the results found by MOGA were dominated by results that were found by MOQEA. On the contrary, there was no solution found by MOQEA which dominated MOGA. Hence, it can be inferred that the developed algorithm was more powerful than conventional genetic and existing evolutionary algorithms. Few of the 26 nondominated solutions are given for the image segmentation in Fig. 13.

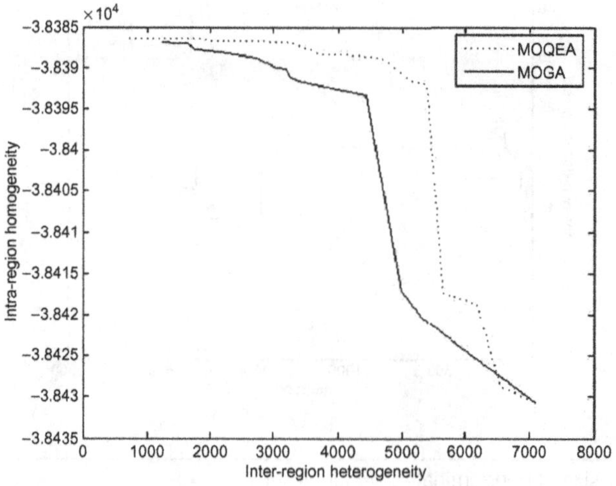

FIG. 12

Nondominated set fitness function values.

4 CONCLUSION

Quantum inspired evolutionary techniques are proven to be the best alternatives in dealing with multiobjective optimization problems. QC for image segmentation is an area which is not much explored and hence provides a platform for an extensive research. With several uncertainty based hybrid clustering algorithms like intuitionistic fuzzy c-means, rough fuzzy c-means, and rough intuitionistic fuzzy c-means, image segmentation with QC will be a field to be worked on in days to come.

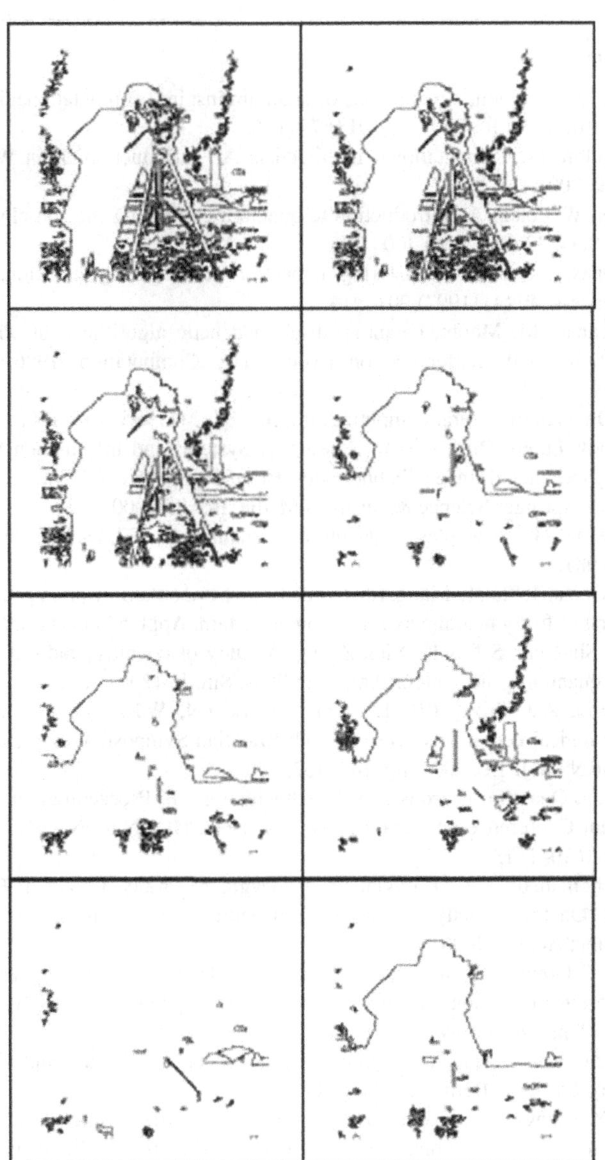

FIG. 13

Some nondominated solutions resulting from MOQEA.

REFERENCES

[1] A. Manju, M.J. Nigam, Applications of quantum inspired computational intelligence: a survey, Artif. Intell. Rev. 42 (1) (2014) 79–156.

[2] A.P. Engelbrecht, Computational Intelligence: An Introduction, John Wiley & Sons, New York, 2007.

[3] E. Rieffel, W. Polak, An introduction to quantum computing for non-physicists, ACM Comput. Surv. 32 (3) (2000) 300–335.

[4] T.N. Pappas, An adaptive clustering algorithm for image segmentation, IEEE Trans. Signal Process. 40 (4) (1992) 901–914.

[5] A. Narayanan, M. Moore, Quantum-inspired genetic algorithms, in: Proceedings of IEEE International Conference on Evolutionary Computation, 1996, IEEE, 1996, pp. 61–66.

[6] S. Kak, On quantum neural computing, Inf. Sci. 83 (3) (1995) 143–160.

[7] N. Kasabov, Future Directions for Intelligent Systems and Information Sciences: The Future of Speech and Image Technologies, Brain Computers, WWW, and Bioinformatics, vol. 45, Springer Science & Business Media, Berlin, 2000.

[8] P.A.M. Dirac, The Principles of Quantum Mechanics, No. 27, Oxford University Press, Oxford, 1981.

[9] S. Zhao, G. Xu, T. Tao, L. Liang, Real-coded chaotic quantum-inspired genetic algorithm for training of fuzzy neural networks, Comput. Math. Appl. 57 (11) (2009).

[10] Z.Z.-J.Z. Shi-Lian, S.J.-N.K. Xian-Zheng, A study of cognitive radio decision engine based on quantum genetic algorithm, Acta Phys. Sin. 11 (2007) 101.

[11] W. Oliveira, A.J. Silva, T.B. Ludermir, A. Leonel, W.R. Galindo, J.C.C. Pereira, Quantum logical neural networks, in: 10th Brazilian Symposium on Neural Networks, 2008, SBRN'08, IEEE, 2008, pp. 147–152.

[12] S. Matsuda, Quantum neurons and their fluctuation, in: Proceedings of 1993 International Joint Conference on Neural Networks, 1993, IJCNN'93-Nagoya, vol. 2, IEEE, 1993, pp. 1610–1613.

[13] G. Purushothaman, N.B. Karayiannis, C. Dagli, M. Akay, C. Chen, B. Fernandez, J. Ghosh, On the capacity of feed-forward neural networks for fuzzy classification, J Appl Funct Anal 1 (2006) 9–32.

[14] Q. Meng, C. Gong, Web information classifying and navigation based on neural network, in: 2nd International Conference on Signal Processing Systems (ICSPS), 2010, vol. 2, IEEE, 2010, pp. V2-431–V2-433.

[15] M. Klusch, Toward quantum computational agents, in: Agents and Computational Autonomy, Springer, Berlin, 2003, pp. 170–186.

[16] D. Nan, Y. Zhang, Predictive modeling based on proportional integral derivative neural networks and quantum computation, in: 7th World Congress on Intelligent Control and Automation, 2008, WCICA 2008, IEEE, 2008, pp. 769–774.

[17] W. Fei-jie, B. Zhong-ying, A novel train traffic control method based on time Petri nets and immune quantum optimization algorithm, in: International Conference on Measuring Technology and Mechatronics Automation (ICMTMA), 2010, vol. 1, IEEE, 2010, pp. 273–277.

[18] X. Wang, J. Chen, Z. Wu, F. Pan, Modeling of fermentation process based on QDPSO-SVM, in: Fourth International Conference on Natural Computation, 2008, ICNC'08, vol. 7, IEEE, 2008, pp. 186–190.

[19] Q. Chen, Flow shop scheduling problem using hybrid quantum particle swarm optimization algorithm (HQPSO), in: Second International Conference on Computational Intelligence and Natural Computing Proceedings (CINC), 2010, vol. 1, IEEE, 2010, pp. 252–255.
[20] S. Zhou, Q. Chen, X. Wang, Deep quantum networks for classification, in: 20th International Conference on Pattern Recognition (ICPR), 2010, IEEE, 2010, pp. 2885–2888.
[21] Z. Ming, J. Weidong, P. Yunwei, H. Laizhao, A novel feature extraction approach for radar emitter signals, in: 2nd IEEE Conference on Industrial Electronics and Applications, 2007, ICIEA 2007, IEEE, 2007, pp. 1785–1789.
[22] R. Seising, From principles of mechanics to quantum mechanics—a survey on fuzziness in scientific theories, in: Fuzzy Information Processing Society, 2008, NAFIPS 2008, Annual Meeting of the North American, IEEE, 2008, pp. 1–6.
[23] V. Kreinovich, L. Kohout, E. Kim, Square root of 'not': a major difference between fuzzy and quantum logics, Int. J. Gen. Syst. 40 (1) (2011) 111–127.
[24] G.G. Rigatos, S.G. Tzafestas, Quantum learning for neural associative memories, Fuzzy Sets Syst. 157 (13) (2006) 1797–1813.
[25] M.S. Hannachi, F. Dong, Y. Hatakeyama, K. Hirota, On the use of fuzzy logic for inherently parallel computations, in: International Symposium on Computational Intelligence and Intelligent Informatics, 2007, ISCIII'07, IEEE, 2007, pp. 89–92.
[26] Q. Hongjian, Z. Dawei, Z. Fangzhao, A new quantum clone evolutionary algorithm for multi-objective optimization, in: International Seminar on Business and Information Management, 2008, ISBIM'08, vol. 2, IEEE, 2008, pp. 23–25.
[27] S. Jie, H. Sheng-nan, Research of fuzzy neural network model based on quantum clustering, in: Second International Workshop on Knowledge Discovery and Data Mining, 2009, WKDD 2009, IEEE, 2009, pp. 133–136.
[28] M.L. Dalla Chiara, R. Giuntini, R. Leporini, Compositional and holistic quantum computational semantics, Nat. Comput. 6 (2) (2007) 113–132.
[29] K.-H. Han, J.-H. Kim, Genetic quantum algorithm and its application to combinatorial optimization problem, in: Proceedings of the 2000 Congress on Evolutionary Computation, 2000, vol. 2, IEEE, 2000, pp. 1354–1360.
[30] K.-H. Han, J.-H. Kim, et al., Analysis of quantum-inspired evolutionary algorithm, in: Proceedings of the 2001 International Conference on Artificial Intelligence, Citeseer, 2001, pp. 727–730.
[31] K.-H. Han, J.-H. Kim, Quantum-inspired evolutionary algorithm for a class of combinatorial optimization, IEEE Trans. Evol. Comput. 6 (6) (2002) 580–593.
[32] A.V.A. da Cruz, M.A.C. Pacheco, M. Vellasco, C.R.H. Barbosa, Cultural operators for a quantum-inspired evolutionary algorithm applied to numerical optimization problems, in: Artificial Intelligence and Knowledge Engineering Applications: A Bioinspired Approach, Springer, Berlin, 2005, pp. 1–10.
[33] G. Zhang, W. Jin, N. Li, An improved quantum genetic algorithm and its application, in: Rough Sets, Fuzzy Sets, Data Mining, and Granular Computing, Springer, Berlin, 2003, pp. 449–452.
[34] G. Zhang, Quantum-inspired evolutionary algorithms: a survey and empirical study, J. Heuristics 17 (3) (2011) 303–351.
[35] H. Talbi, M. Batouche, A. Draa, A quantum-inspired evolutionary algorithm for multiobjective image segmentation, Int. J. Math. Phys. Eng. Sci. 1 (2) (2007) 109–114.

[36] Y. Li, S. Feng, X. Zhang, L. Jiao, SAR image segmentation based on quantum-inspired multiobjective evolutionary clustering algorithm, Inf. Process. Lett. 114 (6) (2014) 287–293.
[37] J.G. Vlachogiannis, K.Y. Lee, Quantum-inspired evolutionary algorithm for real and reactive power dispatch, IEEE Trans. Power Syst. 23 (4) (2008) 1627–1636.
[38] D. Deutsch, Quantum theory, the Church-Turing principle and the universal quantum computer, in: Proceedings of the Royal Society of London A: Mathematical, Physical and Engineering Sciences, vol. 400, The Royal Society, 1985, pp. 97–117.
[39] P.W. Shor, Algorithms for quantum computation: discrete logarithms and factoring, in: Proceedings of 35th Annual Symposium on Foundations of Computer Science, 1994, IEEE, 1994, pp. 124–134.
[40] D.N. Chun, H.S. Yang, Robust image segmentation using genetic algorithm with a fuzzy measure, Pattern Recognit. 29 (7) (1996) 1195–1211.

CHAPTER

8 Fuzzy evaluated quantum cellular automata approach for watershed image analysis

K. Mahata[a], A. Sarkar[b], R. Das[b], S. Das[b]

Government College of Engineering and Leather Technology, Kolkata, WB, India[a] Jadavpur University, Kolkata, WB, India[b]

1 INTRODUCTION

The image segmentation method is a low-level image processing method to partition an image into homogeneous regions. No universal approach exists to support all image types, as this subjective method fails to detect uncertainty. The segmentation methods mainly depend on the application, with no uniformity for all color spaces. Prior information on the image is necessary to analyze solutions of this psychophysical perception approach. The property of handling uncertainty in image processing is the important feature to choose fuzzy theory as a soft computing method. Therefore we have used fuzzy set theory to analyze the uncertainties arising in the image analysis of the Tilaiya catchment area of the Barakar River by a quantum cellular automata (QCA) approach.

Remote sensing is the approach used to obtain information on one object without any direct physical contact with the object. Many methods have been used to classify pixels among homogeneous regions, such as urban regions and turbid water, in satellite images. Theoretically, a set can define a remote sensing image as shown below:

$$P = \{p_{ijk} | 1 \leq i \leq r, 1 \leq j \leq s, 1 \leq k \leq n\} \tag{1}$$

of dimension $r \times s \times n$ for pixels, where $p_{ij} \in \{p_{ij1}, p_{ij2}, \ldots, p_{ijk}\}$ defines the set containing values from n spectral bands on the (i,j)th pixel. To find similar regions, we segment this image set by fuzzy clustering to analyze both the spatial data and their relevant imprecisions.

Let P (usually R^n or Z^n) denote the space of the remote sensing image. Consequently, the points of P (pixels) are x, y spatial variables. Let $d_P(x,y)$ defines the spatial distance of two pixels $x, y \in P$. d_P is generally taken as the Euclidean distance on P.

Quantum Inspired Computational Intelligence. http://dx.doi.org/10.1016/B978-0-12-804409-4.00008-5

In a satellite image, C is a crisp subset of $P, C \subseteq P$. So a fuzzy subset F is P, $F \subseteq P$. The membership function bijectively defines F as $\mu_F(x) \in (0, 1]$ to represent the membership degree of x to F. Higher membership shows $\mu_F(x)$ as closer to 1. The problem of mapping the mixed pixels in overlapping areas in the satellite image of the river catchment area can be solved with this method. If F contains all fuzzy sets on P, then for two pixels x, y, $d_F(x, y)$ denotes their fuzzy perspective distance. A new method using the CA on fuzzy segmentation solutions is proposed in this work.

Clustering, an unsupervised classification method, is based on maximum intra-lass similarity and minimum interclass similarity. The graph theoretic approach [1], K-means clustering [2,3], a self-organizing map [4], and fuzzy C-means (FCM) clustering [5] are state-of-the-art clustering methods for pixel classification in satellite images. Different approaches such as symmetry-based clustering [6] and multiobjective classification [7] are efficient in detecting arbitrarily shaped land cover regions in satellite images.

The membership functions of soft computing approaches such as rough sets and fuzzy sets also efficiently detect overlapping partitions. Fuzzy set theory is an approach to handle uncertainty as well as imprecise data. Several fuzzy methods have been tested for land cover detection in remote sensing images and pattern recognition [8,9]. The mixed-pixels problem in satellite images has been solved by the application of concepts of fuzzy entropy [10], a fuzzy membership function [11,12], fuzzy integrals [13], fuzzy-rule based systems [14], and fuzzy clustering algorithms [15].

In earlier work the spatial information was not considered to compute fuzzy membership values in satellite images [16]. The existence and nonexistence of a pixel in a cluster can be computed with use of the entropy function in the fuzzy method. Luca and Termini [10] developed the fuzzy entropy pseudometric as the objective in their method. This norm fails to detect the separability as a condition. The entropy functions are also used with membership values as in the earlier combined approaches. Coppia and D'Urso [17] defined an approach on fuzzy divergence, which mimics Kulback's approach, but this distance cannot support triangular inequality.

Earlier work on the application of quantum theory to remote sensing images has also shown significant advancements in analyzing images with high precision. A motion-blur parameter estimation method was tested on remote a sensing image with use of two-bit-controlled NOT quantum gate [18]. Casper et al. [19,20] proposed several quantum-implemented state-of-the-art clustering methods for satellite image segmentation—namely, K-means, FCM, and artificial bee colony algorithms.

A CA is defined to be a discrete and dynamical system composed of very simple, uniformly interconnected cells. The CA approach is a popular approach to detect states in cellular spaces. Consequently, to predict remote sensing image segmentation, we introduce a two-dimensional CA to fuzzy set-based initial clustering.

The present work tests the incorporation of fuzzy set theory-based clustering with CA-based neighborhood priority upgrading for mixed-pixel allocation in satellite images.

We test our new model for pixel classification of a chosen LANDSAT image of the catchment area of Barakar River. The quantitative evaluation over two existing validity norms shows the efficient solution produced by our new hybrid fuzzy set-based partitioned quantum cellular automata (FPQCA)-corrected algorithm to detect mixed pixels in clusters. We evaluate our classification result comparatively with the solutions from K-means and FCM methods and also verify it with the ground truth information. The statistical tests also demonstrate the significance of the solution of our proposed FPQCA algorithm over state-of-the-art FCM and K-means algorithms.

2 FUZZY *C*-MEANS ALGORITHM

Clustering is a well-known unsupervised approach among the existing pattern recognition methods based on maximum intraclass similarity as well as minimum interclass similarity. In the state-of-the-art partitional clustering approach (i.e., fuzzy clustering), the belongingness of a point to a cluster may be greater than zero and less than one. Therefore for one pixel in a remote sensing image, one set of membership values is associated with all clusters. These values denote the amount of association of a pixel with the clusters. The most popular soft computing clustering algorithm based on a fuzzy set is the FCM approach. Fuzzy sets were introduced by Zadeh [21] to model the vagueness as well as the ambiguity in the real-world complex systems. Fuzzy sets theory follows the idea of partial membership of one set for a point, with membership degrees in the range from 0 to 1.

Ruspini [22] introduced and later Dune [23] and Bezdek [24] improved the FCM method to be partitioning method on a finite dataset $X = x_1, x_2, \ldots, x_N$ for K fuzzy clusters [25]. Let m be the exponential weight of the membership value, $m \in (1, \text{inf}\}$. The objective function $W_{m\mu}$ of the FCM method is as follows:

$$W_m(U, C) = \sum_{i=1}^{N} \sum_{j=1}^{K} (\mu_{ij})^m (d_{ij})^2, \tag{2}$$

where μ_{ij} is the membership value of point x_i to centroid c_j, and d_{ij} is the Euclidean distance of x_i and c_j. Let $U_j = (\mu_{1j}, \mu_{2j}, \ldots, \mu_{Kj})^7$. Therefore $U = (U_1, U_2, \ldots, U_N)$ denotes the membership value matrix and $C = \{c_1, c_2, \ldots, c_K\}$ denotes the cluster centroids set. W_m represents the compactness as well as the uniformity measure of clusters. In general, a smaller W_m denotes more compact clusters.

The FCM algorithm can be described mathematically as follows:

1. Initialize m, M, and initial cluster centroids C^0. Therefore $U = (U_1, U_2, \ldots, U_N)$ denotes the membership value matrix. Set ϵ to a small value as the terminating threshold. Let iteration $q = 0$. Calculate U^0 according to C^0 as follows:

$$\mu_{ij} = \frac{1}{\sum_{k=1}^{K}\left(\frac{d_{ij}}{d_{ik}}\right)^{\frac{2}{(m-1)}}}, \tag{3}$$

where $\sum_{j\in C_k,k=1,2,\ldots,K}\mu_{ij} = 1$. If $d_{ij} = 0$, then $\mu_{ij} = 1$. Similarly, sets $\mu_{ik,k\neq j}$ shows membership of nonallocated clusters for one pixel.

2. The set of centroids C^{q+1} is updated depending on U^q as shown below:

$$c_j = \frac{\sum_{i=1}^{N}(\mu_{ij})^m x_i}{\sum_{i=1}^{N}(\mu_{ij})^m}. \tag{4}$$

3. Again U^{q+1} is calculated according to C^{q+1}.
4. Finally, U^{q+1} is compared with U^q. If mod $(U^{q+1} - U^q)$, the iteration stops, otherwise the algorithm is executed again from step 2.

3 CELLULAR AUTOMATA MODEL

Cellular automata (CA) models are defined to be discrete spatially extended dynamical systems to study physical systems [26]. They evolve the computational devices in discrete space and time. A CA is initialized with one state with all 0's and a single 1 at different locations. It can generate some fixed unique patterns. Wolfram [27] proposed the simplest CA in the form of a spatial lattice of cells. Each cell holds one discrete value at time t. This is called the "present state of a cell." The next state of this cell at $(t+1)$ depends on the present state and the neighbors' states at time t. In this work we use a three-neighborhood (left neighbors, self, and right neighbor) CA, where a CA cell has two states, either 0 or 1. The next state of a cell is defined as

$$S_i^{t+1} = f\left(S_{i-1}^t, S_i^t, S_{i+1}^t\right), \tag{5}$$

where f denotes the next state function. S_{i-1}^t, S_i^t, and S_{i+1}^t are the present states of the left neighbor, self, and the right neighbor of the ith CA cell at time t; f is shown as a lookup table in Table 1. The decimal equivalent of eight outputs in Table 1 is called "rule R_i" [28]. In a two-state, three-neighborhood CA there can be a total of 28 (=256) rules. One such rule is rule 30 in Table 1. A rule 30 CA can generate a sequence of random patterns. Scientists observed in their experiments that an n-cell rule 30 CA seeded with a state with single 1 and rest 0s, generates a state with a fair

Table 1 Lookup Table for Rule 30

Present state	111	110	101	100	011	010	001	000
Rule	(7)	(6)	(5)	(4)	(3)	(2)	(1)	(0)
Next state	0	0	0	1	1	1	1	0

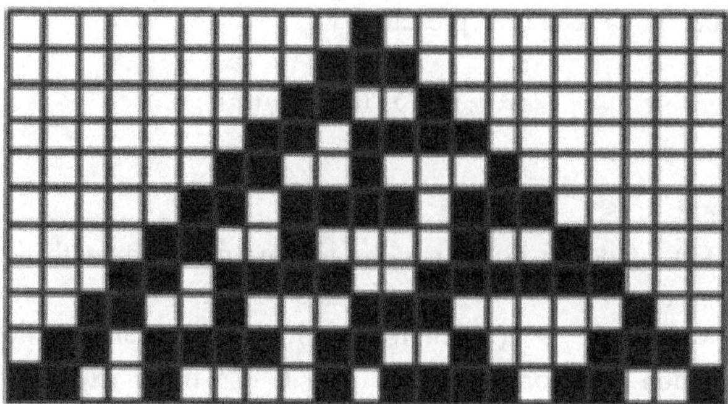

FIG. 1

Example of Wolfram rule 30.

distribution of 0 and 1 after n iterations. However, it is not guaranteed that in more than n iterations no all-0 pattern will occur. It can be proved that for every $n > 1$, an n-cell rule 30 CA seeded with a state with single 1 and rest 0s, at different positions generates a nonzero state after $n/2$ iterations.

By Wolfram's classification scheme, rule 30 is of class III [27]. It shows aperiodic and chaotic behavior. When initialized with one black pixel, it generates a pattern behavior with a randomly patterned center, as shown in Fig. 1.

When the leftmost and rightmost cells are neighbors, the CA has a periodic boundary; in other cases it has a null boundary. Both deterministic and probabilistic (or stochastic) CA are also possible. Our elementary CA is also a deterministic approach.

4 QUANTUM CELLULAR AUTOMATA

John Watrous introduced QCA [29]. He showed how one quantum Turing machine is simulated efficiently with a QCA in 1995. A CA containing quantum cells is called "well formed" if it has global unitary functional transitions. By definition, if the cells of one standard CA are quantized, it does not become a QCA. The difference lies in the fact that the general model of a CA does not recognize the property of reversibility. Kenichi Morita and Masateru Harao [30] showed that the reversible CA can be modeled by the partitioning of one cell into three subcells. This partitioned CA can simulate the model of a nonpartitioned, but no trivial inclusion relation exists between a partitioned CA and an nonpartitioned CA [31].

A quantum state is defined by a transition function of the finite set Q to the complex set C^Q. For $x \in Q$ the quantum state value $[q] \in C^Q$ can be defined as follows:

$$[q](x) = 1(x = q), 0(x! = q). \tag{6}$$

Any inner product on C^Q can be represented by

$$\langle q_1, q_2\rangle = \sum_{x \in Q} \langle q_1(x).q_2(x)\rangle, \tag{7}$$

where $q_1, q_2 \in C^Q$.

A classical CA model in Q defines the transition system with the function of global transitions as $F : Q^N \to Q^N$. In this model, $F(q)_t = f(q_{t-1}, q_t, q_{t+1})$, where $f : Q \times Q \times Q \to Q$ denotes the local transition function. To define the global transition function $F : Q^N \to C^{(Q^N)}$ more explicitly, $F(q,x) = f((q_0, q_1, q_2), x_1).f((q_1, q_2, q_3), x_2)\ldots f((q_{n-1}, q_n, q_{n+1}), x_n)$. If the local transition function is defined as $f : Q \times Q \times Q \to C^Q$ and F is unitary, then the transition system forms a QCA.

5 PARTITIONED QUANTUM CELLULAR AUTOMATA

PQCA are defined to be the most canonical description of QCA. To define PQCA the operational functions $G : Q^n \to C^{(Qn)}$ and $\lambda : Q \times Q \to C$ by $G(q)(x) = g(q_1).g(q_2)x_2.\ldots g(q_n)x_n$ and $\lambda(p,q) = g(p)(q)$ for a function $g : Q \to C^Q$ are defined.

In the PQCA the state of one cell consists of three subcells. One cell with subcells (α, β, γ) [32] is shown in Table 2.

Theoretically, the transition function depends only on the three subcells, consecutively the right subcell of the left neighbor cell, the middle subcell of itself, and the left subcell of the right neighbor cell. Anthropomorphically, a cell views only the right subcell of its left neighbor cell, the middle subcell of itself, and the left subcell of its right neighbor cell to define the transition in the timeline [32]. The update rule for the transition function of PQCA is shown in Fig. 2.

A PQCA simulates a QCA. Fig. 3 shows a one-dimensional QCA with unitary U. Instead of using unitary evolution U_0 and U_1, in Fig. 3, considering the intrinsic universality, one can transform any U_0U_1 QCA into UU-structured QCA [33]. In this PQCA, one line shows one quantum cell, and one box scattering U connected to two cells. The flow of time is upward here.

Table 2 Dependency of transition amplitudes of a partitioned quantum cellular automata.

	Q	1
α	β	γ (6)
$\in Q_L$	$\in Q_M$	$\in Q_R$ (6)

$Q = Q_L \times Q_M \times Q_R$.

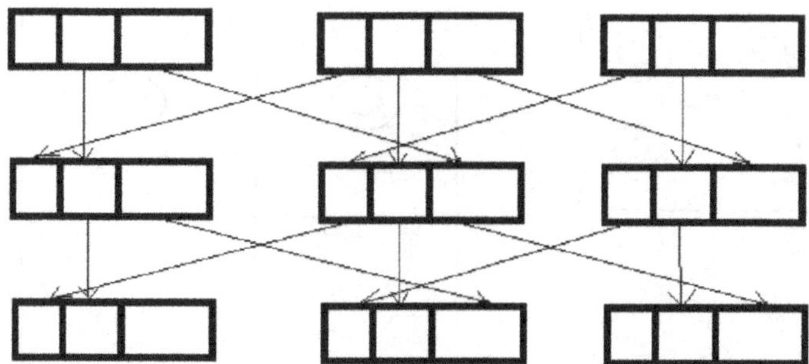

FIG. 2

Partitioned quantum cellular automaton update rule as a permutation of subcells.

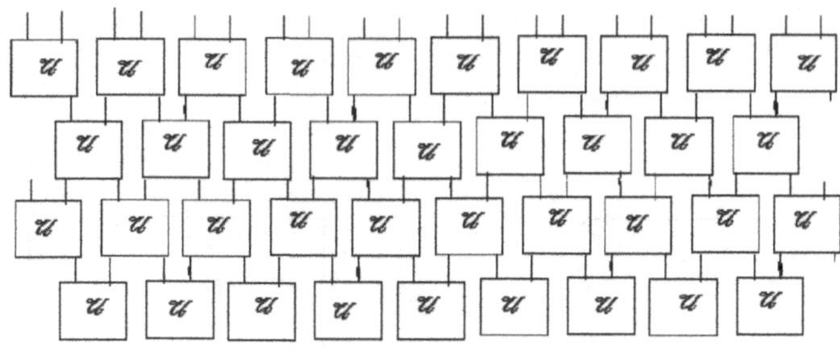

FIG. 3

Partitioned one-dimensional *UU*-structured quantum cellular automaton with scattering unitary *U*.

Based on P. Arrighi, J. Grattage, Partitioned quantum cellular automata are intrinsically universal, Nat. Comput. 11 (1) (2012) 13–22.

To give a formal completion of the proof, it has been shown that any n-dimensional QCA can be expressed as a PQCA. Therefore we can flatten this infinitely repeating (e.g., U_0U_1 circuit) with two layers. Theoretically, initially all the signals with qubit information implement the U_0 value of scattering unitary in the first layer. Next, all signals exit synchronously and implement the U_1 value for scattering unitary in the second layer. This continues for all levels of the n-dimensional QCA to flatten it.

Similarly, a good method for flattening a two-dimensional PQCA is shown in Figs. 4 and 5. Consecutively, the same method can be followed in n dimensions.

6 QUANTUM-DOT CELLULAR AUTOMATA

Quantum-dot CA models use the encoding and further execution of that binary information as stored in the charged arrays of charge-coupled quantum dots.

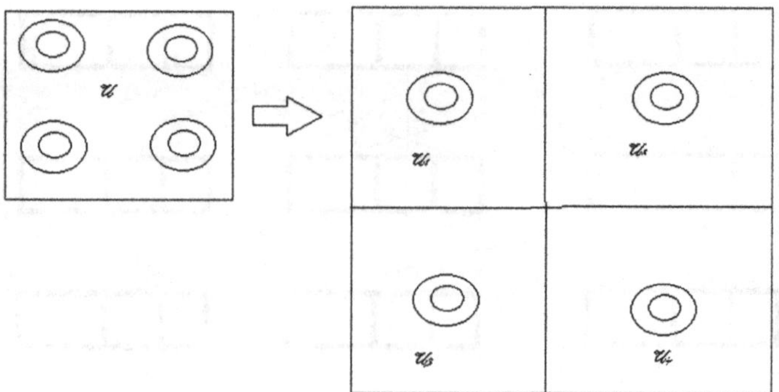

FIG. 4

First two layers for flattening a partitioned quantum cellular automaton into a Universal QCA.

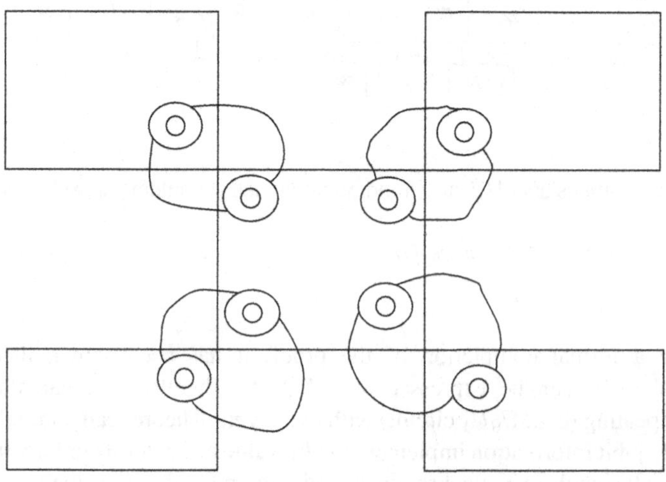

FIG. 5

Second layer for flattening a partitioned quantum cellular automaton into a Universal QCA.

A quantum dot is the region where an electron is thought to be quantum mechanically localized, as shown in Fig. 6. One quantum cell has four dots, at four corners of the square cell. Each cell has two extra electrons. According to the quantum computing theory, these two electrons can quantum mechanically tunnel among the dots. However, they never come out of the cell boundary. Therefore two types of polarization, either $P = -1$ or $P = +1$, as shown in Fig. 6 are possible within one quantum cell. These two stages represent binary logic values, 0 or 1 respectively. This phenomenon is utilized in nanotechnology to develop fast electronic devices. The required power consumption for this tunneling of electrons is significantly less than that for existing mechanisms.

The basic QCA logic elements in an implementation of a majority voter gate are shown in Fig. 7. In QCA wires, information or signal flows like displacement of charges either horizontally or diagonally carrying charges. The truth table of a QCA majority voter gate is shown in Fig. 8. In diagonal tunnels, binary signals change polarization in successive quantum cells.

The basic structural realization of a QCA to develop the majority voter gate is shown in Fig. 8. The gate is defined as $M(P,Q,R) = PQ + QR + RP$. The output of this gate is 1 if two or more inputs have value 1. The standard AND and OR gates can be developed with use of this majority voter gate by the fixing of one input to 0 and 1 respectively. This majority voter gate cannot be defined as a universal gate because it cannot realize the standard logical NOT gate. Therefore, for any universal realization, the functionally complete set can be developed as a combination of a majority voter gate and a NOT gate. So, one needs to implement a logical NOT gate needs separately by arranging QCA cells.

The basic structure implemented with QCA cells in this work is a three-input majority voter gate ($M(P,Q,R) = PQ + QR + RP$ as shown in Fig. 8. An NNI gate can be used as the basic logic element for QCA-based devices. In the next subsection, we introduce a hybrid fuzzy-PQCA clustering algorithm that uses the majority voter gate with QCA cells in the second phase of the proposed method to correct the pixel allocations on the basis of neighborhood values.

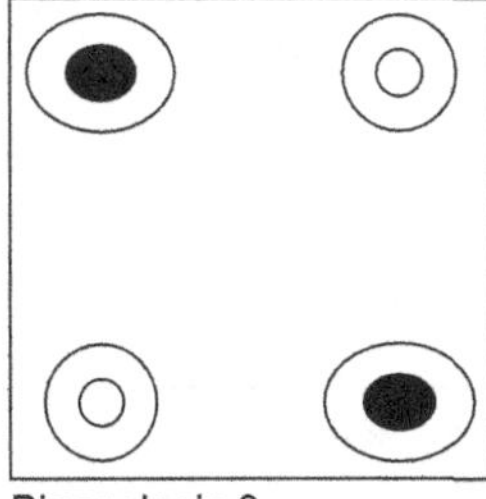

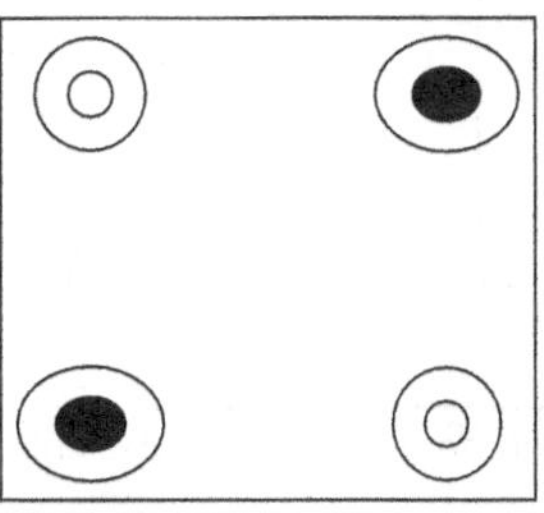

FIG. 6

A quantum cellular automata cell and its binary logic.

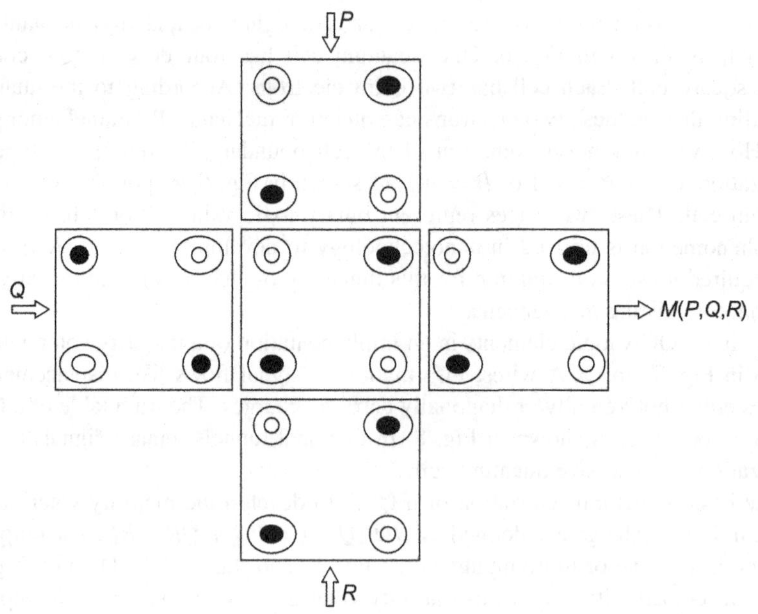

FIG. 7

Cell structure of a quantum cellular automaton majority voter gate (M).

P	*Q*	*R*	*M(P,Q,R)*
0	0	0	0
0	0	1	0
0	1	0	0
0	1	1	1
1	0	0	0
1	0	1	1
1	1	0	1
1	1	1	1

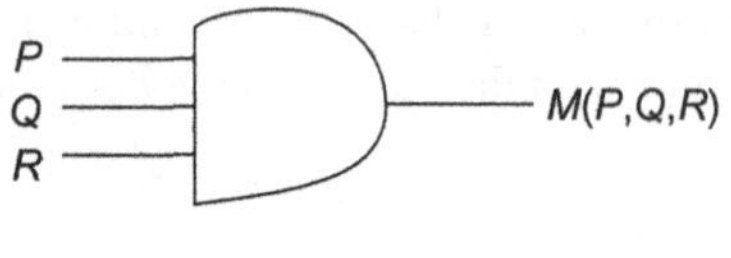

P
Q
R
M(P,Q,R)

FIG. 8

Truth table of the quantum cellular automaton majority voter gate (M).

7 HYBRID FUZZY-PARTITIONED QUANTUM CELLULAR AUTOMATA CLUSTERING APPROACH

This proposed hybrid FPQCA approach implements two consecutive phases: initial FCM clustering on the chosen remote sensing images over the timeline to generate fuzzy membership matrices U based on the allocation of pixels, and the fine-tuning, using the PQCA-based neighborhood priority correction method using majority voting, as depicted in Fig. 9.

Initially N pixels are randomly assigned to k clusters in the initial FCM method. This is done following the steps of the FCM algorithm. From these initial allocations, the initial cluster centroids set C^0 is generated. The threshold level for exiting iterative loops is set to 1×10^{-5}. Then the initial membership value matrix U is generated from these initial allocations. Then we perform the centroid upgrade approach q times and recompute U^q for each iteration. Finally, the difference between the membership value matrices in the previous and the present iterations becomes smaller, and at the terminating threshold value these iterations stop.

After the initial phase in our hybrid algorithm, we perform the new the PQCA-based neighborhood priority correction method over all pixels as described in the next subsection. After the second phase we obtain the final FQPCA-corrected solutions, and on these solutions the final quantitative and statistical evaluations are performed.

8 CELLULAR AUTOMATA-BASED NEIGHBORHOOD PRIORITY CORRECTION METHOD

In our two-dimensional CA model for neighborhood-based priority correction, we have considered the states of the cells in each CA according to the clustering allocations from the fuzzy set-based initial clustering phase. The cells in the CA denote the pixels in their positions in the chosen satellite images. The state numbers of the cells in the model initially denote the assigned clusters from the first phase of our algorithm. State 0 denotes that the pixel has been assigned to cluster 0 in the first phase. In this work, we adopt CA satisfying a periodic boundary condition. We have used deterministic CA for our experiments. Our two-dimensional QPCA model is depicted in the flowchart in Fig. 5.

The first phase of our proposed approach applies the cluster allocation outputs from the initial fuzzy set-based clustering method (FCM) on the chosen remote sensing image. In the second phase of our algorithm, if among four neighbors (namely, on the left side, on right side, on the top side, and on the bottom side) at least two neighbors exhibit the same cluster values, the priority of the present cell changes to that of a similar cluster value. Consequently, the current state of the present cell changes its allocation to reduce the number of outliers in the final solution. Similarly,

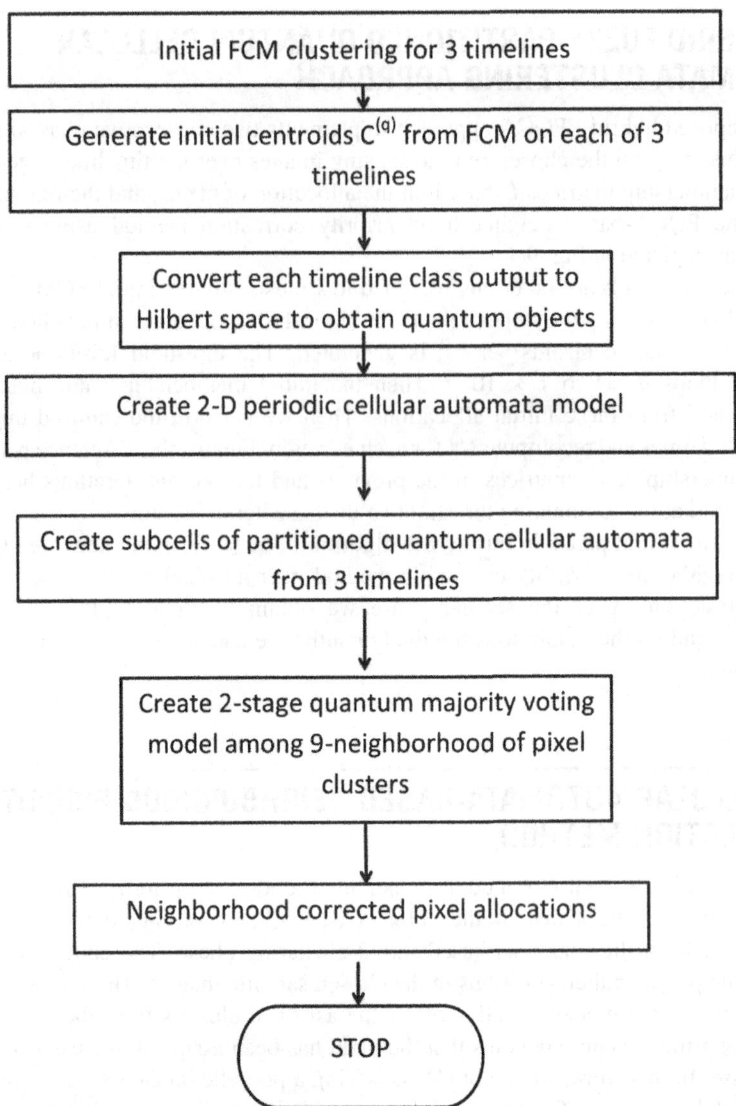

FIG. 9

The flowchart for the fuzzy set-based partitioned quantum cellular automata-corrected algorithm for mixed-pixel classification in remote sensing imagery. *FCM*, fuzzy *C*-means.

if more than four neighbors in an eight-neighbor CA have similar cluster value in the present cell, that value is assigned to the next state of the present cell, to allocate it to similar clusters depending on neighborhood pixels and to reduce the number of cluster outliers. We perform the second phase through the CA timeline matrices to obtain proper neighborhood corrections for pixels in the chosen remote sensing image.

9 PARTITIONED QUANTUM CELLULAR APPROACH USING MAJORITY VOTING

To implement two-dimensional PQCA with periodic boundaries, we convert our state-space matrix output from the FCM clustering solution to Hilbert space to create a quantum object from each of the solutions. As there are three subcells in each cell of the PQCA, we need to convert solutions from three images from the timeline as initially chosen for this experiment. The solution for the Tilaiya catchment area from 2005 is allocated to the left subcell, and the solution for 2015 is allocated to the right subcell. The middle subcell denotes the clustering solution for 2010. Subsequently, following the rules of PQCA, each next state can view only the right substate of its left neighbor, the middle substate of itself, and the left substate of its right neighbor. Again we need to implement the priority correction method based on the CA model. Therefore we implement a majority voter gate with three inputs to create the rules for the CA, which is universal in its logic.

To implement the majority voting function in this model, we convert each allocation initially to binary matched or mismatched in its nine-neighborhood. Then these inputs are passed to the combine gate of a quantum toolbox to obtain the majority voting result for three inputs. After use of a two-stage majority voting using four gates, we get the final output, whether there exists majority voting in the nine-neighborhood or not. According to this result, the rule of the CA has been decided to change the present allocation of a pixel to the majority class in the neighborhood.

10 APPLICATION TO PIXEL CLASSIFICATION

The new FPQCA algorithm was implemented in MATLAB 7.0 on an HP 2 quad core processor with clock speed of 2.40 GHz. State-of-the-art *K*-means and FCM algorithms were also compared with this new method. The quantitative evaluations of Dunn [34] and Davies and Bouldin [35] validity indices was done with the FPQCA, *K*-means, and FCM methods. The FPQCA solutions were verified with the ground truth information on land cover regions.

The LANDSAT image of the Tilaya catchment of the Barakar River was extracted in 2005, 2010, and 2015 for further research. Three bands are available (ie., green,

FIG. 10

Original remote sensing image of the Barakar River catchment area in 2005.

red, and blue bands), with some satellite noise as shown in Figs. 10, 13, and 16, which show the original LANDAST image of the Tilaiya catchment area using histogram equalization on the years 2005, 2010, and 2015 respectively. There are seven classes—namely, turbid water, pond water, concrete, vegetation, habitation, open space, and roads (including bridges).

The Barakar River flows from the top-left corner of the image to the middle-bottom part. The Tilaiya Dam is shown as a deep gray color in upper-left corner in Figs. 10, 13, and 16.

Figs. 11 and 12 show the segmented solutions of those original images obtained by the K-means and FCM methods respectively ($K = 7$) for 2005. In Fig. 11, the K-means method fails to detect the middle higher regions properly. The solution in Fig. 12 also fails to detect the middle-right higher area properly as in original Fig. 10.

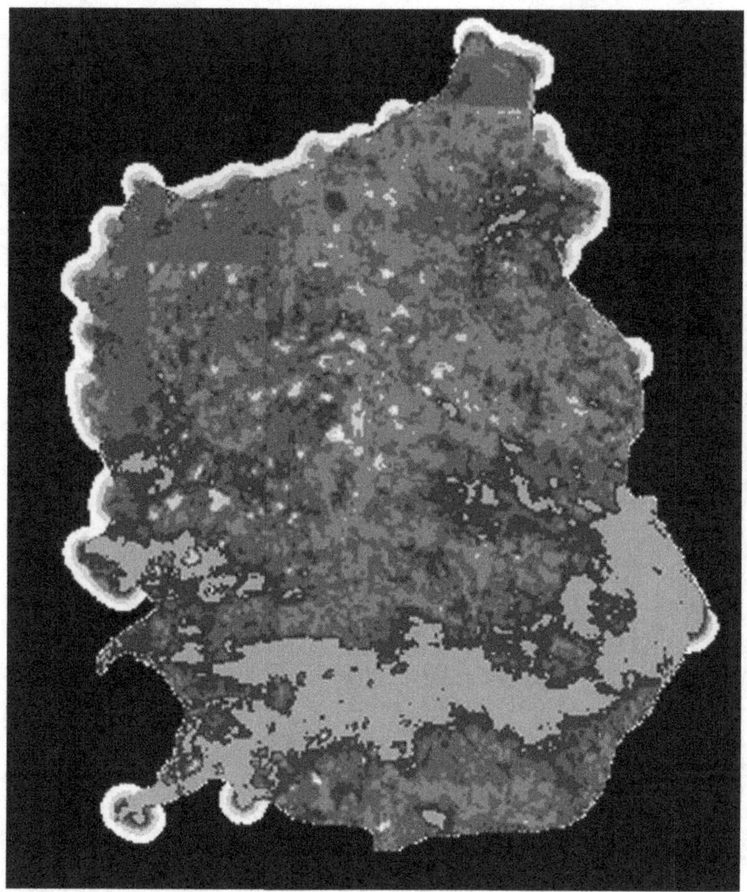

FIG. 11

Pixel classification solution for the Barakar River catchment area in 2005 from the K-means algorithm (with $K = 7$).

Similar improper detection of regions is shown in Figs. 14 and 15 respectively for K-means and FCM segmentations in the upper half of the images as in original Fig. 13. Similarly, in Figs. 17 and 18, the K-means and FCM clustering algorithms also fail to detect Tilaiya Dam properly from the middle higher regions. However, our new FPQCA algorithm (see Fig. 19) classifies the Barakar River catchment area considering the segments across 15 years of the timeline from three images using our hybrid CA model. This indicate that FPQCA method classifies the overlapping regions efficiently across the timeline, whereas the K-means and FCM algorithms segment the images at a fixed time.

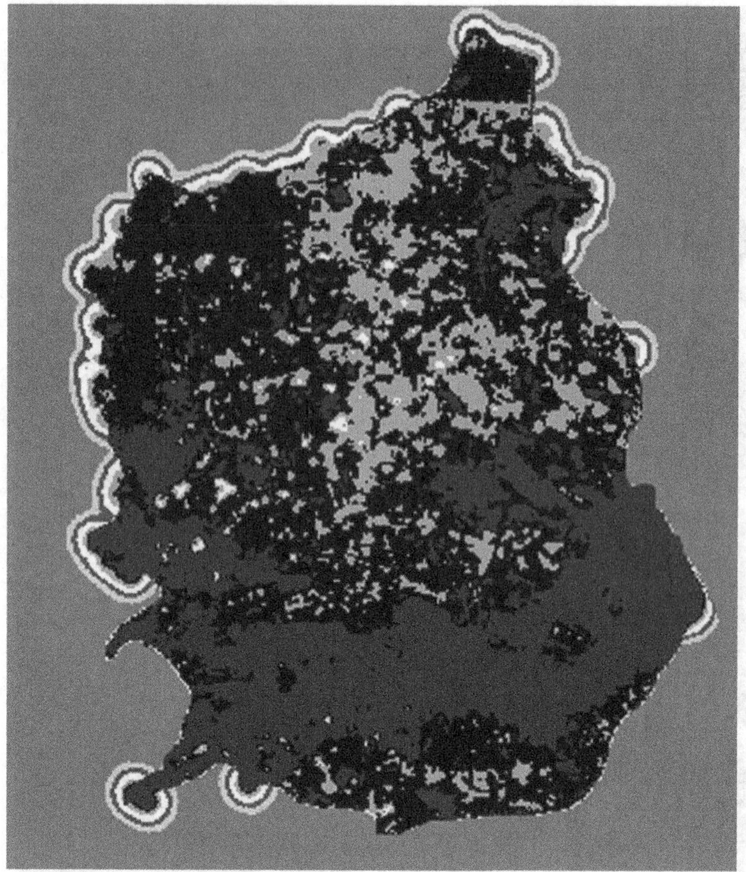

FIG. 12

Pixel classification solution for the Barakar River catchment area in 2005 from the fuzzy *C*-means algorithm (with $K = 7$).

11 QUANTITATIVE ANALYSIS

The quantitative evaluation was done with two validity index values—namely, the Davies-Bouldin [35] and Dunn [34] indices. The evaluation was performed with the *K*-means, FCM, and FPQCA methods on the Barakar River Tilaiya catchment area images (see Table 3). The FPQCA produces the lowest value of the Davies-Bouldin index (0.4232), the *K*-means method produces 0.6029 for 2015, and the FCM method produces 0.5155 for 2015. The FPQCA algorithm produced the largest value of the Dunn index (1.6650), and the *K*-means and FCM methods produce smaller Dunn index values of 1.2846 and 1.3822 respectively for 2015.

FIG. 13

Original remote sensing image of the Barakar River catchment area in 2010.

This quantitative evaluation implies that the FPQCA produces better Davies-Bouldin and Dunn indices than the existing *K*-means and FCM methods. So it shows that the FPQCA produces comparable solutions in terms of goodness as the *K*-means and FCM algorithms. Sometimes the FPQCA outperforms them with more efficient fuzzy regions.

12 STATISTICAL ANALYSIS

Wilcoxon's rank sum test, which is a nonparametric statistical significance test on independent samples with 5% significance level [36], was applied. Three sets of

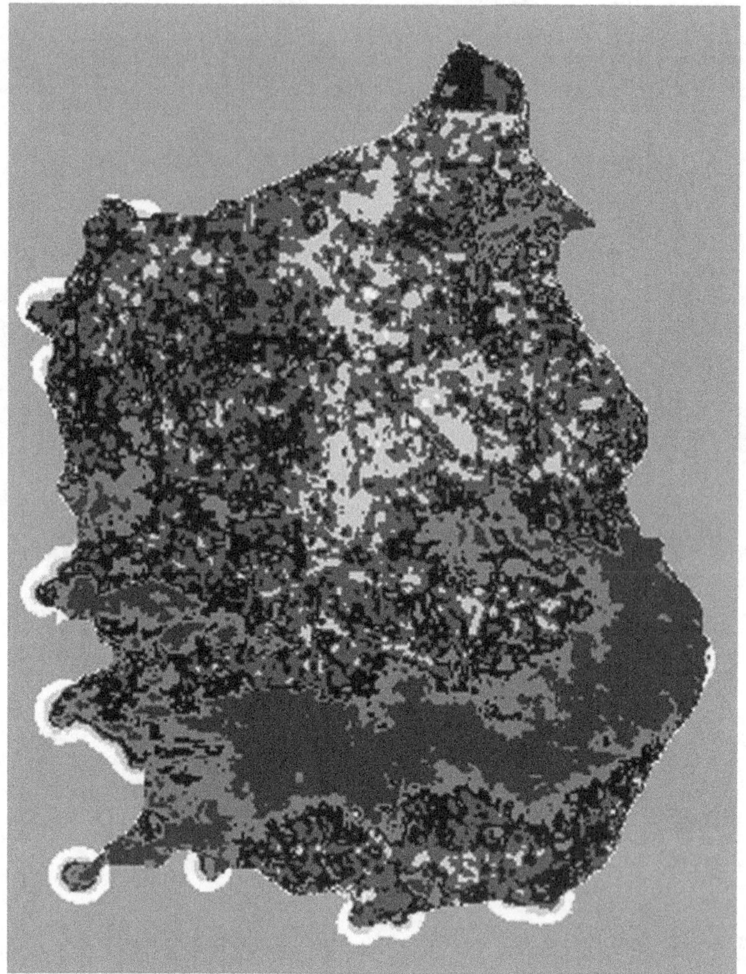

FIG. 14

Pixel classification solution for the Barakar River catchment area in 2010 from the K-means algorithm (with $K = 7$).

Davies-Bouldin indices from 10 consecutive runs obtained by the K-means, FCM, and FPQCA methods were prepared. The median values of each group (see Table 4) show that the FPQCA produces higher median values in comparison with the K-means and FCM methods.

Table 5 shows P values and relevant H values from Wilcoxon's rank sum test obtained from the comparison of two groups, the FPQCA and the K-means method

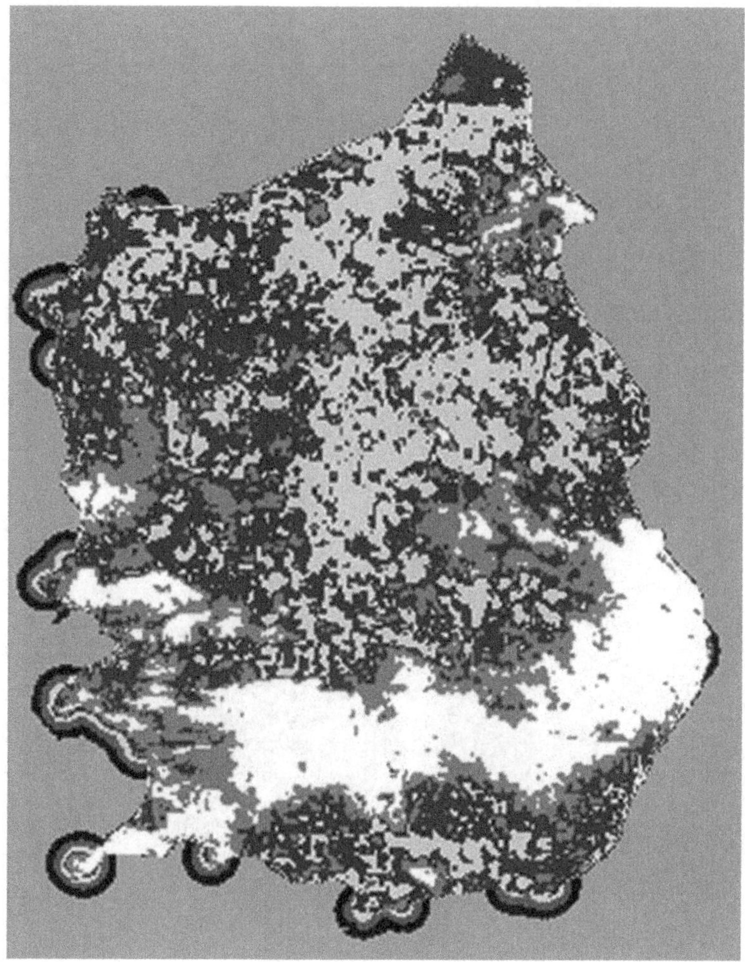

FIG. 15

Pixel classification solution for the Barakar river catchment area in 2010 from the fuzzy *C*-means algorithm (with $K = 7$).

as well as the FPQCA and the FCM method. The *P* values shown in Table 5 exists with a 5% significance level. For the Tilaiya catchment area, the *P* value for the FPQCA and the *K*-means method is 2.00×10^{-3}, indicating the statistical significance of the solutions obtained by the FPQCA. Those solutions did not occur by chance. Similar results were obtained with the FCM method. Hence all values show significant efficiency of the FPQCA in comparison with the *K*-means and FCM methods.

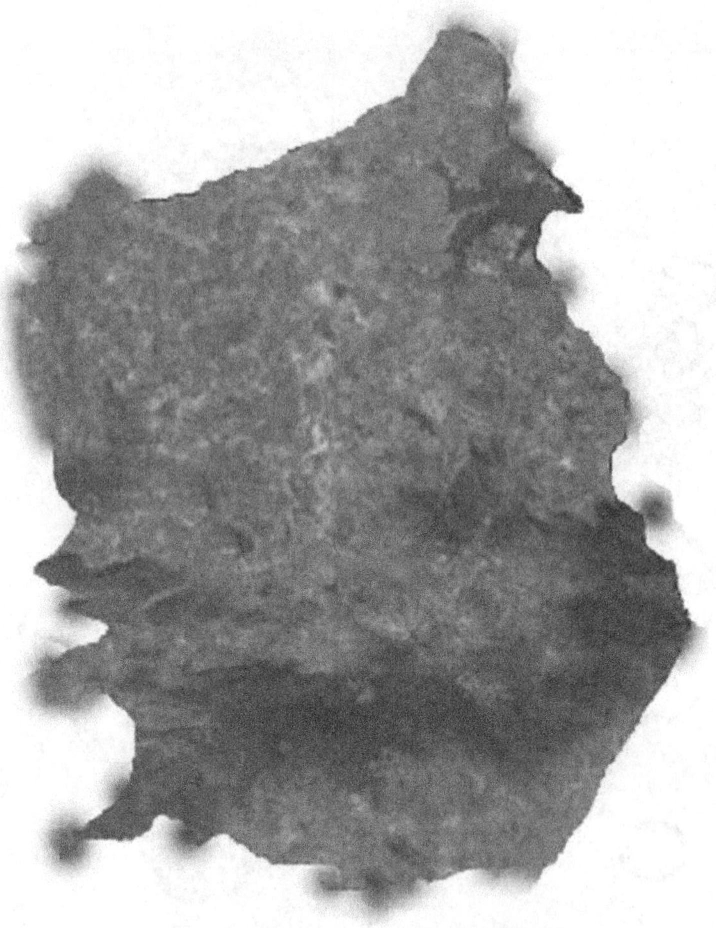

FIG. 16

Original remote sensing image of the Barakar River catchment area in 2015.

13 FUTURE RESEARCH DIRECTIONS

In future work we may implement the FPQCA algorithm on a distributed platform to improve its time efficiency [37,38]. Moreover, including spatial information in a feature vector [8] instead of band intensities in a dataset is an important approach for further work.

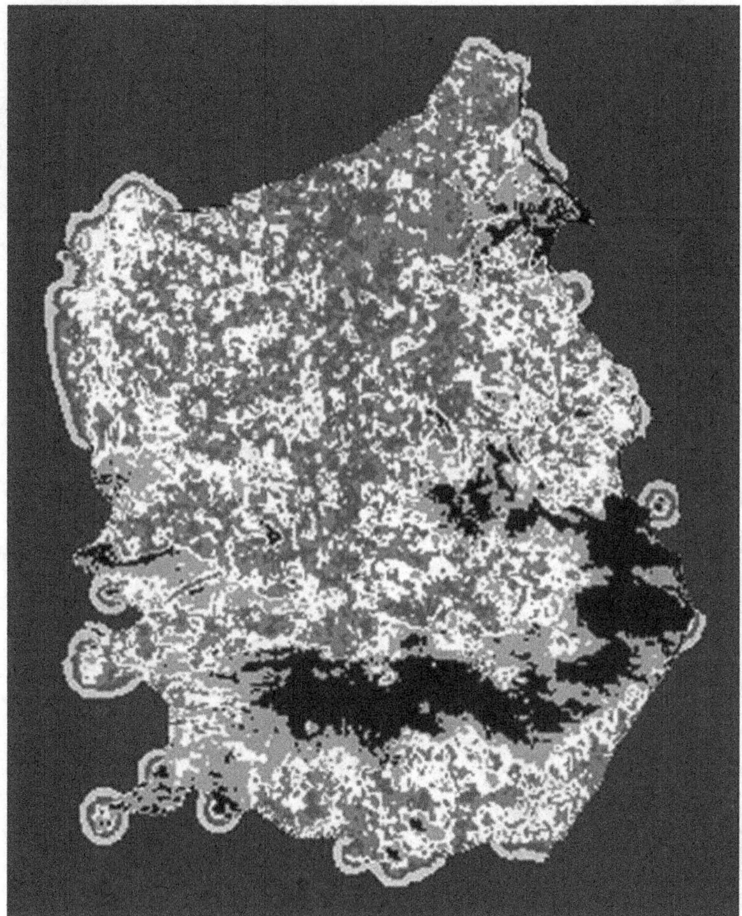

FIG. 17

Pixel classification solution for the Barakar River catchment area in 2015 from the K-means algorithm (with $K = 7$).

14 CONCLUSION

In the analysis of remote sensing imagery, problems with mixed pixels are common. This challenge is because of the existence of multiple as well as partial class memberships of pixels. Therefore standard crisp methods cannot map land covers in overlapping areas. The soft computing approach addresses this problem. Therefore in our work we used fuzzy sets to solve mixed-pixel problems.

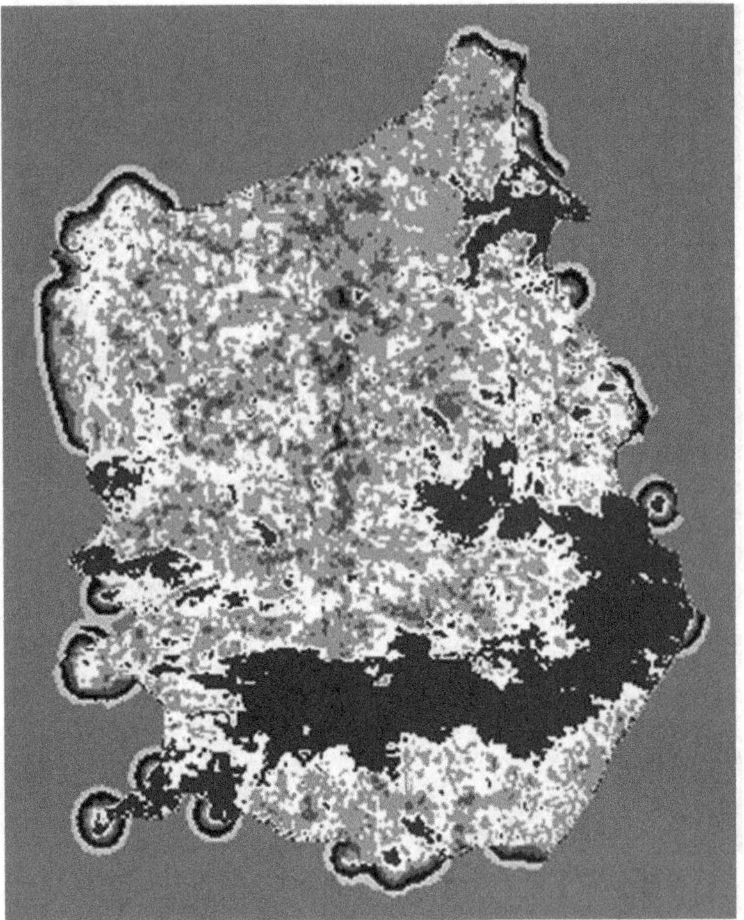

FIG. 18

Pixel classification solution for the Barakar River catchment area in 2015 from the fuzzy *C*-means algorithm (with $K = 7$).

One contribution of our work lies in its use of fuzzy set-based pixel segmentation to detect overlapping regions in our new FPQCA algorithm. The primary features of our proposed method are to incorporate CA-based neighborhood correction over fuzzy-based initial soft clustering. The neighborhood correction phase helps to reduce outlier problems. It corrects the pixel allocations considering the neighborhood.

FIG. 19

Pixel classification solution for the Barakar River catchment area in 2005, 2010, and 2015 from fuzzy set-based partitioned quantum cellular automata-corrected algorithm.

Table 3 Quantitative Evaluation Measures on the Classified Images in Solutions Obtained by the *K*-Means Algorithm, the Fuzzy *C*-Means Algorithm, and the Fuzzy Set-Based Partitioned Quantum Cellular Automata-Corrected Algorithm

	Barakar Image 2005		
Index	***K*-Means Algorithm**	**FCM Algorithm**	**FPQCA**
Davies-Bouldin index	0.4936 (2005) 0.5109 (2010) 0.6029 (2015)	0.4195 (2005) 0.4171 (2010) 0.5155 (2015)	0.4232
Dunn index	1.1667 (2005) 0.8610 (2010) 1.2846 (2015)	1.5173 (2005) 1.1853 (2010) 1.3822 (2015)	1.6650

FCM, fuzzy C-means; FPQCA, fuzzy set-based partitioned quantum cellular automata-corrected algorithm.

Table 4 Median Values of the Davies-Bouldin Index for 10 Consecutive Runs of All Methods

Data	Algorithms		
	K-Means	FCM	FPQCA
Barakar River catchment area	0.5425	0.4572	0.4232

FCM, fuzzy C-means; FPQCA, fuzzy set-based partitioned quantum cellular automata-corrected algorithm.

Table 5 *P* and *H* Values Produced by the Rank Sum Test for Comparison of the Fuzzy Set-Based Partitioned Quantum Cellular Automata-Corrected Algorithm With the *K*-Means Algorithm and the Fuzzy *C*-Means Algorithm

Algorithm	Comparison With the FPQCA	
	H	*P*-value
K-means	1	2.00×10^{-3}
FCM	1	3.90×10^{-3}

FCM, fuzzy C-means; FPQCA, fuzzy set-based partitioned quantum cellular automata-corrected algorithm.

The performance of the proposed FPQCA approach was demonstrated in remote sensing images of the Tilaiya catchment area of the Barakar River. The efficiency of our FPQCA approach was quantitatively evaluated for comparison with the existing *K*-means and FCM algorithms by means of two validity measures. The comparison with the ground truth information also revealed the efficient performance of our FPQCA algorithm. The statistical significance of our new FPQCA algorithm was also evaluated in comparison with *K*-means and FCM methods.

REFERENCES

[1] Y. Xu, V. Olman, D. Xu, Clustering gene expression data using a graph theoretic approach, an application of minimum spanning trees, Bioinformatics 17 (1999) 309–318.

[2] S. Tavazoie, J. Hughes, M. Campbell, R. Cho, G. Church, Systematic determination of genetic network architecture, Bioinformatics 17 (2001) 405–414.

[3] M.J.L. Hoon, S. de Imoto, J. Nolan, S. Miyano, Open source clustering software, Bioinformatics 20 (9) (2004).

[4] R. Spang, Diagnostic signatures from microarrays, a bioinformatics concept for personalized medicine, BIOSILICO 1 (2) (2003) 64–68.

[5] D. Dembele, P. Kastner, Fuzzy c-means method for clustering microarray data, Bioinformatics 19 (8) (2003) 973–980.
[6] U. Maulik, A. Mukhopadhyay, S. Bandyopadhyay, Combining Pareto-optimal clusters using supervised learning for identifying co-expressed genes, BMC Bioinformatics 10 (27) (2009).
[7] U. Maulik, A. Sarkar, Efficient parallel algorithm for pixel classification in remote sensing imagery, GeoInformatica 16 (2) (2012) 391–407.
[8] S. Bandyopadhyay, Satellite image classification using genetically guided fuzzy clustering with spatial information, Int. J. Remote Sens. 26 (3) (2005) 579–593.
[9] R.N. Dave, Use of the adaptive fuzzy clustering algorithm to detect lines in digital images, Intell. Robots Comput. Vis. VIII 1192 (1989) 600–611.
[10] A.D. Luca, S. Termini, A definition of non-probabilistic entropy in the setting of fuzzy set theory, Inf. Control 20 (1972) 301–312.
[11] C.P. Pappis, N.I. Karacapilidis, A comparative assessment of measures of similarity of fuzzy values, Fuzzy Sets Syst. 56 (1993) 171–174.
[12] W.J. Wang, New similarity measures on fuzzy sets and on elements, Fuzzy Sets Syst. 85 (1997) 305–309.
[13] A.S. Kumar, S.K. Basu, K.L. Majumdar, Robust classification of multispectral data using multiple neural networks and fuzzy integral, IEEE Trans. Geosci. Remote Sens. 35 (3) (1997) 787–790.
[14] A. Bardossy, L. Samaniego, Fuzzy rule-based classification of remotely sensed imagery, IEEE Trans. Geosci. Remote Sens. 40 (2) (2002).
[15] C.C. Hung, W. Liu, B.C. Kuo, A new adaptive fuzzy clustering algorithm for remotely sensed images, in: Geoscience and Remote Sensing Symposium, vol. 2, 2008, pp. II-863–II-866.
[16] Y.L. Chen, H.L. Hu, An overlapping cluster algorithm to provide non-exhaustive clustering, Eur. J. Oper. Res. 173 (2006) 762–780.
[17] R. Coppia, P. D'Urso, Fuzzy unsupervised classification of multivariate time trajectories with the Shannon entropy regularization, Comput. Stat. Data Anal. 50 (6) (2005) 1452–1477.
[18] K. Gao, X.X. Li, Y. Zhang, Y.H. Liu, Motion-blur parameter estimation of remote sensing image based on quantum neural network, in: Proc. SPIE 8200, 2011 International Conference on Optical Instruments and Technology: Optoelectronic Imaging and Processing Technology, 2011, p. 8201L.
[19] E. Casper, C.-C. Hung, E. Jung, M. Yang, A quantum-modeled K-means clustering algorithm for multi-band image segmentation, in: Proceedings of the 2012 ACM Research in Applied Computation Symposium (RACS '12), ACM, New York, NY, USA, 2012, pp. 158–163.
[20] C.-C. Hung, E. Casper, B.-C. Kuo, W. Liu, E. Jung, M. Yang, A quantum-modeled artificial bee colony clustering algorithm for remotely sensed multi-band image segmentation, in: Proceedings of IGARSS 2013—2013 IEEE International Geoscience and Remote Sensing Symposium, 2008.
[21] L.A. Zadeh, Fuzzy sets, Inf. Control 8 (1965) 338–353.
[22] E. Ruspini, Numerical methods for fuzzy clustering, Inf. Sci. 2 (1970) 319–350.
[23] J.C. Dunn, A fuzzy relative of the ISODATA process and its use in detecting compact, well separated clusters, Cybernetics 3 (1974) 95–104.
[24] J.C. Bezdek, Pattern Recognition with Fuzzy Objective Function Algorithms, Plenum Press, New York, 1981.

[25] S.S. Reddi, S.F. Rudin, H.R. Keshavan, An optimal multiple threshold scheme for image segmentation, IEEE Syst. Man Cybern. 14 (1984) 611–665.
[26] A.R. Smith, Two-dimensional formal languages and pattern recognition by cellular automata, in: IEEE Conference Record of 12th Annual Symposium on Switching and Automata Theory, 1971.
[27] S. Wolfram, Cryptography with cellular automata, Lect. Notes Comput. Sci. 218 (1986) 429–432.
[28] S. Wolfram, Statistical mechanics of cellular automata, Rev. Mod. Phys. 55 (3) (1983) 601–644.
[29] J. Watrous, On one-dimensional quantum cellular automata, in: Proceedings of the 36th Annual Symposium on Foundations of Computer Science, Milwaukee, WI, IEEE Computer Society Press, 1995, pp. 528–537.
[30] K. Morita, M. Harao, Computation universality of one-dimensional reversible (injective) cellular automata, IEICE Trans. E72 (6) (1989) 758–762.
[31] P. Arrighi, J. Grattage, Generalized partitioned quantum cellular automata and quantization of classical CA, Int. J. Unconv. Comput. (2005) 0312102.
[32] J. Horowitz, An Introduction to Quantum Cellular Automata, 2008.
[33] P. Arrighi, J. Grattage, Partitioned quantum cellular automata are intrinsically universal, Nat. Comput. 11 (1) (2012) 13–22.
[34] J.C. Dunn, A fuzzy relative of the ISODATA process and its use in detecting compact well-separated clusters, J. Cybern. 3 (3) (1973) 32–57.
[35] D.L. Davies, D.W. Bouldin, A cluster separation measure, IEEE Trans. Pattern Anal. Mach. Intell. PAMI 1 (2) (1979) 224–227.
[36] H.M., D. Wolfe, Nonparametric Statistical Methods, Wiley, New York, 1999.
[37] A. Sarkar, U. Maulik, Parallel point symmetry based clustering for gene microarray data, in: Proceedings of Seventh International Conference on Advances in Pattern Recognition—2009 (ICAPR, 2009), Kolkata, IEEE Computer Society, Conference Publishing Services (CPS), 2009, pp. 351–354.
[38] A. Sarkar, U. Maulik, Parallel clustering technique using modified symmetry based distance, in: Proceedings of 1st International Conference on Computer, Communication, Control and Information Technology (C3IT), 2009, pp. 611–618.

CHAPTER

9 Quantum-inspired evolutionary algorithm for scaling factor optimization during manifold medical information embedding

S. Samanta[a], A. Choudhury[a], N. Dey[b], A.S. Ashour[c], V.E. Balas[d]

University Institute of Technology, Burdwan, WB, India[a] Techno India College of Technology, Kolkata, WB, India[b] Tanta University, Tanta, Egypt[c] Aurel Vlaicu University of Arad, Arad, Romania[d]

1 INTRODUCTION

Nowadays, focus is directed toward telemedicine to support remote diagnosis, consultation procedures, and treatment of patients using telecommunication technology. Telemedicine is the process by which visual, electronic, and audio communication files are transferred. Such files include medical images/records and personal medical files [1,2].

Furthermore, the information evolution in the last decade has led to an explosion in the health care information management field [3]. This has led to successful combination of biomedicine and information technology to save biomedical images in a digital format. This has resulted in easy archiving, searching, and retrieval of digital images in comparison with compared with their analog counterparts. Additionally, editing and viewing of electronic patient records has become increasingly common for a health professional using a tablet PC [4]. The progress in the e-health services allows novel practices designed for transmission of the hospitals' and patients' medical images/records, remote access, and interpretation for diagnosis purposes. This advancement in information and communication technologies results in new chances for telemedicine. It facilities medical data transmission through mobile networks and from different geographical places through the Internet and other wired/wireless communication channels. Thus coverage of remote/rural areas and hospitals is guaranteed.

Quantum Inspired Computational Intelligence. http://dx.doi.org/10.1016/B978-0-12-804409-4.00009-7

Nevertheless, there are various threats to medical data transmission via communication channels/media. This severely affects its integrity, confidentiality, and authenticity. Moreover, the transmission of a large amount of medical information through common channels leads to extreme memory consumption as well as high transmission cost and increased time being required [5].

Consequently, protecting patient's privacy and ensuring the security of medical file transfer is becoming a progressively more imperative problem. Information protection is becoming more vital with the integration of modern technology into existing medical services [6]. To achieve the required security, constraints and laws are legally regulated regarding access to the medical data contained in different forms. This requires a secure authentication system to access the patient records [7]. This necessitates the implementation of a medical watermarking system to prevent access to the information and avoid it being read by an unintended/unauthorized recipient.

Therefore digital watermarking of medical images/data is a paramount solution to the security and authorization issues [8–10]. Digital watermarking has extensive applications in the telemedicine domain via its hiding the electronic patient record data within the medical images, while preserving the diagnostic quality of the medical images. For security, authentication, and tamper detection as well as cost reduction of storage/transmission, watermarking techniques for hiding data are used to embed the patient's information in the medical images.

Artifacts in the patient's image from image watermarking can lead to diagnosis and treatment errors, which can be life-threatening [11]. Therefore there are strict constraints on the image reliability which severely forbid any image distortion that may result during watermarking in the medical imaging applications [12]. To overcome the artifact problem from watermarking, different watermarking schemes were established by researchers to provide authentication of the hospital logo or to hide patient information without affecting the original image.

Watermarking methods can be categorized into different groups on the basis of the visibility, domain or permanency. In accordance with the watermark domain, the image watermarking techniques presented are divided into spatial and frequency domains. The spatial domain approaches embed the watermark by adjusting the image pixel's values directly with low computational cost and easy implementation. The most frequently used approaches in this domain involve the spread spectrum [13] and the least significant bit [14]. These spatial domain schemes have the disadvantage of not being robust against attacks and have relatively low capacity. Afterward, the watermark is embedded by the coefficients of frequency transformation. Subsequently, the watermarked image is obtained by inverse transformation. The discrete wavelet transforms (DWT) [15], the discrete cosine transform (DCT) [16], the discrete Hadamard transform [17], the discrete Fourier transform [18], and the Ridgelet transform [19] are such frequency transformation schemes. Typically, frequency watermarking schemes are more robust, more complex and more widely applied than the spatial domain schemes.

Moreover, to resist attacks which attempt to eliminate/destroy the watermark in the watermarked image, robust watermarking is designated [20]. To achieve greater robustness, significant modifications to the host image are required. However, such modifications are discernible, which does not satisfy the imperceptibility requirement. This trade-off between the robustness and imperceptibility can be controlled by the embedding strength [21]. To accomplish the upper performance bound of watermarking algorithms, the optimal embedding strength, called the "scaling factor," should be determined [22]. However, it is complicated to empirically establish the embedding strength. Thus obtaining the scaling factor's optimum values can be considered an optimization problem to solve the optimal watermarking problem.

Consequently, metaheuristic optimization techniques, including a genetic algorithm (GA), particle swarm optimization (PSO), and ant colony optimization, can be used to solve this optimization problem. Generally, a quantum-inspired evolutionary algorithm (EA) is a category of evolutionary algorithms (EAs) which is inspired by quantum computing (QC). An EA is basically an optimization method as well as a stochastic search that is based on natural biological evolution principles [23–25]. Generally, EAs are more robust and global compared with the traditional optimization methods. Nevertheless, the performance of EAs is influenced by these heuristics. Typically, the three foremost schemes of evolutionary computation are GAs, evolutionary programming, and evolution strategies.

In this chapter, frequency watermarking schemes are obtained by the combination of DWT-, DCT-, and singular value decomposition (SVD)-based watermarking technique-based optimization algorithms. The optimization algorithms used are a GA, a quantum-inspired GA (QIGA), and a quantum-inspired EA (QIEA). They are used to discover the best possible scaling factors for embedding a watermark within various medical images. The GA, QIGA, or QIEA are applied separately to optimize the selection of the embedding factor's level to achieve a compromise between the robustness and the perceptibility of the watermarking technique. The watermarked image can then be transferred through a wired/wireless communication channel, where the optimal scaling factors are sent. At the receiver terminal, the watermarked image is used to extract the embedded logos.

The rest of this chapter is structured as follows. Section 2 describes work related to that in the present study. Section 3 provides a brief introduction to the mathematical transformation schemes used in watermarking. Section 4 includes an overview of the EAs and quantum-inspired algorithms. The proposed system for various medical images watermarking is described in Section 5. The results are presented and discussed in Section 6, and the conclusions follow in Section 7.

2 RELATED WORK

Miscellaneous studies based on biomedical content authentication using optimization methods to support watermarking techniques have been conducted [26–30]. Ganic and Eskicioglu [31] suggested a hybrid algorithm using DWT and SVD. The SVD was used with each band of the decomposed original image. The original image singular values are modified with the watermark singular values in all frequencies, which provides a watermarking scheme that is robust against a broad range of attacks. A comparative study of the proposed hybrid algorithm and a pure SVD-based scheme proved the greater robustness and reliability of the proposed method. Huang et al. [32] introduced a watermarking approach based on progressive transmission-based GAs. They implemented a watermark embedding and extraction scheme in the transform domain. The watermark robustness and imperceptibility were optimized with the GA with an accurate fitness function in the watermarking scheme. Simulation results evaluated the robustness/efficiency of the transmission with various attacking scenarios and various bandwidth variations.

Loukhaoukha et al. [33] suggested a novel optimal watermarking system based on both SVD and lifting wavelet transform using multiobjective GA optimization. The watermark's singular values were embedded in a detail subband of the host image. Multiple scaling factors were used to realize the greatest probable robustness deprived of losing the watermark transparency. Therefore, to determine the optimal values of the multiple scaling factors, multiobjective GA optimization was used. The experimental results indicated a superior improvement in the watermarking performance with respect to the transparency and robustness of the proposed method compared with DWT watermarking and the SVD-lifting wavelet transform watermarking scheme with a single scaling factor. Additionally, the false positive detection problem which affects most SVD watermarking algorithms was solved with sue of one-way hash functions. Ramanjaneyulu and Rajarajeswari [34] proposed a robust image watermarking scheme based on DWT. The DWT was applied to the original image and the LH2 and LH3 sub-band coefficients were grouped into different blocks. A GA was applied to optimize the parameters by maximizing the peak signal to noise ratios (PSNR) of the watermarked image and the normalized correlation of the extracted watermark.

Mingzhi et al. [35] presented a combined DWT- and DCT-based watermarking scheme to embed the watermark. A GA was used for embedding and extraction the optimal parameters. The optimization fitness function was used to maximize the PSNR of the watermarked image. The results indicated that this system was robust against many image attacks. Several studies have conducted for medical watermarking applications. Dey et al. [36] suggested a scheme to embed a hospital logo in the electrocardiogram signal. The cuckoo search optimization algorithm was used to optimize the scaling factors of the embedded watermark. Soliman et al. [37] presented an authentication method to secure the patient medical images in order to enhance the confidentiality, security, and integrity of the transmitted images through the Internet. PSO with its modifications (i.e., quantum-behaved PSO and weighted quantum-behaved PSO) was invoked in adaptive quantization index modulation and SVD in conjunction with the DCT and the DWT. The results demonstrated that the proposed algorithm created a watermark which is invisible to the human eye, reliable for tracing colluders, and robust against different attacks.

Singh et al. [38] studied a secure multiple watermarking scheme based on the DWT, the DCT, and SVD to authenticate of the medical images/records and the personal information of patients by means of image and text watermarks. The cover medical image is decomposed up to the second level of the DWT coefficients in the embedding process. The low-frequency band (LL) of the host medical image and the watermark medical image was transformed by the DCT and SVD. The singular value of the watermark image was embedded in the singular value of the host image. Moreover, the text watermark was embedded at the second level of the high-frequency band of the host image. The results were obtained by variation of the gain factor, the text watermark size, and medical image modalities. Krishnamurthi et al. [39] proposed a hybrid algorithm which combined the DWT and the DCT with PSO for authentication and copyright protection of medical images. PSO was applied on the host image to determine the intensities for embedding the watermark bits by the best global solution from the objective function and the fitness function. The embedding procedure was adopted with an intensity level. The simulation results proved the suitability of the suggested method when tested for different medical images and subjected to various attacks.

From the preceding survey it is seen that several image watermarking techniques combined three transform methods, whereas others included optimization techniques for optimized watermarking. However, to our knowledge, no work has been conducted on medical watermarking using DWT-DCT-SVD-based optimization algorithms; namely, a GA, a QIGA, or a QIEA. These optimization algorithms are used separately to find the optimal scale factor values used during the embedding of the watermark within various medical images.

3 MATHEMATICAL TRANSFORMATION

In the current study, the DWT, the DCT, and SVD along with a GA, a QIGA, or a QIEA are applied to embed multiple medical data within various medical images. The transformations used are described in the following sections.

3.1 DISCRETE WAVELET TRANSFORM

The wavelet transformation is a mathematical approach which can simultaneously represent an image in both the time domain and the frequency domain [40]. A wavelet transform allocates the signal decomposition in narrow frequency bands. The DWT is a fast and simple transformation that can be used to translate the image from the spatial domain to the frequency domain [41,42]. Decomposition of an image by a two-level wavelet transformation is performed by a two-level analysis filter bank, which results in four nonoverlapping subband images. Thus the original image is decomposed into an approximate image (coefficients) (LL) and three detail images (coefficients); namely, the vertical details (LH), the horizontal details (HL), and the diagonal details (HH) [43].

3.2 DISCRETE COSINE TRANSFORM

The DCT is an general orthogonal transformation for digital signal/image processing that can be used for high-compression applications, good information integration ability, and small bit error rate. It is a Fourier-related transform similar to the discrete Fourier transform. The DCT turns over the image edge to transform the image into an even function form [44]. In digital signal processing, the DCT is considered one of the most widespread linear transformation technologies. It breaks the image into different frequency bands so it is easier to embed watermarking information into the middle frequency bands of the image. The middle frequency bands are selected because these bands have the most visual vital image parts [45].

3.3 SINGULAR VALUE DECOMPOSITION

The SVD transformation is invoked mainly in several applications, such as image compression, image hiding, watermarking, noise reduction, and image watermarking [46]. The SVD of an $M \times M$ matrix referred to as R_m, which represents the input image, is a decomposition of the form $R_m = USV^{\mathrm{T}}$ [47]. Here U and V are orthonormal matrices, and S is a diagonal matrix consisting of the singular values of R_m. The singular values $s_1 \geq s_2 \geq \cdots \geq s_m \geq 0$ are in descending order along the main diagonal of S. These singular values are obtained by calculation of the square root of the eigenvalues of $R_m R_m^{\mathrm{T}}$ and $R_m^{\mathrm{T}} R_m$. The singular values are unique; however, the matrices U and V are not unique. In the current work we combine the DWT, the DCT, and SVD to obtain the advantages of each in the proposed medical watermarking scheme.

The DCT is used to capture the low-frequency information of the watermarked image as well as to increase the robustness and concealment. Furthermore, the DWT-SVD-based approach and the DCT-SVD-based approach are both much better than the traditional watermarking techniques. Thus the hybrid DWT-DCT-SVD approach has the ability to resist attacks unlike conventional techniques with efficient robustness and concealment.

4 EVOLUTIONARY ALGORITHMS AND QUANTUM-INSPIRED ALGORITHMS

EAs are robust, practical search and optimization techniques inspired by evolutionary processes occurring in molecular genetics and natural selection. The foremost characteristics of EAs are the population dynamics, representation/evaluation of individuals, and evolutionary operators, including selection, crossover, and mutation [48]. Quantum computing (QC) is the discipline that uses the laws of quantum mechanics to solve computational problems. It provides the ability to perform simulations of quantum mechanical processes in chemistry, physics, and biology which could never be done within the range of classical computers. The most significant difference between the classical computing and QC techniques lies in the way in which the calculations are performed. Typically, in the classical approaches, the evaluation time does not increase very quickly with the input data size. Conversely, the calculations in QC are performed by unitary transformations on the state of the quantum bits (qubits). Combined with the principle of superposition, this translates into more efficient algorithms for searching, factoring, and simulation of quantum mechanical systems and furthermore any system that uses QC. Although theoretically the application of unique quantum mechanical phenomena can solve selected computational problems extremely efficiently. Recently, extensive research on hybridization led to the opening a new field—namely, QIEAs.

The evolutionary computing study is depicted by the principles of quantum mechanics, including interference, coherence, and superposition states. This improves the domain of computing combinatorial optimization problems and provides superior results compared with any standard heuristics or EAs. Although the convergence rate in the QIEA is slow and sometimes it gives premature convergence, the QIEA still maintains a good balance between exploration of the search space and exploitation of best solution. Simultaneously, quantum-inspired algorithms are considered a new class of metaheuristics, which obtained their inspiration from both biological evolution and the unitary evolution of quantum systems.

In the current work a GA, a QIGA or a QIEA is used to support the watermarking of various medical images Overviews of EAs and QC are presented next.

4.1 OVERVIEW OF EVOLUTIONARY ALGORITHMS

EAs work on a population of potential solutions, which use the survival of the proper principle to construct consecutively better approximations to a solution. A new approximation set is produced by the selection of an individual process the basis of the fitness level in the problem field and reproduction with use of variation operators in each EA generation. EAs are a population set-based optimization which use bio-inspired mechanisms, including mutation, crossover, natural selection, and survival of the fittest to refine a set of solution candidates iteratively [49]. EAs [50] definitely find the optimal solution within the least amount of time. EAs include GAs [51–53], genetic programming [54], evolutionary programming [55], and evolutionary strategies [56,57].

The basic generic EA first initializes a population of solution candidates (initial population), then the following three procedures are repeated, which are: (1) assesses the population individual's fitness, (2) uses this fitness information to breed a new population of children, and (3) combines the solutions for the parents and children in some way to form a new generation of the population, and the cycle of the process continues iteratively. The generic classical EA pseudocode can be given as in Algorithm 1.

ALGORITHM 1 CLASSICAL EVOLUTIONARY ALGORITHM

```
Initialize random population;
Evaluate the population;
Select fittest solution and store it;
Generation= 0;
while () do
    Evaluate the population;
    Select fitter chromosomes using a survivor selection process;
    Upgrade the population by upgrade operators (genetic operators);
    Recombine the population with the fittest solutions;
    Generation = Generation + 1;
end while
```

The first phase in Algorithm 1 is the selection of the population size and the proper encoding method. A large population size leads to an increase in the diversity in the initial population. Thus to implement the EA with an optimal solution, a suitable population size is to be selected. However, it requires more computational attempts as well as more execution time.

The EA performance depends on the balance between the exploration and exploitation methods. "Exploitation" refers to the use of the accessible knowledge to realize the best solution, whereas "exploration" is defined as the investigation of a new and indefinite area in the search space.

4.1.1 Complexity analysis of evolutionary algorithms

A large number of combinatorial optimization problems can be solved with use of EAs. However, few theoretical concepts exist that can analyze the average time complexity of the EAs for such combinatorial optimization problems. EAs are stochastic, and thus the complexity depends on the representation of the individuals and the population size (P), the maximum number of generations (G), individual length (L), and obviously the fitness function, selection process, crossover, and mutation (i.e., the genetic operators) functions. The parameter settings are as follows: population size (P) of 20, maximum number of generations (G) of 100, crossover probability of 0.5 (fixed), mutation probability of 0.01 (fixed), and chromosome length (L) of 6 multiplied by the number of parameters (K) (i.e., $6 \times 3 = 18$). Moreover, we have one-point crossover (the crossover point is randomly selected), one-point mutation (randomly change one gene), and the termination criterion: maximum generation (G). Hence the worst-case time complexity of the EA for the proposed optimization problem is

$$O(O(\text{fitness}) \times (O(\text{mutation}) + O(\text{crossover}) + O(\text{selection}))) = O((G \times P \times K) \times ((G \times P \times L) + (G \times P \times L) + (G \times P))) = O(G \times P \times L).$$

Furthermore, when all the parameters are constant and the values are predefined, the best-case time complexity of the EA for the proposed problem is $O(1)$.

4.2 OVERVIEW OF QUANTUM COMPUTING

Quantum-inspired algorithms are a set of a new class of optimization algorithms which are inspired by QC. This hybrid concept is actually the combination of some significant features from both evolutionary computing and QC. QC is as a computer science branch which is concerned with applications of unique quantum mechanical effects to solve different computational problems [58].

The hybrid bio-quantum-inspired algorithms are basically intended for classical computers instead of quantum-mechanical computers with the highly efficient characteristics adopted from the original quantum algorithms to solve hard real-world optimization problems. There are various hybrid algorithms, such as QIEAs [59] and QIGAs [60–63], which are described in later sections.

Before we describe the above-mentioned quantum-inspired algorithms, we briefly describe the basic concept of QC. In QC machines, computations are performed on the basis of the laws of quantum mechanics. Quantum mechanics is known the theory that predicts and explains the behavior of particles at the subatomic level. QC is a new class of computing which explores the computational power and other computer characteristics on the basis of the laws of quantum mechanics.

The main objective of QC is to discover quantum algorithms which are much quicker than classical algorithms [64]. Thus QC can be applied in several domains of computer science because of its rapid development. Researchers have become interested in quantum data security because quantum data such as images will suffer from abuse when classical computers are used. Recently, digital image watermarking has been applied for copyright protection and material description on classical computers. With the intention of protection against abuse, extending analogous methods to use quantum-inspired algorithms is necessary.

Generally, a quantum computer is considered a physical machine which recognizes input states to signify a consistent superposition of numerous various possible inputs and then develop them into an equivalent output superposition. Computation is defined as a unitary transformation sequence which concerns concurrently each superposition element, generating a huge parallel data processing [65]. A qubit is defined as a unit vector in a two-dimensional complex vector space, where a particular basic state can be indicated by $|0\rangle$ and $|1\rangle$.

On the basis of the fundamental concept of the superposition principle, if a quantum system is represented by one of these two basic states, then it can also be in any linear combination of these two states, such as $\alpha_0|0\rangle + \alpha_1|1\rangle$, where the coefficients α_0 and α_1 are called the "amplitudes" of the states $|0\rangle$ and $|1\rangle$ respectively. These coefficients give the probabilistic measure of the occurrence of state $|0\rangle$ and state $|1\rangle$ respectively. The superposition $\alpha_0|0\rangle + \alpha_1|1\rangle$ is the basic, or the smallest, unit of encoded information in quantum computers or quantum systems. The qubit representation is given by [65]

$$|\psi\rangle = \alpha_0|\,0\rangle + \alpha_1|1\rangle. \tag{1}$$

According to the superposition principle, the α are arbitrary complex numbers and the squares of their norms add up to 1, as indicated in the following expression:

$$|\alpha_0|^2 + |\alpha_1|^2 = 1. \tag{2}$$

The α are the probabilistic amplitude of the qubit that may exist in one of the two states (state "0" or state "1") and ensure the normalization condition is met.

In a quantum computer, qubits are quaternary in nature. They have three states, unlike the binary bits in classical computers. The states are state 0 or state 1 and the linear superposition of these two basic states. Quantum mechanics establishes that a bit can exist in both of the two basic states at the same time in the superposition state.

4.2.1 Qubit representation

The equation for the superposition state of a qubit can be expressed by the sum of the two basic states corresponding to their probabilistic amplitude coefficients α_0 and α_1 respectively, where α_0 and α_1 are complex but are generally considered real without any loss. An example of a qubit state is given in the following equation and it satisfies the normalization condition:

$$|\psi\rangle = \frac{1}{\sqrt{2}}|0\rangle + \frac{1}{\sqrt{2}}|1\rangle\,. \tag{3}$$

Thus a qubit can be in a coherent superposition of states $|0\rangle$ and $|1\rangle$ until it is measured. Once the measurement has been done, there is one state: 0 or 1 [59]. Suppose we have two qubits. These can be in one of the four computational fundamental states; namely, 00, 01, 10, or 11. Similarly, a qubit pair can be in a superposition of these four states given by

$$|\psi\rangle = \alpha_{00}\,|00\rangle + \alpha_{01}\,|01\rangle + \alpha_{10}\,|10\rangle + \alpha_{11}\,|11\rangle\,. \tag{4}$$

These four states have the normalization condition which is given by

$$|\alpha_{00}|^2 + |\alpha_{01}|^2 + |\alpha_{10}|^2 + |\alpha_{11}|^2 = 1. \tag{5}$$

Thus a qubit string (quantum chromosome), which is set of some individual qubits (quantum genes), can be represented by

$$q = \begin{bmatrix} \alpha_1 & \alpha_2 & \cdots & \alpha_m \\ \beta_1 & \beta_2 & \cdots & \beta_m \end{bmatrix}, \tag{6}$$

where an individual qubit is given by

$$\begin{bmatrix} \alpha \\ \beta \end{bmatrix} \tag{7}$$

and m refers to the length of the quantum chromosome q. Therefore the whole quantum population state $Q = q_1, q_2, \ldots, q_N$ can be depicted by a matrix of vectors as illustrated in Fig. 1 [64].

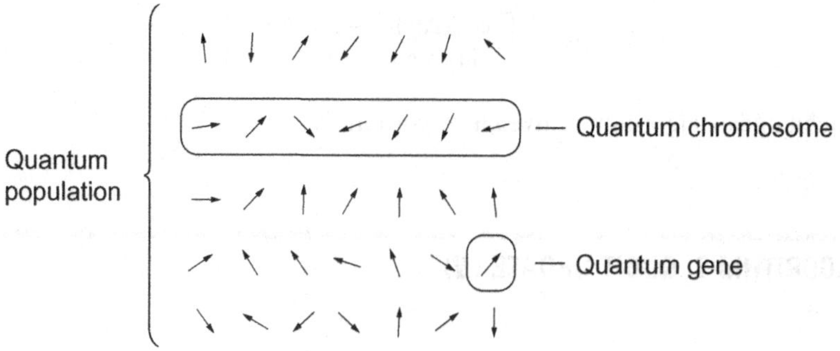

FIG. 1

Population of quantum chromosomes.

Quantum logic gates are used in quantum mechanics and are basically quantum circuits. The quantum circuit is a quantum computation model where computation is performed through a quantum gate sequence. Quantum gates are reversible, such as the inverter (NOT) gate, the output of which can be undone, and thus the input data can be obtained from the output data. Quantum gates are used for the updating of qubits to obtain a better optimal solution.

Additionally, the updated qubits can provide a better convergence rate if the updating operation is performed properly. Quantum gates mostly operate on one or two qubits like the classical logic gates. Thus the gates are symbolized by 2×2 or 4×4 unitary matrices. A matrix is unitary if and only if its inverse equals its conjugate transpose, which is expressed by

$$U^{-1} = U^{+}, \tag{8}$$

where U^{-1} and U^{+} are unitary and $U^{+}U = 1$. This property ensures that any quantum gate is always logically reversible.

4.2.2 Quantum operator

For the updating of a individual qubit, a quantum update operator is used, which in particular is a quantum rotational gate. A rotation gate $U(\Delta\theta_i)$ is used to update the qubit individual as a variation operator. The coefficients (α_i, β_i) of the ith qubit are updated by

$$\begin{bmatrix} \alpha_i' \\ \beta_i \end{bmatrix} = U(\Delta\theta_i) \times \begin{bmatrix} \alpha_i \\ \beta_i \end{bmatrix}, \tag{9}$$

$$\begin{bmatrix} \alpha_i' \\ \beta_i' \end{bmatrix} = \begin{bmatrix} \cos(\Delta\theta_i) & -\sin(\Delta\theta_i) \\ \sin(\Delta\theta_i) & \cos(\Delta\theta_i) \end{bmatrix} \begin{bmatrix} \alpha_i \\ \beta_i \end{bmatrix}, \tag{10}$$

where the rotation gate is given by

$$U(\Delta\theta_i) = \begin{bmatrix} \cos(\Delta\theta_i) & -\sin(\Delta\theta_i) \\ \sin(\Delta\theta_i) & \cos(\Delta\theta_i) \end{bmatrix}. \tag{11}$$

The qubit update algorithm is given in Algorithm 2.

ALGORITHM 2 QUBIT UPDATE (*Q*)

start
$i \leftarrow 0$
while ($i < m$) **do**
  Begin
  $i \leftarrow i+1$
  Establish ($\Delta\theta_i$) using Table 1
  Obtain (α'_i,β'_i) using
  if q is located in the first/third quadrant **then**
    $[\alpha'_i, \beta'_i]^\top = U(\Delta\theta_i)[\alpha'_i, \beta'_i]^\top$
  else if then
    $[\alpha'_i, \beta'_i]^\top = U(-\Delta\theta_i)[\alpha'_i, \beta'_i]^\top$
  end if
  $q \leftarrow q'$
end while

In Algorithm 2 the qubit individuals in the quantum chromosome are updated by use of quantum gates described as a variation operator of a QIEA, where the updated qubit operation should ensure the following normalization condition is met:

$$|\alpha'|^2 + |\beta'|^2 = 1, \tag{12}$$

where $\alpha\prime$ and $\beta\prime$ are the updated qubit values and the rotation gate used is given in Eq. (11), which is used as a quantum gate in the QIEA. The rotation angle of each qubit toward either the 0 or 1 state depending on its sign is denoted by $\Delta\theta_i, i = 1, 2, \ldots, m$. Fig. 2 presents the rotation gate polar plot.

The value of $\Delta\theta_i$ should be fine-tuned as per the application problem domain. A high value of $\Delta\theta_i$ can increase the divergence rate and hence the convergence rate decreases or the solution may converge to a premature local optimum. A fine-tuned magnitude of $\Delta\theta_i$ affects the speed of the convergence. The magnitude of $\Delta\theta_i$ is must be maintained between 0.001π and 0.05π. Table 1 is used to determine the rotation

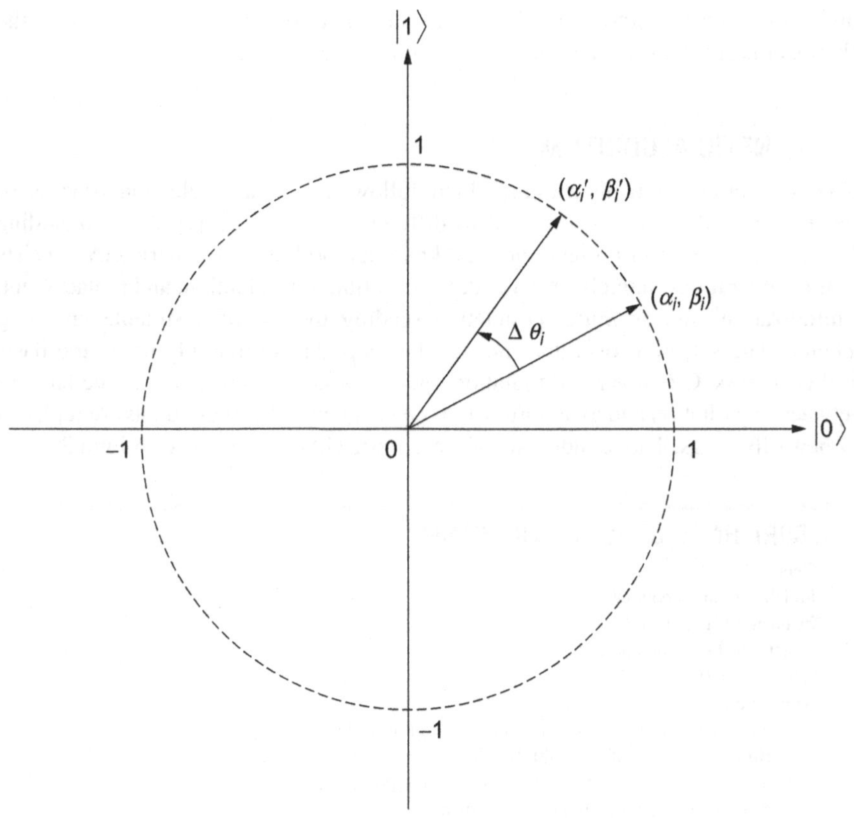

FIG. 2

Rotation gate polar plot.

Table 1 Angle Parameters for the Rotation Gate

x_i	b_i	$f(x) \geq f(b)$	$\Delta\theta_i$
0	0	False	θ_1
0	0	True	θ_2
0	1	False	θ_3
0	1	True	θ_4
1	0	False	θ_5
1	0	True	θ_6
1	1	False	θ_7
1	1	True	θ_8

angle $\Delta\theta_i$; $f()$ is the fitness function of the individual solutions, and b_i and x_i are the ith bits of best solution b and the binary solution x respectively.

4.3 GENETIC ALGORITHM

GAs are optimization algorithms which follow the natural selection process of genetics [66]. They can be applied to different optimization problems, including the traveling salesman problem and the knapsack problem. A generic GA consists of some operations; namely, initialization, selection, reproduction, and replacement. "Initialization" means initial population seeding by use of a suitable encoding scheme. The selection operator chooses the individuals randomly or on the basis of their fitness. Crossover and mutation operations are used to preserve the balance between exploitation and exploration. On replacement, older individuals are replaced by new offsprings. The pseudocode of the generic GA is given in Algorithm 3.

ALGORITHM 3 GENETIC ALGORITHM

```
Genetic Algorithm()
Initialize random population;
Evaluate the population;
Select fittest solution and store it;
Generation= 0;
while () do
   Select good chromosomes (using reproduction procedure);
   Perform crossover with probability of crossover (PC);
   Select fitter chromosomes by survivor selection procedure;
   Perform mutation with probability of mutation (Pm);
   Evaluate the population;
   Generation = Generation + 1;
end while
```

The first step in the GA pseudocode is to choose an appropriate encoding method and the population size. To get a better optimal solution, the proper population size can chosen for GA implementation. A large population size increases the diversity in the initial population but it requires more computational and execution time.

The small population size limits the individual diversity in the solution space. The GA performance depends on the balance between the exploitation and exploration procedures, as for EAs.

4.3.1 Complexity analysis of genetic algorithms

To discuss the complexity analysis of the GA, the following parameter settings are used: a population size (P) of 20, a maximum number of generations (G) of 100, a crossover probability of 0.5 (fixed), a mutation probability of 0.01 (fixed), and a chromosome length (L) of 6 multiplied by the number of parameters (K) (i.e., $6 \times 3 = 18$). Moreover, we have one-point crossover (the crossover point is randomly selected), one-point mutation (randomly change one gene), and the termination criterion: maximum generation (G). Thus the computational complexity is given by O(population size $\times$ maximum generation $\times$ O(fitness) $\times$ (crossover probability $\times$ O(crossover)) + (mutation probability $\times$ O(mutation))).

Therefore the complexity is dependent on the population size, the number of generations, and the computation time per generation. If the population size (P), maximum number of generations (G), crossover probability, and mutation probability are constants as described above for the parameter settings, then the computational complexity of the proposed GA can be simplified to $O(O(\text{fitness}) \times (O(\text{mutation}) + O(\text{crossover})))$. In addition, if the fitness, mutation, and crossover functions take a known amount of time in the proposed problem, then the big O is $O(1)$; that is, the proposed GA takes a constant amount of time to complete the execution. This is the best-case computational complexity of the proposed GA for optimizing scaling factors.

On the other hand, when the parameters are not constant and the values are not predefined as described, then the time complexity of the proposed GA is $O(O(\text{fitness}) \times (O(\text{mutation}) + O(\text{crossover}) + O(\text{selection})))$, where the complexity of evaluating the fitness of each chromosome in the population (P) is $O(G \times P \times K)$, the complexity of computing the crossover function where one-point crossover takes place for the proposed GA is $O(G \times P \times L)$, the complexity of computing the mutation function where there is one-point mutation for the proposed GA is $O(G \times P \times L)$, and the complexity of the selection procedure when roulette-wheel selection is applied for the proposed GA is $O(G \times P)$. Hence the worst-case computational complexity of the proposed GA for optimization of scaling factors during the embedding of manifold medical information is $O(G \times P \times L)$.

4.4 QUANTUM-INSPIRED GENETIC ALGORITHM

The QIGA is a hybrid optimization algorithm enriched with the efficient computing characteristics of a GA and QC. The bio-quantum-inspired optimization algorithm QIGA adopted features from QC, such as qubit representation, superposition of state, quantum state measurement, and qubit updating.

Simultaneously, the GA adopted features including population initialization, selection, crossover, and mutation. The QIGA uses features such as qubit updating, selection, crossover, and mutation as functional operators of the algorithm to resample the population of solution candidates. The QIGA uses binary quantum chromosomes to represent solutions, encoded as

$$q = \begin{bmatrix} \alpha_1 & \alpha_2 & \cdots & \alpha_m \\ \beta_1 & \beta_2 & \cdots & \beta_m \end{bmatrix}. \quad (13)$$

Here each column represents a binary quantum gene $|\psi_1\rangle, |\psi_2\rangle, \ldots, |\psi_m\rangle$. Hence a state of the whole quantum population $Q = q_1, q_2, \ldots, q_N$ can be demonstrated by a matrix of vectors, where $q_1, q_2, \ldots, q_N$ are binary quantum chromosomes. The complete pseudocode of the QIGA is given in Algorithm 4.

ALGORITHM 4 QUANTUM-INSPIRED GENETIC ALGORITHM

Start
$t \leftarrow 0$
Initialize $Q(0)$
while do
  $t \leftarrow t+0$
  Evaluate $Q(t)$
  Perform genetic operations on $Q(t)$
end while
End

Initially, in Algorithm 4 the genes of all individuals in the quantum population $Q(0)$ are initiated by linear superposition $|\psi\rangle = \frac{1}{\sqrt{2}}|0\rangle + \frac{1}{\sqrt{2}}|1\rangle$. Thus whole search space sampling with equal probability is produced. Throughout phenotype creation, states of all genes in quantum chromosomes are detected.

The individual's fitness evaluation is based on the observed population matrix $P(t)$. The genetic operators applied in the algorithm are based on quantum rotation gates [49], where the rotate state's vectors are in the quantum gene state space [63]. The genetic operators applied in the algorithm are inherited from biology, and are selection, crossover, and mutation. In Algorithm 4, qubit individuals in a population of individuals $Q(t)$ are updated by use of some quantum gates as introduced in Section 4.2.

Recently, the field of QIGAs has been one of the fastest growing areas of research. Numerous extensions of QIGAs have been proposed in several fields. Early research examples of a QIGA with a binary quantum representation based on qubits are presented in [60–63,67].

4.4.1 Complexity analysis of the quantum-inspired genetic algorithm

For the QIGA, the following parameter settings were used: a quantum population size (Q) of 20, a maximum number of generations (G) of 100, a crossover probability of 0.5 (fixed), a mutation probability of 0.01 (fixed), a chromosome length (L) of 6 multiplied by the number of parameters (K) (i.e., $6 \times 3 = 18$), and number of parameters equal to the number of scaling factors (K) of 3 ($K1$, $K2$, $K3$). Moreover, we have one-point crossover (the crossover point is randomly selected), one-point mutation (randomly change one gene), the termination criterion (maximum generation, G), and the quantum update operator (quantum rotation gate, U). Thus the worst-case computational complexity of the proposed QIGA for optimization of the scaling factors problem is analyzed as follows:

- To generate the initial quantum population, the computational complexity of the QIGA is $O(G \times Q \times L)$.
- For the quantum state measurement by observation of each qubit in each quantum chromosome, the time complexity of the QIGA is $O(G \times Q \times L)$.
- For evaluation of the fitness of each chromosome in the quantum population (Q) the time complexity of the QIGA is $O(G \times Q \times K)$.
- The time complexity of the QIGA for selection of the best or fittest solution using the roulette-wheel selection process is $O(G \times Q)$.

- The complexity of the QIGA for the updating of the quantum population (Q) using a quantum rotation gate (U) is $O(G \times Q \times L)$.
- The complexities of the genetic operators, such as the crossover and mutation, are $O(G \times Q \times L)$ for each function.
- Hence the overall execution time complexity of the proposed QIGA is $O(G \times Q \times L)$ in the worst case.
- If all of the above parameters are constant and their values are known for the proposed problem, then the best-case time complexity of the QIGA is also constant, and is $O(1)$.

4.5 QUANTUM-INSPIRED EVOLUTIONARY ALGORITHM

Another hybrid optimization algorithm is the QIEA, which was developed with the combined concept of the two most important domains of computing—namely, evolutionary computing and QC. These two types of computations are implemented by the algorithms named "evolutionary algorithms"(EAs) and "quantum algorithms."

Quantum algorithms are mainly intended for quantum mechanical computers and not for classical computers. To utilize the advantages of QC in classical computers, researchers introduced a new concept of computing algorithms named "quantum-inspired evolutionary algorithms" (QIEAs). For various hard and real-world optimization problems, researchers use this new type of computation, which provides more efficient solutions than any classical EAs.

The first proposed EA based on the concept of QC was introduced in 1996 [60]. Other early research examples of QIEAs with a binary quantum depiction based on qubits were presented in [59]. In the past few years, several other studies on QIEAs have been also presented [68–70]. The complete pseudocode of the generic QIEA is presented in Algorithm 5, were $Q(t)$ denotes the tth generation of a quantum population.

ALGORITHM 5 QUANTUM-INSPIRED EVOLUTIONARY ALGORITHM

Start
$t \leftarrow 0$
Initialize $Q(0)$
Construct $P(0)$ by observing $Q(0)$
Evaluate $P(0)$
Store the best solution among $P(0)$ in $B(0)$
while do
  Begin
  $t \leftarrow t + 0$
  Construct P(t) by observing $Q(t-1)$ states
  Evaluate $P(t)$
  Update $Q(t)$ using quantum gate $U(t)$
  Store the best solution among $P(t)$ and $B(t-1)$ in $B(t)$
  Store the best solution b among $B(t)$
end while
End

The QIEA is a population-based probabilistic algorithm resembling other EAs. Therefore it maintains a population of qubit individuals, $Q = q_1, q_2, \ldots, q_N$ at generation t, where N is the population size and q_i is a qubit individual (quantum chromosome).

In the current work, initially the genes of all individuals in the quantum population $Q(0)$ were initialized with linear superposition $|\psi\rangle = \frac{1}{\sqrt{2}}|0\rangle + \frac{1}{\sqrt{2}}|1\rangle$. This results in sampling of the whole search space with equal probability. An individual's fitness is evaluated on the basis of the observed population matrix $P(t)$. The quantum update operator used is based on quantum rotation gates [63]. It rotates state vectors in the quantum gene state space [63]. In Algorithm 5, qubit individuals in a population of individuals $Q(t)$ are updated by the application of some quantum gates. The update procedure was discussed in Section 4.2.

4.5.1 Complexity analysis of the quantum-inspired evolutionary algorithm

The parameter settings used with the QIEA are as follows: a quantum population size (Q) of 20, a maximum number of generations (G) of 100, a chromosome length (L) of 6 multiplied by the number of parameter (K) (i.e., $6 \times 3 = 18$), and number of parameters equal to the number of scaling factors (K) of 3 ($K1$, $K2$, $K3$). Moreover, the termination criterion used is equal to the maximum generation (G) and the quantum update operator is considered to be the quantum rotation gate (U). Thus the worst case for the computational complexity of the proposed QIEA for optimization of the scaling factors problem is analyzed as follows:

- To generate the initial quantum population, the computational complexity of the QIEA is $O(G \times Q \times L)$.
- For the quantum state measurement by observation of each qubit in each quantum chromosome, the time complexity of the QIEA is $O(G \times Q \times L)$.
- For evaluation of the fitness of each chromosome in the quantum population (Q) the time complexity of the QIEA is $O(G \times Q \times K)$.
- The time complexity of the QIEA for selection of the best or fittest solution using the roulette-wheel selection process is $O(G \times Q)$.
- The complexity of the QIEA for the updating of the quantum population (Q) using a quantum rotation gate (U) is $O(G \times Q \times L)$.
- Hence the overall execution time complexity of the proposed QIEA is $O(G \times Q \times L)$ in the worst case.
- If all of the above parameters are constant and their values are known for the proposed problem, then the best-case time complexity of the QIEA is also constant, and is $O(1)$.

5 PROPOSED METHOD

The GA, QIGA, or QIEA is used in the current work to improve the performance for solving complex optimization task. The optimization approaches are used to select proper scaling factors for the DWT-DCT-SVD watermarking process. The proposed system is applied on various medical images to embed the watermark. We performed the watermarking procedure by gathering the image embedding with the optimal scaling factors using the GA, QIGA, and QIEA for secure biomedical image authentication and information hiding. The DWT-DCT-SVD-based proposed watermarking approach using the optimized scaling factors can be outlined as described in the following.

5.1 WATERMARK EMBEDDING

The watermark is embedded in various medical images by means of the DWT-DCT-SVD-based approach. Fig. 3 demonstrates the watermark embedding process, where three different gray watermarks having the same size as the original image are embedded into different DWT subbands; namely, the HH, HL, and LH subbands. Consequently, the DCT and SVD of the cover image using three embedding factors are performed.

The robustness level of the watermarking technique can be improved by optimization of the embedding factors used for singular value modification for the finest results. The optimum embedding factors set is selected for singular value modification by separate use of the GA, QIGA, or QIEA. Because of the variation in the size/resolution of the cover image, the optimal value of the embedding factor should vary from one cover image to another. Thus the security and robustness of the proposed algorithm may be affected by the watermark strength.

The watermark embedding procedure is given in Algorithm 6.

ALGORITHM 6 WATERMARK EMBEDDING PROCEDURE STEPS

Start
Calculate the original gray cover image size.
Select three grayscale watermark images of the same size as the cover image.
Decompose the cover image into four subbands, LL_1, LH_1, HL_1, and HH_1, by applying the DWT.
Apply the DCT on the HH_1, HL_1, and LH_1 subbands individually.
Apply the SVD on all the resultant subbands.
Decompose each watermark image into four subbands (LL_1, LH_1, HL_1, and HH_1) by applying the DWT.
Apply the DCT on all subbands of the decomposed watermark images.
Apply SVD on each resultant subband after applying the DCT on the four subbands of the decomposed watermarks.
Apply both the DWT and the DCT on the image using optimal scaling factors ($K1$, $K2$, $K3$).
Singular values of all the resultant subbands obtained from the cover image are modified using the singular value of the corresponding HH_1 subbands of the watermark images.
Generate the final watermarked image by using the inverse DCT followed by the inverse DWT.
End

After transmission of the watermarked image, the reverse process is required at the receiver terminal. Thus a watermark extraction procedure is required at the receiver as described in the next section.

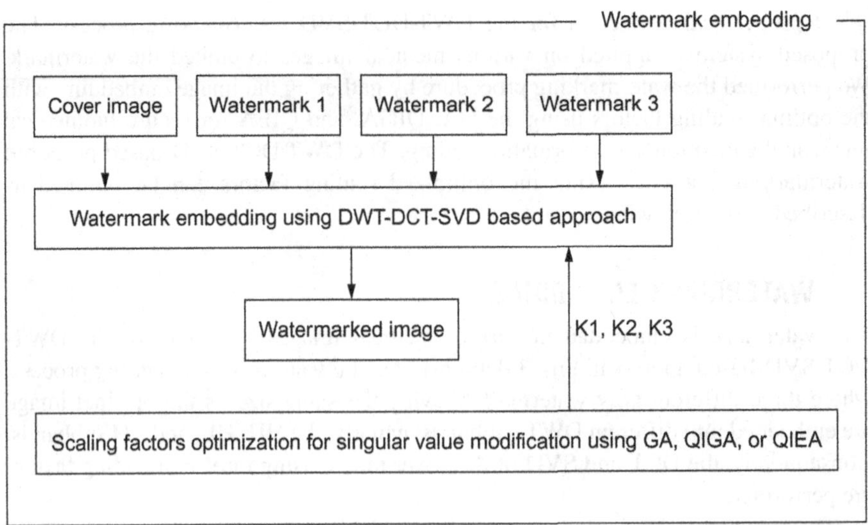

FIG. 3

Proposed method of watermark embedding. *DCT*, discrete cosine transform; *DWT*, discrete wavelet transform; *GA*, genetic algorithm; *QIEA*, quantum-inspired evolutionary algorithm; *QIGA*, quantum-inspired genetic algorithm; *SVD*, singular value decomposition.

5.2 WATERMARK EXTRACTION

The watermark extraction approach has the same embedding algorithm steps, but at the receiver terminal. Fig. 4 illustrates the proposed watermark extraction block diagram. The input to this process is the watermarked image. The DWT-DCT-SVD combination is used to extract the watermark with the optimized values of the scaling factors of the singular value modification.

The watermark extraction procedure is given in Algorithm 7.

ALGORITHM 7 WATERMARK EXTRACTION PROCEDURE STEPS

Start
Decompose the watermarked image into four subbands by applying the DWT on the LL_1, LH_1, HL_1, and HH_1 subbands.
Apply the DCT on the HH_1, LH_1, and HL_1 subbands.
Apply SVD on the resultant subbands.
Modify the singular values of the watermarked image using the optimal scaling factors ($K1$, $K2$, $K3$) to extract the watermarks from the modified singular values of the watermarked image.
Apply the inverse DCT to extract the watermark image from the watermarked image and then apply the inverse DWT on the resultant image.
End

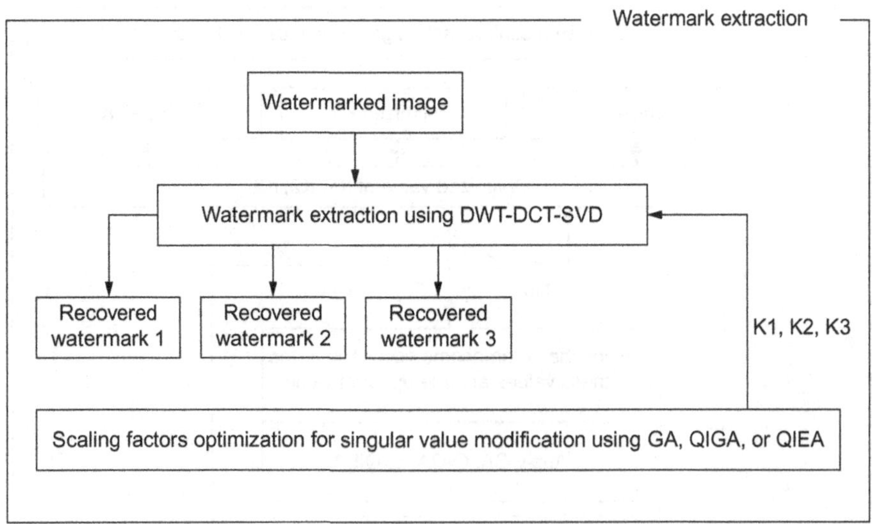

FIG. 4

Proposed method of watermark extraction. *DCT*, discrete cosine transform; *DWT*, discrete wavelet transform; *GA*, genetic algorithm; *QIEA*, quantum-inspired evolutionary algorithm; *QIGA*, quantum-inspired genetic algorithm; *SVD*, singular value decomposition.

An optimization procedure is used in both the watermark embedding at the original source of the image and in the watermark extraction at the receiver end. There follows a detailed description of the optimization phase to determine the optimal scaling factors with use of the GA, QIGA, or QIEA.

5.3 GENERATION OF OPTIMAL SCALING FACTORS WITH USE OF THE GENETIC ALGORITHM, QUANTUM-INSPIRED GENETIC ALGORITHM, OR QUANTUM-INSPIRED EVOLUTIONARY ALGORITHM

In the current work the watermark strength is assessed with three embedding factors set; namely, $K1$, $K2$, and $K3$. Manual selection of these factors for optimality is a complicated and challenging process, and thus they are used for singular value modification-based optimization algorithms. This process requires an automated selection strategy of embedding factors in an optimized approach. The selection of the optimal embedding factors for singular value modification is performed with use of optimization algorithms (GA, QIGA, or QIEA). The PSNR is used as a fitness function for optimization. A block diagram of the scaling factor optimization process using the GA, QIGA, or QIEA during the watermark embedding in various medical images is illustrated in Fig. 5.

The steps used for scaling factor optimization with any of the proposed optimization algorithms (GA, QIGA, or QIEA) are given in Algorithm 8.

Figs. 6 and 7 provides the detailed explanations of the proposed algorithm for watermark embedding and watermark extraction respectively.

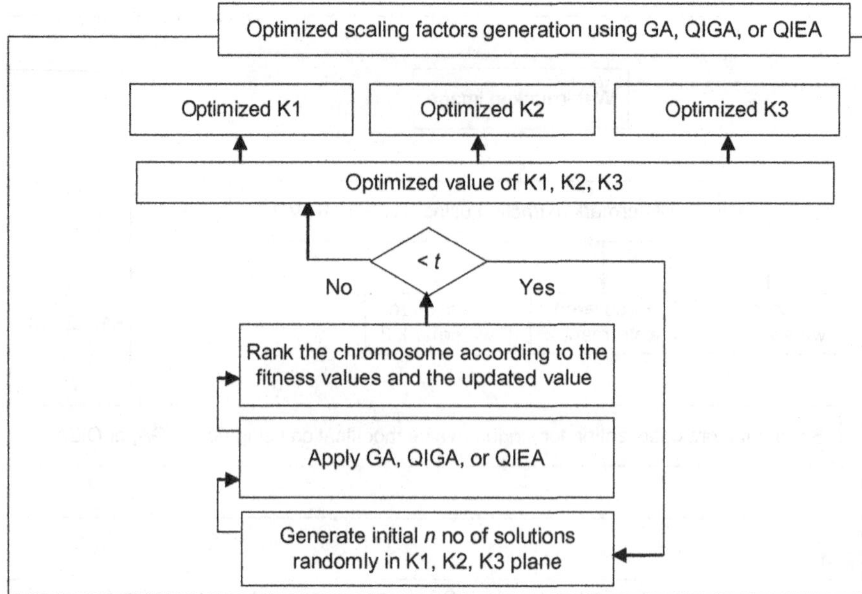

FIG. 5

Optimized scaling factor generation for watermark embedding. *GA*, genetic algorithm; *QIEA*, quantum-inspired evolutionary algorithm; *QIGA*, quantum-inspired genetic algorithm.

ALGORITHM 8 DETERMINATION OF THE OPTIMAL VALUES OF THE SCALING FACTORS BY MEANS OF THE GA, QIGA, OR QIEA

```
Begin
Generate initial population of n chromosomes (quantum chromosome) of K1, K2, and K3 within
a specific range
Calculate the best fitness and corresponding best chromosome from the
initial population by applying the watermarking algorithm
while t < MAX_GENERATION do
   Apply the optimization algorithm (GA, QIGA, or QIEA)
   Calculate the best fitness_l chromosome_g of the tth generation
   if fitness_l > fitness_g then
      fitness_g = fitness_l
      chromosome_g = chromosome_l
   end if
   Update the population according to the chromosome and optimization algorithm
   t ← t + 1
end while
End
Optimal scaling factors are determined by the final value of chromosome_g (K1, K2, K3)
End
```

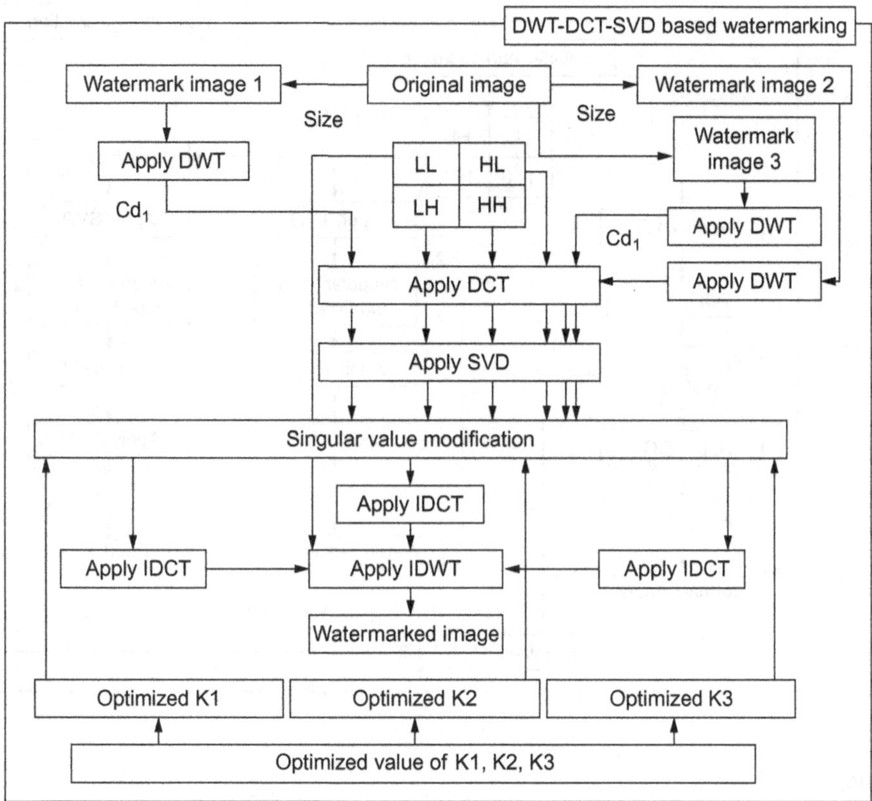

FIG. 6

Detailed description of the proposed method for watermark embedding. *DCT*, discrete cosine transform; *DWT*, discrete wavelet transform; *QIEA*, quantum-inspired evolutionary algorithm; *IDCT*, inverse discrete cosine transform; *IDWT*, inverse discrete wavelet transform; *SVD*, singular value decomposition.

6 RESULTS AND DISCUSSION

The proposed method was implemented in MATLAB 7.0.1. The proposed algorithm was successfully tested on various medical datasets; namely, microscopic, ultrasound, and magnetic resonance imaging dataset images. The ultrasound and magnetic resonance imaging dataset images can be found at http://vimeo.com/groups/ultrasound and http://www.medinfo.cs.ucy.ac.cy/, and the microscopic dataset images were obtained from the Anatomy Department Laboratory, Faculty of Medicine, Tanta University, Egypt. Three different logos for the watermark embedding process are illustrated in Fig. 8.

Samples from the original dataset images used are illustrated in Figs. 9–11.

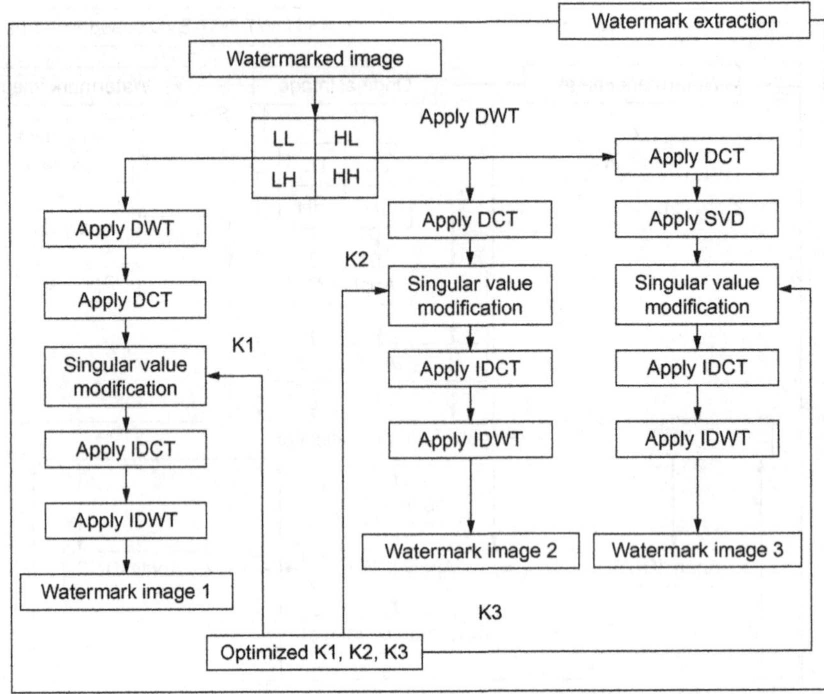

FIG. 7

Detailed description of the proposed method for watermark extraction. *DCT*, discrete cosine transform; *DWT*, discrete wavelet transform; *QIEA*, quantum-inspired evolutionary algorithm; *IDCT*, inverse discrete cosine transform; *IDWT*, inverse discrete wavelet transform; *SVD*, singular value decomposition.

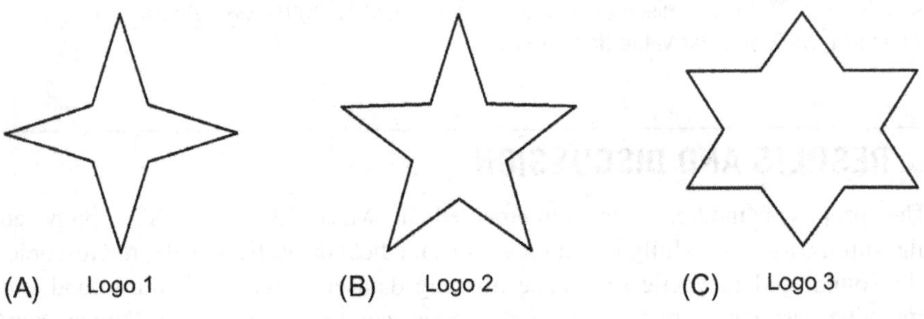

FIG. 8

The logos used for the embedding process. (A) Logo 1; (B) Logo 2; (C) Logo 3;

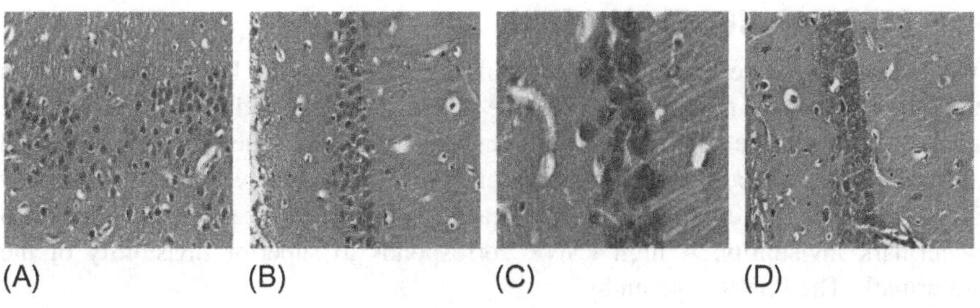
(A) (B) (C) (D)

FIG. 9

The microscopic medical images.

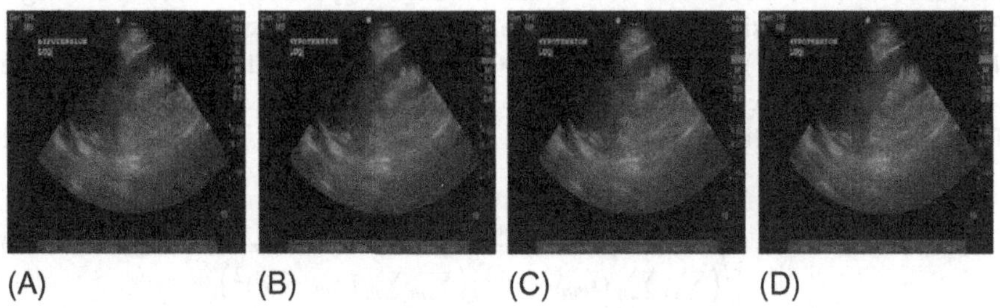
(A) (B) (C) (D)

FIG. 10

The ultrasound medical images.

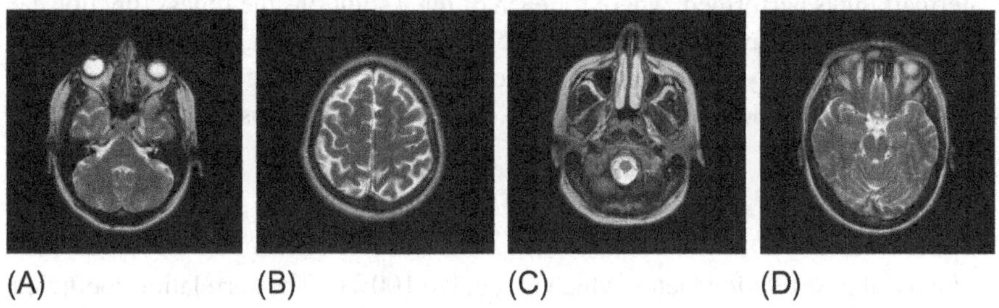
(A) (B) (C) (D)

FIG. 11

The magnetic resonance imaging medical images.

6.1 PERFORMANCE EVALUATION

We assessed the watermarked image quality by measuring the PSNR. The PSNR is the ratio between the maximum achievable power of a signal and the corrupting noise power that affects the reliability of the signal representation. Therefore it can be used as a performance metric to find out the perceptual transparency of the watermarked image regarding the cover image. Consequently, the PSNR measures the embedded watermark invisibility. A high PSNR corresponds to superior invisibility of the watermark. The PSNR is given by

$$PSNR = \frac{XYmax_{x,y}P_{x,y}^2}{\sum_{x,y}(P_{x,y} - \bar{P}_{x,y})^2)}, \tag{14}$$

where X and Y are the number of rows and columns respectively in the input image, $P_{x,y}$ is the original signal, and $\bar{P}_{x,y}$ is the watermarked image. The similarity of the recovered logo (x') to the original logo (x) can be determined by application of the standard correlation coefficient (C) when the logo embedding process is complete. This correlation coefficient is given by

$$C = \frac{\sum_m \sum_n (x_{mn} - x\prime)(y_{mn} - y\prime)}{\sqrt{\left(\sum_m \sum_n (x_{mn} - x\prime)^2\right)\left(\sum_m \sum_n (y_{mn} - y\prime)^2\right)}}, \tag{15}$$

where y and y' are the transforms of x and x' respectively, and m is the size of the image. With use of any of the proposed quantization algorithms (GA, QIGA, or QIEA), a set of n distinct solutions is dislocated randomly in the three-dimensional ($K1$, $K2$, and $K3$) plane search space (S) within a specific range. For each solution, watermarking is performed, where for each of the n solutions the fitness function can be calculated with use of the PSNR and the C values. Afterward, the solution set with the best light intensity (fitness value) is chosen and stored as the best solution for the scaling factors obtained ($K1$, $K2$, and $K3$). The following fitness function is used:

$$FT = PSNR + \rho, \tag{16}$$

where ρ is the correlation factor, which is equal to $100 \times C$. The correlation coefficient (C) is normally within the range of 0 to 1, and thus C is multiplied by 100, whereas PSNRs [71] may reach 100. The simulation results indicated proper selection of this fitness function. The population is updated according to the best-fit chromosome and the new population is updated accordingly to obtain the best solution. This process is repeated for t iterations, and finally the optimized $K1$, $K2$, and $K3$ values (scaling factors) are obtained. The following result sets are obtained for a population size of 20, where the maximum number of iterations is 100 and $K1$, $K2$, and $K3$ range between 0 and 1.

6.2 COMPARATIVE STUDY OF THE CONVERGENCE GRAPHS

A performance comparison of the three optimization algorithms—the GA, the QIGA, and the QIEA—with respect to the number of iterations versus the fitness function was conducted. Fig. 12 shows the graph of the number of iterations versus the fitness for the three algorithms with the images in Fig. 9. The same convergence graphs are illustrated in Figs. 13 and 14 for the medical images in Figs. 10 and 11 respectively.

Fig. 13 illustrates that the GA has the lowest fitness value, which is the worst case, whereas the QIGA achieved the highest fitness value compared with the other optimization algorithms. Fig. 14 illustrates that the GA has the lowest fitness value, which is the worst case, whereas the QIEA achieved the highest fitness value compared with the other optimization algorithms.

The preceding results are tabulated in Tables 2, 3, and 4, which correspond with Figs. 12, 13, and 14 respectively. Additionally, Table 2–4 contain detailed results for the optimized scaling factor values that were used further during the watermarking process. In addition, the PSNR, the fitness values, and the correlation between the original logo and the extracted logo are also reported.

From these extensive results, it is established that both the QIEA and the QIGA achieved almost outstanding results compared with the GA. Additionally, in terms of the average execution time in minutes, a comparison was conducted for each of the medical image datasets (see Table 5), where the processor used to run the proposed program had the following specifications: i5-3230M processor 2.60 GHz, 4GB RAM. MATLAB version R2012b was used.

Table 5 establishes that use of the QIEA as the optimization algorithm required the least amount of execution time compared with use of either the GA or the QIGA. The preceding experimental results revealed that the QC-based watermarking system outperformed the GA in terms of achieving the maximum fitness value with faster convergence. This results in a lower average execution time compared that when the GA is used for optimization. Consequently, the proposed system based on the QIEA and QIGA reported an accurate authentication for information exchange accompanied by robustness and imperceptibility compared with the system based on the GA. However, as a future task, different watermark structures can be considered, and other QC approaches can be applied.

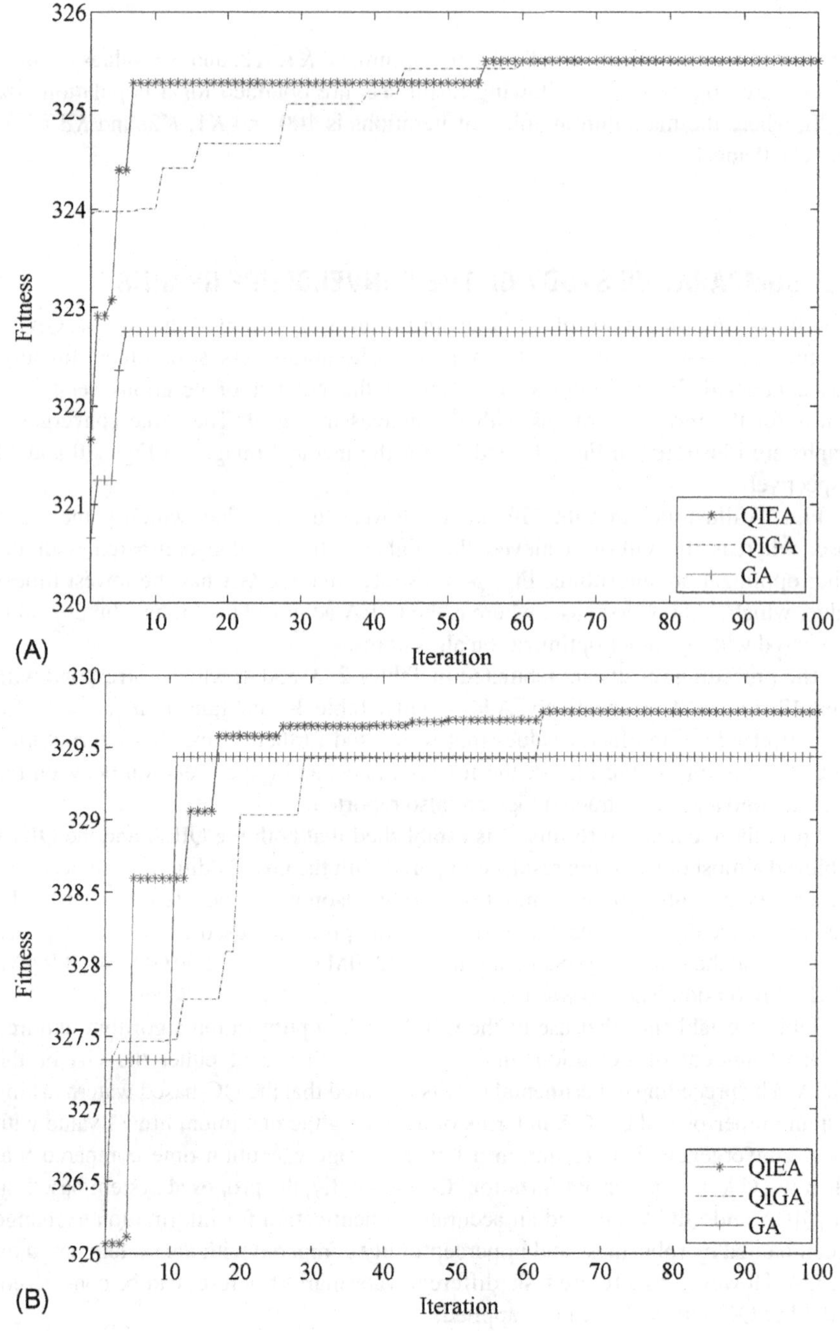

FIG. 12

The convergence graphs of the number of iterations versus the fitness obtained with the images in Fig. 9 by application of the genetic algorithm (GA), the quantum-inspired genetic algorithm (QIGA), and the quantum-inspired evolutionary algorithm (QIEA): (A) for the image in Fig. 9A; (B) for the image in Fig. 9B;

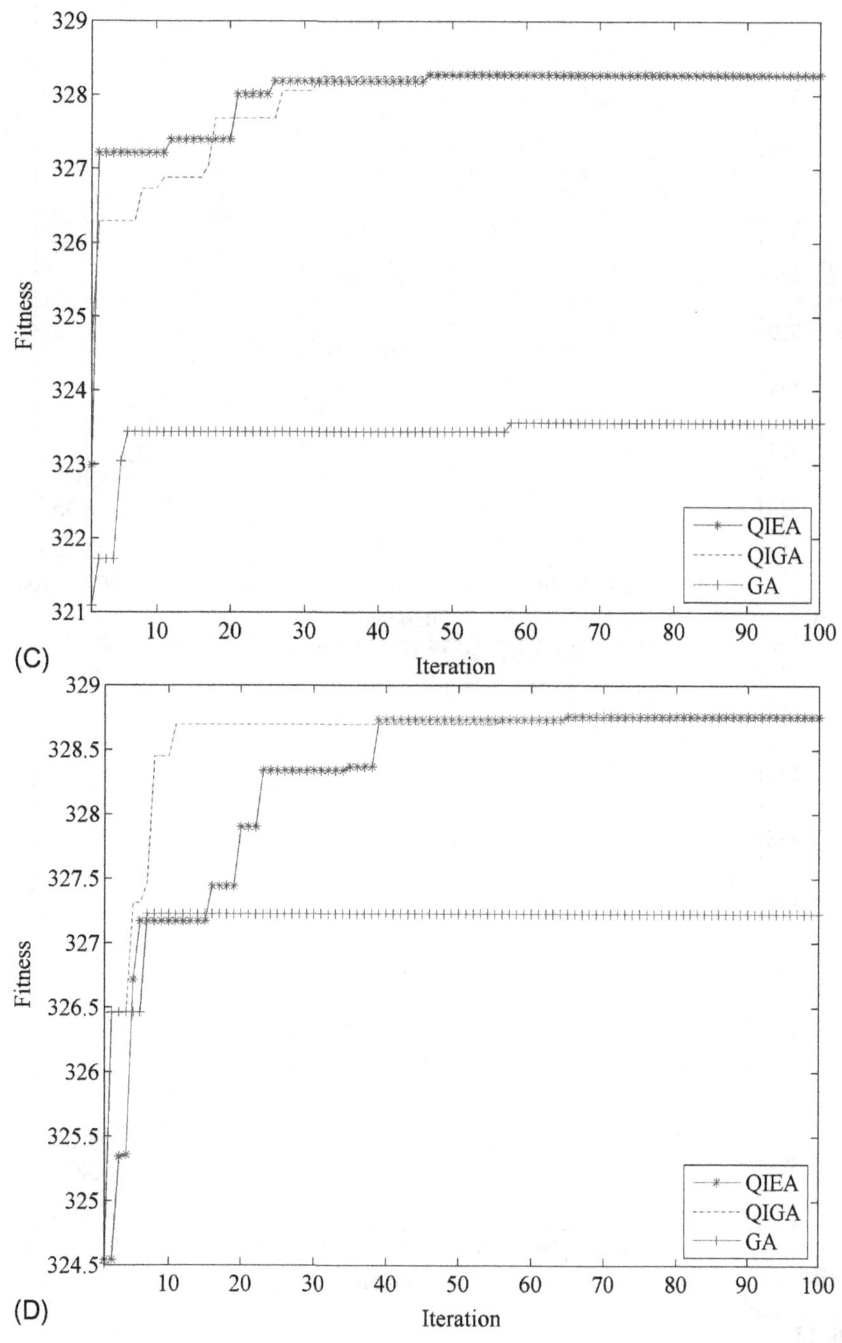

FIG. 12, CONT'D

(C) for the image in Fig. 9C; (D) for the image in Fig. 9D.

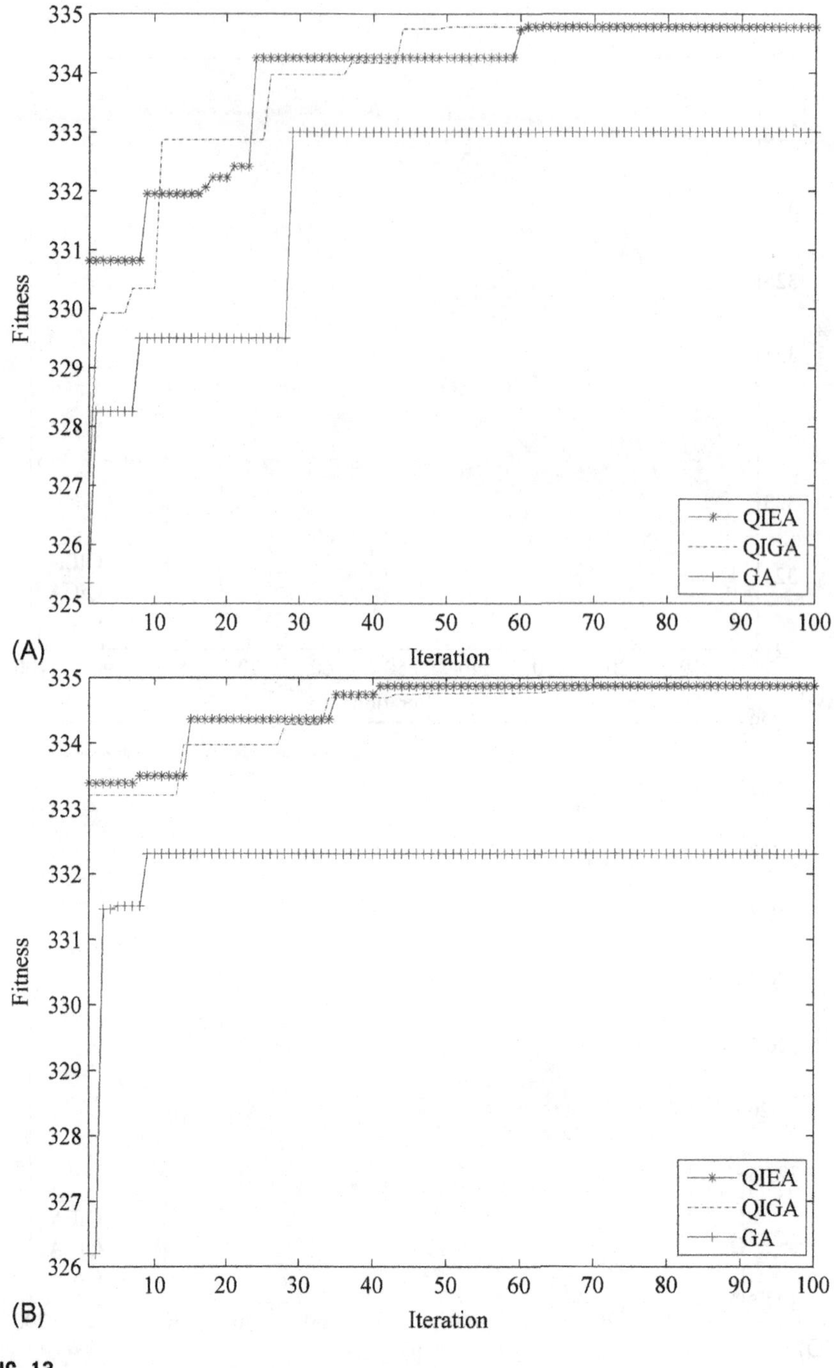

FIG. 13

The convergence graphs of the number of iteration versus the fitness obtained with the images in Fig. 10 by application of the genetic algorithm (GA), the quantum-inspired genetic algorithm (QIGA), and the quantum-inspired evolutionary algorithm (QIEA): (A) for the image in Fig. 10A; (B) for the image in Fig. 10B;

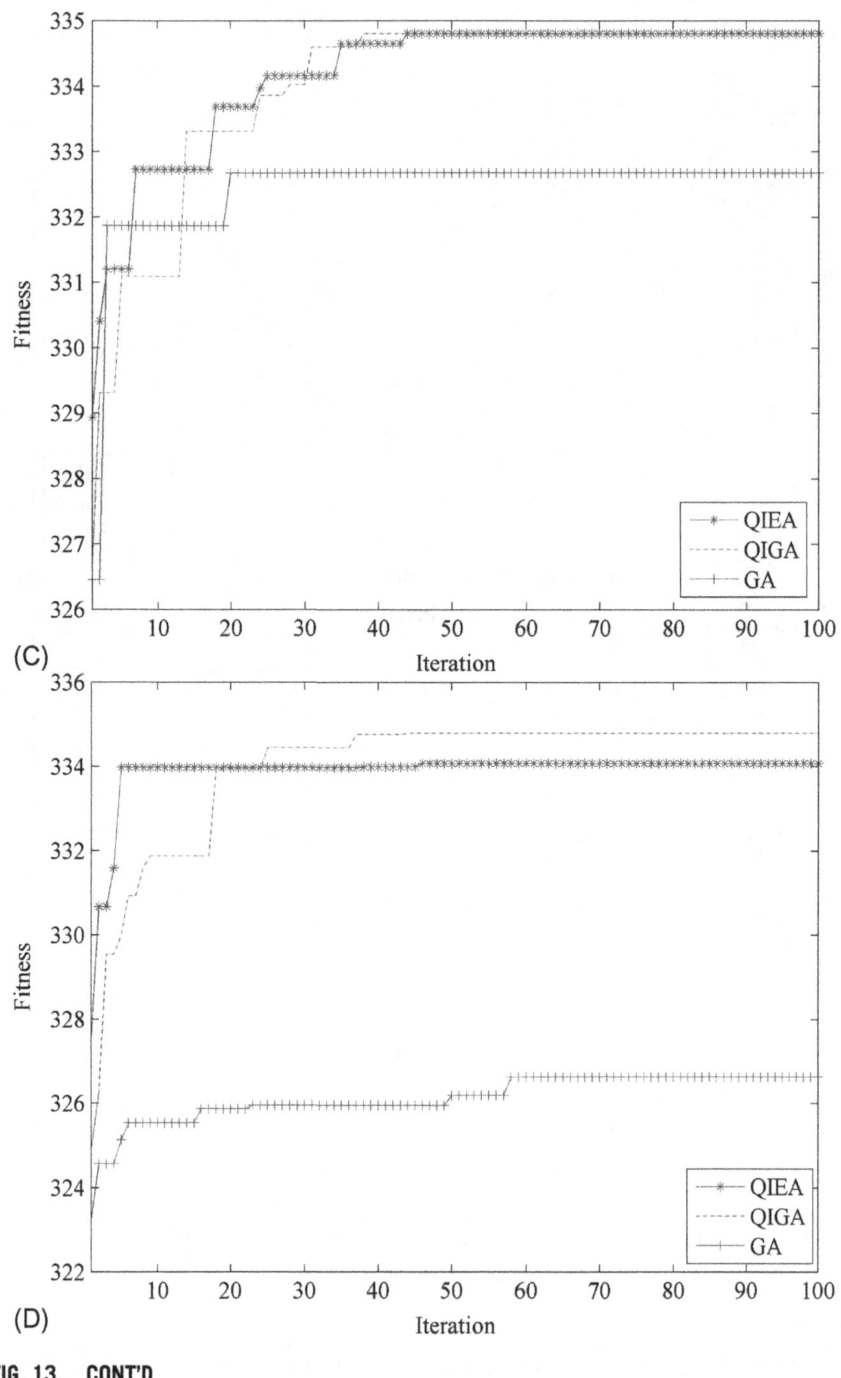

FIG. 13, CONT'D

(C) for the image in Fig. 10C; (D) for the image in Fig. 10D.

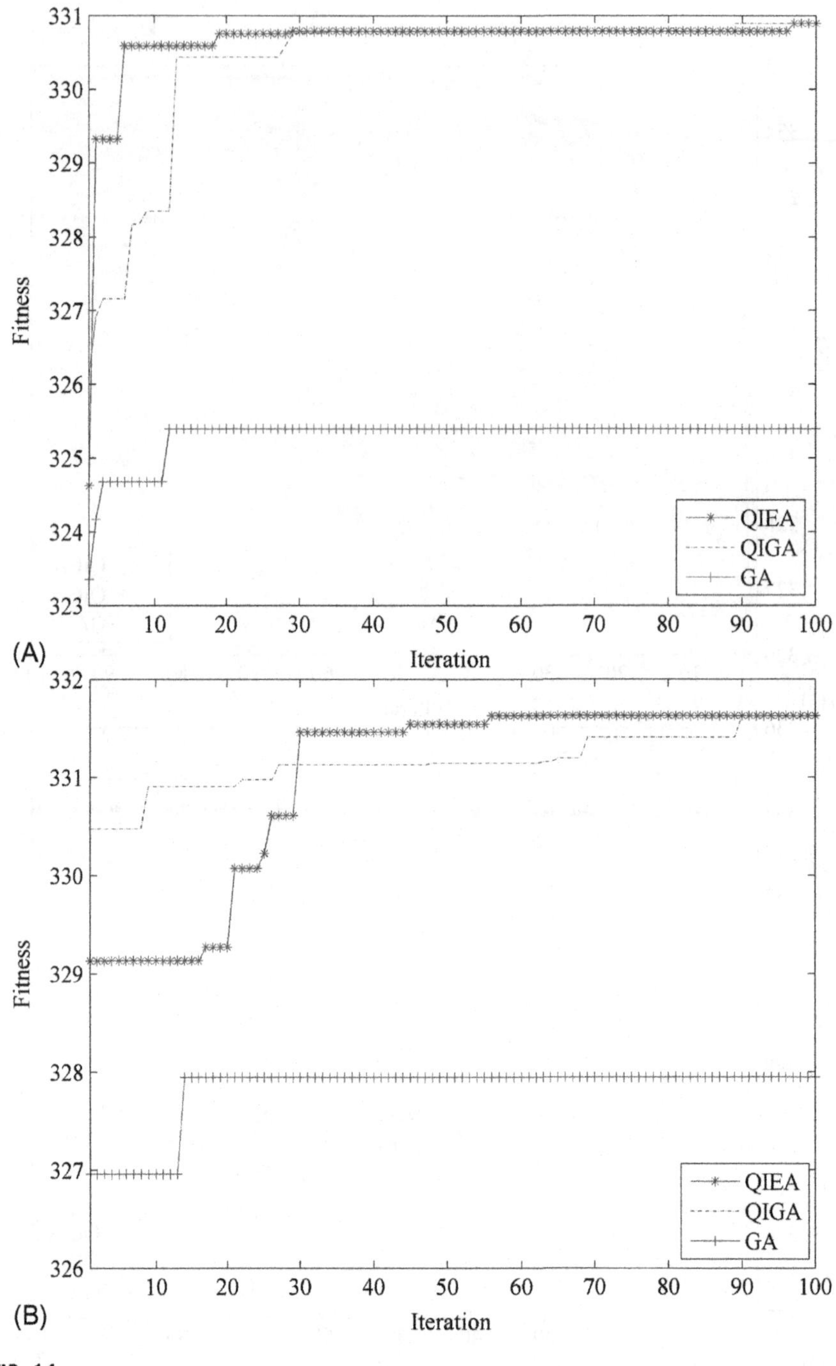

FIG. 14

The convergence graphs of the number of iterations versus the fitness obtained with the images in Fig. 11 by application of the genetic algorithm (GA), the quantum-inspired genetic algorithm (QIGA), and the quantum-inspired evolutionary algorithm (QIEA): (A) for the image in Fig. 11A; (B) for the image in Fig. 11B;

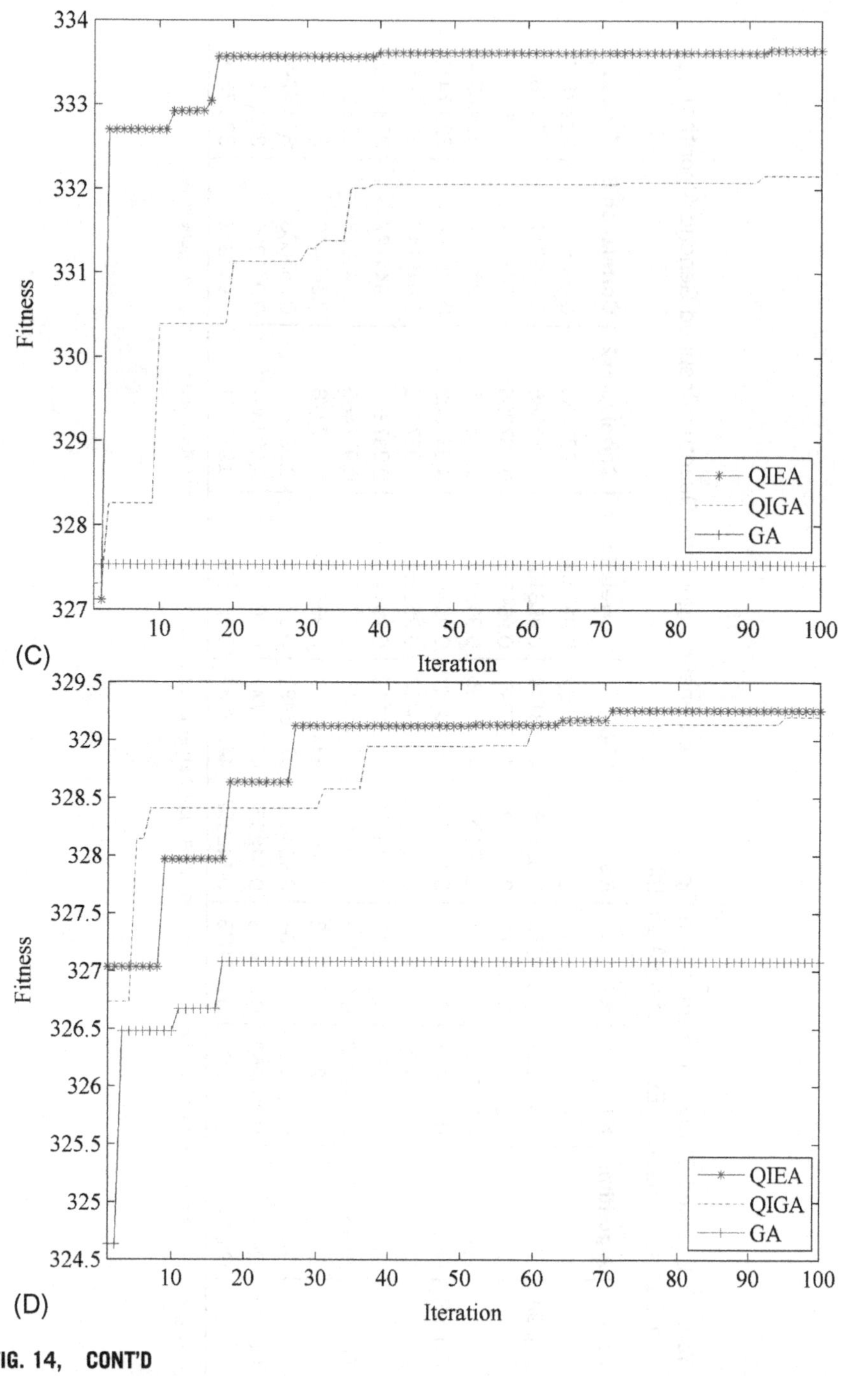

FIG. 14, CONT'D

(C) for the image in Fig. 11C; (D) for the image in Fig. 11D.

Table 2 Detailed Study of the Images in Fig. 9 With the Genetic Algorithm, Quantum-Inspired Genetic Algorithm, and Quantum-Inspired Evolutionary Algorithm

Image	Algorithm	*K*1	*K*2	*K*3	PSNR	Correlation 1	Correlation 2	Correlation 3	Fitness
	GA	0.814724	0.09754	0.632359	34.72722	0.987428	0.937263	0.955599	322.7562
Fig. 9A	QIGA	0.492063	0.015873	0.301587	40.53144	0.968161	0.937685	0.943711	325.4871
	QIEA	0.507937	0.015873	0.301587	40.36397	0.969845	0.937853	0.943712	325.5050
	GA	0.347496	0.004442	0.174261	43.99135	0.965443	0.935385	0.953592	329.4334
Fig. 9B	QIGA	0.317460	0.015873	0.126984	45.23463	0.958858	0.937508	0.948747	329.7459
	QIEA	0.317460	0.015873	0.126984	45.23463	0.958858	0.937508	0.948747	329.7459
	GA	0.970593	0.157613	0.278498	36.21119	0.991415	0.937352	0.944727	323.5605
Fig. 9C	QIGA	0.380952	0.015873	0.190476	43.11618	0.970787	0.937466	0.943178	328.2592
	QIEA	0.349206	0.015873	0.174603	43.84667	0.966080	0.937778	0.940449	328.2774
	GA	0.531102	0.032261	0.494025	37.46482	0.977517	0.937627	0.955003	324.4795
Fig. 9D	QIGA	0.380952	0.015873	0.142857	43.7574	0.965217	0.937301	0.947215	328.7307
	QIEA	0.349206	0.015873	0.142857	44.32887	0.959634	0.937441	0.947213	328.7576

GA, genetic algorithm; PSNR, peak signal to noise ratio; QIEA, quantum-inspired evolutionary algorithm; QIGA, quantum-inspired genetic algorithm.

Table 3 Detailed Study of the Images in Fig. 10 With the Genetic Algorithm, Quantum-Inspired Genetic Algorithm, and Quantum-Inspired Evolutionary Algorithm

Image	Algorithm	*K*1	*K*2	*K*3	PSNR	Correlation 1	Correlation 2	Correlation 3	Fitness
	GA	0.326574	0.041599	0.093234	45.39362	0.985736	0.943132	0.94716	332.9963
Fig. 10A	QIGA	0.206349	0.015873	0.079365	48.6275	0.971932	0.944768	0.944801	334.7776
	QIEA	0.206349	0.015873	0.079365	48.6275	0.971932	0.944768	0.944801	334.7776
	GA	0.205614	0.002601	0.260369	44.0912	0.972391	0.952542	0.957192	332.3037
Fig. 10B	QIGA	0.190476	0.015873	0.095238	48.71937	0.967411	0.944443	0.949657	334.8705
	QIEA	0.190476	0.015873	0.095238	48.71937	0.967411	0.944443	0.949657	334.8705
	GA	0.247121	0.054295	0.178478	45.35434	0.976513	0.941407	0.955283	332.6745
Fig. 10C	QIGA	0.174603	0.015873	0.079365	49.57039	0.961783	0.944525	0.945995	334.8007
	QIEA	0.174603	0.015873	0.079365	43.57039	0.961783	0.944525	0.945995	334.8007
	GA	0.970593	0.157613	0.278498	37.2429	0.995293	0.942605	0.955983	326.6310
Fig. 10D	QIGA	0.206349	0.015873	0.079365	48.6279	0.971058	0.944643	0.945920	334.7900
	QIEA	0.253968	0.015873	0.126984	46.41556	0.979485	0.943842	0.953324	334.0807

GA, genetic algorithm; PSNR, peak signal to noise ratio; QIEA, quantum-inspired evolutionary algorithm; QIGA, quantum-inspired genetic algorithm.

Table 4 Detailed Study of the Images in Fig. 11 With the Genetic Algorithm, Quantum-Inspired Genetic Algorithm, and Quantum-Inspired Evolutionary Algorithm

Image	Algorithm	*K*1	*K*2	*K*3	PSNR	Correlation 1	Correlation 2	Correlation 3	Fitness
	GA	0.664113	0.156113	0.500471	37.34927	0.986698	0.937409	0.956365	325.3965
Fig. 11A	QIGA	0.285714	0.015873	0.126984	46.47312	0.958226	0.93761	0.948353	330.8920
	QIEA	0.285714	0.015873	0.126984	46.47312	0.958226	0.93761	0.948353	330.8920
	GA	0.546789	0.028699	0.320592	40.15498	0.984159	0.936008	0.957732	327.9448
Fig. 11B	QIGA	0.301587	0.015873	0.095238	46.6347	0.958332	0.938562	0.953035	331.6277
	QIEA	0.301587	0.015873	0.095238	46.6347	0.958332	0.938562	0.953035	331.6277
	GA	0.290846	0.014978	0.228960	44.39386	0.942911	0.937587	0.950908	327.5344
Fig. 11C	QIGA	0.285714	0.015873	0.095238	47.00264	0.966501	0.936022	0.949017	332.1567
	QIEA	0.222222	0.015873	0.095238	48.62152	0.963561	0.93552	0.951147	333.6443
	GA	0.396573	0.005322	0.361729	41.02205	0.969489	0.93497	0.956090	327.0770
Fig. 11D	QIGA	0.349206	0.015873	0.142857	44.92650	0.961435	0.937349	0.943964	329.2013
	QIEA	0.349206	0.015873	0.158730	44.69458	0.961435	0.937612	0.946571	329.2564

GA, genetic algorithm; PSNR, peak signal to noise ratio; QIEA, quantum-inspired evolutionary algorithm; QIGA, quantum-inspired genetic algorithm.

Table 5 Average Execution Time for the Genetic Algorithm, Quantum-Inspired Genetic Algorithm, and Quantum-Inspired Evolutionary Algorithm

Dataset	Execution Time (min)		
	GA	QIGA	QIEA
Microscopic	6.5524	11.5196	5.5201
Ultrasound	6.0773	11.5003	5.3015
MRI	7.5952	11.7481	5.7238

GA, genetic algorithm; MRI, magnetic resonance imaging QIEA, quantum-inspired evolutionary algorithm; QIGA, quantum-inspired genetic algorithm.

7 CONCLUSION

The value of $\Delta\theta_i$ should be fine-tuned as per the application problem domain. A high value of $\Delta\theta_i$ can increase the divergence rate and hence the convergence rate decreases or the solution may converge to a premature local optimum. A fine-tuned magnitude of $\Delta\theta_i$ affects the speed of the convergence. The magnitude of is $\Delta\theta_i$ must be maintained between 0.001π and 0.05π.

Modern hospitals investigate and monitor patients through various digital modalities, which produce various immeasurable amounts of medical images/files. In addition, technological progress facilities transmission of patients' medical information. Therefore, the authenticity of the medical images is an urgent challenging issue to guarantee that the image related to the specific proper patient is not modified (integrity check) and is safely transferred.

Digital watermarking is being used in many fields for security, such as in broadcasting, forensic tracking, Internet monitoring, authentication, copy protection, copyright transfer, and e-commerce applications. In medical applications, to guarantee secure transfer of patient data, medical images, and reports, digital watermarking can embed a watermark signal/image into the host data for copyright protection and authenticity.

Recently, researchers have been interested in improving the performance of the watermarking techniques. One approach to achieve this goal is to consider the watermarking process as an optimization problem. In the current work, a GA, a QIGA, and a QIEA were employed to optimize the scaling factor for embedding, in order to support the hybrid DWT-DCT-SVD-based approach of watermarking. We proposed an authentication and secure medical image scheme to enhance robustness, imperceptibility, and payload of medical images that can be transmitted through the Internet. Three logos were used for the embedding watermark in three different medical image datasets—namely, microscopic, ultrasound, and magnetic resonance imaging data sets. A comparative study of the three optimization algorithms was conducted in terms of the convergence, PSNR, fitness values, and execution time. The experimental results established the superiority of both the QIEA and the QIGA over the GA.

ACKNOWLEDGMENTS

We appreciate the efforts of Ahmed Salah Ashour, Department of Human Anatomy and Embryology, Faculty of Medicine, Tanta University, Egypt, in providing us with the rats hippocampus microscopic dataset.

REFERENCES

[1] A. Manu-Marin, E.P.R. Center, Telemedicine as an alternative model for delivering healthcare services: preliminary results of the MultiMED project, Mod. Med. 22 (4) (2015) 342–345.

[2] Z. Kirtava, T. Gegenava, M. Gegenava, G. Simonia, I. Andronikashvili, e-Health/m-health applications for cardiac patients telemonitoring, VI Latin American Congress on Biomedical Engineering CLAIB 2014, Paran, Argentina, 2015, pp. 825–828, http://dx.doi.org/10.1007-978-3-319-13117-7-210.

[3] D. Gans, J. Kralewski, T. Hammons, B. Dowd, Medical groups adoption of electronic health records and information systems, Health Aff. 24 (5) (2005) 1323–1333, http://dx.doi.org/10.1377/hlthaff.24.5.1323.

[4] C. Wen, M.F. Yeh, K.C. Chang, R.G. Lee, Real-time ECG telemonitoring system design with mobile phone platform, Measurement 41 (4) (2008) 463–470, http://dx.doi.org/10.1016/j.measurement.2006.12.006.

[5] D. Anand, U. Niranjan, Watermarking medical images with patient information, in: Proceedings of the 20th Annual International Conference of the IEEE Engineering in Medicine and Biology Society, 1998, pp. 703–706, http://dx.doi.org/10.1109/IEMBS.1998.745518.

[6] R. Schoenberg, C. Safran, Internet based repository of medical records that retains patient confidentiality, BMJ 311 (7270) (2000) 1199–1203.

[7] D. Masys, D. Baker, A. Butros, K.E. Cowles, Giving patients access to their medical records via the Internet, J. Am. Med. Inform. Assoc. 9 (2) (2002) 181–191, http://dx.doi.org/10.1197/jamia.M1005.

[8] S.A.K. Mostafa, N. El-sheimy, A.S. Tolba, F.M. Abdelkader, H.M. Elhindy, Wavelet packets-based blind watermarking for medical image management, Open Biomed. Eng. J. 4 (2010) 93–98, http://dx.doi.org/10.2174/1874120701004010093.

[9] G. Coatrieux, L. Lecornu, C. Roux, B. Sankur, A review of image watermarking applications in healthcare, IEEE Eng. Med. Biol. Soc. 1 (2006) 4691–4694, http://dx.doi.org/10.1109/IEMBS.2006.259305.

[10] A. Giakoumaki, S. Pavlopoulos, D. Koutsouris, Multiple image watermarking applied to health information management, IEEE Trans. Inf. Technol. Biomed. 10 (4) (2006) 722–732, http://dx.doi.org/10.1109/TITB.2006.875655.

[11] N. Dharwadkar, B. Amberker, B. Supriya, P.B. Panchannavar, Reversible fragile medical image watermarking with zero distortion, in: International Conference on Computer Science and Communication Technology, 2010, http://dx.doi.org/10.1109/ICCCT.2010.5640444.

[12] J. Zain, A. Fauzi, A. Aziz, Clinical evaluation of watermarked medical images, in: Proceedings of the 28th IEEE EMBS Annual International Conference, 2006, pp. 5459–5462, http://dx.doi.org/10.1109/IEMBS.2006.260245.

[13] I. Cox, J. Kilian, F. Leighton, T. Shamoon, Secure spread spectrum watermarking for multimedia, IEEE Trans. Image Process. 6 (1997) 1673–1687, http://dx.doi.org/10.1109/83.650120.

[14] K. Tanaka, Y. Nakamura, K. Matsui, Embedding secret information into a dithered multi-level image, in: Proc. IEEE. Military Communications Conference, vol. 1, 1990, pp. 216–220, http://dx.doi.org/10.1109/MILCOM.1990.117416.

[15] W. Lu, W. Sun, H. Lu, Robust watermarking based on DWT and nonnegative matrix factorization, Comput. Electr. Eng. 35 (2009) 183–188, http://dx.doi.org/10.1016/j.compeleceng.2008.09.004.

[16] J. Hernandez, M. Amado, F. Perez-Gonzalez, DCT-domain watermarking techniques for still images: detector performance analysis and a new structure, IEEE Trans. Image Process. 9 (2000) 55–58, http://dx.doi.org/10.1109/83.817598.

[17] S. Maity, M. Kundu, Perceptually adaptive spread transform image watermarking scheme using Hadamard transform, Inf. Sci. 181 (2011) 450–465, http://dx.doi.org/10.1016/j.ins.2010.09.029.

[18] T. Tsui, X. Zhang, D. Androutsos, Colour image watermarking using multidimensional Fourier transforms, IEEE Trans. Inf. Forensics Secur. 3 (2008) 16–28, http://dx.doi.org/10.1109/TIFS.2007.916275.

[19] H. Yu, J. Fan, X. Zhang, A robust watermark algorithm based on Ridgelet transform and fuzzy c means, in: International Symposium on Information Engineering and Electronic Commerce, 2009, pp. 120–124, http://dx.doi.org/10.1109/IEEC.2009.30.

[20] D. Simitopoulos, D. Koutsonanos, M. Strintzis, Robust image watermarking based on generalized radon transformations, IEEE Trans. Circ. Syst. Video Technol. 13 (732) (2003) 745, http://dx.doi.org/10.1109/TCSVT.2003.815947.

[21] H. Qi, D. Zheng, J. Zhao, Human visual system based adaptive digital image watermarking, Signal Process. 88 (1) (2008) 174–188, http://dx.doi.org/10.1016-j.sigpro.2007.07.020.

[22] M.M. Soliman, A.E. Hassanien, H.M. Onsi, Bio-inspiring techniques in watermarking medical images: a review, in: Bio-inspiring Cyber Security and Cloud Services: Trends and Innovations, Springer, Berlin/Heidelberg, 2014, pp. 93–114, http://dx.doi.org/10.1007-978-3-662-43616-5-4.

[23] L.N.D. Castro, Fundamentals of Natural Computing: Basic Concepts, Algorithms, and Applications, CRC Press, Boca Raton, 2006, ISBN, 9781584886433.

[24] F.J. Rodriguez, C. Garcia-Martinez, M. Lozano, Hybrid metaheuristics based on evolutionary algorithms and simulated annealing taxonomy, comparison, and synergy test, IEEE Trans. Evol. Comput. 16 (6) (2012) 787–800, http://dx.doi.org/10.1109/TEVC.2012.2182773.

[25] I. Zelinka, Evolutionary algorithms: principles and applications, in: Wiley Encyclopedia of Electrical and Electronics Engineering, 2015, http://dx.doi.org/10.1002/047134608X.W8264.

[26] F.Y. Shih, Y.T. Wu, Robust watermarking and compression for medical images based on genetic algorithms, Inf. Sci. 175 (3) (2005) 200–216, http://dx.doi.org/10.1016/j.ins.2005.01.013.

[27] V. Aslantas, S. Ozer, S. Ozturk, Improving the performance of DCT-based fragile watermarking using intelligent optimization algorithms, Opt. Commun. 282 (14) (2009) 2806–2817, http://dx.doi.org/10.1016/j.optcom.2009.04.034.

[28] M.M. Soliman, A.H. Hassanien, N.I. Ghali, H.M. Onsi, An adaptive watermarking approach for medical imaging using swarm intelligent, Int. J. Smart Home 6 (1) (2012) 37–50.

[29] M. Arsalan, S.A. Malik, A. Khan, Intelligent reversible watermarking in integer wavelet domain for medical images, J. Syst. Softw. 85 (4) (2012) 883–894, http://dx.doi.org/10.1016/j.jss.2011.11.005.

[30] N. Dey, S. Samanta, S. Chakraborty, A. Das, S.S. Chaudhuri, J.S. Suri, Firefly algorithm for optimization of scaling factors during embedding of manifold medical information: an application in ophthalmology imaging, J. Med. Imaging Health Inf. 4 (3) (2014) 384–394.

[31] E. Ganic, A.M. Eskicioglu, Robust embedding of visual watermarks using discrete wavelet transform and singular value decomposition, J. Electron. Imaging 14 (2005), http://dx.doi.org/10.1117/1.2137650.

[32] H.C. Huang, J.S. Pan, Y.H. Huang, F.H. Wang, K.C. Huang, Progressive watermarking techniques using genetic algorithms, Circ. Syst. Signal Process. 26 (5) (2007) 671–687, http://dx.doi.org/10.1109/CCST.2003.1297536.

[33] K. Loukhaoukha, J.Y. Chouinard, M.H. Taieb, Multi-Objective genetic algorithm optimization for image watermarking based on singular value decomposition and lifting wavelet transform, Image Signal Process. (2010) 394–403, http://dx.doi.org/10.1007-978-3-642-13681-8-46.

[34] K. Ramanjaneyulu, K. Rajarajeswari, Wavelet-based oblivious image watermarking scheme using genetic algorithm, IET Image Process. 6 (2012) 364–373, http://dx.doi.org/10.1049/iet-ipr.2010.0347.

[35] C. Mingzhi, L. Yan, Z. Yajian, L. Min, A combined DWT and DCT watermarking scheme optimized using genetic algorithm, IET Image Process. 3 (2013) 299–305.

[36] N. Dey, S. Samanta, X.-S. Yang, A. Das, S.S. Chaudhuri, Optimisation of scaling factors in electrocardiogram signal watermarking using cuckoo search, Int. J. Bio-Inspired Comput. 5 (315) (2013), http://dx.doi.org/10.4304/jmm.8.3.299-305.

[37] M.M. Soliman, A.E. Hassanien, H.M. Onsi, An optimized approach for medical image watermarking, in: Bio-inspiring Cyber Security and Cloud Services: Trends and Innovations, 2014, pp. 71–91, http://dx.doi.org/10.1007-978-3-662-43616-5-3.

[38] A.K. Singh, M. Dave, A. Mohan, Hybrid technique for robust and imperceptible multiple watermarking using medical images, Multimed. Tools Appl. (2015) 1–21, http://dx.doi.org/10.1007/s11042-015-2754-7.

[39] A. Krishnamurthi, N. Venkateswaran, J. Valarmathi, Swarm optimization based dual transform algorithm for secure transaction of medical images, in: Proceedings of the 3rd International Conference on Frontiers of Intelligent Computing: Theory and Applications (FICTA) 2014, 2015, pp. 483–491, http://dx.doi.org/10.1007-978-3-319-12012-6-53.

[40] M. Ouhsain, A. Hamza, Image watermarking scheme using nonnegative matrix factorization and wavelet transform, Expert Syst. Appl. 36 (2) (2009) 2123–2129, http://dx.doi.org/10.1016/j.eswa.2007.12.046.

[41] T. Bhattacharya, N. Dey, S.R.B. Chaudhuri, A novel session based dual steganographic technique using DWT and spread spectrum, Int. J. Mod. Eng. Res. 1 (157) (2012).

[42] T. Bhattacharya, N. Dey, S.R.B. Chaudhuri, A session based multiple image hiding technique using DWT and DCT, Int. J. Comput. Appl. 38 (18) (2012).

[43] P. Mangaiyarkarasi, S. Arulselvi, A robust digital image watermarking technique based on DWT and Fastica, CIIT Int. J. Digit. Image Process. 4 (2) (2012) 100–105.

[44] M. Jiansheng, L. Sukang, T. Xiaomei, A digital watermarking algorithm based on DCT and DWT, in: International Symposium on Web Information Systems and Applications, WISA 2009, 2009.

[45] M. Eyadat, S. Vasikarla, Performance evaluation of an incorporated DCT block-based watermarking algorithm with human visual system model, Pattern Recognit. Lett. 26 (10) (2005) 1405–1411, http://dx.doi.org/10.1016/j.patrec.2004.11.027.

[46] N. Dey, B. Nandi, P. Das, A. Das, S.S. Chaudhuri, Retention of electrocardiogram features insignificantly devalorized as an effect of watermarking for a multimodal biometric authentication system, in: Advances in Biometrics for Secure Human Authentication and Recognition, 2013, p. 450, http://dx.doi.org/10.1201/b16247-10.

[47] A.K. Singh, M. Dave, A. Mohan, Hybrid technique for robust and imperceptible image watermarking in DWT-DCT-SVD domain, Natl. Acad. Sci. Lett. 37 (4) (2014) 351–358, http://dx.doi.org/10.1007/s40009-014-0241-8.

[48] K.H. Han, J.H. Kim, Quantum-inspired evolutionary algorithm for a class of combinatorial optimization, IEEE Trans. Evol. Comput. 6 (2002) 580–593, http://dx.doi.org/10.1109/TEVC.2002.804320.

[49] M. Sharma, S. Tyagi, Novel knowledge based selective tabu initialization in genetic algorithm, Int. J. Adv. Res. Comput. Sci. Softw. Eng. 3 (5) (2013).

[50] J. Holland, Adaptation in Natural and Artificial Systems, University of Michigan Press, Ann Arbor, 1975.

[51] A. Fraser, Simulation of genetic systems by automatic digital computers, Aust. J. Biol. Sci. 10 (1957) 484–491.

[52] H. Bremermann, Optimization through evolution and recombination, in: M.C. Yovits, G.T. Jacobi, G.D. Goldstine (Eds.), Self-Organizing Systems, Spartan, Washington, DC, 1962, pp. 93–106, http://dx.doi.org/10.1016/S0031-8914(53)80099-6.

[53] J. Holland, Adaptation in Natural and Artificial Systems, University of Michigan Press, Ann Arbor, 1975.

[54] Z. Jan, A.M. Mirza, Genetic programming-based perceptual shaping of a digital watermark in the wavelet domain using Morton scanning, J. Chin. Inst. Eng. 35 (1) (2012) 85–99.

[55] L. Fogel, A. Owens, M.J. Walsh, Artificial Intelligence Through Simulated Evolution, Wiley, New York, 1966.

[56] I. Rechenberg, Evolutionsstrategie: Optimierung technischer Systemenach Prinzipien der biologishen Evolution, 1973.

[57] H. Schwefel, Evolution and Optimum Seeking, Wiley, New York, 1975.

[58] M.A. Nielsen, I.L. Chuang, Quantum Computation and Quantum Information, Cambridge University Press, England, 2000.

[59] K. Han, J. Kim, Quantum inspired evolutionary algorithm for a class of combinatorial optimization, IEEE Trans. Evol. Comput. 6 (6) (2002), http://dx.doi.org/10.1109/TEVC.2002.804320.

[60] A. Narayanan, M. Moore, Quantum inspired genetic algorithms, in: Proc. 1996 IEEE Int. Conf. Evolutionary Computation, Piscataway, NJ, 1966, pp. 61–66, http://dx.doi.org/10.1109-ICEC-1996-542334.
[61] G. Zhang, W. Jin, N. Li, An improved quantum genetic algorithm and its application, in: Lecture Notes in Computer Science, 2003, pp. 449–452.
[62] S. Zhao, G. Xu, T. Tao, L. Liang, Real-coded chaotic quantum-inspired genetic algorithm for training of fuzzy neural networks, Comput. Math. Appl. 57 (11–12) (2009) 2009–2015, http://dx.doi.org/10.1016/j.camwa.2008.10.048.
[63] K. Han, J. Kim, Genetic quantum algorithm and its application to combinatorial optimization problem, in: Proceedings of the 2000 Congress on Evolutionary Computation, vol. 2, 2000, pp. 1354–1360, http://dx.doi.org/10.1109/CEC.2000.870809.
[64] H. Buhrman, I. Newman, H. Rhrig, R. Wolf, Robust quantum algorithms and polynomials, Theory Comput. Syst. 40 (4) (2007) 379–395.
[65] D. Deutsch, Quantum theory the Church-Turing principle and the universal quantum computer, Proc. R. Soc. Lond. A 400 (1985) 97–117.
[66] D. Goldberg, Genetic Algorithms in Search Optimization and Machine Learning, Addison Wesley Longman Inc., Reading, MA, 1989.
[67] R. Nowotniak, J. Kucharski, Building blocks propagation in quantum-inspired genetic algorithm, Sci. Bull. Ac. Sci. Technol. Automat. 14 (2010) 795–810.
[68] A.V. Cruz, M.A.C. Pacheco, M.B. Vellasco, C.R.H. Barbosa, Cultural operators for a quantum inspired evolutionary algorithm applied to numerical optimization problems, in: J. Mira, J.R Alvarez (Eds.), IWINAC(2), Lecture Notes in Computer Science, vol. 3562, 2005, pp. 1–10, http://dx.doi.org/10.1007/11499305-1.
[69] A. da Cruz, M. Vellasco, M. Pacheco, Quantum inspired evolutionary algorithm for numerical optimization, in: IEEE Congress on Evolutionary Computation, 2006, pp. 2630–2637, http://dx.doi.org/10.1109/CEC.2006.1688637.
[70] K. Fan, A. Brabazon, C.O. Sullivan, M. Neil, Quantum Inspired evolutionary algorithms for financial data analysis, EvoWorkshops (2008) 133–143, http://dx.doi.org/10.1007/978-3-540-78761-7-14.
[71] P. Surekha, S. Sumathi, Implementation of genetic algorithm for a DWT based image watermarking scheme, ICTACT J. Soft Comput. 2 (224) (2011).

CHAPTER

Digital filter design using quantum-inspired multiobjective cat swarm optimization algorithm

10

A.K. Dwivedi[a], R.N. Patel[b]

Bhilai Institute of technology, Durg, CT, India[a] SSTC, Bhilai, CT, India[b]

1 INTRODUCTION

Finite impulse response (FIR) filters are widely used in communication [1], consumer electronics, audio [2], and other signal processing applications [3]. One of the important applications of FIR filters is as a Hilbert transformer. Hilbert transforms are very useful especially in detecting the instantaneous frequency and envelop amplitude of the signal. For synthesis of a Hilbert transformer, FIR filters are preferred because they can have exact linear phase, their stability is guaranteed, and they are less sensitive to the rounding of coefficients.

In spite of the advances in the development of design algorithms for FIR filters, there are some challenges faced by design engineers. Although FIR filters are stable, have linear phase, and are easier to implement than infinite impulse response filters, they require higher filter order. Therefore the minimization of passband ripple (PBR) and stopband ripple (SBR) at smaller order has always been challenging. For filter design, various evolutionary algorithms have been widely used because of their ability to converge to the global optimum. The various techniques reported are simulated annealing [4], genetic algorithms [5,6], particle swarm optimization [7–10], differential evolution [11–14], hybrid differential evolution and particle swarm optimization [15], an orthogonal harmony search algorithm [16], and cat swarm optimization [17]. An evolutionary algorithm should possess proper exploration and exploitation capability. Binary representation-based algorithms have been proved to have better exportability than their continuous versions [18,19]. Improvement in the convergence behavior of binary representation-based algorithms motivated the use of a quantum representation. The basic element in quantum computing is the quantum bit (qubit), which represents superposition of the two states 0 and 1 [20]. Quantum theory allows a physical interpretation of Hilbert space and

Quantum Inspired Computational Intelligence. http://dx.doi.org/10.1016/B978-0-12-804409-4.00010-3

its basis. Therefore it increases the global search space in evolutionary optimization [21]. The operations in these algorithms are performed with use of a quantum gate. In this regard, various quantum-inspired evolutionary algorithms has been reported, including quantum annealing [22], a quantum-inspired genetic algorithm [23], quantum-inspired particle swarm optimization [10,24], quantum-inspired differential evolution [25], a quantum-inspired artificial bee colony algorithm [26], and quantum-inspired gravitational search [27]. Quantum-inspired evolutionary algorithms have been used in digital filter design and have been found to outperform their continuous and binary versions [10,24]. However, none of the above-mentioned algorithms is able to meet all the filter specifications simultaneously. If one specification is considered with higher importance, then the algorithms perform poorly in meeting other specifications. For applications such as high-fidelity audio systems and Hilbert transformers, filters with smaller PBR are required. On the other hand, in applications such as denoising of biomedical signals and image denoising, greater stopband attenuation (smaller SBR) is important. Minimizing both the PBR and the SBR simultaneously is not possible at smaller filter order. Similarly, filters which are optimized with regard to PBR and SBR require a greater filter length and greater area and consume more power at the time of execution. Higher power consumption reduces device life and battery life. High power consumption increases cooling and packaging costs and the chances of electromigration. Power consumption in FIR filters can be reduced by filter implementation architecture [28] or by reduction of transition activities [29] between filter coefficients in their digital form during execution. The average signal transition activity can be reduced by use of the information theoretic measure entropy [30–32]. Gray code addressing is used to reduce switching activity in the control path of the embedded processor [33]. Entropy has also been considered as a power sensitivity measure for FIR filters [34]. In the present work, minimization of entropy between consecutive filter coefficients was used for filter design, which results in power consumption minimization. It has been observed with single objective optimization that filters optimized for ripples have higher entropy, whereas filters optimized for smaller entropy have greater ripple content. The filter design problem with low power can be solved by multiobjective optimization. A multiobjective optimization-based asymmetric FIR filter design using a genetic algorithm has been proposed [35]. In previously reported work, symmetric FIR filter design has not been considered as a multiobjective design problem. In this chapter filter design is used for a Hilbert transformer design application. Motivated by quantum mechanics principles, we propose in this chapter a quantum-inspired version of the multiobjective cat swarm optimization (MOCSO) [36] and referred to as "Q-MOCSO." The applicability of the proposed Q-MOCSO was validated by our designing FIR low-pass filters. The designed filter response is compared with that of the classical MOCSO and other multiobjective evolutionary optimization approaches, including multiobjective nondominated sorting genetic algorithm II (NSGA-II) [37,38], a multiobjective particle swarm optimization (MOPSO) algorithm [39], and a multiobjective differential evolution (MODE) algorithm [40,41].

To validate the power consumption reduction in real-time applications, the designed filters were synthesized with Xilinx ISE 14.7 and power was analyzed with an X-power analyzer. The power consumption results obtained with the proposed approach are compared with results obtained without power consideration in other multiobjective evolutionary optimization algorithms.

The chapter is organized as follows. In the next section the formulation of an FIR filter as a multiobjective optimization problem is discussed. Application of FIR filters for a Hilbert transformer is discussed in Section 3. Section 4 presents MOCSO and Q-MOCSO step-by-step. Other state of the art optimization algorithms applied for Hilbert transformer design are described in Section 5. Section 6 describes the simulation and comparison of designed filters with the state-of-the-art algorithms. Section 7 concludes the chapter.

2 FINITE IMPULSE RESPONSE FILTER DESIGN AS A MULTIOBJECTIVE OPTIMIZATION PROBLEM

It has been observed that at lower filter order there are more ripples. The ripple content can be minimized in either the passband or the stopband by providing it with more weight in the objective function, but both PBR and SBR cannot be minimized simultaneously. As PBR and SBR are conflicting in nature, they can be formulated as a multiobjective optimization problem. In this regard, two different objective functions have been formulated related to minimization of PBR and SBR. In this section FIR filter design is discussed as a multiobjective optimization problem in detail. A multiobjective optimization problem can be stated as

$$\min_{h} J = \{j_1(h), j_2(h), \ldots, j_n(h)\}, \tag{1}$$

where $h \in H$, where $h_1, h_2, \ldots, h_n$ represent optimization parameters (filter coefficients), and $H \subset S$, where H is the variable space, S is the objective space, and $J : H \to S$. The proposed Q-MOSCO has been applied to find Pareto-optimal filter designs, which together are referred to as the Pareto set. The Pareto front for the above-mentioned problem can be represented as

$$PF = \{J(h) \in S | h \in PS\}, \tag{2}$$

where PS is the Pareto set. In Section 1 we mentioned that the primary requirement of a properly designed filter is smaller PBR, smaller SBR, or both. However, both objectives cannot be achieved simultaneously for filters of smaller order. In this context, in the present work the first objective function is formulated with the deviation in the response of the designed filter from the desired specifications in the passband and second objective function is formulated with the deviation in the stopband. The objective functions can be given as

$$J_1(h) = |(\max |E(\omega)| - \delta_{\mathrm{p}}) - 1)| \text{ for } \omega \leq \omega_{\mathrm{p}}, \tag{3}$$

$$J_2(h) = |(\max|E(\omega)| - \delta_s)| \text{ for } \omega \geq \omega_s, \tag{4}$$

where δ_p and δ_s are the maximum PBR and SBR, and $E(\omega)$ is the deviation between the desired and the designed frequency response:

$$E(\omega) = [H_d(e^{j\omega}) - H(e^{j\omega})], \tag{5}$$

where $H_d(e^{j\omega})$ and $H(e^{j\omega})$ are the frequency responses of the desired and actual filters. The desired response for a low-pass filter, a high-pass filter, a band-pass filter, and a band-stop filter can be represented as

$$\text{Low-pass filter}: H_d(e^{j\omega}) = \begin{cases} 1 & \text{for } 0 \geq \omega \geq \omega_p, \\ 0 & \text{otherwise;} \end{cases} \tag{6}$$

$$\text{High-pass filter}: H_d(e^{j\omega}) = \begin{cases} 0 & \text{for } 0 \geq \omega \geq \omega_s, \\ 1 & \text{otherwise;} \end{cases} \tag{7}$$

$$\text{Band-pass filter}: H_d(e^{j\omega}) = \begin{cases} 1 & \text{for } \omega_{pl} \geq \omega \geq \omega_{ph}, \\ 0 & \text{otherwise;} \end{cases} \tag{8}$$

$$\text{Band-stop filter}: H_d(e^{j\omega}) = \begin{cases} 0 & \text{for } \omega_{sl} \geq \omega \geq \omega_{sh}, \\ 1 & \text{otherwise.} \end{cases} \tag{9}$$

As discussed earlier, motivated by the importance of low power filter design, we have considered a third objective function for filter design in multiobjective filter design problem (7) for power minimization using the entropy of the filter coefficients:

$$J_3 = \sum_{i=1}^{N} E(Coef_i, Coef_{i+1}), \tag{10}$$

where $[Coef_1, Coef_2, Coef_3, \ldots, Coef_{(N+1)}]$ are the coefficients represented in their IEEE 754 floating point representation, and N is the order of the filter. Entropy is a measure of the randomness carried by set of discrete events observed over time. The information content of the system is the sum of the information content C_i weighted by its occurrence probability P_i:

$$E(p) = \sum_{i=1}^{m} p_i \log_2 \frac{1}{p_i}, \tag{11}$$

where p_i is the event occurrence probability, which is related to information content C_i as

$$C_i = \log_2\left(\frac{1}{p_i}\right). \tag{12}$$

Since $0 \le p_i \le 1$, the logarithmic term is nonnegative and therefore $C_i \ge 0$. Eq. (10) reflects the overall switching in the binary values of the successive coefficients of the filter. A filter with smaller entropy J_3 will have smaller switching activity and hence the power consumption during filter execution will be low. The relation between dynamic power consumption and switching activity in an FIR filter is given as

$$P_{dy} = \alpha_{(0\leftrightarrow 1)} C_L V_{DD}^2 f_{clk}, \tag{13}$$

where $\alpha_{(0\leftrightarrow 1)}$ is the node switching activity factor, C_L is the load capacitance, V_{DD} is the supply voltage, and f_{clk} is the operating clock frequency. Thus we have formulated FIR filter design as a multiobjective design problem by considering three objective functions: J_1, J_2, and J_3 . In the next section, application of FIR filters in the design of Hilbert transformers is discussed.

3 HILBERT TRANSFORMER DESIGN USING FINITE IMPULSE RESPONSE FILTERS

The major challenge in Hilbert transformer design is to achieve a very small PBR and a sharp transition band. Classically Hilbert transformers can be designed with an FIR filter by providing a higher weight factor to the PBR. To define a proper weight for this application is very challenging. Selection of the weight factor can be avoided by use of a multi-objective optimization. Hilbert transformers have impulse response $h(n)_{HT}$ for $n = 0$ to $L - 1$, which is given as

$$h(n)_{HT} = \begin{cases} \frac{2}{n\pi}\sin^2\frac{n\pi}{2} & \text{for } n \neq 0, \\ 0 & \text{for } n = 0. \end{cases} \tag{14}$$

The impulse response of Hilbert transformers is not absolutely summable and thus they are unstable. However, approximations to the ideal Hilbert transformers can be obtained with FIR filters. For positive and negative values of n, it can be seen that the impulse response of Hilbert transformers is antisymmetric. Therefore FIR Hilbert transformers can be designed as either type III or type IV FIR filters.

Assuming we have a length N FIR filter with real impulse response coefficients $h(n)$, the transfer function of the FIR filter is given by

$$H = \sum_{n=0}^{N-1} h(n). \tag{15}$$

In the z domain

$$H(z) = \sum_{n=0}^{2M} h(n)z^{-n}, \tag{16}$$

where M is an odd integer and $2M$ is the filter order. A Hilbert transformer filter can be designed with an FIR filter. First, a sample with value 1/2 located at $n = M$ is replaced by the value 0. For this 1/2 is subtracted from all the coefficients values. The subtraction of this coefficient shifts $H(\omega)$ downward by 1/2. To obtain the Hilbert transformer from this, a shift of $\frac{\pi}{2}$ is required horizontally rightward. This shift is accomplished by multiplication of the remaining coefficients $h(n)$ by $(-j)^{-n}$. The transfer function of a Hilbert transformer can be given as

$$H(z)_{\mathrm{HT}} = 2 \sum_{n=0_{nM}}^{2M} = h(n)(jz)^{-n} = 2\left[H(jz) - \frac{1}{2}(jz)^{-M}\right]. \tag{17}$$

Thus the impulse response of an FIR filter is related to the impulse response of a Hilbert transformer by

$$h_{\mathrm{HB}}(n) = \begin{cases} 0 & \text{for } n = 2k+1, \\ 2(-1)^{k-1}h(n) & \text{for } n = 2k, \text{with } k = 0, 1, 2, \ldots, M. \end{cases} \tag{18}$$

To obtain the optimal Hilbert transformer, the FIR filter must be optimal. An optimal FIR filter is possible only by use of a global optimization technique. Further, a Hilbert transformer should have the smallest possible PBR for a specified filter length, which is obtained by multiobjective optimization-based FIR filter design. The next section details how multiobjective optimization can be applied for the design of FIR filters by means of cat swarm optimization.

4 QUANTUM-INSPIRED MULTIOBJECTIVE CAT SWARM OPTIMIZATION ALGORITHM

In this section the MOCSO algorithm [36] is discussed first and then the proposed Q-MOCSO algorithm is discussed. There is also an analytic discussion of the proposed quantum-inspired algorithm to prove its convergence to Pareto-optimal solutions.

The main difference between the multiobjective and single-objective algorithms is in their selection scheme. In this chapter a Pareto dominance-based selection scheme is used for multiobjective optimization. In the seeking mode and the tracing mode of the single-objective cat swarm optimization algorithm, the solutions are selected on the basis of roulette wheel selection. In this regard, in multiobjective optimization algorithms, Pareto optimality is usually used. The concept of Pareto optimality in filter design problem (1) can be stated as follows: a filter coefficient vector h^* is said to be Pareto optimal for a multiobjective filter design problem if all other vectors $h \in H$ have a higher value for at least one of the objective functions J_i, with $i = 1, 2, \ldots, n$, or have similar values for all the objective functions. The conditions for a solution set to be Pareto optimal [42] can be stated as:

1. For the multiobjective optimization problem a point h^* is said to be weakly Pareto optimal if and only if there is $h \in H$ such that $J_i(h) < J_i(h^*)$ for all $i \in \{1, 2, \ldots, n\}$.
2. A point h^* is said to be strictly Pareto optimal for the multiobjective problem if and only if there is no $h \in H$ such that $J_i(h) < J_i(h^*)$ for all $i \in \{1, 2, \ldots, n\}$.

For the locally Pareto-optimal points the definition is same as above except a feasible neighborhood of h^* is also considered. Otherwise it can be said that if $B(h^*, \in)$ is a ball of radius $\in > 0$, no $h \in S \cap B(h^*, \in)$ exists such that $J_i(h) < J_i(h^*)$ for all $i \in 1, \ldots, n$ with at least one strict inequality.

The curve containing all the efficient solutions is represented as a Pareto front (see Fig. 1). The points on a Pareto-optimal front are called "nondominated" or "noninferior points." On the basis of the above criterion, a Pareto dominance-based sorting is used to select nondominated optimal points or an external archive.

4.1 MULTIOBJECTIVE CAT SWARM OPTIMIZATION

This algorithm is based on the strong attentive behavior and hunting capacity of cats. Cats always remain attentive even while sleeping. Whenever they sense food, they

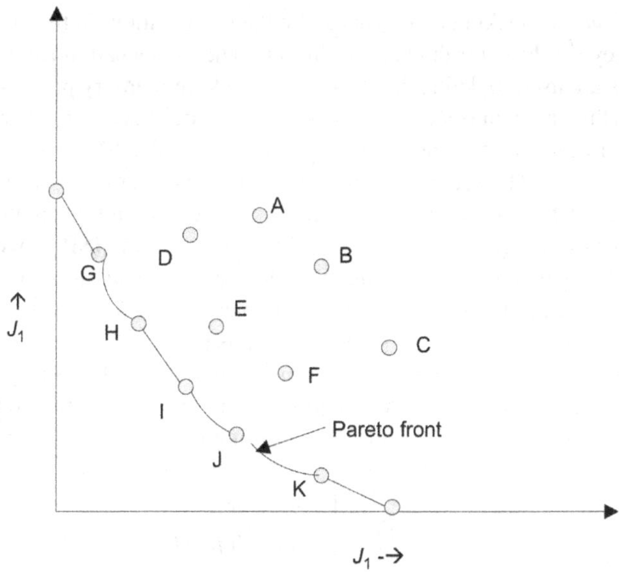

FIG. 1

Illustration of the Pareto front.

immediately come into action and put a lot of energy into hunting the prey. Cats usually move very slowly and attentively in the search of prey; this mode of cats in relation to their food search is termed "seeking mode." Whenever food is sensed, they increase their speed and use a lot of energy; this mode of their behavior is called "tracking mode." Seeking mode enhances the global exploration capability of the proposed algorithm, whereas tracing (tracking) mode enhances exploitation of the global search provided by seeking mode for efficient local search. In the cat swarm optimization algorithm, before it goes to seeking mode or tracing mode, initialization is performed. The positions of cats are initialized as x_id, representing the position of the ith cat in the dth dimension. The velocity of cats is also randomly initialized and represented as v_{id}.

$$x_{id} = X_{i1}, X_{i2}, \ldots, X_{iD} \tag{19}$$

and

$$v_{id} = V_{i1}, V_{i2}, \ldots, V_{iD}. \tag{20}$$

The total population of cats is divided into two groups. One group is for seeking mode and other group is for tracing mode. A mixture ratio defines the ratio of the number of cats in seeking mode to the number of cats in tracing mode. According to the mixture ratio some of the cats are labeled as being in seeking mode and the others are labeled as being in tracing mode. These two modes can be detailed as:

A. *Seeking mode:* In seeking mode cats are in the rest position. In this mode they are alert to prey and look for the next position to where they can move. Essentially four terms are used to define this mode. The seeking memory pool (SMP) is used to define the memory capacity size of each cat. This parameter represents the number of locations explored by a particular cat. The SMP can be different for different cats. The seeking range of the selected dimension (SRD) represents the mutation ratio for the selected dimensions. The other terms are the counts of dimensions to change (CDC) and self-position considering (SPC), which is a Boolean flag which decides whether a particular cat is ready to move or not.

1. If the Boolean flag SPC is 1, the SMP copies of the present cat are produced, otherwise only one copy of the present cat is produced.
2. For every cat CDC is produced and thus a population of cats is generated.
3. For the entire cat population, mutation is performed according to the SRD.
4. The fitness is evaluated for all cats according to

$$fit_i = \begin{cases} \frac{1}{1+f_i} & \text{if } f_i \geq 0, \\ \text{abs}(f_i) & \text{if } f_i < 0, \end{cases} \tag{21}$$

where f_i is the cost of the objective function.

5. Nondominated selection is used to select nondominated cat locations on the basis of their fitness values. The nondominated cat locations are stored in the external archive.
6. Flags of cats are updated according to their modes (i.e., seeking mode or tracing mode).

B. *Tracing mode:* After sensing a target in seeking mode, the cat tries to trace the target. In this mode the energy of cats is high and they are very active and readily move very fast. Tracing mode can be summarized in the following steps:

1. The new velocity of the cat is dependent on its current location and the best location found among all the members of the cat population. The new velocity is updated as

$$v_{i,d} = wv_{id} + cr(X_{gd} - X_{id}), \tag{22}$$

where w is the inertia weight, c is the acceleration constant, and r is a random number uniformly distributed in the range [0,1]. The global best X_{gd} is selected randomly from the external archive.

2. The new position of the cat is updated as

$$x_{i,d} = X_{id} + v_{id}. \tag{23}$$

In Eq. (23), if the updated location touches the boundary of the search space, then the nearest boundary value is assigned to the cat's location and the corresponding velocity is multiplied by -1 to change the search direction.

3. Now the fitness in tracing mode is evaluated (Eq. 22). The external archive is updated by new locations of those cats which represent nondominated solutions.

The flowchart for the MOCSO is shown in Fig. 2.

4.2 QUANTUM-INSPIRED MULTIOBJECTIVE CAT SWARM OPTIMIZATION

The improved version of cat swarm optimization is reported as binary cat swarm optimization [19]. In this chapter a quantum-inspired cat swarm optimization is proposed. The quantum-inspired cat swarm optimization is extended for multiobjective optimization with use of Pareto dominance-based selection, and is abbreviated as Q-MOSCSO. The Q-MOCSO algorithm is based on qubits and superposition of states [43].

Qubits in quantum computing are the basic elements of information that represent superposition of the two states 0 and 1. The state of a qubit can be represented as

$$|\psi \geq \alpha\,|0\rangle + \beta\,|1\rangle, \tag{24}$$

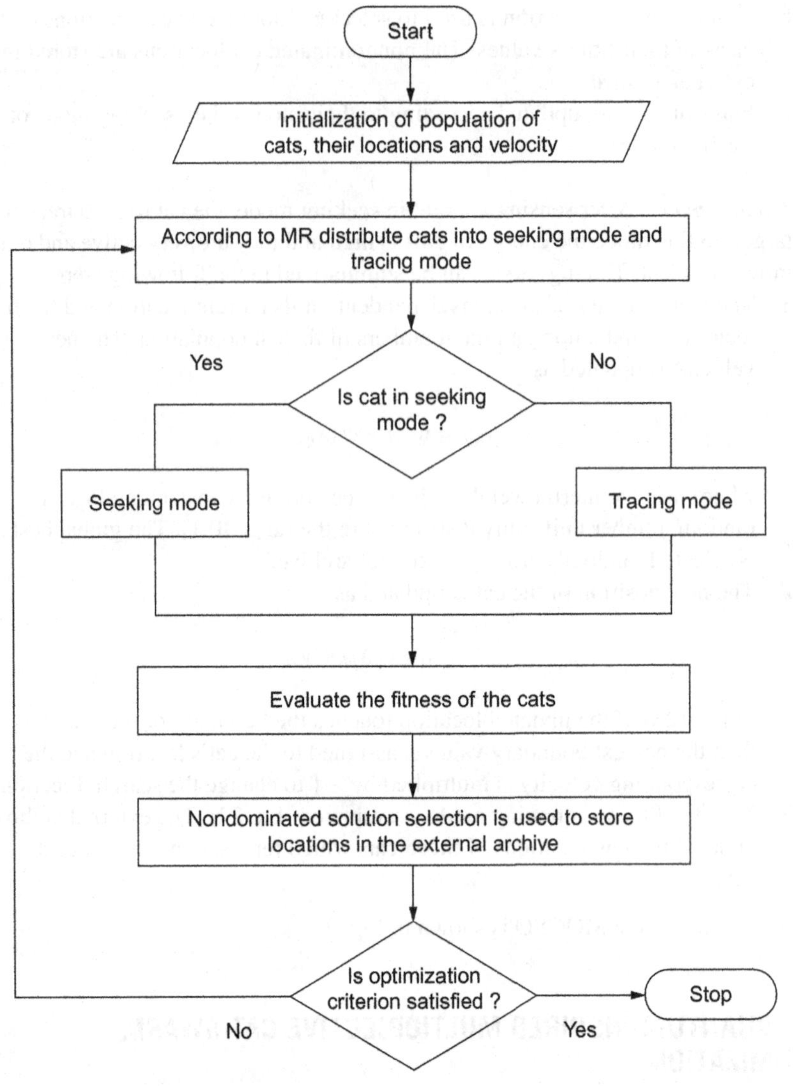

FIG. 2

Flowchart of the multiobjective cat swarm optimization algorithm. *MR*, mixture ratio.

where the probability of getting $|0\rangle$ after measurement is $|\alpha|^2$ and that of getting $|1\rangle$ is $|\beta|^2$. $|0\rangle$ and $|1\rangle$ represent the classical bit values 0 and 1 respectively and α and β are complex numbers satisfying the condition

$$|\alpha|^2 + |\beta|^2 = 1. \tag{25}$$

In the proposed algorithm a qubit representation is used, which is defined as a pair of α and β. A cat in the algorithm is represented as a string of m qubits as

$$M = \left| \begin{array}{cccc} \alpha_1 & |\alpha_2 & \ldots & \alpha_m \\ \beta_1 & |\beta_2 & \ldots & \beta_m \end{array} \right|, \tag{26}$$

where $\alpha_i^2 + \beta_i^2 = 1$ and $i = 1, 2, \ldots, m$. As stated in [43], the advantage of the qubit representation is that only one m-qubit individual can represent 2^m states, whereas in the binary representation 2^m states are represented by 2^m strings only. The locations and velocities in Q-MOCSO are initialized as qubit individuals (Eq. 27). The locations and velocities of the initial population are represented by linear superposition of all possible states with the same probability:

$$\psi_{xid}\rangle = \sum_{k=1}^{2^m} \frac{1}{\sqrt{2^m}} |X_{k,d}\rangle, \tag{27}$$

$$\psi_{vid}\rangle = \sum_{k=1}^{2^m} \frac{1}{\sqrt{2^m}} |V_{k,d}\rangle, \tag{28}$$

where $X_{k,d}$ is the kth state represented by the binary string $(x_1, x_2, \ldots, x_m)$, where $x_i, i = 1, 2, \ldots, m$ and $d = 1, 2, \ldots, D$ is the dimension (number of filter coefficients). Similarly to MOCSO, Q-MOCSO also has two modes: seeking mode and tracing mode:

A. *Seeking mode:* The seeking mode in Q-MOCSO is the same as in the classical MOCSO except for a change in the representation of cats' locations and velocities in the form of qubit individuals. The quantum representation of the population increases diversity in the population and thus improves the exploration capability of cat swarm optimization. The fitness values (Eq. 21) are evaluated by consideration of the decimal equivalent of quantum states. On the basis of the fitness values obtained, a Pareto dominance selection operator is applied to save nondominated solutions in the external archive.

B. *Tracing mode:* The tracing mode of Q-MOCSO is also same as that of MOCSO. The major change in tracing mode is that the variation in location and velocity is performed with a quantum gate. The quantum gate produces variation in qubits which satisfies the normalization condition, $\alpha'^2 + \beta'^2 = 1$, where α' and β' are the values of updated qubits.

$$v_{i,d}\begin{bmatrix} \alpha'_{i,d} \\ \beta'_{i,d} \end{bmatrix} = w \times V_{i,d}\begin{bmatrix} \alpha_{i,d} \\ \beta_{i,d} \end{bmatrix} + c \times r \times X_{gd}\begin{bmatrix} \alpha_{i,d} \\ \beta_{i,d} \end{bmatrix} - X_{id}\begin{bmatrix} \alpha_{i,d} \\ \beta_{i,d} \end{bmatrix}, \tag{29}$$

where w, c, and r have the same meaning as in Eq. (22). Similarly, the locations of cats are updated by means of a quantum gate for locations which is given as

$$x_{i,d}\begin{bmatrix}\alpha'_{i,d}\\ \beta'_{i,d}\end{bmatrix}=x_{i,d}\begin{bmatrix}\alpha_{i,d}\\ \beta_{i,d}\end{bmatrix}+v_{id}\begin{bmatrix}\alpha'_{i,d}\\ \beta'_{i,d}\end{bmatrix}. \tag{30}$$

Except for these changes, the remaining the steps of MOCSO and Q-MOSCO are the same. Because of more diversity represented by quantum individuals and their probabilistic operators, they perform better than their continuous versions. The proposed approach is compared with other state-of-the-art multiobjective optimization approaches for filter design, which include a nondominated sorting genetic algorithm (NSGA), multiobjective particle swarm optimization (MOPSO), and multiobjective differential evolution (MODE). These algorithms are discussed in brief in the next section.

5 OTHER MULTIOBJECTIVE OPTIMIZATION ALGORITHMS USED

Three other state-of-the-art multiobjective optimization algorithms considered for comparison are NSGA-II, MOPSO, and MODE.

5.1 NONDOMINATED SORTING GENETIC ALGORITHM II

The NSGA, proposed in [44], was one of the earlier proposed multiobjective algorithms. The algorithm is used for classification of individuals according to their dominance with use of ranking. Each individual in the population is assigned a rank on the basis of nondomination. Each dominance class is assigned a dummy fitness value proportional to the population size. Since the process of Pareto ranking is repeated in each run, this algorithm is not very efficient. There is lack of elitism in the classical NSGA and there is a need to specify a sharing parameter. An improved version of this technique has been proposed, and is known as NSGA-II [38].

5.2 MULTIOBJECTIVE PARTICLE SWARM OPTIMIZATION

This algorithm is based on the study of a model of bird community behavior simulation [39]. The initial population in MOPSO is initialized from random vectors and every vector is termed a "particle." MOPSO also uses an external archive to store nondominated solutions. A special mutation operator is incorporated to enhance the exploration capability of the particles. MOPSO is able to solve multimodal nonconvex optimization problems easily.

5.3 MULTIOBJECTIVE DIFFERENTIAL EVOLUTION

The MODE algorithm is based on the idea of evolving the populations over the generations; they are known as "individuals". The individuals are encoded as

$$x_{ig} = \{x_{1g}, x_{2g}, \ldots, x_{Dg}\}, \quad \text{where } i = 1, 2, 3, \ldots, Np. \tag{31}$$

A mutated vector v_{ig} corresponding to the target vector x_{ig} is generated. The evolution is continued until the best value is obtained starting from random values:

$$v_{i,g} = x_{i,g} + F(x_{\text{best},g} - x_{i,g}) + F(x_{r1,g} - x_{r2,g}). \tag{32}$$

The crossover in MODE is performed to generate a target vector $u_{i,g}$ with use of a random number for $j = 1$ to D:

$$u_{j,i,g} = \begin{cases} V_{j,i,g} & \text{if } \text{rand}_{i,j}(0,1)¡\ (C_r), \\ X_{j,i,g} & \text{otherwise,} \end{cases} \tag{33}$$

where $i = 1, 2, 3, \ldots, Np$. The external archive in MODE is saved with use of nondominated sorting-based selection.

6 RESULTS AND DISCUSSION

This section discusses the results obtained to evaluate the effectiveness of the proposed Q-MOCSO. The evaluation of the proposed algorithm was done in three stages. In first stage, we evaluated its performance in meeting the desired Hilbert transformer characteristics in terms of two objectives: minimization of PBR (Eq. 3) and minimization of SBR (Eq. 4). In the second stage the proposed optimization technique was applied with an additional objective: minimizing power consumption (Eq. 10). In the third stage the statistical significance of the proposed Q-MOCSO was evaluated by a t test.

STAGE I: APPLICATION OF THE PROPOSED QUANTUM-INSPIRED MULTIOBJECTIVE CAT SWARM OPTIMIZATION IN HILBERT TRANSFORMER DESIGN

The filter order considered for Hilbert transformer design in every case is 20. On the basis of reported work [17,19,36] and a number of pilot runs, the control parameters for MOCSO and Q-MOCSO were as follows: population size 50, number of iterations 500, SMP 5, CDC 0.6, SRD 2, mixture ratio 0.1, w 0.4, C 1.5, and limits for filter coefficients -1 to 1. The filters were designed and simulated with use of MATLAB SIMULINK 8.5 and further implemented with use of Xilinx ISE 14.7 on an xc7vx485t-2ffg1761 device. After implementation, the dynamic power consumption during execution was measured with a Xilinx X-power analyzer. To evaluate the effectiveness of the proposed quantum-inspired algorithm, a low-pass

FIR filter design was attempted with the following specifications: normalized passband frequency 0.35 rad/s, normalized stopband frequency 0.45 rad/s, normalized PBR 0.01, normalized SBR 0.01, and filter length 21. The coefficients of the filters were updated iteratively with the aim of minimizing J_1 and J_2. Fig. 3 presents the Pareto front obtained after convergence of Q-MOCSO with two objective functions and compared with MOCSO. In the Pareto front, each circle (or cross) represents a set of filter coefficients.

From Fig. 3 the ability of the proposed Q-MOCSO algorithm to provide a dominating solution as compared with the conventional MOCSO is clearly seen.

The coefficients of the three selected filters from the Pareto front are shown in Table 1. The first filter provides minimum PBR, the second provides minimum SBR, and the third maintains a compromise between minimum PBR and minimum SBR (J_1 and J_2) . The frequency responses of the Hilbert transformers designed with use of low-pass FIR filters from Table 1 are shown in Figs. 4–6 respectively. These frequency responses are compared with the frequency responses of the respective Hilbert transformers obtained with MOCSO.

The proposed Q-MOCSO algorithm was also compared with other state-of-the-art multiobjective evolutionary techniques: NSGA-II [37,38], MOPSO [39], and MODE [45]. Selected control parameters are shown in Table 2. The filter coefficients obtained after convergence of the algorithms are given in Table 3. The algorithms are compared in terms of their ability to meet the desired frequency domain specifications. The comparison is outlined in Table 4. The proposed Q-MOCSO

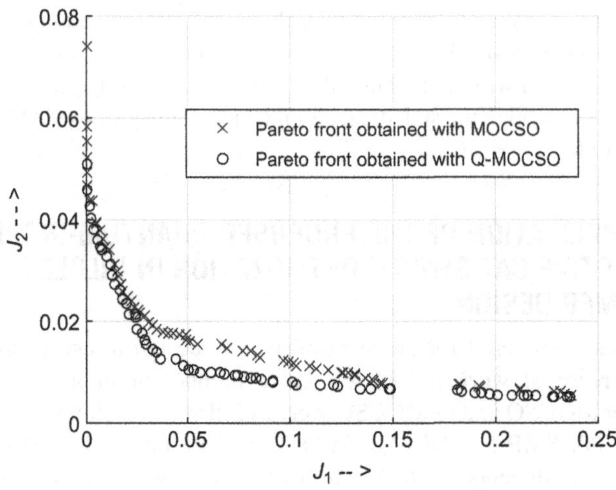

FIG. 3

Pareto front obtained for low-pass filter design using multiobjective cat swarm optimization (*MOCSO*) and quantum-inspired multiobjective cat swarm optimization (*Q-MOCSO*).

Table 1 Optimized Coefficients of the Finite Impulse Response Filter Designed With Multiobjective Cat Swarm Optimization and Quantum-Inspired Multiobjective Cat Swarm Optimization

	MOCSO			Q-MOCSO		
***h*(*n*)**	**min(J_1)**	**min(J_2)**	**cmp(J_1 and J_2)**	**min(J_1)**	**min(J_2)**	**cmp(J_1 and J_2)**
$h(1) = h(21)$	3.64E−02	−2.47E−02	5.30E−03	3.67E−02	−2.36E−02	6.21E−03
$h(2) = h(20)$	−3.66E−02	−3.05E−02	−3.80E−02	−3.60E−02	−2.57E−02	−4.62E−02
$h(3) = h(19)$	−1.16E−02	−1.82E−03	−1.14E−02	−1.16E−02	3.37E−03	−2.07E−02
$h(4) = h(20)$	8.72E−04	4.39E−02	2.44E−02	5.60E−04	4.86E−02	2.13E−02
$h(5) = h(17)$	4.12E−02	5.55E−02	4.86E−02	4.18E−02	5.82E−02	4.33E−02
$h(6) = h(16)$	3.69E−02	3.77E−03	1.27E−02	3.54E−02	5.42E−03	6.46E−05
$h(7) = h(15)$	−8.22E−02	−6.47E−02	−7.06E−02	−8.08E−02	−6.09E−02	−7.07E−02
$h(8) = h(14)$	−7.92E−02	−4.37E−02	−5.94E−02	−7.91E−02	−3.95E−02	−6.01E−02
$h(9) = h(13)$	9.73E−02	1.06E−01	9.83E−02	9.51E−02	1.11E−01	9.19E−02
$h(10) = h(12)$	3.12E−01	3.05E−01	3.08E−01	3.13E−01	3.06E−01	3.01E−01
$h(11)$	3.88E−01	3.95E−01	3.94E−01	3.89E−01	3.97E−01	4.00E−01

cmp, compromise; MOSCO, multiobjective cat swarm optimization; Q-MOCSO, quantum-inspired multiobjective cat swarm optimization.

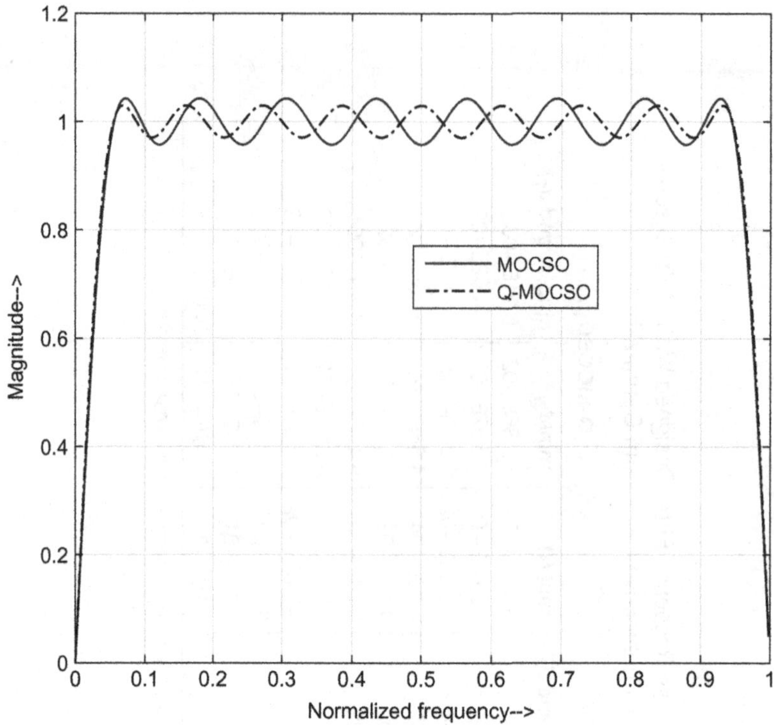

FIG. 4

Normalized frequency response of the Hilbert transformer designed with a finite impulse response filter having minimum passband ripple. *MOCSO*, multiobjective cat swarm optimization; *Q-MOCSO*, quantum-inspired multiobjective cat swarm optimization.

found outperforms the other multiobjective algorithms in digital FIR filter design application.

STAGE 2: APPLICATION OF THE PROPOSED QUANTUM-INSPIRED MULTIOBJECTIVE CAT SWARM OPTIMIZATION IN LOW-POWER FINITE IMPULSE RESPONSE FILTER DESIGN

Considering the importance of low-power consumption, as discussed earlier, the third objective function was included in the multiobjective optimization. All the control parameter settings were the same as those considered earlier. The three-dimensional Pareto front is shown in Fig. 7. To clarify the relation between J_3 and the other objective functions J_1 and J_2, other Pareto fronts are depicted in Figs. 8, 9, and 10 respectively. The efficiency of the Q-MOCSO over the classical approach is clearly

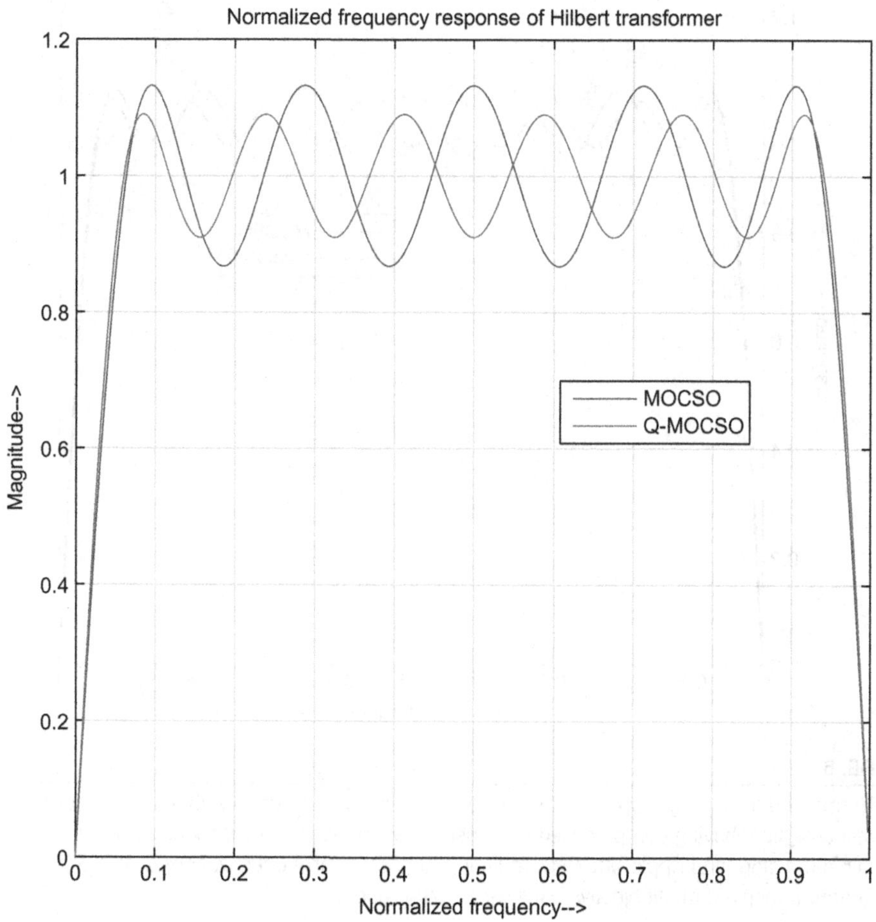

FIG. 5

Normalized frequency response of the Hilbert transformer designed with a finite impulse response filter having minimum stopband ripple. *MOCSO*, multiobjective cat swarm optimization; *Q-MOCSO*, quantum-inspired multiobjective cat swarm optimization.

seen. The filter coefficients obtained with MOCSO and Q-MOCSO are shown in Table 5. The frequency responses of the Hilbert transformers designed with use of filters at corners of the Pareto-optimal front are depicted in Figs. 11–14. The filters designed with the proposed approach are also compared with those designed with other state-of-the-art evolutionary approaches. From the Pareto-optimal fronts shown in Figs. 8 and 9, it is clearly seen that Q-MOCSO performs better than the classical MOCSO. The filter coefficients selected from the Pareto-optimal front are

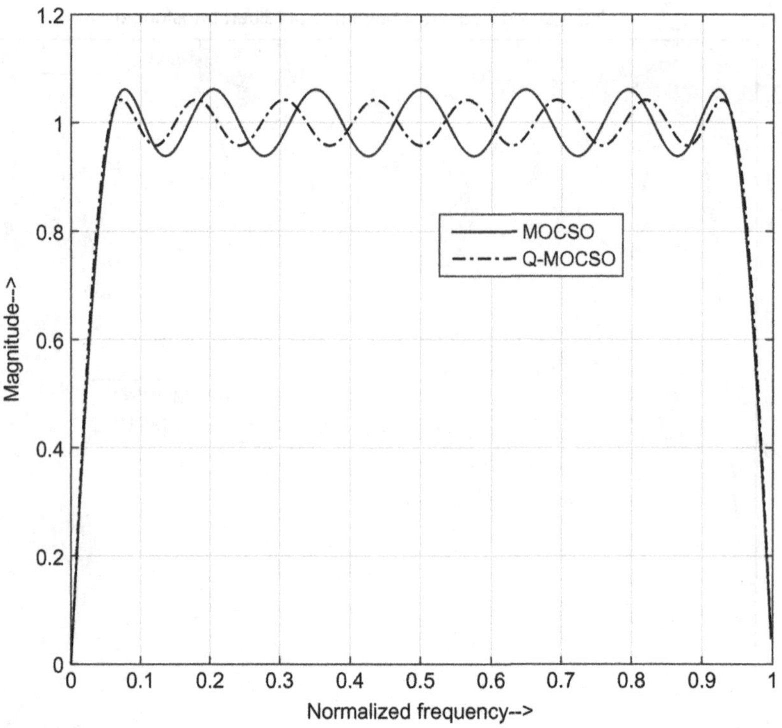

FIG. 6

Normalized frequency response of the Hilbert transformer designed with a finite impulse response filter having compromised response between minimum passband ripple and minimum stopband ripple. *MOCSO*, multiobjective cat swarm optimization; *Q-MOCSO*, quantum-inspired multiobjective cat swarm optimization.

shown in Table 5. The trade-off between power consumption and frequency domain specifications is clearly reflected in Figs. 7–10.

It can be concluded from Table 6 that Q-MOCSO outperforms all the other evolutionary optimization techniques and objective functions J_1, J_2, and J_3 are of conflicting nature.

To test the efficacy of the proposed method for real-time applications, the filters designed were implemented in the digital domain with use of a Viretex-7 field-programmable gate array. Hardware utilization was compared with reported methods (Table 7).

The power consumed during filter execution when the proposed Q-MOCSO was used is compared with the power consumed by the filter designed with MOCSO in Table 8.

Table 2 The Optimized Coefficients Obtained With Nondominated Sorting Genetic Algorithm II, Multiobjective Particle Swarm Optimization, and Multiobjective Differential Evolution

Parameter	NSGA-II	MOPSO	MODE
No. of runs	10	10	10
No. of iterations	500	500	500
Population size	100	50	50
Crossover rate	0.75	–	–
Crossover	2 point	–	–
Mutation rate	0.05	–	–
Selection	Tournament	–	–
Selection probability	1/3	–	–
C_1, C_2	–	1.5, 1.5	–
V_i^{min}, V_i^{max}	–	0.01, 1.0	–
C_r, F	–	–	0.4, 0.5

MODE, multiobjective differential evolution; MOPSO, multiobjective particle swarm optimization; NSGA-II, nondominated sorting genetic algorithm II.

STAGE 3: STATISTICAL ANALYSIS

A *t* test is a hypothetical testing method for determining the statistical significance of the difference between two independent samples of an equal sample size [50];

$$t = \frac{\bar{\alpha_2} - \bar{\alpha_1}}{\sqrt{\frac{\sigma_2^2}{m} - \frac{\sigma_1^2}{n}}}, \tag{34}$$

where $\bar{\alpha}_1$ and $\bar{\alpha}_2$ are mean values of the first and the second algorithm respectively, σ_1 and σ_2 are standard deviations of the first and the second algorithm respectively, and m and n are the sample sizes. The test was performed on the right tail with a significance level of 0.05. In this test, Q-MOCSO was considered as algorithm 1 and the other algorithm was considered as algorithm 2 one by one. The population variances of algorithm 1 and algorithm 2 are considered to be unequal. The p value obtained after the test is the probability of a test statistic being as extreme as or more extreme than the observed value under the null hypothesis. The values of p are in the range between 0 and 1. Larger values of p give more confidence to the validity of the null hypothesis.

From Table 9 it can be observed that the proposed technique outperforms all the other techniques with significant confidence.

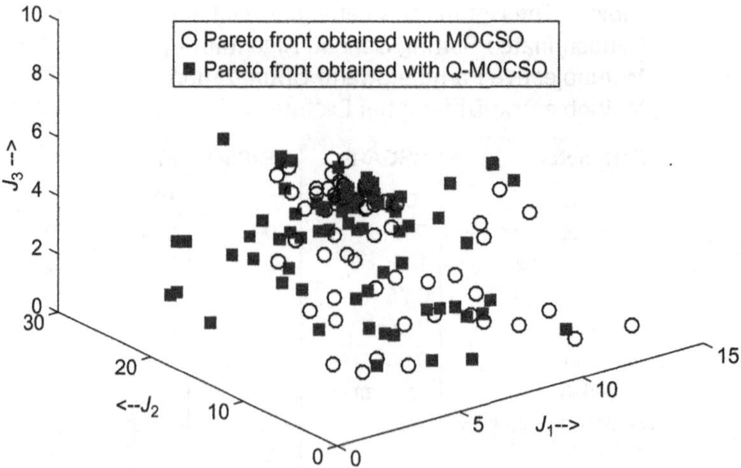

FIG. 7

Pareto front obtained with multiobjective cat swarm optimization (*MOCSO*) and quantum-inspired multiobjective cat swarm optimization (*Q-MOCSO*) after consideration of J_3 as the third objective function for J_1, J_2, and J_3.

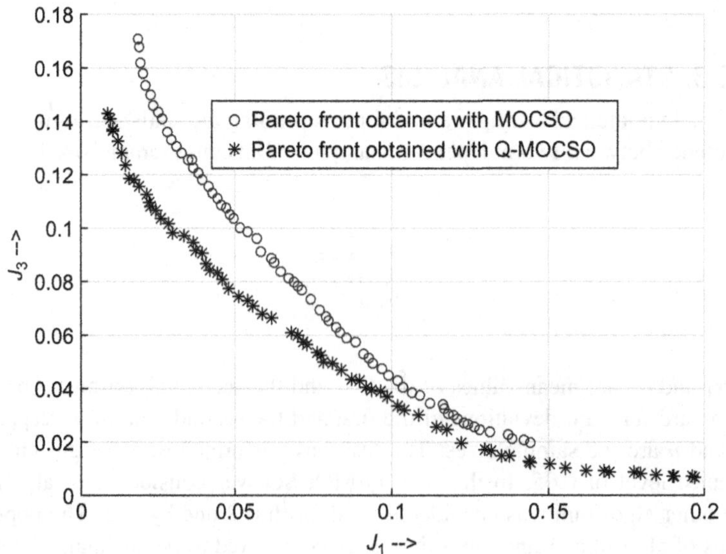

FIG. 8

Pareto front obtained with multiobjective cat swarm optimization (*MOCSO*) and quantum-inspired multiobjective cat swarm optimization (*Q-MOCSO*) after consideration of J_3 as the third objective function for J_1 and J_3.

Table 3 The Optimized Coefficients Obtained With Nondominated Sorting Genetic Algorithm II, Multiobjective Particle Swarm Optimization, and Multiobjective Differential Evolution

	NSGA-II		MOPSO		MODE	
$h(n)$ Technique	**min(J_1)**	**min(J_2)**	**min(J_1)**	**min(J_2)**	**min(J_1)**	**min(J_2)**
$h(1) = h(21)$	1.11E−02	1.10E−02	3.64E−02	−5.80E−04	2.64E−02	−7.40E−03
$h(2) = h(20)$	−3.80E−02	−3.80E−02	−3.66E−02	−2.82E−02	−3.77E−02	−2.83E−02
$h(3) = h(19)$	-1.15E−02	−1.15E−02	−1.16E−02	−2.44E−02	−1.19E−02	−1.54E−02
$h(4) = h(20)$	1.98E−02	1.96E−02	8.72E−04	3.27E−02	1.10E−02	3.83E−02
$h(5) = h(17)$	4.78E−02	4.78E−02	4.12E−02	5.29E−02	4.64E−02	5.37E−02
$h(6) = h(16)$	1.65E−02	1.79E−02	3.69E−02	1.60E−03	2.44E−02	1.36E−04
$h(7) = h(15)$	−7.15E−02	−7.15E−02	−8.22E−02	−6.42E−02	−7.27E−02	−6.44E−02
$h(8) = h(14)$	−6.36E−02	−6.28E−02	−7.92E−02	−5.39E−02	−7.22E−02	−5.16E−02
$h(9) = h(13)$	9.80E−02	9.80E−02	9.73E−02	8.96E−02	9.64E−02	9.32E−02
$h(10) = h(12)$	3.08E−01	3.09E−01	3.12E−01	3.15E−01	3.10E−01	3.12E−01
$h(11)$	3.94E−01	3.94E−01	3.88E−01	3.91E−01	3.93E−01	3.90E−01

MODE, multiobjective differential evolution; MOPSO, multiobjective particle swarm optimization; NSGA-II, nondominated sorting genetic algorithm II.

Table 4 Comparison of the Proposed Quantum-Inspired Multiobjective Cat Swarm Optimization With Other Evolutionary Multiobjective Algorithms

	min(J_1)		min(J_2)		arb(J_1 and J_2)	
	PBR	**SBR**	**PBR**	**SBR**	**PBR**	**SBR**
NSGA-II	0.0633	0.0877	0.0627	0.0879	0.1105	0.0433
MOPSO	0.0461	0.1046	0.0801	0.0697	0.0961	0.0537
MODE	0.0356	0.1233	0.1015	0.0495	0.0979	0.0487
MOCSO	0.0203	0.1719	0.1464	0.0213	0.0746	0.0746
Q-MOCSO	0.0191	0.1655	0.1633	0.0191	0.0679	0.0678

MOCSO, multiobjective cat swarm optimization; MODE, multiobjective differential evolution; MOPSO, multiobjective particle swarm optimization; NSGA-II, nondominated sorting genetic algorithm II; PBR, passband ripple; Q-MOCSO, quantum-inspired multiobjective cat swarm optimization; SBR, stopband ripple.

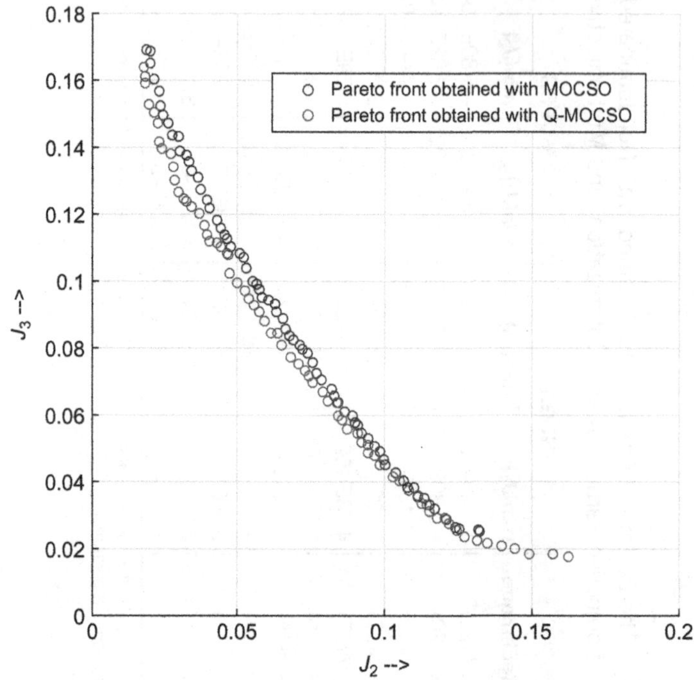

FIG. 9

Pareto front obtained with multiobjective cat swarm optimization (*MOCSO*) and quantum-inspired multiobjective cat swarm optimization (*Q-MOCSO*) after consideration of J_3 as the third objective function for J_2 and J_3.

Table 5 Optimized Coefficients of the Finite Impulse Response Filter Designed With Multiobjective Cat Swarm Optimization and Quantum-Inspired Multiobjective Cat Swarm Optimization for J_1, J_2, and J_3 Simultaneously

	MOCSO				Q-MOCSO			
***h*(*n*) Technique**	**min(J_1)**	**min(J_2)**	**min(J_3)**	**cmp(J_1, J_2, and J_3)**	**min(J_1)**	**min(J_2)**	**min(J_3)**	**cmp($J_1 + J_2 + J_3$)**
$h(1) = h(21)$	−2.60E−02	−2.49E−02	−2.74E−02	−2.74E−02	−2.62E−02	−2.60E−02	3.61E−02	−1.55E−02
$h(2) = h(20)$	−2.36E−02	−2.42E−02	−2.47E−02	−2.47E−02	−2.30E−02	−2.36E−02	−3.66E−02	−3.77E−02
$h(3) = h(19)$	1.96E−02	1.57E−02	2.20E−02	2.20E−02	2.13E−02	1.96E−02	−1.15E−02	−1.00E−02
$h(4) = h(20)$	4.90E−02	4.67E−02	5.15E−02	5.15E−02	5.00E−02	4.90E−02	1.36E−03	3.31E−02
$h(5) = h(17)$	1.13E−02	1.96E−02	7.48E−03	7.48E−03	9.86E−03	1.13E−02	4.12E−02	4.89E−02
$h(6) = h(16)$	−2.27E−02	−4.67E−03	−3.42E−02	−3.42E−02	−2.66E−02	−2.27E−02	3.64E−02	3.60E−03
$h(7) = h(15)$	4.20E−02	5.54E−02	3.25E−02	3.25E−02	3.92E−02	4.20E−02	−8.10E−02	−6.93E−02
$h(8) = h(14)$	1.15E−01	1.13E−01	1.15E−01	1.15E−01	1.15E−01	1.15E−01	−7.89E−02	−4.95E−02
$h(9) = h(13)$	−6.88E−03	−1.45E−02	−3.63E−03	−3.63E−03	−6.18E−03	−6.88E−03	9.62E−02	1.01E−01
$h(10) = h(12)$	−3.01E−01	−3.00E−01	−3.04E−01	−3.04E−01	−3.03E−01	−3.01E−01	3.12E−01	3.06E−01
$h(11)$	−4.63E−01	−4.56E−01	−4.72E−01	−4.72E−01	−4.66E−01	−4.63E−01	3.89E−01	3.94E−01

cmp, compromise; MOCSO, multiobjective cat swarm optimization; Q-MOCSO, quantum-inspired multiobjective cat swarm optimization.

Table 6 Comparison of the Proposed Quantum-Inspired Multiobjective Cat Swarm Optimization With Other Multiobjective Evolutionary Algorithms

	min(J_1)			min(J_2)			min(J_3)			min($J_1 + J_2 + J_3$)		
Algorithm	**PBR**	**SBR**	**Entropy**	**PBR**	**SBR**	**Entropy**	**PBR**	**SBR**	**Entropy**	**PBR**	**SBR**	**Entropy**
NSGA-II	0.051	0.2243	1.23	0.521	0.037	2.34	12.01	6.121	1.89	0.111	0.162	2.13
MOPSO	0.039	0.1865	2.51	0.492	0.021	2.72	11.01	6.951	1.41	0.123	0.141	1.11
MODE	0.043	0.1853	3.56	0.533	0.019	2.61	6.04	8.021	1.32	0.071	0.073	2.91
MOCSO	0.095	0.0608	2.13	0.4265	0.308	1.70	0.223	0.169	0.10	0.1969	0.018	1.10
Q-MOCSO	0.019	0.1713	2.14	0.1445	0.021	2.33	0.020	0.165	0.14	0.1110	0.036	1.33

Q-MOCSO, quantum-inspired multiobjective cat swarm optimization; MOCSO, multiobjective cat swarm optimization; MODE, multiobjective differential evolution; MOPSO, multiobjective particle swarm optimization; NSGA-II, nondominated sorting genetic algorithm II; PBR, passband ripple; SBR, stopband ripple.

Table 7 Comparison of Hardware Utilization of the Proposed Approach With that of Other State-of-the-Art Methods

Methods	Taps	Bits	Device	Slices	Flip-Flops	4-Input LUTs	Maximum Frequency (MHz)
Serial multiplier and serial adder [46]	8	8	Xc4vf100	103	97	162	225
Shift add form [46]	8	8	Xc4vf100	101	48	119	79.171
Multiplexer-based reconfigurable FIR filter [47]	6	–	Virtex	5349	–	9669	–
Dynamic partial reconfigurable FIR filter [47]	6	–	Virtex	4733	–	8427	–
Add shift method [47]	10	12	Virtex-II	474	916	406	–
PDA method [48]	10	12	Virtex-II	781	1480	1103	–
Modified retiming serial multiplier [49]	8	8	Xc4vf100	287	196	379	302.253
Proposed method	11	16	Xc7vx330t-3ffg1761	265	106	288	217.83

FIR, finite impulse response; LUTs, lookup tables, PDA, parallel distributed arithmetic.

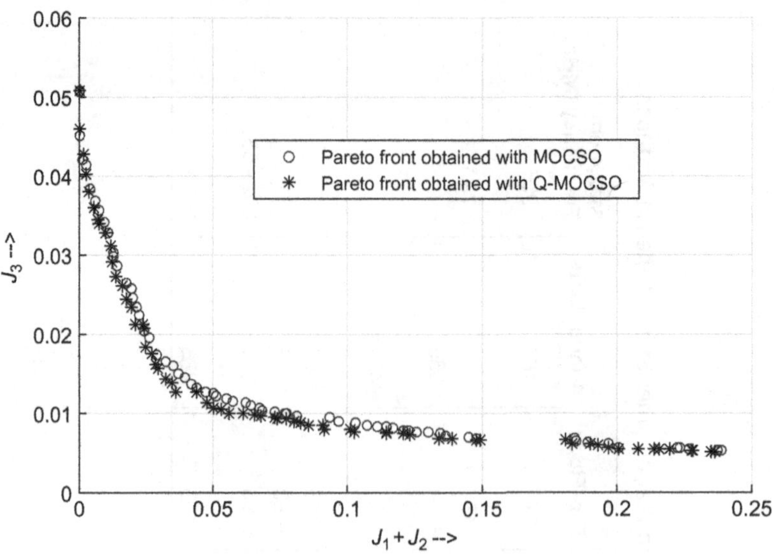

FIG. 10

Pareto front obtained with multiobjective cat swarm optimization (*MOCSO*) and quantum-inspired multiobjective cat swarm optimization (*Q-MOCSO*) after consideration of J_3 as the third objective function for $J_1 + J_2$ and J_3.

Table 8 Comparison of Power Consumed During Filter Execution

Filter Name	MOCSO		Q-MOCSO	
	Entropy	PC (mW)	Entropy	PC (mW)
Table_I_Min_J1	0.51	0.09	0.59	0.08
Table_I_Min_J2	0.23	0.07	2.5	0.09
Table_I_cmp_J1&J2	0.24	0.08	0.5	0.07
Table_III_Min_J1	1.13	0.15	1.38	0.07
Table_III_Min_J2	2.66	0.11	1.75	0.08
Table_III_Min_J3	0.15	0.035	0.12	0.04
Table_III_cmp_J1&J2&J3	0.64	0.05	0.26	0.06

MOCSO, multiobjective cat swarm optimization; PC, power consumed; Q-MOCSO, quantum-inspired multiobjective cat swarm optimization.

7 CONCLUSION

In this chapter a novel approach for digital FIR filter-based Hilbert transformer design with quantum-inspired cat swarm optimization has been proposed. The aim was not only minimization of ripples in the Hilbert transformer but also power

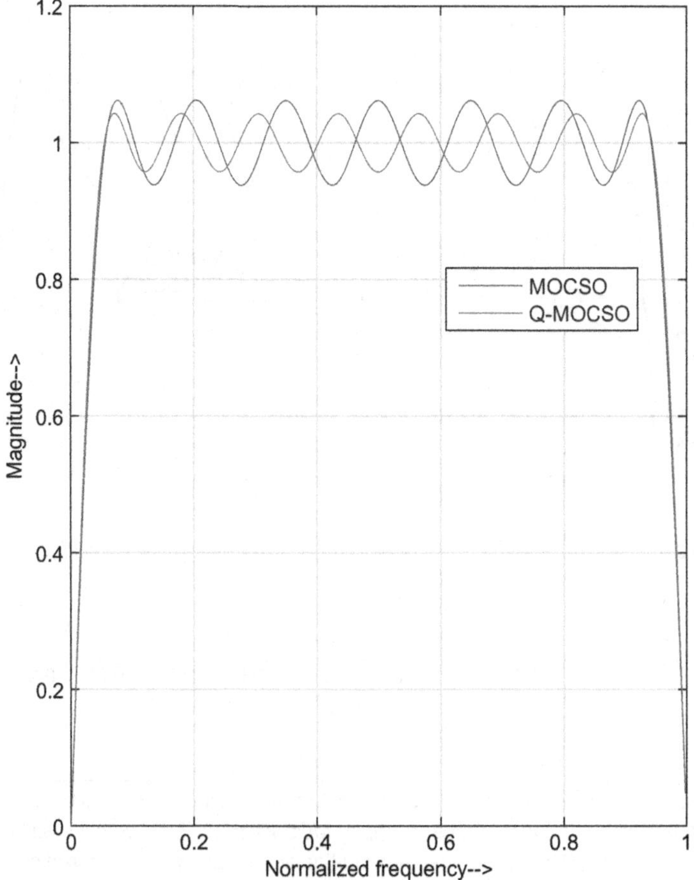

FIG. 11

Normalized frequency responses of Hilbert transformers designed with finite impulse response filters with minimum passband ripple. *MOCSO*, multiobjective cat swarm optimization; *Q-MOCSO*, quantum-inspired multiobjective cat swarm optimization.

minimization. In the existing work on optimization-based Hilbert transformers, the focus was only on minimizing ripples, whereas in the present work, motivated by the significance of reducing power loss, power minimization has been considered as one of the objectives. Hilbert transformer design was performed with FIR filters. Further, the filter design task was formulated as a multiobjective optimization problem and solved with a Q-MOCSO, which improves the convergence by improving the exploration capability of the algorithm. The use of multiobjectives allows one to select a filter from a set on the basis of requirements or the application. The suitability of the proposed algorithm was validated by our comparing it with the

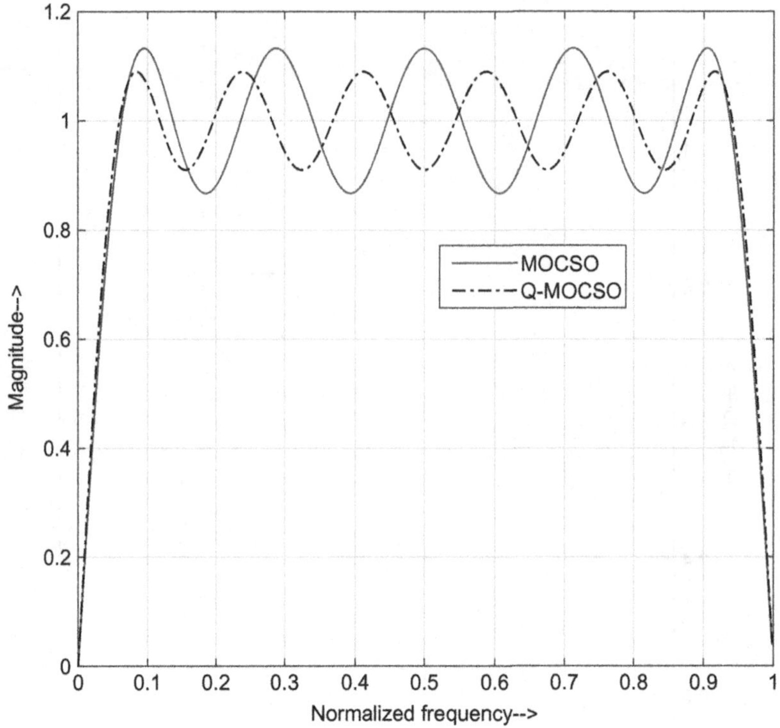

FIG. 12

Normalized frequency responses of Hilbert transformers designed with finite impulse response filters with minimum stopband ripple. *MOCSO*, multiobjective cat swarm optimization; *Q-MOCSO*, quantum-inspired multiobjective cat swarm optimization.

Table 9 *t*-Test Analysis of the Proposed Quantum-Inspired Multiobjective Cat Swarm Optimization for Two Objective Functions J_1 and J_2

	min(J_1)		min(J_2)		arb(J_1 and J_2)	
	PBR *p*	SBR *p*	PBR *p*	SBR *p*	PBR *p*	SBR *p*
NSGA-II	0.8811	0.2011	0.3717	0.9842	0.8563	0.5641
MOPSO	0.9974	0.3910	0.3402	0.8756	0.7781	0.4739
MODE	0.9835	0.5012	0.6581	0.7930	0.7105	0.8138
MOCSO	0.8081	0.7161	0.8643	0.7271	0.6523	0.6398

MOCSO, multiobjective cat swarm optimization; MODE, multiobjective differential evolution; MOPSO, multiobjective particle swarm optimization; NSGA-II, nondominated sorting genetic algorithm II.

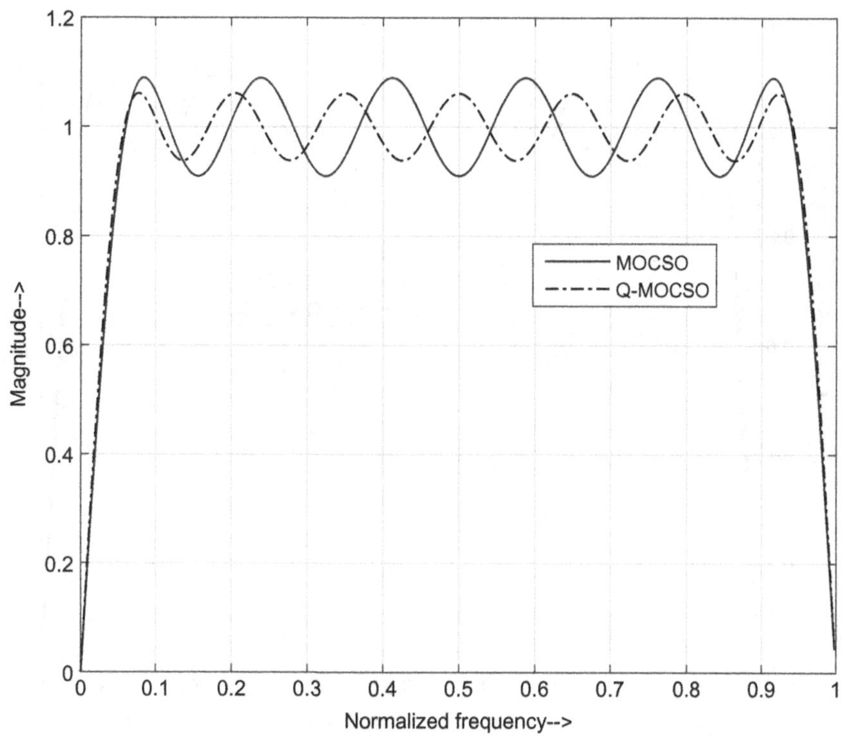

FIG. 13

Normalized frequency responses of Hilbert transformers designed with finite impulse response filters with minimum entropy. *MOCSO*, multiobjective cat swarm optimization; *Q-MOCSO*, quantum-inspired multiobjective cat swarm optimization.

classical MOCSO and existing evolutionary algorithms. Q-MOCSO outperformed all the other algorithms in meeting the specifications for a filter of given order. A trade-off between ripple minimization and power consumption was observed in the Pareto front after convergence (i.e., it is practically impossible to design a filter which minimizes both simultaneously for lower-order filters). The trade-off avoids the use of classical optimization methods involving a single objective. Further, to verify the applicability of the proposed algorithm, for real-time applications, the designed filters were implemented with use of a Virtex-7 field-programmable gate array (xc7vx485t-2ffg1761 device). Both the simulated and the experimental results confirm the usefulness of Q-MOCSO for designing FIR filters with minimum PBR, SBR, and power consumption.

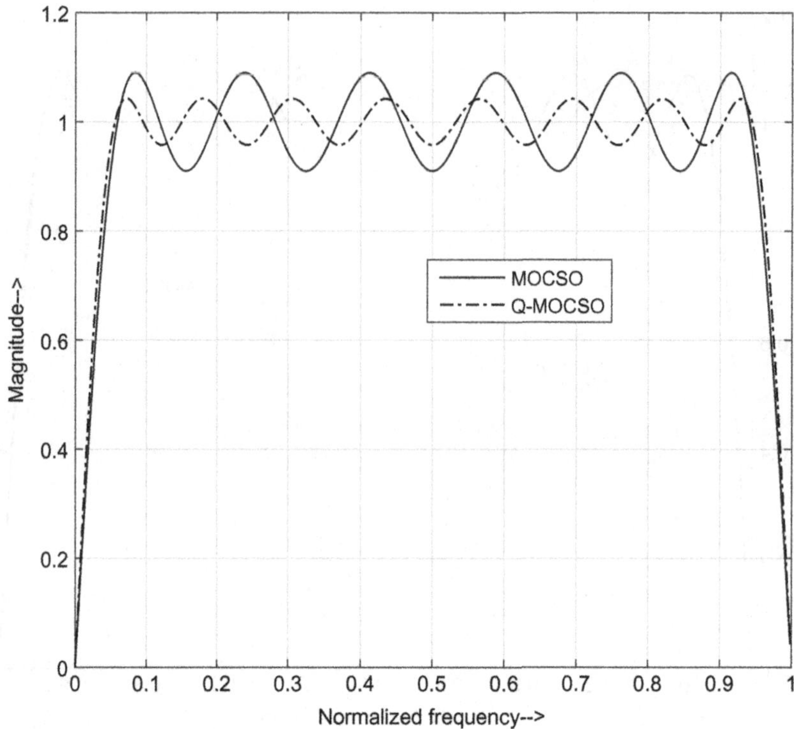

FIG. 14

Normalized frequency responses of Hilbert transformers designed with finite impulse response filters with trade-off between minimum passband ripple, stopband ripple, and entropy. *MOCSO*, multiobjective cat swarm optimization; *Q-MOCSO*, quantum-inspired multiobjective cat swarm optimization.

REFERENCES

[1] L. Lita, D. Visan, I. Cioc, L. Banica, Low-voltage FIR filter for receivers used in communication systems, in: 27th International Spring Seminar on Electronics Technology: Meeting the Challenges of Electronics Technology Progress, 2004, vol. 3, IEEE, 2004, pp. 434–438, http://dx.doi.org/10.1109/ISSE.2004.1490850.

[2] Y. Lian, Y. Wei, A computationally efficient nonuniform FIR digital filter bank for hearing aids, IEEE Trans. Circ. Syst. I: Regular Pap. 52 (12) (2005) 2754–2762, http://dx.doi.org/10.1109/TCSI.2005.857871.

[3] Y. Zhang, C.-H. Chen, T. He, G.C. Temes, A continuous-time delta-sigma modulator for biomedical ultrasound beamformer using digital ELD compensation and FIR feedback, IEEE Trans. Circ. Syst. I: Regular Pap. 62 (7) (2015) 1689–1698, http://dx.doi.org/10.1109/TCSI.2015.2434100.

[4] J. Radecki, J. Konrad, E. Dubois, Design of multidimensional finite-wordlength FIR and IIR filters by simulated annealing, IEEE Trans. Circ. Syst. II: Analog Digital Signal Process. 13 (6) (2005) 424–431, http://dx.doi.org/10.1109/82.392318.

[5] H.-C. Lu, S.-T. Tzeng, Design of arbitrary FIR log filters by genetic algorithm approach, Signal Process. 80 (3) (2000) 497–505, http://dx.doi.org/10.1016/S0165-1684(99)00146-2.
[6] D. Suckley, Genetic algorithm in the design of FIR filters, IEE Proc. G Circ. Devices Syst. 138 (2) (1991) 234, http://dx.doi.org/10.1049/ip-g-2.1991.0043.
[7] J.I. Ababneh, M.H. Bataineh, Linear phase FIR filter design using particle swarm optimization and genetic algorithms, Digital Signal Process. 18 (4) (2008) 657–668, http://dx.doi.org/10.1016/j.dsp.2007.05.011.
[8] K. Boudjelaba, F. Ros, D. Chikouche, Potential of particle swarm optimization and genetic algorithms for FIR filter design, Circ. Syst. Signal Process. 33 (10) (2014) 3195–3222, http://dx.doi.org/10.1007/s00034-014-9800-y.
[9] M. Najjarzadeh, A. Ayatollahi, FIR digital filters design: particle swarm optimization utilizing LMS and minimax strategies, in: 2008 IEEE International Symposium on Signal Processing and Information Technology, IEEE, 2008, pp. 129–132, http://dx.doi.org/10.1109/ISSPIT.2008.4775685.
[10] W. Fang, J. Sun, W. Xu, J. Liu, FIR digital filters design based on quantum-behaved particle swarm optimization, in: First International Conference on Innovative Computing, Information and Control—Volume I (ICICIC'06), vol. 1, IEEE, 2006, pp. 615–619, http://dx.doi.org/10.1109/ICICIC.2006.77.
[11] N. Karaboga, B. Cetinkaya, Design of digital FIR filters using differential evolution algorithm, Circ. Syst. Signal Process. 25 (5) (2006) 649–660, http://dx.doi.org/10.1007/s00034-005-0721-7.
[12] Q. Zhao, G. Meng, Notice of violation of IEEE publication principles design of digital fir filters using differential evolution algorithm based on reserved gene, in: 2010 International Conference of Information Science and Management Engineering, vol. 2, IEEE, 2010, pp. 177–180, http://dx.doi.org/10.1109/ISME.2010.237.
[13] B. Luitel, G. Venayagamoorthy, Differential evolution particle swarm optimization for digital filter design, in: 2008 IEEE Congress on Evolutionary Computation (IEEE World Congress on Computational Intelligence), vol. 2 (2), 2008, pp. 3954–3961, http://dx.doi.org/10.1109/CEC.2008.4631335.
[14] A.S. Chandra, S. Chattopadhyay, Differential evolution based design of multiplier-less FIR filter using canonical signed digit representation, in: 2012 International Conference on Communications, Devices and Intelligent Systems (CODIS), IEEE, 2012, pp. 425–428, http://dx.doi.org/10.1109/CODIS.2012.6422229.
[15] V. Durbadal, M. Rajib, Vasundhara, D. Mandal, R. Kar, S.P. Ghoshal, Digital FIR filter design using fitness based hybrid adaptive differential evolution with particle swarm optimization, Nat. Comput. 13 (1) (2014) 55–64, http://dx.doi.org/10.1007/s11047-013-9381-x.
[16] S.K. Saha, R. Dutta, R. Choudhury, R. Kar, D. Mandal, S.P. Ghoshal, Efficient and accurate optimal linear phase FIR filter design using opposition-based harmony search algorithm, Sci. World J. 2013 (2013) 1–16, http://dx.doi.org/10.1155/2013/320489.
[17] S.K. Saha, S.P. Ghoshal, R. Kar, D. Mandal, Cat swarm optimization algorithm for optimal linear phase FIR filter design, ISA Trans. 52 (6) (2013) 781–794, http://dx.doi.org/10.1016/j.isatra.2013.07.009.
[18] R. Haupt, S. Haupt, The binary genetic algorithm, in: Practical Genetic Algorithms, John Wiley and Sons, Inc., Hoboken, NJ, USA, 1998, pp. 27–50, http://dx.doi.org/10.1002/0471671746.ch2.

[19] Y. Sharafi, M.A. Khanesar, M. Teshnehlab, Discrete binary cat swarm optimization algorithm, in: 2013 3rd IEEE International Conference on Computer, Control and Communication, IC4 2013, 2013, http://dx.doi.org/10.1109/IC4.2013.6653754.
[20] A. Manju, M.J. Nigam, Applications of quantum inspired computational intelligence: a survey, Artif. Intell. Rev. 42 (1) (2014) 79–156, http://dx.doi.org/10.1007/s10462-012-9330-6.
[21] J.T. Tsai, J.-h. Chou, W.-h. Ho, Improved quantum-inspired evolutionary algorithm for engineering design optimization, Math. Probl. Eng. 2012 (2012) 1–27, http://dx.doi.org/10.1155/2012/836597.
[22] A. Ghosh, S. Mukherjee, Quantum annealing and computation: a brief documentary note, 2013, arXiv:1310.1339.
[23] S. Bhattacharyya, S. Dey, An efficient quantum inspired genetic algorithm with chaotic map model based interference and fuzzy objective function for gray level image thresholding, in: Proceedings—2011 International Conference on Computational Intelligence and Communication Systems, CICN 2011, vol. 6, 2011, pp. 121–125, http://dx.doi.org/10.1109/CICN.2011.24.
[24] W. Fang, J. Sun, W. Xu, A new mutated quantum-behaved particle swarm optimizer for digital IIR filter design, EURASIP J. Adv. Signal Process. 2009 (2009), http://dx.doi.org/10.1155/2009/367465.
[25] L.M. De Melo, G.A.O.P. Da Costa, R.Q. Feitosa, A.V.A. Cruz, Quantum-inspired evolutionary algorithm and differential evolution used in the adaptation of segmentation parameters, in: GEOBIA-2008, GEOgraphic Object Based Image Analysis for 21st Century, 2008, pp. 1–5.
[26] A. Bouaziz, A. Draa, S. Chikhi, A quantum-inspired artificial bee colony algorithm for numerical optimisation, in: 2013 11th International Symposium on Programming and Systems (ISPS), IEEE, 2013, pp. 81–88, http://dx.doi.org/10.1109/ISPS.2013.6581498.
[27] M. Soleimanpour-Moghadam, H. Nezamabadi-pour, M.M. Farsangi, A quantum inspired gravitational search algorithm for numerical function optimization, Inf. Sci. 267 (2014) 83–100, http://dx.doi.org/10.1016/j.ins.2013.09.006.
[28] T. Arslan, A.T. Erdogan, D.H. Horrocks, Low power design for DSP: methodologies and techniques, Microelectron. J. 27 (8) (1996) 731–744, http://dx.doi.org/10.1016/0026-2692(96)00010-9.
[29] M. Nemani, F.N. Najm, Towards a high-level power estimation capability, IEEE Trans. Comput.-Aided Des. Integr. Circ. Syst. 15 (6) (1996) 588–598, http://dx.doi.org/10.1109/43.503929.
[30] S. Ramprasad, N.R. Shanbhag, I.N. Hajj, Information-theoretic bounds on average signal transition activity, IEEE Trans. Very Large Scale Integr. Syst. 7 (3) (1999) 359–368, http://dx.doi.org/10.1109/92.784097.
[31] N.R. Shanbhag, A mathematical basis for power-reduction in digital VLSI systems, IEEE Trans. Circ. Syst. II: Analog Digital Signal Process. 44 (11) (1997) 935–951, http://dx.doi.org/10.1109/82.644047.
[32] P.P. Sotiriadis, V. Tarokh, A. Chandrakasan, Energy reduction in VLSI computation modules: an information-theoretic approach, IEEE Trans. Inf. Theory 49 (4) (2003) 790–808, http://dx.doi.org/10.1109/TIT.2003.809601.
[33] C.L. Su, C. Tsui, A.M. Despain, Saving power in the control path of embedded processors, IEEE Design Test Comput. 11 (4) (1994) 24–31, http://dx.doi.org/10.1109/54.329448.
[34] V.E. DeBrunner, L.S. DeBrunner, C. Stephanie, X. Hu, Using entropy to build efficient FIR digital filters, in: 3rd IEEE Signal Processing Education Workshop. 2004

IEEE 11th Digital Signal Processing Workshop, 2004, IEEE, 2004, pp. 97–101, http://dx.doi.org/10.1109/DSPWS.2004.1437919.

[35] S.U. Ahmad, A. Antoniou, A multiobjective genetic algorithm for asymmetric FIR filters, in: 2007 IEEE International Symposium on Signal Processing and Information Technology, IEEE, 2007, pp. 525–530, http://dx.doi.org/10.1109/ISSPIT.2007.4458200.

[36] P.M. Pradhan, G. Panda, Solving multiobjective problems using cat swarm optimization, Expert Syst. Appl. 39 (3) (2012) 2956–2964, http://dx.doi.org/10.1016/j.eswa.2011.08.157.

[37] G. Fiandaca, E.S. Fraga, S. Brandani, A multi-objective genetic algorithm for the design of pressure swing adsorption, Eng. Opt. 41 (9) (2009) 833–854, http://dx.doi.org/10.1080/03052150903074189.

[38] K. Deb, A. Pratap, S. Agarwal, T. Meyarivan, A fast and elitist multiobjective genetic algorithm: NSGA-II, IEEE Trans. Evol. Comput. 6 (2) (2002) 182–197, http://dx.doi.org/10.1109/4235.996017.

[39] C. Coello, G. Pulido, M. Lechuga, Handling multiple objectives with particle swarm optimization, IEEE Trans. Evol. Comput. 8 (3) (2004) 256–279, http://dx.doi.org/10.1109/TEVC.2004.826067.

[40] B. Babu, M. Jehan, Differential evolution for multi-objective optimization, in: The 2003 Congress on Evolutionary Computation, 2003. CEC '03, vol. 4, 2003, pp. 2696–2703, http://dx.doi.org/10.1109/CEC.2003.1299429.

[41] T. Robič, B. Filipič, DEMO: differential evolution for multiobjective optimization, in: Lecture Notes in Computer Science, vol. 3410, 2005, pp. 520–533.

[42] Y. Wang, Y.-W. Leung, Multiobjective programming using uniform design and genetic algorithm, IEEE Trans. Syst. Man Cybern. C: Appl. Rev. 30 (3) (2000) 293–304, http://dx.doi.org/10.1109/5326.885111.

[43] K.-H. Han, J.-H. Kim, Quantum-inspired evolutionary algorithm for a class of combinatorial optimization, IEEE Trans. Evol. Comput. 6 (6) (2002) 580–593, http://dx.doi.org/10.1109/TEVC.2002.804320.

[44] N. Srinivas, K. Deb, Multiobjective optimization using nondominated sorting in genetic algorithms, Evol. Comput. 2 (3) (1994) 221–248, http://dx.doi.org/10.1162/evco.1994.2.3.221.

[45] M. Varadarajan, K. Swarup, Solving multi-objective optimal power flow using differential evolution, IET Gener. Transm. Dis. 2 (5) (2008) 720, http://dx.doi.org/10.1049/iet-gtd:20070457.

[46] B. Rashidi, B. Rashidi, M. Pourormazd, Design and implementation of low power digital FIR filter based on low power multipliers and adders on xilinx FPGA, in: 2011 3rd International Conference on Electronics Computer Technology, vol. 2, IEEE, 2011, pp. 18–22, http://dx.doi.org/10.1109/ICECTECH.2011.5941647.

[47] H. Lee, C.-S. Choi, Knowledge-based intelligent information and engineering systems, in: Lecture Notes in Computer Science, vol. 4253, Springer, Berlin/Heidelberg, 2006, pp. 108–115, http://dx.doi.org/10.1007/11893011.

[48] S. Mirzaei, A. Hosangadi, R. Kastner, FPGA implementation of high speed FIR filters using add and shift method, in: 2006 International Conference on Computer Design, 2006, pp. 108–115, http://dx.doi.org/10.1109/ICCD.2006.4380833.

[49] B. Rashidi, High performance and low-power finite impulse response filter based on ring topology with modified retiming serial multiplier on FPGA, IET Signal Process. 7 (8) (2013) 743–753, http://dx.doi.org/10.1049/iet-spr.2013.0153.

[50] M. Patrick Allen, Understanding Regression Analysis, Springer US, Boston, MA, 1997, pp. 61–65, http://dx.doi.org/10.1007/b102242.

CHAPTER

11 A novel graph clustering algorithm based on discrete-time quantum random walk

S.G. Roy[a], A. Chakrabarti[b]

Techno India College of Technology, New Town, Kolkata, WB, India[a] A.K. Choudhury School of Information Technology, University of Calcutta, Kolkata, WB, India[b]

1 INTRODUCTION

Graph clustering is an important subject, and deals with clustering with graphs. The data of a clustering problem can be represented as a graph where each element to be clustered is represented as a node and the distance between two elements is modeled by a certain weight on the edge linking the nodes [1]. Thus in graph clustering, elements within a cluster are connected to each other but have no connection to elements outside that cluster. Also, some recently proposed approaches [2–4] perform clustering directly on graph-based data. Some important approaches toward graph-based clusters are contiguity-based clusters and clique [5]. Fig. 1 [6] shows a cluster structure.

The clustering concept is very useful in various fields of computer science such as image segmentation and complex network analysis [7,8].

In biology and medicine, the clustering concept is also frequently used to analyze data; for example, in the fields of gene expression [9,10] and protein structure analysis [11,12]. The clustering concept is also used in astronomy [13].

2 CLASSICAL APPROACH OF CLUSTERING

The classical clustering approach generally categorizes clustering algorithms into hierarchical or partitioned clustering algorithms. The different categories of classical clustering algorithms are shown in Fig. 2. In the hierarchical approach, a nested set of clusters is created. Every level of this creates a separate set of clusters. At the lowest level, all items belong to their own unique cluster, and at the highest level, each item

Quantum Inspired Computational Intelligence. http://dx.doi.org/10.1016/B978-0-12-804409-4.00011-5

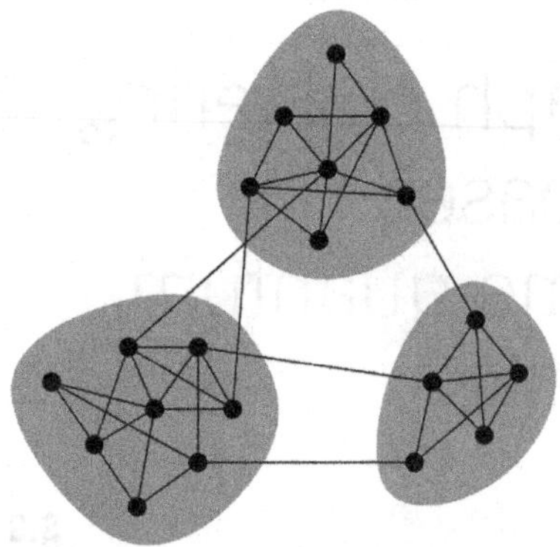

FIG. 1

Structure of a cluster.

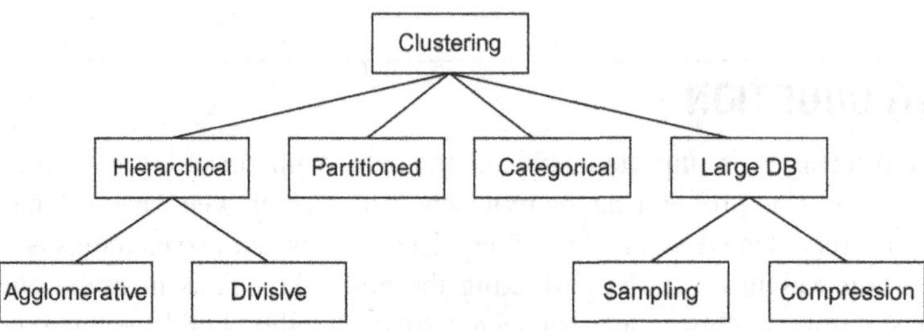

FIG. 2

Classification of clustering. *DB*, database.

is in the same cluster [14]. In hierarchical clustering the desired number of clusters is not given as input. The hierarchical clustering algorithms can be further classified into agglomerative algorithms (use a bottom-up approach) and divisive algorithms (use a top-down approach). In the partitioned clustering approach, only one set of clusters is created. This approach results in a final cluster set based on the desired number of clusters. To implement any clustering algorithm a mathematical model is used. One such model is a graph theoretic approach, which is used in this work.

2.1 HIERARCHICAL CLUSTERING ALGORITHMS

Hierarchical clustering algorithms are classical clustering algorithms where sets of clusters are created. In hierarchical algorithms an $n \times n$ vertex adjacency matrix is used as input and the adjacency matrix contains a distance value rather than a simple Boolean value [14]. If the number of elements to be clustered is represented by n and the number of clusters is represented by k, then the time complexity of hierarchical algorithms is $O\ (kn^2)$. An agglomerative algorithm is a type of hierarchical clustering algorithm where each individual element to be clustered is in its own cluster. These clusters are merged iteratively until all the elements belong to one cluster. It assumes that a set of elements and the distances between them are given as input.

2.2 NEAREST-NEIGHBOR ALGORITHM

This algorithm iteratively merges elements into the existing clusters that are closest. On the basis of a threshold value, elements can be added to existing clusters or a new cluster can be created.

3 QUANTUM GATES AND QUANTUM CIRCUITS

The basic unit of a quantum logic circuit is the quantum gate. Different quantum gates are required to design a quantum logic circuit. A quantum logic gate operates on quantum bits (qubits) to build a quantum circuit model of computation.

The most important difference between a classical and a quantum logic gate is that classical logic gates are not reversible but quantum logic gates are reversible. However, quantum reversible gates are implemented to perform classical computing. For example, all Boolean functions are implemented by the reversible Toffoli gate. Thus a quantum circuit can perform all the operations performed by a classical logic circuit. Any linear transformation of a complex vector space can be described by a matrix. Quantum logic gates are represented by unitary matrices. Matrix M is a unitary matrix if $MM^\dagger = I$, where I is an identity matrix and $M^\dagger$ is the transpose conjugate matrix of matrix M. In other words, we say M is a unitary transformation. The most important property of it is that any unitary transformation is reversible. Like the common classical logic gates, the quantum gates operate on one or two qubits. This helps quantum computing to represent quantum gates by 2×2 or 4×4 unitary matrices. Some useful, simple, single qubit, quantum state transformations are explained in the following, each with an example:

Commonly used gates

A quantum gate operating on n qubits is represented by a $2^n \times 2^n$ matrix. Any quantum gate is represented by a unitary matrix. In a quantum gate the input qubit numbers and output qubit numbers must be equal. The action performed by the quantum gate is defined by multiplication of the unitary matrix (represents the quantum gate) with the vector (represents the quantum state).

3.1 THE CONTROLLED NOT GATE

The controlled NOT (CNOT) gate acts on two qubits. The first one is the control qubit and the second is the target qubit. A CNOT gate inverts the target qubit if the control qubit is 1. The 4×4 unitary matrix for the CNOT gate is shown below:

$$\begin{pmatrix} 1 & 0 & 0 & 0 \\ 0 & 1 & 0 & 0 \\ 0 & 0 & 0 & 1 \\ 0 & 0 & 1 & 0 \end{pmatrix}$$

The upper left of the unitary matrix is the identity and the lower right is an inversion. A graphical representation of the CNOT gate is shown in Fig. 3. The first line in Fig. 3 is the control line and the second line is the target line.

FIG. 3

Controlled NOT gate.

3.2 THE TOFFOLI GATE

The Toffoli gate is named after Tommaso Toffoli and is an extension of the CNOT gate. It is often called a "controlled-controlled NOT gate" (CCNOT gate). The Toffoli gate is a CNOT gate with two control qubits and one target qubit. That is, the target qubit (third qubit) will be inverted if the first and second qubits are both 1. Sometimes an n-Toffoli gate is encountered; this is a CNOT gate with n controlling qubits. Any classical gate can be simulated by the Toffoli gate. So any conventional classical circuits can be implemented with use of Toffoli gates in a quantum computing environment. The Toffoli gate can also be implemented with two-qubit gates.

The 8×8 unitary matrix shown below is for the Toffoli gate.

$$\begin{pmatrix} 1 & 0 & 0 & 0 & 0 & 0 & 0 & 0 \\ 0 & 1 & 0 & 0 & 0 & 0 & 0 & 0 \\ 0 & 0 & 1 & 0 & 0 & 0 & 0 & 0 \\ 1 & 0 & 0 & 1 & 0 & 0 & 0 & 0 \\ 0 & 1 & 0 & 0 & 1 & 0 & 0 & 0 \\ 0 & 0 & 0 & 1 & 0 & 1 & 0 & 0 \\ 1 & 0 & 0 & 0 & 0 & 0 & 1 & 0 \\ 0 & 0 & 0 & 0 & 0 & 0 & 0 & 1 \end{pmatrix}$$

The upper left of the matrix is the identity and the lower right is an inversion, almost like the CNOT gate. A graphical representation of the Toffoli gate is shown in Fig. 4.

FIG. 4

Toffoli gate (controlled-controlled NOT gate).

3.3 THE HADAMARD GATE

The Hadamard gate is named after Jacques Hadamard, a French mathematician. The Hadamard gate is one of the most useful gates in quantum computing. This gate creates a superposition state out of a normal 0 or 1. The 2×2 unitary matrix for the Hadamard gate is shown below:

$$H = \frac{1}{\sqrt{2}} \begin{pmatrix} 1 & 1 \\ \mathrm{i} & -1 \end{pmatrix}.$$

A graphical representation of the Hadamard gate is shown in Fig. 5.

FIG. 5

Hadamard gate.

4 QUANTUM COMPUTATION AND QUANTUM RANDOM WALK

Quantum computing is one of the most promising areas of interdisciplinary research in the modern era. The primary objective of the quantum computation field is to solve classical problems much faster. There are many cases [15,16] where the complexity of the derived quantum algorithm of a problem is faster than it's classical counterpart. There are many classical algorithms that are based on classical random walks. This led to the proposal of a new concept, the quantum random walk. In quantum computing, quantum walks are the quantum analogue of classical random walks [17]. The basic difference between quantum and classical random walk is that in the quantum random walk the walker is in a superposition of positions but in the classical random walk the current state of a walker is described by a probability distribution over positions. There are two types of quantum random walk: discrete-time quantum random walk (DTQRW) and continuous-time quantum random walk (CTQRW). Ambainis et al. [18] give a concise description and comparison of these two quantum random walks.

The DTQRW was introduced after the CTQRW. As a result of quantum interference, the quantum walk has speed advantages. Quantum interference allows paths that have the same final destination to reinforce or cancel each other out.

A quantum walk requires a deep analysis of its simulation. Kendon [19] showed that it is relatively difficult to obtain tight bounds analytically for certain properties of quantum walks compared with numerical simulation. Moreover, independent simulations of quantum walks have yielded improved quantum walk algorithms: one example is the discovery by Shenvi et al. [20] of a quantum walk structure by numerical simulation that allowed Ambainis et al. [18] to develop a grid search algorithm with polynomial speedup; another example is Kempes [21] exponentially faster-than-classical hitting time algorithm which was simultaneously found in [22].

But on the other hand only a few of these algorithms have been simulated effectively by researchers. Thus helpful and comprehensive software packages are required that simulate quantum walk structures and would encourage researchers to use quantum walks for the development of new algorithms.

In this work we will restrict ourselves to the discrete-time formulation, since it shows the most algorithmic potential. Moreover, the discrete-time quantum walk formulation can be used effectively to simulate the continuous-time quantum walk as shown by Childs et al. [23].

5 CONTINUOUS-TIME QUANTUM RANDOM WALK

The continuous-time quantum random walk (CTQRW) can be easily defined from the continuous-time classical random walk. The difference between the continuous-time classical random walk and the CTQRW is that the classical probability in the continuous-time classical random walk is replaced by quantum amplitudes in the CTQRW. In the CTQRW, no coin is tossed and no coin space is required. Consider a quantum walker starts from a state $|\psi\ (0)$. After time t of the quantum random walk, the walker reaches a state $|\psi\ (t)$. Then we can define $|\psi(t)$ as: $|\psi\ (t)\rangle = \exp^{i\mathbf{H}t}\,|\psi\ (0)\ \rangle$. This random walk can be described by generator matrix **H** and the matrix elements of **H** are defined as in [24].

6 DISCRETE TIME QUANTUM RANDOM WALK

6.1 DISCRETE TIME QUANTUM RANDOM WALKS ON A LINE

In a discrete-time quantum random walk (DTQRW) on a line, a quantum particle is considered as a quantum walker. This quantum walker consists of two quantum states representing two coin states. To maintain quantum dynamics, which must be reversed, the coin value is affected by a unitary operator. We denote the basis states for the quantum walk as an ordered pair of labels in a ket $|x, c\rangle$, where x is the position and $c\epsilon\{0, 1\}$ is the state of the coin [25]. We place the walker at the origin with an initial coin state of 0 as shown in Fig. 6. At each time step the quantum walker shifts on the basis of the coin operator value. If the coin operator is the Hadamard H, then $H|x, 0\rangle = \frac{1}{\sqrt{2}}\,(|x, 0\rangle + |x, 1\rangle)$ and $H|x, 1\rangle = \frac{1}{\sqrt{2}}\,(|x, 0\rangle - |x, 1\rangle)$. The shift operator S operates on the basis states. Thus $S|x, 0\rangle = |x-1, 0\rangle$ and $S|x, 1\rangle = |x+1, 1\rangle$. The coin operator generates a superposition of coin states. The conditional shift operator shifts the walker to the desired position on the basis of the coin value. Mathematically [25], the first two steps of a discrete-time quantum walk on a straight line starting from the origin 0 in coin state 0 are shown below:

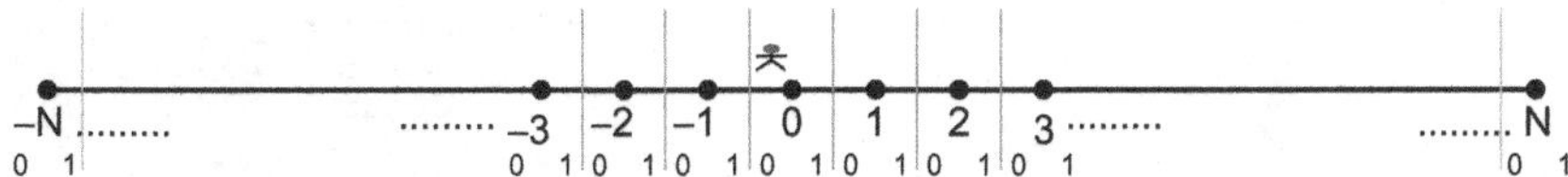

FIG. 6

A discrete-time quantum walk on a line starting from the origin with an initial coin state of 0 [25].

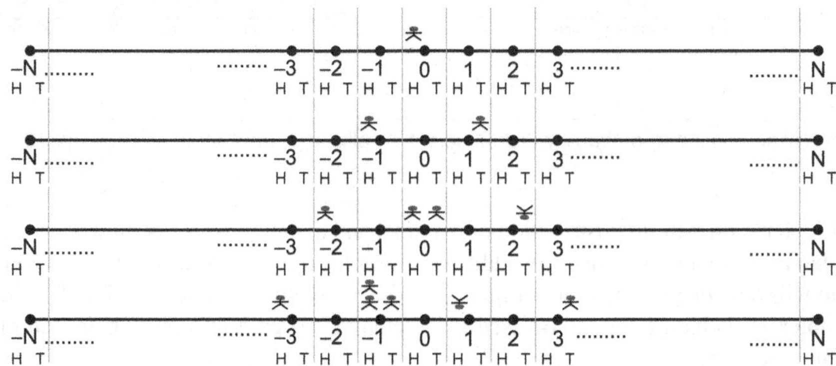

FIG. 7

Representation of the first three steps of a discrete-time quantum walk. The walker starts at an initial state of $|0, 0\rangle$. Quantum interference occurred as the walker traversed the line and walkers with a negative coefficient are shown upside down [25].

$$
\begin{aligned}
(SH)|0,0\rangle &= (SH^2)\, S\frac{1}{\sqrt{2}}\,(|0,0\rangle - |0,1\rangle) \\
&= (SH^2)\,\frac{1}{\sqrt{2}}\,(|-1,0\rangle - |1,1\rangle) \\
&= (SH)\, S\frac{1}{2}\,(|-1,0\rangle + |1,1\rangle + |1,0\rangle - |1,1\rangle) \\
&= (SH)\,\frac{1}{2}\,(|-2,0\rangle + |0,1\rangle + |0,0\rangle - |2,1\rangle).
\end{aligned} \tag{1}
$$

Quantum interference occurs as the walker walks, and may be constructive or destructive. Because of constructive interference some probabilities are amplified and for destructive interference some probabilities are decreased as shown in Eq. (1). This leads to the different behavior for classical and quantum random walks (Fig. 7).

When one step of the entire walk finishes, we obtain a probability distribution of the quantum walker, which is now in a superposition of positions on the line.

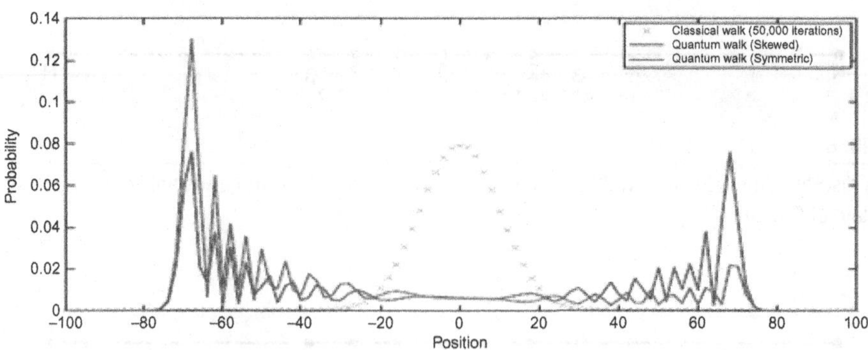

FIG. 8

Classical and quantum probability distributions for walks on a line after 100 time steps [25].

In Fig. 8 the probability distribution of classical and quantum walks is shown. As the Hadamard coin does not give any additional complex terms of coin state 0, each coin state will remain either real or complex, and thus they will not interfere. Finally, the complex Hadamard coin can be used if we change the coin to a more balanced or symmetric coin:

$$H_C = \frac{1}{\sqrt{2}}\begin{pmatrix} 1 & \mathrm{i} \\ \mathrm{i} & 1 \end{pmatrix}.$$

The progress of the quantum walk is controlled by a coin operator, which is in a superposition of quantum coin states [26]. The most general expression for a unitary coin operator $C_2^{(\mathrm{gen})}$ with two degrees of freedom is given as [26]

$$C_2^{(\mathrm{gen})} = \begin{pmatrix} \sqrt{\rho} & \sqrt{1-\rho}\mathrm{e}^{\mathrm{i}\theta} \\ \sqrt{1-\rho}\mathrm{e}^{\mathrm{i}\phi} & -\sqrt{\rho}\mathrm{e}^{\mathrm{i}(\theta+\phi)} \end{pmatrix},$$

where $0 \leq \theta, \phi \leq \pi$ are arbitrary angles, $0 \leq \rho \leq 1$. In this expression ρ, θ, and ϕ determine the bias and the phase angles of the coin. If $\rho = 0.5$ and $\theta = \phi = 0$, then the following expression, called the "Hadamard coin operator," is obtained [26]:

$$C_2^{(\mathrm{Hada})} = \frac{1}{\sqrt{2}}\begin{pmatrix} 1 & 1 \\ 1 & -1 \end{pmatrix}.$$

The phases (θ, ϕ) in the general coin operator appear in the evolution of the walk on the line as $(\theta + \phi)$. Without loss of generality, the coin operators take the form given below [26]:

$$C_2^{(\mathrm{bias})} = \begin{pmatrix} \sqrt{\rho} & \sqrt{1-\rho} \\ \sqrt{1-\rho} & -\sqrt{\rho} \end{pmatrix}.$$

6.1.1 Grover operator

Moore and Russell [27] first introduced the Grover operator, which is based on Grover's diffusion operator. The Grover operator is shown below [26]:

$$C_d^{(G)} = \begin{pmatrix} \frac{2}{d}-1 & \frac{2}{d} & \cdots & \frac{2}{d} \\ \frac{2}{d} & \frac{2}{d}-1 & \cdots & \frac{2}{d} \\ \cdot & \cdot & \cdots & \cdot \\ \cdot & \cdot & \cdots & \cdot \\ \cdot & \cdot & \cdots & \cdot \\ \frac{2}{d} & \frac{2}{d} & \cdots & \frac{2}{d}-1 \end{pmatrix}.$$

If $d = 3$, we get [26]

$$C_3^{(G)} = \frac{1}{3}\begin{pmatrix} -1 & 2 & 2 \\ 2 & -1 & 2 \\ 2 & 2 & -1 \end{pmatrix}.$$

The $d = 4$ Grover coin is the only unbiased Grover coin since all the entries are $\pm\frac{1}{2}$ [26]:

$$C_4^{(G)} = \frac{1}{2}\begin{pmatrix} -1 & 1 & 1 & 1 \\ 1 & -1 & 1 & 1 \\ 1 & 1 & -1 & 1 \\ 1 & 1 & 1 & -1 \end{pmatrix}$$

6.2 DISCRETE FOURIER TRANSFORM COIN

This is an unbiased coin. For $d = 3$, it is [26]

$$C_3^{(DFT)} = \frac{1}{\sqrt{3}}\begin{pmatrix} 1 & 1 & 1 \\ 1 & \omega_3 & \omega_3^2 \\ 1 & \omega_3^2 & \omega_3 \end{pmatrix},$$

where $\omega_3 = e^{\frac{2i\pi}{3}}$ and $\omega_3^2 = e^{\frac{-2i\pi}{3}}$ are the complex cube roots of unity. The d-dimensional discrete Fourier transform coin is denoted by [26]:

$$C_d^{(DFT)} = \frac{1}{\sqrt{d}}\begin{pmatrix} 1 & 1 & 1 & \cdots & 1 \\ 1 & \omega & \omega^2 & \cdots & \omega^{d-1} \\ 1 & \omega^2 & \omega^4 & \cdots & \omega^{2(d-1)} \\ \cdot & \cdot & \cdot & \cdots & \cdot \\ \cdot & \cdot & \cdot & \cdots & \cdot \\ \cdot & \cdot & \cdot & \cdots & \cdot \\ 1 & \omega^{d-1} & \omega^{2(d-1)} & \cdots & \omega^{(d-1)^2} \end{pmatrix}$$

6.3 DISCRETE-TIME QUANTUM RANDOM WALKS ON GRAPHS

The DTQRW was discussed in [28]. DTQRW is conducted in a discrete space of positions. The quantum walk is caused to progress by the tossing of a coin and shifts of the walker on the basis of this coin toss in discrete time steps. We can define the DTQRW on a k-regular graph. This can be done with the position Hilbert space ($\mathcal{H}_P$) and the coin Hilbert space ($\mathcal{H}_C$). The total Hilbert space is defined by $\mathcal{H} = \mathcal{H}_C \otimes \mathcal{H}_P$. If in a k-regular graph the total number of vertices is represented by n, then $\mathcal{H}_C$ and $\mathcal{H}_P$ are given by $\mathcal{H}_C = \{|e_i\rangle : i = 1, 2, \ldots, n\}$ and $\mathcal{H}_P = \{|i\rangle : i = 1, 3, \ldots, n\}$. At each time step the shift operator ($\hat{S}$) shifts the position of the quantum walker, depending on the value of the coin flip operator ($\hat{C}$) the walker traversed, thus transferring the particle into the new superposition state in position space. All the outgoing edges coming from each vertex are labeled as $1, 2, \ldots, k$.

The conditional shift operator moves the quantum walker from vertex v_1 to vertex v_2. If the edge between v_1 and v_2 is labeled by l on v_1's side, then

$$\hat{S}|e_l\rangle \otimes |v_1\rangle = \begin{cases} |e_l\rangle \otimes |v_2\rangle & \text{if } e^l_{v_1} = (v_1, v_2) \\ 0 & \text{otherwise.} \end{cases}$$

We can define a total operator $\hat{U}$ acting on the quantum walker at each discrete time step by $\hat{U} = \hat{S}(\hat{I}_p \otimes \hat{C})$, where $\hat{I}_p$ is the identity operator on the position space. If the initial state is represented by $|\psi\ (0)$ and the state after t steps is represented by $|\psi\ (t)$, then, $|\psi\ (t)\ \rangle = \hat{U}^t|\psi\ (0)\ \rangle$.

The final probability distribution is [29] $P\ (x, t) = \sum_{i=1}^{k} |\langle e_i, x|\psi(t)\rangle|^2 = \sum_{i=1}^{k} |\langle x| \otimes \langle e_i|\psi\ (t)\ \rangle|^2$.

There are different types of coin operator $\hat{C}$ for k-regular graphs. Different types of coin operators are discussed in Section 7.1. The DTQRW behavior is dependent on the types of coin operator $\hat{C}$ and it's initial state.

7 QUANTUM COMPUTING LANGUAGE

Quantum Computing Language (QCL) is a quantum programming language which is used to write programs for quantum computers. A quantum program has to be run on a classical computer, which in turn controls a quantum computer. The quantum program takes classical input and produces classical output like classical programs. The quantum instruction consists of elementary gates, measurements, and initialization instructions, which are passed over a well-defined interface to the quantum computer. The computational model of a quantum programming language is a classical computer with quantum oracle. QCL [30–32] was created by Bernhard Ömer and it is the first realization of a language dedicated to quantum computing. Since every quantum computer has to be controlled by a classical computer, QCL includes features of classical programming languages, such as control structures, variables, loops, procedures, subroutines, functions, and conditional branching, and allows them to operate on classical and quantum data. Fig. 9, illustrates the simulation model for a quantum random walk on a graph obtained with QCL.

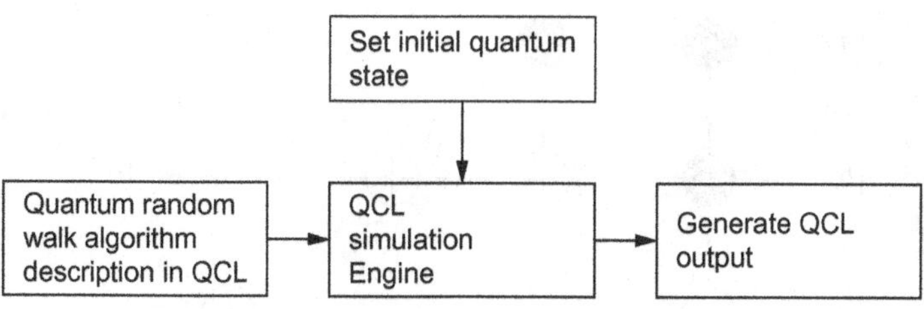

FIG. 9

Quantum random walk simulation model obtained with Quantum Computing Language *(QCL)*.

7.1 FEATURES OF QUANTUM COMPUTING LANGUAGE

QCL can be defined as a high-level programming language for quantum computing. The main features of QCL are discussed in [30] and are as follows:

- Like any classical programming languages, QCL supports flow control and also define functions. Different data types which are used in classical languages are also used in QCL. Some data types which are used in QCL are int, real, complex, boolean, string.
- The quantum operators are unitary operators and quantum gates are reversible gates.
- QCL allows on-the-fly determination of the inverse operator by inverse execution.
- It has various quantum data types (qubit registers) for compile time information on accessing the modes (qureg, quconst, quvoid, quscratch).
- It can manipulate quantum registers.
- It supports quantum memory management to allow local quantum variables.
- It provides Bennet-style scratch space management.

In QCL, qureg is used to define a quantum register. The qureg is one of the basic built-in data types in QCL. It can be realized as an array of qubits.

The following shows the register concept used in QCL:

```
qcl>qureg q[6]; allocates a six-qubit register
qcl>qureg b[4]; allocates another qubit register
```

Fig. 10, shows a quantum circuit used in this work.

The QCL code for the circuit in Fig. 10, is given below:

```
qcl>qureg q[3];// allocates a three-qubit register
qcl>toffoli(q[2],q[3],q[4]);//q[3],q[4] are control qubits and q[2] is a target qubit
qcl>CNot(q[3],q[4]);//q[4] is a control qubit and q[3] is a target qubit
qcl>Not(q[3]);
qcl>Not(q[2]);
```

In the above QCL code q[4] = $|a\rangle$, q[3] = $|b\rangle$ and q[2] = $|c\rangle$.

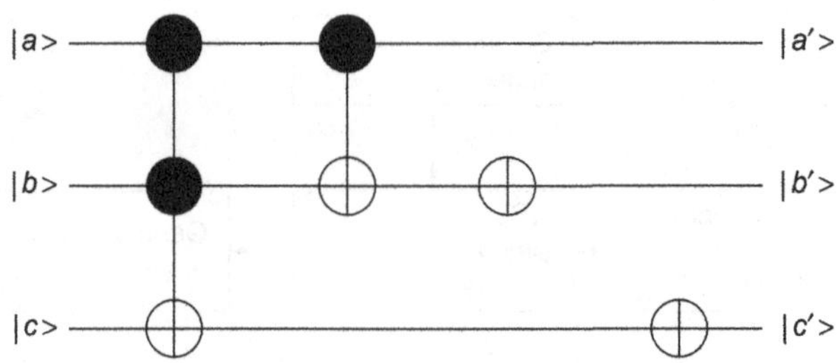

FIG. 10

Quantum circuit implementation by means of Quantum Computing Language.

8 ENCODING TEST GRAPHS FOR DISCRETE-TIME QUANTUM RANDOM WALK

We have considered three test graphs and analyzed clusters within these test graphs with the help of the proposed quantum random walk algorithm for clustering. The three test graphs are shown in Fig. 11.

The three test graph structures are different from each other. For testgraph1 the node set is $V = \{0, 1, 2, 3, 4, 5, 6\}$ as shown in Fig. 11A. This test graph consists of two subgraphs. Each subgraph is a complete graph. One is a complete graph with four vertices or nodes (complete graph K_4) and another is a complete graph with three vertices or nodes (complete graph K_3). That is, testgraph1 consists of strongly connected structures.

For testgraph2 the node set is $V = \{0, 1, 2, 3, 4, 5, 6, 7, 8, 9, 10, 11\}$ as shown in Fig. 11B. This test graph consists of three subgraphs, K_4, K_3, and a subgraph that is a connected general graph not a complete graph.

For testgraph3 the node set is $V = \{0, 1, 2, 3, 4, 5, 6, 7, 8, 9, 10, 11, 12, 13, 14, 15, 16, 17\}$ as shown in Fig. 11C. Testgraph3 is an extension of testgraph2 and contains a cycle of six vertices (cycle C_6).

The test graphs shown in Fig. 11 are encoded as shown in Fig. 12 to implement the quantum random walk circuit model. These encoded test graphs are used to design the quantum circuit which performs the desired DTQRW on the test graphs.

Let us consider a general undirected graph $G\ (V, E)$, where V represents the set of nodes and E is the edge set. This general graph (as shown in Fig. 11) is considered as a test case and the graph structure is obtained from its adjacency matrix, which is given by the user.

A subnode space is associated with each vertex v_i. This subnode space consists of k_i nodes connected to v_i. The degree of v_i is k_i as shown in the test graphs in Fig. 12. Moreover a constraint is assigned. The constraint is that the graph must be a k-regular graph and k is a power of 2 [33]. This constraint must be satisfied if a self-loop is added and helps to encode edges in binary values. As discussed in Section 11.6.2, a DTQRW can be defined by $U = SC$, where U is the unitary operator, S is the shift

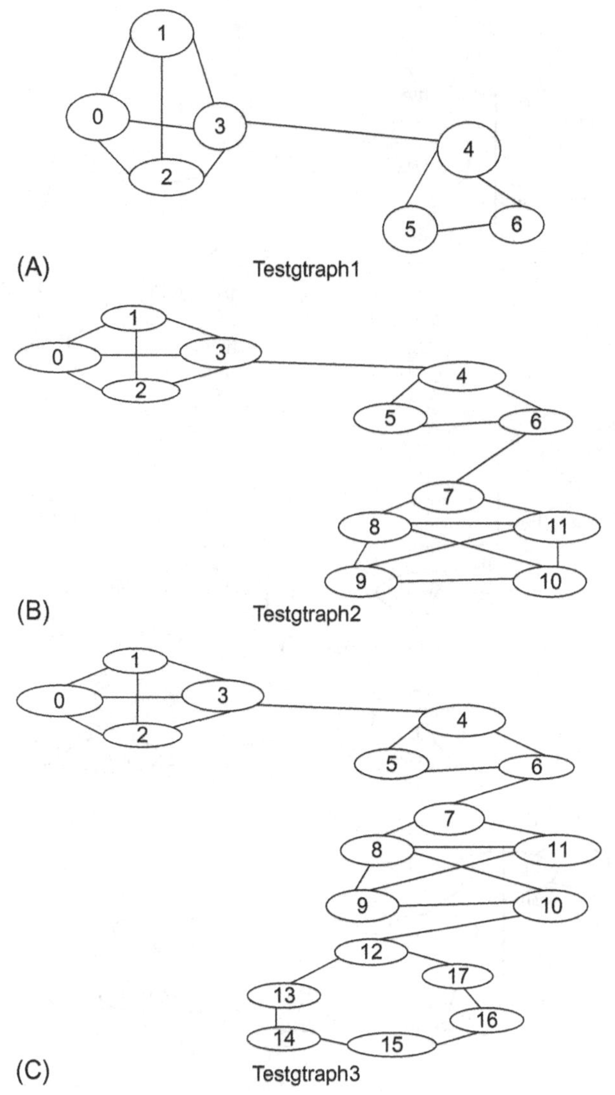

FIG. 11

Example graphs: (A) testgtraph1, (B) testgraph2, (C) testgraph3.

operator, and C is the coin operator. The quantum walk is defined by the coin register $|c\rangle$ and the state register $|v\rangle$ corresponding to the ith vertex of the graph.

If the number of vertices is denoted by n and the degree of the vertices is denoted by k, then we require $\log_2 k$ qubits for coin register $|c\rangle$ and $\log_2 n$ qubits for state register $|v\rangle$. As in Fig. 11, considered as a test case, the degree of the vertices is 4.

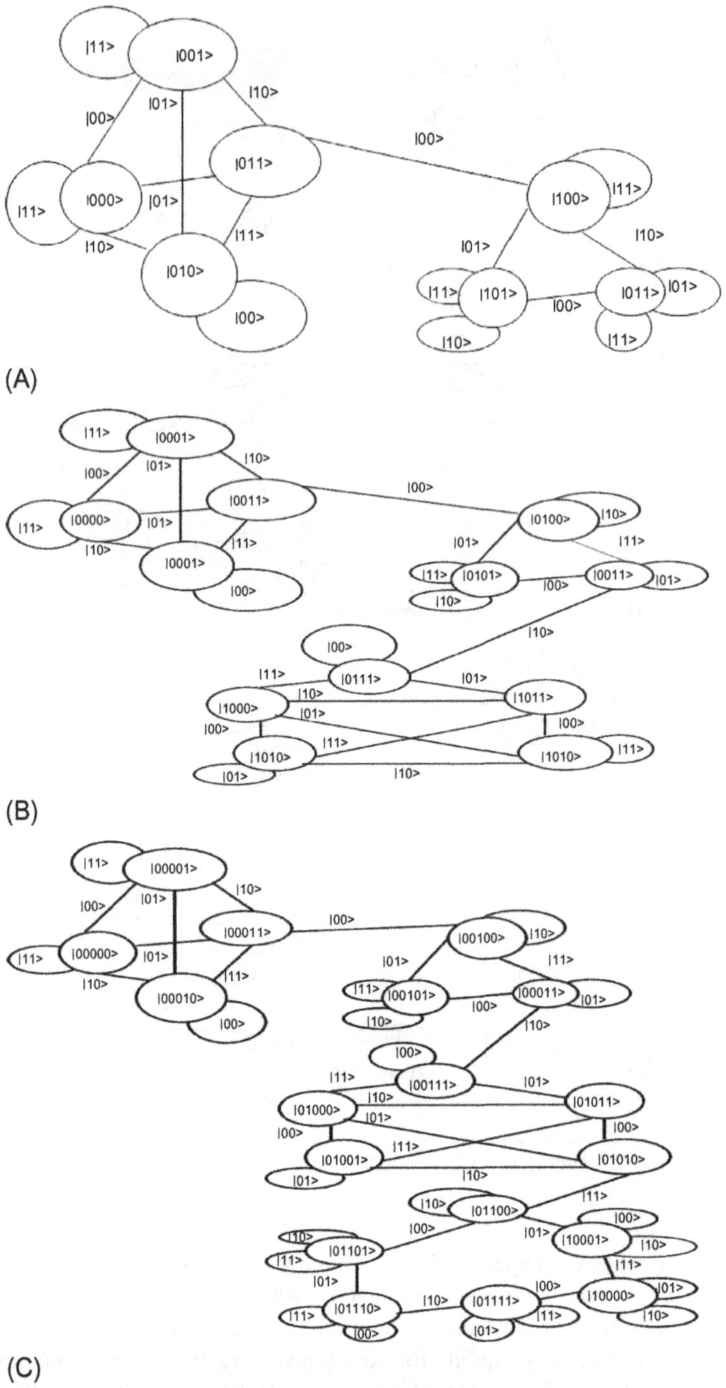

(A)

(B)

(C)

FIG. 12

(A) Testgraph1 and its node/edge labels, (B) testgraph2 and its node/edge labels, and (C) testgraph3 and its node/edge labels.

For the vertices, which are not connected , we add a self-loop to the vertices to make their degree 4 as shown in Fig. 12. The coin value defines the transition from one node to another along an edge. So a particular edge between two nodes is labeled by a particular coin value. Coin operator C gives a superposition of the probability amplitude values for all the nodes. The shift operator moves the quantum state of $|v_i\rangle$ to its neighboring quantum states on the basis of the coin operator value.

In Fig. 12 the degree of all the nodes or vertices for all the three test graphs is 4 , and thus we require two qubits for register.$|c\rangle$. The degrees are obtained from the superposition of these two qubits. Thus the labels on the edges are coin values obtained by the superposition of the coin register. The four coin states are $|00\rangle, |01\rangle, |10\rangle$, and $|11\rangle$.

For testgraph1 as shown in Fig. 12A, to represent the nodes we need three qubits as there are seven nodes in the test graph. The quantum walk is caused to progress by our shifting the quantum state of $|v_i\rangle$ to its neighbor node states depending on the coin value. The detailed step for one iteration of the quantum random walk on testgraph1 (see Fig. 12A) is shown in Eq. (2):

$$\begin{aligned}(SC)[|00\rangle|000\rangle] &= {}^{1}\!\sqrt{2}S[|00\rangle|000\rangle + |01\rangle|000\rangle + |10\rangle|000\rangle + |11\rangle|001\rangle] \\ &= {}^{1}\!\sqrt{2}S[|00\rangle|001\rangle + |01\rangle|011\rangle + |10\rangle|010\rangle + |11\rangle|000\rangle]\end{aligned} \quad (2)$$

The quantum walk starts from the node state $|000\rangle$ and the initial coin state is $|00\rangle$. The coin operator C is a Hadamard coin. Eq. (2) states that the walk starts from $|000\rangle$ and if the coin state is $|00\rangle$, the shift operator causes a transition from $|000\rangle$ to $|001\rangle$, if the coin state is $|01\rangle$, then transition from $|000\rangle$ to $|011\rangle$ occurs, if the coin state is $|10\rangle$, then transition from $|000\rangle$ to $|010\rangle$ occurs, and if the coin state is $|11\rangle$, then there is no transition (i.e., state $|000\rangle$ is retained). In the next iteration the next coin states are obtained from the superposition of the previous coin states. Thus the walk progress.

For testgraph2 as shown in Fig. 12B, four qubits are required to represent the vertices in the test graph. The detailed step for one iteration of the quantum random walk on testgraph2 (see Fig. 12B) is shown in Eq. (3):

$$\begin{aligned}(SC)[|00\rangle|0000\rangle] &= {}^{1}\!\sqrt{2}S[|00\rangle|0000\rangle + |01\rangle|0000\rangle + |10\rangle|0000\rangle + |11\rangle|0010\rangle] \\ &= {}^{1}\!\sqrt{2}S[|00\rangle|0001\rangle + |01\rangle|0011\rangle + |10\rangle|0010\rangle + |11\rangle|0000\rangle]\end{aligned} \quad (3)$$

The quantum walk starts from node $|0000\rangle$, and the initial coin state is $|00\rangle$. C is a Hadamard coin.

For testgraph3 shown in Fig. 12C, the quantum walk progresses similarly as explained for testgraph1 and testgraph2.

8.1 DISCRETE-TIME QUANTUM RANDOM WALK ON TESTGRAPH1

The basis states of the quantum random walk are defined as an ordered pair of labels in a ket $|x, c\rangle$ [25]. Here the position is denoted by x, and c is the coin state,

$c \in \{0, 1\}$. We place the walker at the origin with an initial coin state. At each time step, depending on the output of a coin operator, the conditional shift operator shifts the quantum walker. The coin operator gives the walker a superposition of coin states. Then the conditional shift operator shifts the walker to the actual position on the basis of the coin state. The first two steps of a discrete-time quantum walk starting from the origin in testgraph1 in coin state 00 are shown mathematically below:

8.1.1 Result for the first iteration

$$\begin{aligned}(SH)|00000\rangle &= S\frac{1}{2}\left(|00000\rangle + |00001\rangle + |00010\rangle + |00011\rangle\right)\\ &= \frac{1}{2}|00100\rangle + 01101\rangle + |01010\rangle + |00011\rangle\\ &= \frac{1}{2}|4\rangle + |13\rangle + |10\rangle + |3\rangle. \end{aligned} \tag{4}$$

The above mathematical result is same as we got from the QCL simulation.

It is clear from the above that after the first iteration the walker has traversed nodes 0, 1, 2, and 3. The nodes, which are directly connected to the start node, are all visited at the same time.

8.1.2 Result for the second iteration

$$\begin{aligned}&(SH)\left(|00100\rangle + 001101\rangle + |01010\rangle + |00011\rangle\right)\\ &S\frac{1}{4}\left(|00100\rangle + |00110\rangle + |00101\rangle + |00111\rangle + |01100\rangle + |01110\rangle - |01101\rangle - |01111\rangle\right.\\ &\quad\left. + |01000\rangle - |01010\rangle + |01001\rangle - |01011\rangle + |00000\rangle - |00010\rangle - |00001\rangle + |00011\rangle\right)\\ &= \frac{1}{4}\left(|00000\rangle + |01110\rangle + |01001\rangle + |00111\rangle + |10000\rangle + |00110\rangle - |00001\rangle - |01011\rangle\right.\\ &\quad\left. + |01000\rangle - |00010\rangle + |00101\rangle - |01111\rangle + |00100\rangle - |01010\rangle - |01101\rangle + \langle 00011\rangle\right)\\ &= 0.25\left(|0\rangle + |14\rangle + |9\rangle + |7\rangle + |16\rangle + |6\rangle - |1\rangle - |11\rangle + |8\rangle - |2\rangle + |5\rangle - |15\rangle + |4\rangle\right.\\ &\quad\left. - |10\rangle - |13\rangle + |3\rangle\right)\\ &= 0.25(|0\rangle - |1\rangle - |2\rangle + |3\rangle + |4\rangle + |5\rangle + |6\rangle + |7\rangle + |8\rangle - |9\rangle - |10\rangle - |11\rangle - |13\rangle\\ &\quad + |14\rangle - |15\rangle + |16\rangle) \end{aligned} \tag{5}$$

The above mathematical result is same as we got from the QCL simulation for the second iteration (the negative terms are due to the use of the Hadamard coin operation). It is clear from the above simulation that after second iteration the walker has traversed nodes 0, 1, 2, and 3 again and has traversed a new node (i.e., node 4). That is, all nodes which have previously been visited are visited again and the probability distribution values of these previously visited nodes are amplified.

8.1.3 Result for the third iteration

$$
\begin{aligned}
&(SH)\frac{1}{4}\left(|00000\rangle + |01110\rangle + |01001\rangle + |00111\rangle + |10000\rangle + |00110\rangle - |00001\rangle - |01011\rangle\right. \\
&\quad \left. + |01000\rangle - |00010\rangle + |00101\rangle - |01111\rangle + |00100\rangle - |01010\rangle - |01101\rangle + \langle 00011\rangle\right) \\
&= 0.5|00000\rangle + 0.375|00001\rangle + 0.5|00010\rangle + 0.5|00011\rangle - 0.125|00110\rangle - 0.125|01011\rangle \\
&\quad + 0.125|01100\rangle - 0.125|10000\rangle + 0.125|10011\rangle + 0.125|10101\rangle + 0.125|11010\rangle \\
&= 0.5|0\rangle + 0.375|1\rangle + 0.5|2\rangle + 0.5|3\rangle - 0.125|6\rangle - 0.125|11\rangle + 0.125|12\rangle - 0.125|16\rangle \\
&\quad + 0.125|19\rangle + 0.125|21\rangle + 0.125|26\rangle
\end{aligned} \tag{6}
$$

The mathematical result in Eq. (6) is same as we got from the QCL simulation for the third iteration.

It is clear from the above simulation results that after the third iteration the walker has traversed nodes 0, 1, 2, 3, and 4 again and has also traversed new nodes (i.e., nodes 5 and 6). That is, nodes 0, 1, 2, and 3 are visited again and the probability distribution values of these previously visited nodes are amplified again.

9 QUANTUM CIRCUITS FOR THE PROPOSED QUANTUM ALGORITHM

Fig. 13, presents the quantum circuits used to perform the proposed DTQRW on testgraph1 shown in Fig. 12A. Quantum permutation circuits are required to shift the quantum walker from one node to another, depending on the different coin values.

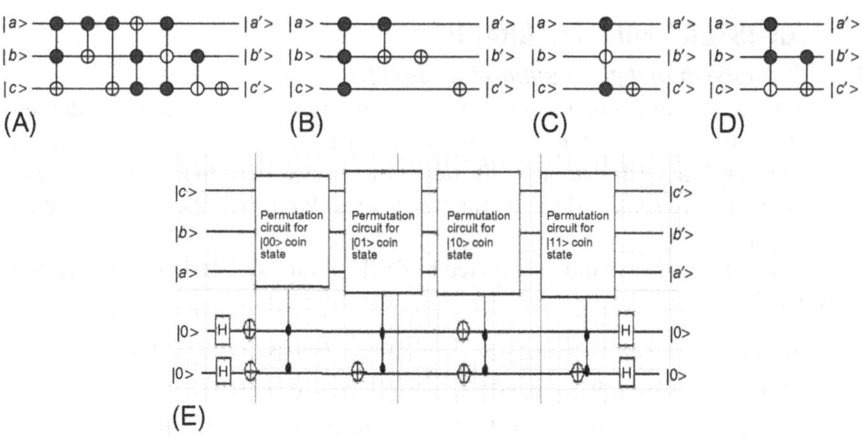

FIG. 13

Quantum permutation circuits for testgraph1: (A) for $|00\rangle$, (B) for $|01\rangle$, (C) for $|10\rangle$, and (D) for $|11\rangle$. (E) Complete circuit for one walk iteration.

To implement the quantum circuits we need suitable quantum gates. The quantum permutation circuits designed to shift the node states on testgraph1 are shown in Fig. 13. These circuits are designed from the permutations shown in Fig. 12. We verified the circuits shown in Fig. 13A–D using QCL simulation.

To implement the permutation circuits we need single-qubit quantum gates and multiqubit quantum gates. The single-qubit quantum gates used in the permutation circuit were a Hadamard sate and a NOT gate, and the multiqubit quantum gates used in the permutation circuit were a CNOT gate and a Toffoli gate.

10 MATHEMATICAL APPROACH

The Hadamard gate transformation matrix is denoted by H:

$$H = \frac{1}{\sqrt{2}}\begin{pmatrix} 1 & 1 \\ 1 & -1 \end{pmatrix}.$$

We can generalize H for an n-qubit register, where $H : |i\rangle \rightarrow 2^{\frac{-n}{2}} \sum_{j \in B^n} (-1)^{(i,j)}|j\rangle$ [30].

If $\rho(i,j)$ is the probability of visiting all the neighbors of a node within a graph with use of DTQRW, where i is the starting node and $\pi(i)$ is the set of all neighbors of i, then $\rho\ (i,j)\ , j \in \pi(i)$.

We can define $\rho\ (i,j)\ = H : |i\rangle \rightarrow 2^{\frac{-n}{2}} \sum_{j \in B^n}(-1)^{(i,j)}|j\rangle$.

11 QUANTUM CLUSTER ANALYSIS

11.1 CLUSTERS FOR TESTGRAPH1

11.1.1 Analysis using the simulation results

We use the QCL simulation results of the quantum random walk circuit to demonstrate the method for finding clusters within the test graphs. We observe the simulation result in each random walk step. In each step new nodes are discovered and these nodes are traversed by the random walker. We repeat the steps until there is convergence.

The probability distribution generated by QCL simulation after the fifth iteration is given below:

$$\begin{aligned}
&0.5625|0\rangle + 0.03125|1\rangle - 0.0625|2\rangle - 0.0625|3\rangle + 0.0625|4\rangle - 0.0625|5\rangle \\
&+ 0.03125|6\rangle + 0.4375|7\rangle - 0.0625|8\rangle + 0.4375|9\rangle - 0.0625|10\rangle - 0.09375|11\rangle \\
&- 0.03125|12\rangle - 0.0625|13\rangle + 0.4375|14\rangle + 0.0625|15\rangle + 0.03125|16\rangle \\
&+ 0.15625|17\rangle + 0.15625|18\rangle + 0.09375|19\rangle - 0.03125|20\rangle + 0.03125|21\rangle \\
&- 0.03125|22\rangle + 0.03125|23\rangle - 0.03125|24\rangle - 0.03125|25\rangle + 0.03125|26\rangle \\
&+ 0.03125|27\rangle. \qquad (7)
\end{aligned}$$

It is clear from Eq. (7) that after the fifth iteration the quantum random walker has visited all nodes with all coin states within testgraph1. The proposed quantum algorithm stops here. In each iteration the probability distribution values of already visited nodes are amplified further. The probabilities of each node after the fifth iteration are as follows:

$$0.5625|0\rangle, 0.4375|7\rangle, 0.4375|9\rangle, 0.4375|14\rangle, 0.15625|16\rangle, 0.03125|21\rangle, 0.03125|26\rangle.$$

Now if we consider the quantum states we get $|0\rangle, |7\rangle, |9\rangle, |14\rangle, |16\rangle, |21\rangle, |26\rangle$; that is

$$|00000\rangle, |00111\rangle, |01001\rangle, |01111\rangle, |10000\rangle, |10101\rangle, |11010\rangle. \quad (8)$$

To design the QCL circuit a five-qubit register is used to implement the walk with a quantum random walk circuit through QCL simulation.

Thus if we consider the node values from the quantum states we get;

$$|\mathbf{000}00\rangle, |\mathbf{001}11\rangle, |\mathbf{010}01\rangle, |\mathbf{011}11\rangle, |\mathbf{100}00\rangle, |\mathbf{101}01\rangle, |\mathbf{110}10\rangle$$

that is, 000, 001, 010, 011, 100, 101, 110

Thus, from Eq. (7) it can be observed that some nodes have the same probability values. Thus a cluster can be formed with nodes with the same probability values according to the proposed quantum algorithm. If we apply the proposed quantum algorithm on testgraph1, the clusters formed are $Cluster_1 = \{0\}$ with probability 0.5625, $Cluster_2$=$\{1,2,3\}$ with probability 0.4375, $Cluster_3 = \{4\}$ with probability 0.15625, and $Cluster_4 = \{5, 6\}$ with probability 0.03125.

Thus an initial set of clusters is found at this stage.

11.1.2 Merging clusters

We may have clusters which consists of a single node after the convergence of the proposed quantum algorithm. We may not require a single-node cluster, so we can merge the clusters with a threshold value ϵ. If $\epsilon = 3$, this implies that each cluster contains at least three nodes. We can take any value of ϵ. The merge and split model is used to meet the threshold criteria. This model may split or merge the initial cluster sets, which are obtained from the analysis of the QCL simulation results.

We consider the set P, which denotes the probability distributions values for each cluster N. For testgrapg1, $N = 4$. Thus $P = \{0.5625, 0.4375, 0.15625, 0.03125\}$.

With use of the merge and split model the average probability distribution value

$$P_{\text{avg}} = 1/4(0.5625 + 0.4375 + 0.15625 + 0. + 0.03125) = 0.296875.$$

Divide the set P into two subregions in accordance with their average probability distribution value. One region is P_1, whose values are greater than P_{avg}, and the other is the region P_2, whose values are less than P_{avg}:

$$P_1 = \{0.5625, 0.4375\}, P_2 = \{0.15625, 0.03125\}.$$

So the resultant clusters are $Cluster_1new = \{0, 1, 2, 3\}$ and $Cluster_2new = \{4, 5, 6\}$. Now the threshold criteria is fulfilled. So no further merging is required.

Because of the advantage of superposition states in quantum computing, the walker repeatedly visits the strongly connected portion of the graph and simultaneously visits new nodes. As the quantum walker progresses, quantum interference occurs. This may be constructive or destructive. Constructive interference amplifies the probabilities and destructive interference decreases the probabilities at each time step. The visiting probability distribution values of nodes which are repeatedly visited are increased. These nodes are repeatedly visited because they are strongly connected nodes. The proposed quantum algorithm forms a cluster of nodes which have the same or nearly the same visiting probability distribution values. Some probability distribution values may be negative because of the use of the Hadamard coin operator on the qubit. The negative probability distribution values may not create any issue as the proposed quantum algorithm uses the absolute values of the visiting probability distribution for each node only.

From the QCL simulation results it is seen that testgraph1 consists of two strongly connected regions (subgraphs): one is K_4 and the other is K_3. These two regions are connected by an edge (nodes 3 and 4). According to the observed results node 3 belongs to cluster 1 and node 4 belongs to cluster 2. This is because node 3 is connected to nodes 0, 1, 2, and 4. Furthermore, nodes 0, 1, and 2 are connected to each other. Node 4 is connected to only node 3, and there are no edges between node 4 and nodes 0, 1, and 2. Node 4 is connected to nodes 5 and 6, which are connected to each other. Node 3 has no connection to nodes 5 and 6. Thus the strongly connected region (subgraph K_4), which consists of nodes 0, 1, 2, and 3, formed a cluster. Similarly, nodes 4, 5, and 6 formed another cluster. The graphical output generated by QCL simulation on testgraph1 after the fifth iteration is shown in Fig. 14.

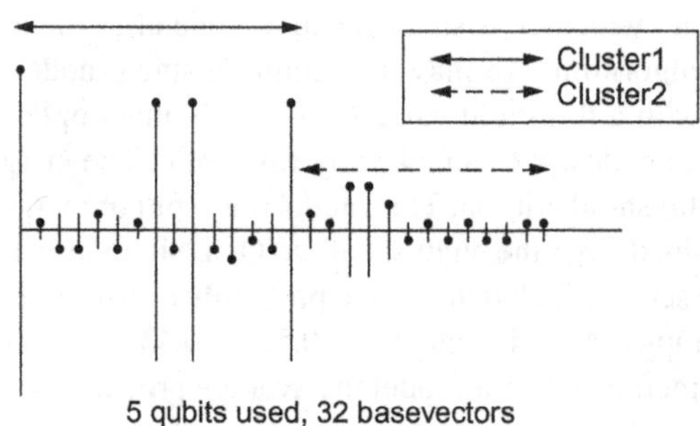

FIG. 14

Graphical output generated by Quantum Computing Language simulation for testgraph1 after the fifth iteration.

In the probability distribution shown in Fig. 14, each vertical line represents a quantum state, which was produced as a result of QCL simulation of the discrete quantum random walk circuit. In Fig. 14, 4 consecutive vertical lines represent quantum states of node 0 for four different coin values. The next four consecutive vertical lines represent quantum states of node 1 for four different coin values, and so on. Thus from the cluster results and graphical results it is seen that nodes with the same or nearly the same visiting probability distribution values tend to lie within the same cluster.

11.2 CLUSTERS FOR TESTGRAPH2

11.2.1 Analysis using the simulation results

The probability distribution generated by QCL simulation after the tenth iteration is given below:

$$\begin{aligned}
&+0.24609|0\rangle - 0.25586|1\rangle - 0.30859|2\rangle + 0.25391|3\rangle + 0.24609|4\rangle + 0.19141|5\rangle \\
&+0.24414|6\rangle + 0.25391|7\rangle + 0.19922|8\rangle + 0.38672|9\rangle - 0.11328|10\rangle - 0.17773|11\rangle \\
&+0.029297|12\rangle - 0.15234|13\rangle + 0.34766|14\rangle - 0.16016|15\rangle + 0.087891|16\rangle \\
&+0.021484|17\rangle + 0.064453|18\rangle - 0.074219|19\rangle + 0.054687|20\rangle - 0.048828|21\rangle \\
&-0.091797|22\rangle \\
&-0.048828|23\rangle + 0.10352|24\rangle - 0.17578|25\rangle - 0.056641|26\rangle - 0.013672|27\rangle \\
&+0.044922|28\rangle - 0.039062|30\rangle - 0.0097656|31\rangle + 0.011719|32\rangle + 0.019531|33\rangle \\
&-0.017578|34\rangle \\
&-0.033203|35\rangle + 0.0058594|36\rangle - 0.019531|37\rangle - 0.019531|38\rangle + 0.025391|39\rangle \\
&-0.0097656|40\rangle + 0.0097656|41\rangle - 0.0039062|42\rangle \\
&+0.019531|43\rangle - 0.019531|44\rangle + 0.021484|45\rangle - 0.0058594|46\rangle - 0.035156|47\rangle. \quad (9)
\end{aligned}$$

If we apply the proposed algorithm on testgraph2, the following clusters are formed: $Cluster_1 = \{0, 1\}$ with probability 0.25391, $Cluster_2 = \{2\}$ with probability 0.38672, $Cluster_3 = \{3\}$ with probability 0.34766, $Cluster_4 = \{4\}$ with probability 0.087891, $Cluster_5 = \{5\}$ with probability 0.054687, $Cluster_6 = \{6\}$ with probability 0.10352, $Cluster_7 = \{7\}$ with probability 0.044922, $Cluster_8 = \{8, 10\}$ with probability 0.019531, $Cluster_9 = \{9\}$ with probability 0.025391, and $Cluster_{10} = \{11\}$ with probability 0.021484.

The resultant clusters after application of the merging model are

$$Cluster_1 = \{0, 1, 2, 3\}, Cluster_2 = \{4, 5, 6\}, \text{and } Cluster_3 = \{7, 8, 9, 10, 11\}.$$

The graphical output generated by QCL simulation, which gives the probability distribution after ten steps for testgraph2, is shown in Fig. 15. From the cluster results and graphical results it is again seen that nodes with the same or nearly the same visiting probability distribution values tend to lie within the same cluster.

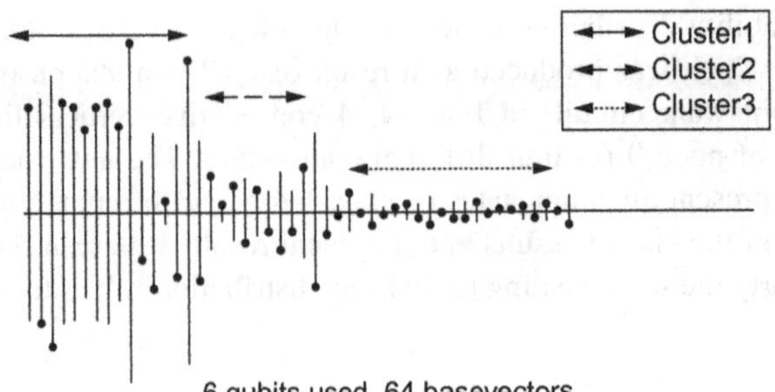

FIG. 15

Graphical output generated by Quantum Computing Language simulation for testgraph2 after the tenth iteration.

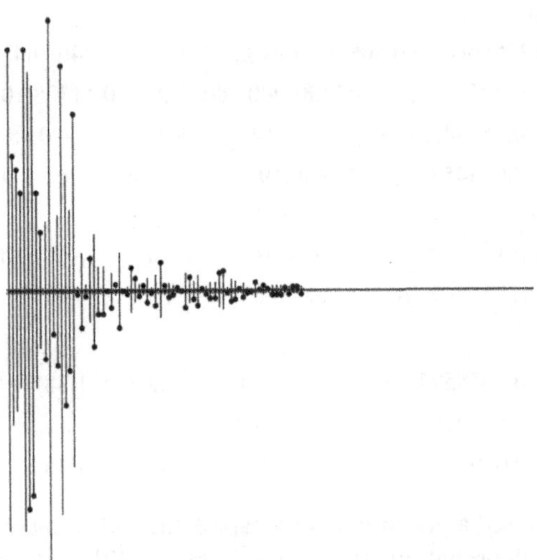

FIG. 16

Graphical output generated by Quantum Computing Language simulation for testgraph3 after the twenty-second iteration.

11.3 CLUSTERS FOR TESTGRAPH3

11.3.1 Analysis using the graphical output

Similarly, the probability distribution after the twenty-second iteration for testgraph3 is shown in Fig. 16.

After application of the proposed algorithm the following clusters are formed: $Cluster_1 = \{0, 1, 2, 3, 4\}$, $Cluster_2 = \{5, 6, 7, 9, 13\}$, $Cluster_3 = \{8, 10, 11, 12\}$, and $Cluster_4 = \{14, 15, 16, 17\}$.

12 PROPOSED GRAPH-BASED QUANTUM CLUSTERING ALGORITHM

We identify clusters within a given general graph $G(V, E)$. If there is any cluster structure present in the graph, the observed QCL simulation result identifies the number of clusters within that graph. The proposed quantum algorithm to identify clusters is given below:

Input: Graph adjacency matrix
Output: Number of clusters within the graph and nodes within each clusters.
Quantum clustering algorithm: Design discrete-time quantum random walk circuit for the graph (as explained below):

1. Start at the origin node: $x = 0$.
2. Choose the coin operator (assumed here to be the here Hadamard coin operator):
$$H|x,0\rangle \rightarrow \frac{|x,0\rangle + |x,1\rangle}{\sqrt{2}},$$
$$H|x,1\rangle \rightarrow \frac{|x,0\rangle - |x,1\rangle}{\sqrt{2}}$$
.
3. The shift operator S helps to move the quantum walker from one quantum state to another state of the superposition states according to the permutation circuit.
4. Apply $U = S(I \otimes \hat{C})$ on the initial quantum state, where I is the identity operator, S is the shift operator, and C is the coin operator. (If U transformation for initial states is repeatedly used, then the resulting superposition state $|\psi\rangle$ will contain more nodes of the graph. The random walker traversed the graph faster.)
5. Repeat step 4 for r consecutive transformations of U until a steady state (convergence) is reached (i.e., all nodes with all the coin states are visited by the quantum walker).
6. Interpret the quantum simulation result for initial clustering. The nodes with the same visiting probability distribution values are now in the same cluster.
7. Step 6 may generate many clusters (the number of nodes is less than the threshold value). Apply the merge and split model to fulfill the threshold criteria and to identify the actual cluster sets.
8. End.

12.0.2 Merge and split model

1. Let p_i be the probability distribution values of node $i = 0, 1, 2, n$. Depending on the QCL simulation result, group the nodes into different sets of cluster $Cluster_j$, where $j = 1, 2, \ldots, n$, according to their visiting probability distribution values.
2. The k-dimensional tree method is discussed in [34,35]. We use the one-dimensional tree method (as our nodes are one-dimensional) in our merge and split model to identify the clusters.

3. Assume we have set P, which consists of visiting probability distributions values for each cluster $Cluster_j$, where $j = 1, 2, \ldots, n$.
4. Set P is divided into two subregions in accordance with their average probability distribution values: $\frac{1}{N}\sum_{i=1}^{N} P_i$ (N denotes the number of clusters obtained in step 6 of the proposed quantum clustering algorithm and P_i is the visiting probability distribution values for each cluster). One region has values greater than the average probability distribution value (p_{avg}). The other region has values less than the average probability distribution value.
5. Repeat until threshold criteria are reached.

Observation of the proposed algorithm shows that the nodes with the same or nearly the same visiting probability values tend to lie within the same cluster.

13 EXPERIMENTAL RESULTS

We tested our proposed quantum algorithm on a real-world network, where a known community structure is already present. This proposed quantum clustering algorithm is applied on the Zachary Karate Club [36], a real-world network. This network is a friendship network of 34 members of a karate club. There are 74 edges in this network. The network is converted into a graph model, where members are represented as nodes. This network structure was developed by Zachary. The Zachary Karate Club network is originally divided into two communities as shown in Fig. 17.

QCL simulation is applied on this social network to find the number of clusters within it. After the third iteration, all the nodes with all coin states are covered by the quantum walker. QCL simulation is repeated for more iterations, but no more significant states are generated. Thus a steady state is reached (convergence). The experimental results are shown in Fig. 18, where vertical lines represent visiting probability distribution values of each node. From the QCL graphical output it is clearly seen that two clusters are found. One cluster is formed by nodes with high or nearly high probability distribution values, and the other cluster is formed by nodes with lower probability distribution values. In Fig. 17 the neighbors are not sequentially labeled, so in Fig. 18 nodes which are repeatedly visited have high visiting probability values, which are denoted by high-rising vertical lines.

14 PERFORMANCE ANALYSIS OF CLASSICAL CLUSTERING ALGORITHMS AND THE PROPOSED QUANTUM CLUSTERING ALGORITHM

Here we compare classical clustering algorithms and the proposed quantum clustering algorithm and observe a speedup over the classical algorithms. The proposed quantum clustering algorithm has a fast rate of convergence as shown in Table 1.

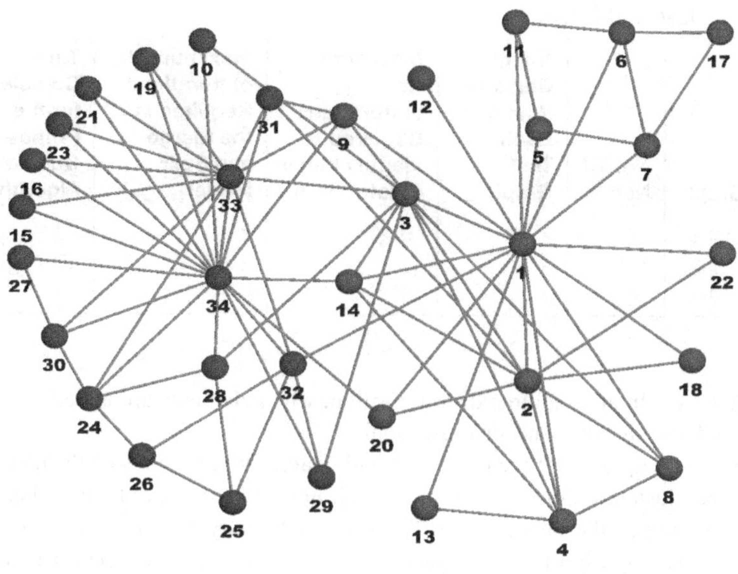

FIG. 17

Zachary Karate Club network.

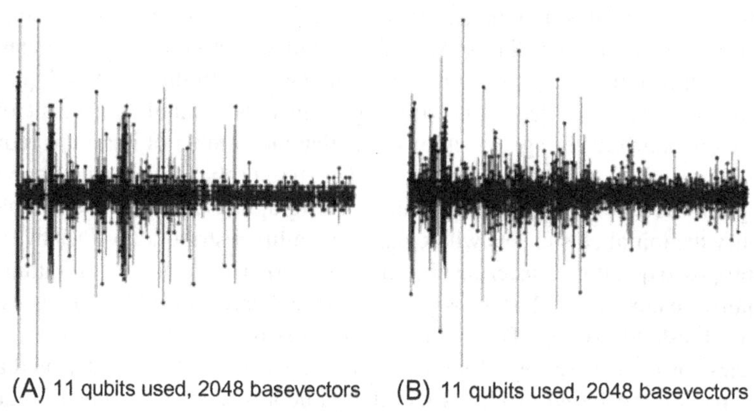

(A) 11 qubits used, 2048 basevectors (B) 11 qubits used, 2048 basevectors

FIG. 18

Graphical output generated by Quantum Computing Language simulation applied on the Zachary Karate Club network: (A) the after third iteration; (B) after the fifth iteration.

The time complexity of hierarchical classical clustering algorithms is $O(n^2)$, where the number of items to be clustered is denoted by n. All agglomerative algorithms experience excessive time and space constraints. The space required for the adjacency matrix is $O(n^2)$, where n represents the number of items. Because of the iterative nature of the algorithm, the matrix (or a subset of it) must be accessed

Table 1 Observed Results

Test Graph	No. of Nodes	No. of Clusters Within Each Test Graph	Maximum No. of Iterations Required to Identify Initial Cluster Sets	Maximum No. of Iterations Required in the Merge and Split Model	Time Complexity for the Proposed Quantum Algorithm
Testgraph1	7	2	5	2	
Testgraph2	12	3	10	3	$O(n \log n)$
Testgraph3	18	4	22	5	

multiple times. In an agglomerative algorithm, when elements are added, removed, or changed, the algorithm needs to run again.

The time complexity of the nearest-neighbor algorithm depends on the number of items to be clustered. For each iteration, each item was compared with other items already existing in the cluster. Thus the time complexity is $O(n^2)$. In most of the classical clustering algorithms as discussed above, the adjacency matrix is used to identify the clusters within a graph structure, but in the proposed quantum clustering algorithm superposition states of all nodes with their visiting probability distribution values are considered simultaneously to identify clusters within that graph structure. Because of the advantage of this mixed state or superposition state, the quantum walker exists in all nodes simultaneously and from each node it can reach its neighbor nodes at the same time but this superposition state is not possible in the classical approach. Thus initial clustering is much faster ($O(n)$) with this proposed quantum algorithm than with classical clustering algorithms. The simulation result of the proposed quantum clustering algorithm shows that the number of iterations required to identify the initial set of clusters with equal visiting probability distribution values for testgraph1 is 5, for testgraph2 is 10, and for testgraph3 is 22. The time complexity to identify the initial cluster sets with equal probability distribution values by means of the proposed quantum clustering algorithm is $O(n)$. This quantum algorithm does not require the number of clusters as an input, but a merge and split model is used to meet the threshold criteria. The k-dimensional tree discussed in [35] uses k keys and cycles through these keys for successive levels of the tree. If the median of n elements is to be found in $O(n)$ time, then a depth-balanced k-dimensional tree is built in $O(n \log n)$ time [37]. Another approach is discussed in [37] to build a balanced k-dimensional tree for which the worst-case time complexity is $O(kn \log n)$ for n points and k dimensions. In this work the merge and split model uses a one-dimensional, as all the nodes are one-dimensional. So the time complexity for merging nodes with equal or nearly equal visiting probability is $O(n \log n)$. We tested our quantum clustering algorithm on a real-world network structure. We found that our proposed quantum algorithm can efficiently detect the cluster structure present in this network. Thus the total time complexity of the proposed quantum algorithm is $O(n) + O(n \log n) \approx O(n \log n)$.

All these observations provide an indication of the effectiveness of the proposed quantum algorithm approach. The observed results are given in Table 1.

15 CONCLUSION

We verified the proposed quantum clustering algorithm, which is based on DTQRW, on different test graphs. We showed that if two nodes are in the same cluster, the probability of getting to a third one located in the same cluster through a quantum random walk should not be very different for both of them. Moreover, like classical random walk, the quantum walker did not get trapped within a cluster [38]. The quantum walker visits clusters and other nodes within the graph simultaneously because of the superposition principle. The QCL simulation results show that our proposed quantum clustering approach performs better than some of the classical clustering algorithms such as hierarchical algorithms and the nearest-neighbor algorithm. The proposed quantum algorithm was used to detect the clusters in the Zachary Karate Club network, the benchmark network to test clustering algorithms. The proposed quantum algorithm approach has the capability to detect clusters within social networks and so can be used to analyze complex networks, social networks, community detection problems, largely on the basis of graph theory. We plan to focus on quantum clustering algorithms using DTQRW that can deal with more complex networks and to design a quantum algorithm to implement the k-dimensional tree to minimize the complexity of its classical counterpart.

REFERENCES

[1] X. Jiang, N. Petkov, Computer Analysis of Images and Patterns: 13th International Conference, CAIP 2009, Münster, Germany, September 2–4, 2009, Proceedings, vol. 5702, Springer, Berlin, 2009.

[2] S. Günter, H. Bunke, Self-organizing map for clustering in the graph domain, Pattern Recognit. Lett. 23 (4) (2002) 405–417.

[3] F. Serratosa, R. Alquézar, A. Sanfeliu, Synthesis of function-described graphs and clustering of attributed graphs, Int. J. Pattern Recognit. Artif. Intell. 16 (06) (2002) 621–655.

[4] B. Luo, A. Robles-Kelly, A. Torsello, R. Wilson, E. Hancock, Clustering shock trees, in: Proceeding of 3rd IAPR-TC15 Workshop Graph-Based Representations in Pattern Recognition, 2001, pp. 217–228.

[5] P.-N. Tan, M. Steinbach, V. Kumar, khdaw.com, 2006.

[6] M.E. Newman, Modularity and community structure in networks, Proc. Natl. Acad. Sci. 103 (23) (2006) 8577–8582.

[7] S. Zhang, R.-S. Wang, X.-S. Zhang, Identification of overlapping community structure in complex networks using fuzzy c-means clustering, Physica A: Stat. Mech. Appl. 374 (1) (2007) 483–490.

[8] S. Boccaletti, M. Ivanchenko, V. Latora, A. Pluchino, A. Rapisarda, Detecting complex network modularity by dynamical clustering, Phys. Rev. E 75 (4) (2007) 045102.

[9] J.C. Mar, C.A. Wells, J. Quackenbush, Defining an informativeness metric for clustering gene expression data, Bioinformatics 27 (8) (2011) 1094–1100.

[10] A.E. Bayá, P.M. Granitto, Clustering gene expression data with a penalized graph-based metric, BMC Bioinformatics 12 (1) (2011) 2.

[11] B. Chen, J. He, S. Pellicer, Y. Pan, Protein sequence motif super-rule-tree (SRT) structure constructed by hybrid hierarchical K-means clustering algorithm, in: IEEE International Conference on Bioinformatics and Biomedicine, 2008. BIBM'08, IEEE, 2008, pp. 98–103.

[12] J. Zhu, L. Xie, B. Honig, Structural refinement of protein segments containing secondary structure elements: local sampling, knowledge-based potentials, and clustering, Proteins: Struct. Funct. Bioinf. 65 (2) (2006) 463–479.

[13] D. Munshi, A.L. Melott, P. Coles, Generalized cumulant correlators and hierarchical clustering (of galaxies), Mon. Not. R. Astron. Soc. 311 (1) (1900) 149–160.

[14] M.H. Dunham, Data Mining: Introductory and Advanced Topics, Pearson Education India, Bengaluru, 2006.

[15] P.W. Shor, Algorithms for quantum computation: discrete logarithms and factoring, in: Proceedings of 35th Annual Symposium on Foundations of Computer Science, 1994, IEEE, 1994, pp. 124–134.

[16] L.K. Grover, A fast quantum mechanical algorithm for database search, in: Proceedings of the Twenty-Eighth Annual ACM Symposium on Theory of Computing, ACM, 1996, pp. 212–219.

[17] Wikipedia, Quantum walk—Wikipedia, The Free Encyclopedia, 2015, [Online; accessed 05/03/16], https://en.wikipedia.org/w/index.php?title=Quantum_walk&oldid=654602668.

[18] A. Ambainis, J. Kempe, A. Rivosh, Coins make quantum walks faster, in: Proceedings of the Sixteenth Annual ACM-SIAM Symposium on Discrete Algorithms, Society for Industrial and Applied Mathematics, 2005, pp. 1099–1108.

[19] V. Kendon, Quantum walks on general graphs, Int. J. Quantum Inf. 4 (05) (2006) 791–805.

[20] N. Shenvi, J. Kempe, K.B. Whaley, Quantum random-walk search algorithm, Phys. Rev. A 67 (5) (2003) 052307.

[21] J. Kempe, Discrete quantum walks hit exponentially faster, Probab. Theory Related Fields 133 (2) (2005) 215–235.

[22] C. Calude, M.J. Dinneen, F. Peper, Unconventional Models of Computation: Third International Conference, UMC 2002, Kobe, Japan, October 15–19, 2002, Proceedings, vol. 2509, Springer, Berlin, 2003.

[23] A.M. Childs, R. Cleve, E. Deotto, E. Farhi, S. Gutmann, D.A. Spielman, Exponential algorithmic speedup by a quantum walk, in: Proceedings of the Thirty-Fifth Annual ACM Symposium on Theory of Computing, ACM, 2003, pp. 59–68.

[24] A.M. Childs, E. Farhi, S. Gutmann, An example of the difference between quantum and classical random walks, Quantum Inf. Process. 1 (1–2) (2002) 35–43.

[25] N.B. Lovett, Application of Quantum Walks on Graph Structures to Quantum Computing, University of Leeds, Leeds, 2011.

[26] I. Carneiro, M. Loo, X. Xu, M. Girerd, V. Kendon, P.L. Knight, Entanglement in coined quantum walks on regular graphs, New J. Phys. 7 (1) (2005) 156.

[27] C. Moore, A. Russell, Proceedings of the 6th International Workshop on Randomization and Approximation Techniques in Computer Science (RANDOM'02), 2002.

[28] Y. Aharonov, L. Davidovich, N. Zagury, Quantum random walks, Phys. Rev. A 48 (2) (1993) 1687.
[29] X.-P. Xu, Discrete-time quantum walks on one-dimensional lattices, Eur. Phys. J. B 77 (4) (2010) 479–488.
[30] B. Ömer, Quantum Programming in QCL, 2000.
[31] B. Ömer, A Procedural Formalism for Quantum Computing, 1998.
[32] B. Ömer, Structured quantum programming, Inf. Syst. (2003) 130.
[33] A. Chakrabarti, C. Lin, N.K. Jha, Design of quantum circuits for random walk algorithms, in: 2012 IEEE Computer Society Annual Symposium on VLSI (ISVLSI), IEEE, 2012, pp. 135–140.
[34] Q. Liu, X. Pang, Y. Li, Y. Pan, Advanced route design based on properties of nodes in opportunistic networks, in: Electrical, Information Engineering and Mechatronics 2011, Springer, Berlin, 2012, pp. 1437–1446.
[35] J.L. Bentley, Multidimensional binary search trees used for associative searching, Commun. ACM 18 (9) (1975) 509–517.
[36] W.W. Zachary, An information flow model for conflict and fission in small groups, J. Anthropol. Res. (1977) 452–473.
[37] R.A. Brown, Building a balanced k-d tree in O (knlog n) time, J. Comput. Graphics Tech. 4 (1) (2015).
[38] B. Ribeiro, D. Towsley, Estimating and sampling graphs with multidimensional random walks, in: Proceedings of the 10th ACM SIGCOMM conference on Internet measurement, ACM, 2010, pp. 390–403.

CHAPTER

The Schrödinger equation as inspiration for a client portfolio simulation hybrid system based on dynamic Bayesian networks and the REFII model

12

G. Klepac
Raiffeisenbank Austria d.d., Zagreb, Croatia

1 INTRODUCTION

In quantum mechanics the Schrödinger equation is used as a tool for prediction of the behavior of a system based on a wave function, which is used for calculation of the properties of the system [1,2]. This mathematical intermediary is known as a wave function, defined as the average value of $A(x, y, z)$, which represents a property of the system as

$$\langle A\rangle(x, y, z, t)\psi(x, y, z) = \int dxdydz\psi' A(x, y, z)\psi(x, y, z, t).$$

The probabilities of finding a particle at time t at location x (for one dimension), at location x, y (for two dimensions), and at location x, y, z (for three dimensions) are calculated [1,3]. This approach does not give the precise location of the observed particle; it gives the probabilities for all possible locations, more precisely the probability density for finding the particle at some position at time t. In light of the Hamlitonian system, we can define possible Ψ for a time-dependent system as [1,4,5]

$$H(x, y, z, t)\psi(x, y, z) = \frac{ih}{2\pi}\frac{\partial\psi(x, y, z, t)}{\partial t}.$$

This approach in which we calculate possible states of the complex system is the inspiration for a client portfolio simulation hybrid system in which we can with

Quantum Inspired Computational Intelligence. http://dx.doi.org/10.1016/B978-0-12-804409-4.00012-7

respect to the initial state of the portfolio calculate future time-dependent trends in the client portfolio. The Schrödinger equation has a role in calculating the "expectation value" of the system properties [6–8]. If we wish to develop a system for evaluation of portfolio states with respect to initial values in a noisy environment such as market conditions, the Schrödinger equation can be used as inspiration and can be emulated with several concepts from data mining. The proposed system is based on dynamic Bayesian networks and the REFII (Rise Equal Fall, second generation) model for time series. The main purpose of the REFII model is to automate time series analysis, through a unique transformation model of time series. An advantage of this approach of time series analysis is the linkage of different methods for time series analysis, which gives us the opportunity to connecting time series analysis for probabilistic calculation with dynamic Bayesian networks. The REFII model combines the trends of discrete functions and the area on the time segment level and creates a basic pattern. The basic pattern is represented by three core values [9,10]:

1. growth trend code Rise Equal Fall part (REF);
2. angular deflection coefficient, which can be classified into categories with the aid of the classical crisp or fuzzy logic;
3. time segment area, which can be classified into categories with the aid of the classical crisp or fuzzy logic.

The basic pattern becomes an element of a chance node within a dynamic Bayesian network. Such defined complex systems have their roots in the Schrödinger equation because its main purpose is to calculate states of the trend with respect to the initial states of the complex system. It also gives the opportunity to perform a simulation regarding a client portfolio by our changing the initial states as well as the chance nodes within a defined dynamic Bayesian network. The first part of this chapter is conceptually oriented, and second part presents a case study on a real client portfolio in the retail domain. The case study presents simulation and calculation regarding buying habit trends during a defined period, taking into consideration changes in pricing policy for one item and interaction between trends for other items with consideration of changes in pricing policy for other items. The chapter contain code in SPSS script language as well as a model of a dynamic Bayesian network with an integrated REFII part for the case study and simulation results for the observed portfolio.

2 BACKGROUND

Portfolio management as a discipline has an important role in everyday business [11–13]. Understanding of customer behavior is a key factor of market success, especially in competitive market conditions. Client portfolio analysis can be done in many ways by the building of predictive models based on logistic regression models [14]. Extraction of important behavioral information from transactional customer data and enabling better decision-making throughout an organization is one of the aims when a company wants to understand its customers. Real data-mining projects require the use of several data-mining methods to achieve defined goals. In the process of building predictive models based on logistic regression or neural networks, or Bayesian networks, or some other supervised learning method, it is important to make attribute relevance analysis the basis for profiling and understanding the nature of the most important factors which have an influence on the target variable [15–17]. The main task of attribute relevance analysis is to reduce the number of predictors, which entered the model by predictive power criteria. A robust and stable predictive model has a few attributes incorporated into the model. These could be 6–10 of the most predictive attributes. Attribute relevance analysis has two important functions: recognition of the variables which have the greatest impact on the target variable, and understanding the relations and the logic between the most important predictor and the target variable. Understanding the relations and the logic between important predictors is important to reveal important behavioral patterns. Recognition of most important variables, which has greatest impact on target variable, reduces redundancy and uncertainty at the model development stage. It provides model robustness and model reliability. Besides measuring importance, attribute relevance analysis evaluates attribute characteristics. Evaluation of attribute characteristics includes measuring the impact of attribute values on target variables. It helps us to understand the relations and logic between the most important predictors and the target variable, and to understand the relations and logic between the most important predictors from the target variable perspective. In a situation when the target variable has two states, as an attribute relevance analysis method information value calculation could be used. There are different approaches regarding attribute relevance analysis when we have two or more output states for the target variable. For attribute relevance analysis of target variables with more than more output state we use measures such as information gain [18,19]. The problem is that those models often do not reflect a real portfolio situation because they represent only a small piece of the portfolio without taking into consideration interaction regarding the current state of the portfolio. On the other hand, temporal influence demands specific modeling approaches [20–22]. Regarding consolidation of modeling temporal aspects with a predictive aspect of a portfolio, dynamic Bayesian networks can be used [23,24]. Generally, Bayesian networks can be very efficient tools for probabilistic modeling [25–27] but often Bayesian networks are used as pure probabilistic models, which are substitutes or alternative models for logistic regression or neural networks.

Traditional simulation models [28,29] do not give an appropriate solution for how to connect the temporal aspect of a portfolio, the most important factors within a portfolio, and competitors and their activities on the market. The proposed model aims to unite all those aspects, taking into consideration all the aspects described.

3 BASIC CONCEPT OF THE PROPOSED MODEL

A client portfolio within companies such as retail companies, insurance companies, and banks which operate with numerous clients/buyers can be observed as a complex system. Complexity is a direct result of a huge client or buyer number, numerous product and services which the company offers, client profiles, client behavioral characteristics, market conditions, changes in market conditions, competition, market trends, and numerous other factors. Changes in company policies, market condition changes, portfolio structure changes, client profile changes, and behavioral characteristic changes can result in different states of the observed portfolio characteristics. As already mentioned, the Schrödinger equation is used as a tool to predict the behavior of a system, which is used for calculation of the properties of the system. The probabilities of finding a particle at time t at location x are calculated. This approach gives the probabilities of finding the particle at some position at time t for all possible locations. This idea has been used as inspiration for the construction of a complex analytical method to calculate the probabilities of portfolio parameters at time t. The probabilities of portfolio parameters at time t are predetermined by the current characteristics (portfolio characteristics, market characteristics) as well as their changes. In that way, the proposed analytical method can provide answers about the expected probabilities on the observed parameters which determine the portfolio status. This is in line with idea of the Schrödinger equation in quantum mechanics as a tool for prediction of the behavior of a system. The proposed model provides the portfolio parameter probability states for predetermined parameters. The model also measures the influence of the parameters in the design phase with the intention to optimize learning processes and probability calculation. Parameters can be temporal or nontemporal, with potential connectivity between them. The first important thing is recognition of the influences between variables and their importance, as well which variable has a great influence on another variable. This is important for model optimization regarding combinatory explosion within the developed Bayesian network.

3.1 SENSITIVITY ANALYSIS

Attribute relevance analysis has two important functions or characteristics:

1. recognition of the variables which have the greatest impact on the target variable;
2. understanding the relations and the logic between the most important predictor and the target variable and understanding the relations and the logic between the most important predictors from the target variable perspective.

Both functions and characteristics are aligned with recognition of portfolio characteristics, especially in the situation when we are developing a predictive model for probability calculation of portfolio states given some initial values. Apart from measuring the importance, attribute relevance analysis also evaluates attribute characteristics. Evaluation of attribute characteristics includes measuring the impact of attribute values on target variables. This helps us to understand the relations and the logic between the most important predictor and the target variable, and to understand the relations and the logic between the most important predictors, taking into consideration the target variable variable. In this case we can talk about many potential target variables, and predictors are variables from their neighborhood if we are talking about Bayesian networks, where evidence can be initially defined in each node within the network.

From the perspective of predictive modeling there are two basic types of predictive models important from the profiling point of view:

1. predictive models with a binomial target variable
2. predictive models with a multinomial target variable

In the case of predictive models with a binomial target variable, a common approach for attribute relevance analysis is the use of weight of evidence and information value calculation. In the case of a multinomial target variable, which is much more complicated, information gain calculation can be used. Information gain can be calculated by the following formula [30]:

$$\text{Info}(D) = -\sum_{i=1}^{n} p_i \log_2(p_i),$$

where p_i is the probability that an arbitrary tuple in D belongs to class C_i. This measure is recommended for use in situations where the output variable has more than two states for prediction. Many measures can be used for this purpose. Information gain is presented as one possible solution for attribute relevance analysis in situations where we are operating with more than two states for the output variable.

In that case we do not have clear separation of impact zones, and the zones overlap. This makes sensitivity analysis more complicated and it is hard or even impossible to perform sensitivity analysis in the same way as in the situation with binary output. Different output classes for the same predictor in the same zones could have significant influence for several output classes. Also, those zones (bins) could be different for different output classes with different information gain values through observed zones. Information gain is a valuable measure for attribute relevance analysis and for finding appropriate predictors, and will be the basis of the predictive model.

Sensitivity analysis provides important information about the significance of influences among observed variables, as well as information about their predictive power. If we have pool of observed variables which can be used for a portfolio simulation model, the idea is to put all potential variables (predictor) in a list. For the first variables, information gain should be calculated taking the remaining variables from the list. Information gain should be calculated for all the variables in the list with exclusion of variables for which we previously calculated information gain. The next step is to define connections between variables regarding the results from the information gain calculation. That means variables can be linked with those variables which show good performance as predictors for the observed variable, and that procedure can be applied recursively for all variables. An alternative approach is the design of linkage between variables on an expert level and use of information gain calculation as an auxiliary tool to prove the hypothesis about correct links between nodes within the portfolio simulation model. Nodes can have nontemporal and temporal characteristics. This exercise is extremely important for correct setting of the initial model. It gives the initial design of the model on the basis of previous experience which can be recognized through history data. Information gain an appropriate tool for measuring the influence between observed variables. Information gain also has an important role in continuous variable discretization, as on the basis of the information gain results, continuous variables can be discretized. This is in line with the Bayesian network concept because Bayesian networks demands discrete values as inputs for variables (nodes).

3.2 ROLE OF BAYESIAN NETWORKS AND DYNAMIC BAYESIAN NETWORKS

Taking into consideration the nature of Bayesian networks, we these concepts share common idea with the Schrödinger equation as a tool for prediction of the behavior of a system on the basis of empirical data by means of conditional probability calculation.

Variables connected within a Bayesian network make a complex system with many interconnections stored within conditional probability tables. The values within conditional probability tables can change depending on new evidence which can be entered into the model. New evidence is a trigger for recalculation of portfolio states expressed as probabilities for each node.

A Bayesian network model for portfolio simulation should be constructed in a way that each node contains some portfolio characteristic. Important nodes for portfolio model building should be recognized in attribute relevance analysis, as described earlier. This is very important because we want to include only predictive and highly interconnected nodes (variables) which show good performance in sensitivity analysis. These approaches guarantee that the final model will show dynamics and reliability learned from empirical data.

Parental nodes contain crucial characteristics recognized in attribute relevance analysis on the portfolio level. Formally, we can express this as [25]

$$Pr[P_j] = [node\ parents],$$

or more precisely as [25]

$$Pr[P_j] = \prod_{i=1}^{n} P_r[P_j \mid Y_i, \ldots, Y_n],$$

where $Pr[P_j]$ represents the probability for the jth instance and Y_i represents the probability of the ith characteristic within the Bayesian network expressed as a state value of a Bayesian network node.

As previously stated, in quantum mechanics the Schrödinger equation is used as a tool for prediction of the behavior of a system based on a wave function, which is used for calculation of the properties of the system. The focus here is on the wave function. Bayesian networks can be used for client portfolio simulation, but they do provide an answer for the wave function. In the case of client portfolio simulation, the wave function can be expressed as a temporal node within a defined Bayesian network. This means that recognized nontemporal variables in attribute relevance analysis can be connected with temporal elements (temporal nodes). In that case we are talking about dynamic Bayesian networks.

For the modeling of temporal processes we should extend the definition of the Bayesian network with a *k*th-order Markov process. For this purposes we should define the transition model as [23,24]:

$$p(Z_t \mid Z_{t-1}, Z_{t-2}, \ldots, Zt - k) = \prod_{i=1}^{N} P(Z_t^i \mid Pa(Z_t^i)),$$

where Z_t^i is the *i*th node at time *t*, and $Pa(Z_t^i)$ are the parents of Z_t^i.

If we are talking about Bayesian networks, or dynamic Bayesian networks, we should be aware that Bayesian networks operate with categorical values. In the case of inclusion of nontemporal attributes as elements of Bayesian networks, it is not difficult to include them in the model. Categorical attributes can be included with their original values, and continuous variables should be categorized. There can be a problem with temporal variables, which make a dynamic Bayesian network.

Because of the nature of temporal data, it is not easy to perform simple transformation of temporal data in way that they can be used for dynamic Bayesian network construction. For this purpose we will use the REFII model.

The REFII model is designed to combine various concepts in time series analysis and traditional data-mining methods so as to construct a new algorithmic procedure for automatic preprocessing of time series. These solutions can be realized by means of hybridization of existing data-mining methods or directly by use of data-mining methods on transformed time series in REFII notation.

3.3 REFII MODEL

The main purpose of the REFII model is to automate time series analysis through a unique transformation model of time series. An advantage of this approach of time series analysis is the linkage of different methods for time series analysis, linking traditional data-mining tools in time series, and constructing new algorithms for analyzing time series. The REFII model is not a closed system, which means that we have a finite set of methods. First, this is a model for transformation of values of time series, which prepares the data used by different sets of methods on the basis of the same model of transformation in a domain of the problem space. The REFII model is a new approach in time series analysis based on a unique model of transformation, which is the basis for all kinds of time series analysis.

The algorithm for time series transformation into the REFII model is comprises several steps [9,10]. A time series can be defined as a series of values $S(s_1, \ldots, s_n)$, where S represents a time series and $(s_1, \ldots, s_n)$ represents the elements of series S.

1. Step 1: Time interpolation. Format of an independent time series $V_i(vi_1, \ldots, vi_n)$ on the interval $\langle 1, \ldots, n \rangle$ (days, weeks, months, quarters, years) with values of 0. It is necessary to implement the interpolation of values missing from $S(s_1, \ldots, s_n)$ on the basis of the series V_i. The result of this process is the series $S(s_1, \ldots, s_n)$ with interpolated values from the $V_i(vi_1, \ldots, vi_n)$ series.
2. Step 2: Time granulation. In this step we define the degree of summarization of the time series $S(s_1, \ldots, s_n)$ that is located within a basic unit of time (day, week, month, etc.). Time series elements are summarized by use of statistical functions such as sum, mean, or mode on the level of a granular slot. That way, the granulation degree of the time series can be increased (days to weeks, weeks to months), and the result is a time series $S(s_1, \ldots, s_n)$ with a greater degree of granulation. We can return to this step during the analysis process to fulfill the analysis goals, and that includes the mandatory repetition of this process in the following steps.
3. Step 3: Normalization. The normalization procedure implies the transformation of a time series $S(s_1, \ldots, s_n)$ into another time series $T(t_1, \ldots, t_n)$ where each element of the array is subject to a min-max normalization procedure to the $\langle 0, 1 \rangle$ interval. Time series T is made up of elements $(t_1, \ldots, t_n)$, where the t_i are calculated as

$$t_i = \frac{s_i - \min(s)}{\max(s) - \min(s)},$$

where $\min(s)$ and $\max(s)$ are the minimum and maximum values of time series T. The time shift between basic patterns (a measure of time complexity) in a time slot on the x-axis is defined as $d(t_i, t_i + 1) = a$.
4. Step 4: Transformation to REF notation. This is done according to the formula

$$T_r = t_{i+1} - t_i,\ T_r > 0 \Rightarrow \text{“}R\text{”},\ T_r = 0 \Rightarrow \text{“}E\text{”},\ T_r < 0 \Rightarrow \text{“}F\text{”},$$

where the Y_i elements are members of the N_s series.
5. Step 5: Slope calculation based on the angle angular deflection coefficient:

$$\begin{aligned} T_r > 0 &\Rightarrow R\ \mathit{Coefficient} = t_{i+1} - t_i, \\ T_r < 0 &\Rightarrow F\ \mathit{Coefficient} = t_i - t_{i+1}, \\ T_r = 0 &\Rightarrow F\ \mathit{Coefficient} = 0. \end{aligned}$$

6. Step 6: Calculation of the area below the curve. Numerical integration by the rectangle theory:

$$p = \frac{(t_i \times a) + (t_i \times a)}{2}.$$

7. Step 7: Creation of time indices. The creation of a hierarchical index tree depends on the nature of the analysis, where the element of the structured index can be located, and an attribute such as the client's code.
8. Step 8: Category creation. Creation of derived attribute values based on the area below the curve and the deflection angles. It is possible to create categories by application of crisp and fuzzy logic.
9. Step 9: Connecting the REFII model's transformation tables with the relational tables that contain attributes with no time dimension.

These nine basic steps are the foundation of the algorithmic procedure underlying the REFII model, whose ultimate goal is the formation of the transformation matrix. The transformation matrix is the foundation for our performing future analytical procedures whose goal is time series analysis.

The REFII model combines the trends of discrete functions and the area on the time segment level and creates a basic pattern. The basic pattern is represented by three core values:

1. growth trend code (REF);
2. angular deflection coefficient, which can be classified into categories with the aid of the classical crisp or fuzzy logic;
3. the time segment area, which can be classified into categories with the aid of the classical crisp or fuzzy logic.

Basic patterns can form complex structures of a series of samples, and as such can be part of the analysis process. The basic pattern defined through the REFII model is its fundamental part. Time series transformed with the REFII model can be used for dynamic Bayesian network construction.

3.4 HOLISTIC SOLUTION: THEORETICAL FOUNDATION

After problem space determination and definition of the analytical aims, the next step is variable selection appropriate for finding an analytical solution. As previously mentioned, attribute relevance analysis should be conducted first for variable importance recognition. For the problem of client portfolio simulation without a clearly determined target variable, the idea is to apply attribute relevance analysis on selected variables with the intention of sensitivity analysis. This approach helps us in Bayesian network design, as well as in categorization of continuous variables. With this approach we can recognize the variables which have the greatest impact on the target/observed variable, and more importantly we have the opportunity to understand the relations and the logic between variables from which the model is designed.

To be in line with the Schrödinger concept and the wave function, the model should contain temporal elements/variables on which nontemporal variables/nodes can have an influence. As temporal variables cannot be included in a Bayesian network in a way as can be done with nontemporal variables, they require a different approach in the transformation process: use of the REFII model. Bayesian models with integrated temporal variables are dynamic Bayesian networks.

Such a designed solution should learn from the empirical data to be ready for client portfolio simulation. A dynamic Bayesian network can learn from empirical data, where time series are expressed through the REFII model. Good practice is to extract a recent sample for model evaluation purposes. This means extraction on predefined case studies/scenario analysis from the recent period which will be the basis for challenging the model developed. The reason why we simply cannot extract a sample in a 80:20 ratio is that we do not have a single target variable and the model is constructed with many variables where each of them can potentially be the target variable. If we predefine the scenario analysis in a way that we know the outputs on the basis of a recent period, we can challenge the model developed. We can extract a sample in a 80:20 ratio for validation purposes, but this means also extraction on predefined case studies/scenario analysis of 20% sample. Validation on a recent-period sample is much more accurate. The problem is that we have to wait for a certain period to collect enough data for validation purposes. That leads us to the conclusion that the model cannot be validated immediately after development. If we wish to validate the model immediately after development on a recent sample, the development sample could be shorter for the needed validation sample on which predefined case studies/scenario analysis can be tested. There is no unique answer as to which validation approach is the best. Also, several approaches could be combined to find the model performance. Because a single target variable does not exist, model validation is not an easy task.

4 CASE STUDY: IMPLEMENTATION OF THE PROPOSED MODEL ON A RETAIL PORTFOLIO

4.1 MOTIVATION FOR APPLICATION OF THE MODEL

The presented solution based on the Schrödinger equation allows us to perform complex client portfolio simulation. The solution takes into consideration that numerous variables can be temporal or nontemporal. In practice, it is very hard to make an appropriate simulation model when we are dealing with numerous attributes with connections which represent influences among them. Also, temporal attributes with the same characteristics contribute to the complexity of such systems. Client portfolios such as retail client portfolios, insurance client portfolios, and telecommunication client portfolios share the same characteristics. The method presented is perfectly suitable as a simulation solution for systems of this kind. It is unrealistic to expect that developed systems will contain all variables and relations which exist in a real business, but the idea is to recognize most important variables and relations and to perform portfolio simulation on the factors and relations which have the highest importance in the portfolio.

By applying this model, companies can make complex *what if analysis* in conditions of high complexity. Most importantly, *what if analysis* can be done with the influence of future trends in the portfolio, as well as with measuring the influence of future trends of some events expressed through time series on some observed temporal and/or nontemporal event.

4.2 PROBLEM DESCRIPTION

The case study shows the application of described model on data from one Croatian retailer. The main idea was to create a model to help in decision support. The model created was also used to help in the better understanding of customer behavior. The retailer has shopping centers with grocery stores across Croatia. The retailer wants to find out the effects of its tactical and operative decisions regarding pricing policy. Some of the shopping centers have strong competition, some of them have moderate or weak competition, and in some shopping centers it is evident that buyers prefers specific items. Also, market basket analysis in previous analysis revealed that buyers prefers to buy some items together with other items, but this is not the rule for each region/shopping center. It depends on the region, as well on the season and other factors. The retailer wants to find out the optimal pricing strategy for each shopping center or cluster of shopping centers on the basis of region, competition, items, and/or other factors which will increase profit. Previous analysis also showed that some competitors are very dangerous market players, reacting quickly when retailer has discounts on some products, some competitors are not very dangerous market players, reacting slowly, and some competitors are not very dangerous market players, having moderate reactions to the retailer's pricing activities. Taking into consideration all this information and numerous items on offer, as well as the tendency for buying items in pairs or group on the basis of seasonal factors, the tendency for buying specific items in different regions, and other factors, the complexity of the portfolio simulation model is evident.

4.3 SOLUTION DESIGN

After analysis target determination, the first step was sample selection. This is not a trivial task because sample size as well as the observed period for portfolio simulation has a great influence on model quality and reliability. A small sample with a short observation period is unusable because it does not reflect the real current situation within the portfolio regarding neglecting a longer period of observation. This means that we can avoid seasonal effects, or we can capture data at some specific period which is not representative, with concentration on some shorter period which does not cover enough time to learn behavioral portfolio characteristics. On the other hand, we also have a problem if we have a huge data sample which covers too much time. In that case we face the problem of data sample dilution. There is no simple and unique answer as how to perform appropriate data sampling for this purpose, and the solution is mostly a combination of experience, use of techniques such a survival analysis, taking into consideration market conditions, and use of trial-and-error methods. In this stage a 2-year observation period as chosen as the sampling period, with determination of a few target variables in relation to frozen food, beverages, children's cosmetics and women's cosmetics. The reason for such target variable selection was inspired by previous results from market basket analysis projects, as well as the fact that competitors on targeted markets show some activities regarding pricing during discount periods.

During the data cleaning stage the data sample was cleaned of missing data and bad values. Bad data and missing values were replaced by unique values which can be recognized as missing data. That means that .null. values as well as empty fields and suspicious values were replaced by unique values. In that stage extreme data values were recognized as were other illogical values within the data set.

Attribute relevance analysis was conducted regarding target variables in relation to frozen food, beverages, children's cosmetics, and women's cosmetics. As a result, attribute relevance analysis provided information on the most important predictors regarding the selected target variables, and was the basis for dynamic Bayesian network development.

The next step was transformation of time series data into the REFII model. Target variables were expressed through time series as the propensity for buying target items or a set of items within a 2-year period. "Propensity" in this situation means the number of items bought within a 2-year period on a monthly basis.

All previous steps was done in service of dynamic Bayesian model development. As will be shown in the next section, some of the dynamic Bayesian model was developed regarding some findings during the development process.

The developed model was validated, and after validation it was ready for use. All described stages are presented in Fig. 1.

The presented solution design describes the required activities and the necessary steps for client portfolio simulation hybrid system development.

4.4 RESULTS FROM EMPIRICAL DATA

After sample selection and data cleaning, attribute relevance analysis was done. The focus was on frozen food, beverages, children's cosmetics, and women's cosmetics as target variables regarding company strategy. The information gain measure shows potential predictor importance, taking into consideration the determined target variables. When we are talking about frozen food, beverages, children's cosmetics, and women's cosmetics as target variables, this does not mean that items in these groups were declared as target variables. The idea was to select items within those groups and to perform attribute relevance analysis regarding a specific item.

Table 1 shows the results for calculated information gain for the target variable diaper in the category of children's cosmetics

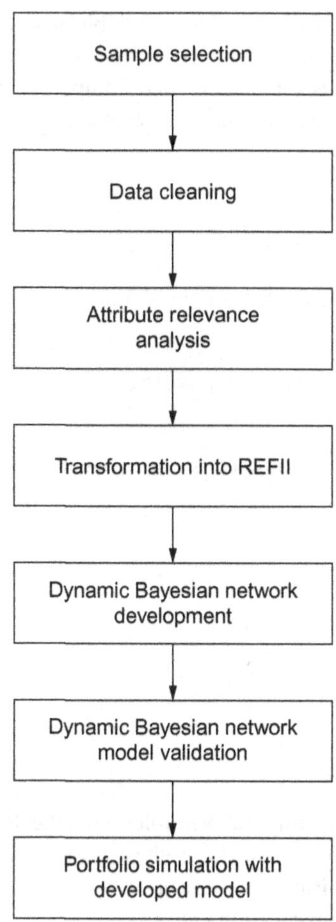

FIG. 1

Solution design.

Table 1 Results for Calculated Information Gain for Target Variable Diaper

Variable Name	Information Gain
Region	1.0034
Season	0.8832
Gender	0.8753
Age	0.7253

A recognized predictor for each target variable was the initial point for model development. Temporal variables such as buying trend for diapers, buying trend for cosmetics, competitor prices for diapers, and competitor prices for cosmetics were transformed to the REFII model by the following code in the SPSS script language:

```
STRING REF (A2).
NUMERIC TREND (N8,2).
NUMERIC TRANSFORM (N8,2).
NUMERIC AREA (N8,2).
COMPUTE transform=(Target_variable-min_target)/(max_target-min_target).
EXECUTE.

COMPUTE trend=transform-LAG(transform,1).
EXECUTE.

COMPUTE area=ABS((transform-LAG(transform,1))/2).
EXECUTE.

DO IF (trend GT 0).
compute  REF = 'R'.
ELSE IF (trend EQ 0).
compute  REF= 'E'.
ELSE IF (trend LT 0).
compute  REF= 'F'.
END IF.
EXECUTE.
```

After transformation of temporal variables into the REFII model and attribute relevance analysis, predictors with the highest impact on the target variable were included in the model (the Bayesian network was constructed with GeNIe Modeler, BayesFusion, http://www.bayesfusion.com).

Fig. 2 shows a dynamic Bayesian network structure for portfolio simulation, the design of which is based on information gain calculation and expert knowledge. This model provides an answer for portfolio behavior for buyers of diapers and cosmetics. Other combinations of products or a single product was used for other models, and this model will be explained in detail as an illustration of the method. As an element of attribute relevance analysis, information gain shows that good predictors for buying diapers and cosmetics are the region, gender, season, and age. This seems logical because buyers in some life periods will have small children and will wish to buy diapers, and there tends to be a gender bias among buyers of diapers. This could also be the case for cosmetics. Season and region are not so easy to explain as predictors, but thing will be clearer after analysis. The retailer collects data on the reactions of its competitors after it has changed prices for certain items, and collects those data in databases. The main tool which can cause buyers or competitors to react is pricing strategy. A company can raise or decrease prices for specific items, and the model has to calculate the states of each node (particle if we are talking about

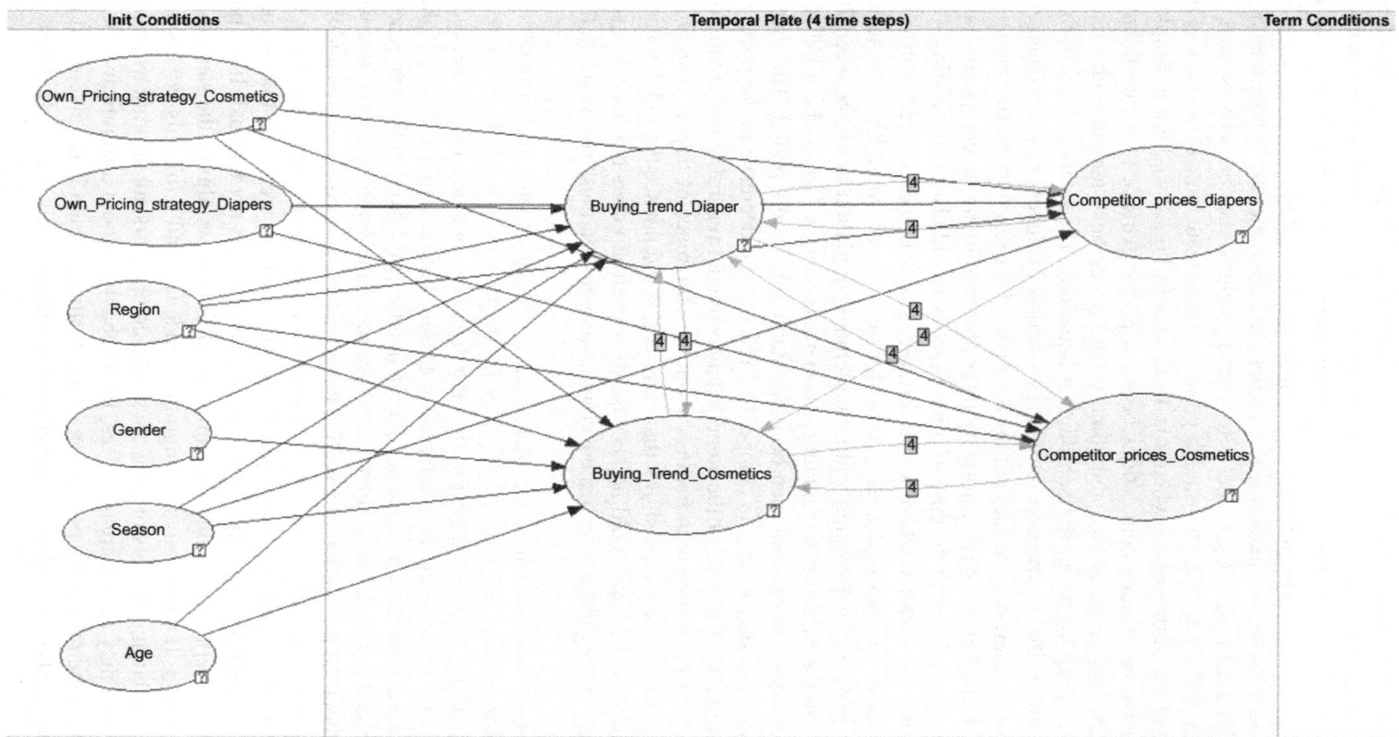

FIG. 2

Dynamic Bayesian network model for client portfolio simulation.

the Schrödinger equation). The reason why cosmetics and diapers are included in same model is because those two groups of items are recognized through market basket analyses as complementary items which buyers like to buy in pairs in a certain number of cases. The purpose of the model is also to find relations such as if competitors have the same situation where diapers and cosmetics are complementary items. An additional task of the model is to investigate how fast competitors react to price changes, and we are used a 4-month period to investigate that. This is visible in the temporal phase of the model where t is 4. As seen in Fig. 2, we have a complex model where we have many connections between nodes (particle if we are talking about the Schrödinger equation), and some of the nodes have temporal character (waves if we are talking about the Schrödinger equation). The retailer wants to find out the reaction of the competitors as well as reaction of buyers to price changes. Also, it would be interesting to find out the time period for reaction to price changes for competitor and buyers. Also, information for observed items are complementary in way of buying in group in the case of price changes would also be interesting.

Fig. 3 shows the situation where we performed a simulation on a recent portfolio when the company decides to decrease prices for diapers and would like to observe the behavior in the northern region within the female population of age between 20 and 40 years in the period not including summer. As seen in Fig. 3, the trend for buying diapers starts to rise and then becomes stable after some period. The rising trend is assumed to stop when the competitors react to the decrease in the price of diapers. Customers show almost the same behavior model regarding the buying of cosmetics, and this is in line with findings about the preference of buying cosmetics and diapers in pairs. The model shows that competitors did not see the link between cosmetics and diapers. This could be because their portfolio does not have a buyer profile, or they simply did not realize the connection between these two items in the portfolio.

Fig. 4 shows situation where we performed a simulation on a recent portfolio when the company decided to decrease prices for diapers and would like to observe the behavior in the northern region within the female population of age between 20 and 40 years in summer. It is interesting to see that in summer the portfolio changes its characteristics. The same population in different periods of the year reacts differently from the simulation results. If we take into consideration the fact that we are talking about the population of Croatian buyers from the northern region and the fact that this is traditionally a period of summer holidays when people are going to the seaside (southern part of Croatia near the sea), and if we are aware that we are talking about a younger population with children, then this is not unusual. If we put evidence for southern Croatia into the same model, it behaves almost the same as a model from Fig. 3. It shows buyers' migration tendency, and remaining buyers are not interested in buying diapers or cosmetics. The competitors are also not aware of that fact because they also decrease prices, but probably without a significant effect because as seen the remaining population in the northern region is not interested in that. The same analysis was done for other combinations of items or single items.

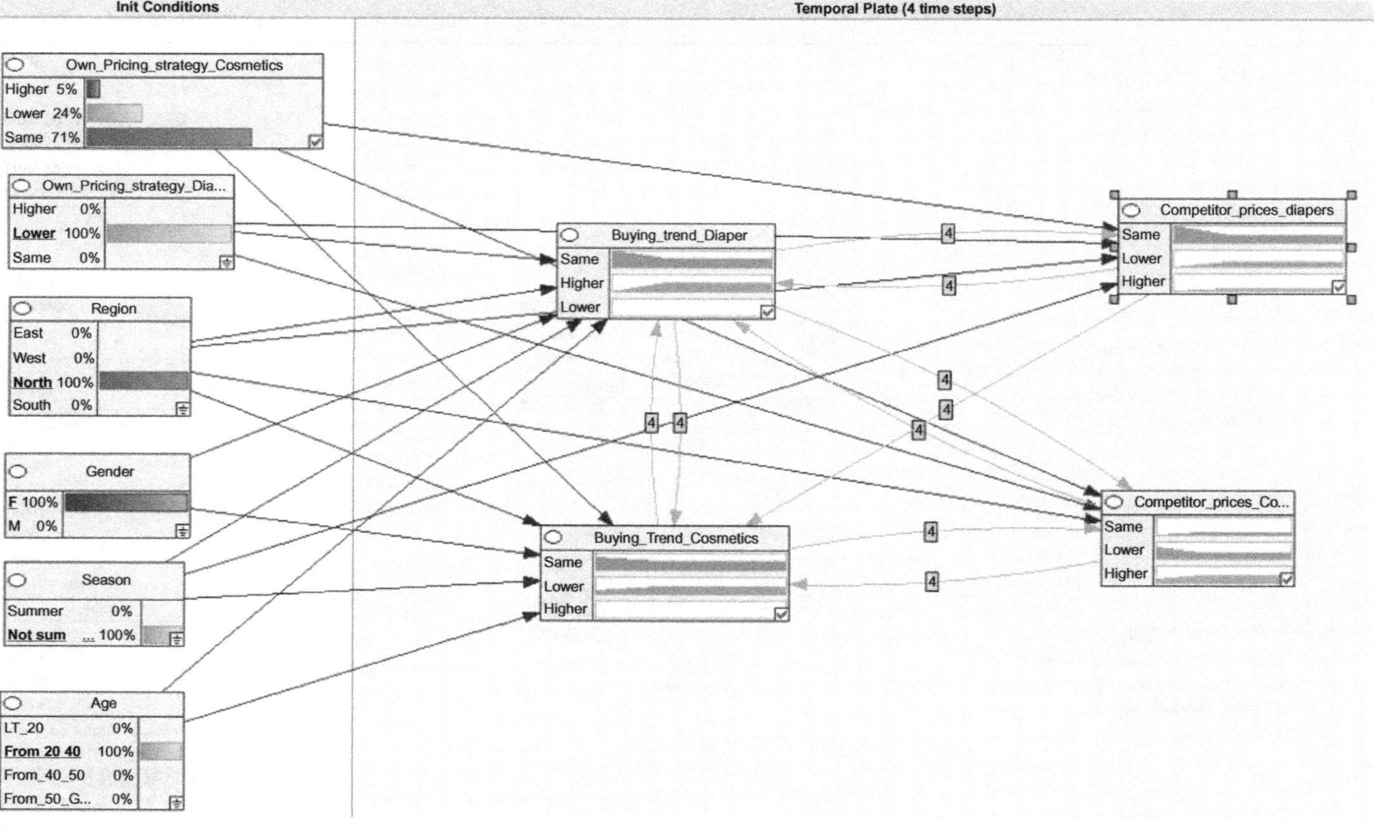

FIG. 3

Dynamic Bayesian network model for the northern region in the period not including summer.

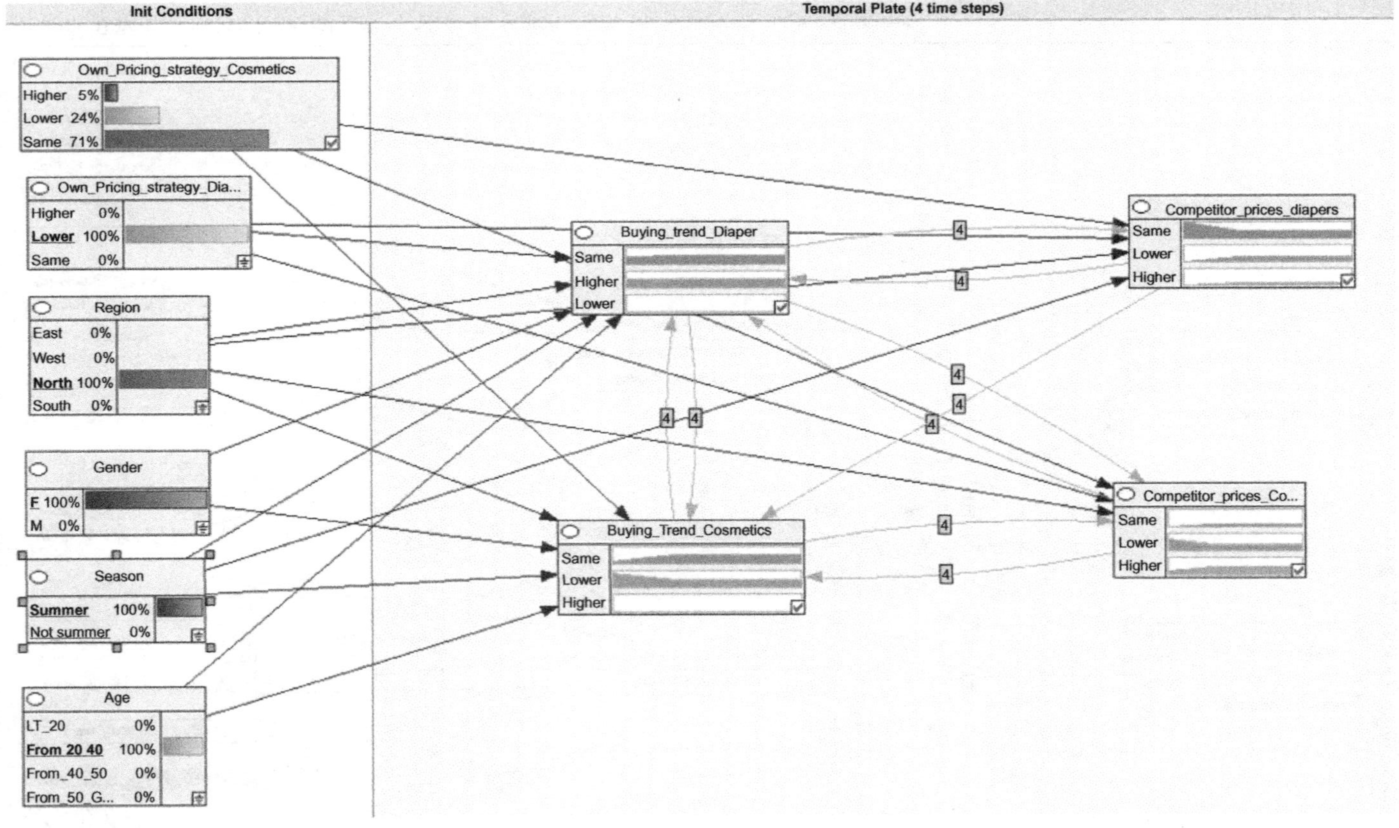

FIG. 4

Dynamic Bayesian network model for the northern region during summer.

The same concept was used for client portfolio simulation where target variables were other items such as frozen pizza, milk, and several other products. A decreasing pricing strategy for milk does not have a significant impact on the reaction of competitors in all regions where there is a shopping center. Obviously it is not a strategic product and this product is not the focus of selling. Also buyers do not show great interest in buying more milk in the period when the shopping center has campaigns with the lowest prices for milk. Obviously competitors are faced with the same situation and they do no react in a situation where the retailer decreases milk prices. Deeper analysis shows that the reason for insensitivity to decreasing milk prices is probably customer habits of buying significant milk supplies once during a 2-month period. A decreasing pricing strategy for frozen pizza shows that the northwest and eastern region is more sensitive to price changes than other regions. The most sensitive population which shows increasing interest for that product in the period of lower prices is the male population between the age of 40 and 50 years. It is interesting that this population shows increasing interest in buying prepared food, which was the trigger for making an additional model with frozen pizza and prepared food. The model shows that this population regarding camping, depending on which of those two item groups currently has the lower prices, prefers to buy items with lower prices. The model shows that competitors are obviously not interested in decreasing their prices for prepared food and frozen pizza in the period when the retailer decreases its prices for these products. That explains the high sensitivity in the portfolio and the changing buying habits with regard to frozen pizza and prepared food. Another explanation could be that this population does not exist in the portfolios of the competitors and the competitors does not see benefits in decreasing prices for those items in the period when the retailer decreases prices for these products. It is clear that portfolio simulation models can raise new questions which can be the basis for additional analysis. It is also purpose of simulation models to discover unusual patterns and set new hypothesis. Also, each hypothesis can be accepted or rejected depending on additional analysis and results from additional analysis. The knowledge revealed about competitor behavior and buyer behavior can be used for strategic and tactical market planning. Also, it can be the basis for finding potential opportunities on the market, and as tool for recognition competitor weak points. Weak point recognition in a competitor portfolio means finding some market segment which is mutually targeted by one's own company and competitors, and competitors are not aware of buyers' buying habits or their propensity to buy a specific product under certain conditions.

5 FUTURE RESEARCH DIRECTIONS

The model presented, inspired by the Schrödinger equation, could be the basis for further improvement and extension. The main idea was to develop a simulation tool for a complex system in the domain of client portfolio simulation where we would like to determine trends in the portfolio caused by some business decisions or by observing clients' dominant characteristics. It would also be interesting to understand which decision should be made in a situation where we would like an increasing trend for buying some items, as well as dominant characteristics of the clients which can contribute to achievement of that objective. In a system which is already complex we should introduce another layer of complexity by using methods such as genetic algorithms or practical swarm optimization algorithms to achieve the objectives. As is evident from the model presented, there are too many combinations and interactions between variables, even in relatively small systems. Each dynamic temporal element and each nondynamic nontemporal element has great potential for generating numerous combinations through states within conditional probability tables and their interactions expressed as bilateral or unilateral ties. Searching for the optimal solution within the developed simulation model without an additional tool is a time-wasting process. The number of combinations rises exponentially with the number of nodes, the number of categories within nodes, and the number of observed periods within dynamic temporal elements. Genetic algorithms or practical swarm optimization algorithms have the task of finding the combination of evidence which will satisfy the defined conditions within the selected target variable or target variables. Fitness function evaluation will be done by maximization of the probability of the targeted state. The proposed solution based on evolutionary computing could be a fast and easy way of finding targeted states of the market as well as dominant characteristics of the clients which can contribute to this aim. In the case where sociodemographic characteristics are included in the model, the same method can be used as a profiling tool [30] which includes not only sociodemographic characteristics but also behavioral client characteristics as well as the propensity for buying during the observed period.

Customer profiling is one of the most important techniques in customer relationship management. Campaign planning, new product development, cross-selling activities, upselling activities and many other activities related to customer portfolio management are closely related to customer profiles. The same is true in the same situation where we would like to measure the risk of insurance company clients. It is unrealistic to expect that the whole customer portfolio has similar or even the same profile characteristics regarding the risk. Risk characteristics are very dependent on behavioral characteristics and their relation to the probability of some unexpected event occurring which will result in additional cost to the insurance company. For insurance companies that have a small number of products and services in their portfolio, risk profiling is an easier task than for insurance companies with a large number of products and services.

Even in a situation where a company has a limited set of products and services, risk profiling is not a trivial task. Profiling is not (an should not be) concentrated solely on sociodemographic characteristics. Risk profiling should also take into consideration customer behavioral characteristics. Customer behavioral characteristics are not obvious and recognizable as sociodemographic variables . Although sociodemographic characteristics could be represented by a set of standard variables such as age, gender, and region and companies can use those profiles within those variables (which is not recommended), risk profiling is still not an easy task. It should be done considering the target variable, which represents use of some products or a group of products. Considering customer behavioral characteristics as a part of profiling makes profiling more complicated. The first problem in the situation when companies decide to include behavioral characteristics as a profiling element is related to recognition of relevant behavioral characteristics, which is significant for profiling. Behavioral characteristics are more powerful determinants for profiling than sociodemographic characteristics. The problem with this approach is that it is not easy to recognize key behavioral characteristics which will show a typical risk profile. The model presented, which was inspired by the Schrödinger equation, has great potential not only for taking into consideration behavioral characteristics but also for taking in consideration temporal behavioral characteristics, which can depend on numerous external or internal factors.

6 DISCUSSION

Bayesian networks are a method commonly used in risk modeling but they are not a purely statistical predictive model (as, e.g., neural networks or logistic regression) because their structure can also depend on expert knowledge. Bayesian network structure could be settled in an algorithmic way, but from the business perspective or the perspective of model efficiency and overall performance, it is recommended that Bayesian network structure be modified by expert knowledge.

Expert involvement in network structure cannot be a guarantee that the network will be optimal but it will be aligned with the business perception of the problem space.

From the perspective of portfolio simulation, the use of dynamic Bayesian networks with the REFII model in predictive modeling is complex. Finding the optimal combination of nodes with corresponding evidence which will maximize the final output is not a trivial task.

The method presented has practical value for decision support, especially in business where information about customer risk profiles is valuable for future portfolio planning, as was shown in the example of an insurance company. An additional advantage is profile similarity calculation based on given results. Additionally, the method described can be used frequently (e.g., on a quarterly basis) for determination of changes in risk profiles, which implies changes in customer behavior or preferences over time.

It is important to keep in mind that the method presented does not guarantee success for each defined product/group of products. It is not surprising that for some defined product/group of products it is not possible to find a reliable risk profile. It depends on the data itself, as well as on the type of the predictive model used. A situation in which adequate profiles are recognized with a certain threshold for the most of the product/group of products is acceptable. Real data-mining projects require the use of several data-mining methods to achieve defined goals and often hybridization, also in the situation where the Schrödinger equation became inspiration for a portfolio simulation model. The approach presented showed good results for the specific company, taking into consideration its market position, data sources, and market conditions.

Predictive models should not be used only as a probabilistic calculator because in that case the business background remains unknown and hidden. Understanding of the business background is a crucial factor for strategic management. Knowledge of typical users of insurance company products is the basis for strategic business activities. Profile changes demand changes in marketing strategies and marketing planning, as well as changes in company policies. Significant profile transformation demands greater changes in marketing strategies. Portfolio management demands continuous portfolio monitoring, especially when a company operates with a large number of products on the market which are covered with some predictive models which calculate the probability that some bad event will happen.

Profiling in a situation where predictive models are used for calculation of the probability of N possible states is a very hard task which demands lots of manual work with doubtful results. In contrast to the situation with binomial states of an output variable in a predictive model, attribute relevance analysis for multinomial output regarding overlap in impact zones and combinatory expansion could not provide clear information for the setting input variable values for profile determination. In this case the target variable within the predictive model should reach the criterion of maximum probability "to belong in the bucket" by use of a particle swarm optimization algorithm. The final result will give optimal values of the input variables for each product/service, such as behavioral characteristics or sociodemographic characteristics, and from which models are developed on the basis of attribute relevance analysis.

Each type of data models developed, as well as presented, could be affected by market changes. Predictive models could lose their predictive power because of some other type of customers and their behavior becoming different because of some reasons different from those in the previous period. This could be explained simply by the fact that competitors could target different market segments from the company portfolio as a result of changing their market strategy. Changes in a competitor's strategy will not cause loss of predictive power in predictive models immediately; it will be a relatively long process. It is important to realize those trends at an early stage, which could a company which is threatened by such changes the opportunity to the make right decisions on time and to calibrate and redesign existing models. If model validation is performed very often (e.g., monthly), these trends will not be so explicit as when model validation is performed less often. Frequent validation ensures recognition of early warning systems. Changes in a competitor's strategy could also affect developed segmentation models, prospective customer values, and all other developed models, which are an integral part of the modeling solution. Regarding all facts, it is important to perform periodic validation, which ensures a solution which is applicable for the current market situation.

Frequent validation is welcomed, but t within a short time span there could be too few sample elements for analysis to capture new trends in the portfolio. One technique uses part of the period on which model was developed (the most recent one) to achieve a reliable data sample. This technique has a weakness because it does not capture a real recent sample only; it combines it with part of the sample on which the model was developed. A mitigating circumstance is that it takes the most recent periods and it shows a real picture of the current portfolio state. Some of the tools which analysts have to perform validation (mostly for predictive models) are:

- the receiver operating characteristic curve
- the Kolmogorov-Smirnov test
- the stability index

With the receiver operating characteristic curve and the Kolmogorov-Smirnov test are applied on a recent sample for existing predictive models, it is possible to realize if the model lost predictive power or not. Also, it is possible to monitor trends in the predictive power of the model, if it loses power with time, or if a different type of trend is evident. Continuous loss of predictive power of the model implies evident changes in portfolio structure. It could be an early warning signal for significant changes in the market which could be caused by the activities competitors or some other reasons. It does not mean that the predictive model should lose its predictive power in way that it is unusable. The predictive model could still have great predictive power, but the fact that it continuously loses power implies that some other characteristics of churners have become much more significant. To find out the reason for that, it is recommended to repeat attribute relevance analysis (weight of evidence, information value). Regarding satisfying predictive power, for sure there would not be dramatic changes in results, but indications of rising trends which cause predictive power drop will be visible. Regarding those trends, the company can make or redesign the churn strategy for a further period. It can also focus on revealed (now relatively weak) indicators, especially on periodic validations to reject or accept some hypothesis about market changes, a competitor's new strategy, or macroeconomic influences on the existing portfolio. Use of weight of evidence and information value measures could also be useful during validation, even if the churn solution does not contain a predictive model. In that way a company could recognize the mentioned trends, the churner's profile, motivation, and behavior, and changes in them. The stability index is another good tool for recognizing changes in portfolio structure (churner's structure). It could be used in combination with predictive models, where some classification regarding churn probability exists, and the portfolio is categorized within churn probability by binned probability scales. That is a common way in which the stability index could be applied. In the case where the predictive model is not part of the churn solution, the stability index could be applied on some other categories/groups, such as clusters from self-organizing maps, or prospective customer values expressed as categories from, for example, a fuzzy expert system. The stability index shows potential layering within a recent sample (freshest one) and an existing portfolio.

7 CONCLUSION

The model presented provides a solution for how to integrate different aspects of a client portfolio and their interaction, as well as the temporal aspect of portfolio, the most important factors within the portfolio, and the activities of competitors on the market. As a final result, we have an analytical tool which takes into consideration different aspects; internal, external, and temporal. This approach is not one-dimensional such as in situation when we are making a predictive model with limited scope which does not take into consideration all enumerated factors. The Schrödinger equation was the inspiration for our developing such a complex model which is in line with real-life complexity and which should take into consideration not only internal factors but also external factors, such as competitors' reactions and activities on the market, taking into consideration the temporal aspect of the problem.

The client portfolio simulation model inspired by the Schrödinger equation gives much realistic insight into internal portfolio factors, external (market) factors, and temporal aspects of both types of factors, as well as their interactions. An empirical example based on data from one Croatian retailer showed the efficacy of the proposed model. The solution presented based on empirical data proves that the proposed method can be used for portfolio simulation purposes, as well as for knowledge extraction and pattern recognition within one's own portfolio.

Extracted knowledge and recognized patterns can be used as a decision support system for business purposes. This is direct connection how some postulates and principles from quantum mechanics can be direct inspiration for business decision support systems. Obviously more than this part of quantum mechanics can be applied for similar purposes or as inspiration for business decision support systems.

REFERENCES

[1] R. Hilborn, Chaos and Nonlinear Dynamics: An Introduction for Scientist and Engineers, Oxford University Press, Oxford, 2004, doi:10.1002/aic.690410719.

[2] J. Honerkamp, Statistical Physics an Advanced Approach With Applications, Springer-Verlag, Berlin/Heidelberg, 2012, doi:10.1007/978-3-642-28684-1.

[3] R. Lapkiewicz, P. Li, C. Schaeff, Experimental non-classicality of an indivisible quantum system, Nature 474 (2011) 490–493, doi:10.1038/nature10119.

[4] S. Akama, Elements of Quantum Computing, Springer International Publishing, Berlin/Heidelberg, 2015, doi:10.1007/978-3-319-08284-4.

[5] D. Bes, Quantum Mechanics, Springer, Berlin/Heidelberg, 2013, doi: 10.1007/978-3-642-20556-9.

[6] K. Hecht, Quantum Mechanics, Springer, New York, 2012, doi: 10.1007/978-1-4612-1272-01.

[7] N. Zettili, Quantum Mechanics: Concepts and Applications, Wiley, New York, 2009, doi:10.1007/978-0-387-88698-5.

[8] F. David, The Formalisms of Quantum Mechanics: An Introduction, Springer, Berlin, 2010, doi:10.1007/BF02058098.

[9] G. Klepac, L. Mrsic, R. Kopal, REFII model as a base for data mining techniques hybridization with purpose of time series pattern recognition, in: S. Bhattacharyya, P. Dutta, S. Chakraborty (Eds.), Hybrid Soft Computing Approaches, Springer India, 2016, pp. 237–270, doi:10.1007/978-81-322-2544-7_8.

[10] G. Klepac, Time series analysis using a unique model of transformation, J. Inf. Organ. Sci. 31 (2) (2007) 1–13.

[11] W.V. Kumar, Customer Relationship Management, Springer-Verlag, Berlin/Heidelberg, 2012, doi:10.1007/978-3-642-20110-3.

[12] J. Cryer, K. Chan, Customer Relationship Management, Springer-Verlag, New York, 2008, doi:10.1007/978-0-387-75959-3.

[13] F. Rajola, Customer Relationship Management in the Financial Industry, Springer-Verlag, Berlin/Heidelberg, 2013, doi:10.1007/978-3-642-02532-7.

[14] F. Harrell, Regression Modeling Strategies With Applications to Linear Models, Logistic and Ordinal Regression, and Survival Analysis, Springer International Publishing, Berlin/Heidelberg, 2015, doi:10.1007/978-3-319-19425-7.

[15] F. Gorunescu, Data Mining, Springer-Verlag, Berlin/Heidelberg, 2011, doi: 10.1007/978-3-642-19721-5.

[16] D. Yeung, I. Cloete, D. Shi, W. Ng, Sensitivity Analysis for Neural Networks, Springer-Verlag, Berlin/Heidelberg, 2013, doi:10.1007/978-3-642-02532-7.

[17] M. Kunh, K. Johnson, Applied Predictive Modeling, Springer-Verlag, New York, 2013, doi:10.1007/978-1-4614-6849-3.

[18] D. Murray-Smith, Testing and Validation of Computer Simulation Models Principles Methods and Applications, Springer International Publishing, Switzerland, 2015, doi: 10.1007/978-3-319-15099-4.

[19] G. Klepac, L. Mrsic, R. Kopal, Developing Churn Models Using Data Mining Techniques and Social Network Analysis, IGI Global, Hershey, PA, 2015, doi: 10.4018/978-1-4666-6288-9.

[20] G. Klepac, Discovering behavioural patterns within customer population by using temporal data subsets, in: S. Bhattacharyya, P. Banerjee, D. Majumdar, P. Dutta (Eds.) Handbook of Research on Advanced Hybrid Intelligent Techniques and Applications, Information Science Reference, Hershey, PA, 2016, pp. 216–252, doi: 10.1007/978-3-642-20110-3.

[21] P. Brockwell, R. Davis, Introduction to Time Series and Forecasting, Springer-Verlag, New York, 2002, doi:10.1007/b97391.

[22] P. Cowpertwait, A. Metclafe, V. Andrew, Introductory Time Series With R, Springer-Verlag, New York, 2009, doi:10.1007/978-0-387-88698-5.

[23] W. Ching, X. Huang, M. Ng, T. Siu, Markov Chains Models, Algorithms and Applications, Springer International Publishing, Switzerland, 2013, doi: 10.1007/978-1-4614-6312-2.

[24] N. Privault, Understanding Markov Chains, Springer-Verlag, Singapore, 2013, doi: 10.1007/978-981-4451-51-2.

[25] F. Jensen, T. Nielsen, Bayesian Networks and Decision Graphs, Springer, New York, 2007, doi:10.1007/978-0-387-68282-2.

[26] U. Kjarluff, A. Madsen, Bayesian Networks and Influence Diagrams: A Guide to Construction and Analysis, Springer, New York, 2013, doi:10.1007/978-0-387-68282-2.

[27] K. Lange, Applied Probability, Springer-Verlag, New York, 2010, doi: 10.1007/978-1-4419-7165-4.

[28] O. Topcu, U. Oguztuzun, H. Yilmaz, Presents a Modeling-Driven Software Engineering Approach for Distributed Simulation, Springer International Publishing, Switzerland, 2015, doi:10.1007/978-3-319-03050-0.

[29] A. Byrski, Z. Oplatkova, M. Carvalho, M. Kisiel-Dorohinicki, Advances in Intelligent Modelling and Simulation Tools and Applications, Springer, Berlin/Heidelberg, 2012, doi:10.1007/978-3-642-28888-3.

[30] G. Klepac, L. Mrsic, R. Kopal, Efficient risk profiling using Bayesian networks and particle swarm optimization algorithm, in: D. Jakbczak (Ed.) Analyzing Risk Through Probabilistic Modeling in Operations Research, IGI Global, Hershey, PA, 2016, pp. 19–124, doi:10.4018/978-1-4666-9458-3.ch004.

CHAPTER

A quantum-inspired hybrid intelligent position monitoring system in wireless networks

13

D.V. Medhane, A.K. Sangaiah

School of Computing Science and Engineering, VIT University, Vellore, TN, India

1 INTRODUCTION

Position-based services have gradually become popular by means of pervasive positioning and rapid growth of the use of mobile devices such as smartphones and other handheld devices. A variety of position-based services, such as real-time position monitoring, responding to position-based queries for nearby source locations in smart city management systems, position tracking of people in supermarkets, and conveying exact driving directions to a car driver, are now available, and these position-based services are made available to consumers with the help of in-built a position monitoring system (PMS) in cell phones and similar devices [1]. Smartphones and other handheld devices play a vital role in real-time position tracking and monitoring of humans, vehicles, computers, and other Global Positioning System devices in spite of the fact that all of these are moving [2].

Over the past few years, many researchers and practitioners came up with numerous PMS frameworks and architectures. There are typically several position monitoring tools in our pockets or purses. However, only a few of them converge at the confidentiality issue of the geographically distributed objects or components. Confidentiality provision to the entities involved within a wireless range area is a serious issue and hence has become a design challenge in the construction and development of a PMS. The real-time position information used by a PMS may expose private and confidential information about an individual; for instance, current position information of an individual; that is, what he/she does, where he/she goes, etc. [3]. So it is essential to protect individuals against several confidentiality extortions and threats while they are using position monitoring tools [4].

In view of that, we propose a hybrid intelligent PMS with the aim of conserving confidentiality of an individual in real-time position-based services. We

Quantum Inspired Computational Intelligence. http://dx.doi.org/10.1016/B978-0-12-804409-4.00013-9

have reviewed the available position monitoring tools thoroughly and come up with several design issues and challenges regarding PMS frameworks and architectures. The proposed quantum-inspired hybrid intelligent PMS will solve the position confidentiality issue and will preserve the confidentiality of an individual while that individual is moving from one geographical location to another.

The quantum computation theory offers a unique framework for the development and implementation of several modern intelligent systems and is undoubtedly one of the most systematic theories of the twentieth century [5]. Hence we are proposing a hybrid intelligent PMS from the perspective of quantum computation theory. Basically, distributed quantum computation theory motivated us to come up with the proposed PMS. The motivation behind distributed quantum computation theory is that the physical mobile resources are used for simulation and control of a large-capacity quantum computer system. Also, several secure communication protocols are proposed in quantum computation theory and are available in the literature. So we can adopt the available secure communication protocols and can extend them for conservation of confidentiality of mobile objects/people in a particular wireless search space area. Various classical algorithms are available in the literature for preservation of privacy of objects in a wireless range area, but no algorithms can accurately and confidentially provide the position-related information. So we proposed a quantum algorithm for conservation of confidentiality in a PMS to overcome with the problems involved in the available PMSs. The proposed quantum algorithm can produce confidential and exact position information in polynomial time.

Moreover, the proposed hybrid intelligent system will come under the hybridization class of problems from fuzzy neural networks. Basically, in the hybridization class of problems more focus is given to interaction between the available approaches for solving the given problem and finally the global system scenario to come up with an effective and efficient outcome [6]. The hybridization of intelligent computing systems is an encouraging research area and is essential for the progress of the next generation of hybrid intelligent computing systems [7]. Many novel intelligent computing systems available today are the result of hybridization since hybridization allows integration of various learning and adaptation strategies to overcome discrete limitations of individual techniques or mechanisms reported in the literature[8,9]. Hence we have planned and designed the hybrid intelligent PMS with hybridization. In recent years, hybrid intelligent computing frameworks have been developed for and used in many systems, such as process control, decision support, robotics, mechatronics, image processing, video segmentation techniques, and data mining [10]. Most of these approaches use various decision making archetypes, learning strategies, and knowledge representation tactics. Such integration of systems is intended to overcome the limitations of specific techniques by means of hybridization. However, the development of hybrid intelligent computing systems by use of hybridization is a flexible and unrestricted concept. Hence we are proposing a PMS with an intelligent hybridization tactic. The use of hybridization in designing a PMS allows the integration of several available mechanisms for position monitoring along with confidentiality-conserving object monitoring [11].

The benefits of the proposed hybrid intelligent PMS include value-added position monitoring, robustness, augmented query solving capabilities, noise tolerance, and confidentiality conservation in a wireless search space area.

This chapter will mainly describe an innovative PMS. The concepts mentioned in this chapter include technical aspects of traditional PMSs and all-purpose position-based services and a quantum algorithm for confidentiality conservation in a PMS. Also, aspects of fuzzy neural networks in hybrid intelligent PMS are discussed briefly along with the proof of correctness.

1.1 CONTRIBUTION OF THIS WORK

In this chapter we examine the problem of a moving object's position confidentiality in wireless networks. The foremost contributions of this work are as follows:

- We present the novel idea of a quantum-inspired hybrid intelligent PMS and explain how the problem of a moving object's position confidentiality can be mapped to fuzzy logic and quantum-inspired computational theory.
- We offer a quantum-inspired algorithm for a hybrid intelligent PMS.
- We map the problem of a moving object's position confidentiality to the problem of a confidentiality-conserving PMS.
- We analyze and evaluate the proposed quantum-inspired hybrid intelligent PMS framework in comparison with the traditional PMS.
- We prove the intelligence and importance of the proposed quantum-inspired PMS algorithm over the traditional PMS algorithm by means of parameters such as the number of queries and confidentiality requirements, the number of moving objects in the wireless range area, user mobility, and the anonymity threshold value used to achieve the moving object's position confidentiality in a wireless network.
- The proposed quantum-inspired PMS algorithm offers strong user anonymity for mobile users.
- We design and develop the simulation environment in Java for evaluation of the performance of the proposed quantum-inspired PMS algorithm and present case studies.

1.2 ORGANIZATION OF THIS CHAPTER

The chapter is organized as follows:

- *Related work*: PMS background, fuzzy logic in PMS;
- *Problem identification*: open research problems in PMS;
- *The proposed quantum-inspired hybrid intelligent PMS model and algorithms*: detailed system architecture, method used, and phasewise detailed algorithms;
- *Mathematical model and complexity analysis*: detailed mathematical model of the proposed PMS framework and time complexity analysis;
- *Proofs of correctness*: theorems with proofs proving the efficiency and correctness of the proposed quantum-inspired PMS algorithm;

- *Performance evaluation*: simulation setup and result analysis;
- *Case studies*: (1) tourist guide; (2) nearest friend finder;
- *Conclusion*: concluding remarks.

The results in this chapter highlight possible research and development in PMSs for conservation of confidentiality of an entity while it is moving in the wireless range area. Also, this chapter offers basic guidelines to researchers and practitioners to adopt and implement a modest and economical PMS for smart and confidentiality-conserving position-based services in 2020.

2 RELATED WORK

In this section the basics of PMSs, fuzzy logic in position monitoring, quantum computation theory, and quantum-inspired intelligent systems are reviewed.

2.1 POSITION MONITORING SYSTEM

In recent years a PMS has been flaunted as one of the killer applications in geographical information systems. In the last decade, position-based services have been incorporated into most mobile applications. People, vehicles, cell phones and other handheld devices are interconnected via the convergence of several technologies, such as the Global Positioning System, radio-frequency identification, location sensing, and geographical information systems. A PMS is basically a system that offers position-based services in association with mobile service providers, and the context-related information is communicated to end users on the basis of their position (latitude and longitude) in real time. In a traditional PMS the position of a particular object or an individual is traced with the help of smartphones or other handheld devices in association with satellite systems. PMSs are broadly categorized into two types: device-oriented PMSs and person-oriented PMSs [12]. A device-oriented PMS is external to the end user, and an object or device is responsible for real-time monitoring and tracking of an individual or a group of people. A person-oriented PMS is end user based and works on the basis of the position of the individual. A typical PMS has applications such as military surveillance, position-based advertising, nearby friend alert, user mobility, tourist guide, position-based news, real-time weather and traffic information, patient monitoring, and emergency services, but PMS are used mainly in three areas: government and military industries, the commercial sector, and emergency services. The position parameters are made available freely through satellite positioning systems and Global Positioning System [13]. So the ordinary end user may use position-related information in real-time tracking and monitoring and hence for coordination and control of different kinds of applications in mobility. Two critical issues involved in the development of a PMS are accuracy of position-based data and conservation of confidentiality of position-related information of an individual in a ubiquitous computing environment. The accuracy of position-based information is a critical issue and has become a big challenge because of interference by intruders and adversaries in the communication environment. Position-aware content delivery and position-sensitive resource management are the basic types of emerging position-based services [14]. On the basis of these two categories, various PMSs such as Gowalla, Loopt, Foursquare, Brightkite, and GyPSii were designed and developed to deliver position-based services to mobile end users. All of these PMSs are meant for provision of position-based services. But several issues such as position cheating and preservation of position confidentiality are still convoluted in the existing PMSs. To achieve the confidentiality of position-related data and hence to offer confidentiality-conserving position-based services, it is essential to provide an intelligent technique for real-time position monitoring in a wireless network with the help of several intelligent and emerging trends in quantum computation theory and fuzzy logic.

2.2 FUZZY LOGIC IN THE POSITION MONITORING SYSTEM

The concept of fuzzy logic was first presented by Zadeh [15] that allows translation of our qualitative knowledge to a reasoning system. The proposed quantum-inspired hybrid intelligent PMS is designed with the help of fuzzy logic. As far as the PMS is concerned, we used fuzzy logic as a problem solving control system approach. Fuzzy logic offers a modest way of solving position-related queries containing ambiguous, vague, and imprecise input information [16]. Moreover, instead of applying a mathematical model to a particular system, fuzzy logic integrates a rule-based IF A AND B THEN C approach to solve position-based queries. So in the proposed PMS framework we incorporate a rule-based tactic to solve position-related queries in real time and to offer confidentiality protection of the end user's current position. Furthermore, the notion of a fuzzy inference system from fuzzy logic is used; this is basically the process that formulates the mapping from a specified input to an expected output. It comprises IF-THEN rules, logical operations, and membership functions. Fuzzy inference systems may be executed with the help of two techniques: Mamdani-type and Sugeno-type techniques. The fuzzy inference system process consists of five steps: input variable fuzzification, fuzzy operator (AND or OR) application, inference from the predecessor (antecedent) to the consequent, aggregation of the consequents through the rules, and defuzzification [17]. We integrate the concept of a fuzzy inference system along with fuzzy logic in the proposed PMS framework. The position-based query forwarding and answering is implemented by means of the concept of a fuzzy inference system.

2.3 QUANTUM COMPUTATION THEORY AND QUANTUM-INSPIRED INTELLIGENT SYSTEM

Quantum computation is the scientific field that fundamentally studies the use of subatomic particles such as electrons and photons to perform and solve computational problems and ultimately big data processing. In quantum computation, data is warehoused in quantum registers, which comprise a series of quantum bits (qubits). Qubits are the quantum analog of bits. Quantum gates in quantum computation are the set of operators that are defined and designed to perform modest qubit-based computations on quantum registers. Quantum computation is capable of accomplishing a fast search over discrete data sets and parallel data processing. The classic computer system used for performing such quantum intelligent activities is termed a "quantum computer system." Quantum computation theory is allied with various scientific fields such as fuzzy logic and artificial intelligence, and promising substantial improvements in the respective fields. To achieve computational intelligence in terms of communication cost and computational cost, a quantum logic along with a fuzzy logic is adopted in the proposed quantum-inspired hybrid intelligent PMS. Basically, the physical implementation of a single qubit might be represented as the energy state of an electron in an atom, the division of a photon, or any other two-state quantum-inspired intelligent system. When a solitary qubit is considered, its state can be established in one of two clearly distinct states, typically transcribed as $|0\rangle$ and $|1\rangle$. These are direct analogs of the 0 and 1 states of a classical bit; however, they are also orthogonal states of a two-dimensional Hilbert space and they are called "basis states" for the qubit [18]. Before the qubit is measured, its state can be in a superposition of its basis states signified as

$$|\mathrm{q} = \mathrm{x}\,|0\rangle + \mathrm{y}\,|1\rangle = x\begin{bmatrix}1\\0\end{bmatrix} + \mathrm{y}\begin{bmatrix}0\\1\end{bmatrix} = \begin{bmatrix}x\\y\end{bmatrix}. \quad (1)$$

In Eq. (1), x and y are complex numbers known as probability amplitudes; $|\mathrm{x}|^2$ is the probability of the qubit appearing in state $|0\rangle$ when perceived, and $|\mathrm{y}|^2$ is the probability of it appearing in state $|1\rangle$. Also, the matrix representation of the qubit states is illustrated in Eq. (1). A series of qubits is called a "quantum register." An n-qubit quantum register can be represented as [18]

$$|\mathrm{Q}_n\rangle = \mathrm{c}_0\,|0\ldots00\rangle + \mathrm{c}_1\,|0\ldots01\rangle + \cdots + \mathrm{c}_{2^n-1}\,|1\ldots11\rangle = \sum_{i=0}^{2^n-1} \mathrm{c}_i\,|i\rangle. \quad (2)$$

From the states in Eq. (2), there are 2^n observable states having a probability of $|c_i|^2$. As mentioned in [18], this can be considered as a vector of an n-dimensional Hilbert space with $\sum_{i=0}^{2^n-1} |\mathrm{c}_i|^2 = 1$.

Furthermore, a single qubit may be delineated as a trivial quantum register with $n = 1$. The quantum register may be represented as a sequence of qubits when $n > 1$:

$$|\mathrm{Q}_n\rangle = |\mathrm{q}_{n-1}\rangle \otimes |\mathrm{q}_{n-2}\rangle \ldots |\mathrm{q}_i\rangle \ldots |\mathrm{q}_1\rangle \otimes |\mathrm{q}_0\rangle = |\mathrm{q}_{n-1}\mathrm{q}_{n-2}\cdots\mathrm{q}_i\cdots\mathrm{q}_1\mathrm{q}_0\rangle. \quad (3)$$

In Eq. (3), $\otimes$ indicates the tensor product.

In 1996 Narayanan [19] started the research into quantum-inspired computational techniques. The first quantum-inspired genetic algorithm was provided by Han and Kim [20] in 2000 [21]. This algorithm is a standard combination of evolutionary computing [22] and quantum computing [23,24], and was discussed for the solving of the well-known 0-1 knapsack problem (NP-complete problem). The basic unit of representation used in this algorithm is a qubit. Furthermore, many researchers and practitioners have presented their work on quantum-inspired intelligent algorithms in the literature but, to the best of our knowledge, none of the authors have provided a quantum algorithm for real-time secure position monitoring. Because of this, the aspects of quantum computational intelligence are mapped to a PMS for preservation of the confidentiality of roaming users as demonstrated in this chapter. The proposed quantum-based mathematical model and the quantum-inspired five-phase algorithms for confidentiality-conserving position monitoring in a wireless network are explained in subsequent sections.

3 PROBLEM IDENTIFICATION: OPEN RESEARCH PROBLEMS

The following issues are involved in the management and control of the roaming object's position confidentiality:

(1) *False position monitoring*: As far as the anonymity concept for preservation of confidentiality is concerned, instead of reporting the monitored object's exact position; the object reports several positions where only one of them is the object's actual position and the rest of them are false.
(2) *Space transformation*: Sometimes during the movement of an object from one search space to another, an object seems to be present in the old search space and in the new search space as well. So it is difficult to locate the actual object in the search space area. Moreover, a PMS raises issues of network architectures and computational geometry.
(3) *Social issues*: Several position monitoring applications permit third parties to avail themselves of the facility of real-time position monitoring to locate the user even though such access to the user's current position is illegitimate. Adequate data mining techniques are available to achieve position confidentiality but secure mining techniques should be introduced and implemented for social science promises.

4 SYSTEM MODEL AND ALGORITHMS

The quantum intelligent PMS is planned on the basis of fusion of a PMS with quantum technology. A quantum intelligent PMS is fundamentally a complex quantum-standard hybrid autonomous system that comprises three components:

(1) position server
(2) anonymous server
(3) quantum-inspired position-based services application

Fig. 1 depicts detailed components and the working of the proposed quantum-inspired hybrid intelligent PMS in a wireless network. We will define the problem

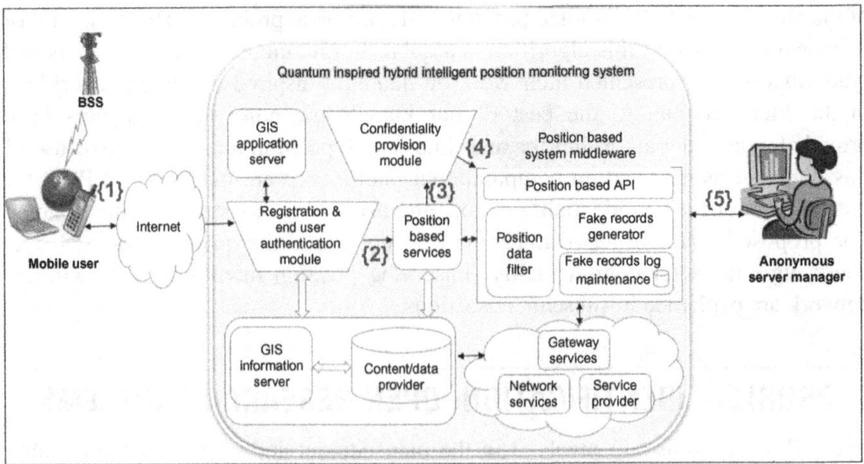

FIG. 1

Proposed quantum-inspired hybrid intelligent position monitoring system framework. *API*, application programming interface; *GIS*, geographical information system.

addressed by the proposed PMS framework and then illustrate details of each component and the confidentiality model of the proposed PMS.

4.1 PROBLEM DEFINITION

With a set of wireless objects $o_1, o_2, \ldots, o_n$ accompanied by a set of wireless range areas $r_1, r_2, \ldots, r_n$, a set of moving objects $m_1, m_2, \ldots, m_n$, and a mandatory anonymity level k, we discover an aggregate position of an individual wireless object o_i as, $R_i = (Area_i, M_i)$, where $Area_i$ is a quadrangular region covering the wireless search space area of a set of wireless objects o_i and M_i is the total number of moving objects positioned in the wireless search space areas of the wireless objects in o_i such that $M_i \geq k$. An aggregate query Q (enquiring into the number of moving objects in a definite area $Area_i$) is responded to with confidential position information in the form of qubits on the basis of the aggregate positions conveyed by wireless objects o_i.

4.2 BUILDING BLOCKS OF THE PROPOSED POSITION MONITORING SYSTEM

The position server is the basic module responsible for the provision of latitude and longitude values of the user's or the object's current position. The position server works on the basis of a simple geographical information system which used for tracking, monitoring, and controlling the user's position in real time when user is moving. The anonymous server offers a platform for selection of either a traditional position monitoring approach or the quantum-inspired hybrid intelligent position monitoring paradigm. The quantum-inspired position-based services application offers a graphical user interface to end users. With the help of the quantum-inspired position-based services application, the end user may forward position-based queries to and from the anonymous server and position server. This module is incorporated in the proposed framework and hence the end user may communicate and coordinate several position-based activities in a distributed wireless network scenario more securely.

4.3 CONFIDENTIALITY MODEL

Following is the detailed stepwise procedure for attaining confidentiality of mobile users with the help of the proposed quantum-inspired hybrid intelligent PMS:

- *Step 1.* The mobile end user will be given access to the system through the first module (i.e., the position server, which comprises two basic building blocks—namely, a registration unit and a position-based services unit). Every end user must register with the system so that, at the initial level, access to position-related information of the end user will be given to authorized users only.
- *Step 2.* In the next stage, each user in the search space area should form his/her own list of authorized users with the aim of his/her current position being accessed by authorized users only (those who are enlisted in his/her list).
- *Step 3.* After the creation of a list, the respective users should communicate to the listed users through a message passing mechanism, which is the basic way of communication among the scattered wireless nodes as far as a distributed system is concerned [25]. Hence all mobile end users present in a particular wireless range area forward a quantum message to their respective neighbor objects [26]. This quantum message is especially a combination of three elements: the unique id of a wireless object (end user) for identification of a wireless object (end user) distinctively, the wireless range area, and the total number (count) of wireless objects (end users) involved in that wireless range area.
- *Step 4.* The next step is the determination of the search space area. It is too expensive for any wireless object to assemble the information of all the wireless objects for calculation of its relative least cloaked area for the wireless object since a classic wireless network has a large number of wireless objects.
- *Step 5.* The fourth step is followed by the process of approximate least cloaked area conformation. In reality, this step plays a key role in computation of the approximate least cloaked area of the respective wireless object in the network. In this step the basic task is the formation of groups of at least four wireless objects. Why at least four objects? The reason is that at least two wireless objects are required to describe the width of the least cloaked area and at least

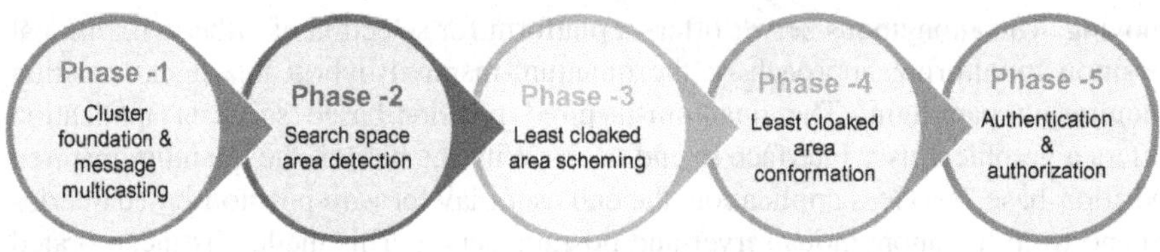

FIG. 2

Phases of the proposed framework.

two wireless objects are required to describe the height of the least cloaked area. So at least four objects will be required for the formation of least cloaked area in the specific wireless search space area. Adding wireless objects *o* to the search space area should not decrease the area of the least cloaked area of a respective search space or the number of objects contained in the least cloaked area of the search space.

The detailed method integrated in the proposed framework is illustrated in the next subsection.

4.4 PROPOSED METHOD

The proposed method is a five-phase procedure (see Fig. 2) for provision of confidential position-related information:

- phase 1: cluster foundation and message multicasting;
- phase 2: search space area detection;
- phase 3: least cloaked area scheming
- phase 4: least cloaked area conformation;
- phase 5: authentication and authorization

4.5 PHASE 1: CLUSTER FOUNDATION AND MESSAGE MULTICASTING

This is the primary phase in which all spatially distributed wireless objects contained in a particular wireless range area transfer a quantum message to near wireless objects. These near wireless objects can be treated as neighbor nodes. As mentioned earlier, the quantum message consists of the unique id of the wireless object, the wireless range area, and total number (count) of wireless objects involved in that particular wireless range area. It is mandatory for all wireless objects to have their own neighbor objects list and to form a cluster of respective neighbor objects (see Fig. 3 and Algorithm 1).

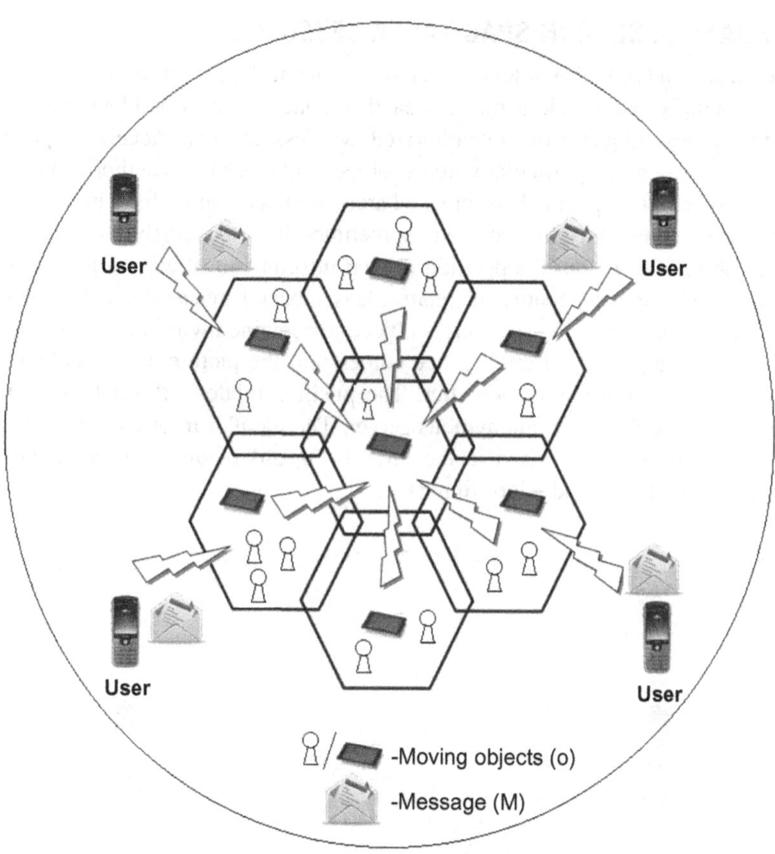

FIG. 3

Phase 1: cluster foundation and message multicasting.

ALGORITHM 1 CLUSTER FOUNDATION AND MESSAGE MULTICASTING

1: **procedure** CLUSTERFOUNDATION&MESSAGEMULTICASTING
2: WirelessObjectList *WOL* ⟵ NULL
3: Forward a quantum message Q_M with the unique identity of WirelessObject *o (o.id)*, Wireless-RangeArea *(o.WRA)*, and ObjectCount *(o.OC)* to all neighbors of WirelessObject *o*.
4: *loop*:
5: **if** WirelessMovingObject *m* receives a quantum message Q_M from WirelessObject *o* **then** add WirelessMovingObject *m* to WirelessObjectList *WOL*
6: **if** WirelessObject *o* got a satisfactory number of WirelessMovingObjects *m* **then** forward an announcement (warning) message to NeighborObjects *n*
7: **if** a satisfactory number of WirelessMovingObjects *m* has not been found **then** forward a quantum message Q_M to NeighborObjects *n*

4.6 PHASE 2: SEARCH SPACE AREA DETECTION

At the outset, individual wireless object should form their own least cloaked area, which is simply the wireless range area that conceals the confidentiality of the specific wireless object from unauthorized wireless objects. Access to position-related information of a particular wireless object will be given to authorized wireless objects only within a specific least cloaked area. So it is essential for wireless objects to form their own least cloaked area. Sometimes it is too costly for a particular wireless object *o* to gather the position-related information of all wireless neighbor objects *o* to calculate and confirm its relative least cloaked area as a definitive wireless network has a large number of wireless objects *o* contained within it. From this step the quantum computational intelligence comes into the picture as we make use of quantum computation theory hereafter. The position-related information is stored in the form of qubits at the anonymous server. The parallel information processing and fast search tactics are used in the PMS by means of quantum computational intelligence (see Fig. 4 and Algorithm 2).

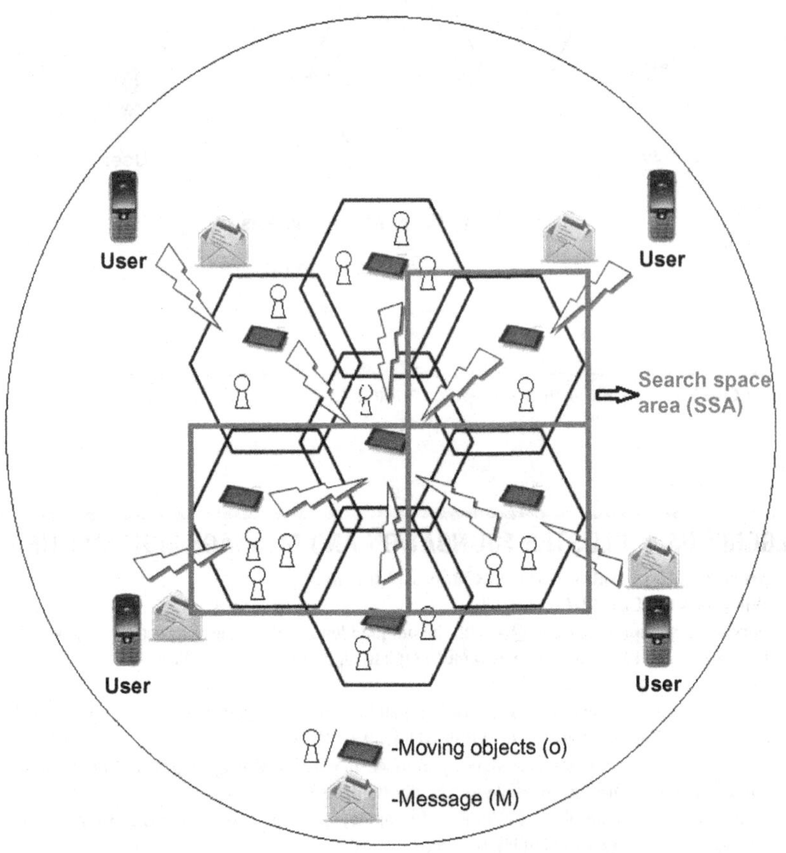

FIG. 4

Phase 2: search space area detection.

ALGORITHM 2 SEARCH SPACE AREA DETECTION

```
procedure SEARCHSPACEAREADETECTION
    SearchSpaceArea SSA ⟵ NULL
    Evaluate each NeighborObject n appearing in WirelessObjectList WOL
    NeighborObject n with highest AnonymityThreshold k from WirelessObjectList WOL
  to SearchSpaceArea SSA unless and until aggregate count of NeighborObjects n in
  SearchSpaceArea SSA is at least AnonymityThreshold k
    Detect and calculate SearchSpaceArea SSA on the basis of AnonymityThreshold k and
  WirelessObjectList WOL
```

4.7 PHASE 3: LEAST CLOAKED AREA SCHEMING

A group of wireless objects contained in the wireless search space area are treated as an input in this phase. This phase plays a vital role in calculation of the least cloaked area of a wireless object o. It is essential to inspect all the permutations and combinations of the wireless objects in a search space area. At least four wireless objects must be clustered because a minimum of two wireless objects is needed to designate the width of the least cloaked area and a minimum of two wireless objects is needed to designate the height of the least cloaked area. The least cloaked area has the property of monotonicity since accumulation of wireless objects o in a particular wireless search space area should not diminish the search space area itself or the number of moving objects m contained in least cloaked area of the search space area (see Fig. 5 and Algorithm 3).

ALGORITHM 3 LEAST CLOAKED AREA SCHEMING

```
procedure LEASTCLOAKEDAREASCHEMING
    LeastCloakedArea LCA ⟵ NULL
    Assemble the information of WirelessMovingObjects m positioned in SearchSpaceArea SSA
    Add individual WirelessMovingObject m positioned in respective SearchSpaceArea SSA to
  LeastCloakedArea LCA
    Add WirelessMovingObject m to WirelessObjectList WOL
loop:
    for x = 1; x ≤ 4; x++ do
        for WirelessObjectList WOL = {o1, . . . , on} in LeastCloakedArea LCA[x] do
            if WRA (LCA(WOL)) < WRA (LCA) then
                if MOC (LCA(WOL)) >= k then
                    LCA ⟵ {WOL}
                    Eliminate WOL from LCA[x]
            else
                Eliminate WOL from LCA[x]
```

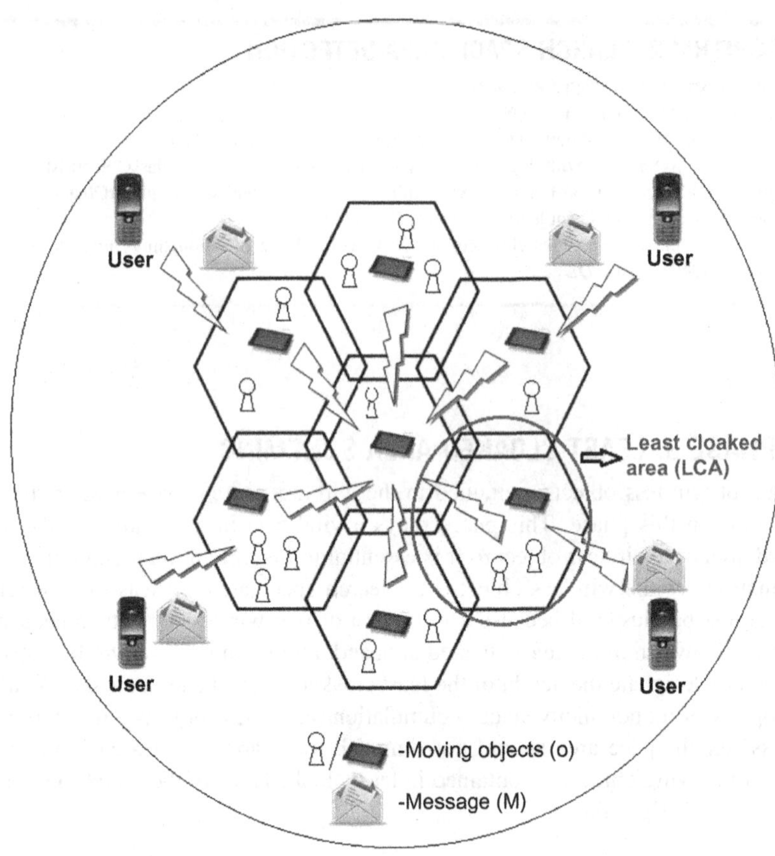

FIG. 5

Phase 3: least cloaked area scheming.

4.8 PHASE 4: LEAST CLOAKED AREA CONFORMATION

Individual wireless object *o* transforms its wireless range area into a least cloaked area containing a minimum of *k* objects for sustaining the prerequisite of *k*-anonymity confidentiality. Each wireless object *o* sets a search space area and discovers a value for individual wireless moving object *m* in its own neighbor list. This value of wireless moving object *m* is simply the ratio of the moving object's count of a particular wireless object *o* to the distance between wireless object *o* and wireless moving object *m*. Finally, wireless object *o* conforms its least cloaked area, and this least cloaked area conceals the total number of moving objects *m* in the neighbor list and the wireless range area of wireless objects in the search space area (see Fig. 6 and Algorithm 4).

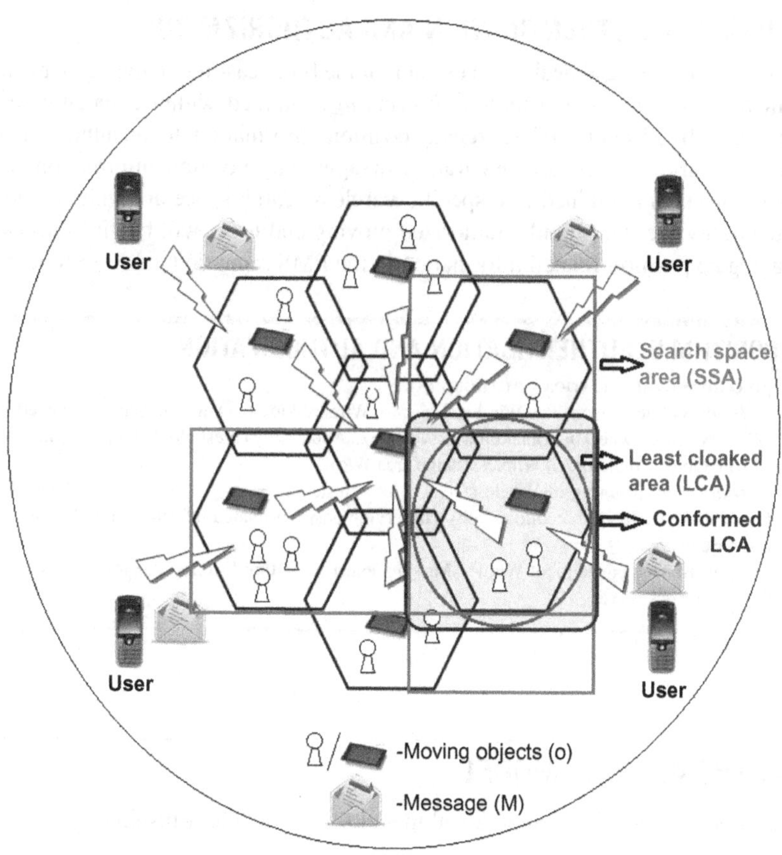

FIG. 6

Phase 4: least cloaked area conformation.

ALGORITHM 4 LEAST CLOAKED AREA CONFORMATION

procedure LeastCloakedAreaConformation
loop:
  if $x < 4$ **then**
    for each $WOL; A = \{a_1, a_2, \ldots, a_{x+1}\}, B = \{b_1, b_2, \ldots, b_{x+1}\}$ in $LCA[x]$ **do**
      if $a_1 = b_1, \ldots, a_x = b_x$ and $a_{x+1} \neq b_{x+1}$ **then**
        Add $WOL\{a_1, b_1, \ldots, a_{x+1}, b_{x+1}\}$ to $LCA[x+1]$
  WirelessRangeArea *WRA* ⟵ LeastCloakedArea *LCA*
  MOC ⟵ Total number of WirelessObjects *o* in LeastCloakedArea *LCA*

4.9 PHASE 5: AUTHENTICATION AND AUTHORIZATION

This is the last phase and deals with evasion of the broadcasting of aggregate position information to unauthorized moving objects m contained within a specific search space area. Broadcasting of aggregate position information to unauthorized end users is not allowed because integration of aggregate position information of all moving objects m contained in a specific wireless search space area might leads to confidentiality breach. So only authorized moving end users will be given access to the aggregate position-related information in the PMS scenario (see Algorithm 5).

ALGORITHM 5 AUTHENTICATION AND AUTHORIZATION

1: **procedure** ATHENTICATION&AUTHORIZATION
2: *Input:* PublicNetwork *PN*, WirelessObject o, WirelessMovingObject m, WirelessObjectList *WOL*, NeighborObject n, QuantumMessage Q_M, AnonymityThreshold k, ObjectCount *OC*, MovingObjectCount *MOC*, WirelessRangeArea *WRA*.
3: *Output:* A clustering of WirelessObjects into clusters of size $\leq k$, SearchSpaceArea *SSA*, LeastCloakedArea *LCA*, confidentiality-conserving position-related information in the form of response to query Q.
4: Forward message M to all WirelessMovingObjects m within WirelessRangeArea *WRA* and the anonymous server

5 MATHEMATICAL MODEL

This section explains the mathematical model for the quantum-inspired PMS framework.

- ***Variables:***
  - R, the required object's position $[r = 1, 2, \ldots, R] \geq 0$;
  - P, position $[p = 1, 2, \ldots, P] \geq 0$;
  - Q, qubits $[q = 1, 2, \ldots, Q] \geq 0$;
  - T, time $[t = 1, 2, \ldots, T] \geq 0$;
  - C, end user's current position $[c = 1, 2, \ldots, C] \geq 0$.
- ***Decision variable:***
  - A_m, if position p is selected, the value is 1, otherwise it is 0.
- ***Independent function:***
  - NC_{pq}, net confidentiality attained in the PMS;
  - FI_p, fuzzy inference value for the quantum-inspired hybrid intelligent PMS.
- ***Parameters:***
  - UCC_{qpt}, communication cost per unit of the qth qubit at position p at time t;
  - Q_{qpt}, number of qubits in association with position p at time t;
  - CC_{qt}, communication cost of a single qubit q at time t;

- Q_t, number of qubits forwarded at time t;
- RTP_{qt}, regular time production of the qth qubit at time t;
- MT_t, maximum threshold value considered for generation of fake records at time t in order to achieve confidentiality in the PMS;
- RTP_{qpct},regular time production of the qth qubit produced in the pth position for current position c of the end user at time t;
- D_{qct}, demand for position-based qubit q from current position c of the end user at time t;
- CAP_{pt}, capacity of position p at time t;
- $PROCAP_q$, processing capacity for qubit q;
- $TCAP_p$, total capacity of position p;
- $PMSU_t$, PMS use per qubit by end users at time t;
- TEU_t, total number of end users using the PMS at time t;
- UCC_{qpct}, unit communication cost of the qth qubit from position p to current position c of the end user at time t;
- A_{qpct}, total number of qubits from position p to current position c of the end user at time t;
- TE_{qct}, total communication cost of qubit q to current position c of the end user at time t;
- UCC_{rpt}, unit communication cost of the required object's position r to position p at time t;
- TQ_{rpt}, total number of qubits sent from the required object's position r to position p at time t;
- TCT_{rt}, total transportation cost of the required object's position at time t;
- IC_{qt}, investment cost of qubit q at time t.

- ***Model:***

$$Max \sum_{m=1}^{P} FI_m \mathrm{A}_m + \sum_{m=1}^{P} \sum_{n=1}^{Q} \mathrm{NC}_{mn} \mathrm{A}_m \tag{4}$$

subject to

$$\sum_{m=1}^{P} \sum_{n=1}^{Q} \mathrm{UCC}_{qpt} \cdot \mathrm{Q}_{qpt} \leq \sum_{n=1}^{Q} \mathrm{CC}_{qt} \cdot \mathrm{A}_m, \tag{5}$$

$$\sum_{n=1}^{Q} [\mathrm{Q}_t \cdot \mathrm{RTP}_{qt}] \cdot \mathrm{A}_m \leq \mathrm{MT}_t, \quad t = 1, 2, \ldots, \mathrm{T}, \tag{6}$$

$$\sum_{m=1}^{P} \sum_{n=1}^{Q} \mathrm{RTP}_{qpct} > \mathrm{D}_{qct}, \quad t = 1, 2, \ldots, \ \mathrm{T}, c = 1, 2, \ldots, \mathrm{C}, \tag{7}$$

$$\mathrm{TCAP}_p \geq \mathrm{CAP}_{pt} - \sum_{n=1}^{Q}[\mathrm{PROCAP}_q \cdot \mathrm{Q}_{qpt}], \quad t = 1,2,\ldots,\mathrm{T}, \tag{8}$$

$$\mathrm{TEU}_t \geq \sum_{n=1}^{Q}[\mathrm{PBSU}_t \cdot \mathrm{RTP}_{qt}] \cdot \mathrm{A}_m, \tag{9}$$

$$\sum_{n=1}^{Q}\sum_{o=1}^{C}[\mathrm{UCC}_{qpct} \cdot \mathrm{A}_{qpct}] \leq \sum_{n=1}^{Q}\mathrm{TE}_{qct} \cdot \mathrm{A}_m, \tag{10}$$

$$\sum_{l=1}^{R}[\mathrm{UCC}_{rpt} \cdot \mathrm{TQ}_{rpt}] \leq \mathrm{TCT}_{rt} \cdot \mathrm{A}_m, \quad t = 1,2,\ldots, \quad \mathrm{T}, l = 1,2,\ldots,\mathrm{R}, \tag{11}$$

$$\sum_{t=1}^{T}[\mathrm{TCT}_{rt} + \mathrm{TE}_{qct}] \cdot \mathrm{A}_m \leq \mathrm{TCT}_{rt}, \tag{12}$$

$$\sum_{n=1}^{Q}[\mathrm{CC}_{qt} + \mathrm{TE}_{qt}] \leq \mathrm{IC}_{qt} \cdot \mathrm{A}_m. \tag{13}$$

The independent function (4) maximizes the net position confidentiality achieved and the qualitative factor of the position on the basis of quantitative factors. Functions (5)–(13) demonstrate the communication cost, maximum anonymity threshold value, request for position-based qubits, capacity of a particular position, number of online roaming users, total communication cost of an individual qubit, unit communication cost from the user's perspective, unit communication cost from the qubit's perspective, and total investment cost of position-based qubits respectively. The proposed quantum-inspired PMS framework is a standard combination of fuzzy logic and quantum computation theory.

5.1 TIME COMPLEXITY ANALYSIS

Assume that there are o wireless objects in the wireless range area. As every wireless object has $o - 1$ peers, we have to consider

$$\sum_{x=1}^{o-1}\mathrm{CommunicationCost} = 2^{o-1} - 1 \tag{14}$$

wireless search space areas to find the least cloaked area. In the quantum-inspired PMS algorithm, the second phase (search space area detection) determines the search space area and reduces the number of wireless objects positioned outside the search space area. Let M be the moving wireless objects in the search space area satisfying the condition $M \leq (o - 1)$. The communication cost can be reduced to

$$\sum_{x=1}^{M} \text{CommunicationCost} = 2^M - 1. \tag{15}$$

In phases 3 and 4 of the quantum-inspired PMS algorithm, it is proved that the least cloaked area can be defined with the help of a minimum of four wireless objects. Since we have to consider the arrangements of at most four wireless objects, the communication cost is reduced to

$$\sum_{x=1}^{4} \text{CommunicationCost} = (\text{M}^4 - 2\text{M}^3 + 11\text{M}^2 + 14\text{M})/24 = \text{O}(\text{M}^4). \tag{16}$$

In the proposed PMS framework, the wireless range area is reduced to the search space area comprising only three wireless objects; consequently, we have to calculate and determine $2^3 - 1 = 7$ least cloaked areas.

6 PROOFS OF CORRECTNESS

In this section we show the accuracy of the quantum-inspired PMS algorithm.

Lemma 1. *The proposed PMS framework delivers mobile user anonymity.*

Proof. In the proposed PMS framework the anonymity of a particular mobile user in the wireless search space area can be attained by means of the anonymity threshold value (k). On the basis of this anonymity threshold value, fake records are generated by the anonymous server. For instance, if the anonymity threshold value $k = 5$, then five fake records will be generated in the same wireless search space area of the end user's current position. Because of these fake records, intruders cannot detect the user's exact position, and hence confidentiality of position information of a particular user is conserved. In the initial state, mobile users make use of their user credentials to get authorized access to the PMS. The user credentials are communicated to the anonymous server and then authorized access is given to mobile users. □

Lemma 2. *A search space area calculated with use of the quantum-inspired PMS algorithm incorporates the least cloaked area.*

Proof. Let us assume that A is the least cloaked area of size less than or equal to the search space area. It is prerequisite that the least cloaked area A should entirely cover the search space area. Assume that the least cloaked area A is not completely covered by the respective search space area; the least cloaked area A should encompass at least one prolonged search space area, SSA_i, where $1 \leq i \leq 4$. This shows that the least cloaked area A is greater than the total area of a prolonged search space area. This disagrees with our supposition that A is the least cloaked area. Hence the search space area incorporates the least cloaked area. □

Lemma 3. *A minimum of four objects is sufficient and can be used for formation of the least cloaked area.*

Proof. As far as the concept of least cloaked area is concerned, an individual edge of the least cloaked area touches the search space area of some wireless objects.

In some extreme situation, there may be a wireless object that touches all edges of the least cloaked area but it does not touch other edges of the search space area. The least cloaked area can be defined with the help of minimum four wireless objects that touch different edges of the least cloaked area. For any edge of the least cloaked area, if several wireless objects touch the same edge of the least cloaked area but no other edges of the search space area. Then we can choose any one wireless object from the available wireless objects. Hence it is proved that the least cloaked area can be defined with the help of a maximum of four nodes. □

7 PERFORMANCE EVALUATION

The proposed PMS framework is analyzed and evaluated in terms of the number of queries and confidentiality requirements, the number of moving objects in the wireless range area, user mobility, and the anonymity threshold value. These parameters and their values are provided as an input to the simulation setup explained in the following subsection and then the results obtained are discussed.

7.1 SIMULATION SETUP

We implemented the quantum-inspired PMS algorithm in Java to simulate the performance of the proposed PMS framework and compare it with a traditional PMS. All work was done with a Windows 10 laptop computer. For the simulation, 500 mobile users were considered within the simulation area of 2 km × 2 km. Table 1 describes the parameters and their corresponding substantial values.

7.2 NUMBER OF QUERIES AND CONFIDENTIALITY REQUIREMENTS

The following experimental parameters were used to show that the proposed quantum-inspired PMS algorithm promises strong confidentiality protection. Initially, we evaluated the average size of the least cloaked area (in kilometers) and the number of points of interest by varying the anonymity threshold value k in the range from 5 to 10. The number of online mobile users was fixed to 500 while we executed each dataset of simulations. When the anonymity threshold value k increases, the average size of the least cloaked area becomes broader.

Table 1 Parameters and Their Values

S.No.	Parameter	Value
1	Simulation area	2 km × 2 km
2	No. of users	500
3	No. of queries	In a range from 15 to 500
4	User mobility technique	Plus mobility (Roaming)
5	Time interval	2 h
6	Anonymity threshold value	Low (5), medium (7), and high (10)

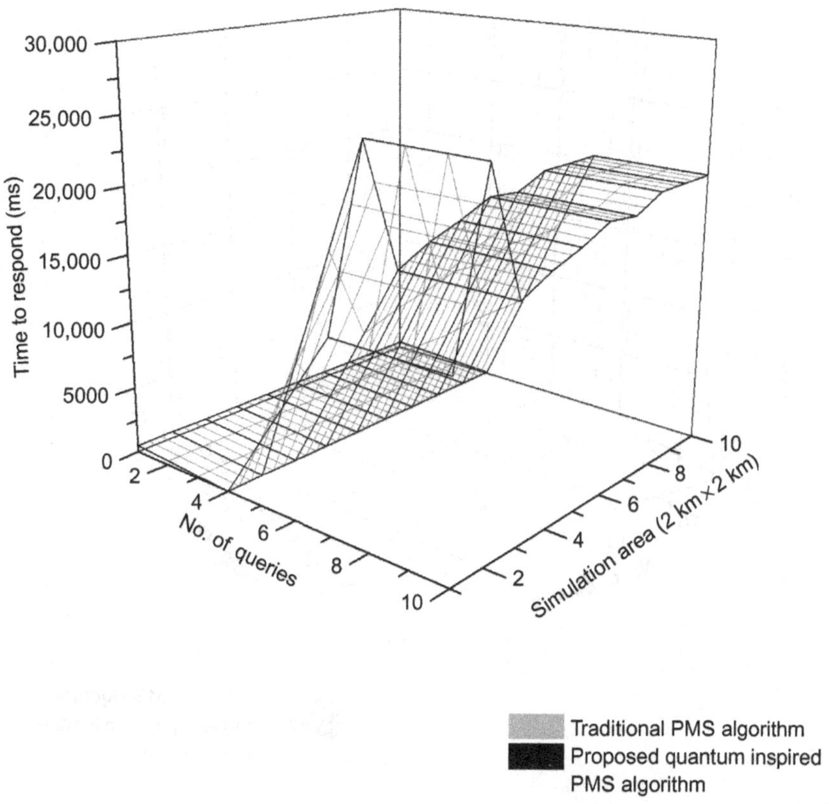

FIG. 7

Impact of the proposed quantum-inspired position monitoring system (*PMS*) algorithm on the number of queries, the simulation area, and the time to respond.

Furthermore, the quantum-inspired hybrid intelligent PMS accomplishes better confidentiality protection while segregating the wireless range area with a larger cell size. Normally, the average least cloaked area is less than 2 km × 2 km and strong position confidentiality is statically preserved. In Fig. 7 we validate that the number of queries (points of interest) within a particular least cloaked area is significantly affected by the anonymity threshold value k and is less affected by the number of fake records generated. Fig. 7 depicts the impact of the proposed quantum-inspired PMS algorithm on the number of queries, the simulation area, and time to respond.

7.3 NUMBER OF OBJECTS IN THE WIRELESS RANGE AREA

Fig. 8 illustrates the performance of the proposed PMS framework pertaining to increasing the number of wireless objects from 50 to 500. As shown, the

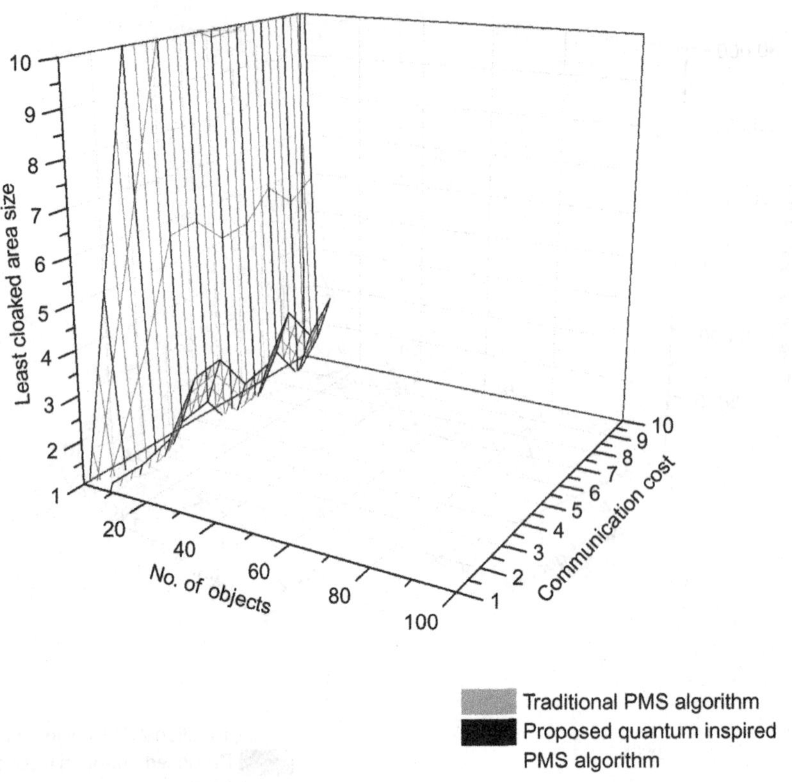

FIG. 8

Impact of the number of objects on the communication cost and the least cloaked area size. *PMS*, position monitoring system.

communication cost increases slightly when the number of wireless objects in the search space area increases. When there are more wireless objects, the mobile object discovers a smaller least cloaked area sustaining the property of anonymity confidentiality since phases 2 and 3 of the proposed quantum-inspired PMS algorithm permit an individual wireless object to find a satisfactory number of neighbor nodes to form the least cloaked area.

7.4 USER MOBILITY

Fig. 9 presents the performance of the proposed PMS framework with regard to aggregate wireless object (user) mobility within a specified wireless range area. The results indicate that the increasing user mobility affects the least cloaked area size and the communication cost of the proposed algorithm to some extent. Hence

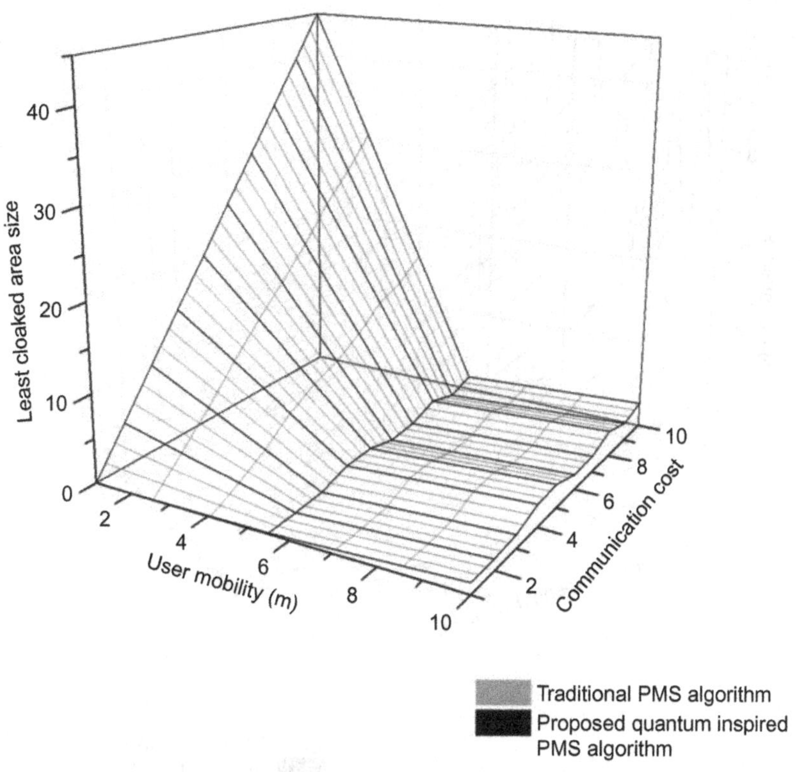

FIG. 9

Impact of an increase in user mobility on the least cloaked area and the communication cost. *PMS*, position monitoring system.

there is very small effect on search space area determination and conformation of the least cloaked area.

7.5 ANONYMITY THRESHOLD VALUE

We analyzed the performance of the proposed PMS using the anonymity threshold value k. We used different least cloaked areas and values of k from 5 to 10 to validate the total number of mobile users in a particular least cloaked area that comprises at least k mobile users mentioned in the position confidentiality framework. In all circumstances, the average number of mobile users exceeds the anonymity threshold value k. In the case of a simulation area of 2 km $\times$ 2 km, the number of mobile users is nearly 100 times greater than k as is shown in Fig. 10. From the results obtained, we can say that the proposed PMS framework accomplishes anonymity for conserving confidentiality of position-related information of mobile users.

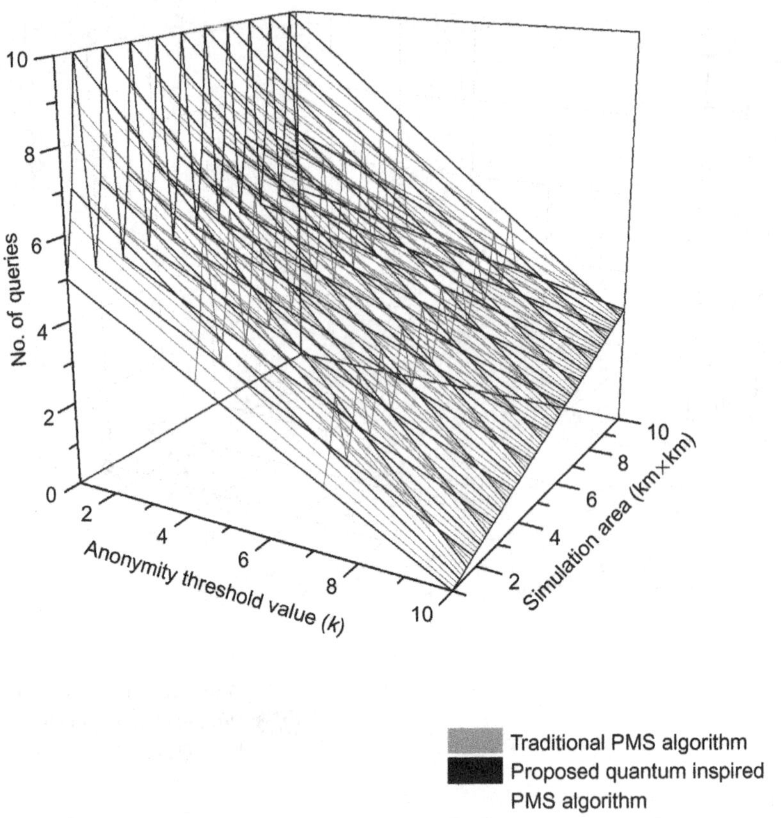

FIG. 10

Impact of the anonymity threshold value (*k*) on the simulation area and the total number of queries (by users). *PMS*, position monitoring system.

8 CASE STUDIES

8.1 TOURIST GUIDE

Position-based services and applications are one of the most evolving trends in mobile commerce. Several position monitoring applications ranging from friend finders to position-based games are empowered by the Global Positioning System and geographical information systems. These position-based services are intended to offer customers immediate access to their local and personalized data. In this case local data contents are present along with the current position of a particular end user. Such position-based applications or services can be used to deliver position-based appropriate alerts to roaming users when a particular user is near a preselected position.

This case study concerns a classic position-based smartphone tourist guide application. Google offers smartphone users several position-based services and applications. So when a particular smartphone user types a search query into Google Maps, the detailed directions from the user's current position to the required place are provided. In the same manner, we have implemented the tourist guide application in Java incorporating the proposed quantum-inspired hybrid intelligent PMS algorithm for attaining position confidentiality in wireless networks. This case study explains the tourist guide application using the proposed PMS framework in detail.

8.1.1 Goals of the quantum-inspired tourist guide application

The quantum-inspired tourist guide application aims for two confidentiality goals: nonframeability and rate limitation. The nonframeability characteristic of confidentiality promises that any authenticated user who is genuine as per the authentic anonymous server may connect to an anonymous server so as to get directions to a particular location (e.g., a bank, restaurant, hospital, or movie theater) in a specific region. This prevents an invader from framing a valid authentic user of the application. Rate limitation guarantees for any authentic anonymous server that no valid user can connect to it more than once in a single period of time.

8.1.2 Quantum computational intelligence in the tourist guide application

The proposed five-phase procedure for attaining confidentiality of the user's current position (see Section 4.4) is applied to the tourist guide application. In the tourist guide application, anonymous user U carries a confidential qubit Q_i which he/she wishes to share among u authorized users in such a way that in any case k users (these k users will be the fake users [records] generated so as to attain nonframeability and rate limitation) are required to rebuild the confidential position-related information. The problem of achieving the confidentiality of a specific user's current position is well known in conventional sceneries and is decipherable for all (u, k). As far as quantum computational intelligence is concerned in this circumstance, the (U, u) case is resolved with the help of the least cloaked area.

For further discussion, let us consider the least cloaked area as it is depicted as a graph containing seven wireless roaming nodes in Fig. 11. This is appropriate for

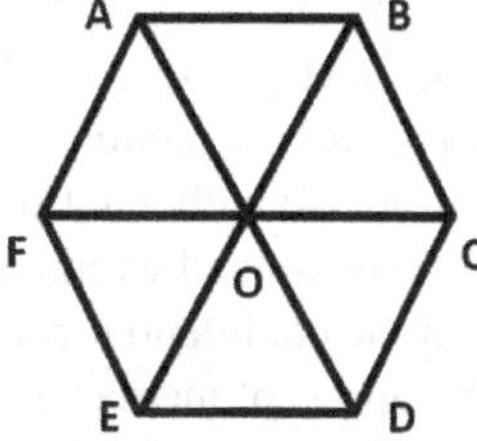

FIG. 11

Wireless range area containing seven roaming nodes depicted in the form of a graph.

better understanding of the proposed quantum-inspired tourist guide application. We evaluate and show the nonframeability and rate-limiting features of the quantum-inspired tourist guide application by applying the five-phase procedure on the graph shown in Fig. 11. The scenario considered here is that any authorized wireless roaming node among the seven nodes shown in the graph (see Fig. 11) may broadcast the authentication message to authorized nodes of a specific least cloaked area and hence confidentiality can be achieved in terms of forwarding the secured position (latitude and longitude) values by means of following procedure:

(1) The authorized user forwards a qubit Q_i along with its own unique identity i to all authorized wireless users. The authorized user is then responsible for its individual search space area detection and should outline its own least cloaked area.

(2) The user should then broadcast his/her message (containing the user id, wireless range area, and count of valid users within the respective search space area) to all authenticated users of his/her least cloaked area. The quantum message $Q^A_{D_x}$ is a message transferred from node A to node D, where node D comes with its neighbor nodes, which can be represented as a set $D_x = \{D1, D2, D3\}$, which exemplifies that three neighbor nodes will receive the confidential announcement received from node A.

(3) Furthermore, the necessary resources required to achieve confidentiality in communication can be calculated as

$$\mathrm{G}(u,k) = \otimes_{x=1}^{7} \mathrm{Q}_i(\mathrm{U}_1;\ldots;\mathrm{U}_6;\mathrm{U}_7;\prod_{e_{xy}} \mathrm{E}_{xy})\pi, \tag{17}$$

where u is the count of authorized users in the respective least cloaked area, k is the total number of fake users generated, and e_{xy} is the set of edges. The value of π varies as per the phases from the five-phase procedure and can be represented as:

(a) $\pi = (U_1;\ldots;U_7;\prod_{e_{xy}} E_{xy})$ (cluster formation and message multicasting)

(b) $\pi = (Q^A_{D_x});(Q^A_{D_y});(Q^A_{D_z});\ldots$ (search space area detection)

(c) $\pi = Q_7^{D,\pm a} Q_x^{U_x,\pm b} Q_y^{U_y,\pm c} \ldots Q_z^{U_z,\pm k}$ (least cloaked area scheming)

(d) $\pi = a^A; b^{D_x}; c^{D_y};\ldots;k^{D_z}$; (least cloaked area conformation)

(e) $\pi = (Q^{D_x}_{D_y}, A_z^{M_x});(Q^{D_y}_{D_z}, A_z^{M_y});(Q^{D_z}_{D_x}, A_y^{M_z});\ldots$ (authentication)

(4) On the basis of the least cloaked area scheming and formation, an individual user regulates the authentication and authorization procedure. If the users involved in communication are contained within a similar least cloaked area ($xyz = x(x+1)(x+2)$), then the confidential conversation among users can be represented as several combinations of messages as $(M_7^B M_x^A M_y^B M_z^A)$, $(M_7^C M_x^C M_y^A M_z^C)$, $(M_7^C M_x^A M_y^B M_z^B)$, and $(M_7^B M_x^B M_y^C M_z^C)$.

(5) Finally, to achieve confidentiality in terms of nonframeability and rate limitation, the final expected outcome (confidential pathways from the source

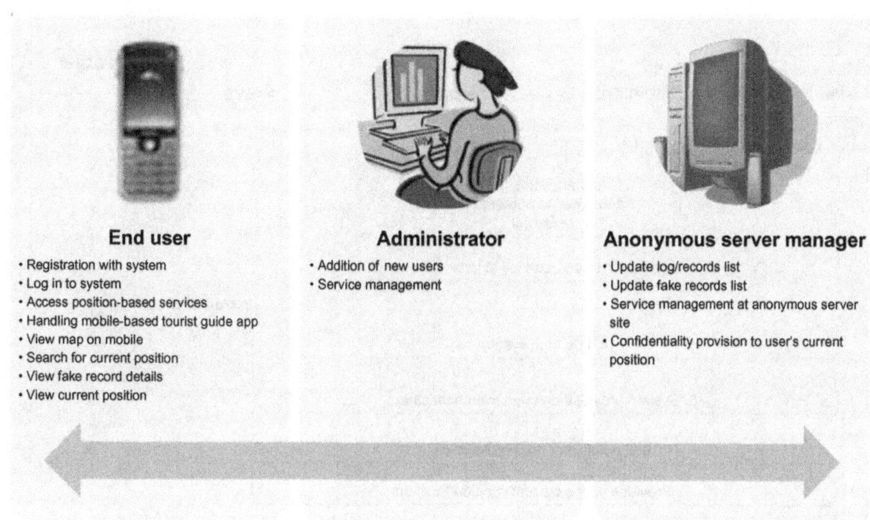

FIG. 12

User profile: tourist guide application.

to the destination) can be estimated as $P_7 = P_x \oplus P_y \oplus P_z$. The valid users contained within a specific least cloaked area make use of fake records (k) generated showing $P = P_7$, henceforth launching the confidentiality preserving quantum-inspired tourist guide application.

Fig. 12 illustrates the users and their individual responsibilities in the tourist guide application. The detailed workflow of the quantum-inspired tourist guide application is depicted in Fig. 13.

8.1.3 Building blocks of the tourist guide application

The quantum-inspired tourist guide application comprises three key components:

(1) position server (server side)
(2) anonymous server (server side)
(3) simulation module (client side; user interface)

Tables 2–4 give a detailed description of all the modules.

8.1.4 User interface

The front-end user interface of the quantum-inspired tourist guide application is shown in Fig. 14.

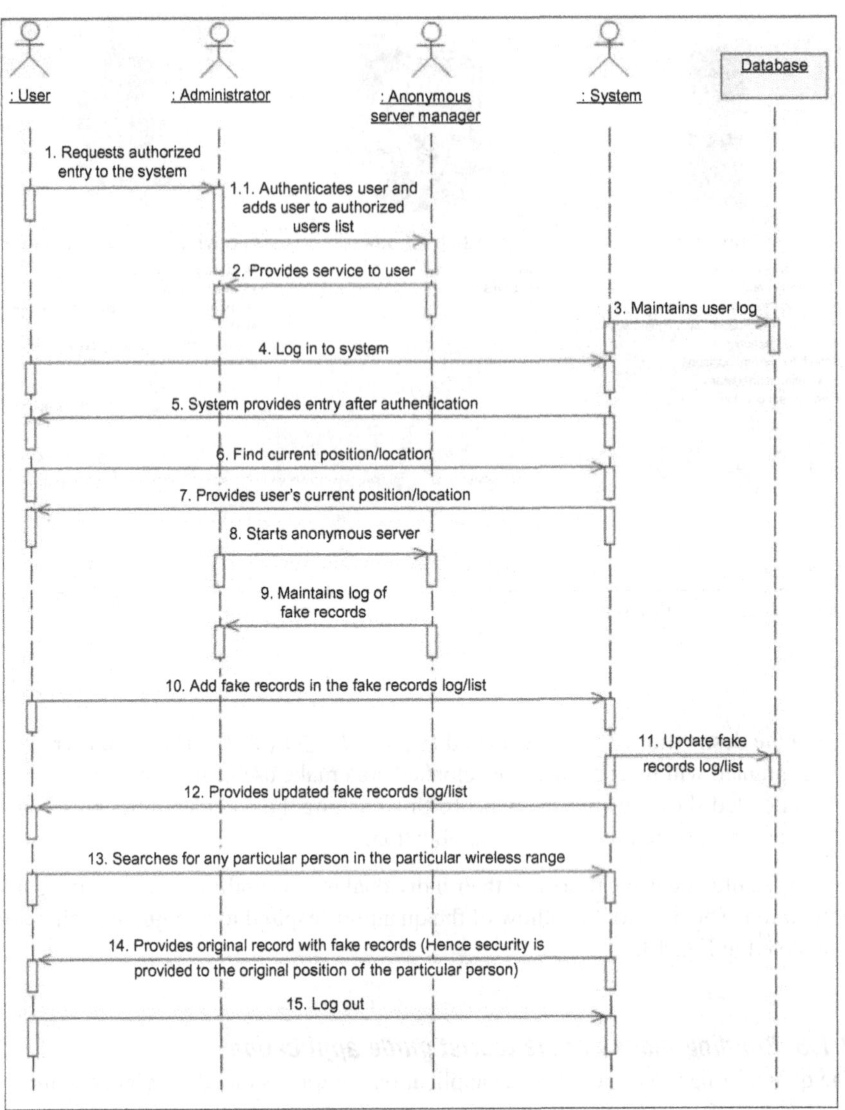

FIG. 13

Sequence diagram for tourist guide application simulation.

Table 2 Position Server Module

Module No.	01
Module name	Position server
Input	Username and password (for login)
Output	Latitude and longitude values of the user's current position.
Frequency of use	*n*
Assumptions	–
Description	The position server is the basic module which is responsible for providing the latitude and longitude values of the user's or object's current position.
Preconditions	The user's computer has sufficient free memory available to the launch task
Postconditions	Authorized access to the system will be provided to the user after registration with the system
Priority	Essential

Table 3 Anonymous Server Module

Module No.	02
Module name	Anonymous server
Input	Username and password (for login)
Output	Fake records (for provision to intruder), directions from source to destination (in textual format)
Frequency of use	*n*
Assumptions	–
Description	The anonymous server provides a platform for the user for selection of either a traditional PMS approach or the proposed quantum-inspired PMS approach so as to preserve confidentiality of the current position of the user or object. Also, the anonymous server detects attack by an intruder and is responsible for providing fake records to the intruder to maintain confidentiality. The user can see the latitude and longitude values of his/her current position in roaming
Preconditions	The user's computer has sufficient free memory available to launch the task
Postconditions	Authorized access to the system will be provided to the user after registration with the system
Priority	Essential

PMS, position monitoring system.

Table 4 Simulation Module

Module No.	**03**
Module name	Simulation module
Input	Username and password (for login), system space (*S*), mobility method (*M*), query (*Q*), anonymity threshold value (*k*), time interval (*T*)
Output	Query response along with directions from the source to the destination in text format
Frequency of use	*n*
Assumptions	–
Description	The simulation module provides a graphical user interface for the user. It allows the user to select values such as system space/simulation area (*S*), mobility method (*M*), anonymity threshold value (*k*), and time interval (*T*). The user can enter his/her query through the simulation module and the simulation module then displays the response to the user's query and also provides directions from the source to the destination in text format
Preconditions	The user's computer has sufficient free memory available to launch the task
Postconditions	Authorized access to the system will be provided to the user after registration with the system
Priority	Essential

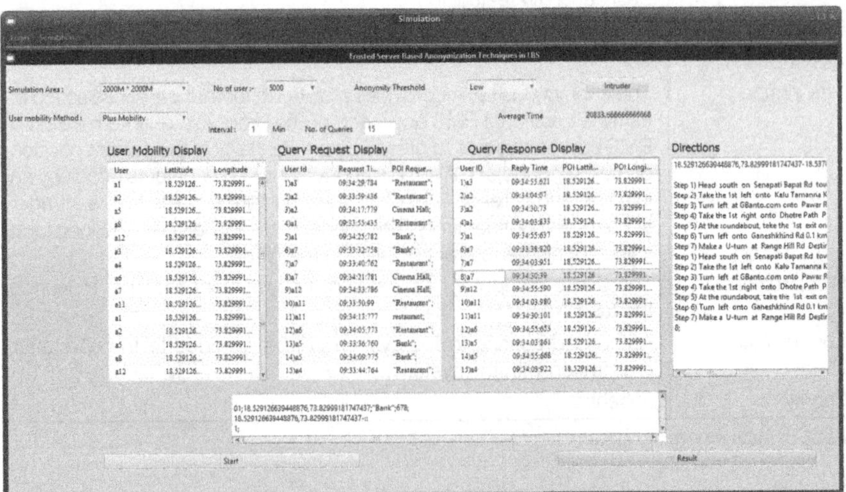

FIG. 14

Simulation setup: tourist guide.

8.1.5 Performance evaluation

Table 5 and Fig. 15 presents the dataset used for performance evaluation of the tourist guide simulation and the results obtained from simulation respectively. The average time for query response display is 2892.55 ms.

8.1.6 Concluding remarks

The proposed quantum-inspired PMS provides more confidentiality to the current position of the roaming than the traditional PMS. The aggregate position

Table 5 Dataset Used for Performance Evaluation of the Tourist Guide Application

S.No.	Name of Element	Value of Element
1	Simulation area	2 km × 2 km
2	User mobility technique	Plus mobility (Roaming)
3	No. of roaming users	500
4	Anonymity threshold value	Low (5), medium (7), and high (10)
5	Time interval	1 min
6	No. of queries	In a range from 15 to 500
7	Algorithms	Traditional PMS; proposed quantum-inspired PMS

PMS, position monitoring system.

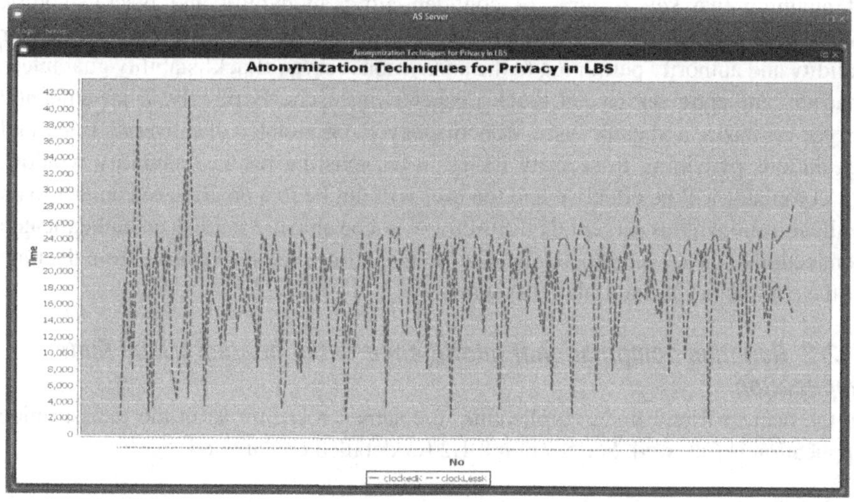

FIG. 15

Comparison of the traditional position monitoring system and the proposed quantum-inspired position monitoring system. *LBS*, location-based services.

information calculated through the proposed PMS framework is more secure in comparison to the traditional framework.

8.2 NEAREST FRIEND FINDER

The next case study is analogous to the usual or typical friend finder application. The main motive is to deliver position-based alerts to users so they can stay in touch with their family and friends. Mobile users are in a position to find each other and to obtain directions to a particular place in a city (e.g., a bank, restaurant, or college). The same simulation setup as used in the previous case study is used here. The following capabilities are offered in the nearest friend finder application:

(1) deliver position-based information of an individual user securely
(2) determine driving directions while roaming
(3) provide position-based alerts to authorized roaming users
(4) localization of authorized end users
(5) routing among users and their points of interest
(6) provide information about travel conditions (e.g., traffic-related information) in real time

Fig. 16 illustrates the data flow between the end user, administrator, and anonymous server manager.

8.2.1 Goals of the quantum-inspired nearest friend finder application

The quantum-inspired nearest friend finder application is proposed with the aim of attaining two key features of confidentiality: anonymity and blacklistability. Anonymity protects the unidentified nature of authentic users irrespective of their validity and authority pertaining to the anonymous server. Blacklistability guarantees that any authentic server can block misbehaving users. Explicitly, if an authentic server criticizes a specific user who disobeyed or violated the overall rules and regulations pertaining to security issues in the existing recent linkability window, the complaint will be effective and the user will not be in a position to connect to an authentic anonymous server i.e., the user will not be able to establish an authenticated connection to the server effectively in subsequent time periods (ensuing from the time of the complaint) of that linkability window.

8.2.2 Quantum computational intelligence in the nearest friend finder application

In the nearest friend finder application, the same procedure as in the tourist guide application is followed. See Section 8.1.2 for detailed explanation.

8.2.3 Performance evaluation

Table 6 shows the dataset used for performance evaluation of the quantum-inspired nearest friend finder application. Fig. 17 compares the results obtained by a traditional PMS and the proposed quantum-inspired PMS.

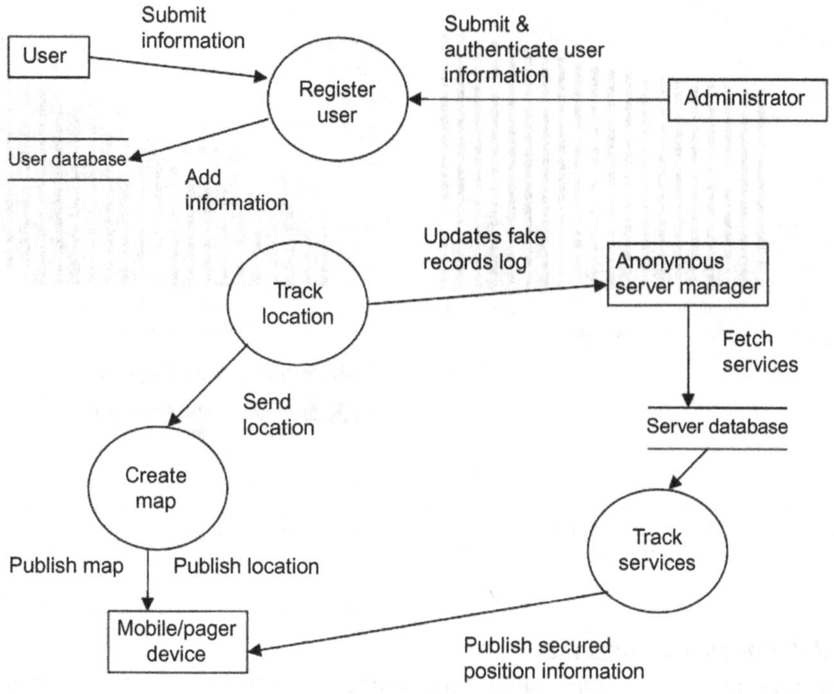

FIG. 16

Data flow in the nearest friend finder simulation.

Table 6 Dataset Used for Performance Evaluation of the Nearest Friend Finder Application

S.No.	Name of Element	Value of Element
1	Simulation area	5 km × 5 km
2	User mobility technique	Plus mobility (Roaming)
3	No. of roaming users	500
4	Anonymity threshold value	Low (5), medium (7), and high (10)
5	Time interval	5 min
6	No. of queries	In a range from 15 to 500
7	Algorithms	Traditional PMS; proposed quantum-inspired PMS

PMS, position monitoring system.

As shown in Fig. 17, the proposed quantum-inspired PMS responds to position-based queries in the minimum time in comparison with the traditional PMS, and the proposed PMS delivers more efficient responses to position-based queries even if the mobility speed of roaming users within a particular wireless range area increases.

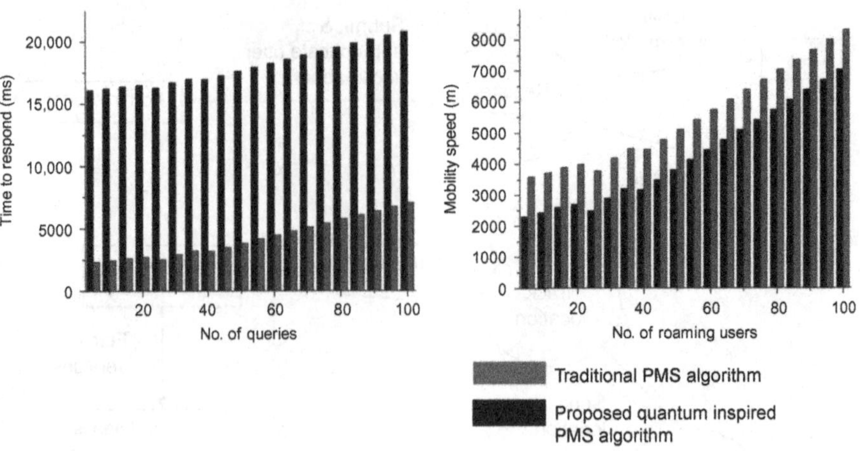

FIG. 17

Comparison of the traditional position monitoring system (*PMS*) and the proposed quantum-inspired PMS.

8.2.4 Concluding remarks

The integration of the proposed quantum-inspired PMS framework in a traditional nearest friend finder application results in securer position-related information when end users are roaming. We can overcome problems such as position cheating, fake record generation, and forwarding by use of the proposed quantum-inspired PMS algorithm. The proposed PMS delivers high-quality position-based capabilities, and the accuracy of the proposed quantum-inspired PMS algorithm is about 90%.

9 CONCLUSION

In this chapter we have described a novel quantum-inspired hybrid intelligent PMS for analysis, modeling, and evaluation of the confidentiality of a moving object's position in wireless networks. The proposed PMS framework is a combination of quantum computation theory and fuzzy logic. The quantum-inspired position-based services application from the proposed framework anonymizes the position-related information on the basis of the anonymity concept so as to conserve the confidentiality of position-based information of roaming users. We have presented a novel quantum-inspired five-phase procedure and algorithms for PMS to achieve confidentiality of the mobile user's position. Furthermore, we have provided a detailed mathematical model for the proposed quantum-inspired PMS framework and evaluated its performance from a position confidentiality perspective. This work suggests source node position confidentiality as an emerging field of research. For future work, we propose formulating the quantum-inspired intelligent versions of *k*-anonymity algorithms available in the literature so as to achieve 100% accuracy in preserving the position confidentiality of roaming users in wireless networks.

REFERENCES

[1] M.S. Ackerman, L.F. Cranor, J. Reagle, Privacy in e-commerce: examining user scenarios and privacy preferences, in: Proceedings of the 1st ACM Conference on Electronic commerce, ACM, 1999, pp. 1–8.

[2] H.W. Hamacher, Z. Drezner, Facility Location: Applications and Theory, Springer Science & Business Media, Berlin, 2002.

[3] S. Lederer, J. Mankoff, A.K. Dey, Who wants to know what when? Privacy preference determinants in ubiquitous computing, in: CHI'03 Extended Abstracts on Human Factors in Computing Systems, ACM, 2003, pp. 724–725.

[4] M.F. Mokbel, C.-Y. Chow, W.G. Aref, The new Casper: query processing for location services without compromising privacy, in: Proceedings of the 32nd International Conference on Very Large Data Bases, VLDB Endowment, 2006, pp. 763–774.

[5] M. Oskin, F.T. Chong, I.L. Chuang, A practical architecture for reliable quantum computers, Computer 35 (1) (2002) 79–87.

[6] T. Tassa, D.J. Cohen, Anonymization of centralized and distributed social networks by sequential clustering, IEEE Trans. Knowl. Data Eng. 25 (2) (2013) 311–324.

[7] C. Lai, H. Li, X. Liang, R. Lu, K. Zhang, X. Shen, CPAL: a conditional privacy-preserving authentication with access linkability for roaming service, IEEE Internet Things J. 1 (1) (2014) 46–57.

[8] M.M. Mahmoud, S. Taha, J. Misic, X. Shen, et al., Lightweight privacy-preserving and secure communication protocol for hybrid ad hoc wireless networks, IEEE Trans. Parallel Distrib. Syst. 25 (8) (2014) 2077–2090.

[9] H.P. Li, H. Hu, J. Xu, Nearby friend alert: location anonymity in mobile geosocial networks, IEEE Pervasive Comput. 12 (4) (2013) 62–70.

[10] B. Alomair, A. Clark, J. Cuellar, R. Poovendran, Toward a statistical framework for source anonymity in sensor networks, IEEE Trans. Mobile Comput. 12 (2) (2013) 248–260.

[11] H.J. Jo, J.H. Paik, D.H. Lee, Efficient privacy-preserving authentication in wireless mobile networks, IEEE Trans. Mobile Comput. 13 (7) (2014) 1469–1481.

[12] S. Zakhary, M. Radenkovic, A. Benslimane, Efficient location privacy-aware forwarding in opportunistic mobile networks, IEEE Trans. Veh. Technol. 63 (2) (2014) 893–906.

[13] R.-H. Hwang, Y.-L. Hsueh, H.-W. Chung, A novel time-obfuscated algorithm for trajectory privacy protection, IEEE Trans. Serv. Comput. 7 (2) (2014) 126–139.

[14] C. Bettini, S. Mascetti, X.S. Wang, S. Jajodia, Anonymity in location-based services: towards a general framework, in: International Conference on Mobile Data Management, 2007, IEEE, 2007, pp. 69–76.

[15] L.A. Zadeh, A computational approach to fuzzy quantifiers in natural languages, Comput. Math. Appl. 9 (1) (1983) 149–184.

[16] K.-H. Han, J.-H. Kim, Genetic quantum algorithm and its application to combinatorial optimization problem, in: Proceedings of the 2000 Congress on Evolutionary Computation, 2000, vol. 2, IEEE, 2000, pp. 1354–1360.

[17] C.-S. Tseng, B.-S. Chen, H.-J. Uang, Fuzzy tracking control design for nonlinear dynamic systems via TS fuzzy model, IEEE Trans. Fuzzy Syst. 9 (3) (2001) 381–392.

[18] K.N. Sgarbas, The road to quantum artificial intelligence, 2007, arXiv preprint arXiv:0705.3360.
[19] A. Narayanan, M. Moore, Quantum-inspired genetic algorithms, Evolutionary Computation, 1996, in: Proceedings of IEEE International Conference on, IEEE, 1996.
[20] K.-H. Han, J.-H. Kim, Genetic quantum algorithm and its application to combinatorial optimization problem, Evolutionary Computation, 2000, in: Proceedings of the 2000 Congress on, Vol. 2, IEEE, 2000.
[21] Z. Michalewicz, Genetic Algorithms + Data Structures = Evolution Programs, Springer Science & Business Media, Berlin, 2013.
[22] M.A. Nielsen, I.L. Chuang, Quantum Computation and Quantum Information, Cambridge University Press, Cambridge, 2010.
[23] A. Amir, M. Lindenbaum, A generic grouping algorithm and its quantitative analysis, IEEE Trans. Pattern Anal. Mach. Intell. 20 (2) (1998) 168–185.
[24] C. Chen, A fuzzy group decision model of location selection for distribution center, J. Manag. Syst. 6 (4) (1999) 459–480.
[25] D.V. Medhane, A.K. Sangaiah, Source node position confidentiality (SNPC) conserving position monitoring system for wireless networks, in: Emerging ICT for Bridging the Future-Proceedings of the 49th Annual Convention of the Computer Society of India CSI, vol. 2, Springer, Berlin, 2015, pp. 347–355.
[26] D.V. Medhane, S.P. Kosbatwar, A K-anonymity confidentiality defending locality examining scheme for wireless networks with Jack secure system, Int. J. Comput. Netw. Wireless Commun. 2 (5) (2012) 615–621.

Author Index

Note: Page numbers followed by *f* indicate figures, *t* indicate tables and *np* indicate footnote.

C

D

H

I

J

K

L

M

N

O

P

T

U

V

W

X

Y

Z

Subject Index

Note: Page numbers followed by *f* indicate figures and *t* indicate tables.

O

P

Q

R

S

T

U

V

W

Z

Printed in the United States
By Bookmasters